S0-ASQ-024

MOSES OF OXFORD

Perez de Cuellar congratulates Mikhail Gorbachev
after his address to the L'Chaim Society

Rabbi Shmuel Boteach

MOSES OF OXFORD

A JEWISH VISION OF A
UNIVERSITY AND ITS LIFE

1

Introduction to Volume 1 by
Professor Norman Stone

André Deutsch

First published in Great Britain in 1994 by
André Deutsch Ltd
106 Great Russell Street
London WC1B 3LJ

ISBN 0 233 98878 5

Cataloguing-in-Publication data available for this title
from the British Library

Printed in Finland
by WSOY

This book is dedicated to the visionary supporters
of the Oxford University L'Chaim Society

Mr and Mrs Edmond Safra

who embody the synthesis that we seek for our
students at Oxford: devoted Judaism and
humanitarianism at the forefront of world
achievement.

Contents

VOLUME ONE

———

Acknowledgements   xiii

Introduction **by Professor Norman Stone**   xv

Author's Foreword   xvii

SECTION ONE   **Social Issues**   1
Chapter One   **Lessons from the Environment: Why**
     Humankind Resembles a Tree   3

Chapter Two   **Sexual Harrasment and 'An Eye for an Eye'** 10
Chapter Three   **Does Homosexuality Differ from**
     Heterosexuality?   24
Chapter Four   **Race Relations and Positive Discrimination**
     at Oxford   45
Chapter Five   **Should Jewish Organizations Ever Have**
     Non-Jewish Leadership?   56
Chapter Six   **Pornography and Passion in Judaism**   63
Chapter Seven   **Does the World Have Too Many Babies?**   71
Chapter Eight   **Why Can't We Live Forever?:**
     Coping with the Death of a Parent   85
Chapter Nine   **Abortion in the Bible**   93
Chapter Ten   **An Innate Optimism for Human**
     Improvement   107
Chapter Eleven   **Enough of Justice, More of Love**   115
Chapter Twelve   **The Case for Modesty in Intimate**
     Relationships   128

Chapter Thirteen	Moses' Spies: Gaining a Sense of Priority	134
Chapter Fourteen	The Agony of Moses and Conflicts in Modern Jewish Identity	141
SECTION TWO	**The Phenomenon of Judaism at Oxford**	149
Chapter Fifteen	**The University of Oxford**	151
Chapter Sixteen	**Religion and the Belief in God in Modern Oxford**	170
Chapter Seventeen	**The Life and Growth of Religion at Oxford University**	175
Chapter Eighteen	**Oxford Reaches the Modern Era**	187
Chapter Nineteen	**The Jews of Oxford**	191
Chapter Twenty	**Jewish Involvement with the University Itself**	196
Chapter Twenty-one	**The Challenge of Modern Oxford**	207
Chapter Twenty-two	**The L'Chaim Society in Oxford**	223
Chapter Twenty-three	**Oxford Gown and Jewish Garb: Similarities between Jewish and Oxford Traditions**	236
Chapter Twenty-four	**Shylock the Jew?**	254
Chapter Twenty-five	**Lessons from Oxford Town and Gown: Interdependency of Lay People and Scholars**	271
Chapter Twenty-six	**Controversy of Chanuka at Oxford**	281
Chapter Twenty-seven	**Noah, Students and Modern-Day Arks: The Ivory Towers of Academia**	291
Chapter Twenty-eight	**Born Anew: Mature Students and Modern Living**	295
Chapter Twenty-nine	**The Evils of Slander: The Central Ingredient in Society's Moral Decline**	299
Chapter Thirty	**Promoting Israel Against Its Critics**	303
Chapter Thirty-one	**Reform and Orthodox Judaism: Are They Equal Expressions of Judaism?**	318
Chapter Thirty-two	**Singles Reject Synagogues Without Separations**	335

SECTION THREE   Judaism and Other Religions in Oxford   339

Chapter Thirty-three   How Kosher was Khomeini?   341

Chapter Thirty-four   Is There a Devil in Judaism?   359

Chapter Thirty-five   Messiahs Came Marching One by One   363

Chapter Thirty-six   Capitalism, Communism and Computers
in Jewish Thought   384

Chapter Thirty-seven   Mormons and Jews at Oxford   395

SECTION FOUR   Relationships   403

Chapter Thirty-eight   When Men and Women Cannot
Understand Each Other   405

Chapter Thirty-nine   Why Do We Marry?   413

Chapter Forty   Can One Lie to Promote Peace?   423

Chapter Forty-one   Are We Bored With Sex?   431

Chapter Forty-two   Two Approaches to Contemporary Judaism
and a New Approach to Intermarriage   441

Chapter Forty-three   Rejecting Judgementalism   453

Chapter Forty-four   A Definition of Loneliness and How
to Overcome It   465

Acknowledgements

═══

This book could not have been completed without the dedicated assistance of some of my closest colleagues and friends.

Foremost among them are Oxford students, Marcus Roberts and Sarah Pengelly, who painstakingly edited the manuscript and offered wonderful ideas and anecdotes; as well as my conscientious assistant, Kathy Brewis. I have known Marcus longer than almost any other student at Oxford, and he served as one of L'Chaim Society's first Presidents. It was he who provided the bulk of the information for the historical descriptive found in Section two, which he co-authored with me.

As both volumes are concerned with the experiences and challenges I face at Oxford University, I could not have written them without the existence of our L'Chaim Society which is generously sponsored by many kind friends. The following names are only some of the many hundreds who make our activities possible: Foremost among them are Mr Alec (o.b.m.) and Mrs Eileen Colman, who provided the initial funding for the Chabad House of Oxford, and which bears their name, Mr and Mrs Edmond Safra (to whom this book is dedicated); my father and my brother Yoav and Chaim Boteach, Mr Charles Colman, Mr and Mrs Sandy Eisenstat, Mr and Mrs Jonathan Faith, Rabbi and Mrs Shneur Zalman Fellig, Mr and Mrs Jonathan Green, Mr and Mrs Michael Gross, Rabbi and Mrs Joseph Gutnick, Mr and Mrs Meir Jungreis, Mr Malcolm Lyons, Mr and Mrs Curtis Maclean, Mr and Mrs Stanley Merran, Mr and Mrs Alex Paul (my aunt and uncle), Mr and Mrs Sam Rosen, Mr and Mrs Sydney Rubin, Mr and Mrs Zvi Rysman, the Saka family, Mr and Mrs Elan Shasha, Mr and Mrs Harris Sidelski, Mr and Mrs Danny Shoskes, Ms Lucy Stone, Mr and Mrs Jonathan Webber, and Mr and Mrs Jeff Zulman.

I pay a special tribute to the man who for the last five years has been my principal guide and wise mentor in all aspects relating to my work, Rabbi Faivish Vogel, director of the Lubavitch Foundation of the UK. Rabbi Vogel is famous as one of the finest Lubavitch representatives anywhere in the world and I consider myself extremely fortunate to work under his direction.

I thank my wife Debbie for being the most trusted and loyal companion in life that any man could ask for. There is nothing I do in this city, no event which we stage and no speaker which we host, in which Debbie is not fully and actively engaged in making a success. A woman of grace and humility, she seeks no mention or tributes of credit, unlike her husband, and I must therefore ensure that she receives it. In addition to the four beautiful children with which we have been blessed, she has ensured that from the day I embarked at the age of twenty-one upon this odyssey at Oxford that I would never lose confidence in myself, amidst many trying times.

I pay tribute to the great teacher of Israel, the Lubavitcher Rebbe, Rabbi Menachem M. Schneerson, who, in the course of a private audience at the time of my Bar Mitzva in his office, convinced a disillusioned thirteen years old that his life and efforts made a difference. In every challenge I have faced at Oxford I have benefitted from the Rebbe's wisdom and guidance, as well as the knowledge that a man of vision and greatness stood firmly behind me. I ask the Almighty for His blessing that the Rebbe regain his full strength and continues to lead and inspire people like myself and my students to ever greater heights.

Finally, I pay homage to the Master of the Universe for His ongoing strength and loving kindness of which I am so unworthy.

Rabbi Shmuel Boteach
November 1993
Oxford, England

Introduction

====

Oxford and the L'Chaim Society

Rabbi Boteach runs a good show. His office, at the top of a street that, in old Oxford, used to be called 'Great Jewry', is at the centre of the university, and, as this book makes plain, he has organized some spectacular events since he arrived in 1988. He has in fact become something of a legend in the place, and it is very good to have these volumes. In them, he raises, in essence, a question that must be of the greatest interest for anyone interested in intellectual life. Where does Judaism fit in? Especially, how can its Absolutes be reconciled with the liberalism that, within disputed boundaries, universities are bound to maintain?

The Church of England faced similar questions, even one and a half centuries ago, and Rabbi Boteach is quite good in outlining the battles that this caused. In response, the Church's control of the university was relaxed; and Rabbi Boteach is not very respectful towards the outcome, what with chaplains who confess to near-disbelief, and who adopt in many cases an anything-goes line in personal conduct. This relationship with religion, and with society in general, is an essential one in Oxford's history, from medieval times to the present day, and it is right that a Chasidic rabbi should look upon this seriously. Nowadays, the anything-goes line has affected the university seriously, and Rabbi Boteach does not conceal the problems that result – fifteen per cent of undergraduates reported to need psychiatric care, or the endless problems over 'relationships'. He himself does quite a bit of good, in an unobtrusive way, in clearing up various resulting 'messes', and in talking about Oxford, past and present, he is a good source of anecdotes and illustration. I disagree with him about one thing: he is, I think, alarmist as to 'sexual harassment', because there is not very much of it, certainly not enough to justify elaborate codes; most Englishmen are, rightly, too scared of women.

Rabbi Boteach says that up to about seven to ten per cent of the student body is Jewish, a figure I had not known, but that Cambridge attracts the Orthodox, where there has been a much more coherent Orthodox body (I can believe this: Cambridge always was more of a puritanical place).

He himself would like to see the Jewish students more conscious of their origins, despite the surface attractiveness of modern liberal ways, and, for instance, the statistic (which again I had not known) that marrying 'out' now accounts for over a third of males. Here, he shows the great power of religion in overcoming the disintegrative tendencies of what, since the 1960s, we have called 'the permissive society'. He does so with considerable, though never overwhelming, learning in Jewish thought upon these matters which, really, are age-old. I have read this book with great interest and admiration and it is good to have great Jewry back again in Oxford.

Norman Stone
Professor of Modern History
at the University of Oxford.

Author's Foreword

Many of my closest friends and colleagues at Oxford warned me not
to use this title because it would only be interpreted as a great symbol
of arrogance. Now, I have certainly never been the most humble man
on earth, as was the first Moses according to the Bible. However, in all
probability I am not the most arrogant either.

The most important disclaimer of this book, then, is: no, I do not have
any pretensions to this glorious title, which is not meant to convey that I
see myself in the seat of Moses at Oxford. Rather, when I first arrived
in Oxford in 1988, and I shall discuss this later in the book, I was overwhelmed by the prevailing Christian culture and history of the university
and wondered whether a serious Jewish contribution could ever be made
to this city because of its Christian identity. But it was not until I delved
more deeply into the very early history of the university that I discovered
that, preceding the Jewish expulsion from England in 1290, Oxford had
once been strongly Jewish with a sizeable Jewish population participating
significantly in the university's founding.

It is more significant, however, that some of the leading early scholars
at the university were Jewish, and one of the greatest, named Moses, was
known as Moses of Oxford. A detailed description of him and his dynasty
is in Section Two.

I fell in love with the memory of this sage as soon as I heard
his name. There could be no greater inspiration of the purpose of my
coming to Oxford and administering as the students' rabbi than the name
Moses of Oxford. My objective is to bring synthesis and orchestration to
the great and ancient traditions of one of the world's leading universities,
and the world's oldest monotheistic religion, Judaism. In short, I arrived
in this city because of the opportunities here to revive the rather neglected
universal aspect of Judaism; I came to this city to bring Moses and Oxford
together, and make them one.

The Jewish faith was never meant to be insular or parochial. Its
spirituality was intended to illuminate the earth, as well as the souls of
the world's inhabitants, not through embracing the Jewish religion as such,
but through accepting its vision of the One God and the requirements of

goodness He makes of humans.

What better place to promote this universal message of Godliness and goodness than in the world's intellectual crossroads, Oxford? But I have been pre-empted in this task by an old Jewish sage who nearly a millennium ago, at a time when religions were fiercely intolerant and exclusivist, had the courage and foresight to bring the spirit and warmth of the Jewish God to this intellectual centre.

It is to the memory of this extraordinary man that this book is offered.

An Invitation to Oxford

It was an early June morning in 1988; I was twenty-one years old, had been married for just five months, and was completing my rabbinical degree in New York. The telephone rang. It was an unexpected long distance call. The man on the line was someone I had heard much about, as he is one of the most eminent of the Lubavitcher rebbe's emissaries in the world. His name is Rabbi Faivish Vogel, director of all Chabad activities in the United Kingdom, and he had called me with a proposition. 'We have obtained funding,' he said, 'to open a new outpost in Oxford, and we are currently searching for someone to run the place. Would you be interested?'

'Oxford?' I asked, trying to contain my surprise and delight. 'Do you mean *the* Oxford, as in the university in England?'

'That's the one,' he replied with some confidence.

So began a fascinating odyssey which largely consumes my every waking moment to this very day. I was soon sent to Oxford as an emissary of Rabbi Menachem Mendel Schneerson, the Lubavitcher rebbe in New York. I do not come from a Chasidic home, choosing first to enrol in a Chasidic (sometimes spelt Hasidic) seminary when I was fourteen years old. Yet seven years later, having just completed a two-year tour-of-duty in Sydney as a founding member of the first rabbinical seminary there, I was given my first major assignment.

My task was a daunting one: to further the teaching of God and impart Jewish tradition and learning in this ancient university. I was to attempt to portray Judaism as exciting and illuminating, and imbue the students with a deep desire to re-embrace their heritage. In particular I was to reach out to young Jews at the university who had lost touch with their Jewish spirituality and were not affiliated to the existing Jewish community or structures in the city. But I also saw it as my task, in accord with the universalism expressed in Judaism and in the philosophy of Chabad Chasidism, to arouse a greater awareness for the need of Godliness in the rest of the university in the way the covenant of Noah urges a belief in God, an ethical life, and the creation and maintenance of institutions to preserve the conditions in which these flourish.

The Glorious Legacy of Oxford

It was daunting because I felt the weight of Oxford's great history and reputation on my shoulders. The university has flourished from at least 1117 (and perhaps from as early as 1094) and in these last eight centuries has seen most of human affairs, particularly in the field of religion. Oxford has had more than its fair share of great religious innovators and religious movements, saints and martyrs, eccentrics and lost causes. It is a bold person who claims to do anything that is truly original in Oxford, and an even bolder person who ventures to suggest that perhaps the great minds of Oxford ought to think or do something not being undertaken at present.

With the benefit of five years of hindsight, I do indeed believe that Lubavitch and the Oxford L'Chaim Society has made an original contribution to the teaching of God in Oxford, and certainly one that is relevant to the continuing needs of the university. Before my arrival there was no resident rabbi in the entire city, and the needs of the Jewish students were being catered to sporadically. My work, then, as a rabbi to the Jewish students has been pioneering in Oxford's religious history because the presence of Chabad-Lubavitch in Oxford in the last five years probably represents the university's first sustained influence by and contact with Chasidic Orthodox Judaism. (The now worldwide Chabad-Lubavitch movement originated among eighteenth-century Jews in the White Russian town of Lubavitch from which the movement obtained its name.) While there probably have been Orthodox Jews in the university since 1854 their profile has been very low, and they have generally avoided disseminating Jewish ideas into the university at large.

Contribution of our Students

Much of my work of teaching God in Oxford has been through the teaching programme and highly varied events of the Oxford University L'Chaim Society. This was set up by students in 1989 under the auspices of the Chabad House in Oxford to provide an appropriate means to further traditional Judaism among our student supporters, and the university at large. The general commitment to the society and contribution of individual talents by our students and community supporters, adding to my own overall direction of the society, have made it a great success. L'Chaim is the fast-growing new society in Oxford. By November 1993, L'Chaim remarkably represented the second largest student organization in the university with over 1,500 members, half of whom are non-Jews. The society has organized and hosted a truly multi-faceted programme of events since it began in 1989 and has enabled me to go some real way towards fulfilling my role to further the teaching of God in Oxford to many different groups of people.

Much of the book that follows is devoted to addressing the serious and most pressing challenges, discussions, and ideas that have arisen in regard to traditional Jewish values over the course of my stay at the university, and the way I believe our response has served to reinvigorate Judaism. If Judaism can live and thrive at as demanding a place as this, it can do so anywhere. Many of the following chapters were originally written for the students, to answer and meet their needs and frequent questions. They were distributed primarily through our weekly student and academic mailing within Oxford. But they were also sent to people throughout the world by electronic mail on the worldwide computer network, Internet, where the essays are posted weekly. Although written with the express needs of my students in mind, it was not long before I discovered that the articles could serve as an invaluable tool in my work of teaching God in Oxford.

Also, they are a high-tide mark of many of the debates I have had with students on various issues, and in some cases they answer pressing pastoral questions that were put to me by students. Overall some of the value of the essays comes from the fact that the students are used to asking the most difficult questions and expecting clear answers. Serving as rabbi at a university like Oxford is a difficult appointment because the students expect to challenge the essentials of what you believe to be true. I have rarely noted intellectual deference to me merely on account of my being a Jewish spiritual head.

The subjects in this book are varied. It will be seen that many of the great themes of Judaism and spirituality are covered, as well as pressing social and ethical problems, which in themselves may not be directly religious questions but can be readily informed by the thoughts of the great Jewish sages and thinkers of the past. All the chapters and themes address questions of general interest but it is important to remember that the context of all the essays is Oxford University, as will be seen.

SECTION ONE

SOCIAL ISSUES

Chapter One

LESSONS FROM THE ENVIRONMENT:
WHY HUMANKIND RESEMBLES A TREE

Of the three Oxford academic terms, Michaelmas, Hilary, and Trinity, it is the third which is most looked forward to by students. In many ways this is surprising since it is Trinity term in which the university's major exams and finals fall. Yet England is often cloudy, in fact too often. The daily routine of waking to a bleak world, coupled with the considerable academic pressures borne by the students, begin to take their toll about midway through the year, in Hilary term. It seems that students experience many low moments and high anxiety at this time. But Trinity term, with its beautiful spring weather, changes all that.

During Trinity, the weather turns from predictably cold, windy and wet to being as consistently warm and balmy as British weather can be. In a matter of a few weeks, or even days, the sights that have seemed so static over winter are transformed: the graveyard of St Giles's Church sprouts first snowdrops, then crocuses, then daffodils and tulips in lush, damp grass. The ancient and crooked almond tree in the High Street (that is biannually saved from being destroyed by the city council because it is supposed to be too old and dangerous) shoots out limp, green buds, then gloriously pink blossom, and finally full leaves, all as though for the first time. The blackbirds in Walton Street, Jericho, a trendy, studenty area of Oxford, start to warble their courting songs and the wood pigeons start to coo placidly from the rooftops.

Students suddenly look forward to waking up in the morning and greeting the early sun. A full day of outdoor activity can also be looked forward to with such diverse activities as punting, rowing, cricket and tennis. The thick winter coats can come off and students can feel more relaxed. Champagne bottles litter the streets as students take to long afternoon picnics in the magnificent University Parks and gardens, complete with strawberries and cream and Pimms.

In addition to heightened outdoor activity, the university and city of Oxford are far more beautiful in spring than at any other time. The superb architecture is more visible than during summer since the new leaves of the trees are barely able to block out the sunlight or the gaze of an observer. Yet the spring light is also softer than that of winter and more flattering to the warm stone from which most of our buildings have been made. Oxford is often referred to as the city of dreaming spires, largely because of its beautiful summits and picturesque towers which achieve a full glow only with the summer sun. As spring progresses, the people's faces light up as they go about their business in the centre of the city, especially on the warm and sunny days that come after periods of rain, the days on which the earth seems to compete successfully with all the smells of modern life.

I too am overtaken in Oxford with the promise of summer. My office is in what is perhaps the very best location, overlooking the city square itself. I am often pestered by photographers from newspapers and travel services who want the perfect picture of Oxford and feel they can achieve it from my window. During the year, however, I find myself looking inwards far more often at the contents of my office and at my computer screen, trying desperately to avoid the bleak, grey sky. But when spring arrives, I turn my computer around and work from the opposite side of my desk so that I am always facing outwards, gazing on the glowing swarm of busy activity. I grow cheerful from the energetic hive of students running to and fro now with smiles on their faces, and from seeing the city centre come alive. In the late winter or early spring, the sap is rising in the trees and all other plants to give a wonderful feeling of new life awakening. Even busy townspeople can share in the renewal of nature going on all around at this time of year.

As a child, Rabbi Joseph Isaac Schneerson was once standing in his home looking out of the window. His father, Rabbi Dov Ber, the rebbe of Lubavitch, walked over to him and said, 'It is better to be standing outside looking in, than to be standing inside looking out.' The reference, of course, was to Judaism, and indeed it is far better to be on the perimeter of Jewish life and harbour a desire to become more involved than to be a regular who was brought up with Judaism who now wants out. But I apply this lesson to myself and Oxford. For most of the year I am looking inside, into my office, and thus I can get much done. But during the summer months I am suddenly on the inside looking out, wishing I could enjoy every moment of sunshine. I grew up in Los Angeles and Miami Beach, Florida, both cities flooded the year round with warmth and sunlight, and I cannot easily slide into and be satisfied with the British grey. This of course leads me to get far less done in the summer than the other terms, and the students tell me that they have exactly the same problem.

Feeling an Affinity with Nature

I cannot help feeling renewed and uplifted at such a time, in touch with nature even in the middle of a busy commercial centre. It is proper and healthy to remember our community with the rest of creation. What most people are unaware of is feeling that such communion with other living things is a mainstay of the Jewish religion. For instance, the Torah prohibits man from cutting down fruit-bearing trees, even during wartime. In addition, the Talmud stipulates that a green belt, within which one is not allowed to build any residences, must surround every city in the holy land. The Talmud also stipulates the exact diameter beyond which the city must not extend so that people are always in touch with the green belt and, hence, nature.

When I arrived in Oxford in 1988, the fight to save the environment was at fever pitch and I found myself delivering lecture after lecture on the subject of Judaism and the environment. This was the period when *Time* magazine went so far as to award the endangered earth its 'Man of the Year Award' because it was the most newsworthy item. The students could not seem to get enough of the subject and the largest crowds we drew was when we sponsored any event connected with ancient Jewish teachings concerning the environment. We even brought the chairman of the largest property development company in Europe, a Jewish philanthropist, Godfrey Bradman, of Rosehaugh, Inc. (who at the time was building the main British terminal for the Channel Tunnel link to France), to speak on how commerce and the environment could coexist.

But perhaps the greatest statement of the Torah demonstrating human-kind's kinship with nature is the verse found in Deuteronomy which reads, '... for the tree of the field *is* man's *life*' (20:19). So seriously is this verse taken in Jewish law that it is cited by the Talmud as the reason the Jews celebrate *Tu Bishvat*, the New Year for Trees. Humans are likened to the trees of the field and so nature's new year affects humans as well.

Remaining Connected to Roots

The lesson we are meant to draw from the Torah's equating man with a tree was once the subject of an inspiring message by the Lubavitcher rebbe. Although a tree grows out into the world, it is constantly connected to its source. Indeed, if it were to be grubbed up from its roots, it would wither and die. Likewise, the purpose of a Jew is not to remain secluded in a Jewish ghetto environment. A Jew must 'go out into the world', gain a profession, fully integrate into society and breathe the fresh air. He must serve as an inspiration in society as well as a source of goodness. At the same time, a Jew must also remain steadfastly connected to the source of Jewish being. After gaining a thorough grounding in Judaism and Jewish living, an individual may indeed be prepared to take their place on the world stage, well outside the strict confines of a Jewish community. But he or she must remember that the fountains of the Torah and Jewish tradition remain the life-source. One dare not be disconnected.

Of course, this message is particularly pertinent to the Oxford Jewish student community, many of whom will go out into the world and lead extraordinary lives. This success should not, and need not, come at the price of losing one's identity. While being fully integrated into mainstream society, a Jew must also remain bound to one's people and tradition.

An inspiring message indeed. Yet something is still missing. The correlation between people and a tree still seems a bit disappointing, largely because of a tree's obviously passive nature. Indeed, a tree does grow out into the world, but its presence, however beautiful, goes largely unnoticed. A tree just stands idly and grows, but does not seem to grab the mind's attention or imagination. It makes no noise. It usually lacks the brilliant colours that would naturally cause the head to pivot automatically in its direction, such as the reaction induced by pretty flowers. To all intents and purposes, the passive contribution of trees to our world is not only often unnoticed, but taken almost entirely for granted.

Harmony in Society

Yet, amidst this passive nature, the tree still makes one of the most significant contributions imaginable to our daily lives. Through the process of photosynthesis, it oxygenates our air and gives us life. Without the trees and other plants, the world would not only be lacking an essential element of its beauty, but life as we know it would not be possible. In this respect, the tree plays the role of the facilitator, the *enabler*. It enables people to undertake a proactive role, being itself quite content to remain in the background. It is the humans who make the headlines. Yet it is the tree that not only provides the paper for those headlines, but provides the very means by which those people live and prosper.

Understood in this way, making humans analogous to a tree is intended to indicate that we must embrace not only an active or leading role, but also the role of the facilitator. We must not content ourselves with being at the forefront of achievement and the professional world, but we must also enable others to do so.

To be sure, one of the prime objectives in our existence is to make something of our lives. This aspect is one which, justifiably, has been given pre-eminence throughout history. There has never been a shortage of human beings who tried to lift themselves up from poverty and destitution to a life of respectability, financial security and power. Unfortunately, this preoccupation with our own goals has often severely depleted the number of people who were watchful for others. What we need are people who are willing to put a significant amount of time and energy into others' lives. We must cultivate the element within us which is likened to a tree. We must not just breathe, but also cause others to breathe. In the course of our inhaling the fresh air we must ensure that we are not suffocating someone else.

Rejoicing in Another's Achievement

I truly believe with all my heart that the world will not be a better place until we learn sincerely to complement our peers and rejoice in their achievements, instead of feeling threatened by them. Until we make it our priority not only to advance ourselves but facilitate the progress of our peers, we cannot honestly speak of equality and love for our fellows.

The time has come for us to find it realistic to demand of ourselves that we be as caring of and sympathetic to someone else's aspirations and ambitions as we are to our own. This message is especially pertinent to Oxford students because of the academic rivalries and jealousies that abound and form part of the reason for individual success.

About a year ago there were two students who were very good friends. They each applied separately for a significant Oxford fellowship that entailed a substantial research grant and much prestige. In spite of the many candidates, one of these friends won it. The young woman was so proud of her achievement that she came immediately to tell me and some friends. Later, the other friend came to my office looking despondent. She was upset that she had not won. I asked her what made her more upset, the fact that she hadn't won or the fact that someone she knew so well had outdone her. 'Well, to be honest,' she replied, 'I don't want to sound arrogant, but I deserved it far more than her. My qualifications were far superior. I am the better student.' Indeed she was. 'But,' I said to her, 'are you a better person? A good person is someone who can negate their nature and find it within themselves to partake of their colleague's successes, even at the expense of their own.' She then left the office to congratulate her friend.

And this is one of the themes I constantly return to when delivering my weekly Friday-night Shabbat talk to the students. I emphasize and re-emphasize, 'If you have a friend who has won a significant scholarship, applaud her genuinely. The world is big enough for both of you to be special. If one of your colleagues becomes engaged to a wonderful young woman, congratulate him from the bottom of your heart. The world has plenty of wonderful marriage partners. If one of your classmates lands a fantastic job, be truly happy for him. Tell him he deserved it. Let him savour the moment. You'll see. Later, he will do the same for you. You will have developed the most beautiful thing that life has to offer: human kinship and fellowship, a lesson we learn from the fact that plants feel it is not insulting but life-affirming to be in the background.

Moses is Held Accountable

Accompanying this sense of fellowship should be our need to feel responsible for our fellow human beings. Life cannot be only about self-development and aggrandizement. Amidst the legitimate concern for our own welfare, there must also be a genuine concern that nobody is left behind and that the road to success is large enough to embrace us all. One should not, indeed need not, feel that one must forgo any ambition in order to be caring or responsible for those around us.

It is no coincidence, then, that *Tu Bishvat* occurs in proximity to *Parashat Beshalach* (Exodus chapters 13–17) every year, in which we read of the exodus from Egypt, and how the Almighty sustained the nation of Israel in the desert by feeding them with bread the Jews called *manna* which rained from the heavens. God made one important stipulation about collecting the manna: they were not to collect it on Shabbat, the day of rest. The Jews were a stubborn people and sure enough, on the first Shabbat morning after God's instruction there they were in the fields to collect manna. The Jewish people, together with Moses, were rebuked for their behaviour. 'And the Lord said unto Moses, How long refuse ye to keep My commandments and My laws? See, for that the Lord hath given you the Sabbath, therefore He giveth you on the sixth day the bread for two days . . .' (Exodus 16:28–29).

Reading the story carefully, though, it is clear that Moses did not himself break the Sabbath, but none the less he was rebuked as the other Jews were. Rashi explains that Moses had not yet taught the Jewish people about their obligation to keep the Shabbat holy (it being prior to the giving of the law at Sinai). Because of his sin of omission and his failure to educate the community, 'Scripture punished him . . . for God did not exclude him [Moses] from the rest of the congregation' (Rashi on Exodus 16:22). Indeed, humankind is one family, one unit. When one from within our midst succeeds, we must all rejoice. And when one of us fails, we are all to be held accountable.

Sharing Our Good Fortune

From here it is evident that sins of omission are rendered as sins of commission. Each and every one of us who has been fortunate in one area of life carries an obligation to share that good fortune with our neighbours. If one has been lucky enough to have had the benefit of a Jewish education, one must never look down on contemporaries who may not have been as fortunate. On the contrary, rather than lamenting the current state of Jewish ignorance, fulfil the obligations which you have to the community. Give of your time and energy to those who, through no fault of their own, have not yet studied Judaism but would savour the opportunity.

Treat them as your equals and show them nothing but the greatest respect and love.

If you are fortunate enough to enjoy financial security, don't look down on those to whom you may have to offer your support. On the contrary. The assistance you offer is not charity, but justice. It is your obligation. Your existence embraces a dual function. Not just your obligations to yourself but your obligations to others. You would never feel that dressing yourself up nicely and warmly is an act of charity to yourself; neither is it an act of charity to another individual. It is the reason that we are here together and we must not allow selfishness to infringe on this innate sense of community. If we do, what will happen the day the trees decide to become selfish?

Lessons from the Moon

When I was just six years old I remember watching one of the Apollo missions to the moon blast off from Cape Canaveral in Florida. So excited was I by the event that I made my mother sit down and tell me all about the space programme. She told me how it had all started just a few years earlier, in 1969, when the first man had walked on the moon. I could see a glimmer in her eye as she described what it was like to sit here on earth and watch, live, as astronauts set the first human feet on the earth's satellite. 'Were you excited?' I asked her. 'Excited?' she said. 'We were not excited, we were ecstatic!' All of us. Everyone in the house, everyone in the city, everyone in the world. Everybody celebrated.'

I remember how as a child this story made such a strong impression on me. Here was a woman, along with the rest of the earth's inhabitants, who was thousands of miles away from the event. Yet they gloried and rejoiced as if it were *they* who were setting foot on the moon. Indeed they were. Because they felt it was the collective effort of humanity as a whole who was setting foot on the moon. In the now legendary words of Neil Armstrong, the astronaut who did first walk on the moon, it was 'one small step for man, and one giant step for *mankind*'. The earth's inhabitants felt themselves at that moment to be a family. We must now endeavour to restore that feeling, employing it in our daily lives and interactions with our fellow humans.

Chapter Two

SEXUAL HARRASSMENT AND
AN 'EYE FOR AN EYE'

I encounter many people at Oxford who I am led to believe actually feel they have their fingers on the pulse of current affairs. In their lofty view of themselves, they imagine they have the answer to every wrong and woe in the world presented to them in their daily newspapers so kindly provided by their college. Of the many virtues and gifts that abound among Oxford students, humility is not often one of them.

But it is not really arrogance that leads students and academics to assume their small round-table discussions can relieve poverty, suffering and Third World debt. Rather, it is also great idealism and a refusal to become disillusioned with the current state of the world. Such vision, as opposed to arrogance, must obviously be applauded and I feel privileged to be a religious individual living in a city brimming with intellectual energy.

Flawed Ivory Towers: Problems with Rape

A problem arises, however, in how cut off from reality the members of such a university can be. An insular institution such as Oxford can still have a highly ambivalent attitude to many issues. For instance, there was a recent outcry here when a judge punished a teenage rapist by ordering him to pay his victim £500 for 'a good holiday', presumably in the belief that two weeks in the sun would erase the memory of the ordeal from the victim's mind. Colleges buzzed with the topic, undergraduates could hardly believe that so mature and socially responsible person as a judge could be so insensitive and trivial. After all, how could a holiday be compared to what the woman had been put through? All the students voiced their approval when the appeal for a more appropriate and stern judgment was successful.

Now the city of Oxford has currently, and has had in the past, a serious problem with rape. Hardly a month goes by without some headline describing how a female student is attacked. For this reason, the young women here will almost never venture out alone at night, even in the busy Oxford thoroughfares. Of course, the seeds of rape lie in not making it clear that sexual harassment, which is a much more common offence at Oxford, as at other places, is completely unacceptable.

In the weeks following the rape case above, at least one college allowed a serious and vicious case of sexual harassment towards a female student to be virtually unpunished. The worst chastisement handed out to one of the male perpetrators was typically Oxonian: 'social rustication', that is, not being allowed to mix with other people in college. This was the most severe punishment for just one of the many people involved. In the past, students had been 'sent down', that is, kicked out of their college for offences far less severe – such as getting a third in preliminary examinations. Again, the college was a hotbed of dissent, with everyone loudly condemning the behaviour of these men. But in this case the outrage quickly subsided. The reason: nearly everyone at the college knew at least one of the harassers as a friend, and to that extent their fate was somewhat sympathized with, as lenient as the punishments were.

Sexual Harassment at Oxford

Sexual harassment of the women at the university is a problem that is gradually being addressed. As the presence of women in colleges has become the norm rather than the exception, their voices cannot be ignored; at the same time the university as a whole is recognizing it as a problem which must be dealt with if Oxford is to retain its credibility. It is not that the problem at Oxford is any worse than any other University but rather that Oxford practises a pretty prescient silence on most matters and especially when they are of this nature. It used to be the case that women found it virtually impossible to denounce those who made unwelcome advances; there was no structure for making complaints, so they were dealt with on an ad hoc basis that made it difficult to ensure justice was done. Added to this was the problem that women in the previously all-male colleges could only complain to a group of men (the Senior Common Room) who had recently emerged from an artificial environment in which women played a more marginal and subservient part.

After all, it was only in 1860 that the (all-male) dons were first allowed to marry, women were only allowed to take degrees from 1920 and the first women were admitted to previously male undergraduate colleges in the early 1970s. There have long been women's colleges at Oxford but they have been segregated from the men. The most important women's colleges were Lady Margaret Hall, St Anne's College, Somerville and St Hilda's, which remain single-sex (although Somerville will be accepting men from 1994). But it was as late as 1974 that leading Oxford men's colleges such as Balliol, Wadham and Christ Church first began to admit women. As this integration progressed, problems arose: men had been used to complete control over their own domain. Typical of the original statutes of many colleges was that of Wadham which decreed that no female should be allowed past the college gate except the laundress and she was to be of 'such age, condition and reputation as to raise no sinister suspicion'. Such codes should not be altogether surprising, since many like them appear in Jewish law as well, such as Maimonides forbidding men to speak to strange women in the street lest people suspect something sinister. But this, of course, was written in an age where there was far less public social interaction between the sexes. So too in Oxford we can be sure that many of the dons enjoyed their artificial seclusion from the real world of which women formed half the population. In a system that had been oriented towards men for so long, women were seen as intruders, and their problems are thankfully now beginning to be taken very seriously. But as one might appreciate, the university does not particularly want the public to discover that there are indeed still some flaws in the system.

Dons Determine One's Future

What compounds the problem, not just at Oxford but at every educational institution, is that tutors and dons exercise considerable say over the academic future of any female candidate. Thus, many women find it difficult to refuse the advances of a particular don, without having to face possible retribution.

Driving Lessons for Dons

I remember how a female student once came to see me about a problem. She felt fortunate that a world-renowned expert in her field was now tutoring her, but she was also concerned. She was quite attractive, and saw that he noticed; she was tutored by him personally, which, because of his speaking engagements around the world, is increasingly uncommon. Matters came to a head when the tutor, who was spending more and more time with her, asked if she would give him driving lessons: she nipped about in a nifty little sports car and he had never learned to drive. She asked me if she should comply, fearing that if she didn't he might stop the tutorials or take retributive action. In the event, I advised her against it but she did not heed my advice. But I did understand her reluctance to think too sinisterly of his motivations, since he was a particularly nice fellow and seemed genuinely sincere.

No Love Lost for the Media

Ultimately, it becomes clear that an institution such as the University of Oxford has so profound a fear of media interest in all its goings on that it cannot hope to prevent its members from suffering from unacceptable behaviour. The eye of the media is very much on Oxford, especially when it comes to things that make the world of privilege look sordid and just like the rest. People love to see a proud person or institution shown up and even I am amazed at how some of the smallest Oxford indiscretions immediately make national headlines, as do its student suicides. The fear that newspapers or broadcasters will get hold of the story often prevents the university authorities from handing out serious punishments as deterrents. This can unfortunately lead, in effect, to *carte blanche* being given to any but the grossest offenders. No institution likes to be seen to have problems with discipline, and the fact that Oxford has for so long been a training ground for the future leaders of the country means that its reputation must be particularly well-guarded. It seems easier to deny there is a problem than to root it out, and one can almost sympathise with the university for its inaction. And yet, something must be done.

Senior Members Can Be Immune

This tendency is of course even more pronounced when the offender is a senior member of staff, as is not unknown; then the college authorities close ranks even more swiftly and with more determination. Even when conduct may be so appalling that the senior member is asked to leave, it is usually unheard of for a warning to be given to the educational institution that is unfortunate enough to have their services next. I heard a story of one male don who was thrown out of an Oxford college (for 'counselling' his male students about their homosexuality and then trying to seduce them) is now teaching at one of the most prestigious universities in the United States. For years, nothing was done to stop him because each time someone complained, they found they were the only one, so it was their word against his, and of course the don was believed. This meant that each year it became harder for people to pluck up courage to denounce the man who would be writing a reference that could affect the rest of their careers. Eventually, though, *three* young men marched into the dean's room to complain, all with the same story to tell, and they had to be believed. However, as he is a brilliant academic and the college was reluctant to publicize his tendency to abuse his position, he found no difficulty in finding a new post.

Of course, the best interests of victims and potential victims of such an unpleasant person may not always be the highest priority: the possibility of the story getting into the media is understandably of great concern and often all other priorities must bow to that. Oxford, like any leading academic institution, is greatly concerned with the preservation of its sacred image as at the forefront of, and cradle to, Western civilization.

Recently, gestures have been made towards opening up a decent process of redress to members of colleges, with codes on sexual harassment being the most publicized. The problem is that however many codes and guidelines are introduced, they can do nothing if people do not feel they will be taken seriously or if they fear that their aggressors will continue to be seen in college every day. Also, it is very difficult to face up to certain aspects of harassment, such as that of a man abusing another man. Even if a man who has been abused plucks up the courage to go public with the indiscretion, it is questionable whether he will be believed. This is what the young men found in the case outlined of the don above; the authorities assumed that male students could defend themselves, forgetting that there was the issue of this don's mental influence over his students as well as his power in determining their academic futures. Whatever their physical strength, they may have felt unable to reject his advances.

Still one wonders how decent and fair any system can be in an institution where the police can enter only if invited in by the correct college authorities; they cannot simply be called on by any member, that is, a student. College members are always asked to take their complaints through the university or college system first so that the situation can be 'controlled', but which the students often interpret to mean so that the media does not get wind of it. At the very least, if the police are eventually called, there may be little valuable evidence left. In his wonderful introduction to this book, for which I am so grateful, Professor Stone tells me that I may be making too much of the existence of sexual harrassment, certainly to justify elaborate codes. Still, my training and schooling was mostly at all-male seminaries, specifically rabbinical. Knowing how powerful the attraction between the sexes is, it seems to me that if men and women are going to study together at a co-educational establishment, and if men are going to tutor females in private settings, then at the very least certain precautions must be taken. I respect Jewish law for actually forbidding a man and a woman who are not married to be locked together alone in a room. Such wise measures preclude the possibility of any compromising situations, and therefore eliminate the necessity for specific codes designed to redress sexual harrassment. It therefore surprises me no end when I hear my students telling me that these codes of Jewish law are sexist and antiquated. The fact is that if these laws were adhered to we might not have, or at least might have drastically reduced, the global tumult concerning sexual harrassment that pervades most western universities, and the resulting enmity that it has caused to exist between the sexes.

Rather than encourage a policy of 'checking' human sexuality and forcing people into situations in which they must continually repress their sexual inclinations, Jewish law advocated a far healthier approach in which people do not get themselves into the kind of situations in which they must repeatedly negate their essential, human selves. Human sexuality is not meant to be repressed. Rather it should be allowed to express itself in carefully constructed and positive settings. Seen in this way the ancient

Jewish aphorism which states that the difference between a wise man and a clever man is that a clever man can extricate himself from a compromising situation into which a wise man could never have allowed himself to be found, speaks for itself.

How Judaism Rehabilitates Its Members

Discussions along these lines and on these issues often lead to my teaching the students of the Jewish alternative to modern western government's punitive measures, which I highly respect. In the book of Exodus, God lays out the essential elements of Jewish civil law for the Jewish people. Having just come out of Egypt, they were already being groomed and primed for higher things. God gave them an extremely thorough and meticulous ethical code by which to live and through which to transform them into a holy nation. One of the most famous and controversial of these laws reads:

> If men strive, and hurt a woman with child, so that her fruit depart *from her*, and yet no mischief follow: he shall be surely punished, according as the woman's husband will lay upon him; and he shall pay as the judge *determine*.
> And if *any* mischief follow [to the woman], then thou shalt give life for life,
> Eye for eye, tooth for tooth, hand for hand, foot for foot.
> Burning for burning, wound for wound, stripe for stripe (Exodus 21:22–25).

Enemies of the Hebrew nation have often used the above verses as evidence in support of Jewish barbarism. But the talmudic interpretation of this verse, 'an eye for an eye', has always been that this does not mean that the eye of the offender must literally be extracted, but rather he must pay monetary compensation. Our rabbis' tradition that 'an eye for an eye' means monetary restitution has preoccupied the commentaries throughout the generations.

Today, as in former times, there are those who do not view this interpretation as God's word, but as if the *Halakha*, Jewish law, were able to change. Obviously, for anyone not deeply imbued with faith in the authenticity of the Torah's oral tradition, a rabbi's interpretation of these words, seemingly so different from the text, is difficult to understand. However, talmudic rabbis have dedicated a number of utterances to proving how much this tradition, that the Torah may not demand physical but only monetary retribution (Bava Kama 83), is respected. This is despite the fact that most of these passages are intended for those who accept that rabbinical tradition stems from Sinai as an axiomatic statement of belief, and so needs no further proof. A few of these utterances read as follows:

The Torah states, 'And he that killeth a beast shall make it good, beast for beast' (Leviticus 24:18). The next verse reads, 'And if a man maims his neighbour, as he did so shall be done to him' (ibid 19). The Talmud acknowledges that there is a need for 'justice when a person kills a beast', and although the Torah explicitly stated 'a soul for a soul', the restitution is still monetary. We never take a human life for the killing or maiming of an animal. By analogy they extend monetary restitution to the maiming of one's fellow man. Just as 'soul for soul' is not to be taken literally, the same is true of 'an eye for an eye'.

Another proof is taken from the fact that the Torah says, 'take no satisfaction for the life of a murderer' (Numbers 35:31). The rabbis comment that no ransom (money) is to be taken for murder, but it is to be taken for the maiming of limbs, and the Talmud does not refute this.

Additionally, the Torah states 'an eye for an eye', and not 'an eye and a life for an eye': losing an eye can sometimes be fatal, and so, if 'eye' meant a real eye, the punishment would not always fit the crime.

Another proof is brought from a seeming repetition. Leviticus 24:19 states that, 'And if a man cause a blemish in his· neighbour; as he hath done, so shall it be done to him.' In the next verse, though, the Torah adds, 'as he hath caused a blemish in a man, so shall it be done to him.' The Talmud concludes that the word 'yinnaten', translated 'shall be done' and meaning shall be given, must refer to money.

Rav Ashi, the redactor of the Talmud, provides yet another proof. He deduces a *gezera shavah* (an analogy between two laws established on the basis of identical expressions in the biblical text) from the section regarding rape: '[the offender] shall give ... fifty shekels ... because he hath humbled her' (Deuteronomy 22:29). Just as the word '*tachat*' ('because') refers to monetary compensation, so does '*ayin tachat ayin*' (an eye for an eye) refer to monetary compensation, since both verses use the word '*tachat*'. *Gezera shavah* is a talmudic model used in cases where two verses use an identical word; the implications of the latter verse can be applied to the former. Rav Ashi's argument is not refuted.

Finally, Rabbi Shimon bar Yochai presents an argument that if 'an eye for an eye' were taken literally, it would be impossible to punish a blind man who had blinded someone. (However, the Talmud refutes this saying with, 'where possible, the law is applied, otherwise it is not'.)

Maimonides Contradicts Himself

Maimonides, in the introduction to his commentary in the Mishnah, writes that there was never any rabbi from the time of Moses until Rav Ashi who ever disputed the fact that 'an eye for an eye' and 'he who blinds another should himself be blinded' means anything but monetary compensation. Similarly, he states in *Laws of Assault and Battery* 16, 'Our ancestors witnessed a monetary execution of "an eye for an eye" in the courts of Joshua, the prophet Samuel, and every other court system from the time of Moses to the present.' In yet another area, Maimonides writes that in the same *Laws of Assault and Battery*, law 3, the Torah states, 'as he hath caused a blemish in a man, so shall it be done to him' (Leviticus 24:20). By this the Torah does not mean that one should be maimed or wounded as he has maimed others, but that he *deserves* to have this done to him. Instead, however, he must pay damages. Maimonides also quotes the talmudic dictum that 'No ransom is taken for murder but ransom is taken for the maiming of limbs', thus establishing clearly that whereas in a murder case the perpetrator is punished with the loss of his own life, in a maiming case a monetary ransom for the life of limbs of the offender is what is taken.

The great length to which Maimonides goes to prove that 'an eye for an eye' refers to monetary compensation illustrates that he was probably engaged in a polemic with those in his day who opposed this view. Maimonides' lengthy arguments against the non-believing Karaites are well known.

It is truly remarkable, therefore, that in his celebrated philosophical treatise, *Guide to the Perplexed* (3:41), Maimonides interprets 'an eye for an eye' *literally*. He writes as follows, 'Do not be disturbed by my interpreting "an eye for an eye" literally . . . my purpose here is to explain a biblical text, not its talmudic commentary. As for the talmudic commentary, I possess an oral tradition.'

An Heretical Statement

This pronouncement disturbed many of the sages. Rabbi Shem Tov asks inquisitively, 'Has not Maimonides taught us that if the Messiah rejected rabbinic tradition to interpret the book of wisdom [the Torah] literally, he would deserve death?'; and he concludes, 'Where has our teacher and luminary gone wrong (may the benevolent God forgive us all!).' Other commentaries such as Akedat Yitzchak were equally perplexed and disturbed at the words of Maimonides. It is possible, however, to postulate an explanation for this mystery.

In his famed philosophical treatise *Guide to the Perplexed*, Maimonides offers a literal meaning of the verse, explaining that in the Torah the punishment always fits the crime: whatever one does will be done to him in return. This is exactly what Maimonides means in *Laws of Assault and Battery* 1:3 quoted above, when he states that 'Whoever bruises or maims someone *deserves* to be maimed or bruised in the same fashion.' In accordance with rabbinic tradition, such a person was *not* physically punished as he might 'deserve'. The rationale for this is given by Maimonides, not in *Guide to the Perplexed*, but in his halachic compendium, *Laws of Assault and Battery*, where he alludes to the explanation he received, as to how essential the words of our rabbis are. Really, this person deserves to have done to him what he has done to another. But rabbinic tradition, which maintains that the Torah cannot allow such inhumane treatment of a human being, serves as the definitive ruling as to how the offender is treated, whether or not he is deserving of worse.

Can a Prison Truly Rehabilitate Offenders?

What Maimonides says here is very significant. Since time began, men have committed heinous crime and generated suffering based on their insensitivity to their fellow men with whom they share this earth. The question has always arisen of how we are to rectify people's misdeeds and uproot crime, acts of assault, battery, theft, rape and murder from our midst.

The solution that has largely been adopted in contemporary western civilization is that of the prison system. A person convicted of a crime in today's world is locked away from society in a penitentiary. The apparent reasons for this are twofold. Firstly, the short-term effect is to remove someone who is a nuisance to society, who may indeed be dangerous and harm others, until such times as he or she learns to better their ways. The second reason is more important in the eyes of contemporary western thinkers. It is rehabilitation: the offenders are removed from society and put in a place where they can be taught to mend their ways and be given the incentive to be released early. Indeed, he or she adopts a new path in life and demonstrates their ability to live in peace with others and to rectify their previous ill ways. It is for this reason that western governments have commonly referred to their penitentiaries as rehabilitation centres or correctional facilities, because the primary purpose is not to rid society of a potential hazard, but to rehabilitate the offender.

Interestingly, the Torah does not offer any punishment in the form of prison: when someone commits a crime they are never locked away from society. The Torah deals with crime in an altogether different fashion whose underlying premise is expressed by Maimonides.

Resensitizing a Deadened Sense of Pain and Misery

To explain, the Torah's punishment for someone who steals is that he must pay *kefel* (double the amount); if a thief stole a watch worth a thousand dollars, he or she must not only return the watch when caught, or give himself up, but must also pay an additional thousand dollars. The reason for this is found in Maimonides' *Laws of Theft* (Mishnah Torah 1:4), 'We do unto him as he was proposing to do unto someone else'. In other words, the idea Maimonides is attempting to impart is that the individual, by virtue of the fact that he has stolen from his fellow man, has demonstrated a general insensitivity to human suffering. The thief apparently did not empathize with the pain which would ensue when his victim discovers that the object he has worked so hard to acquire has suddenly vanished.

From all this, it appears that Judaism believes humans are born with an innate sensitivity, an intuition, for right and wrong, good and evil. This intuition is largely predicated on our ability to discern what hurts us: by extrapolating from the pain *we* feel, we understand the pain our fellow man must feel. For example, one of the reasons Judaic man innately understands not to steal is that he understands the value of his own precious objects and how difficult it is to earn money to buy himself those things he needs.

Maimonides' thief has demonstrated that he is completely insensitive to the value of an object, and the pain caused when it goes missing. What we do in order to rehabilitate the offender is to take away the exact amount of money or the same object from him so that he is resensitized to the idea of loss. Obviously he is pained by the fact that his crime entails paying the identical sum as that he has stolen: the payment will serve to counteract his lack of sensitivity to his victim's anguish. This is true rehabilitation. In this respect, it seems that the Torah's view of rehabilitating criminals is far wiser than contemporary conventional wisdom would suggest. For what leads us to believe that taking a thief, and putting him in a penitentiary with a thousand other thieves, will teach him anything but how to be a better thief? From this viewpoint, the prison system as a correctional facility is intrinsically flawed, for who is to serve as the role model for the convict other than other convicts? This is the other reason why Jewish law opposes incarceration.

Rehabilitation through Rehumanizing and Resensitizing Offenders

For this reason, Maimonides, in the philosophical *Guide to the Perplexed*, takes the verse 'an eye for an eye' literally. In this he is not attempting merely to convey the strictures of Jewish law, but rather the law's philosophical underpinnings. What he is trying to say to the criminal is this: 'Really you deserve to have your eye removed; you have demonstrated while fighting that you have no sensitivity to a person's vital organs and vital human bodily functions; you have demonstrated no sensitivity to them by gouging the man's eye out. What we do is punish you to resensitize you and counteract your inability to feel others' pain, not by doing the same to you but by showing that you deserve the same should happen to you. By this we can counteract the inbalance in your soul and hopefully make you whole again.' What should have prevented him from striking the other combatant in the eye is the thought of how torturous life would be if he himself had to live out his years without an eye. That is the philosophical reasoning and the rehabilitation. But, because the Torah is humane and not sadistic or demonic, it will not allow the actual gouging of the eye from the perpetrator, but rather monetary compensation for the victim which will also serve to rehabilitate the offender because of the pain he will feel from the loss of his own funds.

The lesson from the above is obvious. Even before arguments of goodness prevent us from hurting or offending other people, the mere thought of how much we ourselves would hate the same thing happening to us should prove sufficient to stop us. One should always keep the words of Hillel the Elder before us. When asked to encapsulate the entire Torah into a single precept, he responded, 'That which you hate, do not do unto others. That is the entire Torah, the rest being but commentary' (Talmud Bavli Shabbat 31a).

Is Man Innately Moral?

But this leads to a much broader discussion. The underlying assumption behind the Maimonidean insight is that humans are innately moral and possess an organic conscience, as if we were aware of right and wrong without even being told. From our earliest age, without our parents teaching us better, we understand from our own experiences, our own pain, not to inflict the same kind of suffering on another human being; not to steal from them when we know how badly we hate being stolen from. To be sure, this is one of the ways in which we educate our children: parents with two young children who refuse to share, take away the object from the child who refuses to share and say, 'Now do you see how it feels?' Of course the child cries and learns to share, now that he knows what it is like to live without the object he covets.

This leads to the question of whether Judaism accepts that man is born good. As I say repeatedly throughout this book, the overriding concern of most young Oxford students is somehow to make a better world. That, of course, will only happen when we make a better human. But there are, essentially, two ways of going about it. If we accept that man is innately good, all we must do with a bitter and unpleasant person is remove the obstacles that obstruct his innate goodness from manifesting themselves. But if we accept that man is inherently evil, it is insufficient to place him in a wholesome environment and allow his goodness to shine forth. We must change him through rigorous education and ethics.

It is no secret that the great majority of Jewish individuals in Oxford have been given nothing like a comprehensive or, in some cases, even basic Jewish education. What this often leads to is gross misconceptions about the essentials of Jewish belief. Earlier we spoke of extrapolation. Extrapolating beyond Christianity is one of the most common means of obtaining information about Judaism which most Jews seem to employ. Just by living and being immersed in society, one of course learns far more about Christianity than Judaism. Thus many Jews make this simple error: they assume that if Christianity says one thing, Judaism says the opposite: if Christianity says it is night outside, Judaism says it is day. In other words, many individuals seem to believe that Jewish belief comprises the very antithesis of Christianity, bar the belief in God. Since Christianity, in one of its most central doctrines, that of original sin, seems to believe that man is born flawed and sinful, Judaism must believe that man is born perfect and good.

Man is Not Good, But Innocent

But this is most certainly not the case. There is no single statement to be found anywhere within the Jewish tradition, be it biblical, prophetic, talmudic or embodied in Jewish law, that would suggest man is born good. We do believe, however, that man is born *innocent*, and thus we reject the concept of original sin because we do not believe that man is born in need of redemption or salvation. Rather, man has the choice to do with his life as he pleases: to be good or evil. In fact, there are even statements in the Torah which seem to contradict the concept that man is born good or in a primordial state of goodness, such as 'every imagination of the thoughts of his heart was only evil continually' (Genesis 6:5); and there are other statements which support this view.

Judaism does not suggest we are born into a primordial state of goodness but rather as possessors of an innate state of innocence. Man is not born in need of salvation but neither is he angelic at birth. Instead, he is born innocent, with a whole range of possibilities open for him so that he can choose what shall become of him. In other words, man is born neutral, and he must therefore, in the Jewish view, study and submit his will to Godly teaching and ethical conduct so that he will discern the difference between good and evil and dedicate his life to the pursuit of goodness.

But this just begs the question of what exists that would suggest humanity possesses an untaught sense of morality, an innate way of discerning between good and evil, so that people, of their own accords, would know not to steal. Thus, there seems to be an inherent contradiction in the Jewish view of man. On the one hand Judaism, as expressed by Maimonides, seems to suggest that man is born with the knowledge that stealing is wrong, that certain human actions are unpardonable. On the other hand, from time immemorial there has been no culture, no civilization, no religion, that has emphasized more than Judaism has the need for education. Judaism of course also stresses that an educational system which tries to impart knowledge without values – something which is primarily being offered in today's western schools and liberal arts universities – is ultimately fruitless and will not imbue any proper sense of ethics into its students.

The Humanist and the Altruist

To reconcile this seeming contradiction we must accept that there are two kinds of goodness. One is altruistic goodness which comes as a result of imparting values, educational mores and standards, which comes from parents teaching their children to do the right thing *because it is right*, teaching them to give charity, not because one will be recompensed in heaven or because the person to whom charity is given will one day pay them back or be there in their time of need. Rather, children are taught to be charitable because it is righteous and proper. This is what we refer to as *altruism*, the ability to do that which is proper for the sake of righteousness alone. The ability to sacrifice oneself without any thoughts of recompense or other personal gain. This type of sacrificial goodness can only be handed down from one generation to another. It is not an innate part of human nature, it must be acquired.

Acts of Self-Preservation

But there is another kind of goodness which is not altruistic but rather is best described as an act of self-preservation. This sense of goodness is achieved by examining within ourselves what it is that pains us and by resolving not to do the same to another. No sacrifice or external knowledge on our part is necessary to reach this pinnacle. Rather, it results from introspection and internal examination. Inasmuch as we know ourselves, we also know that there are certain things which we so despise that this itself makes them wrong. In the modern world, this is known as humanitarian goodness and serves as the basis for ethics espoused by secular humanists. We refrain from stealing because we know how much we hate being stolen from. We refrain from humiliating people publicly because we know how badly we ourselves want to avoid being humiliated. One additional corollary is necessary to make this system work: if I steal from Tom, then what is to stop Tom from stealing from me. Thus, by pursuing this illegal course of action, we render the effective workings of civilisation impossible. We understand that if we created a world where people could freely steal from each other, talk behind each other's backs and betray one another, engage in petty rivalries, the world would be insufferable and life would be unlivable.

The difference between the two is clear. Whereas humanism can, at best, inspire a man to *assist* his fellow man in need or refrain from causing pain to him, this is only true so long as the former need not make a sacrifice to help the latter. This is because the goodness itself is merely an expression of self-preservation, based on the theory that if I hurt him, eventually he will hurt me. Since a sense of self serves as the motivating force for the good deed, it is a contradiction to continue this course of action to the denial or detriment of the self. But altruism, based as it is on a Divinely revealed code of ethics at the heart of which is the Will of the Creator, can demand that man make a sacrifice on behalf of his fellow man. It can even demand that he lay down his life for his fellow man, since, in the final analysis, it is God who in the first place gave life. He has the right to specify the ends to which it should be put, even to its negation.

Eternity and Ephemerality

Thus altruism uses spirituality and a Divine imperative as its motivation. Humanism uses human beings as its motivation. The former has its bedrock in Godliness and eternity, the latter in mortal man and ephemeral reality. After all, given that human beings and human society change, it is completely possible, even likely, that what was accepted as being beneficial and detrimental to society in medieval times will not at all be the same in the modern day. Torah law, which does not emanate from human experience, and transcends human designs, is therefore immutable. But humanism, created as it is by and on behalf of human beings, can be modified in accordance with human whim.

It is this kind of goodness, which is an act not of altruism but self-preservation, which Maimonides discusses in the Torah's sense of rehabilitation. The Torah's statement to a thief that 'we will take from you that which you sought to steal is not to teach altruism but decency. This is being done to him solely to teach him the value of another person's property, because from his action it is clear this is a lesson he has forgotten. It is not altruistic goodness we seek to instil within him, but empathy, the very first step in creating a more decent society.

Thus, Judaism recognizes that ethics and morality are the first step towards holiness. Altruistic goodness is holy and is based on what the Almighty set as right and wrong. But empathy for the pain of another serves as the very foundation of a moral society without which the world cannot endure. The difference between the two is the difference between goodness and decency, the latter being the least common denominator bonding two people who both know what hurts and pains them. People cannot thrive and prosper in a jungle. In the words of the prophet: the world was created 'to be inhabited' (Isaiah 45:18). By searching the depths of our soul we are easily able to identify those things which truly hurt. We must ensure we never serve as the agents who visit such pain on another human being. And this is the first and most fundamental lesson a young student about to embark on life should learn.

Chapter Three

DOES HOMOSEXUALITY DIFFER
FROM HETEROSEXUALITY?

In November 1991 I was invited by the Oxford University Medical Society to participate in a panel debate on the subject of homosexuality. The Medical Society is one which caters primarily to the medical students and their faculty at the university but the membership is large and diverse. The purpose of the debate was to help the audience, consisting of young medical students, to formulate their essential professional opinions on the subject of homosexuality. To achieve this objective, the students felt they needed the greatest diversity of opinions and interests engaging in a discussion on the subject. I was asked to represent the Jewish view of homosexuality, and I was told that there would be five panellists in all. The President of the Oxford Gay and Lesbian Society and the President of the Oxford Gay Medical Society would be present, and the other panellists were to be professionals representing their respective approaches within their given line of work. Thus there was me, the rabbi; a Doctor of Divinity who was chaplain at one of Oxford's larger colleges, representing Christian views; and finally a professional psychiatrist whose task was to deliver an unbiased professional assessment of how the mental health establishment viewed homosexuality.

Each speaker was to be given fifteen minutes to deliver his or her opinion, and I was the fourth speaker. The debate took place at St Catherine's College in front of a large student audience and I quickly realized that I had been set up. As the speakers came on, it became apparent to me that I would be the only dissenter. This was partly due to the fact that I was the only heterosexual.

Firstly, the psychiatrist was a militant gay: instead of speaking dispassionately on the way in which homosexuality is viewed by mental health professionals, he began to psychoanalyse all those who are not homosexual, or are opposed to it, explaining the latter attitude as an illness. He maintained that all those who pour scorn and derision on homosexuals do so in order to suppress their own latent homosexuality.

Next, the chaplain spoke. He went to great lengths to damn Christianity's attitude to homosexuality: he advocated a complete change in approach to non-heterosexuality, saying that the Church should begin to view homosexuality as a viable and acceptable alternative lifestyle. In my entire career as a minister of religion, I have never heard another cleric so vigorously disparage his own religion. There he was, sitting in his robe and collar, making fun of St Paul and the Church Fathers ('When one gets right down to it, St Paul's views on homosexuality are really quite silly . . . chuckle, chuckle. . .' It quickly became clear that he was chosen for the debate since he was homosexual himself, a fact he alluded to, but would not publicly avow. Indeed, a few months later he resigned his post as chaplain of his college, citing irreconcilable personal differences with his religious duties.

Then there was me, the last-but-one speaker, and I was about to cause an uproar by my opposition. Because mine was the only dissenting opinion, the entire debate began to focus around me. But my attitudes and opinions on homosexuality are of great importance because I have established long and lasting friendships, over the past five years, with many gay Jewish men who have sought my counsel. It was particularly hurtful to me that other avowed gay men abstained from coming to L'Chaim in the belief that they would not be fully accepted.

By Definition, Sexuality Cannot Be Deviant

My thoughts on this subject, which I articulated at the debate, were developed during some time through many discussions on the subject with Rabbi Manis Friedman, dean of the Beis Chana women's institute in St Paul, Minnesota. Homosexuality cannot be a sexual deviance because the very idea of a sexual deviance is a contradiction in terms. Sexuality is primarily instinctive, and deviation is incompatible with an instinct. Why then should homosexuality be frowned upon? Can we say it is any more objectionable than some of the other forms of sexuality or sexual behaviour that are sanctioned by Torah law? The only explanation we can offer is that it is wrong only because God said so. The Creator of the Universe expressed a preference for heterosexuality and mandated that it alone be practised by humans.

At the conclusion of the speakers' presentations, all questions but two were directed at me. I continually emphasized the point that it was the Torah that gave us the western ideals of morality which have kept people living together, and preserved civilized society, for thousands of years. Therefore, when the Torah frowns upon a certain form of sexual behaviour I believe we must take the disapproval seriously.

At the start of the evening I feared I would be pelted with everything from tomatoes to daggers, but to my surprise, while all the panellists made it clear they could not embrace my position, and would continue in their choice of lifestyle, they also said that my approach was the most acceptable and humane of any religious argument on the subject they had heard. Instead of being the outcast of the evening as I had expected, I was applauded wildly at the conclusion of my presentation. The medical students said they appreciated this approach; it did not make them feel that religion was frowning at them as some kind of anomaly, but rather as people who were perhaps transgressing a Divine law as they would any other law. The following chapter is dedicated in its entirety to this theme.

Intolerance on All Fronts

Before continuing I should mention, however, that interestingly the only people who did not applaud were a few Muslim students in the audience – who later told me I was far too soft on the subject – and the doctor of Divinity, who felt I was being too hard. I think he also felt I was judging him and his approach to religion, which I did not, nor would ever allow myself to do. I am as fault-ridden as the next person and possess no moral justification for looking down on my fellow man. Indeed, subsequently it turned out that I myself was being judged by some Orthodox Jewish groups who got wind of my comments: they too felt I was at best too lenient, and at worst misrepresenting the Jewish view. This response is not unusual: when I was asked by a major Jewish news magazine to contribute an article on my ways of dealing with the most difficult Jewish challenges that arise at Oxford, the entire section dealing with homosexuality was scrapped, without my being informed.

Homosexuality as a Panacea of Life

The issue of homosexuality is an important one for all people, not just those who have to deal with homosexuals, are 'out', or are thinking they may be homosexual. *Every* young person must at some time consider their sexuality and what they intend to do with it. Is it to be an instrument for one particular variety of personal pleasure alone, or is it a part of the whole complement of human qualities that can be used to create a thriving and happy community?

In the course of my duties as a rabbi, students have come to me in great distress about their sexuality. Some are considering marrying non-Jews, some have decided they never wish to marry, still others are pregnant or have got someone pregnant; others have realized that their main attraction is for their own gender. Over the years, I hope that my approach to those who have come to me for help has become as humane and understanding as possible. (I do not use the word 'tolerant', which I find repugnant and connotes 'stomaching' another person's differences.) The main point is that whatever choices one makes in one's life, Jewishness cannot be renounced. God and the Jewish people are prepared to love and embrace every individual, however he may choose to live his life, although there are guidelines set down which are designed to make us happy and to allow our lives to fulfil their potential within the community.

Origins of the Word

A starting point is the word 'homosexual' itself. The present English meanings given to the (originally Latin) prefix 'homo' are fascinating for the insights they give to modern western thinking. The element 'homo' in a word referring to the human species is traditionally interpreted in English as meaning 'Man'. *Homo sapiens* is therefore 'thinking Man', the Man who is supposed to have climbed to the top of the evolutionary tree, the Man we identify with and recognize as human. On the other hand, the element 'homo' in words such as 'homologous' or 'homosexual' is interpreted to mean simply 'the same'. Homosexual love is love for the same gender, as opposed to the apparently more 'natural' love for the other gender that is called 'heterosexual'. It is therefore never suggested that the words 'homosexual love' can only refer to love between two men rather than between two women, nor that 'homosexual love' can be felt by a woman for a man. In this context, the element 'homo' means exclusively 'the same', and not 'Man'.

'Homo' is such a fluid term in modern English that it can convey both a derogatory meaning when applied to those pushed to the margins of society (the nickname applied to homosexuals, 'homo') while at the same time it is our most central and flattering definition of ourselves, homo sapiens. I would like to suggest that awareness of the term's dual meaning (either 'people' and 'Man', or 'the same as') could be usefully applied to broaden our conception of what it means to be human and what it means to be homosexual.

Firstly, it would be splendid if 'homo' were genuinely interpreted as 'the same as me' when used as the definition of humans: 'Homo sapiens', implying to achieve a real inclusion by men (and women) of the other gender in their conception of their species.

Secondly, borrowing some of the connotations of 'homo' in the term 'Homo sapiens' and applying them to 'homosexual' would broaden and humanize the current interpretation of homosexuality. To see homosexual love primarily as the natural act of loving *a person*, someone who is the same as you in the same way that one Homo sapiens is the same as another (rather than as the aberration of loving someone of the same gender), would help mainstream society to accept that there are in fact fewer divides between homosexuals and heterosexuals than are often supposed. This would in turn help homosexuals to be accepted as a part of the whole community, not forced into defining their community as only existing amongst themselves, or for homosexuals to view themselves as aberrations who can do nothing to orient their sexuality.

Traditional Approaches to Homosexuals

The issue of homosexuality is one which has largely been ignored by the Orthodox Jewish community. While various papers have been published offering an halakhic appraisal, I have yet to see a coherent and wholesome perspective being proffered, one which blends into an overall Jewish appraisal of human sexuality. At present, homosexuality in the more traditional sections of the Jewish community is treated as an aberration at best and something deeply shameful, a sickness, at worst.

The problem with this simplistic dismissal of such an emotive issue is its inhumanity. A proportionately high number of Jewish students here at Oxford, as well as throughout the world, are either themselves homosexual or have friends who are homosexual, and this necessitates a humane and coherent message of inclusiveness to be generated by the Jewish community. A recent study by Hadassah, *Jewish Marital Status*, published by Jason Aronson of New Jersey, suggests that as many as eight to ten Jewish men out of every hundred are professed homosexuals, and approximately one out of every hundred women. Even more striking, one of the latest and most respected studies of human sexuality, *The Janus Report*, maintains that 22 per cent of all men admit to having had a homosexual encounter. Of course, there must be many more who would be unable to admit their homosexuality. Just as the world Jewish community would and should never turn away a Jew because of lack of adherence to a specific halakhic precept, so too the issue of homosexuality must never be allowed to be divisive, as I strongly believe it currently is. Many Jewish students have told me they purposely avoid the L'Chaim Centre and our activities because Orthodox Judaism rejects homosexuals.

The Nature of the Jewish Prohibition

Views on homosexuality vary greatly. Although Judaism considers homosexuality to be a sin, this does not resolve the question of whether it is only objectionable behaviour in spiritual terms, or really a manifestation of psychological pathology. The debate continues. There are other possible approaches. Some rabbis seem to concur with the opinion voiced by William Blackstone, a leading eighteenth-century jurist of England, that homosexuality is a 'crime against nature'. To some physicians of the late nineteenth century, it was a manifestation of inherited physiological degeneration. Each conception of homosexuality implies an appropriate spiritual or social response – acceptance, religious penitence, psychoanalysis, or in some cases suggestions as bizarre as imprisonment.

I once sat at a public lecture in Australia delivered by one of the finest rabbinical speakers in the world. The lecture took place in the mid-1980s, and the questions afterwards turned towards the AIDS epidemic. When asked by one of the listeners if the rabbi felt AIDS to be a Divine curse against a sexually explicit generation, he stunned me with his response, 'Who says it has to be a curse? In my opinion it is a blessing.' While some of the members of the audience applauded, a stream of people immediately walked out. He thoroughly alienated the less committed members of his audience. This story is especially tragic because the average person uninitiated in Jewish thought or law will, of course, automatically assume that such is the authoritative Jewish view of the subject. Following the lecture I inquired of my friends who had attended: they told me they assumed his words, coming from such an eminent speaker, represented the definitive Jewish approach to the subject. And this was the second reason it was a tragedy. I knew this rabbi personally, and in every other aspect I can promise you that he was one of the kindest and most caring human beings I had ever met. He just seemed to have no sympathy for homosexuals.

At this point it should be made clear that this approach contradicts everything that Judaism stands for in the form of a good, loving, long-suffering God who asks His creatures to emulate His mercy and compassion.

From my experiences I must conclude that such intolerance is usually caused by an under-exposure to the issue or to the people themselves. One of the reasons I am extremely sympathetic and respectful towards homosexuals is that the problem is extremely close to home. Two of my closest friends whom I grew up with were homosexual, and the cousin I am closest to is an avowed homosexual.

The Humane Jewish Approach

A sympathetic and mature Jewish attitude to this subject must begin with the premise that it is not unreasonable for the Creator to demand that His people regulate their sexual activity. Every civilization throughout history, from the most religious and conservative to the most secular and liberal, has not felt it was sufficient just to advocate certain sexual pathways, but has instituted laws to enforce these pathways.

In an important article on the subject, the contemporary Jewish thinker Dennis Prager points out that one of the first things Judaism set out to accomplish as a religion, contrary to all primitive pagan cults, was the de-sexualization of the Supreme Being, without which organized religion would not have been possible. 'Among the consequences of the unchannelled sex drive is the sexualization of everything – including religion. Unless the sex drive is appropriately harnessed (not squelched – which leads to its own destructive consequence), higher religion could not have developed.'

The first and foremost premise is this: Judaism does not prohibit or in any way look down upon homosexual love. In the eyes of Judaism the love between two men or two women can be as natural as the love between a man and a woman. What it does prohibit is homosexual intercourse.

There is No Logical Sexual Norm

One of the great misconceptions among modern thinkers is the subdivision of human beings into categories: bisexual, homosexual, transsexual, heterosexual ... and more have probably been invented since this was written. In the Jewish view of things, a human being is classified merely as *sexual*. There are no prefixes. People have various outlets for their sexuality which may assume some of the modes of behaviour described by the adjectives listed above. However, rather than these modes of behaviour being seen as intrinsic definitions of a human being's sexuality, Judaism would understand them as expressions or permutations of sexual behaviour, rather than as states of being. In other words, human beings are sexual, and their sexuality is capable of various forms of expression and orientation, depending on society, personal exposure and other factors which may even be genetic and influence one's sexual preferences.

Judaism may indeed accept the notion that certain men, for example, are born with an inherent sexual attraction to other men rather than to women. In a public address on homosexuality, to which I shall refer later, the rebbe, Rabbi Menachem Schneerson, seemed to accept this as a matter of fact. Judaism does, though, reject the habit of labelling these men as 'gay' or homosexuals. Rather, they are sexual beings whose first preference and sexual attraction is for other men. The preference results not from an irreversible genetic condition, but rather from social conditioning and nurturing, although the attraction can be present from the earliest age. This is strongly supported by numerous well-conducted studies into sexuality during the twentieth century. Most recently, there has been the statistic published in *Time* magazine, the source of which is the influential and comprehensive *Janus Report on Human Sexual Behaviour*. A study of men who were confirmed 'heterosexuals' found that 22 per cent had homosexual affairs. Similarly, other studies have found that even 95 per cent of men calling themselves homosexual had affairs with women. These findings hint at the fact that sexuality is much more than a question of preference; it is primarily a question of self-perception. A majority of men who call themselves heterosexual, but have had physical relationships with men, refuse to see their behaviour as homosexual or even bisexual: it is just a part of their sexuality as a whole.

But the greatest proof to the effect that homosexuality is no more an aberration than heterosexuality is shown by history. In the article quoted above, Dennis Prager cites many examples of the widespread practice of homosexuality in virtually every culture and civilization. Unless otherwise noted, these examples are taken from a major work of scholarship published in 1988 by the University of Chicago, *The Construction of Homosexuality*, by David E. Greenberg, Professor of Sociology at New York University. It is the most methodical sociological study of homosexuality throughout history ever written. Greenberg shows how homosexuality was pervasive throughout the ancient world. The uniquely Jewish point of view – the desexualization of God and the channelling of the sex drive – arose in a world full of contrast. Sex actions of the inhabitants of the absolute realms became more valuable than the sexual actions of those of the mundane world, thwarting our spiritual growth. Greenberg writes, 'Other than the Jews, none of the archaic civilizations prohibited homosexuality *per se*.' It was Judaism alone that about three thousand years ago declared homosexuality wrong.

To exemplify the previous remarks, we begin a short trek through the great civilizations of the ancient world, with brief quotes from Greenberg's work.

The Americas: Among the Aztecs, 'sodomy was virtually universal, involving even children as young as six. Cortez also found sodomy to be widespread among the Aztecs, and admonished them to give it up – along with human sacrifice and cannibalism. One of the Aztec gods, Xochipili, was the patron of male homosexuality and male prostitution.'

Ancient Near East: 'In Mesopotamia, Hammurabi, the author of the famous legal code bearing his name, had male lovers. Egyptian culture believed that "homosexual intercourse with a god was auspicious". Having anal intercourse with a god was the sign of a man's mastery over fear of the god. Thus one Egyptian coffin text reads, "Atum [a god] has no power over me, for I copulate between his buttocks." '

Greece: 'Homosexuality was not only a conspicuous feature of life in ancient Greece, it was exalted. The seduction of young boys by older men was expected and honoured. Those who could afford, in time and money, to seduce young boys, did so. Graphic pictures of man–boy sex (pederasty) adorn countless Greek vases.' 'Sexual intimacy between men was widespread throughout ancient Greek civilization . . . What was accepted and practised among the leading citizens was bisexuality; a man was expected to sire a large number of offspring and to head a family while engaging a male lover . . . The male homosexual act usually involved anal intercourse with a boy.' 'Plato makes clear in the *Symposium* that it was perfectly acceptable to court a lad, and admirable to win him.' As Greenberg writes, 'The Greeks assumed that ordinarily sexual choices were not mutually exclusive, but rather that people were generally capable of responding erotically to beauty in both sexes. Often they could and did.' 'Sparta, too, institutionalized homosexual relations between mature men and adolescent boys.'

Rome: Homosexuality was so common in Rome that Edward Gibbon, in his *History of the Decline and Fall of the Roman Empire*, wrote that 'of the first fifteen emperors Claudius was the only one whose taste in love was entirely correct' (that is, not homosexual). 'Greeks glorify and idealize homosexuality, the Romans simply accepted it as a matter of fact . . . Pederasty was just another sexual activity. Many of the most prominent men in Roman society were bisexual if not homosexual. Julius Caesar was called by his contemporaries every woman's man and every man's woman.'

Europe: 'In lists of national characteristics, pederasty was considered the particular distinction of the Gauls.'

England: 'The people of England,' wrote St Boniface in 744, 'have been leading a shameful life, despising lawful marriages, committing adultery and lusting after the fashion of the people of Sodom.' According to Greenberg, this was because 'there was no prejudice against it [homosexuality]'.

Asia: 'During the feudal age, it [homosexuality] flourished among the military aristocracy. A samurai warrior went to battle accompanied by a favourite youth, who also served as a sexual partner . . . Literary sources depict the relationships as highly romantic, sustained by undying loyalty. Sometimes samurai fought battles on behalf of their lovers.'

Arabia: In the Arab and Islamic worlds, 'A de facto acceptance of male homosexuality has prevailed in Arab lands down to the modern era.'

Philosophical Systems

Epicureanism: 'Within the framework of Epicurean philosophy . . . no distinctions were made between homosexual and heterosexual partners.'

Stoicism: 'The Stoics held the sexual function of the body to be morally indifferent, just like other bodily functions – from which it followed that love of men or women was to be viewed strictly from the point of view of expediency.'

Cynicism: The founder of cynicism, Antisthenes, a student of Socrates, 'considered homosexual affairs acceptable provided the partner was worthy, and so did his disciple Diogenes (412–323 BC)'.

After these various observations, Greenberg concludes: 'With only a few exceptions, male homosexuality was not stigmatized or repressed so long as it conformed to norms regarding gender and the relative ages and statuses of the partners . . . The major exceptions to this acceptance seem to have arisen in two circumstances.' Both of these circumstances were Jewish, the reasons for which we are about to explore.

Homosexuality in Youth

Various social studies of homosexual men would seem to support the conclusion that sexual preference for one's own sex is not an inborn characteristic. Many of the men studied were found to possess strikingly similar patterns of relationships during their formative years, such as a detached, harsh, and discipline-oriented father, and usually a mother who compensated for the father's detachment by becoming unusually close to her son.

A lengthy study conducted of male American POWs in Vietnam showed that most of them, having been restricted from contact with women because of many years of incarceration, began to develop homo-erotic tendencies: an overwhelming *majority* engaged in homosexual activity. The same is pre-dominantly true of prison inmates. Greenberg, in his monumental study of homosexuality, also comments that 'high levels of homo-eroticism develop in boarding schools, monasteries, isolated rural regions, and on ships with all-male crews'.

These situations are, as far as the general population goes, highly unusual environments. They are situations where the usual mixture of the sexes does not occur, and where family values are a very minor concern. In his lecture on the subject, the rebbe stated as much by saying that those who prefer homosexual relationships should be told that their sexual preference, although it does not constitute an aberration, would seem to negate the very laws by which the human race propagates itself. A homosexual must therefore be encouraged, the rebbe argued, at the very least to make some effort in the direction of reorienting the sexual attraction he or she feels. They should be told that although they may feel this way of loving best suits them, there is the possibility that they are overlooking some of the benefits of a heterosexual relationship which are simply unavailable in homosexual associations. I shall return to elaborate this argument later.

Do We Possess the Right to Correct Behaviour?

When a parent corrects a child's behaviour, the argument most often used is not that such behaviour is deemed inappropriate by society, but that the behaviour is not what is best for the child. With a significant desire to change, and a society which helps by encouraging change, rather than accepting the child's behaviour, the child can actually reorient its selfish or reckless tendencies from infancy. Similarly, the argument the rebbe put forward did not emphasize any negative associations of homosexuality, but rather the positive aspects of heterosexuality.

Are There Enough Men to Go Around?

In 1990, as part of the International Week of Jewish Woman, seventy students participated in a forum we held at Lincoln College, Oxford, entitled 'Are

Nice Jewish Men a Vanishing Breed?' The subtitle of the event was 'Single Jewish Women Ten Years Later, Their Complaints about Men and the Male Response'. There was a panel that commented on this subject – the participants being Rabbi Shlomo Levin, charismatic leader of one of London's most dynamic congregations; Jennifer Saal, wife of Matt Saal, a Marshal Scholar at Oxford who was one of the L'Chaim Society's founding members, and who married at thirty-one, having survived the American singles' scene; and Rosalyn Baron, a senior financial consultant who became engaged at thirty-two through Rabbi Levin's Jewish singles' group. The purpose of the evening was to address a fundamental problem affecting marriage within the Jewish community: the scarcity of eligible Jewish bachelors. There were just too many nice Jewish girls in Oxford aged twenty-five or over, searching for too few marriageable men. Their despair led to us discussing the problem for the first time openly.

The evening began with me delivering the findings of a five-year study on single Jewish women that was published as part of a Hadassah publication quoted earlier, *Jewish Marital Status*. The statistics told why there are so many more single Jewish women than men. The overall problem is that, as opposed to the general population in which there are now more men than women, in the Jewish population there are simply more women than men. According to the report, there are ninety-two Jewish men for every hundred Jewish women. What the report shows is that in the first three post-World War II decades, the biggest factor contributing to the larger number of eligible Jewish women (as opposed to Jewish men), and made matters much worse, was that there were far more Jewish men than women marrying outside the Jewish community. By the mid-1980s, of those ninety-two Jewish males, thirty-seven were marrying out, a choice that only twelve females took. So males were reduced to fifty-five Jewish men for every eighty-eight women. This is a serious problem, but one on which the world Jewish community has already focused much time and energy. Everybody understands that intermarriage is a problem and there are many individuals and organizations who are committed to doing something about it.

But surprisingly, one of the biggest and often overlooked problems is the number of Jewish men who are homosexual, as opposed to a very small number of women who are lesbian. The numbers which this report lists are at least nine Jewish men of every hundred being openly homosexual, with the possibility that many more are still 'in the closet'. At the same time, there are not more than one or two Jewish women per hundred who are lesbian. Thus, by the time we look at a group of approximately a hundred thousand, the discrepancy has left approximately seven thousand Jewish women without the possibility of a Jewish partner. And while the number may be a bit smaller because of some homosexual men who marry, it still points to a problem of terrible proportions.

Focusing on Communal Responsibilities

This is another element of the argument that homosexual men must look beyond their personal sexual and relational satisfaction. They have to be aware of their Jewish communal responsibilities and the repercussions that their lifestyle choices have: many Jewish women will never have husbands. (This is besides the fact that anyone familiar with the situation knows that women are far more attracted to homosexual men who are found to be unusually kind, loving and patient, and share more in common with women than do heterosexual men.) By making no effort even to try to embrace some of the benefits of heterosexuality, a homosexual man is passively creating an untenable situation for a phenomenal number of Jewish women who will remain alone.

Nature vs Nurture

I would argue that Judaism implies a rejection of the notion, currently being circulated by many mental health professionals, that homosexuality is controlled by nature rather than nurture, and must logically be accepted as an alternative and equally legitimate lifestyle to heterosexuality. This is not to say that homosexuality cannot be genetic, but rather that even if it were it would constitute no more than a natural predisposition towards homosexual tendencies, rather than an irreversible organic state. Judaism is willing to accept that homosexuality represents no more of an aberration than heterosexuality, because sexuality as a whole is naturally instinctive. Not being a contemplative act, it is contradictory to label any sexual behaviour unnatural. However, the Jewish objection to homosexuality is based purely on the fact that God has revealed the forms of sexual behaviour He deems to be holy, and those which are not. This is not to say one form is any more natural than another. It does mean that, besides heterosexuality, God has proscribed all other forms of sexual congress however desirable or gratifying, to humankind.

For all those on the right-wing fringe who argue absurdly that homosexuality is a 'crime against nature', and prove their point by reference to human anatomy and the seeming heterosexual union it would suggest, I ask this: is oral sex or anal intercourse any more natural than homosexuality? And how about masturbation? Is there anything that would lead us to believe that any of the above are any more natural than homosexuality? And if the answer to both these questions is 'no', then why are they only combating 'homosexuality' as an aberration and crime against nature. I put this question to a mean-spirited participant in an Oxford Union debate on homosexuality, who today remains one of England's most popular right-wing journalists. His response was to look inquisitively at me, perhaps to determine if I myself was gay. Seeing the beard and yarmulke, he concluded that I probably was not and then said to me, 'The idea of two men kissing and doing "other things" is the most reprehensible thing that I can think of. We must do everything in our ability to protect ourselves from this disease.' I told him I did not necessarily see the morality or beauty in group sex, for example, and asked if he campaigned as vigorously against that. He just walked off.

Can We Change?

If homosexuality is a product of nurture rather than nature, then there exists the possibility that a homosexual may find sexual fulfilment in a heterosexual relationship. The rebbe's viewpoint clearly expressed the belief that, regardless of one's learned or congenital sexual orientation, one should, indeed must, expend every effort to reorient sexual tendency into something which all humanity can benefit from.

In this respect, there is a twofold response to the young homosexual man or woman who argues that they deserve love in life, which indeed they do, and they did not choose to be this way, but God made them homosexual.

First, God did not make them in any specific way. The homosexual is a sexual being like all others, and chooses his or her sexual preference. While he or she may indeed have been born with a specific sexual disposition, that does not preclude the possibility of finding sexual fulfilment in a heterosexual arrangement, specifically marriage.

Secondly, Judaism does not only concern itself with the happiness of the individual, but with that of the entire society. Even the homosexual has obligations to the rest of civilization which cannot be ignored. Nor does personal contentment and happiness supersede duty to humanity. In this respect, the homosexual is in a similar situation to that of a Jewish bachelor whom Judaism encourages with every power of persuasion to marry. That is an equal obligation that cannot be ignored.

In this scheme of things, acting on the attraction between two people of the same gender would not be referred to by the Torah as an aberration or sexual deviation at all. Rather, it would be referred to as a *sin*, something which the Torah designates as spiritually unsatisfactory and undesirable to God, much as the flesh of a pig is spiritually undesirable. No one could argue that eating pork is a dietetic aberration. It is just as normal as eating anything else. Rather, the only source for its rejection is a Torah pronouncement as to its undesirability in the eyes of God. So too, homosexuality, while not constituting a sexual deviance from the norm (for there cannot be said to be a norm when sexuality is such an instinctive and flexible medium of expression), is proscribed by Torah law, much as a married man is forbidden to all but his wife.

An attraction felt by a man for other men or by a woman for other women would not be described by the Torah as 'disgusting' or offensive. A human is a warm, lovable and attractive being, whatever the gender. Rather, it is *acting* on that homosexual attraction which the Torah forbids in the strongest possible language. A man's sexual attraction to another man would be classified in the same category as being tempted to eat at McDonald's. The Torah is sympathetic to the attraction, but prohibits translating the attraction into action. Judaism opposes pre-marital sex, celibacy, adultery, incest and bestiality. Why should sex between an adult brother and sister be more objectionable than sex between two adult men? And why should 'consensual' adultery not be permitted? Obviously the objection is not that they constitute a 'crime against nature', but that a Divine prohibition has made them morally objectionable. We condemn the actualization of the act, not the urge.

Distinguishing between Motivation and Action

It is most important to distinguish between the act and the motivation for the act. Even those liberal sociologists, for example, who would sympathize with the African-American children who committed rape in the famous episode of the Central Park jogger agree that the action is wrong. They only sympathize with what they would refer to as the uncontrollable reasons for the action, brought about, in their opinion, by the neglect and frustration inherent in the ghetto and inner city. The same applies to the devastating Los Angeles riots that burned large portions of the city. Even those who defended the action referred only to the tremendous frustration experienced by African-Americans in their quest for justice. But none could reasonably excuse the havoc wrought on the city and many innocent victims.

No one would argue that an attraction to a forbidden woman constitutes a sexual aberration. In fact, it may be regarded as absolutely normal for a man to be attracted to someone else's wife. But normality does not render an act permissible. Men are attractive, loving and sensitive beings, and so it is normal for one man to feel an attraction to another. However, its normality cannot remove it from God's list of undesirable actions.

Jewish Society Distinguishes Itself

As before, this approach has the added advantage of being supported by weighty psychological evidence. The psychologist Howard Becker in David Greenberg's *The Construction of Homosexuality* summarized the essence of the perspective neatly: 'Social groups create deviance by making the rules whose infraction constitutes deviance, and by applying those rules to a particular people and labelling them as outsiders. From this point of view, deviance is not a quality of the act a person commits, but rather a consequence of the applications by others of rules and sanctions to an "offender". The deviant is one to whom that label has successfully been applied; deviant behaviour is behaviour that people so label.'

In his study of homosexuality, David Greenberg demonstrates conclusively that throughout history homosexuality was as common, and in many instances more common, than heterosexuality in virtually every culture and civilization: in North America, the ancient Near East, Rome, Greece, Carthage, amongst the Gauls, in Scandinavia, England, Asia, China, Japan, Thailand, and especially among the Arab peoples. Ancient categories of sexual experience differed considerably from our own. The central distinction in sexual morality was the distinction between active and passive roles; gender of the object was not itself morally problematic. The world divided sexuality between penetrator and penetrated.

There was one notable exception to the commonplace practice of homosexuality. That was Jewish civilization. Their restraint from what was widespread sexual practice cannot be said to have resulted from an intrinsic disdain for something seen as repulsive or unnatural, but from the fact that it was prohibited by Jewish law. Greenberg writes, 'Homosexuality was phenomenally rare among Orthodox Jews.' He summarizes the geographic distribution of homosexuality in this way: 'With only a few exceptions, male homosexuality was not stigmatized or repressed so long as it conformed to norms regarding the gender and the relative ages and statuses of the partners . . . The major exceptions to this acceptance seem to have arisen in two circumstances. Both of these circumstances were Jewish.'

What this proves is that homosexuality was as common, as 'normal', as heterosexuality, throughout the ages. But what caused it to be regarded as an aberration, or undesirable behaviour, was only the fact that it had specifically been deemed so in the Bible. Otherwise, it would never have been stigmatized in the first instance.

Society Determines the Extent of Homosexuality

Greenberg makes a point of demonstrating that homosexuality is only stigmatized by society: if a society does not condemn it, then it is perfectly legitimate. 'It is thus the existence of social prohibitions and the response that enforce the prohibitions, that make a behaviour deviant. In a world where no one thought homicide wrong, it would not be deviant, no matter how frequently or infrequently people killed one another, and no matter how immoral or objectively harmful killing is. Deviance, then, is in the eye of the beholder. It is beliefs that homosexuality is evil, sick, or undesirable – and the corresponding efforts to punish, cure, or prevent it

– that make homosexuality deviant. Whether or not these beliefs are true is beside the point.'

Avodah K. Offit, prominent psychiatrist of the Cornell University Medical School, and Coordinator of the Sexual Therapy and Consultation Center of Lenox Hill Hospital, declares, 'In the absence of firm scientific data indicating whether or not homosexuality is biologically predetermined, it seems to me that we should accept it as a choice that people make in much the same way that people decide to become firemen or nurses.' To be sure, there would be many who would disagree with this conclusion. But it does go far in showing the strong diversity of opinion among prominent psychiatrists and a rejection of the biological predetermining view of sexuality.

Although Greenberg is sympathetic to gay liberation, he still feels the necessity to remark, 'Biologists who view most traits as inherited and psychologists who think sexual preferences are largely determined in early childhood, may pay little attention to the finding that many gay people have had extensive heterosexual experience.' Surely the fact that over 80 per cent of homosexuals admit to heterosexual liaisons is proof of a possibility for sexual reorientation, however difficult this may be to achieve. Similarly, a four-year study of 128 gay men by a UCLA professor revealed that 'more than 92 per cent of the gay men had dated a woman at some time, two-thirds had had sexual intercourse with a woman'.

Commenting on the radical feminist Jill Johnson's assertion, in *Lesbian Nation: The Feminist Solution*, that 'the continued collusion of any woman with any man is an event that retards the progress of women's supremacy', Greenberg concludes his study with this: 'By and large it is society, not the individual, who determines whether or not homosexuality will be practised, and the extent of homosexuality in that society.'

This easily buttresses the view that homosexuality is not a deviance, but simply a Divinely proscribed act which becomes wrong because the Torah labels it to be so, and not because it is a minority or anatomically incongruent sexual act. This approach seeks to make the ostracizing or victimization of homosexuals logically impossible, because it recognizes their essential identity with all humans.

Is Homosexuality an Abomination?

Many observant Jews reject this 'soft' view of homosexuality by pointing out that the Torah uses the word *to'evah*, 'abomination', in describing homosexuality. What these individuals, however meritorious, seem to ignore easily is the Torah's use of the same word in describing the prohibition in eating a *sheretz* (creepy-crawly) and other non-kosher foodstuffs: 'Thou shalt not eat any abominable thing' (Deuteronomy 14:3). The same word *to'evah* is used to describe the prohibition of a woman returning to her first husband, from whom she has been divorced, after she has already been married to someone else (Deuteronomy 24:4). Again, the word *to'evah* is used in Deuteronomy 17:1. 'Thou shalt not sacrifice unto the Lord thy God *any* bullock, or sheep wherein is blemish, or any evilfavouredness, for that *is* an abomination unto the Lord thy God.' Similarly, there are many other uses of the word *to'evah* in the Torah which would not depict a social loathing or repulsion of a particular mode of human behaviour.

A poignant example is the many things referred to as an abomination by King Solomon in Proverbs, such as envy and a false heart (Proverbs 3:32, 16:22), or the seven things King Solomon says 'the Lord hates and are an abomination to Him. A proud look, a lying tongue, and hands that shed innocent blood. A heart that devises wicked imaginations, feet that be swift in running to mischief. A false witness that speaks lies and he that sows discord among brethren.'

It would be most helpful if Orthodox Jews could offer an objective view on homosexuality dissociated from their own personal feelings, whatever they may be. If a homosexual comes for advice it is best to concentrate, sympathetically, on the fact that a human being may be in distress, a human being who easily hurts and will in no way tolerate a rabbi who makes moral judgments on their lifestyle. The success of the Lubavitch movement as a potent force promoting Jewish identity as well as social welfare is in no small measure due to its universally applauded and imitated non-judgmental approach, in every aspect of Judaism, and the issue of homosexuality should never be excluded from that openness and caring. More than anything else, this attitude tells the homosexual that their personal life is totally within their own control, and that irrespective of whatever choices they make, they are and will always remain full members of the Jewish community.

Making Room to Embrace Everyone

The advantages to the approach I have outlined above are: homosexuals are not made to feel their preference makes them 'freaks' or outcasts. Secondly, the understanding that every human being is not homosexual or heterosexual, but just sexual, and is capable of reorienting sexual preferences, gives one the hope that indeed the professed homosexual is able to overcome their preferences and in-born inclination to live a life in accordance with halakhic guidelines. The desire of the Jewish establishment should not only be that a homosexual should refrain from sinful activity, but that that person should engage in building a family and in finding a fulfilling life within the holy, heterosexual institution of marriage. Every time an Orthodox representative looks upon a homosexual as being sick, it is simultaneously accepted that the homosexual can do nothing to reorient his or her sexual condition.

To this extent, it may be desirable to encourage homosexuals to see professional guidance counsellors. An Orthodox Jewish psychologist, or someone else who is sympathetic to an Orthodox Jewish lifestyle, might be invaluable in assisting a gay man or lesbian woman to change their lifestyle. Of course, no psychologist can possibly be of any use unless the individual not only desires to change, but believes it is within their capability to change.

Thirdly, it gives the homosexual a genuine belief that, although he or she will be forgoing a lifestyle which at present yields fulfilment and satisfaction, they will not be completely giving up all hope of such joys. Instead they are embarking upon a course that, through sufficient toil, will yield a world which is likely to be even more fulfilling, productive and lasting.

The gain for the non-gay world is also quite substantial. Having been close to a number of homosexuals and having observed them with children, I have always been impressed with the unusual love and patience that a gay man or woman is capable of showing to all walks of life. We need these people as parents. It would be a great example to us all. And the unborn children of this world need to be reared with the kind of love and sensitivity I have seen when my cousin spends time with my children.

Re-embracing Homosexuals in Jewish Communal Life

Despite all the potential for positive action, this does not mean that those homosexuals who find it too difficult to refrain from homosexual life should be discouraged from participating fully in all areas of Jewish communal life. If they point out the contradiction that their private life poses to Jewish observance, and use this as an excuse to remain ostracized, they should be told that homosexuality is a sin like any other sin: because someone eats a ham and mayo sandwich does not in any way impair their ability to participate fully in Jewish life.

I have witnessed too much pain caused to homosexuals by those who claim to speak in the name of God and traditional values. A few years ago there was a student here in England whose father was a Sephardic rabbi. When the boy informed his parents, at the age of twenty, that he was gay, they threw him out of the house and ostracized him completely. As a result of this traumatic occurrence, the boy gave up Jewish observance in its entirety. I approached the father seeking a reconciliation on the son's part. I was amazed to discover that the father was relieved to hear that his son was no longer observant. 'His lifestyle tarnishes and pollutes every *mitzvah* he does. Better, then, that he does nothing.' As if this statement wasn't bad enough, he infuriated me by saying, 'If my son's *neshama* (soul) were able to speak, it would run to the top of Mount Everest and shout to the world, "Please, anyone, release me from this contaminated shell, this body." ' I asked the father if he felt the same way towards his congregants who every Shabbat drove their cars to *Shule* (Synagogue). 'No,' he said, 'it was not as bad.' And yet, desecrating Shabbat in strict Jewish law incurs a penalty. 'Yes,' he said, 'but *my* son will die in this world and the world to come.'

No wonder, then, that once when I walked unexpectedly into the bedroom of this young man, he had the words, 'I hate God' scrawled on the wall above his head. His homosexuality had made him a pariah to his father and those like him. But worse, his father had made him feel that he had lost his God and was removed from his people.

Has the Torah Trapped the Homosexual into a Loveless Life?

The homosexual in question will doubtlessly bring up the argument that the Torah is being unfair, trapping the homosexual in a life lacking passion and fulfilment. They say, 'God made me like this.' But also, the Torah forces the homosexual to live a heterosexual existence, which the homosexual does not find fulfilling. Orthodox Judaism has in fact come under considerable criticism from those who would argue that encouraging a homosexual to marry is deeply unfair, even inhuman, not just to the homosexual, but especially to the spouse.

There are two responses to this. Firstly, the same prohibitions in the Torah apply to homosexuality as they do to a man acting on an infatuation with someone else's wife. The man may argue that he is totally unfulfilled by his own wife and must have this other woman, but this is not an argument that anyone would accept as a justification of adultery. There are certain things which are just plain wrong, regardless of how they affect those who must adhere to them. Would those who argue that Orthodox Judaism is committing an abomination by urging a homosexual to marry, on the grounds that neither partner will find love or satisfaction in the marriage, similarly argue that a husband who claims he has fallen in love with another woman should leave his wife in favour of that woman? Suppose his wife has borne him many children and has now reached middle age. He does not feel that she is as attractive as she once was, and he seeks to find someone new. Is there anyone who would condone such sentiments and action? Here his wife gave him the best years of her life, yet he desires to discard her. For his part, the husband argues that he understands the immorality of his action, but what can he do? 'The woman just fails to turn me on.' In such cases, our instruction to the husband is to make his damnedest effort to be attracted to his wife once again. The fault is in him, not in her. It is he who must change. No one could argue the former – that a homosexual should be allowed to engage in activity proscribed by Jewish law based on his inability to find fulfilment in a heterosexual relationship – without simultaneously embracing the latter, that the husband can find a younger woman once his wife ceases to stimulate him.

The second response to this legitimate question concerns the possibility of sexual reorientation. If it is true that being homosexual is something which we choose, then there is the possibility of choosing something else. I do not seek to be so naïve as to propose that this choice is easy. What I do contend however is that before the homosexual gives up on any possible attraction to a woman, they at least make their damnedest effort. The prospect of a heterosexual lifestyle may not appeal at first to the person being counselled, but the primary concern is not to persuade them to enjoy it this very minute, but at least to try it with a long-term view.

Is There Genetic Evidence for Homosexuality?

The bulk of this essay has seen the subject from the perspective of male homosexuality, mainly because of the bias of research towards investigating gayness rather than lesbianism. I am assuming that the cases are largely similar, but as with the research into gay men, doubts are still raised as to whether sexuality is conditioned or inherited.

Research into homosexuality has recently been conducted in San Diego's prestigious Salk Institute. It was found in post-mortem examinations that gay men possessed a pineal gland, the area of the brain associated with sexual functioning, the same size as that of an average woman, and roughly four times smaller than that of a heterosexual man. If true, this would seem to constitute irrefutable evidence that male homosexuals are genetically different from male heterosexuals. This would indeed be a strong argument against Judaism because the Torah would basically be condemning a homosexual to an unfulfilled life.

Having consulted various experts in Oxford on the subject, with whom I discussed the research, I have been led to believe that there is significant reason to question the conclusions reached at the Salk Institute since the cadavers used for the research were all AIDS victims, the illness having had, as yet, an undetermined effect on the size of the pineal gland. Another problem is that it is unknown whether the size of the gland is a cause or an effect, or an epiphenomenon (that is, a second phenomenon occurring with the first but not necessarily related causally). It may therefore be that the similarity in their pineal gland with that of a woman is entirely coincidental, and is due to the effects of the illness, rather than being evidence of predetermined genetic sexual orientation.

At the present time, the mental health profession has rejected the findings as inconclusive and so no inferences may be drawn from it. Meanwhile, I conclude by reiterating that the humane Jewish approach to homosexuality must be based on a positive appraisal of the benefits of heterosexuality, rather than on deploring homosexuality. There must also be a clear commitment on the part of the homosexual, at the very least, to make a concerted effort to live in accordance with Divine law. Only after a herculean effort has been made in the direction of heterosexuality can he or she make peace with themselves for rejecting the Jewish prohibition against homosexual behaviour.

The Homosexual Gene?

At the time of publication of this article, the world is abuzz with the story of the possible discovery and identification of the 'homosexual gene'. Whether or not this discovery, which has so far drawn a multitude of supporters and critics, will prove to be scientifically acceptable, and what the exact implications of the discovery are, remains to be seen. In the meantime, the media reports that have come to my attention have said that even if the identification of this gene is accurate, it would still not mean that a man or woman is born homosexual, but rather they are born with a greater predisposition, or inclination, towards homosexuality. Nevertheless, the predisposition does not guarantee that they be homosexual. But it is difficult to comment on these findings until more time has elapsed and more information is available.

Chapter Four

RACE RELATIONS AND POSITIVE
DISCRIMINATION AT OXFORD

In 1986, a landmark book of general interest on the state of formal American higher education was published by Alan Bloom, Professor of Political Theory at the University of Chicago. Called *The Closing of the American Mind*, it generated a storm of controversy because it attacked the liberal American education establishment, claiming that educational standards, and especially the standard of students, had much deteriorated during the forty years he had been lecturing in higher education.

I discovered the book during a television interview. A religious British national television programme, *Visions*, decided to do a story on our work in Oxford, with particular reference to my second book on the subject of Jewish messianism. Oddly, they insisted the interview took place in a punt.

Now, in the summer Oxford is a punting city. Oxonians are proud of the fact that punting is a traditional Thames activity, practised for centuries for commerce and, since the nineteenth century, for leisure. The craft was only introduced to Oxford's great rival, Cambridge, this century and, when it was, they chose to punt *backwards*, bow first. For some reason, this always seems to be a great joke for those at Oxford.

The Art of Punting

The ancient art of punting looks, from the bank, a delightfully calm and easy activity, but to accomplish it with grace is rather more difficult. Unlike any other small craft, the punt is manoeuvred from a standing position, with a pole. Matters are complicated further by the Oxford tradition that the punter must face their passenger, who sits in the bow of the boat, so that the person responsible for the balance and steering is positioned in the stern. The first attempt at punting is rather like trying to push a bicycle by holding the saddle rather than guiding it from the front: the punt wobbles all over the river, in a course alarmingly like that of a yacht tacking, until you either fall in or learn how to steer by adjusting the angle of the pole as it enters the water. Once you have this skill, though, there is nothing quite like it. It is so restful to mess about in a boat on a warm, hazy afternoon, and the lush summer greenness of Oxford, with its soft yellow stone buildings peeping through the trees, certainly adds to the experience. Those who are lucky enough have aged relatives who are willing to lend them an old-fashioned wind-up gramophone to play old 78 records of the jazz classics while they eat their picnic and sip their chilled wine.

Punting is such an essential part of an Oxford summer that most colleges own their own boats or have agreements to buy the rights to certain punts during the summer term. One mathematics undergraduate could not bear to be separated from the river when he was supposed to be revising for his examinations, so he hired a punt every day of the week as a place in which to study. He could always be found somewhere along the Cherwell or Isis, as long as there was daylight to read by, his folder on his lap and his pen between his lips as he gazed at the trees pondering infinite lines containing a finite space and suchlike wonders.

Interview on the River

So there we were, a television crew of five people, including the interviewer and myself, all tucked into a small punt winding its way down Oxford's Cherwell River, the small craft uneasily threatening to capsize with its every movement. Even more amusing were the bewildered faces of passing joggers on the river bank who felt that perhaps they had run one mile too many and were beginning to hallucinate.

After the filming, the interviewer asked me if there were any good bookshops in Oxford. *Are there any good bookshops in Oxford?* Oxford prides itself on its great bookshops! The most famous of these is Blackwell's in Broad Street, whose Norrington Room, named after a former university vice-chancellor, is said to contain the most books on sale of any room in the world.

Mission at Blackwell's

As an aside, I should mention that, despite their considerable stock of books, it seemed when I arrived that Blackwell's, at least from my particular vantage point, had a less than adequate Jewish section. It was a chance occurrence in October 1991 that may have helped to reverse this. We hosted the Academy Award-winning actor Jon Voight, star of *Midnight Cowboy, Coming Home* and *The Champ*, when he lectured under L'Chaim auspices at the university examination schools. Jon is a Gentile but very interested in Jewish culture and literature, and he wanted to buy a book called *The Prophets*, by the noted American Jewish theologian, Abraham Joshua Heschel. I took him to Blackwell's in search of it but when we got there it could not be found. We asked a shop assistant but she looked blankly at us. By chance, a member of the Blackwell family was in the shop, being interviewed for television about the rising price of books. I walked over to him, interrupting the interview, and told him that perhaps he would care to include a world-famous actor in the interview to demonstrate the kind of clientele who frequent his store. He was thrilled. Jon took the opportunity to complain to Mr Blackwell about the Jewish section in his shop. Within a week, the store was carrying every Heschel book in print, along with a significantly enhanced Jewish section which remains strong (remarkably strong – they even carry *my* books!).

A similar story dates from the time when we hosted Benjamin Netanyahu, now leader of the Likud Party in Israel, who was then Israel's Deputy Foreign Minister. After having tea at Balliol college, Mr Netanyahu asked me if we might visit Blenheim Palace, the residence of the Duke of Marlborough and birthplace of Sir Winston Churchill (he is a big fan of Churchill). It was five o'clock, the worst time for traffic heading north out of Oxford, and although Blenheim is only a fifteen-minute drive from Oxford, the contingent of four British and one Israeli bodyguards who were protecting him was reluctant to turn on their sirens and whisk him through traffic because it would attract unwanted attention. I therefore suggested it would be a better idea if, instead, we visited the local Blackwell's bookshop as he also loves books. So we wandered into the shop, and it was a sight to see. This very handsome young minister surrounded by a small army of bodyguards and student officers marched in. All eyes were on us as we went into the Middle East section where scores of books, critical of Israel, were sitting on the shelf. I asked Bibi (as he is known) if he saw even one book that he would approve of, but he just smiled.

He picked up one from the second-hand section, written by Lord Balfour, and we went to pay for it. Bibi asked the shocked attendant if they had any more books on Israel. The poor attendant, with sixteen pairs of mean eyes staring at him, replied, 'No, sir. But I promise that we shall get some.'

Quotas and Positive Discrimination

One of the many points for debate in Alan Bloom's best-selling *The Closing of the American Mind* is the assertion that quotas for different ethnic groups along with affirmative action or positive discrimination have led to a breakdown in race relations, specifically between whites and blacks in universities in the USA. He writes: '[The white students] pretend not to notice the segregated tables in dining halls where no white student would comfortably sit down. This is only one of the more visible aspects of a prevailing segregation in the real life of universities – which includes separation in housing and in areas of study, particularly noticeable in the paucity of blacks in the theoretical sciences and humanities.'

According to Bloom, this segregation is the result of the shame and suspicion caused by the effects of positive discrimination and other quota-oriented social programmes. The result, he says, is that blacks by and large tend to keep close to each other and avoid the white students at university. According to Bloom, 'The worst part of all this is that the black students, most of whom avidly support this system, hate its consequences. A disposition composed of equal parts of shame and resentment has settled on many black students who are beneficiaries of preferential treatment. They do not like the notion that whites are in a position to do them favours. They believe that everyone doubts their merit, their capacity for equal achievement. Their successes become questionable in their own eyes. Those who are good students fear that they are equated with those who are not, that their hard-won credentials are not credible. They are the victims of a stereotype, but one that has been chosen by black leadership. Those who are not good students, but have had the same advantages as those who are, want to protect their position but are haunted by the sense of not deserving it. This gives them a powerful incentive to avoid close associations with whites who might be better qualified than they are and who might be looking down on them. Better to stick together, so these subtle but painful difficulties will not arise . . . White students . . . do not believe in the justice of affirmative action, do not wish to deal with the facts, and turn without mentioning it to their all-white or, rather, because there are now so many Asians, non-black society.'

Bloom concludes his section on race relations with a warning: 'Affirmative action [quotas], at least in universities, is the source of what I fear is a long-term deterioration of the relations between the races in America.'

Dearth of Black Students at Oxford

After careful consideration my reaction was to oppose Bloom's position on this issue. My personal support for positive discrimination comes from my observation of the dearth of black British students studying at Oxford. This is little known and I think the university would rather people did not focus attention on it, although recently the university magazine included an article on just this issue. The facts cannot be concealed, though. I have known and become well acquainted with many black students, some exceptionally talented and gifted, but I have encountered very few who are from Britain. I have asked my students and they have confirmed the same thing. They know of a few black students at Oxford but virtually none are from Britain.

This in itself is most peculiar. Even if we were to accept the outlandish supposition that the number of black students qualified in this country for a university such as Oxford is disproportionately low compared with the total black percentage of the population, we would still expect to see a greater number of British black students. But as I said, there are proportionately few. I will not contend, nor do I believe, that the reason is racism. As I have written in other essays about Oxford, apart from one or two isolated incidences I have never encountered institutionalized anti-Semitism or racism in this city or university. I am therefore forced to draw one of two conclusions, or perhaps a mixture of both. Either there are not enough black students who believe they will be accepted if they apply, or those who do feel they are qualified are put off by the paucity and perhaps perceived treatment of other black students, and so refrain from applying. If the latter is true, then their case is similar to that of Orthodox Jews: there are so few of them here primarily because such students prefer to go where they are better represented and better cared for. Thus those observant Jewish students who are good enough to get into Oxford choose to go to Cambridge instead. Because I am sure the truth lies somewhere in between, I have always naturally supported affirmative action. If a significant minority has, through oppression and discrimination, been excluded from genuine opportunity, then the same society which committed the wrongs must undo them through positive discrimination. However, because I respected much of the other material in the book, which is nothing but wise and well-informed, I decided to explore the subject at greater length.

The First Black South African Rhodes Scholar

As I have said, Oxford certainly has far fewer black students than would be expected. All the black students I know, many of whom are regulars at our events and are some of my closest friends in this city, are from abroad, primarily from the United States. There are also a number of African students I have met and who have frequented our society's events. In fact, the first black student I became friendly with was a South African by the name of Isaac who had the distinction of being the first black Rhodes Scholar from South Africa; he was much respected by the other students for this reason, aside from being a talented soccer player on the university's varsity team.

The Jewish festival of Sukkot falls at the beginning of the academic year and a Jewish Rhodes Scholar from Brown University, Katherine Finkelstein, brought Isaac to our *sukkah* (booth) to experience a Jewish holiday and to make him feel welcome. He was a charming young man with whom it was easy to strike up a friendship. Through another Jewish Rhodes Scholar from West Virginia, Brian Glasser (who was simultaneously President of our L'Chaim Society as well as being a member of Rhodes Scholars Against Apartheid, RSAA), I became acquainted with other black

Rhodes Scholars. Brian was a born leader, with exceptional humour and dedication. The conviction he had for the flourishing of Judaism at Oxford, based on his belief in the freedom to be oneself, is what led him to fight apartheid in every way he knew. He did not do so because of feelings of guilt or bleeding-heart liberalism. The other students saw this and as a result they respected his leadership.

Guilt in Taking the Money of Rhodes

Now, one of the lesser known secrets of the otherwise gala life of the Oxford Rhodes Scholar is the guilt many feel in taking the money of Cecil Rhodes. Rhodes was a racist, and although he stipulated that no student would be ineligible for his scholarships because of his race or religion, the selection procedure he instituted in practice excluded blacks, as well as women.

The subject of whether or not it is morally acceptable to take his money is always a subject of conversation amongst the various Rhodes Scholars, but I only know of one so far who has rejected the scholarship. Most argue that the prestige and 'clout' afforded by the scholarship will lend them the opportunity to fight racism and other forms of prejudice, and this is an argument with which I concur. Nevertheless, the Rhodes Scholars are always keen to distance themselves from the ideology of Cecil Rhodes himself. Brian suggested at one point that the Rhodes Scholars should get together, go to the grave of Rhodes in Zimbabwe and collectively shame his grave. It was said as a joke and evoked much laughter, but some present seemed to take it seriously.

Brian used many of the facilities of L'Chaim for the RSAA, and my home was a frequent meeting place. Through these meetings I came to know a female black Rhodes Scholar from Mississippi who had an incredible story of how she rose above a terribly impoverished background to achieve academic excellence. She was the first black Rhodes Scholar from this, the poorest state in the Union.

Relations with Black Students

From then on we easily established very healthy relations with the Oxford black student community. At the risk of generalizing I would say I have always found the black students to be naturally more spiritual than others. This attracts them to our activities and attracts me to them. Ironically, in the light of recent race riots in Brooklyn's Crown Heights, it is my experience that many feel drawn to the warmth of Chasidic Judaism. While the vast majority are committed Christians and have no intention of converting – and we, of course, do not condone proselytizing – they enjoy the very human approach to religion that Judaism has, putting people before doctrines. For example, in 1992 a new batch of Rhodes Scholars arrived, and with them two black Americans, Cory Booker and Greg Gunn. Both were deeply religious but wished to remain themselves, while steadfastly adhering to their beliefs. We spent endless hours discussing possible common ground between religion and secular humanity, and they attended many of the events hosted by L'Chaim. They particularly enjoyed the Jewish festivals, and the two together were largely responsible for the vibrant, joyous celebrations that took place here on Simchas Torah and Purim in 1992 and 1993. Cory is a former Stanford football star Tight End who caught the winning pass when Stanford upset number one, Notre Dame, in 1990, televised nationally in the United States; and on Purim he was carrying four children at once and dancing with them.

Our discussions covered the extremely sad fact of the total breakdown in communication between Lubavitch and the blacks of Crown Heights, and especially the violence which had followed. There was no anger in our conversations, only a desire to extend our friendship beyond its borders and affect our colleagues across the sea.

Common History at the Passover Seder

Yet it wasn't until I invited Cory to attend our Passover *Seder* (supper) that we really discovered how much we had in common, and how senseless the current ill-feeling in New York was. Cory sat through the entire *Seder* and witnessed a people celebrating their release from captivity and their redemption as free men and women. He was deeply moved by all the words contained in the *Haggadah* (*Seder* prayer book). After Passover, he sent me this letter via electronic mail:

Shmuley,
Thanks so much for allowing me to share Passover dinner with you. It was quite an experience and I am still carrying around the Matzo in my stomach to remember it by (smiley face).

In all seriousness though, as I said on the way out, I felt very akin to this celebration – in a sense it made me a little sad to realize how much our two peoples have in common historically but yet how little that helps us bridge present-day problems. Even in looking at the civil rights movement (I have been doing some more reading on the subject this break) the role of Jews as financiers, activists and philosophical contributors to a struggle for justice was overwhelming. Yet today, both of our groups seem to engage in behaviour, and/or take on attitudes which are more indicative of the perpetrators of injustices. Looking back over the Atlantic ocean, I see great imperatives in our country. But very broadly, our country seems to be in great need of healing, both spiritual and physical. Some of the wounds go back to our founding fathers and some are very fresh. My respect for you lies, in brief, in the fact that I see you as one fully dedicated to healing and my hope, my friend, is that presently and in the future our friendship can greatly help us in achieving our mutual goal.

Forgive me for rambling . . .

By the way, I really enjoyed my first ride on your scooter – I hope it still works . . . However, I hear the police have an A.P.B. out on a strange black man riding a probably stolen scooter . . .

Take care, Cory

Indeed, the close association and meaningful discussions which I have with these students is proof that the two communities not only tolerate each other's existence but thrive on it.

The gross under-representation of ethnic minorities at Oxford is a problem that concerns many members of the university, but unfortunately few practical solutions have been suggested and acted on so far. Is it enough simply to say that there is something in the Oxford system that tends to exclude non-white applicants, and to say that we believe this is wrong? Or should we take positive steps to redress the current imbalance? How far are we justified in acting to rectify injustice? Many of our students asked me what I thought the Torah view of affirmative action programmes would be. This was my response. The first step in ascertaining the traditional Jewish view is to explore how the Torah instructs us to deal with those who may be oppressed.

A Severe Divine Warning

'You shall not afflict any widow, or orphan. If you afflict him in any wise; for if he cries at all to me, I will surely hear his cry: My wrath shall become hot, and I will slay you with the sword; and your wives shall be widows, and your children fatherless' (Exodus 12:21–23).

God forewarns against any 'affliction' or ill-treatment of widows and orphans in the most uncompromising terms. An extraordinary degree of Divine wrath will be invoked if the Jewish people do not take extra care to protect and care for these vulnerable individuals.

Interestingly, Maimonides in his *Hilchot Deot* (Laws of Character) formulates the exact instances when this law may not apply. Although smiting or oppressing a widow or orphan deserves severe punishment, there are exceptions to this rule.

The key is to keep a perspective on what the law is aiming to achieve. Its intention is to redress the balance, not to create more injustice by allowing the oppressed to live outside the law. The general principle which Maimonides codifies is that the prohibition only applies to someone seeking to oppress an orphan for personal ends and advantage. If the purpose in rebuking an orphan is for their own good, the prohibition falls away. After all, it would not be right to let an orphan grow up illiterate just because he or she refused to attend school. In essence, the law tries to bring orphans and widows back into the centre of society rather than to push them outside.

One of the examples which Maimonides gives is the case of a teacher who has an orphan in the classroom. Of course there will be instances where, in the interest of discipline, there may be no alternative but to reprimand the orphan, and this is what the teacher would do for any other pupil in the class. Since it is done in the interest of the student, the prohibition against smiting an orphan does not apply.

Leeway in Special Circumstances

And yet Maimonides goes on to rule that even in such circumstances the teacher should be careful to distinguish between his treatment of the other pupils who are fortunate enough to have two parents and this orphan who is not so fortunate.

Even when a teacher seeks to discipline the child and has his/her best interests at heart, the orphan's difficult circumstances cannot be ignored. One must try to give the child extra leeway. If the orphan child is misbehaving, one must remind oneself that perhaps s/he does not have the same discipline at home, since s/he has lost a parent. Perhaps the remaining parent is so preoccupied with generating support for the family that s/he has no time to sit and examine whether the children are learning to be considerate and all the other things that will help them be loving people later in life. This is not to say that such leeway is a licence for orphans to behave as they wish; the purpose is to bring them lovingly to a state where they can be on an equal footing with their peers.

I experienced the need for this kind of tolerance in my second year at Oxford. A woman moved into the city with five young children. She was a single parent, having lost her husband after a long bout of illness. As our two families became closer, and as she and her children began to frequent our Chabad House more and more, she expressed a strong desire that I serve as a kind of older brother to her youngest son. He was eight then and had taken his father's death very badly. Although he was too tender in years fully to appreciate what his father's death meant, he was old enough to notice his absence. Since the two of them had been extremely close, his father's absence left a void in his life.

So, every week, when they came to eat with us on Shabbat, she would place him next to me. The problem was that the boy seemed incorrigible. Now, every Shabbat we have numerous guests who eat with us, often esteemed members of the university. While I was making my utmost effort to talk to those guests, the boy made a circus of everything in my vicinity. He craved my attention so much that he would let no one else get a word in edgeways and spent much of the evening asking me the most obvious questions to which, of course, I had to respond. As my patience began to wear thin, I focused on how unfortunate this poor child was and how, if his father had been alive, he would have had someone else to tell him lovingly that he had to behave. He also would not have been so desperate for the affection and attention of his rabbi-friend. But his present condition rendered him terribly insecure and it was important for him to feel I cared. Had I not constantly reminded myself of this fact, I would never have been able to befriend the boy: I would have treated him as a nuisance, which would have been unjust. In the event, we became very close and I believe that my friendship and affection towards him did help to stabilize his character and behaviour, and he improved considerably. But this came only through setting this principle of Maimonides before me, to remind me of goodness, at all times. It was not easy.

Undoing Injustice

Because the Torah is eternal, its ancient truths have modern application. It is not enough to believe in these principles, as I said to Cory; we must act on them. Debate rages in today's society, especially in the United States, as to whether programmes such as positive discrimination and quota systems should be retained or introduced in order to enable previously disadvantaged groups to advance their educational, social and employment opportunities. This is a highly passionate debate because there are very strong arguments on both sides. Bertrand Russell wrote that, when discussing a question, one is most likely to come near to the truth if one genuinely considers how the opposition may have reached their conclusions, rather than assuming they are idiots. Now, most people agree that we aspire to a just society; the question is, how? For those who oppose, what do they offer in return? And will they also oppose the law set out by Maimonides that orphans and widows, even in an educational setting, must be given special, even preferential treatment?

Who is Better?

What seems clear from Maimonides' principle is that if someone is falling behind the rest of the class, or if they may not appear to be the best possible candidate for the job, their background must be given extra weight. Just as the orphan child's problems at school may be a result of the loss of a parent, the black American applicant, for example, may not appear to be the best candidate only because he or she was not afforded the same educational and developmental opportunities as other applicants. Social and economic background may have prevented them from reaching their fullest potential.

So those who argue, 'This is not the best candidate and therefore why should they be considered before someone else?' are not necessarily making a correct assessment. Whereas one applicant from a privileged background may indeed appear to be more qualified than the minority member before us, it may well be that the latter possesses far greater potential. It is our duty to see that it is developed. This, then, argues that we take an holistic approach to student-candidate evaluation, judging their potential for success alongside their current state.

Alternatively we can say that while it is true this is not the best possible candidate, giving them the job is justice, since we must seek to promote those who were not given the same opportunities and undo the injustices that were practised against them.

Either way, our purpose is to ensure that every stratum of society is always treated in the manner befitting a being 'created in the image of God'. This also means ensuring that not a single fibre of their being is wasted. Human potential will flourish if afforded the correct opportunities and if placed in a conducive environment. Affirmative action ensures that this thought is translated from mere words into action and the policy must therefore be supported.

Chapter Five

SHOULD JEWISH ORGANIZATIONS EVER HAVE NON-JEWISH LEADERSHIP?

When the student members of the L'Chaim Society decided to appoint Cory Booker, a black American non-Jewish Rhodes Scholar, whom I mentioned in the previous chapter, to be one of our two student presidents, the other student members and myself as director of L'Chaim were very proud and felt that Cory's involvement in our activities was a feather in our cap, a source of inspiration to all of our members. Cory received his bachelor's degree in political science and his master's degree in sociology from Stanford University where he became famous as a star player for the varsity football team. Cory was also president of his graduating class and left Stanford with the university's two highest awards for service to the university and community.

Many of Cory's friends were taken aback by his decision to head a Chasidic Jewish organization. To explain his position, Cory wrote the following letter, which appeared in the *Jewish Chronicle* in England, the *International Herald Tribune*, and as an opinion editorial in the *New York Times*:

23 August 1993

Dear Sir,
I was pleased to read in last week's *Jewish Chronicle* that the black and Jewish communities of Crown Heights are reaching out toward one another as a result of the rescue of a black woman by a Chasidic rabbi.

Shmuel Boteach is a young Lubavitch rabbi and I am a young black male. In the United States it is doubtful that our paths would have crossed. Rabbi Boteach attended Rabbinical Seminary in Crown Heights and admittedly in those days was completely uninterested in and apathetic to the black youths in his home town. I grew up 30 minutes outside of Manhattan in New Jersey. My exposure to Chasidic Judaism was very small and my view of Jews reflected the long, often rough, road of black–Jewish relations. As a boy I would often hear about the Jews 'who own everything' or would very simply hear them referred to as 'damn Jews'. While my personal relations with less Orthodox Jews greatly tempered my internalization of these pronouncements, they were still continuously supplemented by the statements of black leaders and often shocking events in the city.

I left for college on the West Coast viewing New York Chasidic Jews as strange extremists who were dangerously narrow-minded, prejudiced and insular. Eventually, Stanford led me to Oxford, England, where I arrived last October on a Rhodes Scholarship. Within a month I was introduced to Rabbi Boteach through a mutual friend. Admittedly, I found our first meeting awkward and I was suspicious of how I would be received and of his initial kindness, but within an hour our conversation raced and we agreed to meet and talk further.

In our subsequent meetings, we discussed issues concerning Israel and the Palestine question, examined Jewish philosophers and black thinkers and explored the realities of race and religion in America. We have exchanged writings, shared meals, recently I have even become co-president of the Oxford L'Chaim Society, but most importantly we have developed a friendship.

And what have we gained? A relationship which thankfully goes beyond shallow cries for tolerance. I have come to see tolerance as a spiritually defunct state. Rabbi Boteach aptly states that 'Tolerance is really a repugnant state of mind. Rather than find any redeeming virtue or positive element of another person, we tolerate, or bear them. We stomach, or suffer, their right to be different. There is something immoral about this approach.'

Reflecting upon my past and the city that both Shmuley and I know best, I can't help but dwell upon the words which W. E. B. Du Bois stated in 1903, 'In a world where it means so much to take a man by the hand and sit beside him, to look frankly into his eyes and feel his heart beating with red blood; in a world where a social cigar or a cup of tea together means more than legislative halls and magazine articles and speeches – one can imagine the consequences of the almost utter absence of such social amenities between estranged races, whose separation extends even to parks and streetcars.'

I need not imagine the consequences of social sequestering, for I fear that I see them within New York city and elsewhere in America and I fear that scarcely six years ago Rabbi Boteach and I, upon meeting, may have been engaged in something far different than intellectual commerce. The efforts of reconciliation by some black and Jewish leaders of recent times as well as the highly beneficent act of Rabbi Shemtov have been greatly inspiring. While these steps are certainly promising there are still a host of negative events and attitudes which desperately need to be overcome. Until then I fear that our peoples, in relation to each other, seem to be caught up in Booker T. Washington's barrel of crabs. A barrel strewn with prejudice and misconception, with each crab, while ardently clawing to get out, pulling the others down with them.

Earlier this year, during Passover, I shared Seder dinner with Rabbi Boteach. As he stood before the large table recounting the story of Moses leading his people out of bondage, I could not deny the poignant feelings of kinship I felt with the people around me, for I had heard this story celebrated before. I heard it celebrated in the songs of my ancestors. Songs sung about Pharaoh, Moses, the Promised Land and struggle. It is painfully obvious that the black struggle continues in America today. Yet, while blacks are grappling with many different community issues than Jews are, I believe Rabbi Boteach and I have come another step closer to realizing fully that we are part of a common humanity, all with the capacity to make worthwhile or detrimental contributions to a common destiny.

Sincerely,

Cory A. Booker
The Queen's College
Co-President, Oxford University L'Chaim Society
Oxford, England

I thought the letter was beautiful and was therefore very surprised that on its publication in the *Jewish Chronicle* there was severe criticism from certain Jewish quarters. Perhaps even more surprising was from where that criticism arose. On the one hand, there was a group of leading Orthodox rabbis in London who felt that it was inappropriate for a non-Jew to be the head of the L'Chaim Society. On the other hand, many of the largely non-observant Jewish students at Oxford complained that they wanted the L'Chaim Society to be a haven from the non-Jewish world, where they could be in totally, or at the very least predominantly, Jewish company. They felt, therefore, that it was inappropriate for our leadership to be non-Jewish. In a radio debate on the subject of homosexuality, I was even attacked by a leading Orthodox rabbi who told me that it was no wonder I took a 'soft' approach to homosexuals when I am the same rabbi who allowed a non-Jew to head a Jewish organization.

This is my reply to explain our motivation and the reasons why Cory became our president.

An Obsession with Goodness

I have always been obsessed with the concept of goodness, and have always seen one of the main functions of religion as being to bring out the good in people. The reason for this on a personal level is that whereas religious observance has been relatively easy to achieve, goodness has never come easy to me. Whereas I have always found it easy to keep kosher, to keep the laws of Shabbat (refraining from eating cheeseburgers in McDonald's and hopping into a taxi on Shabbat), I have always found it very difficult to curb my temper when I feel that someone has wronged me; to smile and be the first to greet every person to walk into my office even when I have had a terrible day and feel miserable (which is an important dictum in the Mishnah); to give my children the time they deserve, having taken on the responsibility along with my wife to bring them into the world. Therefore I have an obsession with making myself a better person, and this passion I bring into my Judaism as well. Although I am far from, as yet, being totally successful, it remains my constant goal.

My affirmations and guiding principles in life can be summed up very simply: first and foremost, I believe there is a God, and this is the first point of knowledge that man must have. Secondly, I believe as a natural result of that knowledge, humankind must lead a good and moral life, a life dedicated to the pursuit of goodness as defined by the ultimate arbiter of goodness and ethics, the Almighty. Anyone who has ever read any of my essays, which are distributed to approximately a thousand local students weekly, to about two thousand Jewish families in London monthly, and also disseminated internationally through the Internet computer services to readers in twelve countries, again weekly, will notice that all my essays are on this subject. I have always found it very difficult to bridge the gap between writing about goodness and actually implementing it in my own life; in the modern vernacular, to practise what I preach.

In the light of the above, when I do find an individual who not only preaches goodness, but actually lives by it, that to me is a very special person who embodies everything that we at L'Chaim are trying to achieve, and so becomes an inspiration to everyone around him, including myself. Such a person is Cory Booker. The first moment I met him, he gave me such warmth, an openness and a non-judgmental approach, that we immediately became friends. Being from the black community, he had heard from other black students about what Chasidic Judaism might represent, and about the deep animosity and divisions that exist between the Chasidic and black communities in New York, and yet he judged me as a person, as an individual. We met on Simchas Torah, the annual Jewish celebration of the completion of reading the Torah, when he came to pick up a friend who was with us on the night. It was a very jolly atmosphere; we were drinking and saying *L'Chaims*, and I invited him to stay with us. He showed no reluctance or hesitation, and there was an immediate friendship.

Respect for All Humanity

Amidst the criticisms I heard later, especially from Jewish students who told him that Chasidic students are overly strict about their religion and are racist with no respect for Palestinians, Cory never accepted anything without discussing the issues with me first. When I refuted these objections, he was prepared to accept the truth, even to the extent of bringing those people who didn't like us or who had never even met a Chasid, along to our meetings to see for themselves what the L'Chaim Society was about. Although this is less important than our friendship, Cory has also served as a tremendous source of recruitment for the L'Chaim Society, especially among the Jewish students who have never been exposed to what we are trying to achieve, and who had a natural ambivalence because of parental or societal prejudices about coming to an officially Lubavitch organisation.

Cory's strengths, and the reason for his continuing success in life, are far more than achievements such as already serving as a football hero, playing in many nationally televised games, and being a student president of Stanford University. His greatest strength is his personality; his love, his caring attitude, his constant refusal to judge other people or to say a bad word against anyone. He has never once criticized or complained about another person, far less betrayed a friend, in my presence. He will always seek to come and cheer me up when I am down. I have never met anyone who has had a bad word to say about him, and the reason, I believe, is that he has never had a bad word to say about anyone else.

I once complained to him that some of the Jewish students don't give me a fair chance, or a fair hearing. It seems that in certain quarters I can't just do my activities and my work here in Oxford without first dispelling their preconceived misconceptions about what I stand for. They see me not as a person but as a cog in an institutional machine. Cory was very surprised to hear my complaint. 'Shmuley,' he said, 'you're the one who always teaches about love and acceptance and non-judgmentalism, so how can you do the same thing? If you always show people love and caring and warmth, then they're bound to reciprocate and reflect that love – maybe not the first time, or the second, but eventually.'

Those words have had a tremendous impact on me and my dealings with these students.

'I am not a Fundamentalist'

That Shabbat evening, I went to pick up Cory outside Queen's College and I couldn't find him. A young female Scottish Jewish student came over to me and said 'Good Shabbat' and kept on walking. So I stopped her and asked her if she was Jewish, she said yes, and I asked her if she had heard of the L'Chaim Society. She said that she had heard they had many great speakers but had never attended. I invited her to come along to the speaker meeting we were having that evening but she said, 'Sorry, I won't come to L'Chaim because I'm not a fundamentalist.' It was a very rude and arrogant remark, and one which normally would have provoked a very hostile reaction on my part. But because of the conversation with Cory the previous night in the same location, I decided to do it differently. I went after her and said, 'Just hear me out. You may not be a fundamentalist, and I don't believe I am either, and in fact what's interesting is that L'Chaim attracts very few observant students; most people who come are non-observant students or non-Jewish, because we are not proselytizing. Rather, we seek to provide a home from home, a place where people can be comfortable and receive warmth, and study Judaism if they so choose. But our agenda is universal because above all we try to impart goodness.' She was very surprised that after her arrogance towards me, I was still very friendly; I wished her Good Shabbat and walked away. She then ran after me to wish me a Good Shabbat too. I would not have acted like this were it not for the conversation I had had with Cory before.

Conversely, but in a similar vein, once on a Saturday morning I was running late to synagogue. Everyone was waiting outside for me (not an uncommon occurrence), as I had the keys. As I galloped through the street with little time to spare, I was stopped by a black Rastafarian man on a street corner. He was smiling from ear to ear and said 'My name is Slim. Today's my birthday, and I see that you, my friend, are Jewish.' After noticing my special Shabbos attire complete with long black kaftan and black Chasidic hat, this was painfully obvious, and I jokingly said to him, 'How did you figure that out?' In a friendly manner, I tried to excuse myself because of my tardiness to the synagogue. But, he pressed me, 'I have a question for you,' he said. 'You claim to be Jewish and you want to be a real Jew. So why do you reject the belief in Jesus as the Messiah.' So I said 'Slim, really this conversation is beyond the scope of what I now have time for . . . but I would quickly answer you that Jews don't believe in Jesus as the Messiah because he never fulfilled the traditional Jewish prophesies. Furthermore Judaism rejects any belief in the corporeality of God, and therefore we cannot accept that Jesus was divine.' Slim responded to me with disgust, 'Well in that case you are not a real Jew,' and he hurried off. Normally, I would have been angered by this encounter, but I stopped to consider how Cory would have reacted in such a situation. I decided to pursue Slim. I ran over to him as he was a half block away from me. I caught up with him: 'By the way, Slim, have a very happy birthday.' He saw the decency of my gesture compared to the treatment I had received from him, and he put his arms around me. 'Thanks, man, you've really brought joy into my day!'

So for all those critics who don't understand why Cory Booker, who is not Jewish, is a president of the L'Chaim Society, it is because he embodies the aims and goals that the L'Chaim Society seeks to achieve. And in general, this is the foremost priority on the Jewish agenda. A nation that that was meant to serve as 'a light onto the nations' must teach goodness and decency, within a Godly framework, to the outside world. Cory is a good, decent human being who never shies away from doing a favour for another person, who is always prepared to give people his time, and who has done umpteen favours for the L'Chaim Society. Some of the largest things may be those which people do not even know about. For example, our educational director Avraham Dubosky and I had to build the Sukkah ourselves, but I simply did not have the time since it was the beginning of term, my busiest time, so Avraham would have had to do it by himself. But Cory came along and spent a whole day banging nails into wood, assembling the Sukkah. Every week he comes to help with the mailings, posters, and negotiations with other societies with which we collaborate.

This therefore is why Cory is one of our two student presidents. The L'Chaim Society is not just a Jewish student organization: it is an organization that seeks to promote the beliefs that there is a God, and that now that we know this, we have to be good, decent people, ushering in the Messianic era, an age in which all people are happy for another person's achievements rather than being threatened by them, in which they are not judgmental, and are constantly seeking to enhance the quality of other people's lives. Cory embodies these aims. We are proud to have him as our president, and I believe his presence has done much even to change my natural doubts about the world's evils, and my feeling that amidst my considerable effort in promoting a message of goodness (and trying to live by it myself), I am just banging my head against a brick wall. He has always given me encouragement in the faith that what I was seeking to achieve would one day take place. In that respect, Cory joined me as a partner; I have gathered from Judaism a vision of the way in which the world can be better, and Cory has actually implemented this in his everyday life. I shall always respect him, and shall watch and applaud with great affection the great things I am confident he will achieve during his life, with all humankind as his beneficiaries.

Chapter Six

PORNOGRAPHY AND PASSION IN JUDAISM

Oxford is too small a city to have its own full-blown red-light district, but what it does have is a couple of underprivileged-looking pornography shops which, oddly enough, are both across the street from the Chabad House. Considering the location, this in itself is not surprising, as we shall see.

Before we opened the Oxford University L'Chaim Society Jewish Student Centre in the middle of the city itself, our first presence in Oxford was in an ordinary family house. Now, there are no houses to be purchased in the city centre since those are lands owned by the colleges of the university for hundreds of years. The only buildings to be found in the centre of Oxford are the colleges themselves, churches and shops. (It goes without saying that there is also a pub on every street corner, a common facet of British town life.) So we bought the next-best thing for our Chabad House, which was a family home in East Oxford on the Cowley Road, about a ten-minute walk from the main centre.

Welcome to Cowley Road

Cowley Road is probably the most diverse and interesting street in Oxford. There's the Inner Book Shop which deals with alternative medicine, meditation, green publications and the like, the Bangladeshi Mosque, scores of Tandoori, Jamaican and Halal restaurants, many second-hand clothing and bookshops, an anarchist tea house, bead shops, avant-garde cafés, the Jehovah's Witnesses' Temple and of course Oxford's only two pornography shops. It made perfect sense that the city's first Chabad House should open in this colourful and multi-cultural district, and we fit in perfectly. Cowley Road itself is a pretty beaten-up part of town and the essential reason for its original existence was as an extension of housing needed for workers in Oxford's famous Rover (formerly Morris) car works, which are found in Cowley proper.

Cowley Auto Works

The works were at their peak of influence in the second and third quarters of this century. William Morris had hit on the innovative idea of making a cheap but reliable car that would appeal to the ordinary person, but his master stroke was to slash the prices of his cars during the recession after the First World War. When other manufacturers were trying to keep prices up to sustain profit margins large enough to survive, Morris made his car even more accessible to the middle-income groups. His sales rose so much that he could buy parts cheaply and in bulk: cars had never been so affordable. Today, although the works have suffered in the industrial decline that has affected the whole of Britain, they still employ a significant percentage of the working population while the rest of the city shows a significant interest in the goings-on at the factory.

The works at Cowley are the biggest reminder that the city does not rely on the university for its status, whatever the guidebooks may imply. The day-to-day reality is, of course, that Oxford is famous for its university but the city would easily survive without it. Therefore Cowley Road, which directly links the ancient city centre to the modern Rover factory, is important physically and symbolically.

Living in Proximity to One's College

For example, students have traditionally lived as close to their colleges as possible, and one of the university statutes enforces this, stipulating that no undergraduate may reside beyond a seven-mile radius of Carfax in the centre of town. Recently, though, students have increasingly found accommodation in Cowley Road, away from the town centre and the majority of colleges. It is relatively inexpensive and the Bohemian atmosphere in the area appeals to many young people: shops and nightclubs stay open extraordinarily late, food and clothes are exotic and unconventional, and there is often a distinct aroma of cannabis as one walks past the small urban park.

Narrowing the Gap Between Town and Gown

However, this influx of students has been interpreted, by long-standing inhabitants, as an invasion. What was once a close, working-class community has been transformed into just another extension of the university. Although there are of course the usual town–gown clashes, so much a staple of historic Oxford, the townspeople's response is not intrinsically hostile, it is more an expression of loss. The one area of the city that remained a potent symbol of the old-style working-class ethic (a man works hard to earn money to feed, house and clothe his family, and everyone stands by their fellow workers and neighbours) has fallen to the alternative values of the university.

The common conception among many of the working-class is that the university is a world of privilege; the government pays for clever and relatively well-off people to study and lead active social lives, and generally 'laze about' for three years, or so it seems from the outside. Ever since my *yeshivah* days when I was supported by my parents while my brothers and sisters worked for a living, I have learned that the average worker does not accept that studying constitutes 'real' work. The student invasion of Cowley Road may well mark the death of the ancient separation between townspeople and students, but we cannot expect assimilation to be entirely painless.

At the moment, however, students and townspeople live in uneasy but relatively peaceful proximity in Cowley Road. Both listen with the same incredulity to the self-styled 'Wise Old Man', a local character who wants everyone he meets to send him the names, addresses and photos of their young female relatives and friends because he says he has been enlightened to the fact that the best marriages are between experienced mature men and very young (about thirteen to fifteen is apparently the ideal age) women/girls. Both buy exotic pickles, spices and Basmati rice cut-price from the friendly shops such as Daud. And both speculate about the rumours that certain pubs are IRA meeting houses and strongholds.

Dark and Private

Returning to the two pornography shops, I should point out that they are both very low-key, standing just one block away from each other as though huddling together for comfort. One, The Private Shop, has no windows and is a strange shade of blue. The other, Adult Book Shop, is directly across the street from Chabad House and advertises itself as selling 'marital aids'. The shop front is entirely of dark glass covered by iron mesh, impenetrable to passing schoolchildren who try to peer through the glass.

The Women Window-Smashers

On one of our first mornings in Oxford I discovered the reason both shops guard their windows so charily. We were startled, while eating breakfast, to hear a terribly loud crash. I ran outside to see the entire glass front of the Adult Book Shop smashed to bits. I have since been told that this had happened many times, and The Private Shop had had its shop-front damaged so many times that the proprietors decided to leave it boarded up with wood.

The window-smashers are radical and not-so-radical feminists and parents' organizations who feel the shops are a cancer in the heart of Oxford. Since the shops are still there after quite a few years of concerted harassment, these groups have tried other tactics, too. Probably the most successful was to videotape every person who walked in, which served as a deterrent to customers until both shops set up rear entrances.

Now, to be honest, the shops are fairly unassuming. Moreover, although

I have not, as yet, been inside, a student who went there to buy me a not-very-amusing birthday present (and which was found to be quite tasteless by most of the people who attended my surprise twenty-sixth birthday party put on by the students) told me the shop is pathetically boring: nothing but shrink-wrapped plastic erotica and magazines, and it was certainly not very threatening.

The women in Oxford, particularly the students, often find the idea of a shop selling pornography, however pitiable its merchandise is in reality, offensive and demeaning. They have made a general crusade against the two shops, which continue to defy their various tactics. Because of this, and because pornography is seen as an important issue in society (with the campaigns of the likes of Mary Whitehouse achieving particular notoriety), I am often asked what the Jewish position on pornography is. This question is particularly pertinent in Oxford since, believe it or not, a high percentage of the male students' twenty-first birthday parties feature strippers or dancers popping out of cakes. This seems at once to delight and offend an equal number of both religious and totally irreligious students, depending on their personal orientation.

Tools to Replace and Not Regain Passion

Firstly, Judaism, as one might expect, tends to oppose pornography, but not for the reasons one might expect. It is not because Judaism toes the prudish line of the religious 'right', opposing pornography purely because it is indecent and immoral. Nor does it take the moral 'left', which argues that it denigrates human sexuality and primarily degrades women. Although *all* these things may in fact often be true about pornography, they are not the root of the problem. The fact is, Judaism supports those things which lead to the enhancement of passion and romance between a married couple, and opposes those which lead to a replacement of passion. However, in most cases, pornography serves not as a means to enhance the sexual excitement of a couple, but rather as an end in itself. And because of that the other problems – indecency and the denigration of women and sexuality – are allowed to flourish.

For example, one of the most precious and important laws within the Jewish guidelines to love-making is that no spouse can think of another individual while making love. If they do, then essentially they are violating the most precious gift given by God to us, the gift of human intimacy. What kind of intimacy is it when you use someone's body as a mere form of friction for self-gratification while you are thinking about, and being excited by, the thought of someone else? There can be no greater degradation of another human being than to replace them with someone else in the mind's eye during the most intimate human behaviour.

In other words, even if the thought of another woman might theoretically get a husband more excited during love-making with his wife, Judaism would not, could not, allow this, even if it led to heightened pleasure in their love-making. The reason, of course, is obvious. These thoughts do not serve as a means for this man to love his wife more. On the contrary, they serve as ends in themselves whereby his wife is completely blocked out of the picture.

Bringing Couples Closer Together

Judaism opposes all kinds of sexual activity which are not an expression of human intimacy or that do not bring a husband and wife closer together. It supports all kinds of external aids, even erotic and bizarre, which enhance the love between husband and wife while preserving sexual modesty. Therefore, Judaism would indeed advocate a wife buying the sexiest lingerie to excite her husband. I even know of a very respected rabbi who, when a husband told him he was losing sexual interest in his wife, suggested to the man that he should obtain whatever sexual aids would lead him to feel more interested. The rabbi said he should try anything within the framework of Jewish law, which is amazingly liberal in what it allows between husband and wife to enhance their mutual passion. The Talmud says that 'a man may do with his wife whatever sexual acts please them', although one must refrain from the purposeful and deliberate destruction of semen (seed). In this respect, Judaism does not oppose pornography, *per se*, but would rather redefine pornography as any form of explicitly sexual material which serves as an end in itself, rather than as a means to achieving enhanced closeness and excitement between two legitimate sexual partners.

Pornographic Videos

An example of this radical redefinition of pornography is the following: while Judaism would allow for marital aids, sexy clothing, new techniques and the like, it would oppose sexually explicit videos. While the former enhances the eroticism of one's partner, the latter replaces it. If a couple watch a pornographic video while making love, they are focusing on that video as the source of their excitement, instead of on each other, and it is those external images which serve as the origin of their passion. While it may indeed excite them, it does not bring them, in any way, closer together, which is what Judaism sees as the purpose and glory of the sexual encounter.

Sex for Pleasure and not Procreation

This constitutes an important rule of thumb. Many people make the mistake of assuming that Judaism, along with other morally assertive religions like Catholicism, only advocates sex for the purpose of procreation. This is entirely false. While Judaism obviously recognises sex as a procreative act, this is just one of its facets.

Judaism sees sex as the ultimate form of human closeness, unity and intimacy, and so precious is this and so susceptible to abuse that it should not be shared with a stranger. Just as you will only share your closest secrets with someone whom you trust and to whom you are devoted completely, so it should be with sex, but infinitely more so. Sex is something that should be shared only with the person to whom we wish to be absolutely closest and with whom we feel good, so that we stay with them for ever. The more it is shared with people with whom we don't feel that kind of closeness, and the more it is done with a multitude of partners, the less effective it later becomes when it is most needed, when that very special person does come along. Sex with many partners becomes like a secret told to too many people. It is no longer a secret and is no longer interesting or special. If indeed sex is the ultimate expression of love, which Judaism certainly believes it is, then we should consider this: How effective an expression of love is it if you tell one person that you love them and only them, but then you find someone else that you want to say 'I love you' to, and another and another and so on? The love which you are trying to express becomes meaningless. And the same is true with sex outside marriage. It cannot mean the ultimate expression of love, but rather the vain pursuit of pleasure and conquest.

Glue Bonding Husband and Wife

Sex should be seen as the very glue which binds a husband and wife together. As long as a couple looks forward to moments of intimacy, then their marriage is still fresh and young. But the moment they become indifferent to their most private encounters, or worse, they share that intimacy with people outside the marriage, then the death knell has been rung for their marriage and something must be done right away.

Marital Aids

Now here, as above, Judaism would support any sexual aids that enhance their passion, which is why, if the shop across the street from us could truly become what it purports to be, a *marital aid* shop, then the existence of such centres should be applauded. Anything which helps keep a husband interested in his wife, and a wife interested in her husband, is praiseworthy. We all have to be realistic about the difficulty of maintaining passion in a monogamous relationship in which one has the same sexual partner. Anything that can be done to help focus sexual energy on one's partner, or make love-making exciting and new, must indeed be done. While intrinsic and internal causes for passion within marriage can of course be said to be far superior to external and artificial aids, this does not in any way limit their assistance in certain circumstances or relationships.

But the type of pornography which replaces one's sexual partner as the source of passion, with magazines, videos or even mental fantasies, must be avoided. We have sex with them and not with our spouses, and then our spouses are just being used and degraded, treated no better than a lifeless piece of flesh. This is where Judaism concurs with the aims of the feminist groups in Oxford who oppose the Cowley Road shops: both aim to channel human sexuality away from abuse and towards respect.

Let's be honest with ourselves. If indeed we abuse our sexuality and replace it with partners outside marriage or with pornographic excitement, or indeed with masturbation, what recourse is left to us as human beings to achieve unity with someone we love? The act of becoming one with the person we eventually choose to live with will be all but lost to us.

Masturbation in Jewish Law

It is for this reason, for example, that Judaism discourages masturbation. It is not just, as is commonly assumed, due exclusively to the prohibition of the wasting of seed (as recorded in Genesis 38:9, 10) because this would not explain the fact that Judaism also discourages female masturbation. Rather, the reason is that masturbation is a form of sexual gratification without a partner; it doesn't bring one closer to anyone else, and in that sense it is an abuse of sex. It is a form of self-gratification independent of a partner. Sex is the ultimate human activity which creates a warm interdependence, not just between human beings but between opposite sexes; masturbation negates this basic premise.

One cannot argue, as it has been in so many places, that masturbation is completely innocent and harmless, serving as a relaxing sedative. These arguments rest on the premise that because masturbation is a solitary practice it should be regarded as a private matter, one with which public pronouncements on morality are unconcerned. However, it is not true that masturbation is solitary, since there is no such thing as masturbation without thinking of something or someone erotic outside ourselves. One must always concentrate on something external; the imagined object is being abused. Furthermore, as mentioned, since masturbation lessens the necessity for physical closeness to another human being, it leaves the realm of the private and personal, becoming an issue which the community at large must take issue with.

An Outward Orientation

This proves the point that the nature of sexuality is something which pulls us outside of ourselves, instilling within us an outward gravitation.

It is not at all something private or solitary, because it is not something we can ever enjoy on our own. We must always contemplate someone else. Sexuality serves as the primary means of bringing two lovers together. By inverting the process and using it for something other than that, even if it is used purely for self-pleasure, we destroy the mechanism of binding two different people as one.

The Place of Erotica in Jewish Life

At the same time, I also insist that blindly to break the windows of 'marital aid' shops, and to declare all forms of erotica degrading to men and especially to women, is as extreme as to disperse one's sexuality amongst many partners. Erotica definitely has its place within Jewish life but, and I reiterate this, only when it enhances the object of one's desire, which should and must be one's chosen, married partner.

Appreciating the Sublimity of Sex

There are no more excuses. The time has come when we must be adult enough to accept that sex by far transcends a sense of pleasure.

Once, when I was delivering a lecture about the place of sex within Judaism, I mentioned to the student audience that, however petty it may sound, now that sex is so readily available, people are finding increasingly little reason to marry. Once, the only way one could get sex was through marriage. Now, it can be obtained anywhere and at any time.

The reaction of the students to this line of reasoning was, predictably, hostile and disparaging. 'Imagine,' one said, 'that of all the shallow reasons in the world to marry, to do so because of *sex*. How degrading.' I couldn't believe my ears. *Sex! Shallow and degrading?* But the fact is that nearly every other student agreed with him. Sex is shallow and degrading. Can you imagine that we have debased and degraded sex to such a point that, whereas Judaism has traditionally explained it as the most profound statement of love, intimacy and holiness between two individuals, today it has become nothing more than an empty physical act and a basic physiological need, whose only virtue is that it brings pleasure?

To reduce the act of love-making to something which brings pleasure like a warm cup of tea, a back rub or a delicious meal, and not recognize it as the only means by which our love for another person is truly translated into a devoted act of unity, is to rid ourselves of one of the most precious activities known to humanity. That is, not just to love, but to bind ourselves to a cherished partner and 'become one flesh'.

Chapter Seven

DOES THE WORLD HAVE
TOO MANY BABIES?

Every Sunday evening the L'Chaim Society sponsors Point-Counter-Point, a debate between myself and a student volunteer on a contemporary issue, usually one of controversy, affecting Jews everywhere. By and large, it is the students who suggest or choose the subjects.

One of the recurrent themes students wish to discuss among themselves is the issue of over-population. It seems that being around a relatively large Chasidic family brings the matter to the forefront of their minds. Various issues are at the heart of this concern, such as the welfare of the woman who must bear and largely look after the children. This, the students are willing to admit, is a private matter, and so they rarely bring it up with me, but it is one which I will address here in any event. (To be sure, Judaism would not only frown upon, but actively oppose, with the force of law, any child-bearing which brings in its wake health risks to the mother, be they physical or psychological. 'Inconveniences', however, are a different matter.) Then, there are the children themselves. The students wonder if the children will be more neglected by having so many siblings. Can any two parents possibly focus enough attention on so many children? Finally, the biggest question of all: Don't parents have a responsibility to the rest of the world not to fill the planet with children who later cannot be fed, God forbid? While it is true that children are a personal and private matter, the supposed over-population of the world is everyone's concern.

Interestingly, the issue of limiting the number of children we bring into the world is one the students avoid discussing *with me*: they are wary of it because of the perceived slight against my wife and me, given our Chasidic propensity for large families. (At the time of writing this, we are, thank God, blessed with four young children, all of whom were born in Oxford.)

A Home Away from Home

Students are often a bit disoriented upon their arrival in Oxford. For the British students it is almost always their first protracted stay away from home, and of course they miss their families. In this respect, my family and I become a home from home, an extended family as it were, for a great many young people. Many of the students become extraordinarily attached to our children. Regularly a number of students come round to take the children to the park, to baby-sit or to read them stories and put them to bed. The children love all the attention and reciprocate the affection. It is not uncommon for me to enter the house accompanied by a number of students when my own children will run up to a student to be lifted into the air, instead of running up to me.

But even amidst this affinity and closeness, I have rarely seen the students express anything but surprise whenever a new pregnancy has been detected. 'But you had one just a few months ago.' They then turn to my wife (especially the women) with a look of compassion as if implying that something deeply undesirable has been forced on her.

While students love the thought of children – and rarely have I encountered a student who expresses anything but praise for the thought of having children – they dislike the thought of having *too many* children.

The Arbitor of Life and Death

But which child is 'too many'? Three years ago, during the festival of Sukkot, we hosted a Lubavitch woman whose husband is one of the Lubavitcher rebbe's most prominent representatives: she stayed with us during the festival because her husband was on a speaking tour throughout the United States. They, thank God, have thirteen children and she brought the five youngest with her. As the students played with her children in the *sukkah* they would gradually ask the question, 'Are these all the children you have, or are there more?' Whenever they heard how many more there were, there was a look of astonishment as their lower jaws dropped and cracked against the rigid stone floor of the shed that makes up our *sukkah*. After a few minutes, the students would regain their capacity for speech, awake from their stupor and invariably say something to the effect of, 'Ummm ... don't you feel that perhaps that's too many?' It was quite amazing that students who were normally compassionate and concerned with the welfare of others, even students I personally held in very high regard, could be so openly inconsiderate, even offensive, to the feelings of this woman.

It reached the point, after this same reaction occurred about thirty times, that, with tears in her eyes and holding her youngest son, she told my wife and me that the Lubavitcher rebbe, who encourages large families, told her in a private audience that she should never be ashamed of having a large family and should always be proud of the blessings that the Almighty had bestowed upon her. Thus she refused to submit to such insensitivity.

It was only after yet another student made some comment about 'too many' that I intervened. I said, 'Please identify the one or the ones who are too many. Just tell us which are acceptable and which cross the border of "adequacy" so that we can do something about it.'

Given the choice to play a Dr Mengele-like role at the gates of Auschwitz, the student backed down and realized that what he had been saying was wrong. But it is sad that it often takes such a confrontation to counter the world's current distaste for large families.

The Malthusian Nightmare of Limited Supply

In one of our weekly Point-Counter-Points in which I debated the issue of over-population with a student volunteer, I opened the discussion with the following argument to curb immediately any diatribes against large families.

First, a definition of the problem: recently, progress in disease control and medical advances that prolong human life has given rise to new fears of the Malthusian nightmare that world population will outstrip world food supply. It was Thomas Malthus who first argued, in his anonymously published work in 1798, *An Essay on the Principle of Population as it Affects the Future Improvement of Society, with Remarks on the Speculations of Mr. Godwin, M. Condorcet and other Writers*, that infinite human hopes for social happiness must be vain, for population will always tend to outrun the growth of production. The increase of population will take place, if unchecked, in a geometrical progression, while the means of subsistence will increase in only an arithmetical progression. Population will always expand to the limit of subsistence and will be controlled by famine, war and ill-health. 'Vice', which included, for Malthus, contraception, 'misery' and 'self-restraint', could alone check this excessive growth. But Malthus was also an economic pessimist, viewing poverty as the human race's inescapable lot.

For better or for worse, the Malthusian theory of population has been incorporated into current theoretical systems of economics. Its predictions discouraged the traditional forms of charity which Judaism has tried over the centuries to cultivate. In Jewish tradition, charity is not determined by minimal necessary subsistence of the poor or impoverished person. Rather, the Talmud has always insisted that charity must be allocated to each person, based on a 'respectable' standard where 'respectable' means, for example, restoring a fallen businessman to his former standard of living. Thus, as codified by Maimonides the law states that even if the impoverished man had a hundred servants and chariots running before him because of his importance, we must provide the same for him. But Malthusian economics is used by Western governments to this very day to justify a theory of wages that makes the minimum cost of subsistence of the wage earner a standard of judgment.

Catastrophic Nightmares of Famine

Ever since Malthus, the prophets of doom who assumed his mantle have argued that unless vigorous action is taken to prevent the worldwide imbalance of a declining death rate coupled with a burgeoning birth rate, humankind is irrevocably committed to a catastrophic famine and a subsequently violent depopulation of the earth.

What is most puzzling is how Malthus's presentation of statistics as fact has been accepted without close scrutiny. In the many publications presented to the lay public, the basic mathematics of the Malthusian nightmare go unchallenged. Historically speaking, the projections Malthus made have turned out to be totally inaccurate. He failed to allow for the technological and scientific advances that have kept increases in food production ahead of the rise of population growth. Indeed, as Rabbi Mordechai Tendler points out in an outstanding article on this very subject, at the World Conference on Population organized under the auspices of the United Nations in September 1965, many expressed the opinion that 'there was no problem of excessive rates of growth in underdeveloped areas and therefore no public or private action was needed'.

Even at a recent international symposium on population, the view that the world faces a choice between strict birth control and famine was not at all unanimous. Many maintained that 'despite the stresses imposed upon our food supply by the unprecedented population explosion, we could feed everyone well'. Similarly, most environmentalists agree that it is not the rise in population which causes the problem, but the rise in wasteful Western consumerism: fears about a global population explosion are largely based on projecting our own guilt for over-consumption on to those we have taught to emulate us, the poor countries of the world. The industrialized west, so to speak, agrees to demonize the poor east for sins that are ours: we tell them that their 'excess' children will destroy the planet, so they'd better not have any more, while at the same time we reach for the next hamburger.

A Final Solution

In an effort to demonstrate just how Malthusian arguments degrade the very notions of life and humanity by quantifying and qualifying them, I, somewhat ironically, offered the following argument to my students. If indeed the high birth rate risks our ability to feed humankind, then a simple solution is in order. We must institute a system whereby every time someone dies, instead of being buried, the corpse is eaten. Instead of lamenting the birth of every new baby, as we now do, we could celebrate their birth in the knowledge that they will be providing a meal for countless others after they grow big and strong.

After I had made this sarcastic proposal, one of the more observant students pointed out that Jonathan Swift had pre-empted me in his satirical tract, *A Modest Proposal*. However, whereas Swift argued that the Irish should eat their babies to solve their food shortages, I maintained that we must eat our *dead*. Now, a baby could hardly make a single satisfying meal for more than three or four adults, and would be like a small plump turkey, so eating babies could not allow the population to grow. Also, it would be totally barbaric to kill children just to eat them. However, if we let the baby go on to a lead a full life, including eating plenty, then by the time s/he dies they will provide a meal fit for a monarch and all his ministers. Surely this is a far more humane method of ensuring food supplies? Furthermore, we could then take whatever inedible portions remain of the old corpse, grind it up into little bits, and sprinkle it out on the fields to fertilize the crops. Thus we have the added advantage of not having to waste scarce planting space as special burial plots.

Of course, all the above is mere satire but it is said to demonstrate a point. Throughout the past century we have been subjected to a constant barrage of ideologies that diminish the quality of human living. These come in the guise of medical 'care', political intrigue and incessant war. Human life is cheap and is becoming cheaper by the day.

Can Killing Ever Be a Mercy?

Britain has recently been roused from its moral stupor by the debate concerning euthanasia and mercy-killing. Doctors, who are entrusted by the Almighty with the preservation of life, are increasingly arguing for its termination in an increasing number of scenarios. Of course, in the minds of those doctors who favour euthanasia, this is the just and merciful thing to do, and it is seen as an act of preservation. They speak of preserving the *quality* of life. They tell us that when a human life has degenerated to such depths that it is only a convulsion of pain, it may be shut down.

In March 1992, our L'Chaim Society sponsored a mega-debate which pitted the former Chief Rabbi of the United Kingdom and Commonwealth, Lord Immanuel Jakobovits, against the surgeon who performed the first human heart-transplant, Dr Christiaan Barnard. The latter is a strong advocate of euthanasia and wrote a celebrated book, *Good Life, Good Death*, in which he argues, as the title suggests, that people have a right to a dignified end.

In the debate he proved a master showman. He charmed his audience with humour and wit, challenged them with coherent arguments in favour of his position, and then trapped them emotionally when he was suddenly reduced to tears. As he made his case for euthanasia, he told a story of how his own mother had been dying in hospital riddled with incurable cancer. There was nothing left for her, except the will to die. She gathered her remaining strength and turned to her son, a physician in the hospital. 'I have one request,' she said. 'Don't let me continue like this.' And, facing the most painful moment of his life with great strength, he garnered the courage to perform his mother's last request. A deep hush descended on the audience as he told us of this. He then sat down in silence, his cheeks wet with tears.

Collective Euthanasia

I do not in any way wish to imply that Dr Barnard was insincere – we could see that he was being completely honest. Indeed, Dr Barnard was extremely gracious to us and demonstrated loving kindness and humility during his stay. He impressed all the officers of the society who were charged with his care with his warmth and wit, and we are lastingly grateful for his acceptance of our invitation. Nevertheless, the debate was now over. His opponent, Lord Jakobovits, had not a chance of beating that display of emotion. He argued eloquently about the sanctity of life, with a truly novel approach to the subject, saying that if we are to agree that once a life has become nothing but pain and despair it is no longer worth living, then the Jewish people should have committed collective suicide centuries ago. The history of the Jews had been one long story of misfortune and misery. Inquisitions, crusades, pogroms and genocide had rocked us throughout a turbulent life: Babylonians, Greeks, Romans, Spaniards and Germans had stormed and thundered against us. If the measure of the worthiness of our national existence had been satisfaction and tranquillity, we should long ago have adopted the way of the defenders of Masada who, in 72 CE, in the midst of certain capture and torture at the hands of their Roman oppressors, also saw no hope in a continued existence.

Despite their oppressors, the Jews had survived all their tormentors because they had had one secret: they knew that every moment of life is a victory, every breath is the winning of another battle. They never despaired and they always understood that life transcends pain and suffering. They also believed that all the promises that their God had made to them through His trusted servants would eventually be fulfilled, and thus they never so much as contemplated collective euthanasia. If there is one thing that could be said about the Jewish people it was that they had instilled within their children the will to survive and prosper, amidst terrible adversity.

Although Lord Jakobovits fought hard with profound eloquence which deeply touched his audience, Dr Barnard, according to those present, carried the day.

A Movement of Life vs. an Eternity of Death

But he got it wrong. In Judaism there is no such thing as a dignified death. Death is never dignified. It is an aberration. Adam and Eve erred in the Garden of Eden and the consequence of their action was that death descended upon the world. The Creator had commanded them to eat of all the trees of the Garden (even the Tree of Life) except one. They were to connect themselves only with holiness and spirituality, but they did not pay attention. Instead, they fastened on to an earthly and material tree, putting their confidence in materialism rather than the God of life, and immediately they began to decay. Everything connected with the Almighty, the Tree of Life, benefits from His eternity. And sin, which acts as a barrier separating each human from the Creator, cuts us off from the fountain of life.

Death is a mistake that must be corrected. Ultimately, it will be cured when the ancient messianic prophecies culminate in a perfect civilization in which every human is immune to accident, old age and disease, living on into an eternal existence. But until that age arrives – and we pray for it incessantly – we combat death by staying alive, by spitting in its face and confronting its challenge. We never yield, and we cultivate an environment in which every living being is a warrior against this, the darkest of foes.

Sanctity, as Opposed to the Quality, of Life

While today's physicians and philosophers speak of the quality of life, the rabbis of old spoke of the sanctity, indeed the holiness of life. Life is everything which is blessed, everything which is Godly. It is goodness and beauty, while death is a black curse by which everything withers. It is defilement in itself. It is the abandonment of hope, the end of success, a poverty of achievement. Death is the ultimate defeat, while every moment of every life is a victory.

One moment of life is infinitely superior to an eternity of death. Thus we must speak of the sanctity of life, the promise of the future. We must never work towards achieving a dignified death, or even seek to preserve the quality of life at the expense of life itself. Rather we revel in the beauty that is life, because even when it appears to be nothing but pain and misery, it is a blessing. Witness the fact that the ancient Jewish toast on alcoholic beverage is 'L'Chaim – To Life!' We do not say, 'Good life!' or 'Successful life!' Life itself is the most profound blessing.

How Life Has Been Degraded

That we can think of life as anything but this is a product of the modern age that has learned to treat life with contempt. We must never forget our place in the infinite spiral of time. We live just fifty years after Hitler exterminated six million innocent Jews. He diminished by half the people who had always refused to die, and part of each one of us died with them.

Later, it was revealed that Stalin too had taken millions with him in his process of collectivizing farms. Millions of Soviet farmers – so many that no one will ever know the exact figures of those who perished – just disappeared from the landscape. Then it was revealed that Mao in China and Pol Pot in Cambodia perpetrated similar massacres of millions in pursuit of their ideological utopias. The phrase which best describes the momentous occurrences of these last generations is 'mass murder'.

No wonder, then, that our sense of the sanctity and special nature of life has been dulled. It is impossible to hear that numbers of that magnitude were killed without becoming desensitized to the idea of the sacredness of life in general. Never in history have so many innocent non-combatants been murdered in a single century. The numbers are simply staggering. We cannot even create one minuscule strand of life, let alone understand what it means to terminate *millions* of lives. It is possible, even after witnessing the Holocaust, to react to hearing news that one ordinary human being has been murdered by saying, 'Wow! Is that it? Only one!' No reason to wonder why, when we read in the newspapers of hundreds dying in everyday natural disasters or terrorist attacks, our only reaction is to turn the page to a more *exciting* story. We are so accustomed to death that we are bored to death with it. Can there be any greater tragedy?

This trend of denigrating human life has continued in the latter half of the twentieth century with the most detrimental explosion of cultural influences ever pervading the earth. Amidst this explosion, when all that is left to us is the beauty of human life and experience, we hear calls to slow down the population explosion. In today's culture, where we are surrounded by ugliness and violence, even in music and drama, we must appreciate the beauty and innocence embodied in our children. What is left to us without them?

Jewish Children vs Converts to Judaism

What is very troubling is that those who are willing to listen most to calls to reduce our numbers seem to be the Jews. The latest population survey has shown that the average Jewish household has 2.1 children, with the numbers in Israel falling to 1.7 per household. But even according to those who would argue that the world must slow down its growth, it is still the Jews who have a vital argument and right for expansion. After the Holocaust, there is a moral imperative upon the Jews to increase radically their numbers and shout in the face of Hitler that they will never die. For every one of our numbers subtracted, we will add two. Who will replace the lost innocents of barbarism if not us?

Two years ago we hosted an internationally famous Jewish thinker, a social and political commentator, with whom I found I had a common language and for whom I have developed a deep respect. His lectures were a great success, inspiring his audience to rethink their entire position on Judaism and its concerns. We instantly became friends and he sent me a collection of his essays. I found myself in agreement with virtually everything he wrote, until an essay appeared advocating that Jews should actively seek non-Jewish converts. The act of proselytizing non-Jews is foreign to Judaism and something that I find deeply offensive. People are fine the way they are, as long as they pursue a life filled with holiness and goodness, and it is absurd to assert that they must become Jewish in order to achieve proximity to God.

The next time I was in the United States, we met again and I argued vigorously against the points he raised in this paper. We argued back and forth until finally the argument came down to this: he believed that the Jewish people have a grand contribution to make to the world and thus they need greater numbers. 'I want us to convert more Gentiles because I want more Jews. Can you argue against that?'

'Certainly,' I responded. 'It is to be done through a population explosion. We need more Jewish *babies*. We need people who celebrate life before they worry about finance. Parents who look forward to their children's marriages rather than fretting over the bills or the hassles.'

The Human Right to Have Children

Missing completely from the arguments of those who encourage a sharp reduction in the birth rate are the philosophical or ethical implications of projected programmes to reduce the birth rate. The conflict of science and religion was once limited to the question of the authenticity of the Torah, so that in the nineteenth century the challenge to the Torah came primarily from the evolutionists. In modern times, however, the challenge comes almost entirely from the methodology of natural science. The challenge to Jewish values stems from the claim that the methods of natural science serve as our only reliable measure to ascertain true reality.

What does this mean? The personal letters of Charles Darwin are fascinating reading. If the God that rested on the Sabbath, after six days of creative activity, does not exist, then the God who took the Jews out of Egypt, who intervened to answer the call of an oppressed population, is equally non-existent. But this completely contradicts the traditional Jewish view. We believe that the regulation of the world's population is relegated unto God. The insistence that God erred in not realizing the mathematical certainty of a geometrically increasing population outstripping arithmetical increases in food supply is but another manifestation of a limited and superficial understanding of God and religion. Inherent in our concept of a personal God is the outlook encouraged by King David in Psalm 145, in which God is praised for providing sustenance for all His creatures. So significant is this one verse that the entire first portion of the daily prayer service is built around it, and, in addition, it is recited three times daily by practising Jews. There must be a point at which we recognize that such necessities as food supply and world population are areas of Divine concern.

Junior Partners in Creation

To be sure, humans have always been encouraged to join the Almighty as partners in the management of this world, although our role is of course always one of subservience, the junior partner as it were. Imbued with the spark of Divine intelligence, mankind is permitted, even required, to use partnership rights to regulate their own affairs, on condition that they do not violate the by-laws of this God–man relationship that are formulated in the Torah. What if the present food supply/population projections prove to be more accurate than those made by Malthus? We are told that at the present rate of increase in world population, four hundred million tons of additional grain annually will be needed by 1995. This is more grain than is now produced by all of North America! What guidelines have been set down for our instruction in this yet hypothetical situation?

Developing the Earth's Full Potential

The Jew as a world citizen is personally concerned with famine in Africa and China. However, the Noachide laws which serve as Torah (instruction) for all humanity demand a proper sequence of actions: to establish courts of justice, to prohibit idolatory, blasphemy, bloodshed, sexual sins, sadism to live animals. Rabbi Mordechai Tendler, the renowned Orthodox Jewish scientist, wrote a learned paper on this subject already quoted above, in which he argues convincingly that before a Jew can support coercive birth control measures in 'overpopulated' areas of the world, he must insist on heroic efforts being made to utilize fully the agricultural potential of the earth. This implies a fair distribution of food supplies as well as the extension of modern farming technology to all parts of the world and a more effective and more morally responsible distribution of food surpluses. It is ludicrous to maintain that Indians will on the one hand allow themselves to be surgically sterilized, or implanted with a plastic loop, bow or spiral, or their children to be aborted, but on the other hand will obstinately refuse to use a better grain seed, add chemical fertilizers to the land or adjust the ploughing pattern so as to minimize water loss. And it is ludicrous for us to ask them to do so when each individual in the rich West consumes as much as an Indian's entire extended family.

It is equally untenable to insist that the logistics of worldwide food distribution present insurmountable obstacles. During the massive Gulf War operation, the Pentagon bragged that it had transported so many troops (over half a million) and so much food and supplies that it served as the equivalent of moving the entire city of Hoboken, New Jersey, to the Middle East. A nation that can transport the people and material needed to wage modern war several thousand miles from home with such efficiency can certainly overcome all obstacles in the way of food distribution. It is a question of adequate motivation. Is it really more immoral to allow a family to lose its political freedom than to sit idly by while it loses its personal freedom to bear children?

Michael Jackson in China

My wife and I were married in Sydney. On the return journey to the United States we stopped in Hong Kong, where I had been invited by a section of the Jewish community, under the direction of Rabbi Mordechai Avtzon, to lecture on Judaism and dreams. While there, we took a one-day trip into mainland China. We were mortified, just three weeks into our marriage, to discover that families were limited to one child each, with significant punitive measures enacted against those who did not comply. As a newly-wed I saw this as the cruellest form of torture, imposing conditions on the loving and intimate union of a husband and wife.

Later in that same trip, we were taken on a bus tour to a small and impoverished Chinese village where we, twenty westerners, were brought into the home of a frail old woman to discover the hardships of the Chinese peasants. There were virtually no furnishings in the house, and almost no food. But to our amazement, there was a picture of the woman together with Michael Jackson, the pop superstar, standing arm in arm. The tour guide explained that Mr Jackson had taken the same tour, alone obviously, and had come to this house. I was told, and being a rabbi I have a feeling for the apocryphal, that the woman's version of his visit was that he was more moved by the plight of her cat, who was as thin as a toothpick, than by her own emaciation. He took out a crisp $100 note and made her promise she would spend the money on food for her cat. She was honest and kept her part of the bargain and fattened the cat up; when she and her family were hungry, they ate their pet.

The point of the story is twofold. The first is, of course, the mistake of feeding a cat before a starving human being. Secondly, we were amazed by the wide-open, beautiful highways and streets which lined this entire area of Canton. What startled us was that, besides our tour bus and perhaps three other cars which we saw the entire day, there was not a single other motor vehicle. Everyone was on a bicycle. 'So for whom did they build the roads?' we inquired of the tour operator. He bent over and whispered in our ear, 'To impress the western tourists.'

Here you see conclusively what we stated at the very beginning. In today's age, human life has been cheapened to such an extent that everything takes precedence over it. Resources are spent on building roads no one will use, rather than on food for the population.

To Save a Dog or a Human Life

My friend Dennis Prager, publisher of the well-known Jewish quarterly, *Ultimate Issues*, who has spoken twice to our students at Oxford, told us that in his lectures to high school students around the world he often asks them this question, 'If your favourite dog and a human being were drowning at the same time, who would you save?' He reports that about a quarter answer, 'the human'. About another quarter say, 'the dog' outright. And the remaining half almost always shrug their shoulders showing their torment over this difficult decision. 'It's a very good question,' they tell him.

At the symposium previously mentioned, a leading professor of political science bravely presented a prognosis that spells the doom of the concept of the integrity and worth of the individual upon which all democratic principles depend. He predicted, 'Inescapably, there will be changes in our most intimate habits and patterns of living. It is not enough to have a pill. People must be willing to take it – in many cases not merely to prevent the birth of unwanted children, but even to prevent the birth of deeply wanted, even longed-for children. The time may not be far off when some societies, at least, may find themselves pressed by unyielding circumstances into an extraordinary invasion of human privacy – the limitation of births by legal ordinance, with severe penalties for infraction.'

The perceived threat of Communism pales in comparison with this summary of the fantasy of *1984* materializing simply because we lack the humility to admit that there are areas immune to our human interference. Rabbi Tendler asks how any moral individual can concern him/herself with forced abortion clinics before s/he has suggested, no demanded, that our resources be committed to increase production of local staples, tap the wealth of the oceans, and then develop new sources of high-quality proteins from the algal and microbial cultures studied experimentally these past few years.

Third World Food Development

The idea that an illiterate African, Asian or South American would rather starve than accept a diet 'strange' to him/her has been fully disproved by the Incaparina Program in South America. Under this programme, teams of nutritionists educated the protein-starved masses to accept a flour composed of corn, sesame or soy oil, peas and vitamin A. New recipes were accepted by the 'illiterate masses' with the resultant upgrading of the national diet of millions of people.

There has to be unanimity in the conviction that we must not dump potatoes, burn excess wheat or cut back on production quotas; only then may we make impassioned pleas for free distribution of contraceptive devices as a humanitarian effort to prevent worldwide famine.

To Poison So That No One Could Eat

The Thatcher and Reagan years are supposed to have taught the vast majority of English speakers to respect the cold hard facts of economics. But what is the result when these 'facts' are applied? Apparently, if the price rises, food is destroyed, and if it drops ... the outcome is still the same.

I recall that when I was a child of about ten I watched television news about how a California-based produce company had dumped many tons of fresh oranges in a landfill outside Los Angeles because there had been a glut of oranges due to the successful harvest that year forcing worldwide prices down considerably. People began to travel outside the city to pick up oranges. The company then returned and sprayed insecticide poison on them so that no one could eat them.

A similar but far more disturbing story was told to me by my office assistant, whose father has a farm in Australia: thousands of sheep were shot on each property, hundreds of thousands altogether in the whole country throughout the 1980s, because the farmers could no longer afford to feed them when the world price for beef dropped. The farmers were deeply upset by what they had to do but there was no way out for them unless other people stepped in. But no one would. Is that what living in the modern world has to be about?

The Gift of Life

This, then, is the tragedy. We have managed to allow every type of concern to supersede that of human life. Money, pain and even war are given priority over our concerns for what Judaism argues is the holiest and greatest blessing in this confused world – the gift of human life. If we do not learn to protect and value it, then the only possible outcome of this devaluation of life is that it will eventually affect us and encroach upon our own freedom.

There is hope, however. About ten years ago the Lubavitcher Rebbe Shlita, who up to that time had encouraged a ten-point *mitzvah* (commandment) campaign comprised of donning *tefillin*, lighting Shabbat candles, giving charity, and other very simple and practical Jewish measures, spoke at a public gathering and encouraged every family, however large or small, to have at least one more child than planned. The response was overwhelming: families who were barely observant were enthusiastically responding to the rebbe's call. They may have hesitated to do something as simple as putting up a *mezuzah*, but a rabbi promoting the beauty of a child warmed their hearts, and many wonderful children were born as a result.

By thinking beyond the calls of prophets of doom and looking for practical solutions to the world's problems, and by putting life before all concerns, we ensure that the quality, indeed the sanctity, of life is established for eternity.

Chapter Eight

WHY CAN'T WE LIVE FOREVER?
COPING WITH THE DEATH OF A PARENT

Even for those with a stable and happy home life, studying at Oxford is often an enormous strain, but it becomes even more formidable for those who have problems outside their studies to cope with in a responsible and adult way. Some of the most difficult times at Oxford involve students who, God forbid, lose a parent or other loved one while far away from home.

A particular student to whom I was very close was one of those who came to Oxford from the United States. One terrible day, he was summoned into the room of his head of college to be told compassionately but as a matter of fact, that his father had died of a heart attack. The student was obviously stricken with grief, but he also had a major examination two days later, which would decide his continued presence at the university. He had to choose whether he should go to the funeral or take the exam. The college was adamant that while they would allow him to sit the papers later in the year, they would have to be taken alongside his final examinations eight months later. This would make it impossible for him to prepare for, or succeed at, both.

Respect for a Deceased Parent

There are certain things in life which are immutable and can never be compromised. Respect for a deceased parent is one of these, and I told him there was no possible way that he could miss the funeral and sit for an exam during the *shivah*, the traditional seven days of mourning. For his part, he insisted that his father would have *wanted* him to take the exam. The father had been so proud that his son had been admitted to Oxford on a scholarship, and he would have objected to his son observing a period of mourning during such a crucial juncture in his academic career. That may be true, I told him, and that is how a father executes his duties as a loving parent towards his child. But a child also has duties, and one of these is to show respect for a parent, even when the parent refuses to accept it, and this is especially necessary where the final respect one can show a parent is concerned. 'Your father can tell

85

you many things which you are obliged to obey and hold precious, but he cannot tell you that he is not your father or to behave towards him in a fashion that contradicts the obligations inherent in the parent–child relationship.'

The student did not heed my advice. He sat the exam with the consent of his mother and obtained one of the best results at the university. But his success had its price. A few months later terrible guilt set in. His self-reproach deepened when he finally arrived home and friends could not believe that he had missed his father's funeral to sit an examination. When he returned to Oxford, he became 'numb', he didn't care any more: he was unable to do any work, and began dating a succession of girls, which even he knew to be unsuitable.

The First Yahrtzeit

His life reached crisis point: his college thought he should be 'sent down' (the Oxford terminology for being expelled). It was now many months since his father had passed away. I sat and spoke to him, telling him there was no reason to feel such a weight of guilt and that he had to pull his life back together again. His father's *yahrtzeit* (anniversary of death) was rapidly approaching: I asked him to undertake to put together a *minyan* (quorum of ten males) for the three-prayer services and to say *Kaddish*. He was not very observant of Jewish law, yet I told him that he *must* be observant of his father's *yahrtzeit*. He must undertake to say *Kaddish* faithfully, light a candle, and even try to put on a *seudah*, a meal, for fellow worshippers at the synagogue. This would be his atonement.

Over the next few months, we began to notice an incredible transformation in his character and religious commitment. He became a far more serious, more devoted, more overtly Jewish student than he had ever been. He also became a far deeper person, engaging anyone in insightful conversation on every facet of life. He also became much more romantic, committing himself to a single girlfriend, writing poetry and sending flowers. Clearly, his father's passing had left an indelible mark on his life. However, his new religious observance marked the greatest change of all, and he began to frequent our synagogue weekly.

We have a custom that on Friday nights the students stand up and toast a *L'Chaim*, a toast to life. And while these always encompass a whole host of subjects, some being very funny and others quite serious, his became increasingly earnest and sincere, many of them deeply moving.

Finally, his father's *yahrtzeit* came around. He made all the phone calls ensuring that there would be a *minyan* three times over that twenty-four hour period, and he recited the *Kaddish*. The way in which he recited it was utterly moving, and he followed up the prayer service with an elaborate spread in honour of his father's *yahrtzeit*, complete with a bottle of Johnnie Walker Black Label Whisky. For a student, this was extravagant indeed: he said to me, 'My father did everything "first class" and I know this is the best way to remember him.'

After he had recited his final *Kaddish*, I sat the congregants down for a few moments to reflect on the events of the day.

An Appropriate Way to Remember

'Surely, we have all witnessed a very touching and moving spectacle. A young man, who loved his father deeply, has shown his father the ultimate respect of reciting the ancient Jewish mourner's prayer in the company of friends and co-religionists. He has taken from a meagre student stipend to provide a festive meal in his father's honour. In short, he has behaved in a manner befitting a son of Israel and a loving human being.

'The first book of Samuel describes the profound love that existed between David and Jonathan. Although they were rivals for the throne of Israel because they were brothers-in-law, they loved each other from the bottom of their hearts. King Saul sought to harm his son-in-law David because he feared that the kingdom of Israel would be taken from his own son, Jonathan. The twentieth chapter describes an exchange between the two young men: Jonathan warned David of impending disaster. His father, the king, customarily invited his entire household to his table to celebrate the first day of each Jewish month, and David was planning to be absent from the next day's festive meal. Jonathan warned him, "Tomorrow is the new moon and you will be remembered, for your seat at the table shall be empty" (Samuel Book I, Chapter 20).

Memories Generated by an Absence

'There are moments when someone is better remembered through their absence than their presence. A *yahrtzeit* is such a time. Although a father may be deceased, his absence is noted and he comes back to life, as it were, through the actions of his children. If on a *yahrtzeit* a family just goes about its normal business as if nothing has happened, if the children do not go to synagogue to recite *Kaddish* or if they do not commemorate the day with any special observances, then their father has died an eternal death. But if they mark the occasion by visiting his tomb and by performing and dedicating good deeds in his honour, they cause their father to live an eternal life. In other words, he is influencing and affecting their lives in death as he did while alive. Thus, he may be said to be "alive".

87

The Patriarch Jacob Never Died

'To understand this, we can turn to the book of Genesis, where the death of our patriarch Jacob is described. Interestingly, the Torah never actually uses the words, "He died", but rather, "He gathered up his feet into the bed; and he departed this life, and was gathered to his people". Because the word "death" is not used, the Talmud makes the spectacular pronouncement that our forefather Jacob never actually died. But if he did not die, what are we to make of the lengthy description in the Torah of his burial that ends with the words, "For his sons carried him into the land of Canaan, and buried him in the cave of the field of Machpelah, which Abraham bought with the field for a possession of a buryingplace" (Genesis 50:13)? Did they really bury a live man?

'"Of course not," responds the Talmud. Rather, the statement that our forefather Jacob "did not die" is not meant to be taken literally, but metaphorically: "Since his children were alive, he lived on through his children."

'The Talmud is saying that Jacob was the last in a tradition of three great men who gave the world monotheism, the most radical and important concept ever set out before humanity. Abraham was the originator of monotheism, but when he died, only one of his two principal children carried it forward. It was as though half of Abraham had died, but the other half lived on through his son Isaac. Abraham was, in effect, still alive because the doctrine which he gave the world continued to flourish and influence mankind's behaviour.

'In his turn, Isaac also had two sons. As in the case of his father, only one of these two proved true to Isaac's principles of holiness and monotheism. Half of Isaac died when he departed the world, but half of him remained alive, and so everything he stood for was carried on nobly by his son Jacob.

'But Jacob had thirteen children, and all of them remained loyal to the God of Israel and His commandments. Therefore, "our forefather Jacob never died". He lived on eternally through the activities and teachings of his many children. Since his children were all alive, and since they carried on their lives according to the traditions he had imparted to them, he lived on for ever through them.

Eternal Life Conveyed through Influencing Actions

'Every time a Jew puts on *tefillin*, keeps Shabbat or performs an act of kindness in accordance with God's will, s/he thereby breathes eternal life into the nostrils of our forefather Jacob. These acts ensure that Jacob is never forgotten, since the doctrines he espoused are never forgotten.

'In Judaism, life is defined as the positive impact which one leaves on one's world. The Talmud states with some confidence that "the righteous, even in death, are said to be alive, while the wicked, even in life, are said to be dead". Because evildoers do not enhance or affect their environment in any positive way, but are actually detrimental to it, they cannot be said to be alive. Their existence may be a reality, but it is not life. Life is defined by our continued ability to have a positive and beneficial impact on our environment. As long as someone's memory serves to bring the world another step forward, they are still alive, even though they may have walked the earth centuries earlier.

NASA Searches for Life on Mars

'It may come as a surprise to know that this ancient way of describing life is also the most basic definition of life that we modern humans have. Scientists use it, as we discovered in February 1990, when we staged a weekend dedicated to the reconciliation of science and religion, featuring internationally prominent scientists. Professor Velvl Greene, currently director of the Immanuel Jakobovits Centre for Medical Ethics at Ben Gurion University of the Negev in Beer Sheva, Israel, was one of the main speakers. One of his lectures focused on his tenure as director of NASA's Life-Science Research Centre. He and a team of specialists were charged with the duty of immunizing the Viking Lander in preparation for its landing on Mars in search of life. The space craft was immunized to ensure that no microbes from earth were present on the lander that could mistakenly be attributed to life indigenous to Mars.

'The most important question that arose in the mission's quest for life was this: supposing they did find life on Mars, how would they identify it as being alive? Perhaps a life-form could be so radically different from life on earth that the instruments would fail to recognize its significance. It suddenly became essential to postulate a universal definition of life, equally binding on all planets. It is uncanny that the approach they adopted resembles the Jewish definition. They decided that anything found on Mars which somehow changes its environment, in other words has an impact on its surroundings, is alive. On earth, plants are to be considered alive because they oxygenate the air. Animals are alive because they constantly change the environment around them. Anything which changes its environment would be judged by the scientists as being alive.

'It follows that something continues to live so long as it is impacting its environment, even long after it has lost that principle which we commonly call life that distinguishes a vital and functional being from a dead body.

Death Catches up with Karl Marx

'Without even realizing it, most of us accept the validity, in essence, of this definition. I recall a political cartoon which appeared in *Newsweek* immediately after the failed coup attempt in the former Soviet Union against President Gorbachev, when he had ordered the Communist Party to disband itself. It showed the angel of death, complete with scythe and all the traditional paraphernalia, leading Karl Marx away. The humour of the cartoon was meant to be the supposed similarity in looks between the apparition and the famed political thinker, but it also underscored the truth of the way we think about life. As long as Communism in the Soviet Union flourished, Karl Marx was alive: however, when Communism finally died, Marx died along with it. He could not be said to have survived the fall of Communism, but similarly he could not have been dead while his political theories shaped the lives of hundreds of millions of people in the USSR.'

Link in an Unbroken Chain

After this lengthy speech (that had appeared to be a digression, but was really connected to the *yahrtzeit* he had just celebrated) I turned to the student and emphasized that as long as he continued along the proper path of Judaism and human goodness, his father would live. His father had served as the unbroken link in a chain extending thousands of generations and had taught him the importance of being a Jew. But the moment any of his progeny did not live by the values he espoused, his father's memory dimmed. Thank God, I emphasized, on this *yahrtzeit* his father's memory blazed like a glowing furnace.

My Family from Europe

This concept of preserving life and tradition is an especially potent one for my family. My mother's relations came from Russia and emigrated to the United States near the turn of the century, one small part of the influx of thousands of Jewish refugees who swept the shores of America in search of religious liberty and economic opportunity. My maternal grandfather arrived with eight brothers. They were all youngsters and deeply religious, but it was not easy to remain an observant Jew in New York in the Twenties, Thirties and Forties. My grandfather, may he rest in peace, often used to tell me that the factories had signs which read, 'If you don't come in on Saturday, don't bother coming in on Monday.' Even Jewish shop owners granted no latitude to their employees for the observance of the Sabbath or Jewish festivals.

For material sustenance, and through no fault of their own, millions of Jews lost their precious heritage. The ignorance of the Jewish immigrants rapidly worsened until the grandchildren of these first-generation pioneers were hardly recognizable as near-relations of their forebears. My family was largely a victim of this trend. While my grandfather himself preserved

Jewish tradition and observances, largely because of my grandmother who was Orthodox, his brothers and their children were able to preserve very little. Although my mother's first cousins, and my second cousins, are Jewish, they are not at all knowledgeable of our glorious family tradition.

Matters came to a head a few years ago when I was visiting my family in Miami Beach. One of my mother's last surviving uncles, who had crossed the Atlantic from Russia seventy years earlier, passed away. Being the only rabbi in the family, I was called upon by his children to conduct the funeral ceremony. However, I was a bit apprehensive, since it was being conducted in a mausoleum. Jewish law stipulates that a person must be properly buried in the ground, and as a mausoleum does not constitute proper interment, it is prohibited by Jewish law. I therefore had reservations about conducting the funeral since I will not compromise on matters of Jewish law. But the deceased was my great-uncle and I desperately wanted to be there for his children and to ensure that there would be significant traditional Jewish content in the ceremony. So I went to the funeral and delivered a eulogy, emphasizing our ancestor's roots and how our family, like so many others, had descended from a line of very prestigious scholars and learned rabbis. I also spoke of how much my great-uncle cherished Jewish things – everything from Jewish friends to Jewish food – and how his children must continue to follow his example so that the family may continue in a celebrated tradition of Jewish activity. I then recited the *Kaddish* word for word, prompting his two sons.

A Traditional Tennis Ball

When I finished my discourse, we began to leave. As we filed out, his eldest son, who was in his forties, leaned forward, took a tennis ball from his pocket and placed it on the mausoleum. I asked my cousin what meaning this gesture had. He answered, 'My father loved to play tennis. He played virtually every day. He loved it so much that when I was young he taught me how to play, and for years hardly a Sunday passed without us on the court having a great time together. This tennis ball reminds me of him. It is a gesture of the love he had for me and I for him.' With that he walked away.

As he went, the full extent of the Jewish tragedy that had befallen my family hit me. To be sure, the fact that a father takes the time to teach his children tennis, to spend time with them every Sunday, is a beautiful demonstration of love and devotion that could be emulated in different ways by every parent. But tennis should not be the only way in which a son remembers his father. At the risk of sounding condescending, I would maintain wholeheartedly that a son reciting *Kaddish* for his father is of infinitely greater value. Tennis only binds you to the here-and-now, but reciting *Kaddish* and keeping up other Jewish traditions in memory of a parent binds you to an eternal people. When you play tennis, you repeat something which your father loved and imparted to you, but when you recite the *Kaddish* you do something which your father was taught by your grandfather, and your grandfather was taught by his grandfather, all the way back for hundreds of generations. Keeping up Jewish tradition is something which links us to a glorious past and an eternal future.

So, teaching your child to play tennis is beautiful and loving, but it must be accompanied by teaching your child to read Hebrew so that if, God forbid, it is ever needed, they are able to recite the *Kaddish* on their parent's behalf of their own accord, without the need for help from another person.

In no way do I judge my relatives. The blame for the lack of observance among American Jews should perhaps be laid at the feet of the Almighty, since it was He who put them into a new and Godless situation. They fled pogrom-infested Russia in search of a country where they could be Jews without having to suffer for it and arrived in a country where in order to eat they largely had to sacrifice their observance.

Still, it is in the end irrelevant to apportion blame. What is important is that we Jews renew our commitment to our traditions, to ensure that Judaism is strengthened in our lifetime so that we and our people are strong, and live to see the fulfilment of the glorious promises of a messianic future.

Chapter Nine

ABORTION IN THE BIBLE

The subject of abortion is not only one of the most controversial in today's society, it is also one of the most misunderstood and misrepresented within Judaism. Many academics and students here at Oxford, in their haste to label religious beliefs as rigid, anti-feminist and contrary on every level to western liberal values, immediately assume that Judaism takes a hardline approach to abortion. Although it is a highly emotive subject, it is also one which can be approached rationally and within the context of a coherent system of beliefs. As is the case with marriage and divorce, secular law does not often attempt to address clearly religious issues (because it has an altogether different emphasis and purpose). Hence I tell students that often such subjects must be viewed through the lens of traditional values.

In Hilary Term (January) 1990, we hosted a debate in the Oxford Union on abortion which was attended by a few hundred students. Prof David Baum of Bristol University was there as well as Prof Arthur Schaeffer, a world-renowned medical ethicist from the University of Manitoba. Their opponents were Catherine Francois, a leading spokeswoman for the Pro-Life movement in Britain, and Anne Widdecombe, a leading woman MP and one of the best female orators in Britain.

It was a very fiery debate and we had not previously staged such a controversial event. About six hundred students attended with everybody holding a personal and passionate view on the subject. The two pro-life speakers were representing the Society for the Protection of the Unborn Child (SPUC). Immediately before the debate there was a crowd of students demonstrating. Many of the women present were holding placards which read 'SPUC OFF' so that it was not too difficult to discern which side they were on.

The abortion debate at the Oxford Union was fraught with many strange and bizarre occurrences. Debates, which are a central staple of Oxford life, always seem to be a bit on the far side. Perhaps one of the strangest events, which left all of the spectators dumbfounded, was one woman's reaction when Prof Arthur Schaeffer rested his pro-choice argument on the premise that abortion was an attempt by the male members of society to gain dominance and control over the female element and dictate what they could and could not do with their bodies. He was making the case that a foetus, especially in its very early stages, is not alive and has no semblance of life whatsoever. It is totally dependent on the mother for its existence and sustenance. Rather, he argued, the real reason men are not allowing women to have abortions is so that they can tell them what to do with their bodies . . . it's another aspect of male domination. He was speaking primarily as a medical ethicist. While he was speaking a very angry young woman stood up and made an objection (allowed in the rules of debate of the Oxford Union), very loudly. She shouted at the top of her voice. She pointed out that she was sitting on the anti-abortion side of the house, and that to claim that the women on the other side were any more liberated and that the pro-life women were under male domination was 'nauseating and repugnant in the extreme.' She proceeded to tell everyone that she was a religious Catholic and goes to church every Sunday, and that she believes deeply in Jesus Christ. Amidst all of that she also said that she is very promiscuous and enjoys having sex with a variety of men. At this point she pulled out a packet of birth control pills to illustrate her point. She said 'I take these because I am going to be with him tonight,' pointing to the man sitting on her left. He immediately buried his head in his hands. A deep hush fell over the audience. But, no one was so startled as her boyfriend, who sat for the rest of the debate with his head between his hands just shaking it backward and forward. Occurrences such as these are not unusual in the Oxford Union. The debates thrive on these spectacles. They are what the students expect most. (In fact, this same girl later participated in a debate on the place of pornography in society. She was clad in modest attire to express the way women are imprisoned by the strictures of society and tonight she was going to liberate herself . . . at which point she removed the dress revealing only a bikini. This was a televised debate in the Oxford Union. Indeed, Oxford does have its moments.)

Caught Unwittingly in History

The debate was equally divided, with half the students supporting the pro-life and half supporting the pro-choice side. There was a wide range of views. Coincidentally, Elgar Smith, who works for the pro-life lobby in the USA and has written a book entitled *When Choice Becomes God*, was present. What we didn't know at the time was that he planned to include in his book a description of how our baby daughter, Chaya Mushka, had to be taken out of the hall because she was crying. He used this incident to make a strongly pro-life argument.

'Just as one of the speakers was making a crucial point, from out of nowhere came the totally unexpected whimper of a tiny baby. More wondrous than either crying or screaming, her faint little voice caught this audience of university students by surprise. At first there were curious glances, wondering what a baby was doing in the Debating Chamber. She became quiet again and all eyes returned to the front of the room. Within a few moments, however, came a second whimper, this time evoking glances less curious than cutting.

'We all know that look. It's the one people give when a baby cries during a wedding or screams out during a graduation ceremony. It's the look that says, "Get rid of that baby! It's getting in our way!"

'By now you must surely suspect where I am headed with this illustration. As the baby's mother bolted for the door, already sensitive to glances she never saw, it occurred to me that the statement being made by many women having abortions (and sometimes by their partners as well) is very much the same: "Why did you have to bring that baby into my secure world at this point in time? It's ruining my life!"

'At the end of the evening, the analogy proved to be even more appropriate than I had first thought. When I introduced myself to the child's parents, a pro-life rabbi and his wife, I learned that their lovely daughter's name was Chaya Mushka. "Chaya" is Hebrew for "life"! It was life that was interrupting the proceedings – life that had to be "gotten rid of".' (*When Choice Becomes God*).

Ever since that we have had many debates on abortion, none of which seems to have dispelled the myriad misconceptions that people, including the above-mentioned author, have about the Jewish attitude towards abortion. When people discuss this most sensitive of issues they assume I take a rigidly pro-life and completely-opposed-to-women's-choice line, which is why I have given numerous classes delineating the exact halakhic (Jewish legal) guidelines on the subject, showing that there is a tremendous amount of moderation in the Jewish viewpoint on abortion.

Receiving a Thorough Education about Abortion

Before I arrived in Oxford, abortion meant nothing more to me than an academic debate, albeit an emotive one. It was only when I assumed my place among the students that the issue came alive with frightening frequency. The first instance occurred virtually upon my arrival, when a first-year Jewish student, barely eighteen years old, thought his non-Jewish girlfriend was pregnant. He wasn't very observant but it seemed that the thought of having non-Jewish children, especially at eighteen, did not particularly appeal to him. He wanted my advice, but not necessarily a halakhic opinion, on whether he should agree to the young woman having an abortion, which it seems she was anxious to have in any case. After a few very tense days, they discovered it was a false alarm.

But it was certainly not the last time that this type of scare forced me to face the issue. It was to occur many times at Oxford and abortion remains a highly charged issue here as elsewhere.

One of the most difficult scenarios I faced was when an academic at the university, divorced and with a child from her first marriage, got seriously involved with another academic. After a few months they decided to marry and honoured me by asking if I would perform the wedding. As we began discussing the marriage plans, it emerged that she did not yet have a *get*, a Jewish divorce. This was a serious development and we immediately began working on procuring her *get*. The problem was, as in most cases, that as soon as her first husband discovered how badly she needed the *get* and that Jewish law could never allow her to remarry without it, he began to blackmail her for a large sum of money. He was financially (and morally) bankrupt and tried to make some quick cash from his wife's predicament.

She was desperate to acquire the *get* quickly, especially as Jewish law stipulates that a woman cannot remarry for three months after she obtains her *get*. The reason for this proviso is to ensure that the woman marrying again is not pregnant from her first husband, as this would cause problems for her and her new family as well as present a difficulty in identifying the baby's father. In this case it was impossible for her to have become pregnant by her husband since she had been separated from him for many years. Jewish law, however, does not distinguish between circumstances. Every woman who obtains her *get*, notwithstanding how long she has been separated from her former husband, must wait ninety days before she can remarry.

Difficulty in Obtaining a Get

They were both becoming quite unnerved at the entire process and told me that they had decided to be married at a registry office. After all, they said, the law that a woman cannot obtain a *get* from her husband unless he wishes to give it, is unfair: why should they suffer because of it? In the United States, they have already begun to enact legislation which will make it a criminal offence for a husband to refuse to grant his wife a Jewish divorce, once a civil divorce has been awarded. But Britain is not as advanced in these matters, and her husband's refusal really was a problem. I endeavoured to explain to them, through many nights of conversation, the very serious consequences if they were to marry without first obtaining a *get*. Their children would be *mamzerim*, 'bastards', and in Jewish law would only be allowed to marry other *mamzerim*.

Now, many people have the wrong presumption that any child born out of wedlock is a bastard in Jewish law. The only bastard in Jewish law is the child born to a married woman but fathered by someone other than her husband, or a child born of incest. 'That's OK,' my friend said, 'later on our child can just convert.' I explained this would be impossible: a child can never undo his or her status as a *mamzer*. In this respect, it is far more serious than a Jewish man marrying a non-Jewish woman, for example, in which case, although the children are not Jewish, they can indeed convert later. In the case of a *mamzer*, they cannot convert at all. They can do nothing. 'Think of your children,' I told them. 'Whatever hardships you are going through now, it is nothing compared to what your children will be forced to undergo when they want to marry.'

This persuaded them for the time being. One night I received a frantic phone call from the woman. 'I have a real problem with regard to my forthcoming marriage and obtaining my *get*. I'm pregnant.'

This caused all sorts of problems. It not only meant that her child would be a *mamzer*, since she was still married to her first husband, it also meant that in Jewish law she would never be allowed to marry her fiancé. Jewish law stipulates that if a married woman has an affair with a man other than her husband, she becomes forbidden to both men, her husband and the lover. We presumed it would become common knowledge that she had had an affair and was now pregnant: no observant rabbi in the world would be able to marry them.

We all panicked. After all my efforts to avert this kind of catastrophe, it seemed it was too late. She asked me if she could have an abortion, and I had to admit this was the first thing that had gone through my mind as well. The prospect of sanctioning an abortion in Jewish law, for the purpose of preventing the birth of a *mamzer* and allowing a woman to marry (rather than for a far more serious reason, such as the health of the mother or even a genetic defect in the baby) seemed daunting indeed. I was forced to inquire into the subject at great length. Various misunderstandings about the Jewish attitude towards abortion begin to fall away when one approaches the subject in a serious manner through Jewish writings, tradition and law.

Abortion in the Bible

There is not a single direct reference in the entire Bible to abortion. The legislation of the Bible makes only one reference to our subject, and this by implication. 'If men strive, and hurt a woman with child, so that her fruit depart *from her*, and yet no mischief follow: he shall be surely punished, according as the woman's husband will lay upon him; and he shall pay as the judges determine. And if any mischief follow, then thou shalt give life for life' (Exodus 21:22–23).

This crucial passage, by one of the most curious twists of literary fortunes, shows the parting of the ways for Jewish and Christian rulings on abortion. According to the Jewish interpretation, if no mischief follow the 'hurt' to the woman (that resulted in the loss of her 'fruit', the foetus), then there is no capital guilt involved, and the attacker is merely liable to pay compensation for the loss of her fruit. The words 'mischief' and 'hurt' refer to the survival of the woman, not the foetus, following her miscarriage. The more serious case occurs if the woman is fatally injured ('And if any mischief follow . . .'): only then does the man responsible for her death have to 'give life for life'. In that event the capital charge of murder exempts him from any monetary liability for the aborted fruit. This interpretation is supported by the rabbinical exegesis of the verse defining the law of murder: 'He that smiteth a man, so that he dieth, shall surely be put to death', which the rabbis construed to mean 'a man [person], but not a foetus'.

These passages clearly indicate that the killing of an unborn child is not considered as murder punishable by death in Jewish law. If it did, then the phrase 'give life for life' would also have to apply to the words 'if no harm follow', meaning that since the foetus was considered a 'life' but has now been killed, even if the mother lives, the man would still incur a capital penalty.

From this it seems we can deduce that the Bible does not define a foetus as being fully and humanly alive.

The Christian tradition disputing this view goes back to a mistranslation in the Septuagint. There, the Hebrew for 'no harm follow' was replaced by the Greek for '[her child be born] imperfectly formed'. This interpretation distinguishes between an unformed and a formed foetus, and brands the killing of the latter as murder. This definition, as well as its consequences in law, was accepted by Tertullian and by later Church fathers. Subsequently, it was embodied in canon law as well as in Justinian law. Hence, until this very day, the Catholic Church defines abortion as murder and lists it as one of the most grievous sins, as serious as murdering a mature adult, perhaps more serious, since the foetus is innocent.

Traditional Responses

In a significant pronouncement on the subject, the Mishnah declares, 'If a woman is in hard travail [and her life cannot otherwise be saved], one cuts up the child in her womb and extracts it member by member, because her life comes before that of the [child]. But if the greater part [or the head] were delivered, one may not touch it, for one may not set aside one person's life for the sake of another.' Once the head comes out, as Rashi explains in the Talmud (Sanhedrin), one life may not take precedence over the other, because we cannot decide 'whose blood is redder'; this is a matter for God (Oholot 7:6).

Here the Talmud appears clearly to follow the direction set in the Bible. The foetus is not treated as being alive since it is not yet born. Once, however, the head of the child appears and it is technically born, it cannot be put to death, even to save the life of its mother, since it is just as much alive as she is.

This ruling is the sole reference in the principal codes of Jewish law that sanctions abortion. Maimonides, in his magnus opus on Jewish law, *Mishne Torah*, explains the logic behind the mishnaic pronouncement. The child, he says, is treated within the law as if it is in 'pursuit' of the mother's life. It may thus be destroyed with impunity since it is treated as an 'aggressor', following the general principle of self-defence. This is a ruling found throughout the Talmud which states that if one individual is pursuing another in order to murder them, the former, or even an innocent bystander for that matter, may strike and kill the pursuer since he is an 'aggressor'. Since he is trying to take another life, he forfeits his own.

The problem with this explanation by Maimonides is that it seems to upset our earlier understanding, whereby the foetus may be destroyed because it is not alive and cannot thus be protected in the face of its mother's life. By stating that the foetus is treated as an aggressor, it would appear that Maimonides is saying the child is alive. It may, however, be killed in the face of the danger to its mother's life because it is perceived in law as trying to kill its mother, although of course this is not deliberate.

The same would be true if, by way of analogy, two people fall out of a window and the first to fall catches hold of the leg of the second, who desperately clasps the window ledge: both will fall unless the latter lets go of the foot. Halakha (Jewish law) states that the one holding the ledge would be permitted to kick the other from his leg in order to save his own life, for the reason given above. The latter individual is treated as an (inadvertent) pursuer, or murderer, and has therefore forfeited his life. Our purpose is not to determine 'whose blood is redder'.

This, however, does not prove conclusively that by treating the foetus as an aggressor Maimonides is actually saying that the baby is alive.

Not Fully Human

Indeed, Rashi (the great Torah commentator) interprets the Mishnah's statement quite differently. He explains that the reason the foetus may be destroyed is that as long as the baby's head does not come out, that is, the baby is not born, the baby is not considered to be a *nefesh*, it is not a human being. It can thus be eliminated. According to Rashi's understanding of the Mishnah a foetus is not alive. The question of the legitimacy of destroying a pursuer does not arise.

There are many leading halakhic authorities, most notably Sefer Meiras Einayim known as Semah (*Chosen Mishpat*, but see also Rabbi Isser Zalman Meltzer and Rabbi Chaim Soloveitchik on the subject), who agree that a foetus does not possess the halakhic status of a human being and would even argue that Maimonides did not suggest that a foetus should be considered alive. Semah brings proof for his view from the same biblical passage describing the fight between two men (which results in a spontaneous abortion to a bystander) quoted above. The Bible, according to the Jewish interpretation, seems to indicate quite clearly that the man is not a murderer and so does not incur a capital penalty.

The problem with this exegesis of the biblical verse by Semah is that he is an *Acharon*, that is, he lived during the last four centuries. Judaism recognizes a general descension in the scholarship of generations, whereby the scholars of today are not considered to be the equal of yesterday. As such, he is not empowered to interpret biblical verses but must be supported by an earlier exegete.

Luckily for Semah, Yad Ramah, a much earlier commentator, holds the same view. He rules unequivocally that if a Jew, even willingly, performs an abortion, he or she does not incur a capital penalty. A Jew is simply never put to death for the performance of an abortion. It is in no way the equivalent of murder.

This still does not tell us whether it is permissible to perform an abortion but only that it is not to be punished in the same way as a murder. If it is not permissible, it is still important to understand the nature of the prohibition.

First, the Hardliners

A very respected and significant analyst, Mizrachi, ruled in his commentary on the Torah that performance of an abortion is absolutely prohibited by Jewish law. Although he ruled that no capital penalty is incurred, he still considered it the equivalent of murder.

If Mizrachi believed that an abortion is the equivalent of murder, why is it not a capital offence?

In Jewish law, a person only incurs a capital punishment for murder if the victim would have survived more than three days, had he or she not been killed. Murdering a terminally ill patient, for example, a day before the doctors expect the patient to die, while of course forbidden as a murderous act, does not incur a capital penalty. The same would apply to abortion. Since the child has never lived, we cannot be sure that it will last once it is born and thereby constitute a fully viable life, the murder of which would elicit a death penalty.

Furthermore the Mizrachi argues that the performance of an abortion does not involve capital punishment because a Jew needs *hatraah*, an explicit warning that the act in question may not be committed, or he or she will be killed for it. When it comes to an abortion, it is impossible to deliver that kind of warning or for it to be valid, since we cannot possibly ascertain whether or not the foetus will be a *bar kayama*, a baby born live and healthy. How can one be warned not to murder a foetus and then incur a capital penalty when it is not known if the child, once born, will survive more than three days? Of course, the implication is that the baby is only alive when born, since Mizrachi counts the three days from the time of birth and not from any time the foetus is still in the womb. This implies again that a foetus is not alive, although Mizrachi intended to prove otherwise.

Not every halakhic authority is willing to attempt to label abortion murder. Maharam Shik (in *Yoreh Deah*) said that while he could not agree that an abortion is murder, chiefly for the reason cited above that it is not known if the baby will survive, it is, however, a derivative of murder, known in the Halakha as an *abisrayu* of murder.

Abortion as a Form of Wasting Seed

While these commentators take a hardline approach and define abortion as murder, with its necessary condition of regarding the foetus as being alive, there are other significant halakhic authorities who take up opposite positions. While they agree an abortion is proscribed by Jewish law, they maintain the prohibition is far less serious than anything approaching the taking of a life.

Thus, in a significant pronouncement on the subject, Chavot Yair (Chapter 31) as well as Yaavetz maintained that the performance of an abortion is certainly not murder. The reason for its prohibition is simply that it comes within the domain of wasting semen, or masturbation. Aborting a foetus, according to these two sages, is the same as destroying seed and is thus forbidden. While this prohibition is taken seriously in Torah law, as can seen from the biblical story of Er and Onan, the children of Judah, who were severely punished for their wasting of seed in their relations with Tamar (see Genesis 38:9,10), nevertheless, it still does not approach the severity of murder.

Other sages would reduce the abortion prohibition to even less serious levels. Teshuvat Maharit, for example, explains that it is neither murder nor wasting seed. Rather, the prohibition against performing an abortion in Jewish law has to do with *chavalah*, the same law that forbids people from mutilating or injuring their bodies. Judaism very strictly proscribes the act of inflicting any injury on a person's body, even if they would maintain that they enjoy it.

Common applications of this concept are the Jewish prohibition of having a tattoo, or even undergoing unnecessary surgery. (This is why, for example, the rabbis seriously debate whether cosmetic surgery would be permitted, although they permit it in many instances.) Since the Talmud has at times declared a foetus to be like 'a limb of its mother', and since abortions have the potential to imperil the lives of the mother or to damage her body, as well as destroying the 'limb', it follows that the foetus cannot be aborted. Of course, if the situation arises where the woman's life is imperilled unless the foetus, 'limb', is removed, the law would allow an abortion because her life is more important than any limb.

What we can gather from all of the above is that there are generally two approaches within the Halakha as to why an abortion is forbidden. One is that abortion is a form of murder. The other, more lenient, is that it is not murder but is forbidden in most cases for other reasons. These major differences on the nature of the prohibition will express themselves in important discrepancies in Jewish law.

A Nazi Soldier Orders an Abortion

One of the most important examples of the way these two approaches yield radically different results is a story told by Rabbi Isser Yehudah Unterman, late Chief Rabbi of Israel. During the German occupation of Poland at the start of the Second World War, a German soldier impregnated a Jewish girl. In panic, the soldier took the girl to a local Jewish doctor and ordered him to perform an abortion, or he would murder him.

Now, although Judaism commands its adherents to forgo the laws of the Torah if death is threatened, there are three exceptions to this rule: murder, idol-worship and illicit sexual acts such as incest and adultery. So, although a Jew must, of course, consume a pork sandwich if an evil anti-Semite puts a loaded gun to his head, he still may not commit murder even if *he* will be murdered for abstaining.

If it is determined that abortion is murder, the doctor must allow himself to be killed rather than perform the abortion. Of course, if abortion is prohibited for reasons other than murder, then the doctor must perform the abortion and not martyr himself.

In reality, however, Rabbi Unterman explained that even according to those authorities who described abortion as murder, there would have been no obligation for the doctor to martyr himself. The reason is that, according to the great Jewish sage Rabbi Moshe Isserles, known as Rama, one of the leading halakhic authorities of all time, the only occasion where the obligation to die rather than commit a murder applies is when it is a direct murder, not an *abisrayu*, that is, any derivative of murder, such as abortion is agreed to be by even the most uncompromising commentators. Only those things stated explicitly in the Torah, such as 'Thou shalt not murder', carry with them the halakhic imperative that one must forfeit one's life rather than commit the offence.

So even if abortion is a form of murder, one is not obligated by Torah law to forfeit one's life, since it is not a direct form of murder, and the Torah does not command against it directly, either.

In a similar vein, Minchat Chinuch said that the law of *'yehareg ve'al yaavor'*, that one must die rather than perpetrate any of the three above offences, would still not apply to abortion, even if we agree it is a form of murder, since we cannot ascertain if the foetus will live after birth. As discussed above, if a person murders someone who is about to die anyway, the transgression is mitigated and the killer does not incur the capital penalty. Therefore, the logic behind the argument of 'whose blood is redder' (which is the reason we force someone to martyr themselves rather than be coerced into murdering someone else) does not apply.

Similarly, the argument sometimes used in the Talmud to describe how one life is not more valuable than another, namely, 'How is one to know which one of them God prefers alive?', does not apply here, because in Jewish law a permanent life, or a life that has already demonstrated its viability, always takes precedence and is more important than a temporary or questionable life.

Therefore, the doctor in the above case, since he is healthy, takes precedence over the foetus whose life is still an unknown quantity.

Abortion By Chemical Means

Teshuvot Geonim Batrai (edited by Shaagat Aryeh) maintains that no less a talmudic heavyweight than Tosafot holds that abortion is not murder. He adds that there is a tentative distinction between abortion by chemical means and direct physical removal of the foetus. While he makes no clear halakhic distinction between the two, he draws attention to the fact that Maimonides found it necessary to state definitively that in cases of danger to a mother while she is pregnant, 'it is permitted to dismember the foetus in her womb, whether by chemical means or by hand'. The implication is that, if not explicitly obviated, a theoretical distinction might have been drawn between physical dismemberment of the foetus and abortion by indirect means (*gerama*), such as imbibing abortifacient drugs in order to induce the expulsion of the foetus. This would seem to permit an abortion with the new abortion drug RU 486. At the time of writing, the French pharmaceutical company which manufactures the drug is attempting to obtain a US government warrant to sell it within the United States, and the Clinton administration is leaning towards its dispensation.

Such a distinction is in fact made by Rabbi Yehudah Eyush in his *Teshuvot Beit Yehudah*. He maintains that abortion induced by chemical potions is of rabbinic proscription, whereas direct removal of the foetus is forbidden on biblical grounds, which are much stronger. On this basis,

Rabbi Eyush grants permission to induce an abortion in a woman who becomes pregnant while nursing her previous child, in order that the life of the nursing infant is not endangered. This too is a familiar topic in the Talmud: since a pregnant mother's milk usually dries up, she will no longer be able to suckle her child, which can sometimes prove injurious to the nursing baby.

What the above demonstrates is that there clearly is a sharp disagreement between the halakhic codifiers on the subject of abortion. While all seem to agree that abortion is indeed proscribed by Jewish law, the nature of the prohibition, as well as the circumstances in which it would be permitted, are the subject of serious debate.

The Jewish Abortion Debate in Contemporary Times

Essentially these two schools of thought, as to whether or not an abortion is deemed by Jewish law to be the equivalent of murder, has continued to the present day, with two of the leading halakhic authorities of our time battling it out.

One of the leading halakhic experts on Jewish medical issues, Rabbi Eliezer Yehudah Waldenberg, who is head of the Jewish Court in Jerusalem as well as the chief halakhic authority for Shaarei Tzedek hospital in Jerusalem, maintains emphatically that abortion does not involve any form of murder.

He quotes Chavot Yair, who spoke of a case where a married woman became pregnant by another man. Since she was carrying a *mamzer* (bastard), she desired an abortion. He wrote that he thought of allowing an abortion only in order to save her from the shame of rearing a *mamzer*, which was a very serious issue for her and the entire Jewish community. He said he was willing even to consider allowing an abortion for no other reason than a face-saving one, since, in his opinion, the prohibition of an abortion was only one of wasted seed. He was therefore prepared for leniency. In the end, however, he decided her embarrassment was not a sufficient criterion to allow an abortion because he feared it would lead to sexual promiscuity. If every woman who got pregnant outside wedlock could simply rid herself of the unwanted baby, the result would be to encourage more illicit relationships. Therefore he would not allow it.

Based on this, Rabbi Eliezer Waldenberg, in his book of responsa, *Tzitz Eliezer*, says that an abortion is not murder, because Chavot Yair entertained the possibility of performing an abortion even because of embarrassment.

Aborting a Tay Sachs Baby

Rabbi Waldenberg continues to say that if there is a great reason for an abortion, it would be permitted. He gives an example of a Tay Sachs baby. If the doctors have determined that the child, once born, will definitely die, then in order to prevent suffering and pain, both for the baby and the parents, it is permitted to perform an abortion. (There is a possibility that this ruling may be complicated by the new genetic test that proposes to eliminate genetic defects, pioneered at Hammersmith Hospital by Professor Robert Winston, Professor of Fertility Studies at the University of London. He has twice spoken for us at Oxford on the subject of fertility and is one of the world's leading experts on the subject. I have discussed the issue with him and it seems that until the technique is proven stable and productive, its existence would not seriously affect the halakhic position.)

Rabbi Waldenberg goes on to say that since the prohibition is only one of *hashchatat zera*, the destruction of seed, it is better for the abortion to be performed by a woman Jewish doctor, since there are some eminent talmudic authorities who are of the opinion that women are not commanded to abstain from destroying semen.

Although Rabbi Waldenberg would permit an abortion in many circumstances, especially in cases of health, he goes to great lengths to emphasize that this is not a light matter and should certainly not be performed or allowed with impunity. He quotes the Zohar (Shemot) which states that many terrible occurrences befall the world because of abortions and he adds that this statement of the Zohar 'should send chills down the spine of any individual who takes this prohibition lightly', such as someone who wishes to have an abortion simply because a child is unwanted and will cramp the parents' lifestyle.

Rabbi Feinstein's Rebuttal

The contemporary ruling does not stop there. This response of Rabbi Waldenberg provoked a sharp attack from the world-renowned halakhic authority, considered by many to be the greatest Jewish legal expert of the post-war era, Rabbi Mosheh Feinstein of New York. While Rabbi Feinstein was known to search for grounds to be lenient in the application of the halakha, he was very exacting when it came to abortion.

The lengthy response he wrote on the subject was written with Rabbi Waldenberg in mind. He first cited a passage from the commentary Tosafot on the Talmud (Sanhedrin), which says that abortion is murder. Rabbi Feinstein held that Tosafot's comment quoted above, which says clearly that abortion is not murder, is a printing error, and he cites convincing evidence to this effect. He vigorously maintained that abortion is indeed murder. As a result he ruled categorically that unless there is actual danger to the mother's life, it is forbidden to perform an abortion. Even in the case where it is known a baby has Tay Sachs, or some other debilitating or fatal genetic disease, he would not permit an abortion. Although the parents will obviously suffer from watching their child wither away, he said this is not a life-threatening danger, and therefore he would not sanction an abortion. He ended his responsum by saying he was particularly and uncharacteristically stringent concerning abortion because it had become largely practised in modern times. He also said one should not rely at all on the legal decision of Rabbi Waldenberg.

The Counter-Offensive

In a further instalment of the contemporary debate, Rabbi Waldenberg wrote in his treatise on Jewish medical law, *Laws of Doctors and Medicine*, a reply to Rabbi Feinstein, saying he vociferously defended his earlier decision, despite the assault by Rabbi Feinstein. He also devoted many lines to refuting the arguments of Rabbi Feinstein. None the less, he reiterated that all rabbis and Jewish judges should be extremely cautious in permitting an abortion.

This is where the debate has reached today. While there is a universal Jewish legal consensus that abortion constitutes a major prohibition, the nature of that prohibition, as well as whether or not abortion is murder, is hotly contested. I should say, however, that there is not a single halakhic authority that would sanction abortion merely because a baby is deformed. Life, they say, is measured by its sanctity, of course, not by its quantity, and not even by its quality. The life of a baby is not degraded in any form by the abnormality of the child's physical features, not even mental retardation. It is important to remember that when our sages prohibit something for the reason of preserving the sanctity of life, this is not a mere safeguard to prevent life becoming generally denigrated. It means that all life, in all forms, is sacred, and we must strive to preserve and sanctify it.

Chapter Ten

AN INNATE OPTIMISM FOR
HUMAN IMPROVEMENT

Early in my stay at Oxford I was fortunate to make friends with Dr Norman Stone, Oxford's Professor of Modern History. As well as being a historian of immense reputation and world renown, he is a true friend of the Jewish people, evidence of which of course is the introduction to this book, although this is just one example of his numerous kindnesses.

In my years here, he has delivered several most interesting lectures under our auspices, one of which was 'The Secret Archives of the KGB'. Through his high-level contacts with the Soviet government, Professor Stone received exclusive access to tonnes of secret KGB documents which only became available at the close of the Gorbachev era and with the break-up of the USSR. Included in these papers were a dozen train carriage-loads of Nazi documents relating to the Holocaust that had been seized by the Red Army at the end of the Second World War. He is just beginning to investigate the treasures and horrors contained in this archive.

Another lecture which Professor Stone delivered on our behalf investigated the Bosnian Muslims' link with the Nazis in the Second World War and its effects on the current conflict in the Balkans. He is an ardent supporter of the Bosnian Muslims in their struggle against the Serbs in the former Yugoslavia, and one day he came to me with one of their leaders, a young man by the name of Favis Nanic. Professor Stone asked if I could assist in bringing awareness of the plight of Favis's people, victims of 'ethnic cleansing', to the British Jewish community. They hoped that Jews in Britain, having faced even worse atrocities under Hitler, would provide aid and political assistance to these people. We arranged for Favis to be interviewed by the *Jewish Chronicle*, in which he was given top billing and an entire page for his story.

Meeting Paul Johnson

During my involvement with this effort I also met Paul Johnson, who has been one of my literary heroes since I read his books, *Intellectuals*, *History of the Modern World* (given the title *Modern Times* in the USA), *A History of the Jews* and *A History of Christianity*. There is probably no historian alive who better illustrates that the untold destruction, mass-murder and atrocities perpetrated in the twentieth century by man against his brothers and sisters are all due to the loss of absolute values in our world. In the closing paragraph of *History of the Modern World*, he writes, 'Towards the close of the century it was not yet clear whether the underlying evils which had made possible its catastrophic failures and tragedies – the rise of moral relativism, the decline of personal responsibility . . . not least the arrogant belief that men and women could solve all the mysteries of the universe by their own unaided intellects – were in the process of being eradicated.'

Professor Stone asked his friend Paul Johnson to write about Favis in his celebrated column in the *Daily Mail*, and he *shlepped* me along to meet him. I was very excited and thankful. I quickly ingratiated myself with Mr Johnson by informing him of a very great compliment paid to him of which he had previously been unaware. Ronald Reagan's most respected speech writer, Peggy Noonan, wrote a memoir of the Reagan years called *What I Saw at the Revolution*. On page 102, in an effort to encapsulate the essence and central staples of life in Reagan's Washington, she writes, 'You'd be in someone's home and on the way to the bathroom you'd pass the bedroom and see a big thick copy of Paul Johnson's *Modern Times* lying half open on the table by the bed. Three months later you'd go back and it was still there.'

He was most flattered and invited me back to his home on my own, which I have to confess is what I had hoped for in the first place. I came with a bottle of Johnnie Walker Black Label, and we drank some *L'Chaim*'s and engaged in discussion. I was curious to know whether his monumental work, *A History of Christianity*, had led to any diminishing of his faith? After all, it was a historical work, and although Johnson is a devout and proud Catholic, it seemed to me that when one scrutinizes a religion from the perspective of history, as opposed to revelation, something might give. 'No,' he told me, 'it strengthened my faith tremendously.'

Johnson had studied at Magdalen College, Oxford, but was most disillusioned with his *alma mater*. 'The vice-chancellor recently sent me a fund-raising letter. "Why don't you continue helping to support your old university?" it read. I'll tell you why. Because, since I left, it has become fashionable for students to be leftist Marxists, and they are so ignorant, they don't even know the serious implications of what this means. Let them read a little history!'

The Age of Slaughter

Immediately after Moses had successfully argued for the preservation of the Jewish people following the sin of the Golden Calf, we read that Moses asked God to reveal himself in all His glory. He wanted to understand the essence of God and not just the way in which God reveals Himself in history. The Talmud explains that Moses was really asking, 'Why are there righteous men who suffer, and wicked men who prosper?' It is indeed fascinating that the Talmud should equate the understanding of the essence of God with understanding the nature of why good people suffer.

No Jewish text has ever answered this question satisfactorily, although the prophets repeatedly insist that because God is good, justice will one day triumph. Contemporary Jews, most of whom lack the prophets' religious faith, do not usually find this response consoling.

The question of suffering and justice is becoming increasingly important as the twentieth century draws to a close. There are so many horrific things going on all around us in the world, and modern technology, with its widespread dissemination of news and current events, does not afford us the opportunity of feigning ignorance of the terrible plight of so many humans. In his best-selling *A History of the Modern World*, Johnson referred to this century as 'the age of slaughter'. Indeed, there is probably no better phrase to sum up the events of the last ninety-odd years. The following is just a brief account of the numbers of people who have died in this century as a result of Godless political ideologies.

In 1915, the Turks deported the entire Armenian population of 1.75 million to Palestine. An estimated 600,000 died of starvation or were killed en route. In western Europe, eight and a half million individuals were killed or died as a direct result of the First World War, with 1.3 million dying at the first battle of the Somme alone. The Red Revolution of 1917 led to the slaughter of unknown millions, and the number of peasants shot by Stalin in his effort to collectivize Soviet agriculture is not yet known, although Stalin himself told Churchill in 1942 that ten million had been 'dealt with'. The Spanish Civil War slaughtered hundreds of thousands more.

Aside from the deaths of the actual combatants in the Second World War, which also numbers in the millions, Hitler was directly responsible for the deaths of twelve million innocent victims, in the most barbaric and gruesome way. In 1942, the Bosnians, backed by the Nazis, massacred the Greek-Orthodox Serbs. In the same war, the Japanese killed more British soldiers in prison camps than on the field of battle; they even allowed cannibalism of Allied prisoners when food was not available. Of the 50,000 prisoners who worked on the Siam railway, 16,000 died of starvation and torture, and Japanese medical officers removed hearts and kidneys from prisoners while they were still alive. There were between forty and fifty million deaths overall in the Second World War, the largest conflict in history.

The Cultural Revolution

Mao Tse-tung's 'Great Leap Forward' policy of August–December 1958 transformed the economic, political and administrative life of 700 million people virtually overnight, and also led directly to famine which killed untold tens of millions; no one knows even today the exact number. Idi Amin in Uganda killed over 200,000 of his own citizens, some with sledgehammers. Then there were the Korean and Vietnam wars, and thirty civil wars in Africa in two decades. Between April 1975 and the beginning of 1977 Pol Pot and his armies of mostly peasant farmers ended the lives of 1,200,000 people, a fifth of the Cambodian population. President Assad of Syria killed 30,000 of his own countrymen in an uprising in Hamas, most of whom were crushed to death under tanks. In the mid-1980s, the United States had close to 30,000 murders a year, mostly by hand-guns. Then there were the numerous Arab–Israeli wars, Central and South American civil wars, wars waged by governments against their own people, such as the Indonesian dictatorship which has claimed more lives than will ever be known, and ideological wars sponsored by western governments, such as the US-funded Contra war in Nicaragua.

How Can We Still Hope?

Because of the above, it has become increasingly illogical for anyone still to believe in the redemptive power of man. What impels us to dream of higher and higher states of perfection while we sit in a tiny air pocket surrounded by such slaughter? We still dare to wish for better, even with the immense weight of the millennia of history posed against us.

People seem to be obsessed with perfecting the world, as if we somehow know, contrary to all the evidence, that it is indeed possible. We are sure this can be achieved and refuse to reconcile ourselves to the apparent fact that there will always be war, famine, tyrannical regimes and mass murder.

Students who Dare to Dream

All day I deal with young and idealistic students who are completely unwilling to accept the injustices of society. They not only dream of the eventual perfection of society, but while they are at university, they devote their time and energy to organizations and efforts which actively seek to rid the world of cruelty. Many of the students I know at Oxford volunteer for the National Society for the Prevention of Cruelty to Children, Rhodes Scholars against Apartheid, or Oxfam, not to mention all the Jewish organizations to which they belong. Something motivates them to divert a significant amount of time from study and achieving the best academic results to a goal that at best seems elusive.

The victorious nations that emerged from the Second World War formed the United Nations. Something led them to believe they could found an international regulating body which could intervene in territorial conflicts and avert war. What served as the inspiration behind the idea of a community of nations? What led these nations to believe, in the wake of the most destructive conflagration in world history, that they could resolve conflicts through diplomacy and protracted negotiations rather than through hostilities and belligerence? Is it mere coincidence that on the Wall of Peace standing in the Plaza of Nations at UN Headquarters in New York, there is a single line from Isaiah, etched in stone, which reads, 'Swords shall be beaten into plowshares . . . Nation shall not lift up sword against nation, neither shall they learn war anymore' (Isaiah 2:4)?

Any cursory glance at twentieth-century history does not bode well for the future of humanity. How, then, against the backdrop of the terrifying crimes perpetrated in the lifetime of many people reading this work, can we still hope for an era of peace and brotherhood between all men?

A Purposeful History

Although the Lubavitch Messianic campaign has met with a certain degree of unease in the international Jewish community and some Jews treat the subject of the Messiah as if it were foreign to Jewish life, I argue that our hope is founded exclusively on messianism and messianic prophecies. Although the traditional messianic expectations have tended to be tossed aside as irrational in Judaism's march into and through modernity, we often fail to recognize that messianic expectations and their promises of a better world have already permeated society and the way we, religious and secular alike, think of ourselves and the future.

The great contemporary Jewish thinker, Rabbi Joseph Soloveitchik, who passed away during Passover of 1993, explained that 'the patriarchal covenant introduced a new concept into history. While universal [non-Jewish] history is governed by causality, by what preceded, covenantal [Jewish] history is shaped by destiny, by a goal set in the future' (*Man of Faith in the Modern World*, p. 70). He explains that in universal history every event is brought about by a preceding cause. Such history develops almost mechanically: origins determine events; the present is precipitated by the past. Most historians are guided by this principle, namely that causality dictates unfolding events.

Jewish history is different. Therefore when secular scholars try to interpret Jewish history from a secular viewpoint, they inevitably arrive at bizarre conclusions and distortions. Covenantal Jewish history is propelled by purpose. The destiny of the Jewish people emanates from a Divine promise about the future, rather than by events from the past impelling them to act in a given way. Jewish history is pulled, as if by a magnet, towards a glorious destiny; it is not pushed by antecedent causes.

Destiny and Destination

The word 'destiny' is of course etymologically related to the word 'destination'. What determines Jewish historical experience is not one's point of departure, but one's destination. The destination of the Jewish people, as foretold by our prophets, is a state of perfection and redemption, not just of the Jew, and even not just of humankind, but of the entire universe. Rabbi Yehudah Loew of Prague, famous as the *Maharal*, creator of the Golem, writes, 'The essential function of the Messiah will consist of uniting and perfecting all, so that this will be truly one world.' The words of the prophet Zechariah still ring in our ears: 'The Lord shall be King over all the earth: in that day shall there be one Lord, and His Name One' (Zechariah 14:9). This is the messianic dream of Judaism and the spiritual goal of Jewish history.

The Jewish writer Peretz proclaimed, 'The ancient Greeks and Romans tell of a golden age in the past ... Our Messiah alone belongs to the future. He still has to make his appearance, and not solely for the benefit of his own people. The whole world must be judged and redeemed' (*Der Dichter*, 1910).

It is this covenantal understanding that accounts for the Jewish obsession with perfecting the world, an obsession that has nagged us throughout history as well being the source of our infectious hope and enthusiasms for the future. There is a passionate determination to lift up the Jewish people by every means possible, be it creating our own homeland in this century after nearly two millennia of exile, or rescuing Soviet, Syrian and Ethiopian Jews from their oppression, or even something as everyday as building Jewish schools throughout the world and promoting Jewish education amidst mass assimilation. These actions bear witness to an innate belief in a glorious destiny and a supra-rational determination to force the millennium. How else can we explain why it is that the very people who suffered most are the most hopeful: people who dedicate so much of their imagination and creative talents towards making a better world, or at the very least dreaming a vision of its possibility? There is no political, sociological or nationalistic explanation which can otherwise account for the intensity and solidarity of the Jews in relation to these goals, despite having been brought up in distant lands, immersed in disparate cultures. Other nations have suffered lesser catastrophes and succumbed to the imperatives of historical decline.

Secular Jewish 'isms' Influenced by Judaism

Judaism, with its vision of a better world, has influenced, even brought into being, many movements and 'isms' which can be referred to as secular messianic utopias.

It is more than sheer coincidence that so many of the world's political ideologies have come from Jews: secular Jews desire to perfect the world through every means because they have been exposed to the teachings of the Jewish prophets and the promises the prophets gave of a perfect world. Even those Jews who have abandoned Judaism are still driven by its vision, but they reject a Divinely ordained messianic epoch in favour of the concept of a secular utopia. The early fathers of Communism spoke of a time, almost straight out of the Bible, when all the earth's inhabitants would have according to their needs, when no one would go hungry, when there would be peace and harmony between all people. No human being would exploit another because of the economic gap that separated them. The only real difference between what Communism promised and the Jewish messianic ideal was that instead of a Jewish Messiah the Communists hailed a Bolshevik messiah who would save the people, a Marx or a Lenin; but what was promised was still a utopia. Jews, even secular Jews such as Karl Marx, have had this overwhelming drive to perfect the world.

Three thousand years of promises of hope hardened the Jew, who emerged from the Holocaust, not depressed and distraught from the blows of the past, but energized with superhuman zeal by a dream about the future which the flames of the crematoria could never extinguish. A Jew feels deep in his or her bones that destiny, not causality, is the mechanism behind the Jewish people and this constitutes the dynamics of covenantal history. The future is responsible for the past, and what this has bred within us is an irrepressible, organic, and innate optimism for the perfection of humanity, and the advance of civilisation.

A Dream that Resulted in Israel

An example of what I am referring to is a group of secular Jews about 150 years ago who began to have a vision of re-creating the Jewish homeland. They believed that although Jews were scattered throughout the world, and although Jews had no political rights or at least no political national rights, they could somehow concentrate and refocus Jewish attention on re-establishing a Jewish commonwealth.

Rabbi Berel Wein tells the story of Theodore Hertzl, the father of modern secular Zionism, who had an audience with the German Kaiser in 1898. He told the Kaiser his idea of building a Jewish national homeland in Palestine. The Kaiser started laughing and said, 'In order for that to happen, you would need three world empires to fall.' The first of course was the Ottoman Empire controlled Palestine prior to the First World War; the second was the Austro–Hungarian Empire that guaranteed Palestine for the Roman Catholic Church; and the third was the German Empire of which the Kaiser was the ruler and which guaranteed it for the Lutheran

Church. Of course, twenty years later all these empires had disintegrated. Before that happened, something gave these Jews the belief that they could somehow reconstitute themselves as an independent entity against all rational odds.

Even secular Jews believed their nation could be revived; even they lived by messianic expectation. No student of history who has read what the Jews have undergone for so many thousands of years would expect we could be a strong, independent and revitalized people. It was the ancient prophecies of people like Isaiah, standing in public squares foretelling of a time when the Messiah would come, that made the Jews again believe that they could change the world. It was this kind of belief, and only this, that led the Jews to hope during their very turbulent history.

Just three years after the Holocaust the people who built the land of Israel found faith in a revitalised nation and acted on that aspiration. But it was an ancient aspiration that had permeated their bodies since the dawn of time. What other nation after that kind of trauma can somehow find the hope to rebuild itself? It is only because there were prophets long ago who said it was possible, no, inevitable. This is the Jewish approach to history. Even now, when we are blessed with our own state, we ask for more. The state of Israel, while certainly a profound blessing, endures many difficulties: therefore we do not accept that it is the beginning of the messianic era, because we still aspire to a land where young soldiers don't die at eighteen years of age defending their people.

Curing Dreaded Diseases

On a more universal plane, the people of the world hope, even know, that they can build a better world. We believe that we shall eventually cure AIDS, cancer and other debilitating or lethal diseases. Billions of dollars, literally, have been and continue to be spent on AIDS and cancer research. Is there no one who believes this to be a complete waste of funds? Perhaps there is no cure? Perhaps this quest is nothing but an exercise in futility? Yet, we somehow possess a congenital belief in our ability to conquer and eradicate deadly disease, even though the world has always been poisoned by one destructive illness after another. What makes us think we can somehow rid society of all of its ills? No one has done it before, yet we still speak in political, social and academic circles as if it is not just a remote possibility but something at hands' grasp, always inducing us to make more of an effort.

This is all the result of Jewish messianism. It is possible only because of the promises of our Jewish prophets. This is what the focus of our attention must be: the Jews are the bearers of a dream which we must translate into reality through the Messiah.

Chapter Eleven

ENOUGH OF JUSTICE,
MORE OF LOVE

It is strange how much dramatic revision some of Judaism's most cherished customs have undergone over the years. Here I am not referring to Reform or Liberal adaptations of halakhic Judaism, but rather changes right across all Jewish denominations.

Perhaps the most powerful example can be found in our celebration of Yom Kippur. No Jewish festival is better observed by so many of the Jewish community and students in Oxford than the hallowed Day of Atonement. In all my five years here I have seen students emerge, as if created *ex nihilo*, for the observances of Yom Kippur. Hundreds of residents, who will in all likelihood vanish into obscurity immediately after the twenty-four hour observance, suddenly appear in all their strength for this, the holiest of Jewish days.

My intention is not to discourage, but to applaud their attendance. It is truly beautiful that so many individuals find the time and commitment to be with their co-religionists on this important occasion. What I lament, however, is the way in which the day itself is observed.

In Oxford, Yom Kippur is viewed by students and academics alike as a solemn and serious holiday. In the day's observances, many find no joy, no celebration, no fulfilment beyond the purging of their guilt. This is very unfortunate, because this is the only Jewish observance of the year for many people. It leaves an unpleasant and uninviting aftertaste; to use the modern vernacular, 'it turns people off': Yom Kippur is the Jewish party-pooper.

It is surprising, then, to discover that traditionally Yom Kippur was a *joyous* day, the merriest of all the Jewish festivals. The Talmud relates that, 'there were never such happy and joyous celebrations for the Jewish people as Yom Kippur, the Day of Atonement ... the young maidens of Jerusalem would take the tambourine, and dance in the city streets in front of the bachelors.' Why did the Jews rejoice with such abandon on Yom Kippur? If the central message of the festival is one of recognizing our errors and seeking forgiveness and atonement, what reason can there be to celebrate?

People before Principles

Yom Kippur is a happy time because it reminds us that people are more important than the abstract concept of justice. Even if you messed up last year, you are still worthy of God's love. *Teshuvah*, repentance, teaches us the intrinsic value and worth of every individual. In essence, the Almighty is saying to us, 'If I were interested in justice or righteousness, then commensurate with your actions I might have given up on you long ago; but because I seek to express my love of humanity, on Yom Kippur I embrace you, flawed as you are, waiting patiently for you to atone.'

The women in the Talmud passage danced with such joy because they were celebrating life. They were praying for and honouring their own and others' existence. They danced because they realized the central theme of the day is that human life is dear and we are precious to our Creator.

Instead of viewing Yom Kippur negatively, I remind the Oxford students that on this threshold of a new and unknown year, they should be filled with joyous reflection. On Yom Kippur, we pray that in the coming year life may be granted to us, to our children and to all those near to us, and that we appreciate unqualifiedly the very existence of one another. Although we may crave many things, we seek life. The kind of life we should embrace is granted out of love, and not because of expediency. We are not merely conduits to justice.

The above principle is so significant to me, and I believe it is so central to the problems of today's society, that it requires further elaboration.

One of the principles I try to follow in my own position is never to use leadership for the purpose of spreading guilt or despondency. There is already too much of that in the world. I want to give people a positive example so they can find a way to live their lives fully. The following is not intended to darken the gloom many people experience but to point out what the problem of modern living is so that we can see how to lighten our lives.

The Quality of Life

If there is one statement that can be made of contemporary society it is that there has been a vast reduction in our perception of the value of life. Last year on Yom Kippur one very ordinary student asked me if, within Judaism, life in and of itself is worth such veneration, and why indeed we were praying for life. Is life still worth celebrating in the current, confusing times?

While humankind is advancing as never before, conquering even the most far-fetched technological frontiers, society does not seem to be advancing at the same rate. Few would even say it is going forward. A cursory glance at the modern world reveals the widest variety of people who all feel justified in their feelings of futility and despair. The problems seem to be worst where modernity most shows its face: friends who live in the 'world capitals' of London and New York tell me their cities are caught in terrifying social and racial clashes.

As a rabbi I frequently meet people who do not find life a blessing but a curse. While a student-rabbi in Australia, I would visit homes for the elderly before each of the major Jewish festivals. I and the others would receive the tearful praise of many old people because we bothered to see them when they had been abandoned by their families. Some felt so useless and rejected that they would say they wanted to die. It was there that I also witnessed a terminally ill patient racked with pain, begging for death's release.

Then there are the young people with terrible problems. In Australia a respectable Jewish school had a teacher who got many of her students hooked on heroin and engaged in illicit relations with them. Pressure from her union and the fear the students had of testifying against her made it impossible for her to be dismissed. But the students I would study with, who at eighteen were heroin addicts, told me repeatedly that they had lost their desire to live.

The Curse of Life

In my second year at Oxford I became friendly with an Oxford resident who detested his drug-addicted life so much that he tried to take an overdose on three occasions. Only miraculous last-minute medical intervention saved him. When I told him in the hospital that I would say a blessing in the synagogue for him to have a speedy recovery, he asked me rather to pray he would find more success in his next attempt to die.

I believe wholeheartedly that this university should be a place where students are shielded, momentarily, from the corruption and abandon of the world. This way they can truly aspire to the greatest things life has to offer, and then go out into the world and apply them. This was also the operative principle in the yeshivahs which I attended. We were there to study while the faculty sought to protect us from anything that would get in the way. In Oxford, though, there are so many suicides that students have become all too familiar with death. On one occasion we heard of another student suicide, once again over academic pressures, but this time it was much closer to home. A regular at the L'Chaim Society had received an electronic mail message from the student who committed suicide just one day before. The message said he felt low and wanted to meet and talk. By the time the former responded, it was too late.

Some years ago there was the tragic story, which no student can forget, of Rachel Maclean, an undergraduate at St Hilda's, who was murdered by her boyfriend. He hid her body under the floorboards of the house. Her housemates lived there for three weeks without being aware of the presence of the corpse. These are the kinds of things which twenty-year-old students are being forced to witness today.

How the World Suffers

More collectively, we read daily of the pollution we have put in our atmosphere, seas and soil. The peace talks in the Middle East and the Balkans are fraught with uncertainty. Is it any wonder that against such a background, many people today seem lonely, sad, lost and hopeless? There is a growing sense of despair and fatigue gripping people, giving them no rest, allowing them no peace.

As we hear of more and more senseless killing in the Balkans, and in other trouble spots, the 'sanctity of life' has become nothing more than an empty phrase belonging to another age. The idea that humans are the 'image of God' is slowly fading as we treat our fellows with fear, suspicion and prejudice.

No Place Like Home?

Nor do we have to gaze on the world scene to see the deteriorating quality of life. It is all about us: in our homes, communities and schools, and even in the heart of mankind.

Crime is seen as an everyday fact. The Talmud maintains that it is our homes which complete us as human beings. Can this be said when we must purchase lock after lock to bolt our doors, making us virtual prisoners in our own homes? We seek security, but to little avail. We forbid our children from walking the streets after dark, we lock ourselves into our fortresses, and still we do not feel safe.

Perhaps the greatest contemporary tragedy of all is that marriage has often failed as an institution. Aside from the fact that nearly half the students I know in this city are children of divorced parents or where marriage is severely strained, I routinely hear people who are prepared to swear they will never get married, or at the very least have no plans to marry. Being a rabbi to students, I do not often perform marriages, but I have sometimes done so. I wish I could convey to you the flippancy with which some of the brides and grooms march to the marriage canopy. It is as though they are saying, 'After living together, this is nothing but a formality. So let's just get it over with.'

The very first time I performed a funeral was at the age of twenty-two in the United States of America. I had known the deceased, although not well. Still, I felt the gravity of the occasion and wished to deal with it seriously. Yet the very first thing the eldest son said to me as we arrived at the cemetery was, 'Rabbi, please make it short!' I complied with his request but it later dawned on me what an insult this was to the dignity of a man who had struggled to provide for his wife and children.

Is It Too Late?

There is a story about the famous Jewish theologian, Rabbi Dr Abraham Joshua Heschel. When he was in *cheder* (primary school) Heschel heard for the first time the story of Isaac being bound by his father Abraham, as a test of his loyalty to God. When Abraham was about to slaughter his son, and God at the last minute called out, 'Abraham, don't do it', Heschel began to cry. His teacher asked, 'Why are you crying? This isn't a sad story: Isaac lived, his father didn't kill him.' Heschel, although he was just a boy, said, 'I'm crying because, although an angel cannot come late, we can come late.' In other words, an angel could stop Abraham in the nick of time to save Isaac's life, but we are human beings. We must immediately become motivated if we and others are not to perish from humanity's indifference to the sanctity of life.

The question that arises from this is, why should we pray for and celebrate life on Yom Kippur? Surely we should now qualify our prayer for life to include the word 'good'. Good lives, meaningful lives, lives with direction – *chayyim tovim*. Without this qualification life can end up 'bad', and a long life is the last thing one would pray for.

And yet, the Jewish tradition has always been to pray for life without qualification. Moreover, if we do indeed qualify our wish, it is as if this qualification in itself reduces the precious concept of life. Life in itself is a blessing, and we must seek to restore this concept in the minds of all the earth's inhabitants. But how so? What is the best course of action for us to pursue in order to restore the world and human life to its original glory?

Why Do We Fail?

From time immemorial the human race has striven to make the world a better place. We must admit that while there have been very significant advances in certain areas, as a whole we have failed. It is in fact interesting to note that whereas society as a whole seems to have improved, in that governments are tolerant, there is religious freedom and a social welfare structure meeting the needs of the people, it is the individuals who comprise that society who appear not to have developed at all. There is still very violent crime, hatred, contention and malice among people, living even in the most stable and civilised western states. The reason for our failure, I believe, is this: we have not worked for a better world, but rather to promote justice. Each and every one of us has a deep-seated indignation against injustice. It shakes us to our very foundation when we witness the wicked prosper or the good suffer. But is this proper? Perhaps it is far more important to help those who suffer than to cry out against injustice.

A simple example will suffice. It is no secret that too many of the thousands of cyclists who use the Oxford streets every day, mostly students going to tutorials, are struck down by careless motorists. Hardly a week passes by without hearing of some tragedy. Suppose one witnesses a drunken motorist, with no regard whatsoever for the safety of others, strike a bicyclist down. We can either run to attack the motorist, who is clearly deserving punishment, or at the very least get his licence plate before he speeds off; or we can run to the aid of the injured cyclist. Justice dictates that the motorist be held accountable for his wickedness but goodness dictates that the welfare of the stricken student comes before anything else. Leave the motorist to his oblivion, and concern yourself with rushing the cyclist off to the hospital. Although justice will definitely suffer through using one's agencies to assist the student, goodness will prevail.

Dennis Prager, who spoke at L'Chaim in February, recently published an article, 'When Anger Overwhelms Love: Reflections on Feminist and Civil Rights Organizations'. He points out that in the late 1970s, when Idi Amin and his followers were butchering about half a million black Africans, almost the only news the world heard from Africa concerned South Africa and the evils of apartheid. To this day, mention to any university student the evil inflicted upon black Africans and you will be told, correctly, about apartheid. But it is questionable whether one out of ten university students can show the same knowledge of Idi Amin and his regime, the greatest murderer of blacks in the last half-century.

Prager attempts to rationalize this emphasis as follows: 'The primary reason, I believe, is that, contrary to their declared goals, it is not the welfare of blacks that preoccupies black and civil rights organizations; it is anger at, and sometimes even hatred of, whites. Their agenda, as they see it, is to fight against white racism, not for black welfare.

'Third World organizations, civil rights and feminist groups, and activists on the left in general, are animated more by anger than by concern for the groups in whose names they claim to speak. Their most passionate members, and especially their leaders, are angry people – and their movements reflect that fact. Some are angry at capitalism and at the Judeo–Christian tradition; some at the West, especially at the United States, some at men, and some at whites.'

I respect so much of what Dennis Prager writes, and while in this case I feel that he makes a point that should be considered, I feel it is somewhat off the mark. Having been in Oxford for five years and met many people who fight for the causes he mentions above, I know the majority of them are far more positively motivated and caring than he asserts. Nevertheless, I do believe they are animated not by negative anger, as Prager asserts, but by the pursuit of justice. They correctly feel that men have subordinated women, and that whites have persecuted blacks. But they are far more interested in correcting or reversing these historical wrongs than they are in helping those who have suffered as a result of these policies. Justice is their first priority, not loving-kindness; as if it were the human imperative to be judges over the earth, rather than angels of mercy.

Workers of Light

The Talmud tells us that the principal calling of humanity is to be candles or 'workers producing light'. Our prerogative in this world is to advance the cause of goodness; only afterwards do we promote justice. Justice is the business of the One supreme Judge. While God does indeed bid us to pursue justice (Deuteronomy 16:20, 'That which is altogether just shalt thou follow'), this never comes before the human imperative to seek out and disseminate goodness and loving-kindness. Our task is not to question how and why good people suffer, but rather to alleviate suffering to the best of our ability. Neither is it our task to seek to punish the perpetrators of injustice before we first assist those who suffer. Our purpose is to help the light shine out, not to attack the darkness.

The Zohar asserts that correcting injustice cannot be humankind's goal, by referring to our world as 'a world of darkness' and as 'a false world'. Ours is not a world where justice *can* truly prevail, at least not yet. The world is still too dark and operates on many false principles. However, by increasing the world's goodness we bring it to a state where justice will one day finally prevail.

So central is this concept to Judaism that one of the first rabbinic teachings concerning the creation of the world is this: 'In the beginning, the Lord desired to create the world through justice. But He saw that the world could not endure, so He added to it mercy and loving-kindness' (Midrash Rabbah).

To pursue the annihilation of all we think evil is to change what God Himself has created to fit human concepts of how the world should be ordered. After all, throughout history different nations have had very different ideas of what is just. Are we really so sure we have got it right: are we prepared to stand up in front of the Judge of the universe and explain our concepts of justice as anything better than cultural imperialism? Worse, if our principal occupation becomes the pursuit of justice, over and above loving-kindness, then God may act in the same way towards us. If we desire to punish more than to be good, and if God decides to emulate our actions, then which of us will be found truly meritorious and worthy of complete preservation in God's eyes? No wonder, then, the Talmud, in a famous passage, asserts that he who quarrels with his fellow and exclaims 'May God judge you for your iniquity,' is immediately judged by God himself. If his purpose is to invoke divine justice, rather than mercy, then it shall first be visited upon him.

Should one's goal, when responding to injustices, be to correct them? Can the correction of 'injustice' be an achievable, ultimate goal? Is this practical? And even more importantly, is it humane?

To celebrate life is not to root out injustice but to help others through love. The legacy of the Jewish people has always been a nation replete with acts of loving kindness. In acts of loving kindness, others' pain becomes our own pain. In the small acts of humanity one can discover the value of life in this tumultuous age. Which brings us to the second lesson of Yom Kippur.

Atonement for Sins

I stated above that people are more important to God than justice or righteousness. We must adopt this same principle. We must focus more of our time on helping humanity and our motivating force must be the love of humanity, even if it means putting aside our own sense of justice. The same is true even if it means sacrificing large, abstract theories on the nature of eradicating evil, by focusing our time on the smaller acts of day-to-day goodness. We must learn to put people before principles and ideologies. Only this way do we become worthy of the honour bestowed each Yom Kippur as God shows us His love by forgiving our sins and re-embracing us. I made this point to a Christian student who became a dear friend and a regular at the L'Chaim Society, until he began to proselytise the Jewish students and pester them about Christianity. Even I did not escape his efforts. One day I pulled him over and told him that he was abusing friendship by using it to further religious convictions, however worthy his agenda might be. He took my words to heart and sent back the following response: 'I was dismayed that I had caused you (and other members of the L'Chaim Society) distress. This was never my intention and I am glad you have told me of anything which you perceive as a problem in my relations to you and the L'Chaim Society in general. I fully agree with you that friendships should come before doctrines, and I will comply with your request to re-examine my priorities as far as friendships are concerned. I do not want to make friends with an ulterior motive of persuading people to think the same way that I do, neither do I want to be seen doing this.'

Recently a man came to me with a problem. A few years ago he had married into a wealthy family. His in-laws assumed he loved money more than their daughter, so they treated him very disrespectfully, both privately and publicly. When it became intolerable, he came to see me with a plan of how to respond to their abuse. 'I will no longer allow them to come to our home or see their grandchildren.' He would seek justice and treat them as cruelly as they had treated him, denying them all contact with their grandchildren. 'But,' I objected, 'then you will become just like them. You and your wife have a Divine imperative, an obligation, to treat your parents with respect, to promote goodness and loving-kindness. We humans must concern ourselves first and foremost with being good people, not with punishing the unjust, or stooping to their level.' Luckily, he continued treating them with respect despite their cruelty, and they began to reciprocate, begrudgingly, and showed him respect as well.

The lesson is that we must live and seek to pursue peace and love, not justice alone. Enough of justice. Why is it that we are naturally so much more judgmental than we are compassionate? We were created to be emissaries of *chesed*, love, not justice, *din*.

Jonah and the Whale

My thoughts on this subject first began to germinate when I read a discourse of the Lubavicher rebbe about one of the central stories read on Yom Kippur, that of Jonah and the whale. In the story, God sent Jonah to the city of Nineveh to warn the people to repent, or He would destroy the city. Instead of obeying, Jonah jumped onto a ship bound for Tarshish. Of course, running away was futile: God, as always, caught up.

Even though Jonah ran away, we still view him as a virtuous man. This is because Jonah fled from God's order not for any selfish reasons, but out of love for the Jewish people. He was afraid his prophecy of the need to repent would not be heeded by the Jews, but only by the non-Jews. This would have been terrible, for God would compare the Jews negatively to the gentiles who had obeyed His order. In other words, Jonah risked every form of Divine wrath and punishment for the sake of the Jewish people. He was motivated by love.

The rebbe explained that this is the reason he later met with such success in his mission to Nineveh; the people did indeed heed God's word and repent. Had justice been more important to Jonah than loving-kindness, he would have gone on his original mission, regardless of its consequences for the Jewish people. His thinking would have been, 'If the Jews are evil and deserving of punishment, so be it.' Fortunately, he was more concerned with their welfare than with their righteousness.

Till today we remember him as one of our greatest and most virtuous prophets. This is why Jonah is referred to as *ben amiti* (truthful son). He understood the real truth; only by being motivated by true love of our fellows can we succeed in helping someone else. This is also what motivated Aaron to feel that he should sometimes even bend what other people call the truth for the purpose of peace and love.

Modern Love

This is a lesson for every one of us today. Many of us, for different reasons, desire to make the world better. It could be because we hate evil, it could be because we hate suffering. Hatred, or the pursuit of abstract concepts, are grossly insufficient for the task. We will fail if we are motivated by the need to vent our anger at injustice, not out of any love for humanity.

Recently I hosted a group of students at my home for dinner. The talk centred around the Major government and the Clinton administration, and how both were failing to address the fundamental social challenges of the age. The talk at the table was entirely political. I broke into the conversation halfway through and reminded everyone, including myself, that it is far easier to talk and complain of political abstractions than to deal with tangible realities.

Surely if I and these students lament a president's inaction, then we too must do something. Let us begin with the little things, like sacrificing time from studies and exams to assist or counsel a fellow student, or refraining from speaking badly about someone behind their back. Let us allow our love of humanity to manifest itself in real activity, rather than just complaints and outrage.

Jonah was willing to sacrifice everything for his love for others – even his life and his relationship with his God. Only such a person is able to help others reveal the virtues latent within them.

The Ultimate Sacrifice

True love of our fellow humans is necessary for us to be able to help others. There is a very beautiful story about Rabbi Elimelech of Lizhensk, who was known for his tremendous love of his community. Not only was he a great scholar, but he did everything he could to promote the welfare of his congregation. One day, he was speaking at the synagogue about how lazy the congregation had become and how much their families were suffering because of this. After the service, he summoned a group of ten men into his study, including Yankel the wagon driver. He suddenly turned to the wagon driver and started to scream at him in front of the entire shule, 'When I speak of laziness I especially mean you! Every day you get up late, leaving no one to drive your carriage. You have lost all your customers. And now that your trade has been destroyed, no one has confidence in you any more. Your wife goes around begging and your children have nothing to eat. You must turn your life around!'

Yankel went red, and ran out of the room. People couldn't believe what Rabbi Elimelech had done. How could he say those things when the Talmud maintains that whosoever embarrasses his fellow in public loses his share in the world to come? No one said a word. They were afraid to challenge the great rebbe, but when everyone had left his son asked, 'Father, how could you embarrass him in public? No one could believe it. You, who are a great lover of Israel, you, who would never even contemplate sinning. You have lost your share in the world to come!'

Rabbi Elimelech turned to him and said, 'Listen, my son, the fact is that he is lazy. He doesn't care for his children and is about to lose his wife because of it. So many times I've told him this, and he has not listened. I knew the only way he would listen to me was by telling him this in public. Now, every time that he oversleeps the entire city will be waiting to see whether he comes on time to work. They'll watch his children, to see if they are indeed beggars. They will look at him with scorn when he doesn't care for his family. I knew this was the only way to motivate him. You tell me that I will lose my place in the world to come. Better that I lose my world to come, than for his children to continue to go hungry.'

This is the ultimate example of love of humanity: being willing to sacrifice everything, even one's place in the world to come, from love for our fellows.

This selfless love is also enacted in the book of Ruth. Ruth, a Moabite woman, shows utter devotion to her mother-in-law Naomi. Even after Ruth loses her husband, she devotes all her energies to her mother-in-law. Instead of abandoning Naomi, Ruth gives her what she desires most: a family and a means of support. Ruth is not motivated by guilt, or by a hatred of the injustice which has left her without a husband. What motivates Ruth is her love of Naomi, and the desire to express it through small acts of kindness.

Kennedy's Peace Corps

In his brief administration, President Kennedy started the Peace Corps, and even today there are young people who dedicate their lives to it, leaving the comforts of American suburbia to care for those who suffer from disease and starvation. I once had a lengthy conversation with one of the early volunteers who was on sabbatical at Oxford. I asked her what had motivated her to join. 'A combination of reasons,' she told me, 'hatred of the evil perpetrated by tyrannical regimes; a guilty conscience for living a privileged life in America. Here I was living an easy life in the world's richest country while just across the ocean there were people starving to death.' After a year, she dropped out and returned to a high-paying job in New York City.

Had she been motivated by love of humanity and the desire to spread goodness, which the rebbe has always insisted is the only motive that will succeed, she would have seen her activities as a never-ending calling, not just a once-only attempt to salve her conscience.

Can Ends Justify the Means?

The original intentions of the twentieth-century tyrants Stalin, Pol Pot and Mao Tse-tung were to improve the lives of their people. They ended, however, bringing untold misery and destruction. I believe that part of the reason for their dismal failure was that they were motivated by abstract theories and a desire for vengeance as the basis on which they attempted to build their idealized civilizations.

The truth of this is borne out by how much of their effort was first directed at punishing their personal enemies and those they labelled 'enemies of the people', both real and imagined. That is why ultimately everything they built crumbled. In the end, what they demanded was sacrifice by everyone but themselves. They sacrificed their own citizens on the altar of abstract ideological principles. Callousness such as this led to inestimable suffering through the Cultural Revolution in China, the Peasant Collectivization in Russia and the evacuation of Phnom Penh in Cambodia.

In my opinion, a political leader who truly loved his people was the late Israeli Prime Minister Menachem Begin. In all the years I have been at Oxford I have met many secular Israeli students who have complaints about many Israeli leaders, especially those from the liked and idealogical right. With Menachem Begin, however, they may not have liked his policies, but they all agreed he was a tremendous human being who had a deep love for the people he led. He wanted his people to live in peace because he loved them. He didn't just want to end war in the Middle East, he thought of the people first and not politics.

I saw an incredible example of this first-hand. I was in Los Angeles in 1983 at the height of the Lebanon war when Israel rid Northern Galilee of the PLO. Israel was under intense, worldwide pressure. Begin flew to the USA to meet President Reagan to discuss this and the war which was dragging on. There were more and more Israeli casualties. It was a Friday afternoon. Begin arrived in Los Angeles prior to his meeting in Washington with Reagan and was going to address the Los Angeles Jewish Federation. We knew he was going to stay at the Century Plaza Hotel in Century City. A few yeshivah students and I heard on the radio that there was a very big demonstration against him waiting at the hotel, so we decided we would go to show him some support because we understood the tremendous pressure on him. An hour before he arrived it was announced on the radio that the biggest casualties of the Lebanon war had just been suffered. The Israeli military headquarters in the city of Tyre in Lebanon had exploded, not in a bomb or terrorist attack, but as the result of a gas leak. About eighty soldiers were killed instantly. That was one hour before Begin arrived.

As we went to the hotel, I saw his motorcade and it was the greatest display of security I have ever seen. There were two helicopters overhead and hundreds of agents emerged from everywhere. People pretending to be painters and gardeners were all part of the security team; you should have seen their eyes flashing. Suddenly Begin arrived, absolutely white; he didn't look anywhere, just straight ahead. He had heard the news of the soldiers' deaths and just couldn't recover from it. I'll never forget the expression he had on his face, the utter pain and anguish for the lives of the soldiers displayed his love for the welfare of his people.

He stayed in the hotel for Shabbat. On Saturday night he was supposed to speak to the Jewish Federation but he received the news that his wife had died and he immediately flew back to Israel. I remember it because I was with my father in the Westin Bonaventure Hotel in downtown Los Angeles where the banquet was supposed to take place. The Israeli ambassador to the USA at the time, Moshe Arens, later to become Israeli defence minister, walked in to announce that Prime Minister Begin would not be attending because his wife had died and he was leaving for Israel. That double blow was the end of his prime ministership. He stayed on a few months, scheduled another meeting with President Reagan, cancelled it and then resigned. Yitzhak Shamir became Prime Minister.

The major lesson of a truly bloody century is that people and human life must once again be seen to transcend principles and abstractions, and this lesson must be heeded first and foremost by the world's political leadership. In a city like Oxford where a disproportionately high number of the students will enter into major positions of leadership, it is an important lesson indeed.

Chapter Twelve

THE CASE FOR MODESTY IN INTIMATE RELATIONSHIPS

I mention in several parts of this book that there is a surprisingly large number of non-Jewish students at Oxford who seek conversion to Judaism, with a significant number translating that desire into reality. In February 1990, Rabbi Manis Friedman, author of the highly acclaimed book about relationships, *Doesn't Anyone Blush Anymore?*, and one of the best-known Lubavitch speaker in the world, was invited to lecture on the subject of 'Modesty, Intimacy and Sexuality' at a televised appearance at the Oxford Union. He had spoken for the L'Chaim Society three months earlier and the president-elect of the Union had been so taken with him that he made him the first Chasidic rabbi to speak at that illustrious venue.

Now, to be fair, coming to a place like Oxford and lecturing about modesty is like going into Iraq with an 'I love George Bush' T-shirt. The students initially find the whole subject very oppressive. But Rabbi Friedman was an incredible hit. In the drinks ceremony in the president's office that followed his lecture, at least nine non-Jewish students came up to me and inquired about conversion, and at least one I know of did convert through the London Beth Din (Court of the Chief Rabbi), through a process initiated at that lecture. What can it possibly be about modern-day relationships which are so painful that a little exposure to traditional teachings about how to make them successful could lead such a large number of students to wish completely to reorient their lives and become Jewish, so they can live by those teachings?

Finding Oneself

As students come to university from their homes and secondary schools, many question for the first time their particular relationship to knowledge others have been imparting to them. For example, those from a religious background, whether it is Jewish, Muslim, Catholic, Anglican or others, often have to address their attitude to the central tenets of their faith and the observance of that faith for the first time. At home and in school we are often told we must behave in a certain way simply because those are the rules. At university, the choice is yours: the University of

Oxford no longer prohibits a man from entering the rooms of a woman, nor insists that a woman is chaperoned while in a man's rooms, as it once did. Each individual must decide for themselves what their personal rules are and whether they agree to live by the convenient ready-made code laid down by God, both in private and in public life.

It is not just that a Jewish student must decide whether to preserve his or her tradition while alone in his or her rooms: each of us must also consider whether we wish to affirm the Jewish faith through our appearance, the way we symbolically relate to the world. This is not just a question of a young man wearing his yarmulka (skull cap) or not; one's faith involves confronting the whole of one's appearance and actions and then assessing them critically, discovering whether they are the best way of behaving in relation to other people.

Punishment for Non-compliance

There is a famous prediction that much grief will come to the Jewish people in the event of wrongdoing. This is the painful *tochacha*, or rebuke. Libraries of nonsense have been written about the 'evil portent' facing the Jewish people in the event of non-compliance with God's law, but there is a more Godly and humane way of looking at the matter.

If one is to understand the 'rebuke' properly, one must understand that the concept of punishment in Judaism is not one of vengeance and vindictiveness on the part of the Almighty. Rather, as we believe the Torah serves as the guide for a good and enriching life, failure to live in accordance with the Torah forces us to tackle life on our own, and there is no telling where we shall end up. We require wisdom in order to traverse the labyrinths of life and to make proper decisions. We believe the Torah to be that source of wisdom. Life without this repository of wisdom can be painful and hurtful.

Pain of Modern Relationships and Peaceful Divorce

Of the many facets of human life with which I deal as a rabbi, I have found that none is more painful, confusing or frustrating than that of intimate relationships. It seems that one of the greatest crises in society today is a deep sense of despair and hopelessness concerning male–female relationships.

As an example, ours seems to be the first generation to experience the phenomenon of peaceful divorce.

In earlier times, a couple would come to a court or cleric bruised and broken. They may have wanted their marriage to last but they simply could not get along. And so it remained after the divorce. This type of divorce did not make one question the viability of marriage as an institution. It was still possible to say, 'Marriage is good, only these two couldn't make it work.' Our attitude would be that the incompatibility of the individuals involved was at fault, not the institution.

Today, in just a few decades, polite and antiseptic divorces have become common. There are no really serious complaints. There's no bloodshed, no anger and no grief over the loss of an important relationship, only regret for the inconvenience of rearranging one's life. Couples are falling out of love and drifting apart. This is not to say I believe it is good for people to suffer in a loveless marriage, rather that abandoning a special relationship has become a very casual matter. There can be no question that ours is a generation of aliens.

The modern rationale for divorce is often this: 'There doesn't seem to be any intimacy between us.' The couple may have been married for ten years. They may have shared the most intimate thoughts and activities. Yet they can turn around to say, 'You know, we just don't feel married,' or, 'We don't feel attracted to one another any more. There are no hard feelings, but we want a divorce. We have nothing against each other, but we're looking elsewhere for an intimate relationship.' The leading surveys of modern-day sexuality, such as Masters and Johnson, the Hite Report and the Janus Report, all show that the leading cause of divorce today is sexual boredom and the loss of passion in a monogamous relationship.

It is this type of divorce that makes our young people consider love and marriage and see them as impotent. They are all convinced that marriage may provide stability and permanence but at the sacrifice of fiery passion and romance. After all, it couldn't even hold together two people who were compatible and were getting along. The problem appears to them to be with the institution, not the individuals involved.

Euphemisms for Romance

Another indicator of the elusive quality of intimacy today is apparent in the circumlocution people use when talking about their closest relationships. 'I'm seeing someone,' 'dating someone' or 'going out' are the terms employed. Now, why do we use these ambiguous euphemisms that can only convey the most distant idea of a real relationship? Either these vague expressions are a form of modesty, a way of preserving the relationship between the two people as a private matter for them alone, or they are a form of embarrassment: 'I don't want to let on that I have a close relationship with anyone – we're just seeing each other.' It is almost as if in today's society our first instinct on getting involved with another person is to protect ourselves. So we use words which minimize the importance or the intensity of the relationship to ensure that in case something goes wrong, or if nothing happens at all, we cannot be hurt because it was never serious anyway. Somehow I doubt that these euphemisms are primarily designed to protect the relationship: the old and respectful term 'courting' seems to convey a far greater idea of a relationship than the modern terms used, but the word has of course fallen out of use. So these expressions are used to protect the people in the relationship. But this is not necessarily healthy. How can one thrive in a relationship and ensure that its full beauty becomes manifest when the very first concern is with personal protection? On the other hand, how can we blame anyone for first concerning themselves with averting personal injury?

The Crisis in Intimacy Derives from our Lack of Modesty

Judaism has long advocated the need for modesty in society: in the way people dress, in the way people speak, even in the way people think. While many thought the purpose of the laws concerning modesty was to prevent sinful thoughts, they were wrong. Modesty is necessary to preserve intimacy, not to prevent sin. Modesty was not made for the benefit of the person who wants to sin, just as laws were not made for people who want to commit crimes. Modesty has to do with something much more subtle.

There is an old question, 'Do you lock your house to keep people out, or to protect what is on the inside?' Similarly, should a person act and dress modestly in order to prevent intrusion from outside or to preserve and maintain what is inside: the delicate and precious ability to have and maintain an intimate relationship?

Defining an Intimate Moment

An intimate moment is one in which two individuals invite one another into their private space. Not just a private room, but a private part of themselves. If every bit of ourselves has already become public property, what part of us is left which is cordoned off and preserved for an intimate moment? Each and every one of us understands that a public venue is the wrong place for a sexual encounter. It would not be conducive to that kind of intimacy because it is not private. Well, the very same applies to our bodies. A spouse or sexual partner cannot possibly feel that their encounter with one is special or what they are being shown is unique, if that area of the body is indeed constantly exposed or 'public'. The current lack of emphasis on modesty has meant that our intimate selves have become like a secret told to too many people. It still may be exciting news, and a lot of people may be interested in hearing it, but in no way is it personal or private. After a while, it becomes stale and boring, however sensational it was to begin with.

In an earlier generation there were many expressions of love outside the bedroom. This was the meaning of romance. A couple would hold hands, dance together or cuddle. In today's society 'uninvolved' men and women kiss and hug even as a form of greeting, and total strangers dance together at parties. What is left to a couple as an expression of affection besides the bedroom? And we are quickly becoming desensitized even to that.

After a very hectic term of events in October and November 1990, I took my family to Amsterdam for a weekend. On Shabbat we were staying in a hotel room overlooking a very busy shopping mall. I decided to put my theory to the test: has this, probably the most sexually explicit city in the world, deadened people's sense of romance? I watched the people below for four hours, and I searched for couples holding hands. In all that time I saw only five. To my mind there is an absolute correlation between the two. Will something as simple yet romantic have any excitement in a city where one can see exposed flesh in every other shop front?

Deadened to Sexuality

Now that sex has become a sort of casual interaction, even with people we are not very serious about, later, when we do care for someone and want to create a bond with them, the strong and potent sexual attraction which is necessary to keep couples together is dulled and deadened. When you add too much water to glue it won't stick. So it is with our sexuality.

A recent article in *Newsweek* told of an established French nudist colony which was now undergoing a rebellion by its young. The reporter quoted one of the girls who explained why, unlike her parents, she was wearing a bathing suit at the beach. 'If I don't put on clothes,' she said, 'the boys don't even look at me.' It seems that attraction can be greater when the person is hidden from view than when openly displayed. This is because modesty is what makes intimacy possible. Modesty affords an area of mystery and imagination, so necessary in sexual relations. One cannot be totally conquered and totally viewed if one is to remain alluring and enchanting. Then one becomes stale in the eyes of the beholder, like yesterday's newspaper.

Here you have the solution to the problem of why so many couples are breaking up and how it is possible one day to fall out of love. In a society where modesty is treated as a nuisance and an imposition, we quickly become desensitized to our partner and must look elsewhere to find passion. No wonder, then, study after study cites sexual boredom as the leading cause for infidelity in marriage and divorce.

Running out of Steam

At the Oxford Union, Rabbi Friedman told the following story. Soon after the steamboat was invented, a captain brought his boat down river and stopped at one of the small villages in Europe to show it off. He was fascinated by his new toy and repeatedly tried to impress the simple peasants with the loud boom of his foghorn. Over and over again, the captain stoked the engines, got up a big head of steam and sounded the horn. But when it was time to show how the boat ran, it wouldn't budge. He had used up all his steam on the foghorn.

If we waste our energy wherever we go, we're left without any when we need it. If we are sexual when it doesn't count, we shall have no steam left when it does.

I was studying with one of the young couples whom I was going to marry. I told them that in Jewish law and thought, even a married couple practise modesty when they are not in a sexual situation, even in the privacy of their own bedroom. The couple looked at me incredulously. The groom asked me angrily, 'Do you mean that my wife and I can't walk around naked in front of one another? I mean, really!'

I replied, 'Look, you can discard this advice if you wish. But,' and here I looked closely at both him and his intended bride, 'you then run the risk of falling into the nightmare scenario. This is when your wife undresses at night while you are reading the newspaper and you *continue* reading the newspaper, unabated.'

According to God's law, a healthy society in which marriage and intimacy can flourish is one which is completely alert sexually. This means a society which knows that if women *and men* don't dress modestly, they will soon become desensitized and less attractive to one another. A healthy society is one in which men and women, while socializing and being a part of the outside world, put up a curtain which separates their inner selves from everyone else. This gives us the ability to have times when we lift that curtain to allow someone else to enter our private space for intimate purposes. Immediately afterwards we replace that curtain.

It is time for us to reconstruct the borders that once existed in society's dress and behaviour and to create again the kind of sensitive environment that once kept our grandparents romantically married and involved until a ripe old age!

Chapter Thirteen

MOSES' SPIES: GAINING A SENSE
OF PRIORITY

Oxford has a long and respected history of amassing works of art, which are all the more fascinating because they are haphazardly housed in various collections: in colleges, the Examination Schools and New Bodleian Library, in the jumble of the Pitt Rivers Museum or the classical grandeur of the celebrated Ashmolean Museum. Most collections grew from humble beginnings, an individual's favourite pieces bequeathed to the university or to a college and added to over the centuries.

The Ashmolean Museum itself is a direct descendant of an early collection of curiosities called Tradescant's Ark, which was considered the best museum in the world in the first half of the seventeenth century. After a dispute about the second John Tradescant's will, the collection passed into the hands of the man who donated it to the university and after whom the current museum is named, Elias Ashmole. The museum today is very different from the assortment it once was, although fortunately the dodo is still appreciated by visitors as it has been for a couple of centuries. Now it is ordered and catalogued; sections which were found more appropriate to other collections were siphoned off (such as the ethnographical specimens transferred to the Pitt Rivers) and it concentrates on the two areas for which it is famous: fine art and antiquities.

Even a lightning dash around this building is enough to mark it as a place of enormous interest. First of all, each painting or sculpture is not housed in bare surroundings, but in a gallery or room that has couches from which to contemplate the finest art and furniture which is part of the museum's collection, such as the exquisite satinwood writing desk with its curved knee-hole. Every stairway is decorated in wonderfully clean colours: apricot and Poussin's characteristic blue (the intense shade of the Mediterranean sky and sea infinitely reflecting one another) or some other happy combination. And then the main collection itself, which is what everyone comes for: from the simplicity of fourteenth-century Christian devotional carvings and paintings, the visitor moves up through the deep layers of complexity in western art and culture finally to reach simplicity again with Picasso's *Blue Roofs*. There are paintings which have been known and coveted for centuries, but I find the objects that could have been lost to us for ever the most fascinating, such as the Rodin sculpture of a dancer twisting to see the sole of her foot which was cast from a discarded mould found in Rodin's studio after his death.

But how important is art in itself? Is it a poor reflection of what human achievements really are, or is it, as Sir Philip Sidney suggested and many a Romantic has thought since, a truer representation of what this world should aspire to than the mundaneness we see every day around us? Should we value each unique piece more than the most ordinary person?

The Uffizi: Mourning For Art Instead of Children

To many people, there is no doubt that world-class art is very important indeed. There was an outcry here in Europe when the famous Uffizi Gallery in Florence was damaged in a bomb attack which happened just as I was completing this manuscript in May 1993. Many members of the university are particularly fond of that repository of some of the world's greatest art treasures: it is an essential stop on the very popular 'Interail' tour around the European continent which many young people take just before or after their university careers. Idealistic undergraduates and ageing dons alike were shocked to hear it had been bombed. 'How dare they do such a thing? Who could be so stupid?' Paintings by the greatest artists and other irreplaceable objects were damaged, and six people were killed.

Paintings Outweigh Human Life

Undergraduates dismissed the idea that the bomb was planted by the Mafia, in favour of speculation that the security forces of Italy might themselves have done it in an attempt to discredit a government which is starting to root out corruption at the highest levels. Whoever was responsible, though, few people took notice of the deaths which the bomb had caused, even though some of the victims were young children.

What is more important: some beautiful pieces of art or six beautiful human lives? The terrorists obviously thought the objects we create are more important to us, otherwise they would have looked for an easier way to kill six people to outrage the world. Every day people die unnecessarily but it is not every day that we see great art blown up.

Perhaps it was the suddenness of the destruction that was so appalling? After all, great treasures of the world are disappearing daily as they decay at an accelerated rate in the polluted atmosphere we have created, showing our reluctance to do anything to preserve them. We are even more reluctant to take effective measures to prevent unnecessary loss of life. It seems our values have been turned upside down by the blinkers we wear: a Picasso is worth a couple of million, but an ordinary person is worth very little in cold hard cash. Given a choice between saving the picture or the person, which would you choose?

Loss of Values

This serves to underscore a fundamental problem of the modern world: we have lost touch with a traditional sense of values. Human life, once regarded as the world's greatest commodity – and there is no end to the pronouncements within Judaism which promote the importance of life above all else – has lost much of its value and is now superseded by art. What bothered me most about the Uffizi bombing was the number of students who expressed their outrage to me while never commenting about incessant terrorist attacks which we hear of continually. When even our youngest, most idealistic citizens are deadened to the importance of human life, what hope is there for humanity?

Therefore we need to return to essentials. We must teach today's young minds that often those things most taken for granted are in truth far more significant than things which have overt splendour associated with them, such as a Rembrandt or a Picasso. In the case of the latter, its importance cries out to us because of its beauty. In the case of the former, we must seek to sensitize ourselves to the greater, yet more hidden, beauty which is associated with humanity and living beings. They are more hidden because they are far more common and we have greater access to them, and can therefore be taken for granted.

The problem of misappropriating values and love is an ancient one, found first and foremost in the Bible. By identifying the reasons for the error, how it is that some of the best and brightest can muddle priorities, we can chart a path forward and get on track.

Students Arriving in Oxford with Parents

At the beginning of each term, those parents who are able to come to Oxford to help their children move into college are seen in the town, carrying suitcases and boxes and hi-fis, and trying to get traffic wardens to let them leave their cars just ten minutes longer on double yellow lines. It's very touching to see them. They're so proud of their sons and daughters, so glad they have made it to one of the greatest academic institutions on earth, but at the same time one can see they are sad to let their children out of their care.

While every parent knows their children must be allowed to grow up and face challenges on their own, it is still very difficult to let each child go out into the dangerous world. A problem which has to be faced in many situations is this: if you stop cotton-woolling your loved ones, will the freedom benefit them or harm them? Children are allowed to grow up to be independent adults, but will they abuse that freedom?

For a parent with strong convictions, the process of letting a child go free to choose his or her own way of living is even harder. What if they reject everything I stand for, and turn upside down the values I have tried to give them – will it be my fault? Will they be wise enough to see which things are important and which should be discarded if the necessity arises? Perhaps they will begin to believe that the things which make us intrinsically human, such as caring for those weaker than us, are less important than the things that just happen to make civilized life a little easier or more beautiful, like money and art.

It is often observed that it is easy to believe that the habits we fall into are more important than the real business of life, but this is not only a problem in the modern world. The Bible tells us that spies were sent out by Moses to discover the nature of both the Promised Land of Canaan and its inhabitants. Ten of those twelve spies returned with very worrying reports: although the land was fertile, its inhabitants were too strong and their cities too well guarded to be defeated by the Israelites. 'We be not able to go up against the people; for they *are* stronger than we' (Numbers 13:31), they argued.

'They Are Stronger Than We'

Why did the spies, so soon after the miraculous deliverance from Egypt, doubt that God would give them victory? The morale of the Jews appeared to be very easily broken.

The explanation given in Chasidic thought is that the spies did not fear any physical subjugation. Instead, they feared a spiritual defeat. In the wilderness, each of their many needs was met by a direct gift from God. They did not need to work for their food: their bread was the manna which fell from the heavens. Their water came from a special well and their clothes did not need repair.

The possession of the land of Israel meant a new kind of responsibility. The manna would cease to appear and bread would be obtained only through toil. The providential miracles would be replaced by labour, and with this physical work would come the danger of a new preoccupation. The spies feared that a concern to work the land and make a living might eventually leave the Israelites with progressively less time and energy for the service of God. When they said, 'It is a land that eateth up the inhabitants' (Numbers 13:32), they meant that the land, its labour and the preoccupation with the materialistic world, would 'swallow up' and consume all their energies. They felt that spirituality flourishes best in seclusion and withdrawal, in the protected peace of the wilderness where even the basic necessities of life were 'from the heavens'.

Sanctifying the Whole World

Yet the spies were fundamentally wrong. God's purpose in creating the world was not the elevation of the individual soul but the sanctification of the whole world. This is seen most clearly in the Jewish concept of a *mitzvah*, or Divine command, almost all of which involve the use of some physical object in their fulfilment. A *mitzvah* seeks to find God in the natural, not the supernatural. It is only our frail misconceptions which understand God as being 'up there', and we humans 'down here', which lead us to conclude that 'heaven' and its pursuits supersede 'earth' and its sublimation. God did not intend that we should ascend to the throne of the Almighty in heaven. On the contrary, we were meant to cause God to descend into this world and so consecrate all material existence. Therefore, the miracles which sustained the Jews in the wilderness were not to be seen as the apex of spiritual experience. They were only a preparation for the real task: taking possession of the land of Israel and transforming it into a holy land.

Consecrating the College

A modern parallel would of course be striving to make all places – home, college and our place of work – more holy than they would have been without our presence. This is the work of the L'Chaim Society and the message we seek to impart to our students. We hope for a sanctification of the secular city of Oxford rather than a withdrawal to established strongholds of faith.

We can now see the rationale behind the spies' argument. The miracles of God's protection and care which they had witnessed did not prevent them saying of Canaan, 'They are stronger than we.' Precisely because the Israelites had been delivered, protected and sustained by miracles, they had been able to dedicate their whole existence to God. They feared their spirituality might decline and be defeated in a land where every benefit had to be worked for. The miracles were not, in their eyes, a reason for being confident about the entry into the Promised Land. On the contrary, they were the reason for wishing to stay in the wilderness. So long as miracles surrounded them, the Israelites could make themselves into vessels to receive His will. Land, labour, natural law (everything that faced them in the land of Israel) were not seen as vehicles of Divine revelation. God, they argued, is higher than the world: 'So let us, too, be higher than the world. As soon as we enter the land of Israel we leave this realm.'

138

Holiness in Time and Space

They did not appreciate that in crossing the Jordan, they were to pass beyond a faith that lives in miracles into a life that would sanctify time and place, turning the finite and familiar world into the home of God. In other words, it was God's will that they should enter the land, and as a result they could remain close to Him there. Instead of being 'a land that eats up its inhabitants' it was to be 'our bread'. Instead of our being reduced to its level, it would be raised to ours.

Caleb's answer to the ten spies was, 'Let us go up, let us indeed go up and inherit the land.' In other words, let us 'go up' twice. We have ascended to the spirituality of the wilderness, we have risen above the concerns of the world. Let us now make a new and greater ascent, finding God within the world itself.

There is perhaps no more important messsage for today's Jewish students, especially for those from observant Orthodox homes. Having to leave, say the yeshivah or an established Jewish community to enrol at a university and pursue a career after obtaining a degree, should not be seen as a compromise, or even an evil necessity, since one must eat and pay bills. Rather, it should be viewed as an opportunity to bring Godliness and goodness to the places it has not yet reached. A Jew must always see himself as an emissary for the Almighty, charged with the special mission of bringing God closer, making Him more manifest in His world. The synagogue is already holy, and there already exists a *mikveh* and other Jewish amenities in the community. But they do not exist in Oxford. The student's role is not just to obtain a degree or to receive an education. It is also to transplant many of the familiar and necessary Godly institutions from his community to Oxford.

Oxford and Cambridge's Observant Communities

Among the Orthodox Jewish students who are accepted by Oxford and Cambridge, almost all choose Cambridge. Whereas in any given year there are about seventy fully observant Jewish students at Cambridge, there are never more than about ten at Oxford, many of whom embrace observance while here. Thus, the Orthodox community at Cambridge, through its reputation for large numbers, perpetuates itself. But this, in my opinion, is not necessarily productive. You see, the numbers of Orthodox students there are sufficiently large for the students to create an autonomous, independent and largely insular community. It is not an exaggeration to say that many of the Orthodox students who go to Cambridge, and even some who come to Oxford, mix only with other observant students. The result is that of course their own spirituality is preserved, perhaps even enhanced by their university experience. But what of their obligation to disseminate the warmth and beauty of Judaism, not among Jews alone, but even throughout that noble and esteemed institution?

Here at Oxford, students do not even have the choice. The observant student community is just too small to offer a full-time or satisfying social milieu. So our students are forced to go out, hopefully while still preserving full identities, and become a beacon to their friends and surroundings. Which is what being a 'Light unto the Nations' is all about.

Chapter Fourteen

THE AGONY OF MOSES AND CONFLICTS IN MODERN JEWISH IDENTITY

As part of our continuous programme of visiting speakers, I search for those who are of the greatest interest to the students and who, preferably, have a Jewish or spiritual orientation. However, because of the extreme competition for international celebrity speakers, of which Oxford has no shortage, one must also search for novel speakers who have not yet been thought of by other organizations.

Extra points are awarded for those reclusive writers whom everybody reads but few people meet or see. So it was with great enthusiasm and a sense of destiny that I wrote a letter of invitation to the renowned science-fiction writer, Isaac Asimov, after finding the address to his upper west-side New York apartment. After about three months, I received a postcard written on what seemed an old, rickety, almost illegible typewriter. (Did he use the same one to write all of his five hundred books?) Anyone who has read Asimov will know he had a unique ability to address very disparate crowds, each according to their own disposition. The postcard he wrote had the unmistakable quality of having been written especially for a rabbi: 'Dear Rabbi: I have your letter of 23 August, and the trouble is that I do not travel. I have never enjoyed travelling and as I grow older, my enjoyment has steadily decreased. Now that I have reached the age of Kind David at the time of his death, I never leave the island of Manhattan voluntarily, so there is no use inviting me to Oxford. I would love the honour to speak there, but for me it is physically impossible.' Two years later he passed away, along with any hope of ever hosting him here, having the pleasure of meeting him and claiming a gigantic coup for our students.

But this missed opportunity of meeting the old master was a sore point for me for another, more important reason. For a long time I had been drawn to Asimov because of the penetrating insight he makes in his seminal work, *A Choice of Catastrophes*. He demonstrates that people seem to be most emotionally touched by the choices which are in reality unlikely to affect their own lives, but they find easy to ignore the small and apparently petty issues which profoundly affect the world we inhabit.

Every person has to make choices about their allegiances in life.

Probably the least momentous here in Britain is the ritual of casting a vote in a general election. Yet people get highly charged and emotional about it. The far more important everyday decisions that will have profound moral, economic and social repercussions, as well as deeply affecting the rest of our community, seem boring by comparison, and so are easily overlooked.

Primary and Secondary Identities

A case in point is people's natural fear of the destruction of the earth. For many years, the greatest fear for the earth amongst westerners was that it would be struck by a meteorite, nuclear war would erupt or the sun would burn out. In the second half of the 1980s the industrialized north at last began to show concern for the environmental destruction caused by its economic policies. Suddenly it was socially less acceptable to wear a fur coat, possess aerosols containing CFCs or dine from a new mahogany table. A few years on, Britain is once again the world's largest importer of tropical mahogany, and the United States vetoes trade agreements designed to protect natural resources. It appears it has become too expensive to change our habits of consumption; people have forgotten that not reacting to problems allows them to persist and in this way they express tacit approval. However, people still mention fear of global warming and loss of environmental quality as though these are things that happen to them rather than something they themselves are partly creating, despite the pressures that consumer action has exerted.

Consumer choices are of course not the only way in which we are asked to change the world. Some Jews feel desperately torn between wishing to remain Jewish and feeling they must conform to what they assume to be the expectations of a secular university or employer. They want to be successful in the non-Jewish world but are reluctant to abandon the Jewish heritage that means so much to them. The question is whether this is the kind of choice in which doing nothing is, in effect, choosing to side with the powerful (but not necessarily good) status quo, as is the case with not casting a vote or not avoiding goods that damage the environment. Do we have to choose whether Jewish or secular allegiances come first?

There has never been any doubt in my mind that the first and foremost purpose of our work at Oxford, and of this organization which I head, is to empower young Jewish students with the ability to choose their Jewishness first. The same applies to many of the non-Jewish students who frequent L'Chaim, many of whom stem from other ethnic minorities. We seek to instill a sense of pride and attachment to their traditions, beliefs and ethnicities. Because the moment one's in-born identity is subordinated to other pressing concerns is the moment it has achieved secondary status, and it will always be treated as such.

Torn Allegiances

In January 1991, at Lincoln College (not named after the American President, as many Americans presume), the L'Chaim Society hosted the forum: 'Are Jewish Public Servants Torn by Dual Allegiances?' The inspiration was the controversial book, *By Way of Deception*, by former Mossad agent Victor Ostrovsky, in which he alleges that Israel maintains *sayyanim*, or helpers, in the form of Jews serving in the military and political establishments of foreign countries. Obviously, this book created possibilities for increased tension between Jews and the rest of the community: Israel even attempted to have the book banned but was unsuccessful. Many within the university phoned me and privately asked that we cancel the discussion. They feared our society's event would foster anti-Semitic feeling and hostility. Even employees at the Israeli embassy, with whom we share a friendly working relationship, advised against raising this touchy issue. But in the end it demonstrated Jewish integrity more than anything else. The speakers were distinguished in their own fields: Mr Solomon Gross, former Deputy High Commissioner in Ghana and minister at the British embassy in Pretoria, and two servicemen from the United States Air Force's Upper Heyford Airbase.

In addition to my duties as rabbi to the students of Oxford University, I serve in an unofficial capacity as rabbi to the Jewish personnel at Upper Heyford, which is near Oxford and is one of the largest US air bases in Britain. This puts me in contact with high-ranking servicemen, and over the years I have become close to a number of them. Colonel Donald Sokol is one of the very fully Jewish colonels in the US military and is deputy commander of the base's hospital, while Major Arnyce Pock was on the shortlist as personal physician to President Clinton. The speakers came to the conclusion that it is possible to remain a committed Jew while serving a country other than Israel. But they recognized that the allegiance to one's people, while not conflicting with allegiance to one's country, transcended nationalist sentiments. This event showed the Oxford students that one can be a devoted public servant, professional in all ways, and yet maintaining fully all one's Jewish identity and affiliation. However, sometimes a choice does have to be made, but fortunately we are not all placed in the same excruciating position as Moses.

'He Saw There Was No Man'

One morning, Moses awoke to an event that would shatter his world forever. In his youth, Moses' fortune had dramatically improved from the danger of being cast into the Nile in a pitched basket, to being rescued and adopted by Pharaoh's daughter and so grow up as an Egyptian prince. Although he enjoyed all the privileges of Egyptian royalty, Moses was brought up knowing he was a Hebrew, a Jew, though the extent of his commitment to his people during his early years remains unclear. The Torah relates an incident which, insignificant as it may initially appear, came to be a radical turning point in the future redeemer's life:

> And it came to pass in those days, when Moses was grown, that he went out unto his brethren, and looked on their burdens: and he spied an Egyptian smiting a Hebrew, one of his brethren.
>
> And he looked this way and that way, and when he saw that *there was* no man, he slew the Egyptian, and hid him in the sand (Exodus 2:11–12).

Moses was obviously a man of great courage, commitment and conviction. He could not tolerate the great injustice of a poor and helpless man, especially one of his own people, being beaten mercilessly. So he took action. We are told, though, that he looked in all directions: was it to discover whether he would be caught? If so, he was a coward, for if intervening was righteous and just, then he should have pursued this course of action regardless of the consequences. Is the Torah trying to tell us that had he discovered a potential witness to his deed, he would have done nothing?

Various commentaries grapple with this problem in different ways, but by far the most pertinent of the explanations is this: when Moses looked 'this way and that way', he was looking *within himself*.

Moses was a young Egyptian prince who had matured knowing he was a Jew but had not done anything about it. His conscience had never been sufficiently stirred, had never been given the exposure, to empathise with the plight of his people or to desire to share their fate and live amongst them as one of their own. On this morning he had woken up and witnessed the intolerable scene of one of his brothers being subjected to sadistic cruelty, and for the first time Moses felt his brother's pain. Because the slave was one of his people, every lash of the whip that fell on the man's back was felt by Moses too. For the first time a passion for his own people awoke within him. Still, he was an Egyptian prince: a part, no, the symbol of the realm that authorized the taskmaster to behave to Hebrews in that way. Suddenly Moses felt torn apart by his conscience; he was agonized by indecision. What was he? A Jew first, or an Egyptian? Could he be both? If he meant to be both, he had once again, somehow, to become apathetic to the distress of the Hebrew slaves, an apathy from which this incident had just woken him.

Before witnessing this it was easy for Moses to remain simultaneously a Jew and an Egyptian. At this point, Moses was forced to take a side. Which would he choose? He could have ignored the situation, minded his own business and suppressed the deep emotions for his people now stirring within him. He did not have to 'rock the boat' or disturb the status quo. And yet he felt compelled to do something. Remaining idle was a de facto acceptance of injustice.

It was then that 'he looked this way and that way and saw that there was *no man*'. In other words, he looked at the Egyptian side of him, then at the Jewish side, and understood that as long as he continued to lead half the life of each, he was not a complete man. He was only half a man. Moses saw himself leading a contradictory existence with each identity counteracting the other. One cannot be an Egyptian prince who sanctions slavery and the abuse of human dignity, and still remain committed to one's people and share their destiny.

Once his hand had been forced, Moses quickly and decisively chose the path of the Jews. His action caused him to be banished from Egypt: he would return not as an Egyptian prince, but as the Israelite redeemer.

Are We Jews First?

In today's society we face many of the same dilemmas. The choices may not be as acute and it is generally true that secular society and Judaism are not incompatible. It is acceptable, even desirable, for an individual to engage in the world fully while remaining totally committed to Jewish heritage. Furthermore, it is proper that this pursuit of professionalism should not be amidst a compartmentalisation of one's religion's identity, but rather that the two should be synthesised. One need not make the same kind of sacrifice that Moses did in order to remain loyal to one's people, or to lead a responsible, moral life.

Still, there can be no question that we must always make choices about what we foremost consider ourselves to be. In the face of intense international criticism of Israel, we must decide where we stand. Even while every Jew has the right, even the obligation, to criticize the Jewish state when its actions are misguided, one must ask oneself whether one's rebuke resembles that of a parent who loves their child and tries to correct its behaviour, or that of a family member who is deeply ashamed of the actions of a relative and tries to pretend they are not related.

With its liberal tradition, and because some sections are supported by Arab contributions, Oxford is not a place that displays a great deal of sympathy for Israel. I have seen too many Jewish students arrive committed to the Jewish homeland, only to become vociferous public critics months later. When I express surprise for the venom in some voices, they look at me as at a right-wing hawk. 'Are you saying, Shmuley, that Israel can do nothing wrong?' 'No, that's not what I am saying,' I reply. 'What I would like to know is why you are expressing such moral outrage for Israel's purported evils only since arriving in Oxford?' Criticism is productive when it comes from the heart, not when its source is looking over one's shoulder.

One must make choices, for example, when student examinations occur on Shabbat or a Jewish holiday. The university has set up a special system of invigilation whereby Orthodox Jewish students stay with a family to ensure they do not discover the questions before sitting the exam after the Sabbath. But too few students take advantage of the university's generosity in trying to accommodate them. Of course it is a terrible inconvenience to be invigilated, but refusing to make the decision means taking the examination on Saturday and breaking God's law unnecessarily.

Modern Chariots of Fire

There is a religious Mormon student at Oxford who is a superb basketball player, probably the best in the university. The greatest accolade that can be accorded an Oxford athlete is to become a 'blue', which means you represent the university in a match against Oxford's age-old enemy, Cambridge. Those who participate in these traditional matches, attended by hundreds and sometimes thousands, receive a special blue-and-white sweater that distinguishes them from all the other students. Some events, such as the annual rowing race, are so famous that they are nationally televised. Yet Mike Benson, a grandson of the leader of the Mormon Church, Ezra Taft Benson, gave up the opportunity of an Oxford blue in basketball because the game was held on Sunday, his Sabbath. Even while I joke with him that his story is a modern repeat of *Chariots of Fire* (and indeed was reported as such in the *International Herald Tribune* and the *New York Times*), I respect him greatly because when he was faced with a difficult choice he remained faithful to his tradition. I and many Jewish students at the time gained strength from his sacrifice.

Confronting Internal Divisions

When the United States was divided between North and South, slavery and non-slavery states, the great American President Abraham Lincoln proclaimed that the country would not endure if it were divided against itself. His words were confirmed when the American civil war erupted. We must accept that there are some elements of one's Jewish identity which will forever remain incompatible with certain aspects of a secular environment. When these situations are encountered, we must not vacillate between two positions and so risk compromising our identity on both fronts, emerging as only half a person, a divided being.

We must expend every effort to achieve inner harmony via an unwavering commitment to our Jewish identity: from which everything else will then flow. Judaism is sufficiently universal, compassionate and humane for us to embrace our Jewish identity and allow it to illuminate our lives.

The choice lies before us and we must choose the path of unity, harmony and light.

SECTION TWO

———

THE PHENOMENON OF JUDAISM AT OXFORD

Chapter Fifteen:

THE UNIVERSITY OF OXFORD

One of the most important things that Judaism and Oxford share is, of course, their esteem for tradition. There is no doubt that Oxford is unique. Oxford is noted for its beauty, stunning buildings and architecture, and its ancient traditions that still survive in large measure, as well as its famous alumni who have found celebrity in every field, including the arts, literature, science, politics, medicine, and of course religion. The only field in which Oxford is underrepresented, especially in light of its rich Christian theological tradition, is in the production of saints: St Thomas More, St Thomas of Hereford and St Edmund Campion; John Sherwin was canonized in 1970 and John Henry Newman might one day be added.

Many people outside Oxford have a romantic view of the university. They have visions of academic spires and ancient stone rising out of dewy meadows. Punt parties and exciting boat races, and time-hallowed ceremonies and traditions. Eccentric and genial old dons who appear as a strange hybrid of Santa Claus and Einstein. These visions are justified in respect of the beauty of the Oxford setting and buildings, and some of the surviving traditions. But the people of the university are thoroughly modern. It may also be observed as a further antidote to unnecessarily sepia-tinted images of Oxford that the very lengthy existence of the university has lent it both virtues (considerable) and vices (not inconsiderable). Beyond anything else, when I arrived, one of the first things I discovered was that the university has a certain 'seen it all, and started it all', time-worn cynicism. Even a Chasidic Jew arriving in Oxford did not initially attract much attention. Some of the problems the students experience come from an unrealistic understanding of what the modern university is, leading to an unfortunate gulf between expectation and reality for many of them.

The University's Student Body

Much of the atmosphere of the university, however, arises from its unique structure and methods of teaching. The university is considered to be the third-oldest in Europe, and is one of the largest universities in

Britain with about 14,280 students in 1992. About 30 per cent of students are graduates, and many of the graduates are from overseas, with the largest proportion coming from the USA (403 graduates in 1993 and 106 undergraduates, though many of these will in reality be doing second Bachelor of Arts degrees). A large proportion of the American students are Rhodes Scholars, with the most distinguished recent Rhodes Scholar being President Bill Clinton. Most of the undergraduates (on average more than 90 per cent) are, however, British students, and most of these come from specific areas of England – London, the south and south-east, and interestingly the north-west, the latter probably because of the traditional links of several medieval colleges with this area. This lends the university both a cosmopolitan and a parochial air. One little-known statistic about the university is that between 7 and 10 per cent of the students are Jewish. Only a far smaller proportion of these students affiliate with the Jewish community. It is this fact that suggested that I might have a constructive role to play in Oxford.

Unique Collegiate System

The University of Oxford is famous for its collegiate system. There are about thirty-six fully incorporated colleges; the university is set to add more colleges and students in the next year or so, including Templeton College for business degrees, as Oxford has recognized the financial virtues of offering two-year MBA courses in business. There are another six so-called permanent private halls, which in some cases are colleges in all but name. This sweeping expanse of colleges, as opposed to one central campus with multiple faculties, as in the American model, can make the realization of my objectives even more cumbersome, as there is no centralized place in which to meet new students and promote our activities. Every time one wishes to advertise a L'Chaim Society speaker meeting, for example, one must literally circle the university and all its thirty-six colleges and put up posters, to ensure the information campaign is effective. Hence the centrality of L'Chaim's offices and student volunteers to our efforts is self-evident.

Private Halls vs Colleges

The smallest college, Corpus Christi, has just 219 students, and the largest is St Anne's with about 435. The question of the nature of permanent private halls often causes confusion. The larger of the permanent private halls are in most respects regular though very small colleges in all but name, and are excluded from full incorporation into the university on the grounds that they are sponsored by religious denominations and so exert a religious test on entrance, which is against British university

Rabbi Boteach presents Edmond Safra, international philanthropist and Chairman of the Republic National Bank of New York, with the dedication for this book.

A large L'Chaim Society speaker meeting at the Oxford Union. L'Chaim Society stages international speaker events at Oxford University several times a year.

Lady Mayoress of Oxford, Mrs Barbara Gatehouse, at a L'Chaim dinner honouring Benjamin Netanyahu at the Oxford Town Hall.

The Lord Mayor of Oxford, John Power, welcomes the Israeli Ambassador, Mr Moshe Raviv to the L'Chaim Centre. They are seated with their wives, Mrs Margaret Power, and Chana Raviv. To the left is Professor Norman Lipman.

Ariel Sharon, former Israeli Defense Minister, walks amidst heavy security in the Oxford City Centre to affix the first mezuzah to the L'Chaim Society's new Jewish Student Centre at Carfax.

Hundreds of students protest Ariel Sharon's visit outside the Oxford Union.

Rabbi Boteach presents Ariel Sharon with a bottle of vodka sent by the Lubavitcher Rebbe for the occasion of his visit to Oxford. The event was recorded by thirty international news organisations.

General Robert Oaks, Commander-in-Chief of NATO Air Forces, addresses the L'Chaim Society. His son, Brock struck up a lasting relationship with Rabbi Boteach while on a Mormon mission at Oxford.

Elyakim Rubinstein, chief Israeli negotiator with the Palestinians, addresses the L'Chaim Society en route to the third round of negotiations in Washington D.C.

Elyakim Rubinstein speaking with Professor Norman Stone, Oxford Professor of Modern History and Dan Raviv, Chief Middle East Correspondent for CBS news, at the L'Chaim Centre.

Natan Scharansky, the Russian dissident and world-famous humanitarian, addresses students in the Oxford L'Chaim Society library.

International Chasidic singer, Shlomo Carlebach, in one of his two large concerts staged by the L'Chaim Society. These concerts were an unusual success, where the normally placid academics got up to dance.

Lord Young, British Minister for Trade and Industry, addresses the L'Chaim Society on retaining a Jewish identity in politics. Seated with him is Ed Lazarus, President of the Oxford Union.

Isaar Harel, founder of 'Mossad', the Israeli Secret Service, lectures about his capture of Adolf Eichmann which led to the famous Eichmann trial, to 800 Oxford students. There was great fascination amongst the students about meeting the man behind the Mossad.

Simon Wiesenthal, legendary Nazi hunter, addressing 2,000 students at the Oxford Town Hall on why he has dedicated his life to pursuing Nazi criminals.

Simon Wiesenthal being questioned by the Press at Rabbi Boteach's home about whether Nazi war criminals should be tried and prosecuted in the UK.

statute. The largest hall is Regent's Park College (with about seventy-five students), which is sponsored by the international Baptist community, with two thirds of students taking Oxford degrees, and many going on to be ordained as Baptist ministers. The small halls are basically monasteries, such as St Benet's Hall which is primarily for members of the Benedictine order. There are some other religious orders-cum-halls which are attached to the coat tails of the university, even if they are not formally part of the university. The best known of these is the Dominican order of the Blackfriars, which has members studying and teaching in the university. Blackfriars will shortly become another permanent private hall in January 1994. Their predecessors in Oxford in 1221 were noted for harassing Oxford's medieval Jews, with conversion sermons by the friars being allowed in the synagogue on the Jewish Sabbath by the Christian authorities.

A Jewish Monk

This is indeed peculiar when one considers that up to a year ago there was actually a Jewish Dominican monk, from South Africa, who was one of the leading theologians at Blackfriars. Michael Schwartz – who converted to Catholicism and became a Dominican while in South Africa because, as he told me, 'I was very concerned with combating the evils of apartheid. The Jews seemed wholly oblivious to the suffering of the black Africans, and were much more preoccupied with material pursuits. It was only the Dominicans who sacrificed all for the abolition of apartheid.' – had previously studied in the prestigious Gateshead Yeshivah (talmudical college) before causing his parents grief and moving to Oxford where, because of his brilliance, he was admitted to Blackfriars. He met me one day in the street, and it was a peculiar meeting indeed. He was wearing his long brown sackcloth frock, complete with rope as a belt, and brown sandals. I was walking home from synagogue in my long black Shabbat coat and black hat. It was the first time since I had lived in Oxford that I had encountered someone who looked more out of place than myself in this academic environment, which serves as a rational temple, promoting the deity of intellect. We instantly became friends, and I shall return to his story elsewhere in this book.

The Lack of a Campus at Oxford

The colleges in Oxford lend the university its distinctive air and account much for its particular course of history. The university is not a campus university, a fact which can cause first-time visitors to Oxford some real confusion, and was a particular source of disappointment for me on my arrival. The classic question some visitors ask students is, 'Excuse me, but where is the main campus?'; the classic reply (in a suitably superior Oxford accent) is, 'Sir, the university is all around you.' In fact it is not unhelpful to consider every college as being in many respects like a miniature campus university unto itself. Each college has its own independent founder, history and traditions, and crucially each college is autonomous. Everybody must be a member of a particular college in order to be a member of the university. Nobody from outside the college can tell a college what to do, excepting perhaps parliamentary reformers. The colleges form collectively a kind of federation of colleges, with representative bodies and officials which help regulate the common concerns and needs of the colleges, and help direct the broadest development of the university. But crucially the university corporation only plays an administrative and steering role in university life. It is not a central authority which can readily override the wishes of individual colleges. Such powers as it has devolve from the democratically expressed wishes of the individual fellows and colleges filtered through a medium of numerous faculties, boards and committees. In reality, however, I have seen little friction between the umbrella organization of the university and the fierce independence of the colleges. We have organized several dinners and speakers jointly with Oxford colleges and, much to my surprise, the system seems to work very well.

Paucity of Female Faculty at Oxford

One writer has said of the university that it has 'an almost Athenian democracy'. Of course it will be remembered that in ancient Greece only freemen, and not women and slaves, had the right to vote on the day-to-day running of the polis. The general lack of women in fellowships in the university, and the almost complete lack of say by students in university matters, means this is an uncommonly accurate assessment. This fact has served me in good stead for, whenever a young Jewish woman complains at a class or lecture of mine that women are discriminated against within Judaism and accorded a secondary role (I shall reply to this later), I always shift their anger by pointing out the paucity of female dons at the university, which is an even greater source of anger for women. The point which I try to make to them is that for all their disgruntlement and frustration with the university, it is still an institution which they respect and wish to be part of. The same should be true of Judaism, although of course it is the responsibility of rabbis to offer a coherent defence. (But Judaism has had stranger bedfellows throughout history than Oxford University.)

The Wholesome Provisions of College

On assuming college membership, collegians would traditionally live in their colleges and find all their needs served there. A college is still a

154

complete academic community providing all the facilities and services needed for a corporate academic life. Every college has the same kinds of buildings and facilities. The range of facilities relates to the present and historical growth and needs of the colleges. Virtually every college will have a chapel, library, refectory or dining hall, accommodation, and junior, middle and senior common rooms, although, to our great regret, the average college still does not possess a synagogue.

The common rooms are the only relatively recent addition to the colleges, with most senior common rooms being instituted from the eighteenth century onwards; the rest are drawn from the model of Merton College, the first Oxford college, founded in 1264. It, like the other early colleges, was essentially a religious academic community, so it is not surprising to find that the basic facilities of a college are still more or less like those of a monastic or clerical organization. Whenever one is in the medieval quarter of the university it is hard to avoid seeing how overwhelmingly Christian and clerical the university was until the mid-nineteenth century. There are certainly no marks and evidences of Jewish religious life in the Oxford colleges, unless one counts the occasional skeletons dug up from the former cemetery of the medieval Jews on the site of St John's quad and the chaplain's quad in Magdalen College.

Once, when I was sitting with Anthony Smith, the illustrious head of Magdalen College and former director of the British Film Institute, he told me how the college was at present expanding their kitchen facilities, but had to stop digging on almost a daily basis. The reason was that they were constantly finding bones, which no doubt were from the Jewish cemetery on which that area of the college was built, a subject I shall return to later. But surprisingly, it was English Heritage, responsible for the preservation of English antiquity, who forced them to stop digging.

Making College Home

Returning to the present, the students living in college still find that there is rarely a need to set foot outside college if they do not want to, as one can generally eat, sleep, study, socialize and worship (if Church of England) within its walls. In practice, students are rarely so reclusive as not to want a wider orbit than that of their college. But in the past colleges were more introverted than now, with students mixing less, and there are famous stories of very retiring members of college. In one case, which is reputed to be true, a student of Magdalen was elected fellow in the 1880s and found life so convivial inside college that he did not bother to go outside it again for nearly fifty years. When for some reason he had to make an excursion outside in the 1920s, he liked little the changes effected by modernity and after returning to college remained there until his death.

The colleges in modern times are not the communities they were. It is observable that students and fellows no longer have the sense of loyalty to their college and fellow collegians that they had in the past.

This lack of loyalty is in some ways even more pronounced among the Jewish students, particularly the observant ones, because of the way in which the strictures of Jewish life, such as not being able to eat in college, force them to spend more time with other Jewish students from a broad range of colleges, rather than with their peers from their own college. This, however, is not a hard-and-fast rule. Indeed there are even many kosher students who make every effort to participate fully in college life and who will even go nightly to the dining hall just to have fruit, but more importantly not to separate themselves from their colleagues. This is a position I encourage and support. I do not believe in and have never advocated Jewish isolationism.

Age-old College Rivalries

But it is the earlier loyalty to college that explains why certain colleges were able to maintain acrimonious feuds with other colleges. Feuds and arguments sometimes lasted decades, even centuries. Historically Brasenose and Corpus Christi were at odds since the years of their founding. Brasenose resented the foundation of Corpus because of the conflict between the old scholastic learning and the new humanist learning. At one point the university court had to bind over the principal of Brasenose to keep the peace because he had attacked and harassed the workmen engaged in building Corpus Christi. Balliol and Trinity have found themselves at odds from time to time over several hundred years. In the sixteenth century the elderly head of Trinity, President Ralph Kettle, was caught gleefully throwing stones at the windows of Balliol in an effort to accelerate the decay Balliol was suffering at the time. Even in the present day drunken members of the colleges (usually from the rugby teams) still hurl ritual abuse at each other in the form of two songs created in 1898. The Balliol song is called 'The Gordouli', and each song merely deprecates the other college.

In 1912 Trinity and Balliol had a joint debate – all forms of debate being a great Oxford tradition – with the motion that 'Balliol exists solely for the innocent amusement of Trinity'. The motion was carried substantially, having been supported by R. A. Knox, a leading Balliol man, showing how some of these rivalries between colleges were and are conducted with a strange and inseparable mixture of great seriousness and tongue-in-cheek humour.

The Chamber Pot on Tom Tower

In this century Pembroke College and Christ Church are said to have fallen out due to a 'climbing' incident. Pembroke has traditionally been in awe of its great neighbour, Oxford's mightiest college, although it has had some very prestigious Masters, perhaps the most notable of whom is their current head, Sir Roger Bannister, who was the first to run the four-minute mile. But Pembroke also suffers the added embarrassment that its master lives in a former alms house that belonged to Christ Church before it was sold to Pembroke. One night in 1923 a Pembroke student, a noted Alpinist, struck a decisive blow for Pembroke pride, when under cover of darkness he ascended Tom Tower, the main entrance and architectural pride and joy of Christ Church. When he reached the pinnacle he placed a chamber pot over the finial, and then climbed down undetected. Morning dawned fair and bright, but horror of horrors the men of the House awoke to see their most famous building profaned by a chamber pot.

The Christ Church men were mortified at the spectacle. Their ire awoken, they were determined to remove it before too much damage was done to their reputation. Yet the best efforts of rifle marksmen failed to shift the well-made Pembroke pot from its place of honour, and eventually a steeplejack had to be employed to take it down. It is said that since this time diplomatic relations between the colleges have never been completely restored, and fellows of Pembroke recall that reciprocal dining rights between the high tables of the two colleges have not been resumed.

Of Jewish interest is the fact that this most famous Christ Church landmark is also the site of the ancient medieval synagogue, which lay immediately to the north of the tower. We do not know, however, the extent of the offence taken by the small Jewish community at this desecration. But then, it is a brave Jew indeed who would be prepared to make any territorial claim to Oxford's greatest college, built by Henry VIII as a gift to the university.

Pressures of Academic Work and Striving for Excellence

Naturally students are here in Oxford to work, and most certainly do work very hard these days. Of those students who are historically aware, there must be a secret yearning to return to the life of the unreformed university in the century and a half before 1840 when the colleges resembled private gentlemen's clubs, and a very good time was had by all, with a little academic work thrown in if one had proclivities in that direction. Since the mid-nineteenth century the colleges have become famous for their high academic standards and unique methods of teaching. Oxford and 'the other place' (that is, 'Cambridge', a word not often spoken in Oxford because of the intense rivalries between the two) are thought to be the best universities in Britain, and to rank with the top universities of the world. Oxford is often compared to the Ivy League Universities of Yale, Stanford and Harvard, but for true academic work I still prefer my yeshivah where the women were not as distracting because there weren't any. And while this is said jokingly, I would venture to say that a great deal of an Oxford's student's time is taken up with male–female relationships – either agonizing, worrying or gloating over them or their lack – a subject I shall have much to say on throughout this work.

The Tutorial System

Oxford students are taught within the famous tutorial system, where each student has one-to-one tuition with his or her personal tutor, who is usually a fellow of the student's college. Tutorials are mostly arranged every five days, and students are normally given an essay question to respond to, with a list of recommended books and articles to read to help them address the question or issue; the students may get their books from the college or faculty library or, failing this, they work in Oxford's main library, the Bodleian, a non-lending library with a huge holding of about six million items occupying ninety miles of continuous shelving. After a hectic reading of books or articles the student must then write an essay: many often work through the night once a week to meet their deadline, and it is almost obligatory good manners in college life to claim to your student friends every week that you are having an essay crisis. It after all makes everybody else feel better about theirs, as Maimonides wrote, 'It is a natural phenomenon that we find consolation in our misfortune when the same misfortune or a greater one has befallen another person.' It is certainly an excuse which I hear constantly from students whenever I ask them why they didn't attend a specific class, lecture or Friday-night dinner for which we had been expecting them. Assuming that the deadline is met, one then proceeds to the tutor's study in college. These academic studies are often rather splendid ancient rooms with mullioned windows, panelling and suchlike. The former Professor of Divinity at Christ Church described his study and attached residence as an 'eight-bedroomed hovel', as his suite was part of the former canon's servants' lodgings. Even more beautiful are the residences reserved for the heads of college, and one of the added benefits for me in visiting some of the distinguished Jewish Oxford college heads, such as Sir Zelman Cowen of Oriel College or Dr Baruch Blumberg of Balliol, was just to have this opportunity of seeing their residences, many of which surpass Oxford's museums.

The Gulf that Separates Tutor and Student

On arrival at the tutor's study one sits down and reads the essay. Alas, praise rarely rolls off the lips of Oxford tutors for, as one senior academic put it to me, the method of the university is essentially one of *negative criticism*: the Oxford student who will become close, to the extent of building a lasting emotional attachment, to his tutor, is therefore very rare. In this respect, the Oxford system of education is extremely foreign to me, having spent my life at Jewish yeshivot, Rabbinical training seminaries, where one of the staples of the environment is the intense and personal relationship between master and disciple. Throughout my yeshivah years it was common for us to be at the homes of our tutors at least once a fortnight, whereas the average Oxford student does not even know where his tutor lives. There can be no question that Oxford, much like the English social system for which it is largely responsible, is one of class, and tutors do not necessarily mix with their students, especially the undergraduates. This however is not a hard and fast rule and indeed one does observe a number of dons who have an incredibly close and caring relationship with their students. Nonetheless, the students seem genuinely satisfied with how they are treated by their tutors, and I rarely hear the students complain about the system. They much prefer the tutorials to lectures, the principal system employed in most other universities.

Oxford dons do enjoy a reputation of being experts in criticism and amateurs in praise, though many do endeavour to resist their more natural instincts and provide a generally sympathetic balance of criticism and encouragement. This, then, is the main method of teaching in Oxford, though tutorials are supplemented by lectures. The lectures, however, are not particularly important in the Oxford system; they are there in the main to provide an overall framework into which the specific tutorials may be fitted. Those who write adequate essays can more or less ignore the lectures, which is fortunate when one considers such lectorial delights as 'The Effect of Hegel's Concept of "Geist" on Nineteenth-century Theology', which one student asked me to attend with him. The only exception to this general scheme of things is that the science students conduct much of their work in the central science area, and they have a fairly heavy burden of compulsory lectures and laboratory demonstrations in addition to their tutorials which deal more with the theoretical side of their work.

Parallels Between Oxford and the Yeshivah

I am personally fascinated with the idea of the one-to-one *viva voce* tutorial because in some respects it is very similar to traditional methods of learning in the yeshivah or Jewish academy. In the yeshivah students usually study in pairs, working orally, and students also work one-to-one with yeshivah teachers, all studying from texts. This system of learning in the yeshivah has underpinned the excellence of the yeshivah system, and guaranteed the survival of Jewish learning. The lecture, or *shiur*, as it is known, is of little practical consequence in the yeshivah, where virtually all knowledge accrued is from one-to-one study partnerships. The main difference between the Oxford and yeshivah systems, of course, is that in the yeshivah the partnerships are usually between equals, whereas in Oxford it involves the mature and professional tutor and the young student.

Nevertheless, the similarity between the Oxford tutorial and the yeshivah methods of learning are not accidental, as they have a common origin in the dialectical systems of teaching used in ancient Greece. In the case of Jewish use of Greek methods, it appears that the Jewish religious hierarchy adopted the Greek teaching used in the academies of the Alexandrian empire after Israel was taken over in the Alexandrian conquest. This was because the Alexandrian empire sought with great success to assimilate all local cultures of their subject lands through a process of Hellenization. They encouraged the use of *koine* Greek (the language of the New Testament) as a lingua franca throughout the empire, and propagated Greek ideas through academies of learning which were of great excellence. The crucial aspect of Hellenization was that there were genuine attempts to create a single Hellenic identity across the empire using these methods and, most importantly, if once assimilated into Greek culture any member of a subject nation would be accorded equality, capable of achieving promotion and status regardless of their origins. This proved a great challenge to Judaism, and religious leaders were vexed by the large amount of assimilation, with many of the young men going so far as to have an operation to uncircumcise themselves so that they would not be mocked at the athletics stadium where competitors competed naked, covered only by a layer of oil. So pervasive was this practice that the Talmud finds it necessary to castigate severely one who 'covers the covenant of Abraham', asserting that 'he has lost his place in the World to Come' (*Ethics of the Fathers* 3:11). To preserve Jewish life and learning the religious leaders decided to educate all levels of Jewish society using Greek methods. In short they decided to beat the Greeks at their own system, and they were not afraid to use their methods.

Oxford's Preoccupation with Classical Culture

As for the Oxford use of Greek methods, this has come from the university's more general and ancient admiration for and preoccupation with classical culture, a notable fact that can be witnessed immediately in the classical architecture of many of Oxford's colleges, an excellent example of which is the Queen's College, on the High Street, complete with its neo-classical columns and statues. Throughout the centuries until the last one, the classical world dominated the university to the extent that students were forced to speak Latin or Greek to the virtual exclusion of English. In Brasenose College students were forbidden to use English under pain of punishment until about 1850. Traditionally most teaching in Oxford was dominated by oral and dialectical methods. All examinations until 1840 were by oral disputation before an audience. After the reforms of the 1840s and 1850s written examinations were introduced for the first time and the modern tutorial was evolved. This was in order to improve standards as the academic system in Oxford became decayed and corrupt between the commonwealth period and 1840, to the extent that few students bothered to be examined for their degrees. Those who did merely appeared at the divinity school to participate in a time-hallowed recitation of set questions and answers, followed by a swift retirement for celebratory food and ale. Thus even though the university uses oral teaching and examining far less than it used to, the idea of dialectic exchange between tutor and pupil as the optimal vehicle of teaching is still enshrined in the tutorial system.

The Shy Oxford Don

The conduct of tutorials over the years has given rise to a rich vein of stories (and folklore) among the students and the academics about the stranger happenings in tutorials, which leads to another interesting similarity between Oxford and Judaism in general, and Chasidism in particular, namely the wealth of tales and folklore associated with both. Oxford dons love telling stories of their eccentric counterparts and predecessors, not unlike the rich Chasidic tales of miracles and excesses of the early mystics. I shall leave a comprehensive examination of the two for another book, but will tell here a few brief stories, said to be true. The first was told to me by a don in one of the colleges who knew the tutor concerned. A well-known history tutor, now retired, was so shy that he would not even face his students when he had tutorials. One day a student arrived for his tutorial at this don's study. He knocked on the door and a voice said, 'Enter.' The student went in and could not see his tutor anywhere. But again the disembodied voice spoke and said, 'Pray read.' So the student dutifully read his essay, trying to behave as if nothing were unusual. The entire tutorial was conducted in this way, with the tutor unseen. Finally the student discerned the source of the voice, for as he looked up to the top of the huge antique bookcase that took up one side of the room, he espied the absent tutor lying along the top of the bookcase almost hidden by the ornate cornice work at the top of the shelves.

Tame by contrast were the antics of Rector Mark Pattison, head of Lincoln College from 1861. Pattison was a noted but stern tutor. He could not tolerate the poor submissions of ignorant students, and on occasion he would take the inferior essays from the hand of a student, screw them up into a ball and throw them into the face of the now quivering student. This technique is no doubt one that modern educationalists would call 'negative reinforcement'.

Learning to Teach Oneself

Taking an overview of teaching in Oxford, the tutorial system is generally effective. The system at its best encourages independence of thought by students, and self-disciplined working. In *Ethics of the Fathers* (2:8), Rabbi Yochan ben Zakkai, one of the greatest sages of the Second Temple era, compares the erudition of his two leading disciples: 'Rabbi Eliezer ben Hyrconus is like a sieve which does not lose even one drop; while Rabbi Eleazar ben Arach is like a spring which constantly grows stronger and stronger.' This accolade is interpreted to mean that, whereas Rabbi Eliezer merely retains every word of his master, he does not learn to think on his own. Rabbi Eleazar, on the other hand, is like a spring because he has learned the methods of intellectual deduction and so is able to teach himself. Students in Oxford possess this quality and the benefit of the tutorial system is that they are essentially taught to teach themselves. The hallmark of an Oxford-trained mind is acute and objective scholarly comprehension and analysis, coupled with originality of thought, and a willingness to question received truths and academic truisms at every juncture. One of the major academic sins in Oxford, as far as students are concerned, is a lack of originality. If a tutor dubs his student as 'worthy but dull', this is a death knell for a student's continued career in the university. Naturally every virtue has its corresponding vice, and at its worst the Oxford mind is renowned for its dusty scholasticism and pedantry, the sort of thing that resulted in a new fellow at Pembroke being sent a two-and-a-half page missive by a former bursar, explaining in unctuous and intricate legalistic detail (as according to the college statutes enacted at various times) and in the most pejorative terms why he could not have an official college car-parking space. To his credit, the new fellow concerned framed the letter, recognizing it as a masterpiece of pedantry worthy of a permanent place on his toilet wall.

The Examination System

Of course a description of tuition is not the end of an understanding of a student's work. At the end of the academic day examinations loom large in an Oxford student's life, and it may be observed fairly that students do suffer at examinations in Oxford. This is because many (but by no means all) are awarded their degrees entirely on the results of their final examination at the end of three years, or four years in some faculties.

The Talmud declares that 'the value of everything is determined by its conclusion', and in the case of Oxford students this is especially true. They may have written the most beautiful and eloquent essays through their time at the university which might even be worthy of publication in the finest academic journals. But to no avail; it counts for nothing in the final analysis of what degree they receive. Everything is determined by exam.

Generally students sit up to eight or nine final examination papers, with each paper lasting three hours and normally consisting of three or four essay-style questions. The entire process takes from a few days (morning and afternoon papers four days in a row) to a few weeks. If this pressure were not enough, students know that if they fail any single paper they will fail their whole degree. One retake (of all the papers, whether failed or not) is permitted, but in the second instance only a pass degree may be awarded, not an honours degree.

It should be added that students do have a variety of intermediate examinations of varying importance. The lesser exams levied periodically at the beginning of terms are called collections, and they usually test the student on their reading in the vacation. Whether or not the students take these exams entirely seriously, it is very definitely in one's interest to pass them, as unpleasant things can happen after failing collections. Certain students can be made to take punitive examinations called 'impositions' if they do badly in their study; you can tell a student doing impositions because they have a certain pallor and cold sweat about them, rather like somebody about to jump out of an aircraft without a parachute and still hoping for a soft landing. The most important examination other than finals is the 'preliminary examination' or the 'first public examinations' taken after the second term of the first year. Most students take these with intense seriousness, as these examinations are the most important academic obstacle between the first year and the final exams, and are a time when most students who are going to drop out (or more likely to be pushed), leave.

Since the university has never been planned but has evolved, there are always exceptions to general rules. So students in certain subjects do not take first public examinations but the grand-sounding 'honour moderations' or 'mods', which in some cases do count towards their overall degree result. These examinations are reputed to be of a very high standard (some students say they are nearly equivalent to a degree elsewhere, but that may be an Oxford exaggeration). Students in Literae Humaniores (that's classics to you or me) take their 'classical honour moderations' first of all, and complete their degree with the so-called 'greats'. The present 'mods' were created in the university reforms of the 1850s. Science students on four-year courses have their exams split into two, with exams taking place at the ends of the third and fourth years.

Achieving Academic Excellence

There can be no doubt that academic excellence and reputations must be created by various means, and the tutorial system with final examinations is how Oxford creates its standards. Excellence does have its price, and this is in widespread examination failure. While most undergraduates tend to get their BAs if they manage to get past the first-year examinations, there is a high, and generally unpublicized, rate of failure among graduates. The Master of Philosophy degree created 25 years ago has an average failure rate of 25 per cent! While figures are not readily available for doctorates, the failure rate in 1964 was a staggering 58 per cent in the arts and humanities. Since the conditions in which graduates work now in the arts and humanities have not significantly changed in the last thirty years, it would be fair to suppose that a large proportion still fail to complete their theses or to produce them to a high standard of originality.

The Counselling Service

The other face of failure in Oxford is the fact that 15 per cent of all students attend its psychiatric counselling service before they leave the university. This is a rate of about 6 per cent more than for their colleagues at the mid-ranking and less stressful redbrick University of Reading, twenty-five miles down the road. This figure underestimates the degree of personal problems, as some students will take counsel or treatment elsewhere or will keep their problems to themselves. To be sure, I was not quite prepared for the amount of counselling I myself would be called upon to perform. To date, there is a constant stream in and out of my office, with the students stopping by to discuss both very serious and far lighter matters. A good friend of mine who is a British graduate student served for two years as junior dean of his college, where he expected his duties would consist primarily of disciplining errant students who played their stereos too loudly at night. He was in for a shock. What he thought would be a fairly easy occupation became a time-consuming gargantuan undertaking which involved non-stop counselling. There is a lot of pressure to succeed at Oxford, which brings dizzying effects to the students. There is no doubt pain hidden behind many confident Oxford student exteriors. The university normally claims in all such negative matters (that is, drop-out rates, suicides rates and other problems) that they have neither more nor less in these things than other establishments, but informed observers tend to think differently. However, since this is such an important matter and is so central to my function at the university, I shall return to it in the following chapters.

A Lack of Support

But briefly, if one is to approach this problem seriously, one must recognize that the greater prevalence of personal problems in the university is caused not just by the extra pressure of work at Oxford compared to less élite universities. One of the contributory factors is the general lack of cohesion and loyalty within the colleges, which means that students and academics do not always receive the acceptance and support they need to help them through the difficulties that can crop up during one's university career, especially in highly pressurized universities like Oxford. At worst, without proper support, students and fellows can be prone to psychological isolation and depression, which can cause academic under-achievement or failure, psychological problems, and sometimes even suicide.

The difficulties are compounded by the fact that students are often reluctant to admit fears of inadequacy to each other because of possible loss of face. Also students are wary of confiding problems to some tutors, particularly worries that affect their work, as an admission of academic problems will often mean the student will be compelled to take an academic suspension (traditionally called rustication, literally being sent to the countryside for a set number of terms, usually two), or worse still, they could be 'sent down' (that is expelled) from their college. The students generally believe that an Oxford degree is vital for their success in life, and failure to get one will alter the course of the remainder of their lives for the worse. This is why most are loath to admit to difficulties as they fear being sent down, which is seen as a mark of Cain, certain to bring permanent disaster in its wake. Therefore, it is imperative that students develop an intrinsic sense of self-worth which is impervious to academic or professional achievement, or failure. To a large extent, I am here to help them find this, and coming to speak to me serves, not just as a temporary escape from the rigours of academic pressures, but as a boost to one's confidence since I am not an academic and am interested in them for their humanity rather than their success. I insist that they call me *Shmuley*, as opposed to Rabbi Boteach. And it is specifically in this kind of absence of formality that they can find a respite from the obsession with their own fates and destinies.

An Oxford Degree is a Passport

To be sure, there is a certain general truth in the student perception of the importance of their Oxford career, in that success in Oxford can be the road to joining the élite or those who excel in the country, but also it is a dangerous and distorting generalization as it is crass to assume an Oxford degree is the measure of all things, and that all other avenues in life pale in comparison. This is an assumption which students are all too eager to make and which I am all too anxious to have them avoid. Often, I am forced to remind my students that many of Oxford's most famous men failed their courses or were thrown out of the university, as true genius may find the tighter restraints and conformities of a university irksome to the spirit. The most famous recent example is, of course, President Bill Clinton who, although he completed two years at Oxford, failed to obtain a degree. To be fair, however, it appears that his protests against the war in Vietnam were a large factor in this.

Coincidentally, this fact of the student's neurotic fear of failure explains the perception of many visitors that the majority of students seem to be radiant and intimidatingly confident. One student arrived at Oxford as a graduate from another university and spent his first week in college fighting off gross feelings of inferiority and inadequacy, and even contemplated leaving college. This was all because he felt he was not up to the elevated standard so glaringly evident around him. Then at the end of the first week certain incidents enabled him to make a crucial discovery that the Oxford ring of confidence was for the most part a sham, and that it was generally assumed by students to cover up their own neuroses about Oxford, and to gain the psychological advantage over their fellow students.

Avoiding the Discussion about Failure

In reality, failure of any kind is virtually a taboo subject among students. It is rarely discussed, and many students assiduously avoid contaminating contact with failure of any kind. One Jewish student arrived at Keble College as an undergraduate. He was charming and successful, and had the most wonderful time as he became the toast of the college. He joined the Air Training Corps at Oxford where you can learn to fly for free, providing you remain a Royal Air Force reservist who, in the event of war, can go abroad and fly for the good of your country. But one day disaster struck. The student was landing the expensive trainer aircraft when he crashed and wrote it off, although he himself emerged unscathed. This was no doubt careless and unfortunate, but he did not anticipate the after-effects. The students at the air corps refused to speak to him for several weeks because of his disaster. But one thing he did not anticipate was that the contagion of failure accompanied him to college, where the other students scented failure and refused to talk to him as well. His social life crashed as surely as the aircraft itself and did not recover until the following term.

This tale is a revealing parable about the university. Students and the university believe in its own superiority and importance, and much of Oxford's continued sway in the world depends on the university continuing to convince others of its overwhelming superiority. In reality the image that Oxford creates for itself is almost as important as its concrete achievements, and it is meat and drink to its continued pre-eminence and success. I myself fell prey initially to the university's colossal, awe-inspiring reputation. I arrived enthusiastic, but accompanied by a tremendous fear of failure. How could I indeed breath life into an ancient tradition that was under repeated assault from minds far greater and more learned than my own? Deep depression and feelings of insignificance followed, and the fear of failure quickly threatened to become a self-fulfilling prophecy. But what began as a curse became a blessing. I quickly discovered that by being open about my own fears, and expressing how I was no different in this respect to the newly arrived undergraduate, I quickly gained the students' confidence. What they were really seeking was not only someone to encourage them, but someone to empathize with their trepidation.

Leisure and Society in a Student's Life

To balance all this talk of hard work it must be emphasized that students are generally in control of their work, and they ensure that they get adequate relaxation, if not rest. There is plenty to do in one's spare time in Oxford, however little one has. In my experience it is difficult to get students to commit themselves to any event or activity more than five minutes before it happens, as most students have such a rapidly moving schedule and so many commitments that they are wary of obligating themselves in advance. Among the extra-curricular activities that are available is much inter-collegiate sport. Rowing is by far the most popular, with a third of students rowing at one time or another, and is also one of Oxford's most cherished traditions. There are also reputed to be up to two hundred university societies, catering for every taste and interest, and one of my favourite events every year is 'The Freshers' Fair' where all the societies set up stalls to attract new student members. The diversity, colour and pageantry are astonishing. There are sporting societies, drinking societies, dining societies, cave-dwelling societies, intellectual societies, the Rocky Horror Society, the Sherlock Holmes Society, the Tiddlywinks Society, to name but a few in addition to all the country's political parties who also run student societies. Also, there are the religious societies, under whose classification the L'Chaim Society falls, which has been the context of much of my work and writing in Oxford. As I mentioned above, the L'Chaim Society has the distinction of being the second largest in the university with approximately 1,200 members. The largest by far is the world-famous Oxford Union society with 9,000 members (past and present students) and with whom we co-ordinate many of our larger events, especially international speaker meetings. But the great majority of the remaining societies usually boast no more than twenty to forty members.

College Social and Drinking Life

For those who are too exhausted to pursue sport or society life, the ultimate fall-back as far as relaxation goes is the junior common room of each college, where the basic amenities can be found, usually with the bar. Beer drinking has been of great importance in the university since the thirteenth century; in fact Brasenose College may even be named after its old 'brasenhaus' or brewery. The tradition of drinking is stoutly maintained by the students today, a fact supported by a recent survey showing that a large number of students drink more than is strictly good for them, with at least a third (men and women) getting drunk at least once a week. In fact, while living in Sydney, Australia, as a Rabbinical student, one of the first things I learned about Oxford was the fact that the then Prime Minister, Bob Hawke, who had been to Oxford's University College as a Rhodes Scholar and who has been a L'Chaim speaker, had broken the world record for beer-guzzling at an Oxford college.

It is specifically Hertford College which has gained pre-eminence in the field of barrelology, and the former custodians of Radcliffe Square dread the Friday-night 'bops' or raves that the Hertfordians reward themselves with for what work they do complete. The aftermath is normally a trail of broken and discarded beer glasses forming an easily followed track to the front door of the college, and bicycles artfully hung from high places. The custodians also dreaded the fateful conjunction of both Hertford and Brasenose having parties on the same night, as they seem to encourage mutual mayhem. Just recently four Brasenosians finished such an evening in a big fight outside college, which led to windows being smashed and other damage. The next morning one of the 'victims' was seen walking to a shop to get his breakfast. He tastefully wore a purple tie beautifully matching the colour of his bruises; obviously the age of elegance and grace has not entirely passed us by in Oxford.

Drinking at the L'Chaim Society

This is not to decry the art of drinking, and indeed the word L'Chaim, while meaning 'to life', is the Jewish expression for 'Cheers'. At Freshers' Fair, student officers who man our booth are routinely confronted with the problem of how best to describe a traditional Jewish student club, headed by a Chasidic rabbi but with very famous speakers and a universalist dimension. One of the hallmarks of our activities is the sincere, meaningful toast, or 'L'Chaim', which the students make every Friday night at the Shabbat table. We invite students to express their most important sentiments, or wishes for friends and humanity, and many of the students' utterances are quite profound.

Chapter Sixteen

RELIGION AND THE BELIEF
IN GOD IN MODERN OXFORD

So far I have given an impression of the university as it is at present, offering a sketch of the sort of life that students have here and how they fill their days. It is relevant to describe how the university attained its present condition and ethos, particularly its attitude to religion and religious life. Today it is a thriving research-based university, which is considered by many to be a bastion of secular-liberal thought and a home of rationalism. In its modern guise it is much at odds with most of its history because until the university became an officially secular organization in 1871, it was completely dominated by its Christian history and heritage. Before the climactic rise of liberal and scientific thought of the Victorian period in the university, with the subsequent transformation of its statutes and ethos, the university was a Christian organization, and matters of theology and the teaching of God were of pivotal importance.

Commonality of Judaism and Liberalism

In my work of imparting knowledge of the Jewish God and tradition at Oxford, the secular and liberal ethos of the university is of great importance, as it is the background of my efforts and necessarily determines to some extent the methods I employ in my work with the students, and the way in which I have taught them Judaism.

Oxford is in some ways a very difficult arena for propagating a religious consciousness because of this ethos, but it is very important to emphasize, contrary to many people's assumptions, that the liberal traditions of the university are ultimately a real help and not a hindrance in what I do. Often enough one will hear religious people of all persuasions denigrating liberalism, and the other 'isms' associated with it, as eroding religion and religious life and being anti-Godly. Yet from a Jewish perspective in the university here this is an unwarranted view and fails to understand that the liberal ethos of Oxford is in a real sense the foundation of my activities. Liberalism is by no means hostile to the teaching of God in Oxford, and in many ways can be said to have made it possible. Indeed, without the liberal movement in Oxford there would be no Jews in the university, as it was the liberal reforms which allowed unbaptized Jews into Oxford University for the first time in 1854.

More importantly, the liberal outlook is essentially in accord with many of the important ideas of Judaism that I have communicated in Oxford. The liberal ethos actually ensures that many students are already familiar with many Jewish religious concepts, albeit in a secularized form, before I raise the issues. Ultimately if one is to teach and to persuade, what better path is there to take than to show one's intended audience that the values which they themselves hold dear are essentially similar to one's own?

Shared Values

On the one hand, universities around the world are at the forefront of assimilation. The average campus is a seedbed of aggressive secularism, acculturation and intermarriage. On the other hand, it is no secret that college campuses tend primarily to lean to the political left, and have the most ardent believers in political correctness and multi-culturalism. This provides an excellent opportunity for my work.

Above all, being a rabbi is about values, or more specifically, imparting values. Whether or not they are cognisant of it, every individual has their own *weltanschauung*, world-view. What I as a representative for Judaism am attempting to do is impart a Torah *weltanschauung* to my community. Thus, whereas a person may not readily understand the importance of donning *tefillin* on a daily basis, or keeping Shabbat on a weekly basis, my mission is to demonstrate the relevance of these eternal truths to my listening audience. The same is true of every other *mitzvah* (commandment), the paragon of which is to impart a longing for the messianic era. The average person has not made room for messianic expectation in his or her personal life and may view messianic expectation as an antiquated Jewish dream of a permanently elusive perfect world. I look to open a window and make space within each person's life so that they have time for Jewish observance.

In this respect, I have a great advantage not afforded the average communal rabbi, because the foremost goals of modern liberalism are similar, and in many ways identical, to Judaism. The reason this serves as such an important advantage, a head start if you will, is that the hardest work has already been achieved. I need not awaken students to my aims; rather, my agenda and the goals which students and academia seek to fulfil are both culled from traditional Jewish sources. So I do not see myself as a foreigner who intrudes on the modern world with an alien, antiquated tradition which has been superseded by the advance of civilization. I and my values are completely consonant with the most noble ideals of higher education and academic living. What one must seek to do, however, is demonstrate that in the most convincing way possible, for it is usually not evident to one's listeners: most people today are convinced that religion in general, and Judaism in particular, is completely at odds with modern liberalism.

The Confidence of Liberalism

I find many advantages result from understanding the consonance of academic liberalism and Judaism. Firstly, one of the most difficult elements of being a rabbi in so awesome a place as Oxford, and the one which serves to hinder one's success most, is developing sufficient courage to execute those functions which just must be done. Much of the time, lack of courage, or an unwillingness to confront difficult situations, is due to questioning whether the time is ripe for it, or even worse, questioning whether one even has the right to promote one's views. Insecurities such as these eat away at the effectiveness of someone in my position.

On campus, I sometimes find it difficult to approach, for example, a Jewish student who is in the company of his many non-Jewish friends, and may thus not wish to accentuate his Jewish identity in their company, in order to speak to him about attending Shabbat dinner. Often, students will even take offence at what they perceive is a specific targetting of them. But if I can convince myself that I am not an intruder, that I actually belong, that what I am offering is identical to what the students themselves identify as supreme values, and I am the guardian of the tradition entrusted with its dissemination, then I can speak to students with great confidence, initiate programmes I never felt myself capable of, and find peace of mind in this reverent location.

Multi-culturalism Includes Being Jewish

Interestingly, the liberal ethos of multi-culturalism serves as a compelling argument for the Jewish students to develop, or at the very least examine, their own heritage. How can an academic argue for the intrinsic worth of Mesopotamian culture when he has already consigned the donning of *tefillin* to the ash-heap of history? How can any student campaign against racism or discrimination when he simultaneously rejects a kosher life or regards being Jewish as archaic and prejudiced. How can a black student be told that he should never be envious of white students and should learn to appreciate and cultivate the intrinsic worth of his own culture and identity, when the same people who are teaching him this, primarily Jewish liberal academics, are assimilating themselves into non-existence as an ethnic minority?

The same applies to the world's current preoccupation with peace, which serves as the best possible argument for Jewish messianic aspirations. Two and a half thousand years before there was a United Nations, Jewish prophets such as Jeremiah and Isaiah were standing in public squares speaking of a time in the future, if man willed it sufficiently, when peace would reign throughout the earth. In an age when military might was everything, and those who excelled in battle were made kings and worshipped, the prophets of Israel were promising a radical new world: a world in which good would conquer evil in a peaceful and harmonious revolution.

Around modern campuses, more so in the United States but Europe is far from immune, there is a preoccupation with peace and multi-culturalism. The underlying premise of multi-culturalism is a belief in the intrinsic worth of every culture and the fact that no culture can be said to be superior to another. For example, Christopher Columbus is no longer praised as having brought civilization to the American Indians because who is to say that his society was any more 'civilized'. It might be argued that the Indians, even with their pagan beliefs and rituals, were more advanced since they were not conducting an inquisition at the same time and burning their colleagues because they entertained the 'wrong', that is, non-Christian, beliefs.

But these contemporary values were pre-empted by three thousand years of Jewish thought, from the earliest days at Sinai, when God spoke of the Jewish people serving as 'a light unto the nations'. Included in this description was a deep-seated belief that there must be distinct nations, and that every nation can make a significant and diverse contribution to society within the framework of their traditions. God did not tell the Jews that their mission was to make everybody Jewish, or that Judaism was the only true path. On the contrary, what He instructed them to do was develop their own innate potential, the only proviso of which was to do so within a Godly framework and values. Since God is infinite, the system He bequeathed humanity within which to prosper is sufficiently broad to embrace disparate cultures and ways of life, all of which, however, must conform to universal truths, such as the evils of murder and theft and the sublimity of charity, love and compassion.

Interpreting 'Peace'

Often in Oxford I am confronted by students who refuse to come to the L'Chaim Society because of Lubavitch concern over Israel's current negotiations for a land-for-peace settlement. Many are secular Israelis, of which there are usually thirty to fifty in any given year, and members of the Peace Now movement. I tell them that firstly, if they are virtuous, I cannot comprehend how they could reject the entirety of the Lubavitch movement, all the good things that even they admit Lubavitch represents, for the sake of one facet of Lubavitch policy. But more importantly I tell them that Lubavitch and Shalom Achshav (Peace Now) represent exactly the same ideals. We say '*Mashiach* (Messiah) now!' and they say 'Peace Now!' There is nothing more rudimentary about a messianic era than the fact that it will be an era of peace and there is nothing new about calling out for peace. Amidst these very laudable efforts, these political activists have been pre-empted by two and a half thousand years by white-bearded Jewish men who promised that all war would cease.

But where Lubavitch does differ is in the belief that peace cannot exist in a vacuum. War will not leave the earth until the causes of war – jealousy, hatred and contention – leave the earth along with it. And it is for this reason that Lubavitch stands for communicating higher moral values to the world. We must share with the world our experience of a God who created humankind and commanded them to pursue justice. And what God said was that we should do whatever we can, and He will add the final touches by sending the Messiah.

So we both want peace. But we have different ways of achieving it. We believe that the Jewish people must take a leading role in nurturing the rule of Divine law: that there is a God who created the world for a purpose and ultimately that purpose was for all nations to join together to worship the Almighty in the way He wants to be served. And He stipulated different means for different peoples, as we shall explore later.

It is clear that the students specifically shun a foreign or alien presence. Therefore, it is of some interest to trace the course of religious history in Oxford University to illustrate and emphasize these ideas, showing the university's Christian origins and ethos, which lasted almost to the modern day, and its consequent Victorian transition to reform and a modern outlook. I will also endeavour to show how until the twentieth century, the university took a deep interest in the students' academic and spiritual welfare and regarded religious orthodoxy and the imparting of religious and ethical standards as part of the ethos and education offered by Oxford, representing an aspect of Oxford education that is singularly and sadly lacking today.

Chapter Seventeen

THE LIFE AND GROWTH OF RELIGION
AT OXFORD UNIVERSITY

The most striking facet of Oxford especially evident to a newly arriving Chasidic rabbi is the fact that virtually half of its colleges have Christian names. On arrival, Jewish students introduce themselves to me from Jesus College, Corpus Christi, Christ Church, Magdalen, All Souls and Trinity College. There then follow so many saints that it takes a great effort to list them all. This overwhelming and overt Christian orientation was the Oxford norm for centuries.

When the university began, almost all students were priests, most having taken minor clerical orders. Generally the purpose and goal of the early undergraduates and members of the academic halls was to become ministers of the Church. The early collegians of the secular colleges such as Merton were usually destined to work in the secular arm of the Church. In addition various monastic and mendicant orders had colleges or houses of theological study in Oxford for their brethren round and about the country. The early university was home to many renowned Christian scholars such as Duns Scotus, Roger Bacon, John Wyclif (who till today has a hall named after him), Bishop Grosseteste, William Ockham, Peter Philardo (later Pope Alexander V) and Erasmus. The university was deeply concerned with both the academic and spiritual welfare of its members. Life in the early colleges and halls had a distinctly monastic flavour, and theological orthodoxy was taken with great seriousness. Apart from the furore caused by the Wycliffian heresy in the thirteenth and fourteenth centuries, one of the *causes célèbres* in Oxford religious history concerns the ill-fated Robert of Reading.

The First Oxford Apostate

Robert of Reading was a thirteenth-century cleric of the university, and like many of the students of his day he studied Jewish biblical exegesis in Hebrew as part of his course of studies. Unfortunately for Robert he was convinced through his study that Judaism rather than Christianity was his salvation, and he converted to Judaism, took a Jewish wife, and lived a while in the Jewish quarter of Oxford. The clerical authorities of the university were affronted, and Robert was tried for heresy. The result was his *auto da fé*. He was burnt alive for heresy in Oxford in 1222. The church authorities claimed he had converted for the love of a Jewish woman. This tragic episode illustrates very well the clerical nature of the early university, and the fact that the university saw itself as both teaching and enforcing Christian orthodoxy. The early students were thus constrained in their belief and practice. It need not be pointed out how great a contrast this is with the modern university, which does not seek to influence the students' spiritual and ethical views.

Admission of Lay Students

From the fifteenth century onwards the university evolved in various respects, widening its intake of students by accepting lay students for the first time. These were usually the sons of gentlemen, or trainee secular lawyers. Yet still the university was a Church-dominated institution, with many of its students going on to be ministers of the Church. This remained the case even until the early part of this century. In addition, the university still maintained a strict Christian ethos and expected its students to conform to the prevailing religious orthodoxy, and to follow the moral and legal code of the university enshrined as the famous Laudian Code instituted in 1636. Undergraduates who contravened the code were liable to flogging and other punishments. The code remained in force until 1854.

Cromwell Readmits the Jews

The sympathy between extreme Protestants and Judaism was of some profit to Jews in England, since Oliver Cromwell's celebrated acquiescence of Mannesah ben Israel's petition to allow Jews back in England (and thus Oxford) in 1650 depended on his being predisposed to Jews and Jewish belief. By all accounts Cromwell found himself convinced by Israel's famous theological thesis that Jews must be allowed to come back to England in order to help complete the Diaspora that would herald the advent of the Messiah as promised in the Old Testament. Perhaps even more pertinently, this sympathy was needed if Cromwell were to allow the Jews back and permit them freedom of religious practice, which in fact he did.

A Celebrated Near-Baptism

In the early seventeenth century there was another famous religious incident, this time directly involving a Jew called Jacob Barnet, who was informally attached to the university. Jacob Barnet was a young and talented Jew who was very well versed in Hebrew literature and Jewish learning. In 1609 he met the famous French Huguenot scholar, Casaubon. The two of them got on very well, and Casaubon enjoyed debating religious questions with him. Casaubon was so impressed by his talents that he soon employed Barnet as his personal secretary. Casaubon came to Oxford a while afterwards with Barnet and both were handsomely received by the university. Barnet was, it seems, a man of real charm as well as learning, and consequently he was well liked and respected by the dons and professors. Everything seemed to be going well for him in the university, and then one day as the result of his conversations he intimated to Casaubon that he would be willing to accept Christian baptism. Casaubon informed the vice-chancellor of the university, who was ecstatic. The rest of the university was delighted too. The university heads decided that Barnet's baptism was not to be a quiet and modest affair; instead it was determined that he would be baptized with great pomp and ceremony before the whole university in a special ceremony in the University Church of St Mary's. The plans were therefore laid, and preparations made. The great day duly arrived, and the people gathered with excitement and expectation in the University Church. But the star of the occasion was nowhere to be found! Jacob Barnet had apparently thought better of his position and flown the nest.

This left the University Church filled with an incensed vice-chancellor and university officials. The vice-chancellor immediately instructed the university police to give hot pursuit to Jacob Barnet on the London Road. Meanwhile the preacher for the occasion had to modify his triumphant sermon to one on 'the perfidy of the Jews'. After a chase the university caught up with Barnet and arrested him, and some months later he was deported under the sleeping edict of expulsion. Casaubon later wryly commented that he thought it was no crime for a man to change his mind on such a religious matter. But it was evident that the university had treated Barnet as if he had committed a significant crime. At the very least he had committed the unpardonable sin of making the university look stupid, as well as offending religious mores of the time. All in all the incident is of great Jewish interest as it illustrates the university's religious attitudes of the time and its pastoral concerns with the students.

Lost Student Piety

The preceding comments on the religious ethos and orthodoxy of Oxford may have created the false impression that students and colleges in the past were necessarily pious. On the contrary, there has always been a vague anarchy rumbling in the depths of the university. In the Middle Ages there was endemic violence in the town, with virtual gang warfare and organized violence in the streets. The town remained under a curfew at night because of the danger of violence and criminal activity. Student disorder was a perennial problem until the nineteenth century, with drinking, gambling and prostitution having to be held in check by the university police, the proctors. The Talmud instructs an unmarried student who cannot contain his sexual lusts to go to a city where no one knows him and find a woman. The commentaries, clearly perplexed at this statement, wisely explain it to mean that the torment and length of the journey will serve to curb the passions of the errant student, so that he can give up his fixation and return to his studies (Babylonian Talmud, *Mo'ed Katan*: 17a). But in Oxford, such a student did not have very far to go. Even in 1878 the proctors considered that their primary task in the university was to keep the streets clear of prostitutes. Amusingly, in the proctors' instructions book, the entry for 'women' in the index is ' "Women", see, "Bad" '. The holding cells for the temporary incarceration of prostitutes still survive in the basement of the eighteenth-century Clarendon building. They are now the ladies' and gentlemen's toilets next to the graduate readers' common room. This is a fact previously known to only a handful of people in the university.

It is also on record that at least two students became part-time highwaymen in the eighteenth century, terrorizing travellers in the environs of the city. They were eventually captured, tried, then hanged at the junction of Longwall Street and St Cross Road, on a private gallows (called the 'Gownsmen's Gibbet') belonging to Merton College. On this note, I tell the students that it is reassuring to know that modern collegians do not now have the shadow of the college gibbet looming over them, otherwise it would add new meaning to the essay 'deadline'.

Secular Awakening at Oxford

It was the nineteenth century which saw the university shift rapidly and decisively from being an exclusively Christian organization to a secular one open to all. Its history in the nineteenth century is one of tensions and contrasts: the university continued to maintain its traditional Christian ethos and to ensure its students' religious orthodoxy (or at least piety) for much of the century, but even in this the university had lost its singular idea of orthodoxy; and at the same time the secular values of the Enlightenment continued to percolate into the university and influence it, along with the radical precepts of the German Romantic movement. Later, more tides of German thought flowed through the university, with the philosophy of Hegel and the scientific-historical criticism of the Bible, a discipline still taken very seriously at Oxford, and which has caused me no end of grief, as I shall return to later.

Scientific Attitudes Permeate the University

Finally and as importantly, the fruit of modern scientific thought on the origins of the world, life and man did much to dissipate ancient Christian verities and create a new intellectual ethos in the university. Vitally, the influx of new ideas and the rise of the liberal outlook came hand in hand with the spirit of reform, meaning that the change in viewpoints became coupled with constitutional changes in Oxford, changes that allowed professing Jewish students into the university for the first time in 1854.

Jewish Influence through Spinoza

It is of great interest to note that many of the liberal intellectual currents which swept traditional Christian beliefs off their time-hallowed moorings in nineteenth-century Oxford and elsewhere originated in part from the teachings of the great Jewish philosopher (and declared Jewish heretic) Benedict de Spinoza. Spinoza's sceptical philosophy and metaphysics are generally credited with initiating modern biblical criticism, as Spinoza was one of the first sceptic thinkers. In addition, Spinoza greatly influenced the leading philosophers of the German Romantic movement including Schleiermacher, the acclaimed 'father of modern theology', and his metaphysics were the point of origin of many of their central doctrines and ideas as definitively expressed by Schelling. Moreover Spinoza substantially influenced Hegel, which was of the first consequence for liberal thought and theology, as Hegel was a giant of later nineteenth-century intellectual life, and most biblical–historical criticism of the period was directly cast in a Hegelian mould. Spinoza's thought was also later synthesized by Marx into his socialist ideology and philosophy. Thus one of the reasons why liberal views are surprisingly assimilable to many traditional Jewish concepts in my experience arises no doubt from the fact that liberalism came in part from a Jewish milieu. This is one thing I share with many of the Jewish philosophy students at Oxford: a fascination with Spinoza and a deep desire to discover more about him, which we shall explore in the chapter examining his excommunication.

Supplanting Liberalism for Christianity

These tensions in the university can be seen clearly in the presentation of a sequence of tableaux from nineteenth-century Oxford life. What is most important is that they show how the Christian hegemony of Oxford was undermined and gradually supplanted by secular and liberal thought, so that while Christianity remained important in the nineteenth century, the conditions of its decline were firmly in place. More importantly still from a Jewish perspective, they show how the university became liberalized, a fact of great significance as the liberalism went together with university reforms that produced Jewish emancipation in the university from 1854.

Shelley and his Milieu

At the very beginning of the nineteenth century Christian orthodoxy remained strong in Oxford, and students were required to conform at least outwardly with the prevailing religious establishment. Yet in the first two decades of the century, Romanticism among other kinds of contemporary ideas started to influence the university from Germany, and started to help effect the intellectual changes in Oxford. Events from the Romantic poet Shelley's life at Oxford conveniently illustrate this. In 1810 Shelley became a member of University College. Apart from his great eccentricities (he indulged in such antics as sailing flotillas of paper boats in a Headington quarry lake in the February snows, and practising with his duelling pistols on countryside walks) he was also an early adherent of Romanticism. This led him to repudiate traditional beliefs in God, religion and Christianity. What was more, in a fit of youthful indiscretion he published his thoughts in a pamphlet entitled 'The necessity of atheism', and circulated it to many senior bishops and heads of the colleges. His actions caused a scandal and aroused the ire of his college so that he was ignominiously sent down, which in the manner of these things did his later career and reputation no harm at all. In fact his posthumous fame led to the college setting up a memorial to his honour which is the apotheosis of Victorian maudlin and lachrymose taste, with a weeping muse and winged lions, variously disported around the effigy of a drowned Shelley. It is certainly effective, if excessive. Apparently this memorial had been due to go over his tomb in the Protestant cemetery in Rome, but made a permanent detour to Oxford instead, by courtesy of his daughter-in-law, Lady Shelley.

The Oxford Movement and Cardinal Newman

The next scenes from nineteenth-century Oxford life concern the famous Oxford Movement (whose members were also known as the 'tractarians') which was led by John Henry Newman, Pusey, Keble, and others, and show immediately how the notion of orthodox conformity and its enforcement had been greatly eroded from the beginning of the century. The Oxford Movement, which began in 1833, sought to revive the Anglican High Church from within by reinstilling it with ancient Catholic values that had been lost in the creation of the Church of England and in its subsequent evolution. The movement was not just an intellectual movement but emphasized the devotional and liturgical side of faith as well. Newman particularly sought to reintroduce to the Church many of its furnishings and vestments that had been ripped out since the sixteenth century, and he wanted to reinstil a sense of awe and reverence in worship as one approached the Divine. Further, he sought to indicate how an awesome experience of the Divine might be attained. The movement was in many respects a reactionary response to the liberalism in religion of the period, such as was typified in the so-called 'broad church' movement which had some powerful proponents in Oxford. Newman vehemently denied the ability and the propriety of an individual to discern what was right and ultimate in matters of faith; he denied that man had the ability to recognize directly and deal with religious first principles in the sense of having a direct apprehension of the Divine, as was the first tenet of Romantic theology. To the contrary he stressed the importance of the authority of tradition and the Church over the individual believer.

In a strange way, I feel almost a kinship with Newman because of the deeply entrenched opposition to him of the entire Oxford establishment, although, of course, one must always be wary of allowing oneself to develop a siege mentality. In his greatest guise, Newman sought to bring a soul to Oxford spirituality, and I often find myself defining my mission here in like terms. Newman was helped in his task by his deep knowledge of the Church Fathers, and his great skills as an essayist and sermonizer. Much of the history and many of the dramas of the movement were played out in the University Church of St Mary's, where Newman was the rector. Many of the milestones of the Oxford Movement's progress were marked by particularly powerful sermons delivered by Newman at various times. The university was held in thrall by the movement, though the students and dons were deeply divided about its validity and whether, as detractors of Newman had said, it was really crypto-Catholic and seeking to drag the Church of England on the road to Rome. Newman delivered sermons every Sunday in the evening, and such were their popularity that the University Church was filled to overflowing. It is said that not a single extra person could be fitted into the church. Students sat on window ledges and in doorways. It is also said that some students gave up their Sunday-evening dinner at college to attend. As to this latter report one can only say that it is an utterly unfounded rumour.

Collapse of Newman's Fledgling Movement

The movement finally collapsed in acrimony and scandal with Newman's famous *Tract XC* of 1841. In this tract Newman said that the thirty-nine articles of the Church of England were political rather than theological in their formulation, as they were designed to allow maximum latitude in belief within the framework of the Anglican Church. Even more scandalously he said that in respect of the fifth-century monophysite heresy the Catholic Church had remained in orthodoxy, whereas the rest of the Church including the Anglican Church was in heresy. The furore that ensued broke up the movement and brought Newman's career in the university to an end. Eventually Newman and the rest of its leaders went over to Rome, and Newman was eventually created a Catholic cardinal.

However, he is still held in very high esteem at the university, and there is an annual dinner held in his memory attended by all the university's highest brass. I should know this, because one of the most important and lavish dinners the L'Chaim Society has thus far staged was in honour of the visit of Elie Wiesel whom we hosted in March 1990. Without knowing it, we had scheduled the dinner on the very same night as that for Cardinal Newman. Thus the university chancellor Lord Jenkins and various other dignitaries who attended our dinner, and there were many, all acccepted on the condition that they could leave early because of Cardinal Newman. It appears that my path in Oxford and that of the good cardinal are hopelessly intertwined.

The Legacy of the Oxford Movement

The Oxford Movement is of great significance to the history of the radical transformation of the university ethos and attitude to religion, as its own internal tensions mirrored many of those in the university, and its own apparently conservative, even reactionary, character concealed a radical shift in religious consciousness. In short, things were not quite what they seemed in the religious life of Victorian Oxford. The Oxford Movement marked times of change, for here was a movement sympathetic to Catholicism that was not only tolerated in the university but even claimed the religious loyalties of many of the collegians. It was a short time before all things Catholic had been reviled and expurgated from the university.

Fragmentation of Religious Faith at Oxford

Still, the existence of the Oxford Movement indicated a religious tolerance in the university that had not existed even thirty years before. The Tractarians themselves, despite their apparent conservative credentials, were in reality deeply influenced by the new ideas of the nineteenth century, and they were trying to find intellectual foundations for their religious lives which were in accord with the modern world. Newman's system of thought as exemplified in his 'Essay in order of a grammar of assent' is very influenced by Coleridge, who brought much of the German Romantic thought to England, except that Newman wanted to deny the ability of the individual to contemplate directly religious first principles. Overall, the Tractarians demonstrated how fragmented Christian faith had become. There was no longer any particular version of doctrine that could be appealed to or pointed to as authoritative. In many ways, this was the important development for the admittance of Jews to Oxford, and the re-emergence of Jewish teaching, since there could no longer be any unified Christian opposition.

Finally and most effectively the collapse of the Oxford Movement marked, and apparently caused, a sea change in the attitude to religion in Oxford. It opened the doors yet wider to the liberalization and secularization of the university, and helped create the permanent changes that define the ideals of Oxford today. The importance of the change is very well summed up in the words of Mark Pattison, a leading disciple of Newman, and later a noted head of Lincoln College. He said of the Oxford Movement and its consequences, 'If any Oxford man had gone to sleep in 1846 and had woken up again in 1850 he would have found himself in a totally new world ... in 1846 Oxford was fiercely debating its eternal Church question ... in 1850 ... theology was totally banished from Common Room and even from private conversation. Very free opinions on all subjects were rife.'

'Sorry, God, I Missed the Bus'

Pattison's personal life was itself almost a history in miniature of the great changes in religious life that Oxford experienced in the nineteenth century. Earlier in his career Pattison was a fervent Tractarian, having fallen under the spell of Froude and Newman. Under their guidance he took holy orders. When the Oxford Movement collapsed he eventually decided to go over to the Catholic Church, but he only failed to convert because he missed an omnibus. Apparently he missed his connection to go to his place of reception into the Catholic faith, and while he was waiting at the stop he decided for the time being at least to stay in Anglican orders. Later still his enthusiasm for all things religious suffered a terminal decline, though he still remained in orders as he felt it would be too inconvenient to relinquish his position.

In his maturity he was noted for his developed self-absorption, cynicism and lack of belief. He is credited with saying, 'Nothing is new, and nothing is true, but it does not much matter.'

He did, however, remain dedicated to scholarship, and had an incredible breadth of learning and an impressive private library. He was thought to be a polymath, and could no doubt have joined Professor Benjamin Jowett, master of Balliol, in saying, according to the lines of a humorous poem, 'There's no knowledge but I know it. I am master of this college. What I don't know isn't knowledge.' He also produced a renowned work on the scholar Casaubon which encapsulated the results of twenty-five years of scholarship. He harboured a contempt for undergraduates, partly engendered by his desire for Lincoln to return to the medieval idea of being a college for graduate fellows only. He thus lived out his life as an enigma to his elders and a terror to his students. Here surely was a man who was a symbol of the century in Oxford; a man who went from fervent faith as a Tractarian to agnostic Anglican.

This story is significant because it encapsulates what has largely been my experience in the university. Oxford, even now, has an unpleasant habit of gnawing away at the faith of the believer, and not just the Jewish one. While there are strong vestiges of religion within the university, they appear as a hollow shell. The only thing certain is that those who are religious do not really flourish at Oxford, and in many cases there may even be said to be contempt for a true believer. Once, at a Sabbath-afternoon lunch at my home attended by about twenty Jewish students, seven Christian students, one Muslim, and one Mormon, the rich variety of religions quickly led to a discussion of the fall of observance at Oxford. The unanimous conclusion, with only my voice in dissent, was that it was 'impossible to retain the same level of commitment at Oxford as before one arrives'.

Penetration of Science and Agnosticism

The changes in Oxford life did not only consist of a liberalization in matters of religion and personal conscience. From 1840 onwards the university increasingly came under pressure from secular-agnostic thought, and the results of the empirical sciences. From the time of Hume onwards the university had been acquainted with agnostic scepticism, but now the advances in the sciences and geology added challenging scientific 'facts' to this philosophical movement. In particular Sir Charles Lyell's *Principles of Geology* of 1830 and Robert Chambers' *Vestiges of Creation* (1844) cast doubt on the biblical view of creation and contradicted Bishop Usher's confident assertion from the biblical chronology that the earth was created on a particular afternoon in 4004 BC. The new Darwinian theory of evolution especially caused great consternation with its speculation that man was descended from, and shared kinship with, the apes.

Science–Religion Debates

The Darwinian controversy led to a celebrated confrontation between the creationists and the agnostic-evolutionists in the University Science Museum in 1860. The fact that the day was resoundingly won by the agnostics, and the moral character of the religious fundamentalists was also brought into question, says much about the intellectual and religious climate. The debate itself was convened in the brand-new Science Museum completed that same year. The building was equally admired and reviled as it was intended as a new shrine to the modern sciences, signifying the victory of 'science over obscurantism'. The museum was built in a churchlike Gothic style, the deliberate significance of which was not lost on its conservative detractors. While the building is still brilliant in its conception, and breathtaking in the interior since it incorporates the world's first glass-roofed atrium, the museum does have an undoubted touch of whimsy: the attached Inorganic Chemistry Laboratory is for some unexplained reason a direct copy of the abbot's kitchen among the ruins at Glastonbury Abbey. Perhaps the architect Woodward thought that chemistry was a superior version of cookery?

Huxley Has His Day

Whatever the dispute the museum itself caused this was nothing compared to the controversy caused by the debate held within it. On the great day the Bishop of Oxford, Samuel Wilberforce, faced Thomas Huxley, often referred to as 'Darwin's bulldog', the famous advocate of the so-called 'agnostic principle' and, on this occasion, evolution. Wilberforce was a brilliant debater, and spoke for half an hour denying evolution, saying that rock-pigeons had always been rock-pigeons and that there was nothing in the idea of evolution. Finally Wilberforce, in his famous ingratiating tone, asked Huxley on which side, his grandmother's or grandfather's, was he descended from apes. This was of course an excellent joke, and a nice debating device. But Huxley, no doubt with the existing sympathy of his audience, turned it into an attack on Wilberforce's character, saying he was not ashamed to have a monkey for his ancestor; but he was ashamed to be associated with a man who used great gifts for obscuring the truth. Poor Wilberforce's character was dragged through the mud by this *ad hominem* argument, and this personal attack on Wilberforce has to this day been taken as an important victory for the principle of evolution, though the defamation of character seems slim scientific evidence for evolution! In reality, this much cited 'victory' was used as propaganda by the evolutionists for a flagging scientific theory, which shows that one should not necessarily believe everything one reads.

The Confrontations between Science and Religion Today

The question of the relationship between religion and evolution is still a hot topic of contention in Oxford. A period of 134 years may have passed since that first debate on evolution but the questions it addressed are as contemporary as ever. Here at the L'Chaim Society we have re-enacted the debate on two occasions in the last three years, employing the expertise of some of the world's best-known scientists to debate the relevance and validity of science and religion. On both occasions we have had audiences of approximately one thousand students packing one of the university's largest lecture theatres, the Gulbenkian, to listen to and participate in the debate. Some of our speakers have defended their views with a passion that would not have been out of place in the original debate of 1860.

The Selfish Gene

Dr Richard Dawkins, world-famous author of *The Selfish Gene* and Oxford

University Reader in Zoology, has particularly distinguished himself by his admirable desire to debate these issues of importance, and by his zeal to decry the complete poverty of religion against the gospel of science and the canon of evolution. He is one of the most vociferous exponents of evolution anywhere in the world and I have easily found religious scientists to oppose him in debate. He is a major force to reckon with, verily the man to beat, and everyone knows it. Dawkins is a skilled debater and often gets the better of his opponents. But in the most recent debate we staged he became very exasperated with Dr David Berlinsky, who for once placed Dawkins on the defensive. Berlinsky cleverly questioned the intellectual soundness of evolution in a way that showed that the issues are as relevant and unresolved in 1994 as in 1860. The audience themselves were suitably inspired by the debate; in the week that followed the first debate, some senior academics were overheard debating the issue on Broad Street, and the questions were widely discussed by the students.

Pains in Putting Together a Scientific Panel

So deep are the clefts between the evolutionists and the sceptics of Darwinism that the preparations for our last debate led to well-publicized acrimony between Richard Milton and Dr Dawkins. At the time Richard Milton, an experienced scientific journalist who claims no religious agenda, had produced a highly controversial book called *The Facts of Life* which asserted that the theory of evolution was at a crisis point and lacked evidence. His book went on to outline the weakness of the evolution evidence and to present contradictory evidence against the theory. The book received an avalanche of publicity, so we invited him to speak in our forthcoming debate. Milton accepted, but when Dawkins discovered he was to be on the panel he said he would refuse to share the panel with him, because, he claimed, his work was not scientific. Dawkins felt that Milton's position de facto ruled him out as a credible and reputable scientist. He could in no way be persuaded to change his mind, and indeed I found most credible scientists refusing to share a platform with an enemy of evolution, especially someone they felt lacked proper scientific credentials. Not long after these events, my Herculean efforts to procure a suitable opponent met with success and we lured perhaps the greatest evolutionist of all, Dr John Maynard-Smith, Emeritus Professor of Biology at the University of Sussex, and author of many of the leading textbooks on evolution, to participate in the debate. But this time Milton pulled out of the debate as he said he doubted that he would be given a fair hearing. In consequence of these disputes one wonders if 1860 is as distant from 1994 as far as the arguments surrounding evolution are concerned. I shall return to the subject of these debates later in Volume Two of this book.

Chapter Eighteen

OXFORD REACHES THE MODERN ERA

The preceding tableaux from Oxford's religious and intellectual life of the nineteenth century clearly illustrate the great changes that occurred. It becomes clear how rapidly the prevailing orthodox Christian religious ethos and its enforcement in Oxford was fragmented, and how thoroughly the monolithic Christian fastness of Oxford was assailed. Vitally, the result of all these changes was that powerful reforming parties grew within and outside the university advocating change and transformation of the university and its constitution. These reforms particularly concerned the emancipation of Catholics and Jews in the university. The Catholics were emancipated in 1829 despite much opposition. The major reforms were effected from the mid-1840s when reform started to gain great momentum under the influence of liberal reformers such as Dr Francis Jeune, the Master of Pembroke, and H. G. Liddell, later Dean of Christ Church. Their endeavours, along with many others, secured the enactment of the University Reform Act in 1854, which ended religious tests being imposed at matriculation (the students' formal induction into the university) and on taking the degree of Bachelor of Arts.

Non-Christian Jews Are Admitted

The consequences of this action were that for the first time in university history professing Jews could be admitted to read for degrees and become student members of colleges. Formerly the only Jews to become members of the university were those who had renounced their faith and become baptized Anglican Christians. This did not mean that Jews were yet entirely free in the university, for most fellowships in the colleges were still for the most part restricted to those who had taken Anglican holy orders. Therefore the path was not yet open for the establishment of Jewish academics. This restriction on fellowships was only removed in 1871, when finally Jews were free to enter fully into Oxford academic life and to pursue an academic career at the university. The 1871 enactment is also important as it officially established that the university was now a secular and modern institution, and had finally shrugged off its ancient Christian ethos and replaced it with a modern and generally liberal world-view. As to the fate of Jeune and Liddell, two of the important originators and architects of these reforms, Jeune is obliquely remembered by a small street named after him off Cowley Road, very close to where I live and Liddell is now best remembered as the father of Alice Liddell, who was immortalized as Alice in Lewis Carroll's *Alice in Wonderland*. Such are the strange devices and memorials of fate.

Enter Jewish Fellows

One of the first Jews to hold a fellowship in Oxford was Samuel Alexander, who held his fellowship in philosophy at Lincoln College from 1882 to 1893. As to early Jewish undergraduates there are few reminiscences of them, yet one rises from historical fog: Goldberg of Lincoln College. William Goldberg was a near contemporary of Oscar Wilde at Oxford, reading for his degree in college from 1881 to 1883. Goldberg was by all accounts a great college character who quickly became known exclusively by the nickname Shifter. He had a ready wit, intelligence and a proclivity to wearing plum-coloured clothing; he also had a strange habit of slopping around the main quadrangle of college in slippers. He is said to have indulged in high jinks and stayed out at night, often coming back into college at dawn with the milk delivery. He is also reputed to have threatened to report the milkman for failing to put rum in his milk delivery to the college! His more conventional brother in St John's College was apparently not able to make head or tail of his idiosyncratic sibling. After leaving college with a gentlemanly third class degree, he carved himself a rather bohemian career in writing for the *Sporting Life*, a very unusual and eccentric job for an Oxford graduate of the day. Goldberg tragically died young.

Other early Jewish students of a more august and aristocratic pedigree include two members of the famous Quixano Henriques family. The Henriques family were originally fourteenth-century Jewish aristocrats from Portugal. After the expulsion of 1490 their wanderings eventually took them to Jamaica in the eighteenth century, where they were leading members of the judiciary. The family came to England in the late eighteenth and early nineteenth centuries and became settled again in prominent positions. In 1840 they established the West London Synagogue, the first Reform synagogue in England. Henry Straus Henriques was at Worcester College in the early 1890s. He was later well known as a lawyer, communal worker, historian and president of the Board of Deputies of British Jews. At present one of the Henriques family lives in Oxford and is a member of the L'Chaim Society, keeping up a family connection with Oxford that is over a century old. In fact this student, Cynthia, is the one person I have known longest in the city, having met her when I first arrived just for a weekend in order to find out whether or not I fitted the position.

Negating Nepotism and Gene Pools

Returning to the subject of the reforms after the 1850s, they were not just regarding religious discrimination but were also concerned with ending various anachronisms and ancient abuses in the colleges. One of the most frequently asked questions I encounter at Oxford is about the position of the Lubavitcher rebbe, Rabbi Menachem Schneerson, and the fact that Chasidic dynasties are often passed from father to son, or in the current rebbe's case, from father-in-law to son-in-law. (I shall return to this issue later.) But interestingly, Oxford has had a very similar tradition, albeit with a greater propensity to abuse. This included the privilege of 'founder's kin' whereby some or all of the fellowships or studentships at various colleges were exclusively or at least preferentially reserved for direct descendants and relatives of the founder of the college. All Souls College was perhaps most noted for its provision of founder's kin. The college was founded by Bishop Chichele in 1438 and was intended primarily for his descendants. By 1840 it is estimated that there were about three thousand descendants of Chichele, and so the college was surprisingly able to appoint some distinguished and worthy men. Several fellowships in these colleges were extremely valuable. In 1890 the senior fellows at All Souls were paid a staggering £2,000 a year, the equivalent of at least £100,000 today. Once a man became a fellow in such a college he enjoyed tenure for life. At the founder's day 'Gaudy' or feast each year at All Souls the stipend for the forthcoming year would be announced at the table, and it would always be greeted with a mighty cheer.

Because such a valuable prize was at stake supplicants for fellowships went to great lengths to prove their pedigree, and highly elaborate 'engrossed' rolls were produced with the applicants' genealogy. Many such items still survive. Students in the present era consider application processes to the university difficult enough, but imagine if the application form included a section headed 'Applicant's Pedigree'! During the 1850s virtually all founder's kin provision was swept away, but some limited provision survived in two colleges, and two more provisions were established later at Keble and Hertford. The three Baring scholarships at Hertford (instituted 1880) are constitutionally speaking the only genuine founder's kin scholarships left in the university and are considered inappropriate in this more egalitarian age.

The preceding description of the university, its history and ethos, has touched on the Jewish history at Oxford at several points, indicating through particular incidents and individuals the fact that Jews have played a formative and interesting part in the history of the town and university.

It is well worth outlining a more unified history of Jewish life in Oxford to complete this picture, especially as Oxford's Jewish history is often unfairly neglected. If one is to typify the character of Jewish life and settlement in Oxford, the constant factor in all Jewish settlement and history has been the university. Many of the Jews in Oxford have come to the city because of the attractions of the intellectual milieu, and for some there was always the added attraction of the economic opportunities presented by the colleges and students.

Chapter Nineteen

THE JEWS OF OXFORD

Jewish life in Oxford falls into three distinct phases. The first concerns the medieval Jews of Oxford, who lived here from after 1080 until the general expulsion of the Jews from England in the year 1290. The early Jews of Oxford played an important part in the economic life of the town, and they also had a formative role in the rise of the university, despite being officially excluded from academic life. The second phase of Jewish life in Oxford is from 1290 until the official resettlement of the Jews in England in 1650. As far as Oxford was concerned there were few if any Jews in Oxford in those years, mostly converts associated with the university, though there is an unsubstantiated tradition that a small community of Jews continued to live on in Pennyfarthing Street after the expulsion. The third phase of Oxford Jewish history concerns the Jews who eventually came to Oxford as a result of the Cromwellian resettlement of the Jews in England after 1650. Initially, individual Jews settled in Oxford in the seventeenth century, though a Jewish community was not established until the mid-eighteenth century. This community remained small until the Reform Act of 1854 brought Jews to Oxford in larger numbers because they could attend the university. The modern Jewish community in Oxford really derives from the community established as the result of the Jewish emancipation, which is of course also responsible for the large numbers of Jewish students who continue to attend the university.

Communicating a Sense of Oxford's Jewish Past

One of the aims of the L'Chaim Society in Oxford has always been to communicate to the students the importance and interest of Jewish history in the city, and in fact the first event which the L'Chaim Society traditionally holds at the start of each academic year is a walking tour of Jewish Oxford, both past and present. This task has been the particular domain of one of our former presidents of the L'Chaim Society, Marcus Roberts, who has undertaken a detailed study of Oxford Jewry and its history and is also a professional tour guide. This has been done for several reasons. Principally many Jewish students feel subliminally that they do not have a historical stake in the university, and are overwhelmed by a sense of its Christian origins and culture, and the fact that even today its values are deeply non-Jewish. One can even claim that at a subtle and deep level Oxford is a vital well-head of Gentile culture in Britain, and has been for centuries. Oxford at this level lacks a Jewish soul and the Jewish student may feel a foreigner at best, or intruder at worst.

Yet when one realizes that in reality Jews have played a significant, if relatively unsung, role in the university, even playing a part in the foundation of Merton College, traditionally believed to be the very first college in Oxford, then this outlook automatically changes. When students realize that Jews have participated in university life on and off for eight centuries, this enables them to experience a sense of historical belonging in Oxford which acts against any feeling of historical inferiority. Further, this realization emphasizes to the students that as Jews they have a potentially important contribution to make to Oxford life, and they should be proud of the fact and seek to make a lasting contribution. One of the vital principles I have constantly conveyed to the students is for them to be proud of their Jewish identity and not to feel a need to hide it, or its expression, for fear of prejudice to their dreams and ambitions.

Great Jewry Street

The same more or less applies to the civic history of Oxford. During the middle ages, before the expulsion, the Jews were of real importance to the economy of the town as they were effectively the town bankers, providing credit and coin for the merchants and townspeople, as well as servicing student debt, that age-old constant of student life. Most students at the L'Chaim Society are fascinated to discover that St Aldate's, one of Oxford's main streets and the site of our L'Chaim Centre, was formerly called Great Jewry Street, as the Jewish community used to live in and dominate the north end of the street. Moreover, the students are usually delighted to discover the sites of the former medieval synagogue and Jewish cemetery. The present L'Chaim Society centre itself is thought to be on the site of the putative medieval yeshivah or talmudic academy that almost certainly existed in the town, and this is one of the reasons for choosing the site (the other being that it is probably the best location in the city) and we are very thankful to the Almighty (and our financial sponsors) for having it. This site for the centre was also chosen as a physical reminder of the continued Jewish presence, religion and learning in Oxford since the Middle Ages.

Riots Under My Desk

While on the subject of symbolic locations, my office is almost exactly over and co-extensive with the site of the famous fifteenth-century Swyndelstock Tavern (the tavern was only nine yards square and would probably have been in a basement as was the custom of the time), which was where the notorious St Scholastica day riot of 1355 started because of an argument over a flagon of wine. Students got into dispute with the publican, a fight erupted after he was hit on the head by the flagon, and this spread to vicious rioting between the Town and the Gown which lasted for three days and nights and led to the demise of sixty-two students. Naturally I make no connection between this historic event and the occupancy of my office, and although some feel that my presence has indeed caused quite a stir to date, no deaths, God forbid, are reported.

Earliest Jews Arrive in Oxford

To turn now to the first Jewish community in Oxford: the first Jews probably arrived around 1090, a while after they had arrived in this country with the retinue of William the Conqueror. These Jews were Franco–Norman with many originating from Rouen in France, but there were also Jews in Britain from the Rhineland and areas west of the Rhine that were part of the Franco–Norman orbit. Almost all were Askenasic rather than Sephardic Jews. The Jews who settled in England were so-called feudal Jews, as they were part of the Norman feudal hierarchy. Importantly they were serfs, and not freemen. The Jews were not ordinary serfs, but they were 'serfs of the royal chamber', which meant they were the exclusive chattels of the king himself rather than of one of his underlords. Within the feudal system there was a carefully defined social hierarchy; every person had their own status and role. All owed ultimate loyalty and obedience to the king, but most were usually vassals of various overlords who were themselves subordinate to the king. The Jews' position as serfs of the king was unusual, and their function as serfs was unprecedented. The Jewish community was required to provide financial service to the king, and not the usual manual service of a serf. In practice this did not mean that all Jews were money lenders; some were in other closely proscribed trades and professions.

Finding Professions as Money Lenders

The Norman economy was very primitive, as were the royal finances. Since the ultimate decline of the Roman empire and trade by the sixth and seventh centuries, little had remained of Roman civilization in Britain, particularly in terms of its economic structures. The Jews were used by the king to enhance the royal economy and finances, and generally to expedite the local and national economies. This increased the personal power of the king. He used the Jews rather than anybody else in this way because canon law forbade Christians to lend money at interest. While talmudic law forbade

Jews to lend to other Jews at interest, it did not prohibit the lending to Gentiles at interest. The king took advantage of this fact, and obliged the Jewish community to lend money at interest.

Usury was vital to the king's economy, as well as the economy at large, because it enabled large capital sums to be acquired and controlled by the king in an economy that was cash-starved and generally ineffective. By usury Jews could gain a control of the supply of money, and acquire capital profits in a way forbidden to Gentiles. The consequent capital raised through these expedients by the community could be commanded by the king, by borrowing or mulcting. These large sums of money could be used to augment the king's power, as it could pay for fortifications, military adventures and suchlike. The Anglo-Jews unwittingly provided the king with money to finance the first Crusade, which caused great suffering and persecution to many Jews in Europe.

The Mechanics of Usury

At a local level the Jewish community provided important financial services to all levels of society. The major money lenders would operate rather like the county bank, and the stone cellars of their homes would be used as bank vaults containing large reserves of coin. The walls of the vault of Jacob of Canterbury, which still partly survive in The County Hotel, Canterbury, were six feet thick. The vault of one of the major money lenders in Stamford yielded in recent years two coin hoards with a total of some 50,000 silver coins. Recent evidence also suggests they were involved in the issue of lead tokens which were widely used as small denominations of local currency. Some of the leading money lenders, such as Aaron of Lincoln, also conducted business across several counties using local agents. Aaron of Lincoln was the richest man in the country after the king. There were money lenders on a smaller scale too, and those at the lowest end of the scale ran what effectively were pawn brokerage shops. The going rate of interest in England was usually 43 per cent, considered to be the fair market rate of interest in the country, though European rates were usually cheaper. Money was lent against collateral, which in practice could be anything from property to clothing, and pledges could be legally sold after a year if not redeemed by the borrower. The majority of customers for the Jews were ordinary people from the middle and lower classes. It is thought that many of the clients of the Jews were from the countryside as well as the town. The upper ranks of society only represented about 8 per cent of the money lenders' business.

The Jews of medieval Oxford fitted into this general pattern of Anglo-Jewish life. Oxford Jewry was one of the largest, richest and most significant Jewish communities in England in the Middle Ages, though at its height there were probably never more than eighty to a hundred Jews in the Jewry. The Oxford Jews were in the town before the university was founded, attracted by the business opportunities of one of England's most important, growing towns, notable from the ninth century onwards; it nearly became the country's capital. Once the university became established in the early twelfth century Oxford's importance was enhanced and the influx of large numbers of students to the town presented excellent new business opportunities.

No Books to Study

From this point the fortunes and history of the Oxford Jewry became inextricably linked with the rising university. The Jewish community provided important financial resources for the students. The early students had few or no official sources of income to finance their study (other than money lent against collateral from the very limited St Frideswide's chest set up in 1262), so they would borrow money from the Jewish community. This was apparently of great importance to the early Oxford students. On one occasion the students claimed that so many books were in pledge to the Jewish money lenders that the work of the university had completely ground to a halt! On another occasion in 1244 a riot was instigated against the Oxford Jews, which led to Jewish houses being looted. After the riot the students complained about the high interest rates levied on them, with the result that the university and Bishop Grosseteste intervened and set interest at a standard 43 per cent.

Jewish Property Owners

Apart from money lending the Jewish community provided a lot of property and accommodation for the early academic halls and the students. It is estimated that up to 10 per cent of the academic halls and accommodation belonged to the community.

One of the most important Jewish landlords in Oxford was Jacob of London, who owned about twenty houses and tenements in Oxford; he also played a part in the foundation of Oxford's first college, Merton, established in 1264. Jacob's involvement with Merton came when he sold a property and plot of land to Bishop Walter de Merton in 1266/7 which became part of Oxford's first true college. This property is thought to correspond to the north side of the present front quad of the college, and specifically Staircases 2 and 3. It points to the not insignificant Jewish roots in Oxford University.

Chapter Twenty

JEWISH INVOLVEMENT WITH THE
UNIVERSITY ITSELF

The preceding chapters show how the Oxford Jewry played a formative role in the growth of the university, in the sense that they partly financed and housed the early university. But the involvement of the Jewish community with the university ran at a deeper level than pure economics. Even though Jews at this period were forbidden formal involvement with the university, it appears that they were intellectually engaged with the Christian scholars. Certainly it is known that early scholars of the university studied the Old Testament and Jewish exegetical texts, and it would have been natural if informal consultations had taken place between Jewish scholars in the town and the clerics. The whole incident of the conversion of Robert of Reading to Judaism in 1222 demonstrates this. Also the noted scholars Roger Bacon and Bishop Grosseteste (who are associated with Merton College) both studied Hebrew and Jewish exegesis, and they read and respected works by Jewish philosophers, including, it is thought, work by Moses of Oxford, who lived and studied in Oxford.

Moses of Oxford was one of the leading scholars of medieval English Jewry; such was his reputation in England and on the Continent that he was known as 'the mighty one'. His interests and writings were very varied. Many of his opinions on problems in Jewish law are preserved in contemporary rabbinic literature. He also produced *likkutim* (an anthology) on Jewish law, and some of his opinions on dietary law survive from this. But above all else he is famous for his definitive work on Hebrew vocalization and accentuation. This work was called *Darchei Hanikkud Vehaneginot*, meaning *The System of Punctuation and Notation*. It was regarded as virtually the standard work on Hebrew punctuation in the Middle Ages. As a work of medieval Jewish scholarship it represents a high point in a tradition of Hebrew philology that came to England from Italy, and ultimately from Israel itself. The object of Moses' work, and this tradition, was to enable the accurate reading of the Torah in the synagogue, and to enable accurate production of the sacred text. In particular it involved the method and execution of the complex and specialized task of introducing vocalization (to indicate vowels) and marks into the text of the Pentateuch. Such was his book's importance that it was published in Bomberg's great Rabbinical

Bible of 1527 to accompany the text. It was last printed in Budapest in 1929 under the somewhat lengthy and intimidating Latin title, *Tractatio de punctis et accentibus quae a Moyse punctuator scripta dictitur.*

Moses was of a very long line of rabbis and scholars who originally came from Germany. A genealogy found in Frankfurt states that he was part of a dynasty of rabbis and scholars stretching over seven generations. Furthermore this genealogy shows that Moses was a relative of the great French Torah luminary Rashi; and that he was related to Rabbi Simeon the Great of Mainz, the renowned liturgical poet who has contributed to our standard prayer books. The family in England descended from the Patron and Rabbi Moses of Bristol, who eventually settled in Oxford. His son, Master and Rabbi Yomtob, wrote a noted text on Jewish law called *Sefer Hatenaim*, or the *Book of Conditions*. Yomtov's son was our Moses of Oxford, known in the administrative records of the time as Master Moses of London, because London was where he lived in later life. Moses was born in Oxford at the beginning of the thirteenth century, probably on the site of the town hall. He died in London in *c.* 1268.

The son of our Moses of Oxford was perhaps even better known than his father. I mention him particularly as he is the namesake of my son; he was called Elijah Menachem of London, described in secular records as Master Elias fil Master Mosse. He was a famous expert on Jewish law, of high repute among rabbinic authorities of the time. He also compiled *Tosafot*, commentaries on the talmudic tractate *Rosh Hashanah*, as well as perhaps a commentary on the talmudic tractate *Shavuot*. In addition he wrote a commentary tractate of the first order of the Mishnah.

While it is thought that most Jews in Britain had an active intellectual life and tradition, with most of the larger communities having formal talmudic academies, Oxford was probably intellectually pre-eminent, with London, among the Anglo-Jewry. Certainly Oxford was host to England's leading medieval rabbinic dynasty.

My Office and Jacob's Hall

One of the non-rabbinic members of this rabbinic dynasty was Jacob of Oxford, who was called *Hanadiv*, meaning 'The Liberal', a formal name indicating that he was a patron of Jewish learning. It is highly likely that he set up a talmudic academy in his large house called 'Jacob's Hall' in the 1270s, the site now under the southern side of the present L'Chaim Society Centre, and next to the office where I work and where most of this book was written. Jacob's Hall was a luxurious residence, one of the best in the town. The houses of the Anglo-Jewish magnates were usually stone-built with fine masonry, architectural details and decoration; they were generally among the outstanding houses of their period in England. Moreover they were defensible against attack by anti-Semites. One of the Jewish houses on the east of St Aldate's (probably the house of David of Oxford) may have had glass in its traceried windows, an almost unheard-of domestic refinement at the time.

The original Jacob's Hall survived until it was burnt by the great fire of Oxford in 1644. By that time it had become one of Oxford's best inns, being used to entertain visiting foreign ambassadors and nobility. By an ironic stroke of fate the fire that destroyed it is said to have been started by two royalist soldiers whose efforts to roast a filched pig sparked the blaze that destroyed much of the western side of the city. However, an extensive range of cellars remained until the turn of this century, and were said to be 'perhaps some of the most curious ranges of cellars in the whole of England', having various fine Gothic mouldings, vaulting and an enigmatic sub-cellar, as well as being connected to several other cellars in the area. It was possible until the early 1900s to traverse the street underground and to re-emerge some way further down St Aldate's. It is quite possible that some of the major Jewish houses had subterranean connections, an extra facility which could have been of use in times of stress and disturbance. This latter fact and the extensive cellarage may well have provoked Oxford folklore about secret passageways in the city. Interestingly a genuine secret passageway was found in 1912 during work at the old city wall in what is now Boswell's store at the end of Cornmarket Street. The passageway provided a secret access to St Michael's Church of the North Gate.

Early Oxford's Jewish Properties

The Oxford Jews had a number of other buildings and facilities which are well worth describing for their intrinsic interest, and because they help give an impression of what Oxford Jewry was like. Including the home of Jacob, the Jewish community owned about twelve to fifteen properties at any one time; there were ten households left at the expulsion. The luxury stone-built dwellings belonging to the leading citizens of the community were mostly concentrated in the north end of the street. These were called 'first-floor halls', where the luxurious living accommodation, a defensible hall, was raised to first-floor level, above a stone semi-subterranean vaulted cellar-cum-strong room. These houses were models of domestic comfort and refinement for their time, incorporating fireplaces with real chimneys. The Jews of western Europe enjoyed a much higher standard of living than their Norman masters because they were virtually the only group in Europe who had maintained the high standards of Roman civilization which had been lost elsewhere during the social and cultural fragmentation of the Dark Ages. This showed in many aspects of their day-to-day life: in accordance with Torah law, which stipulates that one must bathe in honour of the Shabbat, they bathed at least once a week.

The houses of the middle and lower ranks of the Jewish community were further south in St Aldate's; many of these houses would have been constructed with a stone plinth on the ground floor and an oak-framed upper storey. The poorest dwellings would have been miserable affairs, entirely wooden with wattle and daub infilling. This type of dwelling was so flimsy that they could be pulled down with a simple hook and rope to create fire breaks in the event of a conflagration in the town.

The First Synagogue and its Ignominious Aftermath

In addition to domestic accommodation, the community also had a synagogue (*c.* 1228–1290) which was in the rear upper part of a tenement that now belongs to Christ Church; it is the site of the north-west tower of Tom Quad. After the expulsion the synagogue became an inn called 'The Dolphin', or it may have become the chapel for an academic hall, 'Burnel's Inn'. It is also thought to occupy the later site of London College, which was one of the few secular collegiate foundations to fail in Oxford, along with the first foundation of Hertford College, which suffered ignominy when it collapsed into the street on one terrible night in 1819. An event that the present Hertford College would like to forget.

Once the Tom Quad for Christ Church had been developed, the corner of the quadrangle was perhaps the most non-kosher place in Oxford history. This came about because the corner of the quadrangle became the home of the famous and eccentric eighteenth-century geologist William Buckland. Buckland had some novel domestic arrangements: his house was filled with fossils and a veritable menagerie of animals, some domestic, some distinctly not. The menagerie included guinea pigs, fowls, ferrets, a bear, snakes and a jackal. He also had an eagle, which one day decided to gatecrash Divine service in the cathedral, much to the ire of the dean of the time. If this were not enough, Buckland rivalled the Chinese in his breadth of cuisine. He prided himself on having tried to eat almost every variety of animal accessible to man, and is reputed to have eaten horseflesh and crocodile; his children were not infrequently confronted by that delicacy of delicacies – mice in batter. The only dish said to have offended his otherwise iron-clad digestion was that of panther chops acquired from London Zoo after the originating panther had been buried for a couple of days.

The Original Jewish Cemetery

Finally it is well worth mentioning that the medieval Jewish community had a cemetery, one of only ten in England. Originally the Jews of England were permitted only one cemetery, and that was in London. For Jews who lived in

York and other far-off places in England this was a great inconvenience, as well as an added religious indignity. In the summer the state of preservation of the corpse by the time it reached London would have been less than perfect. Some skeletons found during 1986 in the later Jewish cemetery of York, the largest cemetery after London, were disarticulated, suggesting decomposition before their burial. There is also an account from Oxford about the removal to London of the body of Deulecresse, the scoffer, after his suicide. He had killed himself after he was criticized by his father for publicly mocking the miracles at the shrine of St Frideswide next to the Oxford Jewry. The chronicler of the day records with unconcealed glee how the dogs of Oxford bayed and howled horribly as the corpse of Deulecresse came by in its cart bound for London.

Site of the Botanic Garden

After 1177 the king allowed individual Jewrys to buy cemeteries. Oxford acquired its cemetery between 1190 and 1231. The original site occupied what is now the extent of medieval Magdalen College. The discovery of burials in the twentieth century indicates that the burial area was confined within the present-day St John's quadrangle and the Chaplain's quadrangle. In 1231 the Hospital of St John coveted the site of the Jewish cemetery as a new site for their hospital. The king gave it to them with the proviso that a site be reserved for the burial of the Jews near the so-called 'Jew's Garden'. The new site was almost certainly opposite and across the road in a rectangular plot roughly co-extensive with the modern memorial Rose Garden in the Botanic Gardens. This site was used until the general expulsion of the Jews from England in 1290. Both Jewish burial sites were taken over and used as Christian cemeteries by the hospital until it was suppressed to make way for Magdalen College in 1458. A mass of bones were found in 1641 at the Botanic Gardens, but most of the bones were probably Christian. Today there's a plaque, erected only in 1931, at the entrance to the Botanic Gardens, just a little to the right, which identifies the memorial rose garden as having served as part of the site of the Jewish cemetery until the expulsion.

Jewish Tombstones

For those who wonder if any Jewish tombstones have been found at the cemetery, alas they have not. There are only two medieval Hebrew inscriptions surviving in England. The only surviving example of a medieval Jewish tombstone in this country was rediscovered recently in Northampton, having languished long in the vaults of the Central Museum after being dug up in the 1840s. That the stone was recovered is a credit to one of the museum's archaeological curators, Mr Robert Moore. Unfortunately he was not entirely certain what it was, or that it was unique. By pure chance, our former president, Marcus Roberts, visited the museum of his home town where he immediately confirmed its identification as a tomb-stone, and recognized its unique significance. Later on he established it as belonging to a late thirteenth-century *chaver* or scholar, and rabbi, Solomon of Northampton.

Returning to the history of the medieval Jews of Oxford and sum-ming up the general character of their life in Oxford, it is fair to say that they had a generally peaceful existence in the eleventh and twelfth centuries. While there were notable riots and some outrages against the community they generally got on well with their Christian neighbours and prospered. Contemporary accounts of Anglo-Jewish life show that the Jews integrated better than might be expected into Christian society, mixing and drinking with Christian friends and acquaintances, and even attending Christian weddings. Also some Jews enjoyed the thrill of the chase (despite injunctions in Jewish law against hunting); Jews of one town were up in the sheriff's court once for pursuing a hind right into town.

Persecution and the Blood Libel Sets in

However, the Middle Ages of course were not a time when tolerance was ultimately possible for religious minorities. In the thirteenth century the Jews of Oxford and England in general experienced increasing reli-gious persecution, associated in part with the crusading fervour sweeping Europe. Jews were pressured to convert; they were also accused of financial and religious crimes. Many were accused of clipping the coinage to illegally appropriate bullion. Perhaps worst of all, Jews were accused of despicable religious crimes, usually the ritual slaughter of young Christian boys in a mockery of the crucifixion. Scores of Jews were accused and many were executed. A favoured, and generally used method of execution of great brutality was hanging followed by drawing at the horse's tail. This meant the victims would be hanged until half throttled, and then tied by their limbs to horses which would be spurred in opposite directions so that the bodies would be torn to pieces. The remains would be hung up as a gory public display. Geoffrey Chaucer's anti-Semitic 'Prioress's Tale' in the *Canterbury Tales*, while written in the fourteenth century and allegedly set in a distant land, in reality graphically evokes events as they would have happened in England, and the religious hysteria that lay behind them. The story also seems to preserve oral recollections of atrocities in thirteenth-century England which Chaucer was in position to know about. There are some significant parallels in the structure of the story and the recollections of the murder of seventy-three Jews, by hanging and drawing at horses' tails, at

Northampton in 1271, on the trumped-up charge of crucifying a Christian boy. In this Canterbury tale there may be a part-record of one of the most cruel and harrowing episodes in Northampton's history which left many of the Jewish inhabitants of the town murdered and hanging 'like strange fruit' in the trees.

Expulsion

After escalating depredations of many kinds on the Jewish community, Edward I ordered the community to leave the shores of 'The land of the Isle' (the Jewish name for England) on 9 October 1290. In fairness to Edward he had previously made attempts to re-establish the Anglo-Jewry, but his measures were not far-reaching enough, and the times were not auspicious for a social experiment in assimilation. The expulsion was for the most part humanely conducted, though a number of Jews were killed and robbed on the way to the Continent. One group of Jews embarked for Europe found their boat stranded by low tide on a sand bar in an estuary. The treacherous captain of the boat suggested they might like to take some exercise on the sand bar while waiting for the tide to turn. This the Jews did, but when the tide turned the captain refused to let them get back on the boat, and they were all drowned. The captain did not ultimately benefit from his plunder, as the king had him apprehended and, after trial, he was executed for his perfidy.

End of a Prosperous Era

The expulsion marked the end of an era, and the end of a community. Between 1290 and 1650 no Jewish community was officially permitted to reside in England, and when Jews finally came back in any numbers to England the memory and monuments of the country's first Jewish community were all but obliterated. What remained of Jewish property in Oxford eventually passed into the hands of Balliol College, today one of Oxford's most illustrious colleges, and the converts left behind in the exodus eventually died. Any descendants they might have had were absorbed into long forgotten ensepulchred Christian generations.

A Sprinkling of Jews Remain

Between 1290 and 1650 there were few Jews in England other than converts, though it is now known (partly through the records of the Portuguese inquisition at Lisbon) that there were small secret Marrano Jewish communities in London and Bristol made up of Portuguese and Spanish Jewish traders and merchants posing as Christians. Additionally there were a few Jewish individuals who were here officially working for the king or state as physicians or advisers. Edward Brandau, a Portuguese Jew, was an excellent example. He became a prominent military and naval commander under the rule of Edward VI. After the victory of Henry VII at Bosworth field, Brandau patronized the young Flemish boy Perkin Warbeck. Warbeck's later pretence to the throne was based on information gained from Brandau. Back in Oxford there were less than a handful of Jews to be found, all associated with the university, and Jacob Barnet was one of the most notable.

The Jews Return

After the negotiated readmission of the Jews to England in 1650, the return of Jews to Oxford was slow. A small number of individuals gradually came back, with the first Jewish resettlement in London and then spreading to the provinces. One of the very first was a Jew called Jacob, who may also have been known as Cirques Jobson. Jacob distinguished himself by helping to introduce the Levantine custom of coffee drinking to Oxford and setting up Oxford's first coffee house (apparently the first in the country) within the Angel Inn, the most important coaching inn in Oxford. Today a commemorative marble tablet records Jacob's feat high on the western interior wall just inside the door of 84 High Street. In 1654 Cirques Jobson opened another coffee shop directly across the street on the corner of Queen's Lane and the High Street. There is still a coffee shop on the site, 'The Queens Lane Café', which is highly popular with the students, a place where much coffee is still served to fend off student essay fatigue and the ubiquitous hangover.

Famous Collection of Hebraica

Within the university Sir Thomas Bodley employed the services of a Jew to help him catalogue his valuable Hebrew manuscripts. The Bodleian Library has at present one of the most important collections of Hebrew manuscripts in the world, including manuscripts and an extensive treatise by Moses Maimonides, one of the greatest scholars in the history of Judaism: there is an original manuscript of the first volume of the Mishnah Torah with Maimonides' signature on page 164. The library's Hebraica incorporate the famous Oppenheimer Collection, one of the most outstanding collections of Hebrew manuscripts; the Vernon Bible of 1454, one of the most superlative scribal editions of the Pentateuch in the world; the first book printed in Toledo in 1492, and a Hebrew Bible.

In 1622 another Jew, Isaac Abendana, came from Holland and taught Hebrew in the university. In the eighteenth century a Jewish writing master taught in Oxford and established himself as a university personality.

The Modern Day

The first proper Jewish community in Oxford after the return of the Jews in the 1650s did not establish itself until the 1740s, and it remained small. The impetus for the real growth and flourishing of the Jewish community in Oxford was the 1854 Reform Act, which allowed unconverted Jews into the university for the first time. Since that time the Oxford community has grown. There are now about three hundred Jewish families in Oxford, and about 7 to 10 per cent of the students at any time are Jewish. For all this there is one active resident rabbi, myself, although the established community which existed well before I arrived has many volunteers who do extraordinary work and activities for the benefit of Jewish community residents, and have a number of rabbis resident outside Oxford who minister on a part-time basis. There are also, from time to time, various rabbis who take up residence in town, though they are mostly inactive in Oxford. At present, I am the only rabbi working full-time among the Jewish students and community in Oxford, and especially the university, where I concentrate most of my efforts. There is an active and flourishing synagogue in Richmond Road, Jericho, which caters for Liberal, Reform and Orthodox congregations, and which, in its present incarnation, was consecrated in 1974.

The L'Chaim Centre also functions as a synagogue but there is no competition with Richmond Road because we both draw on different sections of the Jewish community. The Oxford community runs the synagogue and its services without a rabbi, and they are proud of the religious diversity of their community, being able to conduct all the religious life of their community (including funerals) without outside help. Coincidentally the modern Jewish cemetery is situated in the south-east corner of the municipal cemetery at Wolvercote, to the north of Oxford, and is attended and cared for devotedly by volunteers and officers of the synagogue on Richmond Road. Similarly, the Richmond Road community provides essential Jewish educational and social activities to many hundreds of people, all through the efforts of their enthusiastic volunteers.

Hebrew Studies at the University

Although there existed a teaching post for Hebrew from 1312, a Regius chair was established in 1540 confirming the study of Hebrew as an academic discipline. Jewish study is strong in the university, with students being able to study Hebrew and associated Jewish studies within the university Oriental department. In addition the Oxford centre for Postgraduate Hebrew Studies was established at Yarnton Manor in 1972, seven miles to the north of Oxford, and also in premises on St Giles in the centre of Oxford itself. The centre is associated with the university, though not an actual part of the university, and specializes in advanced research in Hebrew and Jewish studies. It is known among other things for its Yiddish school held in the summer and enjoys a fine international reputation. Many of the students on the programme use the L'Chaim Centre during their stay to complement a real sense of living and of Judaism with its academic equivalent, which they are studying. The Yiddish revue held by students at the end of their summer course is one of the unpublicized delights of the university, consisting of substantial Yiddish humour, drama and song, all very *heimish* in fact.

Traditional Jewish Learning

At the L'Chaim Centre I have aimed to augment the various Jewish studies available in Oxford with traditional Jewish learning, which has been rather neglected in Oxford. Apart from the courses I have conducted myself, which encompass everything from Talmud, to Jewish law, Philosophy, and the subliminal heights of Jewish mysticism, a number of noted Chasidic scholars have lectured and delivered a series of courses at our centre, including Rabbi Adin Steinsaltz who is world-famous for his Steinsaltz edition and translation of the Talmud, and Dr Tali Loewenthal, author of *Communicating the Infinite* and who is currently one of the leading academic scholars of Chabad mysticism in the world; every term he delivers a seminar on Kabbalah and mysticism.

Rabbi Manis Friedman, noted for his comprehensive understanding of Chasidic thought and his skills in lucid presentation of the essentials of Jewish thought in a challenging and original way, has visited the university twice to the great acclaim of hundreds of students, both Jewish and non-Jewish; he was even invited to address the Oxford Union. I also address various contemporary issues from the point of view of Judaism, as teaching in Oxford somewhat ignores the great need for scholarship and intellectual insight to meet with real life and existence, and the needs of others, if it is to avoid vacuousness or intellectual decadence. Oxford prefers to dissociate scholarship from action in the belief that if the two are related this may lead to a subjective approach to one's subject. In the Oxford model, one must remain thoroughly detached from one's subject if one is to approach it properly.

I once attended a fascinating lecture on the life of Rabbi A. Kook, the first Chief Rabbi of Palestine, given at Yarnton Manor. The speaker, Eliezer ben Shlomo, was riveted by and passionate about his subject. I was amazed that the array of academics were so disdainful of his talk: the response of all was that the lecturer was too involved with his subject.

Yet one of the hallmarks of Jewish thought has always been an insistence on the integration of intellect and scholarship with practical life, as Judaism stresses that we need to exist as holistic beings and not as fragmented individuals divided in ourselves. Ultimately study and scholarship must be about what we can give and dedicate to others, rather than just the way we advance and benefit ourselves.

Chapter Twenty-One

THE CHALLENGE OF MODERN OXFORD

This chapter brings us to the present life and ethos of Oxford, where, to be specific, my purpose is to further the teaching of God in general, to promote the wisdom of traditional Jewish values and learning in particular, and to help people attain the fullest growth of their Jewish identity and spirituality. Perhaps most importantly, consonant with the adage of a 'light unto the nations', my purpose is to disseminate the life-affirming qualities of spirituality and its first demand on people: that they be good. To this end, it is not an exaggeration to say that I spend almost an equal amount of time with non-Jews as I do with Jews.

Oxford does raise challenges to our aim of furthering the teaching of God in the university, as well as give us real opportunities. Some of the challenges are common to any university, but others are perhaps uniquely part of the Oxford setting.

Consonance of Religion and Liberalism

Of these challenges that are peculiarly part of Oxford, I have particularly concentrated on the liberalism and secularism which is very prevalent and provides an important element in its distinctive ethos. For it lends itself to one of the major challenges and opportunities for an exponent of traditional Judaism. Because of its importance it is worth showing more closely how liberalism challenges religion and yet ultimately can provide a real help to the teaching of God as its essential sub-structure is certainly in accord with, and is perhaps in some respects derived from, important Jewish spiritual principles.

The liberalism I have been in contact with in Oxford is very pervasive. Most students in practice entertain genuine historical optimism. They believe in human progress, that humanity can and should better their social and material condition beyond what they have now. Moreover the students particularly believe in the need for and the attainability of peace and justice, and the need to resist evil. Anyone associated with the university will see that Amnesty International is well supported as well as the anti-apartheid campaign, and there is a strong activist element within the student population. Archbishop Desmond Tutu's visit to the university three years ago was notable as the students came in droves to hear his sermon and speech, which concerned his response as a minister of the Church in South Africa. The speech was remarkable for the fact that it was spiritual rather than overtly political in its tone. Many of the students had expected pronouncements in line with his more fiery media coverage, but he himself said his political role as one of the few public voices against apartheid had diminished as the white South African leadership had begun to permit free speech and movement towards negotiated change in South Africa. I enjoyed a very pleasant and impressive conversation with him, which began and ended with his firm 'Shalom'.

Empathy with Chinese Students

After the massacre on Tiananmen Square many of the more politically apathetic students were moved to join a demonstration through Oxford of an impressive two thousand people. The demonstration was memorable for the genuine feeling of sorrow and empathy of the students for their fellow students in China, and there was strong feeling against the outrages and injustice by the Chinese authorities. A plaster copy of the goddess of democracy was also set up by the Chinese students near the city centre at St Giles. It was eventually taken down by the Labour city council, who badly damaged it in the process. It is beyond doubt that many of the students have high ideals which are to be encouraged and congratulated, as they believe in the possibility and need for progress and the betterment of humanity through education, equal opportunity and political means.

The Messiah and a Better World

These ideals are in essential accord with the historic beliefs and aims of Judaism. Judaism has for thousands of years emphasized the necessity for humanity to act morally according to the highest principles for the good of humankind, and to promote justice by formal and institutional means, as well as in one's personal actions. Perhaps even more importantly the Jewish belief in the Messiah, one of the thirteen principles of Judaism, has anticipated and even pre-empted liberal historical optimism: belief in the possibility and reality of human progress, and the perfectibility of mankind. Two and a half thousand years before the United Nations was conceived, Jewish prophets stood in public places and declared there would be a world where justice and peace reigned, and man would be morally and spiritually transformed and free of his historical limitations.

Historical Causation vs Spiritual Development

The important difference between the historical optimism of Judaism and liberalism is in the means by which progress of humanity is gained, and the ultimate good of humanity that is sought. The liberal 'millennium' is sought through secular means and a process of natural historical causation. Thus the secular liberal believes that the ability to change is innate to humanity, that we can advance and evolve through our own efforts and knowledge, and the final goal of historical progress is that of a harmonious and peaceful society where the fullness of human potential can be achieved. Crucially, people are conceived as defining their final telos or goal, and setting in motion the natural historical and causal chain of events that bring it about. In Judaism it is agreed that people's actions and their individual moral responsibility are a vital part of their progress to the millennium, and that we are naturally involved in a pattern of historical causation which we determine as far as possible. In fact, when I arrived in Oxford I was so taken with the keen desire of the students to see a better society, and so impressed with the strong similarities between the liberal and Jewish traditions in regard to the perfection of civilization, that I wrote a book on the subject entitled *The Wolf Shall Lie with the Lamb*, which was very well received in Oxford, especially by the students.

But one of the book's purposes is also to point out the discrepancies between the two traditions, particularly about human limitation and, therefore, the necessity of the Creator for the ultimate betterment of our world. Contrary to liberalism, Judaism stresses that God is central to defining and fulfilling human aspirations, and that humankind is not the measure or the ultimate cause of the millennium. Judaism believes that it is insufficient for people to seek only goodness and progress in isolation from Godliness. It is a principle of Jewish belief that goodness has its source in God and that it has been revealed by God. Indeed, they are largely inseparable. Therefore humanity cannot find its fulfilment just by defining its own notion of the good, and then causing it to be actualized in the individual and society, however laudable it may be. Instead we must define our moral and ethical agenda by reference to the purposes that God has for humanity, and the means He has given us to achieve them.

Joining God as Junior Partner

The traditional Jewish view also differs from the liberal position about the importance assigned to human ability to achieve permanent change and bring about the millennium. While the natural agency of people is of great importance in Judaism, and our actions are held to be significant and effective, it is not our devices alone that finally bring about the millennium. Instead, the messianic era is achieved by a combination of natural and supernatural causation. So humanity precipitates the epoch of the Messiah and global perfection by a long process of propagating goodness and Godliness throughout the earth, and seeking to make itself more Godly, but the final and climactic change of the historical condition of humanity can only be brought about by God sending the Messiah. The assumption is that while we can achieve much in the exterior transformation of the world, we cannot finally excise the interior and spiritual causes of chaos and evil, though the spiritual person can gain control over them. So, for example, while people may be able to work for and achieve cessation of wars, they still find it impossible to eradicate the causes of war, contention, hate and jealousy. Only God can finally remove these human propensities, or better, lead us to harness them for a higher good, and bring a degree of altruism and selflessness even to these selfish human propensities.

In sum, much more than natural cause is at work. There is the natural historical causal sequence of events towards the end of the millennium, but there is also a greater causality encompassing natural causality where events are being drawn by God to the millennium. We see natural history encompassed by and guided in salvation history so that human freedom and God's will may work hand in hand to His desired end.

So the continuities and tensions which exist between traditional Jewish views and the liberal position, the secularism and agnosticism of liberalism, are a challenge to be met, but overall the belief in good and morality and the possibility of historical change are strikingly in accord with Judaism, and it is so because many of the key components of liberalism have originally sprung from the Judea-Christian era.

Finding Existing Common Ground

This situation greatly helps me in my work as emissary in Oxford because many of the students already agree with several key principles of Judaism and teachings of Godliness that I am attempting to further in Oxford. Judaism's teachings in this area are such that students cannot fail to acknowledge that it has contemporary relevance. Once students see the links between their beliefs and those of Judaism, many will naturally examine the significance and value of the original context of the ideas. After all, if one admits the significance of one set of ideas, then it is quite possible that the originating and corresponding framework designed to nurture and make these values prosper will be discovered to be relevant as well.

Obstacles Posed by Liberalism

This is not to pretend that the secular and liberal thought of Oxford is not a serious obstacle at times. Oxford is widely acknowledged to be liberal and sceptical in most matters of religion. People of all kinds of religious persuasions and creeds agree that Oxford is a very difficult place in which to maintain and nurture one's spiritual life. Many people feel Oxford has a very oppressive atmosphere in which to practise their faith. It is a sad fact that many go to Oxford observant or religiously inclined, only to leave Oxford confused and agnostic, or even affirmed atheists. It is that sort of place.

The problem comes from several different quarters: Oxford is very pluralistic and is filled by people with every kind of philosophy and outlook who are all ready to defend and advance their position at every opportunity. A religious person who cannot defend his or her belief intellectually, or who has any religious self-doubts, is easy prey for the intellectual jackals of the Junior Common Room and refectory. The questioners and cultured despisers of religion in Oxford, who abound, assume the validity of their 'enlightened' positions and tend to get a little upset if one accuses them of being intellectually shallow, asking them to justify their position. In Oxford it is assumed and not argued that traditional forms of belief are somehow antediluvian absurdities which have effected a curious and irritating survival in the modern intellectual era where psychology and science reign supreme and have enabled us to understand what religion is really about.

Doubts in the Theology Faculty

In the final analysis these liberal and sceptical attitudes to religion among the students are encouraged by the example of the theological establishment in Oxford. The theology dons in the university are generally theological liberals, and whatever the ultimate validity of their outlook and epistemology may be, it is observable that their example may not always inspire the rest of the university to lives of goodness and religious piety. Furthermore if the theological establishment of Oxford does have a religious passion it is in flushing out and eradicating all forms of literalistic or what they call fundamentalist belief which may rear its ugly head within the rationally purified precincts of the theology faculty. While there are Christian students of a more fundamental persuasion in theology in Oxford, they rarely prosper unless they change their ways and piously mutter J.E.D.P. as the article of faith necessary to pass their examinations in theology, and to show their fitness to dwell in the twentieth century. (J.E.D.P. is the literary hypothesis indicating different literary strands in the text. J. and E. refer to names of God and D. and P. to the alleged redactors of the Genesis tradition.)

Influence of Biblical Criticism

Of course J.E.D.P. is also a stumbling block for Orthodox Jewish students who are engaged in Jewish studies. One highly intelligent student with whom I became close embraced a traditional Jewish religious lifestyle while he was in Oxford but became disturbed by the implications of this literary hypothesis, as it denies the Mosaic authorship of the Pentateuch, one of the foundation stones of traditional Jewish belief. Since he did not have a mature knowledge of theology sufficient to put the hypothesis in its proper perspective, he became very disillusioned with his assumed practices and belief. Eventually he was unable to resolve the problem despite efforts to talk it through, and this played a significant part in his retreating from religious observance and becoming completely cynical about Jewish belief, to the point where he even mocked those who continued practising.

No doubt on this surmise Moses employed 'ghost writers' to create and edit his original manuscript. Some of the very senior members of the theological establishment in Oxford, when away from the lectern, admit that the theory has pronounced weaknesses, but that 'it is the best theory we have got at present'.

Orthodoxy of the Literary Hypothesis

The hypothesis is one of the major bulwarks of the liberal theological positions, and it is maintained despite its inadequacies by the theological establishment as it enables one to avoid completely and pre-empt any theological view of Genesis that gives any credence to traditional views of prophetic inspiration and Mosaic authorship of the Torah. The hypothesis throws a kind of *cordon sanitaire* around the liberal position, a fence around a fence. While Oxford claims freedom of thought on most issues, J.E.D.P. is an orthodoxy of the theology department, and students who wish to question it in their essays or exams are told it is best to avoid confronting the hypothesis as they have 'insufficient opportunity' to elucidate fully their opposition; and in any case the examiners want to see them understanding and engaging with one of the major modern critical positions, not rejecting it. Students who do not take this heavy-handed hint will find that academic success does not follow from a heterodox position. Most doubters of the hypothesis usually pay lip service to it, leasing if not selling their souls for the duration of their exams to keep the peace. So I have been told by some disenchanted students.

Amalgamation of Many Traditions

If one talks to the average theology don in Oxford one is subject to an intellectually strange and vertiginous sensation. Many of the theology dons in Oxford are ordained clergy who profess belief in God and the tenets of Christianity; a number even habitually wear their clerical collars. But if one delves into what some theology dons believe, particularly those of more academic tendencies, one discovers they are using the traditional language of belief but with an entirely modern meaning which is a curious alchemical amalgam of psychology, science, historical criticism, modern existential philosophy, *et al.* This is all in aid of mediating traditional forms of belief with the modern thought world, but it is in reality a rationalist's pastiche that aspires to much but adds up to rather less than the original. All this leads to an often repeated and absurd scene on Sundays when the dons preach sermons in local parish churches to ordinary lay people, where the sermon that the laity think they have heard is not the one the don has actually preached. This is of course a condescending and disingenuous exercise in semiotics as many of the clergy deliberately preach a pseudo-orthodox sermon without bothering to explain that they understand it in an entirely different way to the average lay person. Unfortunately, the net result of liberal theology is that you must have a minimum IQ of 130 to be a player in the modern game of faith, as there are no longer 'transparent' religious beliefs which even a simple person can comprehend. All in all, theological liberalism must be ultimately condemned by its intellectual élitism. If religion is to have any contemporary value, then it must speak to people about their everyday lives. Again, this is the view of more traditionally orientated students who frequent the L'Chaim Society for this reason.

The effect which the above has on my work is very pronounced. The Judaism I espouse is Chasidic and Orthodox (although I much lament the need for a recourse to labels) which, while it absolutely advocates an embrace of the world and sees the religious opportunity of modern-day society rather than the obstacles it poses, nevertheless refuses to compromise on matters of principle with societal change and whim. Thus my positions on many subjects will necessarily be seen as rigid, within the Oxford framework, not necessarily by students, but especially by colleagues and clergy from the Christian side of the fence, who have a vested interest in preserving a watered-down form of *every* religion at Oxford, perhaps so as not to expose their own questionable heterodoxies.

This is not my complaint, but is essentially a recurring complaint which I hear from countless Christian students arriving in the city for the first time. They find the brand of Christianity being offered to them peculiar indeed, this amidst a strong decline in Church of England attendance (now dipping below 2 per cent), and seem to find more in common with me and so come to my classes, though without any desire to convert to Judaism, but rather to be a part of a universal Godly tradition. This commonality is not due to their interest in Judaism, but rather to my approach to religion in general, which is with a strong degree of pride and not just an unwillingness to compromise on matters of tradition, but a strong conviction that the wisdom of age-old spiritual truths can be manifest, given sufficient effort and exertion on the part of the believer.

Oxford Clergy's Belief in God

In passing, it ought to be mentioned that there are a number of theologians and even college chaplains in Oxford whose belief in God is very shaky if existent at all. As remarkable as it may seem, it is quite possible to have a career in theology in Oxford and to be a complete sceptic or agnostic. One of the most notable and pious theologians in Oxford who is definitely not in this category, and is perhaps the leading scholar of the Greek Orthodox Church, is Bishop Kalistos Ware of Diaklesia. A few years ago he commented in a society lecture on Christian mysticism that a study of theology which is not rooted in an active religious life and practice is not true theology at all, but should be considered merely a branch of philology. While the bishop was only making a general point about theology, one can only agree that the inspiration for theological study should be a belief in God, else the intellectual side of religion becomes little more than a vapid and elaborate *Times* crossword puzzle of the spirit, cut off from real existence and unable to help transform the world and make it a better place.

Moving to the subject of chaplains, while most are no doubt sincere believers, I know of at least one chaplain who has serious doubts about the existence of God. A student reports that he once had a liquid lunch of sherry with a certain genial chaplain in his college study. As the lunch wore into the afternoon and usurped afternoon tea, as more and more light was seen through the sherry bottle, the subject of conversation turned to religion. At a certain juncture the chaplain sighed deeply and said, 'Do you know what, I find this God business very difficult sometimes; when I was younger I used to believe in God, but I'm not so sure any longer . . . but please don't get me wrong, I still have very warm feelings towards the idea of Diety.' It must be said that the chaplain concerned did not go out of his way to hide his feelings, and was rarely the flavour of the month with the bright young things of the college Christian Union. But he did have a broad kind of spirituality, he felt a genuine sense of vocation to his students and was a good counsellor, perhaps more so than some other chaplains with the 'correct' beliefs.

An Inter-faith Message

Given the very real intellectual challenge of the liberalism in Oxford, one of the objectives of my work is to provide students with a wider vision of the intellectual and theological problems that may concern them in the university. I emphasize the need for the connection between religious belief and practical action. Also on a simple level there is a role for straightforward Jewish apologetics and polemics in addressing some of the liberal theological challenges, as students are often unable to hear a coherent and alternative perspective on their studies, or questions thrown up in their personal intellectual development.

At a more profound and subtle level I also endeavour to convey to the students the fact that Jewish thought is very deep and multi-faceted, and that it provides an important and genuine alternative intellectual perspective (though one that is also complementary) to the one offered in most universities. The average student is, without knowing it, immersed in a particular tradition of thinking which is propagated in the universities of the western world, and has evolved from European Christian culture. This system of thought, like any system, has its own premises and foundations, and facilitates a particular consciousness of the world. The essence of any *weltanschauung* is that certain things are spotlighted in the consciousness it facilitates, and other things are left in the shadows of the periphery of consciousness and are therefore unrecognizable. In practice this means that people within this culture are able to see particular things very well and other things not at all, and most of all one is not able to see the crucial starting assumptions of one's own world-view. The Jewish 'world-view' is both intertwined and independent of the western intellectual traditions. So students at Oxford who become proficient in Jewish thought and traditional Jewish learning are not just gaining an extra department in their knowledge, but are genuinely facilitated in their intellectual and spiritual self-consciousness and understanding of the academic culture they are taking part in.

Impressed with Judaism

In my observation many students who take time to understand traditional Jewish learning are generally impressed by its range and intellectual power, and the fact that many of the concerns of western philosophy and psychology have often been anticipated and dealt with in sensitive and exciting ways in the Jewish tradition. It is clear that in most cases the western tradition of philosophy and theology is generally ignorant of what is contained in the Jewish tradition. One member of the L'Chaim Society studying in the theology faculty has written a thesis utilizing modern 'existential theology' and 'Process theology', which is a twentieth-century system of 'evolutionary' theology popular among liberal theologians, particularly in North America. Many of the concepts used in these systems of theology have striking parallels to the central ideas of Chasidic philosophy, which has evolved from kabbalistic thought since the seventeenth century, yet most theologians in this field are unaware of the parallels.

To return to the student who was disturbed by the rational and sceptical account of the book of Genesis, it is quite likely that if this student had a profounder understanding of the Jewish tradition he would not have been so hypnotically fixated by the narrow rational spotlight of the documentary hypothesis. Many intellectual and spiritual impasses often stand or fall on whether we accept their motivating questions and attendant methodologies in the first place. If one does not see an alternative to the originating question then one is often destined to remain perplexed. Even if Jewish thought does not always provide a direct alternative or answer to difficult questions, its very existence as an autonomous system of thought can sometimes break the closed circuit of logic in an impasse that declares 'This is the only answer!' which gives it the illusion of veracity.

The Religious Minority

The other main challenge any religious person has to face in Oxford concerns not just the intellectual example of their peers and seniors, but also the example of their actions. Any kind of religious student is in a relative minority in Oxford, and they are likely to be surrounded by people whose day-to-day conduct of their lives contradicts and challenges their beliefs and identity. It is all too easy to go with the flow and to conform to the general university ethos, especially as it helps confer acceptance among most students and is frankly far less effort, perhaps even more 'fun', than the discipline and individualism required to follow most kinds of religious life. While I shall return to this problem repeatedly throughout this book, the difficulty is far worse for Orthodox Jewish students, because Jews are a minority in Oxford and being Jewish does not have the traditional place and institutional status of Christianity within the colleges. Being a Christian student may no longer be so fashionable in Oxford, but on some levels it does still have a certain traditionalist cachet in the older colleges. In some of the more conservative colleges regular attendance at chapel is not required, yet it certainly does not damage one's prospects in college, and it may ease relationships with the senior hierarchy. But being Jewish and religious has none of this acceptability in most quarters, and is calculated to make one stand out.

Special Problems of Observant Jewish Students

On a practical level, being an Orthodox Jewish student in Oxford involves many problems. The colleges do not generally understand or cater for the needs of Jewish students. It is difficult for a student to keep kosher in a college, almost impossible if they wish to use the college refectory. Some Orthodox students would have serious problems if kosher meals were not regularly available at the synagogue on Richmond Road and at the L'Chaim Centre: both provide nightly meals during term.

To be sure, the kosher community in Oxford is very small, particularly among the students, and so we twice tried to operate a full-time kosher

216

restaurant, albeit with a limited menu, only to be thwarted by a lack of patronage. At first the restaurant, which had a full-time chef, was quite a success and the talk of the town. But after a few weeks it became increasingly clear it was not financially viable.

Forbidden Entrance to College

Another problem which illustrates the sort of day-to-day difficulties that Orthodox students can have, concerns the recent installation of electronic door keys or entry systems into some colleges. The devices are rightfully there to improve the security of the colleges, but on the Sabbath they can cause relative havoc for Jewish students wanting to get back to their rooms after Shabbat services and meals, as Orthodox Jews are not allowed to operate electrical equipment during the period of Shabbat.

Problems of Identity

The kinds of obstacle I have outlined do cause some Orthodox students problems, and every so often I have to counsel students having difficulty maintaining their religious practice and identity. Generally the problems are greatest for students who are not so well rooted or educated in their tradition. Most often, if a student knows why they are Jewish and Orthodox, and why it is important, they will not go astray. Much of my work is in encouraging students to see that a Jewish identity is an intensely positive thing, and there is every justification in being proud to be Jewish. If one is to follow any path in life then the motivation for it should only be positive, for I find it difficult to believe that one's Jewishness can be life-enhancing if it flows from negative beliefs and motives. In my observation there are many Jews who remain Jewish because of the continuing fact of anti-Semitism and the Holocaust; the attitude seems to be that people hate me, therefore I am. Others remain Jewish merely because of intense family pressure and guilt. This is ultimately self-destructive, and can only encourage non-Jews to affirm one's self-deprecation. Being Jewish is not about any of these things, as Judaism is about positive and life-enhancing values which bring benefit to oneself and others. If one is rooted in the intensely positive values of Judaism it can only bring sweeter fruit, and as we believe in our own self-worth and we believe that we have a contribution to make in the spread of goodness and Godliness in the world, then others will benefit from us and see us as we see ourselves.

Going Out into the Big City

While some students find themselves with problems because they have a negative Jewish identity, some experience difficulties simply because their Judaism has shallow foundations. There are students who have been brought up as Orthodox, and have lived most of their lives in relatively sheltered Orthodox communities where it is comparatively easy to be religious and being religious is in fact the very passport to social involvement and acceptability. Such students, arriving in Oxford, can have nothing less than a rude shock awaiting them, as they suffer an acute role reversal. Far from their ethos being the comfortable norm, they are suddenly the ones who are different, the outsiders; and Judaism no longer ensures comfort, but discomfort and inconvenience. At such a juncture one either reaffirms one's Jewish identity by centring on the intrinsic positive values of Judaism, or one conforms to the surrounding environment. Where one is in a community with conflicting identities an individual must shift from allowing those around to define their identity, to a position where one is to a far greater extent self-defining and self-determining. While I will have much to say about this phenomenon, it is important here to point out that my essential role for these students is to be a catalyst in their religious and social maturing and to provide encouragement and affirmation where necessary.

Anti-Semitism at Oxford

If there is one problem that students do not normally face in Oxford it is anti-Semitism. Students rarely report problems with overt anti-Semitism. Where it does exist it tends to operate on a more subtle level, for example some students who have had to arrange collegiate venues for various non-Jewish events have reported to me that they can normally get rooms for the purpose with few problems at most colleges. Yet when they have gone to some of the same colleges asking for a venue for a Jewish event, suddenly everything is very difficult, or booked up, or there is some intractable problem. Notably, according to these students, the main culprits in this respect are some of the older and more traditional colleges. There is one college I have in mind which to my knowledge has never allowed its rooms to be used for a Jewish event. Colleges with Jewish heads, such as Wadham, headed by Sir Claus Moser, are usually only too willing to help provide venues for Jewish events.

From my own experiences I can honestly say that I have never faced overt anti-Semitism, even in its subtle forms, although I have watched some within the university express slight discomfort with my Shabbat appearance. The only anti-Semitism I have experienced in the form of slurs and the like comes from the riff-raff of society, occasionally late on a Friday night when they shout verbal abuse as their car passes me on my way home. I take no notice of them.

Having said this, there was quite a serious incident just as this book was going to press. One day after a deranged Israeli doctor massacred fifty Palestinians in Hebron, a firebomb was thrown at the window of one of our bedrooms in a deliberate attack, causing a large fire just a few feet away from the bedrooms of our four sleeping children. Luckily our brave Spanish *au pair* quickly put it out and, thank God, no one was injured. At present, the Special Branch of the Police, responsible for investigating alleged terrorist attacks, are seriously looking into the matter, which has been reported throughout the world on television, radio and in the newspapers.

Ethical and Moral Development

From my observations, then, it is clear that Oxford's liberal ethos offers both clear opportunities and challenges to belief in God and a religious life. The other challenge presented by its liberal ethos to individuals in Oxford is in the acquisition of values and a way of life that seeks to spread Godliness and goodness. I described how in earlier times Oxford sought to have an effect on the moral and religious development of its students rather than just on their intellectual development, and how the university had some pastoral concern for its students. During the Victorian period a number of the college heads, such as Professor Benjamin Jowett of Balliol, gained great reputations for their concern for the welfare and development of their students. These college heads sought to promote an all-round excellence in their students, an excellence they inspired by example.

However, due to liberalizing influences as well as other changes within the university, Oxford now takes little or no interest in the students' moral and ethical development. The university as a whole does not encourage or discourage the students' ethical growth. Since the university in the modern day is a pluralistic organization it would be inappropriate for it to tell the students what to do. Yet surely there would be every justification for the university to encourage students to become, in whatever capacity, good people as well as good students. Just because a university is liberal and caters for people of every ideology and persuasion does not mean it must have complete moral and ethical neutrality. Virtually every Friday-night oration which I deliver to the students includes some mention of the perils of a value-free education and, conversely, the beauty of connecting learning and knowledge to deed and action. What objection could be raised against a university which seeks all-round intellectual and ethical excellence in its students? Surely graduates from such a university would be sought above those who had merely improved their minds?

What is more, it is sad to observe in the university today the poor example set by some academics. It is a shame that a few dons, while intellectual giants, are moral pygmies. I do not say this to be judgmental, and nor do I feel myself to be superior to them. The difference, however, is this: whereas I judge myself and encourage my students to judge themselves by their *actions*, the dons of the university seem to determine their standing by knowledge, tenure and publications alone. Judaism has always had a tradition of great learning but has simultaneously insisted that the purpose of knowledge is to teach us what we are meant to do. The great majority teaching in the university are fine people and not an insignificant number are truly kind and altruistic. But there is an equally not insignificant number providing very poor examples for the younger students, who may leave university under the impression that pettiness, ruthless self-promotion and a lack of fixed principles is normal and perhaps desirable in a successful individual. While the university's previous pastoral interest in students was not necessarily entirely positive, it is clear that an important aspect of an Oxford student's education has been lost. Education should concern the whole person and should be imparted not just by pedagogy but by personal example. An education that seeks only to improve a student's intellect and learning, with no regard to a student's ethical development and how their intellectual development might affect the lives of others, is in many respects incomplete.

Developing a Holistic Philosophy of Life

An attendant problem is that the university does not encourage students to reflect on the values and demerits of the academic culture they are part of, what they are trying to achieve by their study and by their support of the university as an institution of learning within society. This is because Oxford does not generally indulge in this speculation itself. On the whole education in Oxford and elsewhere is conducted and experienced in a very unselfconscious way by students and academics. Yet to some extent one's participation in a university which is the result of a complex history of cultural evolution does demand some self-searching and the formulation of a philosophy of education. Obviously it is crass to believe that universities are only about one's career prospects and providing industrial and social leadership; but unfortunately the signs of recent years suggest that Oxford in particular has fallen prey to this notion, as there is no mention of what the university is hoping to achieve in the wider educational sense, nor does one generally get an impression of great scholarly ardour despite the mountains of theses and publications coming out of Oxford each year. The university is at present content to amass a vast new re-endowment fund of over £400,000,000 and to create an assortment of new readerships and professorships, but to what purpose?

Holistic Educational Attitudes

One of the important aims of my work in the university and the founding of the L'Chaim Society was to provide the students with a Jewish educational organization which embodies a holistic concept of education, where learning, ethics and Godliness form a balanced whole which nurtures and brings forth a fully rounded human being. In all the varied educational programmes and religious activities of the L'Chaim Society, I have sought to provide students with both the vision and inspiration to advance their development as good human beings. Largely I do this by seeking to attain those same goals myself, however elusive they prove to be. I would emphasize that the process of self-development I have in mind is not one of condescension where I tell the students what they should think or do. To the contrary, I seek to provide an environment and influences which help them stimulate their own education and self-development, and where they can discover what is vital and productive for them. What has been important in the founding of the society is the provision of an educational organization that complements the existing ethos of the university (which does have many positive aspects) and compensates for its omissions. Also one must never underestimate the importance of the physical example that society provides; people are most likely to change and advance as the result of the people and community they have spent time with, rather than by what they have read or thought about in isolation.

The Rebbe's Inspiration

In all my efforts in Oxford the encouragement and example of the Lubavitcher rebbe, Rabbi Menachem Schneerson, has been central. If I were to be asked who most embodies the positive human and educational values I have been talking about, then I would say without reservation that the rebbe is a consummate example of all these things. We see in the rebbe a man of great academic accomplishment. Apart from his acknowledged stature as a great Torah scholar, he has also achieved superlative academic distinction in secular universities, with degrees from both the Sorbonne and Berlin universities. Also, in his unstinting work of the last forty-four years to revive the worldwide Jewish community, and his support of general humanitarian projects, as well as being an outstanding religious leader, he has shown himself to be a great and complete human being. While many members of the L'Chaim Society are only slightly aware of the rebbe and who he is and what he represents, the work of myself and the L'Chaim Society in Oxford has been made possible and is constantly inspired by the rebbe. If ultimately the general achievement of the L'Chaim Society and the leadership of the rebbe through it is perceived by the university to consist in invigorating the need for Godliness in all people and their communities, and that a vital part of the purpose of study and learning is to increase knowledge, Godliness and goodness, then I would be able to rest content that my wife and I had helped to achieve something of importance and permanence in Oxford.

Chapter Twenty-two

THE L'CHAIM SOCIETY IN OXFORD

Much of my work in Oxford University has been within the arena of the Oxford University L'Chaim Society. The society came into being as the natural response to the needs of the students and the objectives and expression of my work here. After I had been resident and working in the Chabad House in Oxford for a few months, it became increasingly obvious that a greater integration of the Chabad House with university life was desirable. The Chabad House was well patronized but in some ways it was not in the mainstream of Oxford existence. It was clear that students wanted an organization which they could feel was in a definable and official sense a part of the university structure, and an organization in which they could have influence and active participation.

Centrality of Societies to Oxford Life

Anybody who knows Oxford is aware that clubs and societies are the arteries and conduits of most extra-curricular activities in the university. If someone wants to do something in the university then it is likely that a society will be formed. There are already many religious societies in Oxford which are important in providing for the needs of every religious persuasion; and lest it be forgotten, the origins of the Wesleyan or Methodist Church were in the austerely named 'Holy Club' founded by Charles Wesley in Lincoln College in the eighteenth century. Clubs and societies also cater for the needs of the students to exercise democracy as the clubs and societies are all democratically constituted with a committee of officers appointed by election, and their activities have to fall within guidelines formulated and monitored by the Proctors of the university.

With the establishment of the Oxford University L'Chaim Society, Chabad gained an official place in Oxford University life, and became a Jewish organization recognized by the university authorities, alongside the Oxford University Jewish Society. Since that time the society has grown substantially, despite some trying times, becoming the second largest society in the university with 1,200 members. The society's success has come from the powerful and dynamic inspiration of Jewish Chasidic life and thought itself, meeting the needs and catering for the interests of Jewish students in a new way that has complemented the existing work of the Jewish Society and the local community. A good part of the attraction of the society is that it addresses and compensates for some of the deficiencies in university life.

Since the university is a secular and liberal organization, it does not adequately address the deeper educational and spiritual needs of the students. Also, at a much simpler level, the society provides a friendly and relaxed environment and a sense of community which is generally lacking in the competitive cut and thrust of everyday college life. Finally the success of the society has come from a combination of the commitment and talents of all those concerned with the running of L'Chaim. This has enabled an achievement beyond what I hoped for as a lone rabbi working in Oxford. The word *L'Chaim* means 'to life', and we hope, in words of an advertisement, that we have added 'life' in all its positive aspects to the lives of all those who have come into contact with the society.

History of Chabad at Oxford

The story of Chabad in Oxford started in 1988 when Rabbi Gershon Overlander came to Oxford to set up a Chabad House on the Cowley Road. His task was to found and establish the Chabad House in the city before handing it over to his appointed successor at the end of six months. He did an excellent job of initiating Chabad's work and I and my wife Debbie took over the Chabad House in 1988 after I had been offered the position through the offices and received the blessing of the Lubavitcher rebbe in New York. On settling in, my first task was to arrange links with the local Jewish community, and to establish the Chabad House ethos and a central core of members and supporters.

The local Jewish community was slightly cautious about the arrival of Chabad, and some feared we were possibly going to compete with the community and its leadership. The community was particularly worried that the arrival of an Orthodox rabbi would upset the religious balance of a community which provides facilities for three congregations and sees the absence of a rabbi as important in maintaining this balance. I sought as far as possible to allay these fears, and emphasized that the aim of Chabad was principally to reach and cater for precisely those Jewish students who were not affiliated with the local community; I had no wish to cut across community concerns. This gained the support of some principal members of the local community, who accepted this was our main business in Oxford, but sadly, others remained reserved. I cannot fault them for their suspicion, however. For one hundred and fifty years Oxford had a proud, very active, but quiet, Jewish presence, and my work has sought to promote Jewishness at the forefront of Oxford life. This is not something that everyone will be comfortable with.

In an article commissioned by the *Jewish Chronicle* to report on the changes in Oxford life ever since the opening of the L'Chaim Society, an Oxford student journalist wrote: 'It is increasingly difficult to hide from Judaism at Oxford. The boisterous activities of Chabad House have galvanized attention. All non-Jews in the university have heard of L'Chaim Society; all Jews have an opinion on it. Some cannot lavish enough praise. Chabad's charismatic and charming director, Rabbi Shmuel Boteach, secures top-level speakers and provides excellent hospitality for Orthodox and non-Orthodox alike' (*Jewish Chronicle*, Campus section).

Aside from the 'charismatic and charming' stuff, I would say this report is highly accurate. Not everyone is happy that we have brought Judaism to the forefront of Oxford. Nevertheless the Chabad House gained some important supporters in the university and the local community very early on. Two of our most important early supporters and sponsors were the late Alec Colman and his wife Eileen, who helped endow the Chabad House, and which bears their names, and the previous provost of Oriel College and former Governor General of Australia, Sir Zelman Cowen, in his time one of the most distinguished fellows of the university. My wife Debbie had been a friend of Sir Zelman's son and daughter-in-law in Australia, who are Lubavitcher Chasidim, which is how I first came to know Sir Zelman, and his wife Anna, Lady Cowen.

Australian Connection

Sir Zelman did much to help L'Chaim in its earlier days before he left Oriel College and Oxford, and set us up as a society, serving as our first official university sponsor, known as senior member. In addition we soon came to know Louis Lyons, and his wife Batya, OBM, both senior scientists and academics in the university, who also became important friends and supporters of Chabad. Louis Lyons continues as our senior member, and has furnished much advice and support; the friendship and help of his wonderful wife, Batya is sadly missed.

Centrality of Shabbat

Gradually over the next months the Chabad House was built up as we evolved a characteristic programme of activities and events, acquiring a central core of supporters and regularly attending members. At this stage many of the later hallmarks of the L'Chaim ethos were established. The central feature of the week in Chabad House was the celebration of Shabbat, particularly on the Friday evening. This proved to be very popular and soon we were running out of space to seat students on Friday nights. Apart from the warm conviviality of these evenings which will be remembered by many for the rest of their lives, the toasting of Chasidic toasts to life – *L'Chaims* – captured the imagination of many students. For those unschooled in the intense Chasid celebration of life and spirituality, the experience of the *L'Chaim* is in a literal and metaphorical sense a distillation of Chabad philosophy. The *L'Chaim* is about joyously attesting to the God-given positive nature of existence itself, and humanity's ability to change and transcend their condition for the better. Thus the *L'Chaim* is not to good life, health, or riches, but simply to life itself.

In an article about our society which appeared in the *Guardian* in October 1989, they quoted me summing up our society (although I honestly cannot remember saying this): ' "We teach you to enjoy life through the instilment of spiritual values," interjects Shmuley, as he shows you the dotted line. "We are vodka drinkers." He was standing behind a six-foot inflatable champagne bottle on the stall of the L'Chaim Society, a Jewish drinking club, at the annual Oxford University Freshers' Fair.'

This may be a bit exaggerated, but it does capture the meaning of *L'Chaim* and the joy we try to bring into Jewish observance and everyday life.

L'Chaim – to Life

Making a *L'Chaim* has given many students a first taste of the positive and traditional Jewish values, though obviously one must not overplay the theological importance and example of the vodka bottle. The object of the vodka (preferably Russian) in the *L'Chaim* is to help alert the soul to its transcendental possibilities so as to escape being fettered by a sense of limitation that can handicap everyday life. Obviously one needs to keep the correct balance between freedom and limitation when making a series of *L'Chaims*, else the soul will have a gross deficit of transcendence the next morning. When it came to thinking of a suitable name for the L'Chaim Society, a society of Jewish spirituality, 'L'Chaim' was the obvious and almost inevitable choice as it was virtually a slogan that summed up some of the important Jewish values we wanted to communicate to the university.

Besides the celebration of Shabbat and other religious observances we sought to introduce events during the week that would interest and inform students of many aspects of Judaism and Jewish life in general. These consisted of classes and seminars given by myself on various aspects of Judaism, many of which will be detailed later. One popular class over a period of one term was an examination of Maimonides' Thirteen Principles of the Jewish Faith, which culminated in two books, published by the esteemed Jewish publisher, Jason Aaronson of New Jersey. In addition to my classes there were regular speaker meetings where leading Jewish thinkers and personalities would talk on their area of special knowledge or experience. Some of these meetings were directly concerned with aspects of Judaism or Jewish issues. Others would feature leading and successful Jewish figures in many fields. In some cases these meetings would not necessarily mention or concentrate on any Jewish issues as such. The intention of these meetings was to present to students some of the world's leading Jewish personalities who are models of success in their careers or lives, and especially in how they have adhered to Jewish values, whatever their material success.

A Driving Ambition

Oxford University students are generally very ambitious and many Jewish students fear that openly affirming their Jewish identity may be detrimental to their careers. So the object of presenting major Jewish personalities to them, people who are proud of being Jewish and see their Jewishness as central to their careers and lives, is to show that being Jewish and successful are not conflicting but complementary. I have constantly told the students that being Jewish is a matter to be proud of, and in many walks of life excellence in one's career field and in character and conduct in life will generally outweigh any ambivalence there may be towards Jews in work and public life. In this respect having such an accomplished figure as Sir Zelman as patron of Chabad and L'Chaim was very important. Also it is helpful for students to see that before Sir Zelman left Oriel there were six prominent Jewish heads of Oxford colleges, including Dr Baruch Blumberg at Balliol and Sir Claus Moser of Wadham.

Non-Jews at L'Chaim

Of course it should not be forgotten that Chabad does not only direct itself to Jews. In recent years the rebbe has emphasized to non-Jews the great significance of the seven Noachide laws, given in the covenant to Noah for all mankind. Part of the fundamental importance of these laws is the fact that they are universal and serve to unite all mankind on a level which transcends any ethnic, cultural or religious differences: as mentioned earlier in this book, they are prohibitions of idolatry, blasphemy, bloodshed, sexual sins, theft, sadistic treatment of a living animal, and a positive injunction to establish courts of justice. Consequently many of the programmes at Chabad, and later at the L'Chaim Society, have been provided for a wider audience. This is in addition to the fact that on any given Friday night we have an average of ten to twenty non-Jewish students who come to see a traditional Jewish Sabbath, and about 20 per cent of all our classes are non-Jewish.

Of particular value were the two visits of Rabbi Manis Friedman to the university when he addressed students on moral and theological issues of a very general interest. All the students who heard him, whether Jewish or not, were filled with enthusiasm, or at the very least challenged by his teachings and fascinating arguments. His visit showed how Jews and Judaism have something valuable and unique in regard to Godliness that they must not neglect to impart to the rest of the world. It was specifically the non-Jewish students who were so impressed with him that they invited him to lecture about sexuality and intimacy at the Oxford Union, a lecture which was broadcast on television in the United States. It is vital to emphasize that this contribution of Jew to Gentile is not condescending; instead it pertains to the God-given mission that the Creator has given to the Jews and a recognition of the essential brotherhood and shared essence of all humanity. There is an endless stream of non-Jewish students who come to my office on a daily basis to discover all aspects of life from a religious perspective.

Where one fulfils a Divinely appointed task the relationship cannot be one of superiority, for what servant can be greater than their task or the ones they serve? Additionally, as I have mentioned, I have made it my practice to welcome non-Jews to the events of Chabad, and later of the L'Chaim Society, even to Friday-night meals, ever since I arrived. I have found this in general a mutually fulfilling arrangement; as I will describe later, it is also one that has actually greatly assisted the advance of the society. For example the L'Chaim Society developed close links with Ed Lazarus, a former president of the Oxford Union society. He became a very enthusiastic supporter of the society, and was instrumental in helping us stage one of our most successful terms of events ever, held mainly at the Union society itself. This would never have come about if we had taken a more traditional isolationist policy.

Incorporation of L'Chaim as an Official University Society

These early days of Chabad House in Oxford established the general pattern of life carried over into the fledgling L'Chaim Society. The official foundation of the L'Chaim Society was in September 1989 after it became clear that a more formal integration of Chabad into the mainstream of Oxford life was desirable, one which would also help the students to feel at ease, and where they would have more scope to contribute. The decision to found the society was finally crystallized one late summer afternoon in the computer room of Chabad House in an informal meeting with some of the students most closely involved with Chabad. At the same time we unanimously decided to call the society the L'Chaim Society as it was a cheerful and up-beat name that recalled one of our most characteristic and well-known activities on Friday nights, but nevertheless still communicated the essential Chabad ethos and values of the society. After we completed the formalities of electing a president and student officers for the society, formulating a constitution, making membership lists, and finally appointing our senior member (Sir Zelman), we were ready to face the university and most crucially the Freshers' Fair at the beginning of the academic year where most societies attract their members.

Going High-profile

The newly founded L'Chaim Society continued and extended the earlier style and activities. The major new development was a campaign to increase greatly the public profile of the society in the university and beyond. The rationale for this was simple: the projected constituency for the society was mainly (though by no means exclusively) Jewish students who were not affiliated to existing Jewish organizations in the university, or to the local Jewish community. Given that these students had not been effectively reached by the kinds of publicity and events offered by existing Oxford Jewish organizations, it followed that we would have to use a more dynamic approach.

The first priority was to establish our name. This meant doing large, high-profile activities which were enthusiastically publicized throughout the university. Not only did we want to draw in as many non-affiliated students as possible, we also hoped our name would gain wide recognition. It is quite difficult, to use the English understatement, to be successful when students are unaware of your very existence. I can recall all too often being told by students who sought a place to buy a mezuzah, Chanuka menorah (candelabrum) or attend a Friday-night dinner, that they were ignorant of our presence.

Centrality of Celebrities

The plan evolved was for the society to host and strongly promote major events featuring Jewish, and sometimes non-Jewish, celebrities who would have something to say of great interest which was usually directly relevant to Jewish life. They would in many cases be people of such a reputation that students would want to see them regardless of whether they were Jewish or not. The object of this was to establish L'Chaim in the long term throughout the university, and to be associated with excellence and exciting events. I wanted to dispel any notion of L'Chaim being just another worthy but dull religious society.

My aim is to demonstrate that Jewish students have much to contribute to the university by being proud of their Jewish identity and heritage. The evidence of the success of this was demonstrated when a journalist wrote in a university newspaper that the L'Chaim Society had almost made Judaism 'fashionable' throughout the university.

Also, on a subtle level I hoped that unaffiliated Jewish students would be aware of our society even if they never came to it. When posters are put up throughout the university advertising a future speaker, L'Chaim becomes synonymous with exciting, stimulating and professional activities. The ratio of people seeing the publicity to those attending the events is a hundred to one; so the publicity itself becomes a medium through which to stay in touch, albeit in a roundabout way, with all our students.

An American student who had come to study at Oxford for two years phoned me a week before he had completed his studies to thank me. Although we had never met, and in the course of two years it seems he couldn't be bothered to attend one of our functions, he nevertheless received our weekly mail which includes advertisements for the coming week's activities, as well as an essay adapted from the *sidrah* (weekly Torah reading). 'Your mailing is what kept me Jewish at Oxford for over two years,' he said.

As a university society we had official accreditation, and so we were able to entice many world-renowned Jewish personalities to speak under our auspices, and this in turn has enabled L'Chaim to become the university's second-largest society. Many speakers feel it a privilege to receive an Oxford invitation, but I must add that many of the people we brought were organized via the global Lubavitch network and its connections, which proved incomparably useful.

Mr Spock at Oxford

Actor Leonard Nimoy's visit to Oxford to speak at the Union debating chamber on behalf of L'Chaim showed the value of our planning. When Leonard Nimoy came many students were not even aware that he was Jewish, or in fact that he had made an important new film on the subject of Holocaust denial, and that he was proud of being Jewish. What they did know was that he was their youth idol of *Star Trek*, and a star of several major Hollywood *Star Trek* movies which made hundreds of millions of dollars, and they wanted to see him in the flesh. The student response to Nimoy was astonishing: they packed out the Union, many sitting on the floor in the aisles to hear him. There was a buzz of expectation in the minutes before he came into the chamber, which rose to a great crescendo as he finally arrived. Suddenly, as he got to the L'Chaim podium to the applause of the students, he raised his hand high in the famous Vulcan salute. For the first and last time in my career in Oxford I saw the immemorial, immovable sang-froid of the Oxford student crumble completely, leaving a near-teenage pop concert hysteria. Had it been even a degree closer to uncontrolled adulation I would have had to turn my head away in embarrassment. As it was I surprised myself by wishing that the familiar student cool would soon return.

Vulcans and Priests

Leonard Nimoy went on to address the students on the dangers of histori-cal revisionism about the Holocaust. It was the most receptive audience I have ever witnessed in the Union chamber. His speech was entitled 'The Holocaust: a duty to remember', and he introduced and showed his new film, *Never Forget*, based on a real-life story about the holocaust survivor Mel Mermelstein who has fought against Nazi revisionism in California. The film tells how one concentration camp survivor (played by Nimoy) sought to expose the deception of Nazi revisionists in California, which led to the American judiciary legally recognizing the historical fact of the Holocaust for the first time. After the speech and film, both of which impressed the students, Mr Nimoy took questions: he revealed in answers that being Jewish was very important to him, in his career and personal life, and that he had even gone to eastern Europe to rediscover his Jewish background. He also related how he had been impressed by the synagogue services he went to when younger, and that this had influenced the way he had characterized Spock and Vulcan culture in *Star Trek*! The celebrated Vulcan salute was no less than an imitation of the hand gesture he had seen priests making during the Cohanic blessing in the synagogue service when he was a young boy. Apparently during a service, as the blessing of the congregation by the assembled *kohanim* (priests) was about to take place, he was told by his father not to watch while the blessing was going on. The young Nimoy could not resist looking because he had been forbidden to do so and, as he sneaked a glance at the *kohanim*, he was fascinated to see them with their hands outstretched in the characteristic gesture that has become part of movie history.

The value of this meeting was obvious. Nimoy, the Hollywood celebrity, had appeared at the Union chamber billed as a Jewish film star, and in his speech he had shown how important his Jewish identity was to him. Nimoy demonstrated that you can affirm a Jewish identity and be in the mainstream of success. His appearance encouraged non-affiliated Jewish students to consider exploring their Jewish identity. What is more, a large number of people, many of whom were not Jewish, heard an important message about Nazi revisionism and the reality of the Holocaust. There is no doubt that ordinarily much of the audience would not have chosen to go to a meeting on the Holocaust and, because they heard the message from someone they revered, it is very likely they were receptive to it.

The first objective of using high-profile events was to encourage Jewish students to develop a greater Jewish consciousness, and to feel there was something positive in being Jewish. The second objective was to build on this and to encourage these students to come to the L'Chaim Society itself for a Friday-night meal or perhaps an educational programme where they would be able to discover more about Judaism and Jewish life. In all this it is important to emphasize that at every point the means used to encourage students to develop their Jewish identity is their own interest in Judaism and sense of self-discovery.

Even if attracting high-profile speakers had proved an insurmountable challenge, there were still many other activities available to us which appealed to a wide spectrum of students. There are primarily two kinds of public events. The first is a fascinating speaker, famous, with a recognizable name or face. The second is a fascinating subject.

For example, the L'Chaim Society attempts to stage debates or seminars on subjects that are of interest to all students. An evening of panellists discussing 'Are Nice Jewish Men a Vanishing Breed' attracted a sizeable audience, especially women for some reason. Other seminars we have sponsored which have not featured international celebrities but have proven successful include debates on whether anti-Semitism is a Jewish subject; the morality of Israel's nuclear arsenal; whether Israel should return Judeah, Samariah and the Golan Heights; a panel discussion singling out the most important events in Jewish history; a lecture on the causes of distress and well-being among Jewish women; lectures on the predominance of Jewish personalities in the movie and entertainment industry; the influence of Arab oil money in British politics; and one about the similarities between quantum mechanics and the Kabbalah and psychoanalysis and the Kabbalah.

Then there is the weekly debate on a contemporary social issue in which I am pitted against a student volunteer. I always put the Jewish point of view and the student defends a position which most appeals to him or her. Issues debated have included abortion, homosexuality, the pre-eminence of the rebbe within Lubavitch life, and whether or not there is an after-life. The student is paid £10 for participating, and £18 if he or she wins the vote that follows the debate.

Of course, one must try never to lose sight of the reason for all this. These events serve only as a means to a higher end, a medium to attract students to take part in our activities which are devoted to God. Despite the harvest that can be reaped from high-flying activities, they remain largely external.

The second facet of my work is far more important and is, of course, wholly internal. After one has staged a number of high-profile activities and established (even) a small nucleus of supporters, it is time to impart something wholesome to them, thus establishing a deep, meaningful and long-lasting relationship with those who, in the long run, will count most. There is no more urgent requirement in campus work than to establish an intimate group of committed students. What financial donors are to the community rabbi and his congregation, the core student group is to the rabbi on campus. These are the students who will invite their friends to Friday night, regularly attend classes and events, help with mailings and putting up posters, defend the integrity of traditional Judaism against malicious attack (which one is sure to encounter and is usually commensurate with one's success), and serve to cure the pangs of loneliness and frustration that a job such as this can sometimes bring. The students are not just my students, they are my friends. It is their love, admiration and devotion which keep me going and I try my best to show them equal devotion in return.

A Subconscious Identity

It is a vital tenet of Chabad that Jewish identity is innate in every Jew, and for every Jew returning to their heritage there is merely an uncovering and revitalization of what is already there. Therefore the purpose of the L'Chaim Society is to provide a fertile environment in which this can happen, and where they may find intelligent and coherent answers to the questions that inevitably come up during the course of this process. The worst approach that could be employed in trying to help students discover their Judaism is to try to cajole or argue them into it. This approach is only denigrating to an individual's freedom and self-respect and will eventually cause all but the emotionally needy to turn away from Judaism.

Where Students Can Feel at Home

All the students who have come to L'Chaim value the relaxed and friendly atmosphere of the centre and its activities. At the L'Chaim Society I have concentrated on creating an authentic Jewish experience alongside a friendly *heimish* atmosphere. I think it is important to make people feel comfortable with Jewish practice, so I always provide a full explanation about what is going on in any ritual observance. It is essential to avoid what can arise in some shules, where newcomers may be intimidated by unfamiliar practices and feel alienated from the community because they are not fluent in basic Jewish tradition. In addition, I want students to see that Judaism is a coherent and comprehensive way of life and thought which can synthesize all the modern world and existence, so that one can be part of the modern world and be Jewish as well. It is, after all, Jewish universalism that we constantly seek to promote. Also it is important to make the students feel part of the Jewish community, since Judaism is not just a question of belief and action, or even recognizing an interior spiritual identity and destiny, but is to be part of a spiritual community; in Judaism the idea of a solitary Jew does not exist.

Firm Foundations

In my role as rabbi at Oxford, my ultimate criterion of success in my work is not how many students decide to adopt a Jewish observant lifestyle. While it is pleasing to see students embrace a traditional Jewish way of life, the sign of success is that every student has developed and attained their maximum stage of Jewish development appropriate to their needs and situation in life at that time. In many cases one will perhaps only be helping to lay foundations for things that may come later in a person's life. But it is a noble task to labour on foundations, for while foundations are unseen no fine edifice can rise and stand without them.

Acquiring the L'Chaim Centre

The next vital stage in the growth of the society came when we acquired our new purpose-designed L'Chaim Society centre and shule in premises in Carfax, right in the heart of the historic centre of the city. Originally all our events were held in the Chabad House on Cowley Road, but with the growth of the society the house was bursting at the seams on Friday nights and for events not held in university venues. Unfortunately the acquisition of new premises nearly caused the demise of the society, due to the Reagan–Maxwell débâcle which will be recounted later in this book. Briefly, however, the financing of the new centre rested to a great extent on the late Robert Maxwell, the newspaper and publishing tycoon, providing us with complete sponsorship for the new centre in return for exclusive rights for the *European* newspaper on the visit of former US President Ronald Reagan to Oxford and his speech at the Union debating chamber. This suited Mr Maxwell since, the same week President Reagan was going to address our society Mr Maxwell was launching the *European* in the US. This looked very good on paper but life so often gives the lie to theory and hope. Maxwell was the most challenging person one could negotiate with: he was obviously accustomed to driving hard bargains. He wanted value for money, and demanded it. Yet a suitable arrangement was eventually struck, and after much preparation we awaited the imminent arrival of Reagan. Disaster struck when just seventeen days before he was meant to come the president had to cancel. Despite being able quickly to substitute Israeli Housing Minister Ariel Sharon to speak at what proved to be a major and highly successful speaker meeting in the Union, we suffered a financial calamity. When the celebrations and all the clearing up from the official opening of the centre were over, we were suffering a nasty financial hangover and, to use a Dickensian phrase, a financial embarrassment. We did not have enough capital or pledges to cover the costs of opening, and since then I have been involved in hectic fund raising throughout Europe and the United States to keep the centre open. On one fateful day, at the lowest point of L'Chaim fortunes, even the computers had to go. A sorry day in any Chabad emissary's life!

Hope and Renewal

But since that time the computers have happily returned, and the society has prospered and advanced with the added benefit of experience, though I would like to advise that learning experiences are only good if you manage to survive them. The new centre has been of great importance in my work in Oxford as it is purpose-adapted to our needs, and it is in a fine position in the central crossroads of the city centre. The society is now very much an accepted and established part of Jewish society in the university, complementing existing Jewish facilities and activities in Oxford. The slight frisson of competition that the existence of the L'Chaim Society has created in Oxford has been entirely beneficial to the existing Jewish Society, as they have reinvigorated themselves; they have produced their best term cards and events for some years, as well as reappraised their role with regard to their members.

As we are no longer a new and novel institution in Oxford's life and are an accepted part of the landscape, we hope to continue to build towards the best future for individual Jewish students, the general advance of Jewish life in Oxford and, most importantly, the general increase of goodness and Godliness throughout the university and far beyond, until the times when the Messiah will come and complete what humans have been endeavouring to do from the beginning of time. It is my fond hope that this collection of essays will help provide you with insight and inspiration, and help to speed the dawn of the messianic era, a goal to which all learning should be directed, namely, the perfection of humanity and civilization.

I wish this book to convey that there *is* logic, even profound wisdom, in traditional Judaism, and not cold dogma. What students desire most is to see themselves and their Judaism as sensitive to the many dilemmas facing them in the most important developmental stages of their lives.

Chapter Twenty-three

OXFORD GOWNS AND JEWISH GARB: SIMILARITIES BETWEEN JEWISH AND OXFORD TRADITIONS

It is marvellous that a secular institution such as Oxford University can have such a plethora of traditions and stick to them. Some of the most charming traditions are those which are recognizable as old English country practices that have been taken over and preserved because the university respects all things ancient. Two of these are the May Morning celebration and the Beating of the Bounds on the Christian holy day of the Ascension.

At six o'clock in the morning on the first of May the crowds gather around Magdalen College tower, in the High Street and on the bridge, to hear the famous choir welcome the arrival of spring to Oxford. Many of those who gather have stayed up all night in anticipation, and in most years revellers still in evening dress from a May Day Ball swell the crowds. Students and townspeople alike enjoy the sound and the spectacle, and afterwards they disperse to drink champagne and go punting, and also to watch men Morris dancing, complete with a hobby horse and May King or Queen, bells a-jangling and white cotton handkerchiefs a-flying. Although hi-tech speakers amplify the singing to the listening crowds, it is still possible to imagine the scene happening in any century before the twentieth, and the people seem to sense this as they walk away in a rapturous, trance-like state when the choir finally ends its homage to the warm season. Perhaps one of the less talked-about traditions associated with May Morning is that of students jumping into a freezing cold Cherwell River off Magdalen Bridge – usually stark naked, the photographs of which are always included on the front page of the student newspapers. In our third year in Oxford my wife and I decided to go to witness the May Morning celebrations which we had heard so much of. When a young undergraduate stripped, stood up for all the world to see on the rail of the bridge, and then catapulted into the river, my wife and I thought that perhaps we had had too much to drink and were just seeing things. It was only when I remembered I had just woken up and had not drunk anything, and that my wife never drinks at all, that I accepted what I was seeing was a reality.

Beating the Bounds is a custom dating from medieval times that has been preserved in Oxford only because the city has such a strong regard for tradition and ancient precedent. Representatives of the city and university churches observe the strange practice in the middle of the day, with the vicar, choir and parishioners all walking through the busy streets of Oxford as though nothing unusual were happening, intent on marking in turn each boundary stone of their parish. For the procession of the city church, St Michael at the North Gate, this even means walking into busy shops such as Marks and Spencer which have been built around the old boundaries while still preserving the opportunity to observe this custom. Once there, the vicar makes a chalk cross on the brass plaque that marks the traditional boundary, and then he stands back and lets the choir, undergraduates from Lincoln and his parishioners hit the mark with their canes. Shoppers from outside the area look on amazed as this happens, asking the people next to them what on earth is going on, but those who have seen the ceremony before try to treat it casually and claim to see it as entirely normal. The lucky tourist who stumbles on this has caught a glimpse of old Oxford, where tradition is a more important consideration than almost anything else.

Ducks in Oxford Academia

Perhaps the greatest and most memorable of all Oxford traditions is celebrated at the college which has the best scholarly reputation of the lot, All Souls. The Fellows of All Souls are given enormous academic and social cachet, and every century these illustrious minds take part in what must be one of the world's most extraordinary displays of homage to tradition.

It is said that when the college was being built in the mid-fifteenth century, a mallard was found in a drain, and that this was such an extraordinary event that the college adopted the bird as its totem. Twice a year, on All Souls' Day in November and at the Gaudy, the fellows sing the Mallard Song: this is so special that it is not supposed to be overheard by those unconnected with the college, but none the less many people seem to know its words. However, the most amusing ritual comes but once every hundred years: the fellows have a feast to celebrate the mallard. Apparently they set out around their college in search of the unfortunate duck, led by the Lord Mallard and singing a ditty called 'The Mallard Song', the lyrics of which I include below: the original publication was in M. Burrows's *Worthies of All Souls* (Macmillan, London 1874).

> The Griffin, Bustard, Turkey and Capon
> Lett other hungry mortals gape on,
> and on their bones with stomach full hard,
> Butt lett all Souls men have their Mallard.

The Romans once admired a Gander
More than they did their best commander,
Because hee saved, if some don't fooll us
The placed named from the Scull of Tolus.

The poets faind Jove turn'd a swan
Butt lett them prove it if they can
To mak't appeare it's not all hard
Hee was a swapping, swapping Mallard.

Then lett us drinke and dance a Galliard
In the remembrance of the Mallard
And as the Mallard doth in poole
Letts dabble, dive, and duck in boule.

(Refrain)
O' by the blood of King Edward
O' by the blood of King Edward
It was a swapping, swapping Mallard.

A Spectacle to Behold in the New Millennium

Bearing torches to light their way, they are not even averse to walking the college roof. It is even said they also drink an alcoholic concoction laced with duck's blood, but I don't know if this is true. For those who are interested in seeing their intellectual heroes in such a dashing display, the next Feast is due on 14 January 2001.

There are other such Oxford traditions of privilege, enjoyed only by the designated few. These include the celebrated and extravagant May Balls, and the quiet and free pleasures of swimming in Parson's Pleasure.

A double dining ticket to one of the grand commemorative balls currently costs almost £200, but then it is a night never to be forgotten. You can expect to dance to three famous bands, eat and drink fine fare all night, be entertained by a hypnotist or cabaret, get a massage from a masseur or masseuse, ride on fairground rides ... but most of all, you experience the essence of the ball itself. When five hundred people have paid so much for a ticket, and then more for a dress or dinner suit, they *have* to have a good time! Still, the pleasure is only open to current and former members of the university who pay for it; others who wish to go are accustomed to 'crash' (get in without paying), usually unsuccessfully, but sometimes with hilarious aplomb, pretending to be photographers from *Vogue* and suchlike.

As a stark, if you will forgive the wordplay, contrast, there is the famous stretch of the River Cherwell designated as a male-only bathing place. Nude bathing at Parson's Pleasure was only acceptable to Victorian notions of propriety because it was such a long-standing custom that everyone knew it was happening and ladies therefore avoided the area. Until recently, women punters would disembark from their punts before reaching this delightful spot, and pick up their craft later on so that men were free to indulge in the sunshine and water of that secluded spot. Every year the L'Chaim Society hosts a punting party, and you will have to believe me that we knew nothing of Parson's Pleasure. So that by the time we had turned the bend and set eyes upon it, it was too late. The message then went out for the next few weeks, 'Did you hear where the rabbi took the students on their punting trip?'

In many respects the university traditions are as important as the curriculum itself. Students who come to Oxford expect not just an education but a cultural experience. For many people, even those who have studied here, Oxford is more famous for its culture and traditions than its education. When I asked an American student if he appreciated Oxford more than his Ivy League university, he told me he felt his American education had been rigorous, but there was no substitute for waking up to the sound of students playing violins and sipping champagne with strawberries at dawn. True enough, Oxford is one of the most culturally rich cities in the world and there is never a shortage of student theatre, music, art exhibitions and even operas.

Undeniably, the most stimulating form of culture is provided by the university itself. Its rich traditions are as colourful as they are ancient. Many centre around the privileges inherent in being a university don, the most common of which are the dining privileges. While the students suffer the ordinary slop served in most institutions, the members of the Senior Common Room eat a meal fit for a king from 'High Table' on an elevated dais. They have their own chef and are nightly served a multi-course meal consisting of the most exquisite dishes accompanied by the finest wines. All this comes at the price of learning a tremendously complicated system of etiquette which takes many years to master.

Barbarism at High Table

In November 1990 I was invited by the Doctor of Divinity to deliver a lecture on Judaism at Magdalen College and to attend High Table prior to the meal. I warned the powers that be that under the Kashrut laws there was nothing I could eat except fruit, and this they kindly provided. Unfortunately, I did not mention that for the same reasons I could not really use their cutlery either, but I did not realize this omission until I turned up on the night.

A special procession, led by the president of the college, Anthony Smith, brought us in. Everyone was wearing their academic robes; everyone, that is, except me. I immediately regretted I had not put on my Chasidic Shabbat garb which would have allowed me to blend in perfectly. The president recited the traditional benediction in Latin, and the food was served. Waiters in meticulous dress waited upon our every desire. There were three forks, two spoons and two knives in front of us, as well as an entire collection of glasses, each of which was meant to be used with a different wine. I politely excused myself from indulging in this feast, picked up one of the oranges they set before me, and dug in. My fingers were picking at the skin, pulling it to pieces, and little squirts of juice were making a small fountain in the corner of the table. A sudden silence at the table caused me to lift my head out of the intensity of wrestling with the orange peel, and I noticed I was being stared at – by everyone. Their stare was one of utter horror. They had clearly never witnessed the fingers coming into contact with food, and it was as if my hands were eternally contaminated. I politely excused my unforgivable breach of etiquette and explained I could not use the college cutlery since it was used regularly with non-kosher food. This explanation only served to confound them further, and I thought it best to quit while I was not that far behind. I received a sympathetic smile from my official host for the evening, the Doctor of Divinity, but it was hardly reassuring. In fact, it was the kind of last glance a man might give the world before he sets himself alight.

Although I was not immediately invited back to Magdalen High Table, my host did not lose his job for introducing such an uncomfortable spectacle to the college, nor did he take his own life; so the evening was not as complete a disaster as the faces of the dons had led me to believe. Later, the students who listened to my lecture seemed altogether more sympathetic to my way of life than the senior members of college, but then I have often observed that young people are never completely set in their ways. I say most of the above in jest and the senior members were kind and friendly to me, but they were deeply perplexed as well.

Oxford and Jewish Dress

This incident caused me to take a common complaint more seriously than I had done before. The more observant Jewish students at the university have often told me that observing the Kashrut laws places a restriction on their freedom, and they serve as an impassable gulf in their socializing with the non-Jewish students. It also set me thinking about other traditions, traditions that Judaism and Oxford have somehow come to share, despite their disparate histories.

The Oxford tradition which is by far the most common, most adhered to, most famous, most noticeable to the uninitiated, and most disliked by the students is the wearing of gowns. The majority of universities require their members to wear a formal academic gown or robe on the most important occasions, such as the graduation ceremony and the awarding of honorary degrees to benefactors or statesmen. The difference in Oxford is that students are required to wear a gown virtually every day. Whenever the students eat at formal hall, they must don their academic robes. Formal dinner held nightly during the university term is a sight to behold.

The students wear their gowns draped over their shoulders. Many of the Oxford College dining halls are medieval and this lends an added aura to the occasion. The lights are very dim and the students eat directly from the table, with no tablecloth. They come in in twos and threes, gossiping with friends or discussing metaphysics, and sit in long lines on hard wooden benches. Whatever the conversation, though, it may not concern the college paintings that hang in the dining hall, however breathtaking they are. This is a serious breach of etiquette because it implies that one has nothing better to discuss than an old master. The undergraduates must wait for the senior members of college to enter and take their seats before they tuck in, and while they wait there is a strong atmosphere of expectancy.

The big moment arrives when the dons, or fellows of the college, file in for their dinner at High Table. A brief grace is sung or said in Latin that is unintelligible to the majority of the audience and then, when the head of the college is seated, eating may begin. The students are served a modest but hearty meal, which seems third-world compared with the one the dons are served. Many an undergraduate nowadays is rather embarrassed at being waited on by staff who are often over twice their age. It seems so impertinent to raise the water jug to be refilled when you are perfectly capable of walking over and doing it yourself. However, after three courses even the hungriest students are satisfied with the amount of food they are given. They retire in dribs and drabs just as they came in, while the civilized meal at High Table may go on for a good while yet.

In addition, there are many other occasions when the students must wear their gowns. No student can take any Oxford exam without wearing full academic dress, and as colleges set examinations called collections (not to be confused with the termly report, also called a collection) at the beginning of each term, woe betide the student who forgets this vital piece of clothing when they come back from vacation. Whenever the students are summoned for their reports they must also wear their gowns.

The greatest demonstration of the contempt with which some regard their gowns is the scene at the end of finals. The first thing those who have gone through a gruelling week of important exams do is throw off their gowns as they emerge to a torrent of champagne and flowers being showered on them by their friends. Some do so violently, and I am there every year to witness it. It used to be that 'trashing', throwing a revolting mix of foodstuffs over those who have finished, would take place in the streets near the building where exams are taken, known as the Examination Schools, but now the police patrol the area to make sure that this anti-social practice does not happen in public. The students are not even supposed to pop a champagne cork near Schools nowadays, but their excitement is such that they usually try to get round this rule. Everyone is rushing up and down, calling for friends, smiling at Japanese tourists (who are completely bemused by the spectacle, but still their cameras blaze through hundreds of rolls of film) and letting go of the pent-up emotion they have had inside them for months. The traffic in the High Street slows to a grinding pace because of the number of young people who run across the road in their excitement; perhaps they think the ancient tale that all vehicles must stop for a student in subfusc is true, so they are emboldened to treat cars and buses with more contempt than usual.

What Students Remember

My presence is of the utmost significance on these occasions, since this one day of stupendous relief and catharsis is what students tend to remember most. When they emerge to find me waiting there, along with scores of other friends, they know that they mean much more than a statistic to me, that is to say just another student to fill our numbers. They are leaving Oxford and understand we will not be seeing much of each other after the completion of exams; we may enjoy nothing more than communication over electronic mail, and they know I am sorry for this. Being there also demonstrates to the students the truth that I have repeatedly emphasized throughout this book: we care for the students and try to demonstrate our devotion to them even when this is completely outside a religious framework. The Jewish people are exactly that, a people, and not just a religion; therefore they relate to each other on an essential level which transcends any religious, cultural or sociological differences.

I feel I can best demonstrate this by being present for the students on occasions such as these whose only significance is for the students themselves. Their exams are very important, and when they celebrate their completion we want to be a part of the memory of that celebration, even though students often show the least respect for their university's tradition at this time by throwing off their gowns as quickly as they can.

This peculiarly Oxonian phenomenon has always interested me because it reminds me so much of my childhood. I attended a Jewish day school in Miami Beach which, although itself Orthodox, takes in student population primarily from non-observant homes. It happened to be that the school was one of the finest in south Florida and this, coupled with the fact that many parents wanted their children to have some sort of Jewish education, led them to send their children to the school, although they were not personally observant. Of course, the school forced the boys to wear a yarmulka and *tzitzis*, and if they were caught without them they would receive a detention. If the offence was repeated, they could even be expelled. The image of how, every day at exactly three forty-five, when school ended, they would immediately pull off their yarmulkas and *tzitzis* as they ran to the school buses or even to their own cars to go home, will always remain fresh in my mind, and every time I see the Oxford gowns being thrown into the air, quite soiled, by a gleeful student, the image of my childhood returns.

This is, of course, also the way the Oxford students feel. People from all religious and social persuasions seem to disdain a forced uniform. And yet, precisely because of the similarities of these incidents and because, to an extent, all traditions have something in common in that they are the preservation of a specific heritage, I have always advocated that the students should wear their gowns proudly and not complain about them constantly. Every Shabbat I, like most Lubavitch rabbis, wear a long black coat of silk made especially for the Shabbat holiday. I wear it with pride, and especially so in Oxford because as I walk the streets on Shabbat there are so many gowns passing by that I fit in perfectly. But it is also a statement to all of the onlookers – and there are many who are curious – that Judaism is alive and vibrant.

Hats Off to British Justice

Only once have I ever had a problem with my Shabbat dress, and that was on my second Shabbat in Oxford. I was walking to my home for a champagne Shabbat party, an event we do monthly, with a group of students, when a drunken thug of about twenty years old ran by and grabbed my Shabbat hat. Together with the students, I passed him by. With a maniacal gleam in his eye, he first said that Hitler should have finished us all. But we ignored him and this angered him even more. A few moments later, as we continued walking along the street, he came running to us and stole my hat. We chased him up the street, caught him, tackled and held him until the police came. He was brought to trial and when he was examined he argued that he had really been running to catch a bus, but as he passed me, the friend he was with called out to him and he turned and accidentally knocked off my hat.

The magistrates just made faces at this defence, so his lawyer produced another argument as I was cross-examined which I found deeply offensive. Now this thug was being tried for racial incitement, as well as stealing my hat, because he muttered all kinds of vile abuse at us as he was taken away by the police. The law in England against racial incitement reads that the defendant's words must cause offence to the person to whom they are said.

There were too many witnesses to what he said for him to deny it, so his solicitor asked me how I react when someone mutters an anti-Semitic slur. I said I ignore it. She proceeded to argue that if I ignore it then this means that I do not take offence, and thus a crime has not been committed. I was stunned by what I was hearing in a court of law.

I looked at the solicitor and told her that just forty years ago six million Jews had been murdered. According to her argument, since the world, after hearing of the slaughter of such huge numbers of people, is immune to hearing that another Jew was murdered, nobody seems to take offence. After six million, does one more really make a difference – should it then not be an offence to kill a Jew, either?

I looked at the magistrates and they agreed that the defence council had offered an offensive line of reasoning, and immediately ordered the solicitor to cease the argument. They found the man guilty. His sentence was that he was ordered to pay £100 (US $150), but since he was out of work he was ordered to pay only £4 per week. So much for a stiff penalty to prevent him from doing it again. Considering that he also resisted arrest and hit two policemen in the face, this was an especially lenient sentence. The case got a lot of publicity in the newspapers since, on this occasion, it was a rabbi who had chased and tackled his assailant, and not the reverse.

Now although there are many similarities which may be drawn between the traditions of a 3,300-year-old religion and a nearly thousand-year-old academic institution, the subject of gowns and Jewish garb in general, and clothing in particular, is special. Clothing has always retained a unique position in the Jewish religion. As an example, Orthodox Jews are largely identified by their garb.

The Cloth Maketh Man

If a Martian were to land on earth today how could he, she or it distinguish between human beings and animals? How would it know who it would be worthwhile to communicate with and which are the masters of the planet? It would not know that human beings are different by their speech alone, because animals, like dolphins and whales, also make communicative sounds to each other. The only way the extra-terrestrial would know that we humans are unique as a race is because we wear clothing. No other creatures on this planet dress and adorn themselves as we do.

In other words, our clothing does far more than present us to the world in a specific fashion. Rather, it lends us *dignity*. It is not an exaggeration to say that the single most important ennobling quality we possess is our dress. It is understandable that the first impression people have of us is by the way we dress. Before we have a chance to utter a word to colour others' judgement of ourselves, they have already drawn their first impressions simply from our appearance.

Despite the fact that Judaism emphasizes modesty of dress and has many other laws relating to garb and attire, it has always maintained that dress is something external and should be seen as subordinate in importance to what lies behind the dress, namely the person. A person is far more important than the sum of their garments. On the other hand, Judaism is not blind to the fact that the way we dress bears a direct relationship to how we act and what we think of ourselves. In a nutshell, someone who dresses modestly will probably behave in a like fashion. Thus Judaism demands that men and women dress modestly so that they behave modestly.

The most striking example I have seen occurred when I was a student in Sydney. I was walking on a Shabbat afternoon with an old distinguished Chasidic scholar who came from Israel to raise money for a yeshivah. We passed the home of the local reform rabbi with whom I was friendly. He was outside washing his car dressed in shorts and T-shirt.

I said 'Good Shabbat' to him as we passed, and he walked over and introduced himself to the old Chasid as a fellow rabbi. The Chasid asked me in Yiddish, 'Is this man a lunatic?' because he had clearly never seen someone who passed for a rabbi washing his car on the Sabbath. But the reform rabbi understood Yiddish and turned to me to say, 'He's making fun of me? How about him? Does he call himself a rabbi when he is so abusive to a fellow Jew?'

I replied that he had not meant to offend him. It was just that where he came from rabbis looked rather different. The reform rabbi did not miss a beat. He cut me off in mid-sentence and said, 'But it is you Chasidim who always emphasize that the garb does not make the man and what is beneath the clothes is more important.'

Again, I replied that this was true, but then I said, 'I assume that you wore a suit to your Temple this morning,' and he replied that he had.

'Well then,' I said, 'why did you take it off?' 'Why, do you expect me to wash a car with a suit on and destroy the suit?'

'In other words,' I said, 'if you had still been wearing your suit, you would not have washed the car. Isn't it amazing,' I concluded, 'that something as external as a suit can influence us to keep Shabbat?'

Dress can make a difference, although it is imperative that we never mistake the means for the goal. The goal of proper dress is to behave properly. Judaism does not advocate that people spend all their time involved with dress, or anything else for that matter. Rather, we must dress in a fashion that will influence us to achieve the desired result. For an academic, this means wearing academic robes, while for a Jewish man or woman this means dressing modestly, and not shying away from readily identifiable symbols of Jewishness.

Garments of Shame and Garments of Splendour

To gain a deeper insight into the centrality of dress in Judaism, we must look to the Torah. There are only two instances in which the Torah tells us that God clothed mankind or commanded them to be clothed in a distinct fashion. The first instance is in the book of Genesis. Immediately after Adam and Eve sinned by eating from the tree of knowledge, the Torah tells us they discovered their nakedness. They now needed clothing. Thus, immediately after the Almighty enumerates the curses that will befall them for their sin, the verse reads, 'Unto Adam also and to his wife did the Lord God make coats of skins, and clothed them' (Genesis 3:21). The next and last instance is to be found at the beginning of Parshas Tetzave (Exodus chapters 27–30). In relation to the obligations which Aaron and his sons had in their work as Priests in the Tabernacle, God commanded Moses: 'And thou shalt make holy garments for Aaron thy brother for glory and for beauty' (Exodus 28:2).

These two radically different occasions, and the different types of garments associated with each instance, teach us that there are two kinds of garments: those which are associated with shame, and those associated with beauty.

The first garments which came into the world were associated with shame and sin. Adam and Eve lived a perfect existence in the Garden of Eden. They had no need for clothing because, as Maimonides explains in *Guide of the Perplexed*, they saw the world in objective terms. They were not susceptible to their evil inclinations, nor were they ashamed of themselves or their bodies. They had no reason to be. They were good people surrounded entirely by a Godly environment and felt confident and at ease with their existence and who they were.

But things went awry. They transgressed an explicit prohibition from the Almighty. They were now no longer perfect. They were covered in transgression. They had something to be ashamed of and they became aware of this, of their nakedness, how they were bereft of blessing, and they desired to cover themselves up, to hide their disgrace and humiliation. The Almighty in his kindness provided them with garments, but they were the product of an animal, indicating that Adam and Eve had fallen as a result of their sin. They had behaved impulsively and instinctively, like animals, and they were thus given clothing of shame and contrition.

This is much like the man or woman who puts on clothing, not to enhance their natural beauty, but to conceal their own imperfections. It is like an ageing man who dyes his hair because he feels uncomfortable looking old, or an elderly woman who dons clothing unbecoming for her age because she dislikes the way her appearance has changed. I use these examples because Judaism encourages us to celebrate every stage of life. Old age, like youth, has its blessings and one should never feel abashed by one's age. T. E. Matthews, for example, wrote, 'The girl who felt my stare and raised her eyes,/Saw I was only an old man, and looked away/As people do when they see something not quite nice.'

What a contrast with God's command to Moses to make Aaron clothing of 'glory and beauty'. Nachmanides, the famous Jewish medieval thinker and commentator, explains that the purpose of these garments is to honour and glorify Aaron 'in the same way that Royal Garments bestow grandeur on their bearers'.

God desired to set Aaron apart from the people, and so He instituted that the High Priest should be given special clothing which would distinguish him as the most special human within the Congregation of Israel, and indeed in the world. Far from being clothing of shame, these were garments of royalty and grandeur.

In both events, the item is the same: clothing. However, it assumes a completely different meaning according to the purpose for which it is worn.

A Yellow Badge of Shame

In this century, we have discovered two different ways by which we identify as Jews through our clothing. The first is wholly negative. It consisted of an article of clothing imposed upon us by a Gentile overlord, the purpose of which was to identify the Jews as an object of scorn and derision. The most striking example of this was the Nazi's yellow star, which read 'Juden'. Indeed, this was a means by which to identify millions of Jews throughout Europe, including those who would not have been willing to identify themselves as Jews had this mark not been imposed on them. Could it then be argued that there was a positive dimension to this star since it served as the primary method for many thousands of Jews to identify with their people? Can we even say that it is a 'Jewish' garment?

Of course not. And the reason: because it was an article of shame. Not every article of clothing, even those things which may bring in their wake a positive outcome, is designed to bring honour and dignity to its wearer. The yellow star brought nothing but humiliation to those who were forced to wear it. In this respect, it was akin to the first instance where God gave Adam and Eve clothing to cover their imperfections.

Contemporary Articles of Glory

But then there exists a particular garb which identifies the Jews, in accordance with the Divine Will, which is a symbol of splendour and glory. Just as God commanded Moses to make articles of magnificence for his brother Aaron, so too He commanded that a Jewish man should don garments of magnificence which identify him as a Jew. A Jewish man wears a yarmulka and *tzitzis*, all of which crown him as a member of a holy nation and chosen people. These garments differ from the disgraceful yellow badge of shame in three important respects. Firstly, they are donned voluntarily. It is interesting to note that wearing a yarmulka and *tzitzis* is not obligatory in Jewish law. *Tzitzis* are only obligatory when a four-cornered garment is worn, and a yarmulka is described as an act of piety. By wearing them, the Jew *chooses* to identify publicly with his people and to be identified as a Jew. Secondly, unlike the yellow star, which had the dual purpose of identifying the Jew for the Germans to abuse as well as humiliating the Jews generally, the yarmulka and *tzitzis* are supreme signs of holiness and humility. As its name implies, the yarmulka symbolizes that a Jew is created with a purpose: it is an amalgam of the words *yoreh* (fear) and *malka* (king) so that those who wear it constantly stand with humility and subjugation before their Master, ready to fulfil His Will. *Tzitzis* reminds us of all the commandments of the Torah: the commentators point out that the numerical equivalent of the Hebrew letters which make up the word *tzitzis* is 600, and there are then eight *tzitzis* strings and five knots, which add up to 613, the number of Divine imperatives contained in the Torah. Similarly, there are thirty-two strings on the *tzitzis* (four × eight): the Torah begins with the letter 'beis' with a numerical equivalent of two, and ends with a 'lamed' with the numerical equivalent of thirty. Thus the *tzitzis* reminds us of the entire Torah. In this respect, the yarmulka and *tzitzis* work together, the one reminding us that we serve a higher purpose, the other telling us what that purpose is.

Thirdly, as a consequence of the first two differences, the yarmulka and *tzitzis* become articles of magnificence, bestowing honour and beauty on their wearers, whereas the yellow star brought nothing but horror to those who were forced to display it.

Our Choice to Identify Willingly

This is also the choice that we must make today. We can derive our identity from positive acts of identification like a yarmulka and *tzitzis*, or we can take the route of embracing the yellow star. Although of course no one would voluntarily wear the star today, not just a few Jews derive their *raison d'être* from combating it. We can let the yellow star or, in modern terms, combating anti-Semitism, serve as our chief form of identity. If we do so, then it will be the hatred of Israel which gives rise to the Jewish people. Or we can be identified by the traditional garb of the Jew which transcends any temporal dress codes or fashions.

A yarmulka can be knitted, it can have one's name on it, it can be colourful, or it can be pure black. It can look trendy enough for the times, or it can look more traditional. Amidst all this choice, the important thing is that it is worn, and with pride.

When we choose to be Jews for internal reasons, because of a glorious heritage, then we ensure ourselves and our children a legacy of magnificence. But if we choose to be Jews for reasons external to us, and because social outcasts and misfits hate us, then we guarantee for ourselves only a legacy of shame and humiliation.

Tzitzis *and Key Chains*

Once, after I was privileged to meet the incomparable Sir Isaiah Berlin, one of Oxford's greatest names and veritably its High Priest, in his office at All Souls College, it was a beautifully sunny day and I offered to walk him up 'the High', Oxford's name for the High Street. As I helped him close his door, my jacket lifted and he noticed my *tzitzis* hanging out from my trousers and then said, tongue in cheek, 'I don't know if I should walk with you because, as you know, I object to overt displays of Judaism.' He was half joking, so I told him not to worry since no doubt no one in Oxford knew what they were, and anyway they would mistake them for a strange kind of Oriental key chain (which is what people often say to me).

He laughed and we walked, but in truth, why should anyone have to be ashamed of wearing a yarmulka or *tzitzis*? Is it okay to wear an outlandish key chain, which has no meaning whatsoever, but improper to wear an ancient tradition which reminds one of his obligations to his Creator and humanity? If we are ashamed of them, then what qualitative difference is there between the traditional distinguishing garb of the Jews, and the shameful articles imposed on us by the Nazis? If both must be hidden, then how may we distinguish between them? Our children should be taught that indeed there is a difference between choosing to be a Jew and having it forced on us. And the younger generation should be given positive and tangible reasons to be Jewish. In all my years as rabbi to university students, I have found few who accept that Judaism must be preserved for ethnic reasons alone. Our young people are thirsting for life-affirming reasons to be Jewish. It is our duty to provide them.

To Marry a Jew or a Non-Jew

Once, a Jewish girl who had little affiliation with our activities was sent to me by her parents. She wanted to become engaged to her non-Jewish boyfriend. The only concession her parents got out of her was at least to speak to a rabbi before she pursued this course. She harboured immense hostility toward her parents for being so obstinate. I objected. 'Surely,' I said, 'it is not a crime if your parents wish you to marry a Jew. You can object to their wishes, of course. But why are you so angry?'

'Because,' she said, 'my parents do not want me to marry a Jew. They simply do not want me to marry a non-Jew. That is why I am angry. They are only negative.'

I believe firmly in the need for positive pride in being Jewish infecting today's students; there is nothing more irritating to me than when Jewish students come to Oxford and one of the first things many of the men do is take off their yarmulkas. You see, when I was first faced with the prospect of coming to Oxford and serving as a Chabad rabbi, I always assumed that my task would be to get uninterested and apathetic students more involved in or, at the very least, sympathetic to Judaism. What I did not account for was how much time would be spent simply trying to keep many of the *observant* students observant.

The number of observant Orthodox students who give up much, or in many cases all, of their Judaism during their university years is one of the best-kept secrets in modern Orthodox communities around the world. They brag about how they synthesize tradition and modernity – in the words of the great Rabbi Shamshon Raphael Hirsch, one-time Chief Rabbi of Germany, they strive to amalgamate *'Torah im derekh etretz'*, or the Torah with business and profession – but in many instances this is proving a colossal failure.

Now, I am all for a synthesis of Judaism with the modern world, but I am against compartmentalization. Unhappily, this is exactly what nearly all the Orthodox Jewish students who come to Oxford have striven for. They learn to separate their religious lives from their academic ambitions, especially if the two conflict, be the conflict actual or imagined. One of the first things that goes is the yarmulka, and it goes for a variety of reasons: they fear they will be discriminated against by professors and they will be unable to slide easily into their new social circles. But the most important reason is simply that it is very hard being different. In a university the subliminal pressure to conform exerted by peers is immense, and many succumb to its dictates. It takes a tremendous amount of pride and discipline to wear such a striking distinguishing mark, on the head no less, in such an overtly un-Jewish a place as Oxford.

Their justification for taking it off, and interestingly they always seem to want to justify it to me, is that, 'It is not even a commandment, it is not obligatory, and in any event, whenever I'm in the company of Jews or at Jewish functions I wear it. So it's no big deal.'

But compartmentalization cannot work. Just as no soul can exist outside the body, so too no Jewish identity can be preserved unless there is a sense of pride among its faithful.

As I have said, the principle reason a Jewish student takes off his yarmulka, and there are frightfully many who do, is because he sees it as something to be ashamed of while in Oxford. It seems to have so many negative stereotypes associated with it. If we could get these same students to acknowledge their yarmulkas not as an article of shame, but rather as a source of glory and splendour, then they would never dream of taking them off. And here we come back to the difference in the clothing which the Almighty gave Adam, and that which he gave Aaron. Too many people see the yarmulka, or other distinguishing Jewish features, as the mark of Cain. But it was intended to bestow on the Jews the priestly majesty of Aaron. They would see it as a privilege to wear one. It all comes down to a matter of perspective. If a soldier loves his country and feels honoured to defend it, he will wear his uniform with pride. If he is ashamed of his country, he will wear an overcoat over his uniform when in public. Similarly, if Jewishness is something to be proud of, then a distinguishing Jewish mark like a yarmulka will be worn with pride. But if we cannot inculcate a sense of pride in Jewishness among today's students, then any Jewish demarcation becomes an ugly birthmark.

In my work among students, I have always advocated Judaism as a positive and life-affirming identity; an honour which adorns its members. I have always felt nothing but aggression toward the many 'guilt trips' which are associated with Jewish living and which parents and rabbis try to heap on their children and followers in order to preserve their observance. Either Judaism can compete in the outside world and in the marketplace of ideas, or it is nothing. It's that simple. I believe it can, and I hope to teach my students the same. Whenever any rabbi or Jewish leader argues with a student who has taken off his yarmulka, for example, saying he has discarded three thousand years of tradition, this does nothing more than portray Judaism as weak. It appeals to a person's natural feelings of guilt for abandoning tradition, and cannot offer a sound and positive argument for commitment and identification.

Losing Individualism to Collective Tradition

A more difficult case is of those sincere students who will remove a yarmulka because the primary identification alone as a Jew makes them feel uncomfortable. It is not that they are embarrassed to be Jewish or that they fear discrimination. Rather, they reject the fact that when they wear a yarmulka or other form of principal Jewish identification, their friends relate to them first and foremost as Jews, even before they are people.

I first encountered this form of hostility when a highly intelligent religious Jewish Rhodes Scholar, who graduated near the top of his class at Stanford, arrived at Oxford and within a fortnight had taken off his yarmulka, even though he had worn it for his four consecutive years as a Stanford undergraduate. What had suddenly changed?

I was initially cautious about confronting him with it, because in truth the removal of his yarmulka did not precipitate any further decrease in his religious observance, as I had seen in similar circumstances. He still came to all our activities, many of my classes, and even studied with me privately twice a week. He served as a trusted and loyal friend to me, someone in whom I could confide. He also read the Torah beautifully at our Shabbat services. But while removing his yarmulka did not affect him, it did affect many of those around him who now found ample excuse to remove their yarmulkas at their convenience. The problem was that this student, because of his academic excellence and especially his dizzying knowledge of Judaism, was seen by the students as an example they respected. If he could remain observant without a yarmulka, or he did not feel it was particularly necessary, nor would they.

For one student to be automatically cast as a role model for the less observant students at Oxford is always difficult, and something which is actively resisted by nearly all the knowledgeable and observant students who arrive at Oxford. They oppose taking this position because knowing that a group of people is always looking over your back obviously inhibits your own freedom, and what students crave above all is independence and freedom. However, they primarily shirk the role model because most of these same students, by the time they arrive and are immersed in a secular, liberal establishment like Oxford, are themselves confused about their identities and observance. They feel forced onto an almost hypocritical path by the fact that they must live up to the expectations the other Oxford students have of them.

Nevertheless, after publicly discussing the issue of wearing a yarmulka on a few occasions, this particular student came to discuss it with me. Saying that he assumed his removing his yarmulka concerned me, he explained as follows: 'When I arrived, I planned to wear my yarmulka just as I had done throughout my life. But once after a basketball game, I was walking to my college and wasn't wearing my yarmulka since it was right after the game. One of my closest friends whom I had met at Oxford walked right by me and didn't even notice me. Could you believe it! Because I wasn't wearing a yarmulka he didn't even recognize me. It was like I was a different person. From that moment I decided that I did not want a yarmulka dictating who I was.' From this and other events, he says, he concluded that when people see his yarmulka they first identify him as an Orthodox Jew, before he is even a person. They associate him with certain political, social and of course religious views which he may not even entertain, and they assume this only because of his yarmulka. 'And this,' he continued, 'I just won't stand for. I won't be reduced to a yarmulka, or even that I am an Orthodox Jew, before

I am *me*, before I am even a person. I don't want adjectives added to my essential existence.'

'But what if you were married,' I countered. 'By virtue of your argument, you would object to wearing a wedding ring as well, since that would first identify you as a *married* man, before you were even a man. Every woman that interacted with you would know from the ring that before they even say hello to you, you have obligations to someone else and to a family, and that will colour your every exchange with them. Or, for that matter, you would disagree with any type of uniform, such as that of a policeman, since, if you were wearing a policeman's uniform, that would also identify you with a certain way of life. For instance, your friends would not come up to you to tell you of what a wild time they had at some student's room the night before, smoking marijuana. Should we then abandon any identifying symbol because of the potential baggage which comes with it?'

In truth, what he was objecting to, just as he said, was that he was first being identified as a Jew. Undoubtedly, this is what a yarmulka does. However, is it really unreasonable for God to demand that our first loyalties lie with Him? Or that our first form of identity be that we are His people? By way of analogy, would anyone argue that a spouse was being unreasonable for insisting that their husband or wife did not cavort around as if they were single? Would it be too much to demand that they wear some identifying mark that they are married, that shows that they live with certain obligations, and behave accordingly?

Likewise, can God not demand that the Jews live by some guidelines which show that they are a people who are married to God's Will, which entails privileges but also obligations?

The Ability to Stand up Straight

We mentioned earlier that the primary identification badge by which human beings are distinguished is their clothing. But in addition to this there is one more very significant distinguishing feature between human and animal kind: human beings stand and walk upright, whereas all animals are either bent over completely, or have slightly curved postures.

It behoves us, then, as proud Jews, to exhibit both of these distinguishing characteristics with regards to our Judaism as well. Firstly, to adorn ourselves with the traditional Jewish garb which has been worn by our ancestors for hundreds of generations. And secondly, to wear it with heads held high, standing upright, and with great pride in our traditions recognising that they are unique, and define us not just as a religion but as a nation.

Because a people can only survive if it takes pride in its traditions.

Chapter Twenty-four

SHYLOCK THE JEW?

Ask any group of Oxford undergraduates who they consider to be the greatest writer of all time and the most common reply will be, 'William Shakespeare'. A large part of the appeal of his plays is often said to be that the audience can easily see his characters as more than merely incidental to the plays in which they appear. They develop in significance to become archetypal figures. This is usually said to be so most strongly in the great tragedies, but critics and theatre directors have recently discovered afresh the long-neglected 'Problem Plays', and found that they too exhibit this same characteristic to an exciting degree.

In Oxford, the ever-popular student productions of Shakespeare have turned more and more to the interesting problems and ideas that Elizabethan and Jacobean plays such as *The Merchant of Venice* can present to modern audiences. To say that Shakespeare is 'big' at Oxford is a classic understatement. Oxford is barely an hour's drive from Stratford-upon-Avon, where the celebrated bard was born, and many Oxford students will hop over to Stratford for the magnificent Shakespearean productions which are staged there. These in turn are mimicked in the form of less extravagant, but often equally well-acted, student productions. Student actors love to reinterpret characters, themes and ideas that were once thought to be fully developed and fixed. For example, Shylock, the cold-hearted and miserly usurer, has for centuries served as English society's caricature of the vengeful, vain and materialistic Jew, but recent productions have turned him into the hero of the piece. He is increasingly being interpreted as a radical critic of society, a man who, because of his outcast status, cannot only see 'civilisation' for what it really is, but can convey that knowledge to the audience.

Arnold Wesker at L'Chaim

Our first speaker in Michaelmas term 1990, and the first speaker we ever had at our new L'Chaim Centre at Carfax, was the celebrated British Jewish playwright Arnold Wesker, author of *Roots* and many other acclaimed works. Mr Wesker created a storm for a play he wrote called *Shylock*. In it, he went back to the original historical sources that Shakespeare himself had used to write *The Merchant of Venice*, and rewrote the entire play, but this time emerging with a far more favourable portrayal of Shylock. Mr Wesker did this because of his passionately held conviction that Shakespeare's Shylock is an inaccurate and ultimately anti-Semitic portrayal of the Jew. Furthermore, Mr Wesker, who experienced grave difficulties in staging *Shylock* in different parts of the world, alleged there were dark and sinister motives on the part of those individuals who preferred that Shakespeare's caricature of the Jew should stand, without modification. This was largely the content of Mr Wesker's lectures, which was entitled, 'Why I Wrote *Shylock*', and attracted a sizeable and largely sympathetic audience.

Characters like Shylock are pivotal to the questioning attitude of such plays: they confront the most deep-seated assumptions not only of the society they were originally written for, but also of our own society. So forceful is his personality that, in many productions, it threatens to overwhelm the balance of the comedy and to rob it of all its magic and fantasy. The comedy is replaced with a blow in the face for our most 'civilized' assumptions and attitudes.

Shylock as Hero

Many books and articles have been written examining the personality of Shylock. He seems to exert an extraordinarily strong hold over the imaginations of literary critics. While many of those critics are highly negative in their appraisal of him, particularly those of the old school, some twentieth-century interpretations are full of admiration, sympathy and even praise.

Some see Shylock as an 'outraged hero'. Although subject to extended degrading abuse by Antonio, he kept silent, waiting all the time to seize the moment for his reprisal. Then, with extreme cunning and cleverness, he repaid Antonio with devastating revenge. He was completely willing to forgo a huge sum of money in order to restore his honour and integrity. This places Shylock in the role of the shaper of the play, the controlling personality that is analogous with a hero in a tragedy. After all, heroes are not necessarily good, as Macbeth clearly shows us.

So strong was the sense that Shylock was the essence of the play that in the nineteenth century many producers omitted the last act, in which he does not appear.

Several scholars have even argued that Shylock's unexpected offer of an interest-free loan to Antonio was made in a genuine attempt at friendship, and that the Jew only determined to take his pound of flesh after the outrageous theft of his daughter and his jewels. They see Shylock's offer as at first wholly genuine, an expression of the outcast's yearning to live in harmony with his fellow man. His offer to take no interest on the loan was impulsive; earlier in the play he had been trying to calculate the rate which he should charge.

'Three thousand ducats – 'tis a good round sum. Three months from twelve; then let me see, the rate – '

His sudden offer to forget the shames of the past and become a friend of Antonio is seen as an example of the humane Shylock, the man who gave voice to the brotherhood of men in his great speech: 'I am a Jew. Hath not a Jew eyes? Hath not a Jew hands, organs, dimensions, senses, affections, passions, fed with the same food, hurt with the same weapons, subject to the same diseases, healed by the same means, warmed and cooled by the same winter and summer, as a Christian is? If you prick us, do we not bleed? If you tickle us, do we not laugh? If you poison us, do we not die? And if you wrong us, shall we not revenge?'

The 'Shylock as hero' school of thought is perhaps best summed up by Heinrich Heine. He sees Shakespeare as 'originally intending the character of Shylock to please the mob, to represent a thorough-going werewolf, a hated, fabulous being who yearns for blood . . . But the genius of the poet, the spirit of the wide world which ruled in him, was ever stronger than his own will, and so it came to pass that he in Shylock, despite the glaring grotesqueness, expressed the justification of the unfortunate sect which was oppressed by providence, from inscrutable motives . . .' Amazingly, he goes so far as to say that 'those characters [of the play] who are enemies of Shylock . . . are hardly worthy to unlace his shoes'.

On one note, Heine seems justified. No other Jew in Elizabethan literature has given a more moving expression to the sufferings of his race. The Jew was a remarkably common stage character in England at this time, considering the small proportion of the population that was Jewish. Other playwrights such as Marlowe used the Jew as a ready-made caricature, a character who could obviate the need for any deep or psychologically credible portrayal because the mob would fill in the gaps from its imagination and prejudices. For instance, in Marlowe's *The Jew of Malta*, the Jew is unfathomably bad: the play's structure rests on the assumption that there is black and white, good and bad, and the Jew will fulfil the expected role of the villain.

Shylock the Rough Diamond

Seen in this light, Shakespeare's portrayal of Shylock is remarkable. The Jew is undoubtedly a 'rounded' character and not a caricature designed to elicit a simple and automatic response from an audience. He is clearly an outcast who longs for social acceptance, a hated man who needs to love.

Some productions go so far as to portray Shylock as a 'rough diamond', his gruff exterior concealing a heart of gold. His spiritual condition is symbolized in the first scenes of the play by the hidden treasure which is found to lie within the base leaden casket.

Such interpretations as these engage our feelings for Shylock to the point where the comedy of the play may be lost. The last act is then a meaningless superfluity, or a deliberate mockery and shadow of the happy sense of reconciliation that the audience is supposed to feel at the end of a true comedy. Shakespeare was such a supremely sensitive playwright that it is hard to believe this can have been unintended: he wanted us to think again about our culture's automatic reactions to people.

Shylock as Villain

For most, however, Shylock remains the villain of the piece. A miserly Jew who would willingly sell out his daughter and religious beliefs for a profit. Shylock's first lines in the play are an incoherent tirade about money. 'Three thousand ducats – well . . . For three months – well . . . Antonio shall become bound – well . . . Three thousand ducats for three months, and Antonio bound.'

Such a speech immediately reveals a cold and materialistic mind, as he stubbornly repeats the same blunt phrases to express his narrow range of ideas. He is a miser with words as much as with money and he hoards his phrases as he hoards his ducats. The young noblemen of the play vary their words and images in a musical idiom of pure poetry which expresses sensitivity and open-heartedness. But Shylock's repetitive language shows how obsessive and limited his imagination is. He never uses a metaphor or poetic figure of speech. His idiom is concrete and full of monosyllabic nouns. He is an absolute pedant. There is no poetry in his soul. The repetitive use of the same words, line after line, will be found to govern most of his speeches in the play. These are the utterances of a man whose mind is concentrated, obsessed, focused on a narrow range of fixed ideas.

In discussing the possibility of a loan with Bassanio we read:

SHYLOCK: Antonio is a good man.
BASSANIO: Have you heard any imputation to the contrary?
SHYLOCK: Ho, no, no, no, no; my meaning in saying he is a good man is to have you understand me that he is sufficient . . .

His interpretation of the word 'good' divests it of any moral implications or human value. For him, 'good' simply means that Antonio's resources of wealth are sufficient to justify the risk of giving him a loan. This is not the generous world of the young Venetian aristocrat but the world of a miserly usurer who, far from being the master of his money, has become its slave.

The abduction of Jessica, with her father's ducats, serves only to reveal the human priorities of Shylock at their very worst. When he discovers what he has suffered, we might expect that even a miserly old Jewish usurer would be more distraught at the loss of his daughter to a Christian than at the theft of his ducats. It is not so. Shylock's interest in money is even greater than his concern for his daughter.

'Two thousand ducats in that, and other precious, precious jewels. I would my daughter were dead at my foot, and the jewels in her ear; would she were hears'd at my foot, and the ducats in her coffin!'

Furthermore, his oft-cited loyalty to his Jewish faith is shown to be a great deal weaker than his concern for the lost money.

'A diamond gone, cost me two thousand ducats in Frankfort! The curse never fell upon our nation till now; I never felt it till now.'

Under the pressure of his losses, Shylock reveals himself as a contemptible miser with no human emotions, even for his own daughter. Ironically, his closest relationship in the play appears to be with his servant, who turns out to be more of a rogue than any other character in the play.

Contrasting Christian and Jew

As soon as Antonio enters, the pointed and deliberate contrast between Christian and Jew, and the importance of religion in the play, become apparent. Shylock says that he hates Antonio because he is a Christian who gives free loans to the needy and brings down the rate of interest by which Shylock makes a living. Shylock complains to the audience that Antonio has repeatedly denounced him for lending money at interest and has expressed hatred for the Jews. Shylock vows revenge on Antonio.

'If I can catch him once upon the hip, I will feed fat the ancient grudge I bear him.'

Seen in this light, Shylock is a despicable man, a villain who receives no more than his just deserts from the hands of the court. Sympathy for him is out of place because the villain is supposed to be excluded from society so that it can be transformed by the end of the comedy.

Shylock as a Jew

The debate between the critics on the virtue of Shylock's character is far from settled. Of course it is unlikely ever to be resolved: the emotions an audience feels when watching the play are consciously and violently manipulated by Shakespeare. We are not allowed to make up our minds whether he is to be execrated or sympathized with because there is no simple answer. Similarly, the play does not allow us clearly to decide whether the Venetian Jew is an archetype of all Jews or more nearly represents an outcast whose Jewishness is incidental.

Having considered the critical background, though, it is notable that an important aspect of the analysis seems to have been ignored by the scholars. Shylock brought his contract before a Venetian court which immediately accepted the legality of that contract. Venetian law appeared to legislate that one could use one's very flesh for collateral on a loan; and subject to the forfeiture of that loan, the flesh could be extracted by the lender. It was only the heroine Portia's cunning and expert knowledge of the law that served to free Antonio from the bond, and cause Shylock to lose even his capital.

PORTIA: Tarry a little; there is something else.
           This bond doth give thee here no jot of blood:
           The words expressly are 'a pound of flesh' . . .
           But, in the cutting it, if thou dost shed
           One drop of Christian blood, thy lands and goods
           Are, by the laws of Venice, confiscate
           Unto the state of Venice . . .
SHYLOCK: I take this offer then; pay the bond thrice,
           And let the Christian go . . .
PORTIA: He hath refus'd it in the open court;
           He shall have merely justice, and his bond . . .
SHYLOCK: Shall I not have barely my principal?
PORTIA: Thou shalt have nothing but the forfeiture
           To be so taken at thy peril, Jew.

The point that has been ignored is whether Shylock's contract would have been legal had he brought it before a *Jewish* court. Imagine the situations of the Jew and the Venetians reversed, the Jew feeling secure on his own territory in a Beth Din, court of Jewish law: would the contract have to be honoured, and a pound of flesh recognized as proper collateral?

This question, far from being an intellectual exercise, is of pivotal importance. If standard Jewish law rejects Shylock's contractual clause, then we may conclude that, notwithstanding Shakespeare's portrayal of Shylock as a Jew, his character and actions were influenced, not by Jewish, but Venetian thinking. If it can be proven that Jewish law does not merely frown on such contracts but refuses even to recognize their validity, then obviously the personality of Shylock is essentially a product of his non-Jewish surroundings and not a Jewish upbringing.

Shakespeare has already hinted that we are to interpret Shylock partly as a product of his circumstances; he shows how Shylock is forced to react to the Venetians all the time rather than being able to initiate any action for himself. Far from being a villainous Iago-like character who is in control of the entire cast and plot, Shylock is portrayed as buffeted by the winds of Venetian favour or disapproval. Shakespeare is seen to be blurring the expected distinctions between good and bad, hero and villain, just as he blurs the distinctions between tragedy and comedy. The Venetians are in many ways not at all admirable, and the audience is expected at times to feel a great deal of sympathy for Shylock.

There is a further contemporary benefit in exploring the ordeal of Shylock in Jewish law.

The L'Chaim Society is often strapped for cash. Its funding is entirely dependent on my finding charitable benefactors to support its activities, as well as my own salary. There is, of course, little the students can do to alleviate these difficulties. They are, after all, only students. But here in England there is a serious problem of people redeeming hearts and kidneys on the open market for cash. It can be quite difficult to live without a heart. But the average human needs only one kidney to survive. Press reports in Britain speculate that one can earn as much as $75,000 for a single kidney. So I try to encourage the students into an altruistic gift of allowing us to pawn one of their kidneys in return for a not insignificant portion of our annual budget. All we need is three or four kidneys a year and my fund-raising activities are over. It is important, therefore, to know whether or not Jewish law would permit the use of vital or non-vital organs as collateral in loans, or permit them for outright sale.

Analysis Part I

Contracts which Contravene the Law

Ostensibly, the answer is a simple one. All the man-made contracts in the world are insufficient to lift the prohibitions of the Torah, or to obligate a person to act in contradiction to Torah-law. If a man makes a contract with his fellow, say, obligating him to desecrate the Sabbath, the contract would be thrown out of a Beth Din. It would seem that the same would apply in the case of Shylock's contract. Cutting the flesh of a living being is expressly forbidden by the Torah. Likewise, to inflict injury, or to strike a human being is a Torah-prohibition. This applies even if the blow poses no threat to life, and much more so if there is any possibility of loss of life, in which case the offender will also be guilty of transgressing the injunction not to murder. (A detailed analysis of the reasons behind this prohibition will follow later.)

This basic approach to our investigation matches almost exactly the response of a foremost halakhic authority, Rabbeinu Asher.

'And on this other issue which certain sages have had difficulty with, whether a Jew should be allowed to enslave his body to his lender if he cannot repay his debt, undoubtedly this is forbidden ... And even if the borrower has offered his body as collateral on the loan, he still cannot be enslaved. The clause is null and void. Needless to say that torturing the borrower or physically coercing him to pay is absolutely prohibited.'

After a rabbinic pronouncement so clearly in the negative, it seems an open and shut case. Shylock's contract would have been disallowed by a Jewish court. In reality, however, the law is far more complicated and the discussion is far from over.

Contractual Obligations in the Face of Biblical Prohibitions

What happens when an individual legally owes his creditors money, but, for whatever reason, is prohibited by the Halakha from repaying them? Do we say that the debt is removed by the Halakha? Or is it that, the halakhic prohibition to repay notwithstanding, the debt remains in full force. In most cases, the truth is that the obligation for the individual to repay the debt remains intact, but the Torah restricts a debtor from compensating the creditor because of the extraneous circumstances.

For example, the Torah prohibits lending money for interest. If in spite of the biblical prohibition, a lender and borrower both agree to the payment of interest and write a contract to that effect, must it be paid? According to *Maharit*, the borrower is absolutely obligated to pay the interest, just as agreed. Still, the interest is not paid because the Torah will not allow the borrower to do so. The lender is forbidden to take it, and the borrower is forbidden to give it. This summary, where an obligation that is in force cannot be met because the Torah prohibits it, is referred to in talmudic terminology as '*Aryeh rava alah*', 'the obligation is swallowed by the Torah'. Still, the obligation does remain in force.

A Prostitute's Payment

Another illustration may be derived from the biblical law that forbids an animal that was used to pay a prostitute from being brought as a sacrifice on God's altar, '*esnan zonah*'. What is the law if a man uses an animal for the payment of an immediate relative in exchange for her sexual favours?

An incestuous relationship in Jewish law is punishable by death, and a fundamental talmudic law declares that whenever two halakhic obligations come simultaneously, the lesser obligation is subordinated to the more severe. For instance, a man who shoots his neighbour dead is guilty of both tearing the victim's clothes and murdering him. As two penalties come about simultaneously as the result of a single action, the less severe penalty is absorbed by the greater. Thus, although it may be small compensation, the murderer can die peacefully knowing that the cost of his victim's shirt will not be taken from his estate.

Now, in the case of prostitution with an immediate relative, the same halakhic elements are present as in the murder case above. Through a single act, sexual intercourse, a man incurs two different obligations: (1) the payment of the relative's (the prostitute's) wages, as they agreed; (2) capital punishment for engaging in an incestuous relationship. One would therefore expect that the lesser penalty, paying her wages, is subordinated to, and annulled by, the capital penalty. In this instance, since the obligation for payment is removed and the animal never constituted a prostitute's hire, it would appear that the animal could be used as a sacrifice on God's altar.

Financial Obligations in the Face of Capital Punishment

Yet the Talmud disagrees. A prostitute's hire is forbidden as a sacrifice by the Torah, even in the case of a man who has sexual relations with his mother. The animal is forbidden from becoming a sacrifice, even though it was never used as a prostitute's hire because the son's obligation to pay his mother was annulled by his greater obligation to pay the death penalty. *Rashi* explains:

> Although the son incurs the death penalty for relations with his mother, and thus cannot be held financially responsible to pay her sheep since the penalty is absorbed in the greater penalty, nevertheless the obligation to pay her agreed wages remains in force. If she would demand payment in a court of law, the court would not obligate him to pay since he is to be put to death, but the animal is still considered a prostitute's hire since in reality he does owe her the money. It is only the Torah which prohibits him from making the payment, since it is absorbed in the heavy penalty he has incurred as a result of the incest. Had she not been a relative but another woman, she would certainly have been able to demand payment, even in a Jewish court of law.

What we deduce from the above discussion is that responsibilities which result even from unlawful acts possess the full force of law. While their actual performance is illegal, the commitments associated with them are not.

This conclusion has important implications in our study of the legality of Shylock's contract with Antonio. 'I have changed my mind,' Shylock declares before the Beth Din. 'As cutting a pound of Antonio's flesh is expressly forbidden by the Torah, I choose not to collect my debt from the collateral, his body, but to be repaid in full.' He demands that Antonio returns his 3,000 ducats, but Antonio may refuse to pay the money and could be adamant that Shylock collect his debt in the form of a pound of flesh. After all, this is what they agreed to in the contract. Either money, or the flesh, and Antonio would rather not part with his money. What would Jewish law then stipulate?

This question is not only limited to our present investigation, but has very broad ramifications and would apply in all cases where one person pays another to do something forbidden, and then wishes to retract. Suppose a man hires an assassin to kill his enemy and pays the intended murderer £50,000. Later, regretting his action, he returns to the assassin with the words, 'Murder is forbidden by the Torah. My hiring of you was therefore forbidden and I demand my money be returned.' The assassin for his part argues that a deal is a deal and refuses to return the money. If they came before a Jewish court, in whose favour would it decide? By referring to another talmudic discourse we can find an answer.

Ownership without Payment

In reference, once again, to the law of *esnan*, a prostitute's hire, the Talmud states, 'If one gives a harlot a sheep for her hire, yet before the actual act took place, she takes the sheep and brings it up [to the Altar in the Temple] for a sacrifice, it is permitted and accepted.'

This ruling has perplexed many commentators. It seems extraordinary that she is permitted to bring an unpaid-for sheep to the Temple as a sacrifice. She had not yet fulfilled the obligation for receiving the sheep, that is, they have not yet had relations, so the sheep is not hers. Regarding the gifts people may consecrate for the Temple, the Torah states, 'And when a man shall consecrate his home', concerning which our sages have explained, 'Just as his home is in his possession, so too, only those things presently in his possession may be brought for a sacrifice.'

In explanation, the scholars Rashba and Ritva maintain that in every business transaction, as soon as the buyer and seller conclude an agreement of sale, and the buyer lifts or drags the object, it transfers into the buyer's ownership even before it is paid for. The very fact that one lifts and acts freely with the object in the presence of the previous owner is a proof that the article has changed hands and now belongs to the buyer. To be sure, one must still pay the agreed sum of money, but this is treated as a mere debt. Now that the buyer has acquired ownership of the object, the seller is owed the agreed sum. The money owed does not in any way obstruct the buyer's immediate acquisition. Thus the harlot may offer the sheep for a sacrifice because it does, in fact, belong to her.

No Favours even after Payment

This ruling is deeply significant. Notwithstanding the fact that in this case that which is to be paid to the seller for his sheep is prohibited by Torah law (the woman's favours), Rashba and Ritva still treat this as a normal business transaction. Now, what is amazing is that even after the man has given her the sheep, the harlot is allowed, and even obligated, to refuse to offer her favours in return because prostitution is forbidden by the Torah! Nevertheless, the sheep is still legally acquired by the harlot from the moment the man hands it to her, even before she repays him, and even if she chooses to withhold her payment. If he wishes to retract from the agreement, she may still demand that he go ahead and give her the sheep, and after this she may still refuse to give her favours in return. This is not because her obligation has been annulled. She accepted payment for her favours and owes them. But the Torah does not allow her to fulfil her obligation. So, if she suddenly has a change of heart, sees the lowliness of her actions, and wishes to undertake a different lifestyle, she is not obligated to return the sheep. Even if the man demands it, she does not have to give back her hire because they have agreed to a transaction whereby she was meant to pay by doing something which is superseded by the Torah's commandment not to do so.

Summation

If Shylock and Antonio's bizarre agreement came before a Jewish court, and Antonio refused to repay the 3,000 ducats and instructed Shylock to extract the pound of flesh instead, just as they agreed, the court would rule that Shylock is in truth obligated to take his debt from Antonio's flesh. Still, he is not to do so because the Torah forbids this. Shylock could not then demand his money in place of the pound of flesh since Antonio can legally choose to pay with his flesh, just as they agreed. Either way, Shylock emerges the loser.

Thus far, we have seen that before a Jewish court of law Shylock's insistence on his contract would have caused him to lose everything: his money and his chances for revenge. This is already a strong indication that Shylock's character was cast in the cauldron of Venetian, not Jewish, ideals and principles. Remarkably, the character who best understands and espouses this Orthodox interpretation of the law is Shylock's opponent, Portia.

That is the end of one particular aspect of the case, but it remains to prove that, not only was Shylock's contract incapable of compelling Antonio to repay Shylock either with money or flesh, but it was illegal, null and void from the very beginning.

Analysis Part II

Man's Life is not His Own

Why indeed is Antonio prohibited by Torah law from fulfilling his obligation and repaying Shylock with a pound of his flesh? What is the nature of the biblical injunction prohibiting human flesh from being cut or sold?

Man's life, and the body in which that life is invested and on which it is dependent, are not his own and are not under his jurisdiction. Man is not merely forbidden from taking his own life or cutting his limbs. His life and his limbs are not at all his possession. Therefore, if one sells or makes collateral of one's body, flesh or limbs, to another party, the transaction is void. Not because something illegal has been done: rather, the person has sold or pawned something which cannot be owned. It is as if I agreed to sell the contents of Christ Church Picture Gallery, one of the most beautiful in Oxford, to a visiting tourist: the contract is worthless paper and there is no question that the college should contemplate handing over the paintings. The reason: the collection is simply not mine.

The traditional Jewish response to evil tidings, 'The Lord has given and the Lord has taken. May the name of the Lord be blessed!', is not merely a cute adage, but an accurate statement of what has transpired. God has reclaimed what has always been His.

To be sure, God does give us life so that we may use it to bring about goodness on earth, but not to do with it as we please, or act recklessly. Taking life can be done only on the part of the One to whom it belongs, not the one to whom it was given for use. Man is not the proprietor of his life, body or being.

Inflicting Injury with Permission

The sage who spells this out most clearly is Rabbi Schneur Zalman of Liadi in his *Code of Jewish Law*. Whereas the Mishnah, the Talmud and other halakhic works stipulate that it is merely forbidden for someone to inflict injury on himself, Rabbi Schneur·Zalman writes, 'It is forbidden to hit one's colleague, even if that person gives his permission and wishes to be struck, because his body is not his possession, and thus he cannot allow someone else to inflict bodily injury upon him.'

He concludes even more strongly, 'A human being has no jurisdiction over his body at all.'

One problem with the law of Rabbi Schneur Zalman, that the prohibition to injure another person applies even when permission is granted, is that it is not recorded in any previous talmudic literature. The law must be substantiated within the corpus of Jewish law for it to be valid.

Although there is a Mishnah which states that if one says, 'Gouge out my eye and you will not be held responsible', the culprit is still obligated to recompense the blinded party, this deals only with the monetary obligation to reimburse the injury. There is no mention that it is prohibited to commit the act in the first place. Also, the reason given for the obligation for recompense is different in this instance: the injured man does not forgive the culprit completely. Deep in his heart he resents the wound his fellow has caused him.

What, then, was Rabbi Schneur Zalman's source for his pronouncement that man possesses no jurisdiction over his body whatsoever?

Talmudic Tales Prohibiting Infliction of Wounds

A possible derivation from the Talmud is in Sanhedrin. This asks whether a son is permitted to let the blood of his father. After some deliberation, the Talmud concludes that for matters of health he is permitted. If consent alone can be sufficient to give permission to hurt or injure another human being, then the Talmud would not require health motives in this instance.

After all, it cannot be argued that more mitigating circumstances are required than mere granting of permission because injury to parents is a far more serious offence than injuring anyone else. This is because the talmudic law against striking parents is derived from the same verse in the Torah that prohibits striking any human being: 'They shall not continue to strike him.' This verse, which is a warning to a Beth Din who metes out lashes not to strike the offender even half a lash more than was stipulated or that he can bear, is the source of all prohibitions against striking other people.

Again, in Sanhedrin we read:

> Rav did not allow his son to remove a splinter from his flesh; Mar, son of Ravina, did not allow his son to squeeze out [the puss from] a blister, for in the process a bruise may have resulted, thus constituting an inadvertent sin. If this is so they feared that their children might inadvertently sin by causing them bodily harm, why should they have allowed anyone at all to do it, and not only their sons? The answer is that for others [it is merely a prohibition], for children it would constitute a capital penalty.

This demonstrates conclusively that granting permission to bruise one's body cannot remove the prohibition involved, whether they are the party's children or complete strangers.

Relatives and their Deceased

The logic of Rabbi Schneur Zalman, that this permission is worthless since one is not the master over one's body, also finds precedent in the writings of Maimonides. Writing about the imposed exile on a person convicted of manslaughter, he asserts, 'The court is warned by the Torah not to take money (*kofer*) from the accused in order to redeem himself and avoid exile, even if he offers them all the money in the world. And even if the relative of the deceased is willing to exonerate the murderer, it is still forbidden for the life of the murdered party [for which he is exiled] is not the possession of the relatives, but the possession of the Almighty.'

While the words of Maimonides do not appear necessarily to include the limbs of the body, he does stipulate clearly that a person's life belongs to the Creator, our Master.

Preventing Murder and Suicide

Another supporting text to this principle is again from Sanhedrin. One of the verses from which the Talmud deduces that 'one who sees his fellow drowning at sea, being pulled by a beast, or accosted by bandits, is obligated to save him', is from, 'and you shall return it to him', the verse instructing us to return lost objects to our fellows. The Talmud includes (possible) loss of life among those things which must be returned.

The difficulty with this exegesis is that the talmudic law designating that lost articles must be returned also says that those articles lost willingly by an individual do not have to be returned. This seems to mean that one need not save a person who has willingly cast himself from a bridge. Are we under no obligation to save someone attempting suicide?

A suggested solution is that when it comes to life one may not cast it away willingly, since it is not one's own possession. Suicide constitutes casting away something which is not ours, and thus the observer is under an obligation to rescue the victim since the life is not being discarded with the consent or willingness of its true Master.

God's Demand for Accountability

Moreover, it may well be that Maimonides' concept is derived directly from the Bible. The very first time the Bible prohibits suicide and murder it declares, 'Only of the blood of your own lives will I demand an account (*edrosh*) . . . From the hand of every man, even from the hand of a man's own brother, I will demand an account of every human life.' Nowhere in scripture other than here do we find the word *derisha*, 'a demand of accountability', used in reference to offences between humankind and God. The words usually used to describe such offences are *pekida*, or 'keeping in mind', as in, 'He does not clear [those who do not repent], but keeps in mind (*poked*), the sins . . . God takes note of the offence.' (Exodus 34:7 – 'visiting the iniquity of the fathers upon the children, and upon the children's children . . .')

Except for this instance, *derisha* is used in the Bible only to describe the demand one human being makes of another to return a lost possession, be it money or life. If suicide constituted a mere transgression like all others, the word *derisha* would not properly describe it. The fact that it is used shows that the Bible wishes to convey that self-murder is the same as damaging something not one's own. It is as if the suicide had actually destroyed someone *else's* life. God is demanding an account of life and blood that was entrusted to this individual but which was thrown out and wasted.

Self-incriminating Testimony

The idea of one's life not being one's own is also used in connection with self-incriminating testimony and confession. The law states that whereas confessing to a monetary debt makes one legally liable to repay it, confessing to a crime punishable by death or lashes is ineffectual.

In explanation, the renowned Egyptian scholar, Radvaz, avers that all of Judaism declares that the Lord, not Man, is the absolute Master of the universe. This ultimate title to the world includes every person's life. Man, therefore, cannot dispense with his life or limb if he so wishes; he is bidden to protect and enhance his own life as well as the lives of others. The legal inability to surrender to death even by confessing in court is an instance of the theological principle that a person must answer to God for the disposition of his or her life. The same applies to lashes, which are said to be half of death.

Lack of Compensation for a Lost Limb

A final substantiation of this claim may be brought from the payments one is required to make if one assaults and permanently injures another human being, for instance if a person cuts off a limb, puts out an eye. The Torah requires the offender to make five different payments, none of which is really directed to the lost limb. The five are: pain (payment for the pain one suffers as a result of the injury), medical costs, unemployment benefits (for the amount of time the victim cannot work while injured), humiliation (if the blow came publicly and the victim was shamed), and finally damage (recompense for the lost limb or lost ability).

This damage is decided by the court assessing how much the victim would fetch if he or she were a servant, both before the injury and after. The difference is then paid to the injured party. Of course, it would be ludicrous to suppose that this meagre sum is actual payment for the lost limb or eye. Just look at how much human organs fetch today! Rather, this is a disability payment which is meant to mitigate the difficulty the injured person will surely incur in keeping the same livelihood as before the injury. There is no direct payment for the lost limb or eyesight. As it is not human possession, it simply cannot be evaluated and repaid.

Similarly, Maimonides rules that if a man confesses to striking his fellow and there are no witnesses to corroborate the report, he is obligated to pay for the medical costs, humiliation and unemployment benefits, but not for the damage. Whenever a man strikes another man the Torah states that he must pay 'an eye for an eye, a tooth for a tooth'. Of course, the Torah is not speaking literally, but means that since he gouged out the other person's eye intentionally, he really deserves the same. Since the Torah shuns barbarism, it requires the culprit to redeem his own limb through a payment to the injured party. Thus, when a man confesses to severing the limb of his fellow, although he is required to pay the accompanying medical costs, he does not pay the principal damage. The reason is that one cannot obligate another party's money through one's own confession. As the payment of damage is to redeem one's own limb, which is not one's possession, confession is ineffectual.

Conclusion

From all the above one thing emerges clearly: our body, limbs and life are not our own. One therefore cannot involve them in business transactions. One cannot sell them, nor may one use them for collateral. The only use to which they may be put is to serve the purpose of one's creation – to work to bring justice and goodness on earth, making this world a proper dwelling for the King of Kings.

Therefore, the contract between Shylock and Antonio is halakhically null and void. It possesses no force of law, and never did. By Antonio agreeing to forfeit, and Shylock demanding, a possession which does not belong to any person to give, the contract never assumed acceptable legal status. Even if the pound of flesh could be cut from a part of Antonio's body which would not have endangered his life, the contract would still have remained worthless paper.

This reinforces our previous conclusion. Whether Shylock is a virtuous or an evil character, he is not a truly *Jewish* character. Shylock's contract shows a mind influenced by secular law and values, just as his glee at lending money for interest did. Shylock may have been born Jewish, but his ethics and business practices were a result of the Venetian society into which he was immersed.

In a way, this elicits even more sympathy for him: the Renaissance Venetians allowed Jews no real status in their society. Prevented from entering normal life, they were forced into occupations and ways of living which cast them in the role of social pariah, and they were made to follow the expectations and rules of the Venetians, their reluctant hosts.

Shakespeare covertly explores this strange relationship, where the 'civilized' Europeans assume moral authority over the creature they themselves have created, the Jew who is not allowed to assimilate but is yet not permitted to remain Jewish. The forced conversion of Shylock at the end of the play has broader meaning than merely showing the Christian's complete triumph over the Jew: the Jew is shown that to be tolerated by Venetian mercantile society is the same as to be punished for being Jewish. Therefore, whether or not Shylock is an impressive or sinister character, he is surely not entirely culpable or responsible for negative traits of his personality

Chapter Twenty-five:

LESSONS FROM OXFORD TOWN AND GOWN: INTERDEPENDENCY OF LAY PEOPLE AND SCHOLARS

Recently, I was walking through the centre of Oxford and chanced to come upon the eminent scholar, Sir Isaiah Berlin. I greeted him and the two of us paused at Carfax. This ancient crossroads is the traditional centre of the city of Oxford, the focus for all its long and sometimes acrimonious history, and currently the home of the Oxford University L'Chaim Society, and my office. Carfax is a very different place in the cold months from the place the huge number of tourists see in the summertime. Most tourists come for only a single day, or just a few hours, and only a small minority will stay overnight. But they do come, and in their hordes. Like all other towns and cities that have a regular income from tourism, Oxford is careful to do as much building work as possible during the intervals when our visitors are absent. So this winter and spring, as always, there was the hubbub of building and refurbishing work going on, competing noisily with the press of shoppers and the diesel-fuelled buses.

Perhaps the building work this March was particularly noisy, involving as it did the use of electric drills to break up what looked to my layman eyes like perfectly good paving stones – to be replaced with the same type of stone except that the blocks were a few inches smaller. Perhaps the itinerant beggars were particularly aggressive or saddening as they gathered on the benches outside the tower of St Martin's. Oxford has many homeless who line the streets of the city centre, and they contrast sharply with flowing academic robes which nowadays seem outnumbered. Or perhaps the people, students and townspeople alike, for they are barely distinguishable unless one uses the crude criterion of age, looked particularly depressed and unhappy despite the spring sunshine which had come early this year.

Certainly the contrast between our present environment and the media or tourist brochure images of Oxford, which constitute the popular, romantic perception of Oxford throughout the world, struck me forcefully. I turned to my illustrious companion and could not help wondering how the present-day university town matched his memories of the past, in the days when the *Brideshead Revisited* image of Oxford was apparently a reality eagerly anticipated by undergraduates 'coming up', and not the source for television dramas. I asked him what he felt about present-day Oxford: did it compare at all with the Oxford he first knew so many decades ago? Was there any reason to suppose that modern Oxford still retained its character as a centre for learning so removed from the concerns of everyday life that the phrase 'an ivory tower' was indeed appropriate to it?

Sir Isaiah, who has enjoyed a close association with Oxford since the early 1930s, having been an undergraduate at Corpus Christi, a lecturer in philosophy at New College, a fellow of All Souls, and finally the first president of Wolfson College, is an eminent authority on the old Oxford and how it has changed.

He replied with a great deal of contained nostalgia, I thought, that there was very little in common between the two. 'Oxford has changed very much since the time that I was a student.' It does not appear to be the characteristically academic place it once was. This was not to say that the academic standards have gone down in any way; that is a separate issue for debate. The essential change is that the 'real' world has completely left its mark on the town, so that the long struggle between 'town' and 'gown' has eventually been won, it seems, by the values of the market place.

Town and Gown

From the time the earliest halls were founded, the battle between the university and the city was essentially a struggle for power, often centring on explicitly financial issues such as high rents or the price of bread. The first dated reference to Oxford academic institutions given in C. Hibbert's definitive *Encylopaedia of Oxford* concerns a dispute in 1209 over rents between the townsmen and the masters and scholars: the academics won a resounding victory, earning themselves a half share of all rents from all clerks (students) for the next decade. Little happened over the next seven centuries to modify this deep-rooted opposition between the two factions.

The St Scholastica's Day riots of February 1355 resulted not only in the deaths of many scholars and townspeople but, four months later, in the granting of extraordinary privileges to the university over the town. The mayor's annual penance on behalf of the townspeople, in which he swore allegiance to the university and wore a silk halter around his neck in token of his contrition, was only abandoned in 1825. For nearly five centuries, the university officially lorded it over the town, secure in the knowledge that its rights and privileges were protected by indulgent monarchs and powerful friends in government.

In 1358, when town tailors were skimping on the length of the gowns they made, the university promptly passed an edict to rebuke them. As gowns were an important part of academic dress, they said that it was 'honourable and in accordance with reason that clerks to whom God has given an advantage over the lay folk in their adornments within, should likewise differ from the lay folks outwards in dress' (*Encyclopaedia of Oxford*, p. 2). The academics obviously felt the need to assert their superiority visibly as well as by some undefined inner quality, whether the latter was spiritual excellence (since all scholars were also clerics) or intellectual attainment. To this day, the university controls the dress of its members as much by dictating which manufacturers and purveyors of academic clothing are following the approved code laid down by them as by issuing rules and memoranda to students from the proctors.

This assumption of innate control and superiority over the city has come down to modern times. Sportsmen in many colleges were given something like the status accorded to classical heroes, and their misdemeanours were until recently regarded with indulgence and even encouragement by some college authorities. It is said that as late as the 1970s, scores of students would rampage through the city in search of 'some townies' to 'knock some sense into', overturning cars on their way, but these 'pranks' would largely go unpunished in a system where the university was responsible for disciplining its own members.

Who Owns the River?

Around the city of Oxford, the River Thames is called, by a quirk of local nomenclature, the Isis. The river was the original reason for the existence of the city, there being a ford here for cattle drovers to use in crossing their animals from meadow to meadow across the stream, hence 'oxen ford', a crossing place for cattle, later contracted to 'Oxford'. The city arms show an ox passing over a ford to symbolize this. Since the decline of rivers and canals as routes for trade, the university has appropriated the name and use of the Isis almost solely to itself. The chief social event of the university year uses the river and is the annual Eights Week (rowing races held in the summer so named due to the number of rowers in each boat); Oxford University Boat Club names its second crew 'Isis' after the river. The town presently seems to take a limited interest in the river, confined to hiring out pleasure boats that are impossible to steer, called 'punts', and giving river tours to tourists.

Imagine, then, the surprise of some canoeists from the city who were on the Isis on a bright summer's day, having inadvertently obstructed a rowing Eight and then heard a rowing coach loudly claiming ownership of the city's river. Angered that his crew's training had been momentarily disrupted by the tiny craft, the undergraduate bawled out, 'Get off *my river*, you peasants!'; he ordered his crew to pass through.

It seems unsurprising that resentment on both sides still burns in the town. An anarchist group organized violence last summer on the occasion of an expensive Commemorative Ball: young students were attacked for no provocation other than appearing in the garb of privilege ('black tie' for men, ball gowns for women). Pubs are more often than not sharply divided between catering for students or a 'town' clientele, and an uncomfortable time is promised for anyone who enters a pub frequented by the other faction.

It is therefore encouraging to note that the present set of undergraduates is much more keen to participate in town life than their predecessors. Last summer saw a proctor's memorandum (a new rule circulated by university authorities) issued, accompanied by a note from the local police. It ordered that the traditional revels after examinations should not take place in public areas. Now the High Street comes to a virtual standstill as the finalists pour out of Schools and their friends surge to meet them; no traffic can move until the elated students have finished their celebrations. The university police march up and down getting very red in the face, picking people out to fine for obstructing the pavement, and writing their name and college in a much-hated book. And then of course there is 'trashing', which involves throwing flour, eggs and other foodstuffs over those who have finished their examinations, or spraying them with cans of shaving foam. However, the outcry amongst the students of the university was not against the police restricting celebrations; they were vexed by the police implication that they can never be real inhabitants of the 'town', that their typically three or four years of living in colleges does not qualify them to be counted as real townspeople.

Did Nostalgic Oxford Ever Exist?

Of course, nostalgia is a powerful weapon in the armoury of those who wish to complain about modern life. Supporters of football frequently lament the passing of 'family spirit' from the game, forgetting that the nineteenth century saw crowd violence worse than any displays of modern hooliganism, as well as frequent permanent maimings on the pitch itself. The same, of course, goes for Oxford: those who read Evelyn Waugh and reminisce about 'the good old days' are remembering an Oxford as far removed from the needs of the modern world as Alice's Wonderland.

Oxford was only able to be separated into the two concepts of 'town' and 'gown' because of the arrogance of the academics and the defensive response of the town. The idea that 'clerks to whom God has given an advantage over the lay folk' are superior beings has been hard to eradicate, but is now being recognized more and more as fundamentally wrong.

Religious and Academic Intolerance

However, there are striking parallels between such condescension from those who study for a living and those who live their lives by feelings of religious superiority.

Many who are born Jews are rejected by the Orthodox Jewish community because of the choices they make in their lives: to marry a non-Jew, to have a homosexual lifestyle, or to believe that Jesus was the Messiah. The humanity and community spirit of Judaism is forfeited when such people are treated harshly. In recent times, there have been eminent rabbis who live in Israel, possessors of formidable political muscle and respected by the masses, who have repeatedly poured scorn on Israelis who 'eat pig and rabbit'. They have publicly attacked, on television and radio, those young men and women who form the core of the Israeli Defence Forces and imperil their lives, exposing themselves to repeated danger in their national service years, in order to defend all Israel's inhabitants, including those who make these wretched comments. They are the ones who are prepared to die so that others may study in peace.

Judaism teaches that all Jews form a community, a network ordained by God himself. That network is incomplete if any part is ignored or excluded. The ideal situation would be that the whole community follows the laws of God as one, but given that we are for the moment individuals who often make mistakes in our lives, the best current arrangement is to hold the network as closely together as possible; not by force, but with those most powerful adhesives, love and respect.

A powerful dictate of Judaism is of course the idea that we must find the good wherever we can, even in those people or things we may be tempted to despise. The great commentator Rashi shows that our greatest leader, Moses, was subject to this law: when the ten plagues were inflicted upon Egypt, it was Aaron and not his brother Moses who brought about the blood and frog plagues on the Nile. The reason was that, 'Since the river afforded protection to Moses when he was cast into it, therefore it was not smitten by his hand, neither with the plague of blood nor with frogs; but it was smitten by Aaron' (Rashi 7:19). Even inanimate objects that do us good or that contain good must be respected.

A rabbi or a talmudic scholar cannot pretend to themselves that they are better than their fellows, for this would imply that there is something intrinsic to that rabbi or scholar which has pre-ordained their superiority. After all, who is to say how many poor men and women who had no access to books or learning because of the social divisions before the twentieth century would have been as great, or greater, teachers of truth even than the renowned Maimonides, given the same opportunities as him?

Everyone Deserves an Opportunity

Equality of opportunity is the first basis for equality of people, and since at the close of the twentieth century we are still not all the same in terms of access to learning, there is no reason for those privileged to enjoy knowledge to look down on those who work in the Rover factory in Cowley or by looking after their family. After all, those who pay taxes directly contribute to the public good of education, and should be entitled to expect to benefit from it, and not just as a citizen of a nation, but personally too.

It is so easy simply to withdraw into the world of privilege and pretend that the real world outside is irrelevant to study. But we should step back from our books once in a while to consider what study is really for. Is it to be awarded your BA or whatever, to take part in the degree ceremony in the magnificence of the Sheldonian theatre dressed in your best clothes and with your family looking proudly on? Is it to understand all there is to know about one particular branch of knowledge? It cannot be, because even if you had learned all there was to know about everything, your knowledge would mean nothing unless you had people to share it with and for whose benefit you wanted to know it.

The final examinations at the end of years of intense study and seclusion mark the change from absorbing knowledge to disseminating it. After all, what is the examination system but a parody of what I have just said about the real value of learning? Knowledge is useless until you impart it to others, and the formal examination is a crude test of your ability to convey information. Degrees are not awarded for being the most erudite polymath in the world, they are awarded for condescending to share with your examiners the knowledge you have garnered over three or four years of study.

So when the students are drunk on the freedom from revising for their exams, even before they have downed the bottles of champagne that their friends greet them with on emerging from their last papers, they are in a sense also celebrating their return to the outside world. Even while they are indulging in the last freedoms that Oxford encourages, they are also engaged in a rite of passage that makes explicit their dependence on the outside world for the privilege of learning.

The point of all this is that humility on the part of those who are fortunate enough to be in an 'ivory tower' is a paramount virtue, but it is currently a sorely lacking commodity. It is too easy to assume that we have a right to learn merely for the sake of acquiring knowledge for ourselves, but that attitude neglects the fact that we live in a community.

American Style Fund-raising and Marketing at Oxford

The university has long resisted the style of fund raising preferred in the United States where, for instance, clothing bearing the registered logo of Yale University has become fashionable because of the status of the institution and is sold to raise money. However, fourteen years of Tory government have squeezed all state-funded educational establishments, and Oxford realized that if its hard-earned renown was to be retained it had to look elsewhere than the coffers of the government treasury for its money. So the Campaign for Oxford was instituted in 1988 to raise money for the university independently from the government and without relying on benefactors giving large sums to individual colleges.

Since the nineteenth century Oxford University has gradually and falteringly found the path to acting as a real community with egalitarian aims and ideals, rather than the different colleges acting together out of self-interest alone. It was unfortunate that a lack of money was the main motivation for the gathering of this community spirit. However, there is always some good in the worst situations. The post-First World War cash crisis forced the university to open its doors to more and more young people from less privileged backgrounds, and the current crisis in funding also has some valuable repercussions for the ethos of the university.

Age of the Benefactors is Gone

The Campaign for Oxford has opened the eyes of many academics to their dependence on the goodwill of the rest of the community for their existence. The days of magnificent benefactors able to found whole colleges or give money as if it grew on trees, such as Cecil Rhodes, are slipping away. The wealth of the country is now far more concentrated in the whole community rather than a few individuals' resources. The academics must therefore apply to the community and its representative, the government, rather than cultivating a few wealthy men. Similarly, the university now acts as a community itself: the vastly rich colleges such as St John's give large amounts of money annually to keep other poorer colleges afloat financially.

Issachar and Zebulun

For three thousand years the Jewish people have had a model for the close relationship between scholars and those who hold the purse strings. Of the tribes of Israel, two were ordained for interrelated tasks. The tribe of Issachar were to undertake study, for the good of the community as a whole as much as for themselves, and the tribe of Zebulun were to support them in their scholarship. The Zebulun were to be merchants, people engaged in trade to make money, and it was their wealth which enabled others to study. This partnership was epitomized in the blessing which Moses gave the two tribes just before his death, 'And of Zebulun he said, Rejoice, Zebulun, in thy going out [to commercial endeavour]; and Issachar, in thy tents [studying Torah]' (Deuteronomy 33:18; also see Rashi on verse).

Scholars and Benefactors

This may seem to be a rather uneven relationship: the tribe of Issachar get to study for free and the Zebulun get a rather small return on their investment in learning undertaken by the other tribe. However, there is a counterbalance thrown into the scales on the side of the Zebulun. The merchant tribe are to be acknowledged as the benefactors and patrons of those who study. There is no question of Issachar who are privileged to study being entitled to think they are superior to those who earn money for a living.

The relationship between Issachar and the Zebulun is a living one because neither could exist without the other. The scholars contribute to the community with their learning and expertise, while Zebulun contribute part of their wealth to the benefit of others. If Zebulun withheld money from the scholars, or if Issachar ceased to give their knowledge to others or acknowledge their dependence on others, they would lose a part of themselves.

Distributing Honorary Degrees: the Oxford Encaenia

Returning to Oxford, there seems to be an awakening to this ancient idea of interconnectedness.

The Encaenia ceremony seems to epitomize all that is expected of the ancient University of Oxford. The academics process in their academic dress through the city, colours glowing richly in the summer sun, and when the glorious pageant finally reaches the impressive Sheldonian Theatre, one of the earliest buildings by Christopher Wren, they take part in elaborate ceremonies in Latin. The richness of the gowns and the varieties of colours makes the whole display superb visually, and it looks wonderfully old-fashioned. One can easily imagine that the ceremony of the 1990s is the same as any that was performed one or even two centuries ago.

Since the Middle Ages a ceremony has been performed as the ritual high point of university life. Up to 1733, the ceremony was called the Act; degrees were conferred, a witty and often scurrilous speech was delivered by the Terrae Filius, and everyone appears to have enjoyed themselves enormously. The ceremony has become more serious since then; honorary degrees are given (ordinary graduation ceremonies proceed throughout the year) to people who have made important contributions to the world community, and the ceremony now marks a stately if colourful end to each academic year.

Watching Encaenia, it seems as though academic achievements are the grandest thing in the world; nothing could compare with earning the right to take part in such a wonderful display of splendour. After all, those taking part do not seem at all self-conscious, as though walking en masse in brightly coloured silks through the streets of a busy twentieth-century industrial town were the most obvious and natural thing in the world to do. Usefulness and economy are not at all the suitable criteria for judging the worth of this event: they are completely suspended, and replaced with a concern for beauty, tradition and that very old-fashioned concept of pomp. In fact, an honorary degree from Oxford is a highly regarded accolade; in some people's minds it almost ranks with a Fellowship of the Royal Society or even winning a Nobel prize.

In June 1991 the ceremony went on as usual. The Secretary of State for the Vatican, Cardinal Casserolli, and the New Zealand judge, Robin Cook, were among those presented with honorary degrees. Amidst all this ceremony and tradition it was therefore surprising to hear the main speech at the end of the ceremony. Seamus Heaney is the Professor of Poetry in Oxford, a Chair that is not renowned for its practical or worldly considerations, and his speech concerned the recently initiated Campaign for Oxford. To give money to Oxford University was not an act of charity, he said, but 'an act of magnificence', words recalling the gratefulness traditionally shown to the great individual benefactors of colleges.

At last, the most impractical and unworldly representatives of academia have acknowledged that money is important, not a dirty word or concept that they would rather forget. Later, I discovered that indeed this oration on the part of the Professor of Poetry at encaenia, known as 'Lord Crewe's oration' was specifically designed to pay homage to the benefactors of the university. The ordinary person who contributes to the well-being of those who study is a part of a community as worthy of praise as all the individual Cecil Rhodes and John Balliols that have ever given of their personal wealth to benefit scholars.

We can only hope that this move towards a more positive relationship between academia and the wider community continues to aspire to the inter-relatedness of the tribe of Issachar and the tribe of Zebulun. So that 'town' and 'gown' can together celebrate the joys of scholarship, each aware that they need the other to be whole.

To my mind, the contrasting stories of Noah and Abraham reveal what our relationship with the rest of the people in the world should be. Noah escaped the world and the plight of his generation by withdrawing into an ark. Abraham, on the other hand, engaged the world with his newfound monotheism, and imparted into the world. He was an active participant in society, yet all the while remaining somewhat aloof. We cannot permanently withdraw ourselves into a snug ivory tower, whether it is built of books, money, democratic constitutions or anything else. The real work needs to be done where there is not enough knowledge, wealth or freedom. While students have every right to withdraw into a secluded scholastic environment where they are afforded an opportunity to concentrate on their development, they must enter that environment with a clear objective of emerging more complete into the world and contributing to a society that badly needs their participation.

Chapter Twenty-six

CONTROVERSY OF CHANUKA AT OXFORD

It was five o'clock in the evening on the first night of Chanuka 1991, and I was preparing to light the Chanuka menorah with my family. The children were just setting up their candles when suddenly the phone rang. There was a friend of ours on the other end. He sounded very angry. This was a man who supported us both morally and financially. He had just seen the society's giant menorah in the city centre and he was not pleased. In my line of work, it has always surprised me that things which we would never expect to anger anyone, and which we think would be universally embraced by the Oxford Jewish community, can sometimes stir up terrible controversy.

In my first year here I wrote to the Oxford city council, asking them to permit us to erect a giant menorah in the city centre for the Jewish festival of Chanuka. Oxford has a Labour council, who pride themselves on their openness, and we therefore thought it would pass like a breeze. The response we received boggled the imagination. Here was the governing body of the city that hosts a world seat of intellectual study telling us that while they supported the idea of the display of a Jewish symbol in general in Oxford's ancient city centre, they feared a large obtrusive object would distract motorists from concentrating on the road and cause many accidents. When I wrote back pointing out that every year there is a Christmas tree approximately ten times the size of our proposed menorah, they mentioned that people were already used to it, and it thus did not constitute a 'visionary obstruction'.

There was no time to battle with the city council on this matter as we had just arrived in Oxford and there were other pressing matters. However, the next year we wrote to the city council again, saying we believed we were entitled to erect a Jewish symbol in the city centre, especially since the council themselves always put up such a large Christmas tree; and in a pluralistic democracy we deserved equal public representation. Again, they hummed and hawed: eventually we implied that we would pursue the matter in court, as well as approach the press on the subject. They then became very compliant, and indeed we put up a twenty-foot menorah in the city centre. Ever since, the

Council have been very generous and compliant, for which I am truly thankful.

The Jewish students felt a swelling of pride to witness this ancient Jewish symbol smack in the middle of their university town. I was called on by a large number of students, many of whom I did not even have a close association with, to tell us how much they enjoyed seeing the menorah. Every night of Chanuka a crowd of thirty to sixty gathered to watch it being lit.

The reaction of many of Jewish university faculty was quite different. Outright hostility does not quite sum it up. They were furious. One of the university lecturers, who attends my weekly Parsha class, called it 'the most grotesque display of Judaism I have ever witnessed'. Other academics told me they felt I should have consulted them before enacting a display that 'imposes our religious observances on all the well-meaning Christian inhabitants of the city'. I expressed my surprise at their opposition in light of the fact that Oxford is saturated with Christian symbols, ranging from the names of the colleges, about half of which are directly Christian, to the public monuments and the astounding number of churches dotting the city landscape. In light of this, what was wrong with one menorah? A Professor of Sociology reprimanded me with the words, 'You must remember, Rabbi, that we have no right, living in a country that is not ours, to force our religion on others through brash and overt displays.' I also heard the usual chorus of predictions of an increase in anti-Semitism resulting from the display of our menorah.

I was somewhat shaken by the hysteria. The people who opposed what I had done were not enemies, but many well-meaning friends, sympathizers and supporters. This is not to say that it was opposed by the entire academic community; it was not. There was a good number of dons who supported the measure and were proud of its presence. Yet the overwhelming emotion was one of disapproval.

But why? Chanuka is one of the three Jewish festivals universally celebrated by Jews in Oxford, the others being Passover and the High Holy Days. Furthermore, the response of the non-Jewish community to the menorah measured from curiosity to active displays of approval: on some evenings when we lit the menorah, we had a larger crowd of non-Jews present than Jews. They were very taken with the menorah.

Oxford is not the first place where hostility from the Jewish establishment was incurred because of the erection of a public menorah. Indeed, Lubavitch has fought many legal battles in American courts for the right to erect a menorah in public squares, against actions brought primarily by *Jewish* organizations and Jewish lawyers working for the American Civil Liberties Union.

The greatest of these battles reached the United States Supreme Court where, in Chabad vs the ACLU, Lubavitch won an unprecedented victory against the opponents of the menorah. The right to erect this ancient symbol was defended by Washington lawyer Nat Lewin, who is also an observant Jew.

To lend perspective to the argument in Oxford, it is worthwhile briefly quoting excerpts from the principal parts of the court's ruling. The background to the case was that an eighteen-foot Chanuka menorah or candelabrum was placed outside Pittsburgh's city county building next to the city's forty-five-foot decorated Christmas tree. The Greater Pittsburgh Chapter of the American Civil Liberties Union filed suit seeking permanently to enjoin the city from displaying the menorah on the ground that the display violated the Establishment Clause of the First Amendment. The issue at stake was 'the longstanding constitutional principle that government may not engage in a practice that has the effect of promoting or endorsing religious beliefs'. Government is prohibited 'from making adherence to a religion relevant in any way to a person's standing in the community' because 'endorsement sends a message to non-adherents that they are outsiders, not full members of the political community, and an accompanying message to adherents that they are insiders, favoured members of the political community', as the court expressed it.

The opinion of the court in favour of the menorah was based on the premise that 'The inclusion of the menorah here broadens the Pittsburgh display to refer not only to Christmas but also to Chanuka – a different holiday belonging to a different tradition. It does not demean Jewish faith or the religious significance of the menorah to say that the menorah in this context represents the holiday of Chanuka as a whole (with religious and secular aspects), just as the Christmas tree in this context can be said to represent the holiday of Christmas as a whole (with its religious and secular aspects).' The core of the argument was that the display of a Christmas tree had long been found acceptable, and the message of pluralism and acceptance of others' beliefs was enhanced and not destroyed by the display of the alternative symbol of the menorah.

I showed this ruling to the respective university lecturers and emphasized that the highest court in the world's greatest democracy had recognized the menorah to be a universal symbol of religious freedom. Chanuka, the Jewish festival of lights, celebrates the victory of the Hasmoneans over the Seleucid Greeks, and the subsequent rededication of the Holy Temple. The Seleucid Greeks sought to prevent the Jews from practising their religion. The Jews rebelled and waged a pitched battle to overthrow Greek rule and cultural dominance. The subsequent Jewish triumph over their oppression, which culminated in the lighting of the menorah, was a symbol to the world of religious liberty and observance.

Origins of Chanuka

But this deep-seated hostility to overt displays of Jewishness, which I had now experienced first-hand, awakened me to a far deeper significance possessed by the Jewish festival of lights, something which I subsequently made known to the students.

The central festivities of Chanuka revolve around the miracle of the lamps: there was only enough oil to light the menorah (the Temple candelabra) for one night, but it burned for eight. Chanuka is the newest of all Jewish holidays, being the only festival that came into existence after the closing of the biblical canon. An obvious question to ask would be why it has been made a permanent holiday at all. There are so many miracles recorded in the Bible, as well as numerous great victories. Often the Jews were in great danger, both physical and spiritual, and were saved. Why was the miracle of Chanuka so distinguished that it required a special holiday?

To understand the reason for the festival of Chanuka, we must first review the structure of Jewish history after the destruction of the first commonwealth. There was an ancient tradition that Israel would be sub-jugated by four kingdoms: Babylon, Persia, Greece and Rome. Babylon destroyed the First Temple (in 423 BCE), bringing to an end the era of prophecy in Israel. Persia allowed the Temple to be rebuilt, and it was during the period of Persian dominance (373–339 BCE) that the canon of the Bible was closed and the daily services introduced. It was also the time of the miracle of Purim. Under Greek dominance (339–140 BCE), the miracle of Chanuka occurred. Finally came the period of Roman dominance. During this, the Second Temple was destroyed, and the exile in which we still remain began. This exile will not end completely until the coming of the Messiah.

Greek Enlightenment vs Spiritual Light

The Greek persecution of the Jews was nothing less than a *kulturkampf*, a war between cultures. Greece dominated the world of culture and philosophy; the contributions of such giants as Plato and Aristotle had already changed western thought. In their desire to assert cultural domi-nance, the Seleucid Greeks tried to make the Jews 'forget the Torah' and admit the superiority of Greek thought and worship. Although the Jews may have admired the depth of Greek thinking, they were also aware of its limitations. While Greek philosophy had access only to the worldly, the Jews had a Torah which gave them access to the Divine. While Greek thought sought to explain nature, the Torah could provide insight into that which transcended nature. If the Greek philosophers claimed they could perfect the world, the Jews knew they could also perfect spiritual worlds. Not only were the Jews unwilling to give in to the Greeks, but they were even ready to risk their lives to defend their principles.

Under the leadership of the High Priest Mattathias and his five sons, they rebelled against the mighty Greek empire: miracle of miracles, they emerged victorious. In this entire drama, a very special role was reserved for the Holy Temple (Beth Ha'Mikdash). The Temple was the focus of the extra-mundane, the link of the Jew with the spiritual. It was like a miniature Garden of Eden where the rules of spirit rather than of nature were dominant. In the Holy of Holies in the Temple was the rock upon which the Ark containing Moses' original Torah and the Tablets of the Ten Commandments had stood. It was the 'gate of heaven', the portal through which all spiritual energy flowed to the Jewish people. If the focus of Jewish spirituality could be rendered impotent, then their spirituality itself could be conquered. For this very reason the Greeks saw it as important to defile the Temple. Conversely, when the Jews were victorious, they made it their first duty to purify the Temple and rededicate it. The altar that had been defiled by the Greeks was torn down, and when it was rebuilt the entire Temple was cleansed of idolatrous pollution.

Defilement of the Oil

But the kind of contamination which the Jews battled against on Chanuka continues to this day and has extraordinary contemporary relevance. In a discussion of the miracle of Chanuka, the Talmud states, 'When the Assyrian–Greeks entered the Temple, they defiled all the oil that was to be found there. And when the royal Hasmonean House overcame and defeated them, they searched [for oil] but found only one flask that was imprinted with the seal of the High Priest.' From this statement a few difficulties arise. Firstly, why did the Assyrian–Greeks merely 'defile' the oil? If their desire was to suspend the lighting of the menorah, they should have destroyed the oil altogether. It would have been quite simple to pour it on the floor. Their intention was specifically to blemish the oil, which leads us to believe that they were aware of the laws of '*tumah* and *teharah*', ritual purity.

Secondly, if they were familiar with the laws, then they must have also been aware that their actions would not impede the lighting of the menorah. The law stipulates that if the majority of the population is impure, then ritual impurity is ignored. Thus the Jews would have been allowed to make use of the impure oil for the menorah-lighting. From this we may deduce that the Assyrian–Greeks did not mind that the menorah be lit. Rather, their intention was that it be lit specifically with impure oil! Finally, why does the Talmud emphasize that the flask was found 'imprinted with the seal of the High Priest'? Why not state simply that the oil was impure? The explanation given is that the story of the oil is symbolic of the overall struggle between the Assyrian–Greeks and the Jews, a struggle which was essentially a spiritual one.

Judaism as a Religion vs Judaism as a Culture

Oil is a symbol for intellect, or wisdom. This is stated explicitly in the Kabbalah, and in the Talmud we read, 'Because they were accustomed [to eating] olive oil, wisdom was found amongst them' (Menachot 85b). The wisdom of the Jews is of course the Torah.

The oil in the Temple was used for the lighting of the menorah. It was of pivotal importance that the oil be pure – in other words that the Torah be kept pure. Now, the light of the menorah illuminated the Temple and the windows in the Temple were inverted so that the light went outward, signifying the Temple's radiation of spiritual light. This revealed the essential function of the Temple itself: to illuminate the earth with pure light, the light of the Torah.

The very concept of ritually 'pure' and 'impure' is beyond our grasp. Mortal man cannot ascertain what spiritual thing it is which makes one thing pure and the other impure. Maimonides goes to great lengths to emphasize this point: 'It is clearly evident that categories of ritual purity and impurity are fixed by Divine decree. They are not of those things which man's wisdom determines; rather they are generally "*chukim*", laws which defy logic.'

Thus purity is symbolic of something which transcends intellectual grasp. Therefore, 'pure Torah' would signify Torah which is studied with the underlying knowledge that although the Torah can be intellectually apprehended and appreciated, its true essence lies at a plane where no intellect could reach it. 'Pure Torah' signifies a Torah and set of *mitzvot* (Divine commandments or precepts) which are fulfilled with intellectual and emotional participation and appreciation, and at the same time with the knowledge that it is God's Torah and it is only His command and His will which are served with the fulfilment of Torah.

The Assyrian–Greeks were willing to allow the lighting of the menorah. They were willing to allow the Jews to study Torah. It must be remembered that Greek civilization basked in enlightenment. Intellectual pursuits were encouraged. Moreover, the Greeks accepted that the Torah was a book of profound, enriching ideas and thought. What they objected to was 'pure oil', pure Torah. They found reprehensible the premise that the Torah is God's Torah, whose real essence defies understanding.

In other words, *they sought to reduce Judaism to a mere culture*. So long as Jewish practices were culturally enriching, they were willing to allow them to proceed. But the moment they transcended any cultural or aesthetic significance and served as a vector to bind the Jew with his Father in heaven, the Greeks moved in to sever the Torah from its metaphysical attachments.

This is what I had experienced in Oxford and this is what many of the academics had expressed. It was not an overt display of Judaism which irked them, because there has never been any objection to public demonstrations on behalf of Soviet Jewry, or to remember the Holocaust, or even in support of Israel (albeit when staged by left-wing political groups). Rather, what they objected to was an overt display of the most Jewish kind of Jewishness in Oxford, the irrational part of Judaism, which they could not be proud of and for which they had little sympathy. The glory of culture is something in which Oxford delights and seeks to promote. But subjugation to an invisible God and an embracing of His largely enigmatic commandments is not. Oxford is the seat of intellect, and those who occupy the throne vociferously reject the existence of anything which is said to transcend their apprehension. In this case, the supra-rational element of Chanuka, and its symbol in the form of the menorah, had come under attack. Had we put up a giant matza-ball or bagel and lox sandwich in Oxford city centre, or any other Jewish cultural symbol, I doubt that it would have evoked the same emotional outburst.

The Acquisition of Knowledge as a Goal in Itself

Rabbi Yosef Isaac of Lubavitch found expression for this idea in the special prayer recited on Chanuka, in the words 'when the wicked Hellenic government rose up against your people Israel to make them forget your Torah'. It does not state, 'to make them forget Torah', but 'your Torah'. They had no qualms with the Jewish Torah. Every people has its culture, wisdom and scholars, and the Jews should produce the same. But the Greeks believed in knowledge for its own sake. Amidst the most enlightened culture of all time, the Greeks remained hedonistic and incestuous and worshipped idols. Their knowledge had no effect on their actions. Indeed it wasn't meant to. Wisdom and knowledge were not means for man's inner transformation, but goals in themselves. The Jewish Torah as God's law and as a code of ethics to elevate humanity was repulsive to them. It belittled the whole concept of wisdom and knowledge. They wanted a menorah which would burn with the light of Man. In the same vein, modern educational establishments such as Oxford not only refrain from advocating specific values to their students, but even argue that they have no right to do so. Multiculturalism, which has pervaded so many of the world's campuses, argues that no society has the right to promote their values and ethics above that of any other culture. But implicit in this argument for moral relativism is the belief that the acquisition of knowledge on the part of young minds is not meant to lead to any explicit conclusions. When a yeshivah student studies the 'Torah of life' and discovers the infinite significance associated with human life, he naturally understands that he must now do everything within his ability to promote human life. Certainly, everything which we studied in the yeshivah we knew was for a purpose: to translate principles for the abstract realm of discussion into the concrete realm of action. But the same-aged students I serve as rabbi in Oxford are led to believe that the only reason to study is 'to be educated' and for the purpose of intellectual stimulation. There is no moral imperative which results from their studies of values, morals or ethics.

Compounding the problem is that secularism will stop at nothing to remove God from the scene. The way in which secularism has pervaded Judaism is with arguments that one may be inspired and enthusiastic through the observance of *mitzvot* so long as it results from personal examination and conclusion. The students who come to me and get involved with Judaism all have one thing in common: they are prepared to 'go all the way' and even lead a completely observant Jewish life. However, it all must make sense. They reject almost entirely those things which defy their grasp. There is no room for accepting the yoke of heaven. And while this is highly commendable because it means they gain an appreciation for those things which they study, nevertheless it also means that they remain oblivious to the spiritual, mystical nature of the God–man relationship. Mankind today goes about religion in much the same way as he goes about choosing a house in which to live: it must be comfortable, attractive and, above all, fulfilling.

The High Priest in Each of Us

How can this secularization be overcome and this so-called 'defilement of the oil' be averted? The answer is alluded to in the Talmud's emphasis on 'the seal of the High Priest'. One cannot intellectually debate the fallacy of the Hellenistic approach. On the contrary, that will catch him in its trap. It will submerge him into an intellectual and dialectic argument in order to corroborate the Torah's authenticity, thus demoralizing and making the observance of Torah dependent on intellectual mastery. The only way to be victorious is with the 'seal of the High Priest'. The High Priest is he who is removed from the rest of humanity. He is aloof in holiness and devotion to God. He is the representative of the entire people, but he is set apart from them.

There is said to be a 'High Priest' within each and every Jew. It is what can be called the supreme spark of Jewishness which forms the bedrock of one's connection with God. It is beyond the human elements of the body for, while existing in the body, it has never and can never lose its affinity with God. The 'High Priest' in the Jew is his undetachable umbilical chord to the Divine. This part of the Jew is described as 'clamped and clutching You'. It is the intimate, intrinsic, inseparable bond. One must tap it. To fight off the pollutant of Hellenism, one must be conscious of this bond and completely and unconditionally surrender oneself to it. There can and must be trust in the relationship between humankind and God. Then and only then will all interferences dissolve.

But this is only one part. It is imperative that one have the stamp of the High Priest, but there must be oil within the flask. Nullification to God is essential, but there must be knowledge and understanding as well. Purity without oil is meaningless. Thus the bedrock into which every *mitzvah* is anchored should be man's acceptance of God's laws unconditionally, and at the same time accompanied by investigation and feeling so that he uses all his being in serving the Almighty. These are the two sides of religious worship and both are essential. In this way man transforms himself into a vehicle for the Divine.

Preparing for a Time When All Roads Would Lead to Rome

With the victory over the Greeks and the demise of Hellenist culture, the Jews were still not safe. A new threat, Rome, was on the horizon. Although Roman influence may not yet have reached the Holy Land, the Jews realized it would now be inevitable. Rome was the fourth kingdom of which many dread prophecies had been uttered. The influence of Rome would not be shaken off as easily as that of Greece. The Romans would destroy the Second Temple and drive the Jews into exile; the situation would not be rectified until the coming of the Messiah. It was realized that a period was dawning when the spiritual benefits of the Temple would no longer sustain the Jews. Urgent measures were required if the survival of the Jews during this last long exile was to be ensured, and they would have to be taken immediately. The sages of the time realized that commemorating the miracle of the lamps could fulfil such a function. The great faith that had brought about their victory had opened a spiritual door. It was the spiritual force that had flowed through this door, resulting in the miracle of Chanuka. If this door could be opened even when the Temple was destroyed, the spiritual character of the Jews could be preserved. By a proper celebration of the miracle of Chanuka, this door would be held open, allowing a spiritual influx to sustain the Jews during the long exile to come.

As explored above, a key element in the miracle had been faith. Mattathias's son, Judah, had led his people under the banner of the word 'Makkabee', an abbreviation of the verse, '*Mi Khamokha Be'Elim Hashem*', 'Who is like unto Thee, O Lord, among the gods' (Exodus 15:11). This was a phrase from the song that was sung after the parting of the Red Sea, indicating that God was dominant over all powers, both temporal and spiritual. The Maccabees took it as their battle cry, demonstrating that even in war they considered faith their greatest weapon. There are many miracles recorded in the Bible, but all of them so far had occurred during the time of the prophets.

As a general rule, a miracle does not occur unless there is a prophet available to initiate and interpret it. In the case of Chanuka, however, a miracle occurred without a prophet but as the result of pure faith and dedication to the Torah. Just as the Jews were willing to go beyond the call of duty for the sake of God, so He went beyond the limits of nature for their sake. It was this faith that opened the spiritual door of Chanuka. The sages were also aware of the significance of the flask of uncontaminated oil that had been found in the defiled Temple. It was a clear sign that no matter how much something is defiled, some holiness always remains. Like the oil, this holiness can be used to light the lamp of faith and make it shine forth. Even when the exiled Jew would find himself on the lowest spiritual level, the Chanuka lamp would find the hidden bottle of pure oil and bring it forth in order to produce radiance. Chanuka was thus ordained as a festival of hope and faith. During the long exile, every time they lit the Chanuka lamp, the Jews would remember that even in the defiled Temple there was a flask of pure oil. Even when the Temple had been destroyed, during the long exile to come, faith and dedication to God's law would sustain the Jews.

They would recall that every individual has an innate holiness, a 'High Priest', that can never be defiled by the negative forces lurking in this world. The story of Chanuka is a tale of how the small and weak emerged victorious over the strong and bullish. This year, as always, the holiness and sublimity of the soul await revelation on the part of the individual through the lighting of the Chanuka menorah.

The initial hostility of the established community to the menorah has now receded, and people feel far more comfortable with the idea. Indeed, our menorah has become a common annual staple of Oxford communal life, and everyone knows to expect it. Some have even asked me to erect more public Jewish symbols on Oxford's streets. Which just goes to show that a little bit of light on one street can illuminate the fiery souls of thousands. The rebbe, Rabbi Menachem Schneerson, who serves as the motivation and inspiration for our activities at Oxford, has long said that the purpose of a Jew is to serve as a 'lamplighter', not only concerned with the illumination of goodness in our own lives, but wholly dedicated to kindling the same spark within every person we meet.

Chapter Twenty-seven

NOAH, STUDENTS AND MODERN-DAY ARKS:
THE IVORY TOWERS OF ACADEMIA

The story of the flood that nearly obliterated humanity and most living things occurs early in the Hebrew Bible. Its hero of course is a man named Noah. Only one human family was found worthy enough to be saved from the flood. Noah was commanded by the Almighty to build an ark which could withstand the storm, and so save the few people who were to start the human race afresh.

The rabbis are deeply divided about the correct status to be given to Noah's righteousness. The source of their dispute is one of the first verses which introduces Noah in the Bible: 'These are the generations of Noah: Noah was a just man and perfect in his generation' (Genesis 6:9).

Since the verse explicitly qualifies his righteousness with the words, 'in *his* generation', one group of rabbis maintains that the meaning of the verse is that Noah would have been superlatively righteous had he lived in a more worthy generation, because he was able to withstand the evil of his generation and yet remain righteous. Others maintain that only among the exceedingly wicked people of his generation can he be considered righteous: had he lived in the generation of Abraham he would have been found severely lacking.

The Torah testifies that 'Noah found favour in the eyes of the Lord', but the above is just one small fragment of suspicion cast upon Noah by the Sages of the Talmud. It seems strange, therefore, to attempt to find fault with him. This has always been an area of Jewish scholarship that has startled me. When I began to study Judaism seriously in my early teens, and chanced on these critical statements of Noah made by the rabbis about the Talmud, I was very disappointed. I had been brought up to believe that Noah was one of the most righteous men who ever lived, so righteous that God selected him to be the sole survivor of the human race and father of all future generations of Jews. Now, one of my principal heroes had been lost. Surely, the rabbis must have had a very serious charge to level against Noah if they were to undo the favourable characterization afforded him by the Bible.

A Concern with Self

The reason the Sages were so unimpressed with Noah, amidst his undeniable favour with God, was that he made no attempt to save the rest of his generation. He forsook the welfare of his contemporaries and occupied himself only with his and his family's survival. When God says to Noah, 'Save yourself because this generation has had it,' Noah does not put up a fight but builds his ark. There is no protest against the cataclysm that will befall his generation, only quiet acquiescence.

This is remarkable and easily accounts for why the rabbis pulled Noah down from his pedestal. They clearly could not have Noah as a role model for humanity throughout the ages.

Think for a moment of the magnitude of Noah's neglect. Here was a man to whom the Almighty revealed the ultimate plan for the destruction of the human race. And he did nothing. When God told him to pack his bags, build an ark, and save his own skin, he nodded his head in agreement. And that was all.

But where was his sensitivity? Where was his humanity? He had just heard how tens of millions were to be lost, and he didn't bat an eye!

Risking All for the Sake of Others

Now, contrast Noah's inaction with that of Abraham, the first Jew, and the first role model for love, compassion and caring, and human devotion to all of humanity.

God comes to him in very similar circumstances to His conversation with Noah, and just a few chapters later in Genesis. God reveals to Abraham that He is about to blast Sodom and Gomorrah for their wickedness. Of course, Abraham and his nephew Lot were to be unaffected by this judgement. Abraham, who was not a resident of Sodom, would not be harmed, and his nephew, who was a resident, would be saved. Did Abraham sit back and do nothing? Of course not! He shrilled and complained, and spoke even with insolence to the supreme Ruler of the universe: 'How could you? Nay, how dare you!' 'Shall the Judge of all the earth do right?' (Genesis 18:25). Then, in one of the bravest and most eloquent defences of human life in the history of mankind, Abraham began to spar with the Creator, asking if He would destroy the righteous with the wicked.

Abraham begged, pleaded, attempted everything within his power to force God to rescind the decree, even at great personal risk. He could not have known how the Almighty would have reacted to his refusal to accept the Divine edict, and to go almost as far as challenging God's justice. Abraham was prepared to risk spiritual oblivion, not just for other people, but for the most despicable and wicked of all people, the inhabitants of Sodom, concerning whom the Torah testifies: 'But the men of Sodom were wicked and sinners before the Lord exceedingly' (Genesis 13:13).

Dedication to Others as the Measure of Righteousness

Abraham's righteousness was not merely a question of his ability to enhance his own righteousness, but centred on his care and compassion for all humanity. In other words, the measure of true righteousness lies not in self-development or personal growth, but rather in selflessness, contribution to society, and compassion for one's fellow human beings. The hallmark of the great Sages of Israel has always been their selfless devotion regardless of the personal consequences.

Nearly everyone has had exposure to at least a sprinkling of Chasidic tales and legends. The common theme throughout the stories is not of men who were outstanding in prayer or Torah study, which of course many of them were, but rather of warm and wonderful people who dedicated their lives to those around them.

After the sin of the Golden Calf, God wished to annihilate the Jewish people. This time, it seemed as though they really deserved it. After all, just forty days after they had collectively witnessed the greatest revelation in the history of the world, and heard God personally proclaim, 'You shall not have any other gods before Me', here they were worshipping a foreign god. The Almighty informs Moses of His plans; Moses is even promised by God that he will be the progenitor of a new Jewish race, less rebellious and more devout than the stubborn congregation he is leading. And what is Moses' reaction? He steadfastly insists that God forgive them. So adamant is his demand that he actually has the audacity to proclaim, '. . . if Thou wilt forgive their sin – ; and if not, blot me, I pray Thee, from the book which Thou hast written' (Exodus 32:32). Where in the history of apocalyptic literature do we have any other example of a human risking his entire physical and spiritual being by demanding that God destroy the record of any association the two may have had? Moses actually refuses to be remembered as being a confidant of the Creator. He dismisses an affiliation with a God that cannot forgive and who seeks retribution. He cannot face posterity reading of his failure to save his people, especially if he alone would be saved. That would have been the greatest shame for so great a leader. After all, what is a leader if not someone who concerns himself with the welfare of others before any thought of himself?

Having No Time to Write

The Golden Era of Spain was one of the most scholarly periods in the history of the Jewish people. It was a time of prolific intellectual output, with eminent authors such as Maimonides and poets like Solomon and Gabirol establishing their reputations with great works. I once read a history of the era and chanced upon the name of a great Sage I had never come across before. The book said that he was one of the leading rabbis of his generation, but history had not remembered him. The book explained that this Sage had written only one work but had never completed it. The reason was that he was so preoccupied with communal obligations and shepherding the nation of Israel that he never found the time to finish the book. Indeed, having read this I concluded that he *must* have been one of the leading lights of his nation. But it took an unconventional perspective to unearth him from the rejection of conventional history.

The real worth of the largely unknown Sage in the book I read is not measured in terms of fame or good fortune, but many of us can have the best of both the secular and spiritual worlds.

An Invitation to Enter the Ark

All the students who come to Oxford are entering an 'ark', not unlike that of Noah. It is society itself which invites them into this ark. We tell them, 'You must remove yourselves from the turbulent waters of life and finance, and seclude yourselves in this academic centre for a number of years to gain knowledge.' If the students wonder about the world outside, what they may be missing, and what they might be able to contribute, we tell them they should not concern themselves with that for the moment. Now it is time for them to focus exclusively on personal development. Just as Noah was saved from the tide of destructive rain and forces, so too the student is spared the agony and challenges of the outside 'real' world.

A Right to Grow and Flourish

This is not selfishness. Students have every right, indeed a moral imperative, to spend their formative years concentrating on character development and the acquisition of knowledge. But what is pivotal in this cocoon stage is that they understand they are like 'a sponge that absorbs in order later to expel'. Behind the knowledge students work to gain should be the desire to make a meaningful and lasting effort for the benefit of all people. This way we can be assured that the inhabitants of the earth will always be found guiltless and meritorious. There will be no more floods if people reach out to each other with their own experiences and knowledge.

We dare not simply embrace a 'Noah' attitude, in which saving oneself is sufficient. What is sorely needed today is not so much people who build arks as those who enter in order to break out of them and make the whole world a refuge of sanctity and Godliness.

Thus, every moment which a student spends engrossed in his or her work must be with a firm commitment to develop their fullest potential in order to change and assist the lives of those who are most in need.

Chapter Twenty-eight

BORN ANEW: MATURE STUDENTS
AND MODERN LIVING

Compared with a North American or Australian university, Oxford has a paucity of mature students. In the undergraduate courses this is particularly noticeable, with the one or so older students standing out among about one hundred youngsters.

This demographic anomaly is partly to be explained by the way the university works, or is perceived to work. Despite the repeated assurances that candidates will not be discriminated against, the facts are that those from unusual ethnic or age groups tend not to apply to Oxford. The former polytechnics are seen as far more accessible than long-established universities, not just because it is assumed that the Oxford system will discriminate, but because they offer part-time courses which allow students to support themselves while they study, and child care and similar facilities are usually more of a priority. Also, Oxford undergraduates tend to be fresh from school, or they come after one or maybe two years out; they are easy to teach as their minds are open to instruction and waiting to be filled. On the other hand, the mature student will have his or her mind already shaped by the outside world, something that dons tend to find disconcerting whatever they say about the need for rational argument and mature responses.

How, then, do the mature students cope with the way Oxford works? As soon as they arrive they must decide what being a student will mean to them. There is the stark choice between living in college, away from family and friends and attempting to fit in with the youngsters of eighteen, nineteen or twenty, or living out and treating college life as one small slice of existence in contrast to the rest of the student population, who often tend to forget that there is a world outside college. Each student makes their own choice, and there is no single correct answer, but the secret of success seems to be to make your own decision genuinely, without constantly looking over one's shoulder at either one's previous life or one's younger peers in college.

It may seem flippant to compare a person's decision to renew their studies in a university setting on the one hand, with a profound spiritual repentance on the other, but the similarities are there to be recognized.

Both require a reassessment of one's life to date, while retaining the lessons that have already been successfully learned.

Born Anew through Actions

In his treatise on the Laws of Repentance, Maimonides discusses the proper attitude that should be embodied by the penitent (Chapter 2:1–4). Maimonides goes to great lengths to emphasize that the penitent must view his or her entire life as if beginning anew from the day of their repentance. He says that the penitent should change even their most basic identity, discarding one's former name and adopting a new one. One should move away from the place of one's residence before the return to repentance and find a new home. This applies, he says, even to the friends of the penitent. They are not allowed to call the penitent by his old name or remind him of his previous evil ways. This is not to say that the penitent should overlook their earlier failings and continue to practise them, but they must view them as having never taken place, as having been carried out by quite another person.

Discouraged by One's Past

Now whether or not this should all be taken literally is a matter of debate. What cannot be disputed, however, is that with this statement Maimonides intends to teach us that the most fundamental first step in facing the future is becoming a penitent and never to fear renewal. Whenever someone ponders a radically new change in their life, a shift from everything they have been doing before, almost always they think of an obstacle that impedes their decision to embark on that new course. Perhaps the greatest obstacle to change is how they think to themselves that perhaps it is too late. So much valuable time has elapsed without this significant addition, and the opportunity has been missed. They cannot possibly begin now.

Fear of the Computer Age

One of the contemporary secular areas where I find this kind of thinking most prevalent is in the area of computer literacy. Very often older members of the community or students walk into my office to see me typing a letter or designing a flyer on a large computer monitor. They watch and marvel. When I suggest to them that it is not too late for them to learn to use a computer, they look at me as though I am merely attempting to allay their discomfort. But I'm not. I challenge them to say why they feel they cannot begin now, at whatever age, to acquire greater skills that may well be very useful to them. For these people, the answer is as simple as it is nonsensical, 'After all these years I'm not going to begin working on a computer! Are you mad?'

Am I mad? What if we look at this question from a totally new perspective. A young man reaches the age of, say, thirty-five. His friend encourages him to come to an informative class on Judaism. At the very least, the friend tells him, he should learn how to read Hebrew so that he can follow a synagogue service, or make kiddush on a Friday night for his family. He declines. After thirty-five years of leading his life without any Jewish content, it seems irrational, if not absurd to try to start now.

Let us now imagine that this same man lived a thousand years ago. He is unlikely to live anywhere past his fiftieth, or perhaps even his fortieth, birthday. When he is ten years of age someone invites him to come to learn to read Hebrew and study the Torah; should he decline because he only has forty years left of his life? Of course not. He would view his life as just having begun and would be happy for the opportunity to have exposure to Judaism at this early stage of his development.

Increase in Longevity

Why then, at thirty-five, when modern life expectancy affords him at least another forty years, does he decide that it is too late? He has just as much time in the imaginary scenario I've made up as he does in the reality of the here and now.

The reason, of course, is simple. His complaint about being thirty-five years old is not a statement that he does not have enough remaining years in his life to make the present undertaking tenable and worthwhile. Rather, he is saying that at thirty-five years old he is already too set in his ways to embark on a radically new way of life. Even if you had hundreds of years ahead of you, when you have become set in your ways it becomes quite difficult to extricate yourself from an assumed pattern.

A New Start; a Fresh Identity

Maimonides recognized this difficulty, which is why he went to great lengths to emphasize that the only way to ensure success in penitence is to view life as if it were beginning from new. The penitent is a new person. He or she is not set in any ways that might make it difficult for them to adopt a new path. This is the very first step. Ah, but what about the thirty-five years until now? That was a different 'you'. The new 'you' need not fear the resurgence of any past patterns of behaviour, bad choices or dispositions because they are now non-existent. You are now young and full of new life, and it is imperative that you make the right choices and begin life on the right foot. Focus on a promising future and not a non-existent past.

If a list of the ten greatest Jewish Sages of all time and in all categories were to be compiled, Rabbi Akiva, the great teacher of the Mishnah, would be on that list. The Talmud accredits him and four others for being responsible for the transmission of the oral law. The Talmud further relates that God showed Moses, in a prophetic vision, a vision of Rabbi Akiva. Moses became weak at the sight because he felt himself unable to compete with Rabbi Akiva's piety and scholarship.

The Rise of Rabbi Akiva

And yet, despite his enormous learning, Rabbi Akiva is the greatest inspiration to all 'beginners', regardless of age. He began learning to read and write the aleph-beis, the Jewish alphabet, when he was forty years old. Like so many people today, he had not been fortunate enough to have been given a Jewish education, but he had not had any other form of education either. His parents were too poor, and so he became a shepherd. Fortunately, Rachel, daughter of Kalba Savua, the richest Jew of his age for whom Akiva worked, saw his inner potential and promised him her hand in marriage if he would begin to study. He took her up on her offer and within twelve years he became the leading Sage of his era. After twenty-four years, he had 24,000 students.

Can there be any greater embodiment of this principle of Maimonides? If Akiva the poor shepherd had thought differently, if he had focused on what he did not know instead of what he could come to know, the Jewish people would have been deprived of one of its greatest sons.

Life is constantly being renewed. All our tomorrows are filled with infinite potential. Another great Jewish Sage taught what should be called the human creed for achievement. His name was Hillel, and he said the immortal words, 'If I am not for myself, who will be for me? And if I am only for myself, what am I? And if not now, when?'

We are all the inheritors of an ancient, precious tradition. It is there for the taking. All that is needed is an effort. Therefore, I accord special respect to the mature students I encounter at the university because I respect their courage and determination. We must promote this same resolve that 'it is never too late' in the hearts and minds of all our Jewish brethren, and indeed all humanity, that they explore their own roots and embrace their heritage.

And through this process we will bring renewal to the world and all its inhabitants.

Chapter Twenty-nine

THE EVILS OF SLANDER: THE CENTRAL INGREDIENT IN SOCIETY'S MORAL DECLINE

Like many relatively long-established small and select communities, Oxford University has quirks and prejudices unique to it. In fiction, Evelyn Waugh's novel *Decline and Fall* illustrates the pettiness to which these idiosyncrasies can, when taken to extremes, lead. The socially inept hero inadvertently clashes with the élite students of his college, and when he is victimized by them, the authorities side with the bullies because they fit their idea of what an undergraduate should aspire to. The victim is sent down.

Slippers at All Souls

Nowadays, rules and discipline are a little less arbitrarily imposed, although there are still apocryphal tales of bizarre rituals designed to exclude those who are felt not to belong. For instance, it is said that being elected to a fellowship at All Souls is a matter of negotiating a carefully laid minefield of etiquette as much as passing the tough examination. A tale is circulated of a young man who was clever enough to pass the written examination, but fell flat when it came to having dinner with the fellows, a dinner that was to decide whether he would be given a fellowship or not. On academic ability alone he was sufficient for a scholarship, but he made a fatal error: he relaxed at the meal and kicked off his uncomfortable formal shoes. As soon as he had done so, he found they were at the other end of the hall, having been passed there under the table by the fellows: he did not manage to extricate himself from such a socially embarrassing situation, and did not of course get elected to the fellowship.

Whatever the merits of so demanding a system, such aggression towards those who are felt to be 'not quite the thing' can be interpreted as a measure designed to keep the community close and insular, familiar and safe. If a community is larger or more open, rules have to be instituted to keep that community from breaking into rival factions and cliques. One of the most ancient and obvious ways of doing this is to take sanction against those who attempt to split the community with their words, the slanderers and heretics. Traditionally, punishments for these crimes which threaten the very fabric of a community have been particularly severe.

Students at Oxford enjoy gossiping as much as anyone, which, I guess, is perhaps an expectable staple from exuberant, precocious and curious young minds. For me this can be a big problem because I am often dragged into these petty reports about other people's lives and, although I am also their friend, as a rabbi I cannot afford to portray myself as indulging in petty gossip. Besides, if a student hears me gossiping about a mutual acquaintance, they may walk out of my office thinking, 'I wonder what he says about me when I'm not around.' I work hard to earn the students' confidence. Giving up gossip is quite an easy sacrifice to maintain that trust.

Nevertheless, when refusing to discuss someone else's intimate life with a student who has come into my office, I do not want to take a condescending or 'holier than thou' approach which makes me sound disingenuous. So it is imperative that I find the words to explain rationally why gossip is a destructive refrain which I avoid, and encourage others to do as well. I find myself reverting to this explanation constantly.

Spiritual Causes of Leprosy

In the Bible leprosy was a disease with a special significance. The disease was considered by the Torah and the rabbis to be not only a physiological symptom but a punishment specifically for the sin of slander. It was a punishment that Miriam was given for her tale-bearing against Moses. A leper was isolated from the rest of the people once his or her illness had been diagnosed, and was made to live outside the camp. Since the disease had a spiritual as well as physical dimension, this was not simply a hygienic precaution but also had a moral purpose. Likewise, purification was a recovery of spiritual as well as physical health.

What is it specifically about slander, or speaking evilly about another person, which is so dreadful that it carries with it such a severe physical punishment, that it necessitates the perpetrator being isolated from his native community? Various explanations have been offered as to the gravity of the sin.

Designed for Seclusion

Maimonides explained that the leper or *metzorah*'s isolation is intended to seclude him or her so that the community may be relieved of the damage caused by an evil tongue. This isolation is, according to him, in keeping with what our rabbis wrote: 'As he separated with his *lashon hara*, "evil tongue", between a man and his wife and a man and his fellow, he too is to be separated.'

Sefer Ha'Chinuch did not see the isolation as a punishment but as a means to have the person begin thinking about his or her actions and then to repent. Isolation is for the slanderer's benefit so that they may realize the sin which they committed against society.

Another explanation is found in Parashas Kedoshim (Leviticus 19:16). It is explained that the injunction, 'Thou shalt not go ... as a talebearer among thy people: neither shalt thou stand against the blood of thy neighbour', teaches that one who is a talebearer is considered as if he or she shed a neighbour's blood. Since the slanderer has subjected his or her fellow to a character assassination, it is difficult and sometimes even impossible for the subject of the rumour to continue life normally as before.

Yet another commentator, Oznayin Le Torah, however, saw the purpose of isolation as an educational tool, to teach the *metzorah* or leper the value of society and the importance of it. According to our rabbis, the person who engages in evil speech attacks society. If the slanderer is made to live in isolation, he or she will realize how essential society is for people. Our rabbis therefore say that, 'A leper is considered as dead.' Isolation outside society makes life unbearable since there is no life except within the framework of a human community.

The Enemy of Society

What is specific about an evil tongue, as opposed to all other sins and evils against society, that makes it a corrupter and destroyer of society more than any other deed? I would like to suggest that an evil tongue impedes directly the progression of society and therefore leads to its moral decay.

Firstly, the primary reason why people speak evilly of one another is to belittle their fellows and to minimize their accomplishments. Spreading rumours about one's next-door neighbour, who has become a great teacher and a wise person, or has achieved great financial success, minimizes the need for the individual bearing the tale to face up to these accomplishments. When one person among many proves that obstacles may be overcome and that one may uplift oneself and become a good, decent and successful person, she or he challenges all those around for an explanation as to why they have not done the same. It is this challenge that constitutes the main impetus for the advance of civilisation. By belittling one's fellow, the necessity of answering someone else's accomplishments with similar progress is removed. Here we find the pivotal reason why slander is commonly spoken and listened to with great delight.

Such evil speech directly hinders the progress of society because it removes the challenge for people to be better.

Decay of Society

The second reason why slander is seen to be so dangerous is, perhaps surprisingly, not dependent on the rumour being untrue. In secular English law, a slanderer or libeller can only be successfully sued if it can be proved that the words are untruthful. In Jewish thinking, it is implied that the destruction of a person's reputation is the important factor. Evil speech actually destroys the progress of society and causes it to decay. For example, even if the rumour about a certain individual is true, the fact that his deeds have become known to the entire city will cause him to abandon the attempt to be any better. When his own faults were a personal matter, he was able to change himself, without having to concern himself with the huge task of spreading the news of his improved character. Now that his faults have become public knowledge, and he is shunned by all people, he asks himself why he should in turn desire to transform himself into a better person when everyone knows him to be evil. Even if he does become better, people will only remember his former self. The enthusiasm for advancing one's moral and spiritual integrity is eliminated.

The story is told of how a townsman once said scandalous things about the great rabbi of his city, the world-renowned Chafetz Chaim, Rabbi Yisroel Meir Ha'Kohen. When the man came broken-heartedly before the Chafetz Chaim to beg for forgiveness, the rabbi told the slanderer he would only forgive him if he would take a pillow to the top of the city tower, open it up and let its feathers fall all around the city. After the bewildered man had followed the Chafetz Chaim's instructions, he returned once again to ask for forgiveness. The Chafetz Chaim then said to him, 'Go round the city to collect each and every one of those feathers.' The individual looked at him in great surprise, exclaiming that it would be impossible. The Chafetz Chaim responded, 'Thus it is with slander and evil speech. It spreads so quickly that if one wants to rectify the misdeed, one must go to each person who heard the slander. And now you understand the gravity of evil speech.'

Chapter Thirty

PROMOTING ISRAEL AGAINST ITS CRITICS

Right-wing politics leave a rather bad taste in the mouth of the ordinary Oxonian; four Conservative governments in a row have changed the attitude of the higher education establishments from thinking funding was an almost God-given right to seeing it as something that must be scrabbled for in competition with others who may be equally deserving. Although Oxford has had very few left-wing Members of Parliament representing it, and despite the air of privilege and gentility that pervades the university, nevertheless it is particularly sceptical of right-wing politicians, and rather proud of many of its socialist sons.

For instance, while Oxford is renowned for the strength of its student politics, with a high proportion of former presidents of the Union going on to become Members of Parliament, the most famous political organization associated with the university is of course the ostensibly socialist Fabian Society, a founder member of which was George Bernard Shaw. And the most outrageous of all the student political organizations has for decades been not the Revolutionary Communist Party, but the Oxford University Conservative Association. At one time they were dissociated from the university because their activities were bringing such disrepute to the institution.

The Education Secretary visits L'Chaim

The current MP for the university is actually the Secretary of State for Education, Mr John Patten, who is obviously Conservative. A devout Catholic, he has always been grateful to our L'Chaim Society and delivered a lecture on our behalf on a Friday night at the Shabbat dinner in January 1994.

Heavy police security surrounded the headquarters of our L'Chaim Society when we hosted Mr Patten. While over 200 students came in to hear Mr Patten speak of the importance of bringing values into education, an equal number of students staged a loud and angry demonstration against his appearance at the university.

Mr Patten, who once served as an Oxford Geography don, joined us in the usual prayers and blessing of the bread before dinner, but declined our traditional Shabbat dinner because, as a Catholic, he could not eat meat on a Friday night.

The peace of the Shabbat evening was marred however by the sounds of the 200 student protestors shouting directly outside the building where they were protesting the recent cuts of student grants. Earlier, the demonstration had turned ugly when a circular from the university's Socialist Worker Society threatened 'Patten! You're going home in a little black hearse', provoking strong condemnation from the Minister on the radio prior to the meeting: 'I thoroughly condemn these threats and the neo-Fascist attempts to stop free speech in our university city,' he replied. 'I hope that my meeting with this distinguished Jewish body will not be interfered with in any way.'

In my introduction of Mr Patten I referred to the student notice as 'grotesque in the extreme', and mentioned that I had met with student leaders of the Socialist Worker Society where I had told them that their threats to Mr Patten's life betrayed a serious flaw in their education:'L'Chaim Society invited Mr Patten because of his strong opposition to a value-free education whose by-product is young and innocent students willing to produce this kind of absurd intimidation.' I had to repeatedly intervene to shield Mr Patten from angry student questioners, many of whom directed abusive remarks. I told the students: 'Mr Patten has paid us a great honour by agreeing to be with us this evening and we will accord him the dignity and respect that a Minister of Government deserves.'

While the chants continued unabated, Mr Patten delivered his views on 'Morality and Education in a Changing World'. He listed what he called 'the eleven commandments of education', which serve as the most basic criteria of what children must be taught: an acceptance of responsibility, unselfishness, dignity, courtesy, respect, sensitivity to the abuse of others, fairness, honesty, loyalty, a capacity to look to the future and a readiness to stand up for one's beliefs.

Mr Patten seemed to forge spiritual ideas at the very heart of the engine room of political life, as he spoke of the need for politicians to intervene, especially in the domain of education, against the threat posed to moral values by society. Schools being a microcosm of the wider community, Mr Patten argued strongly in favour of the introduction of an authentic ethical education in all schools, which should include a clear definition of the school's ethos in their prospectus. Mr Patten expressed concern for the role played by the media: television and the press, who should illuminate people's decisions, are instead one of the major factors in the loss of moral consciousness.

At about 10.00pm that evening the police quietly whisked Mr Patten away in an unmarked car so that he would not come into any danger. The student protestors were very upset that they had missed him and were even more incensed the following week when Mr Patten publicly called for the Socialist Worker Society to repay thousands of pounds which it cost the local police to oversee the demonstration and protect Mr Patten.

So right-wing politicians are not automatically assured of a warm welcome in Oxford. The Likud Party is Israel's right-wing response to the left-of-centre policies of the Labour Party. During my first four years at Oxford they were installed in power as the Israeli government, under the leadership of Mr Yitzhak Shamir. Our policy at the L'Chaim Society, in that it tries to avoid politics as much as possible, is to invite as many Israel speakers as possible, from a broad political spectrum. Our purpose in doing so is not just to practice fairness, but to promote Israel as much as possible in a city which, although influential, is unsympathetic. But since all the government ministers were from the Liberal Party, they automatically tended to be from the political right.

One of the most controversial events we staged was the visit of the Israeli Minister for Housing, Ariel Sharon. This was part of a much bigger story.

A Great Opportunity

One morning in the summer of 1991 we received a fax from the offices of President Ronald Reagan confirming that he had accepted our invitation to lecture under the auspices of the L'Chaim Society on 18 October 1991. When I wrote to him I did not really believe that he would accept our invitation, so this fax came as a shock and surprise.

Throughout August I had extensive meetings with Rabbi S. F. Vogel, director of the Lubavitch Foundation in the UK, on the subject of maximizing the potential of the Reagan visit. We decided that we would award him a Chair in our soon-to-be-established Oxford Maimonides Institute of Jewish Studies. It would be known as the Ronald Reagan Chair for the study of the Jewish Code of Universal Ethics and Morality, in recognition of his promotion of the Seven Noachide Laws and his great friendship towards Israel and the Jewish people. The President was instrumental in promoting this code of morality, having issued nine proclamations to the effect that the world's inhabitants should abide by these laws. This was in turn inspired by the Lubavitcher rebbe, Rabbi Menachem M. Schneerson, through a correspondence with the President. We also saw Reagan's visit as a good opportunity to launch our Oxford Maimonides Institute for Jewish Studies by linking sponsorship of the President's visit to sponsorship of the Institute.

The Maimonides Institute was planned as a teaching centre for a variety of subjects, including Jewish literature and the thought of Torah personalities of the last two centuries as well as the longer established fields of halakhic issues and Jewish messianism.

Planning the President's Visit

While in Los Angeles I met the chief scheduler in the President's Office, Mrs Joanne Hildebrand. I told her of my intentions and she said that Mr Reagan would be very pleased. She added that the President always considered himself a friend of the Jews and was very honoured and flattered when the Jewish people accorded him honours for their institutions. After conferring with Mr Reagan she accepted our plan to award the President the Chair.

We were also hoping to use the President's visit as an opportunity to raise enough money to realize our dream, a new centre in Oxford. At the time we used facilities in our own single family home as our Chabad House. The largest room there is approximately 250 square feet, and can accommodate only about thirty people comfortably, so larger facilities were very much in order. We were extremely hopeful that we would be able to raise enough money to open a new centre in the very heart of the city, despite the recession.

Rebuilding the Site of Oxford Jewry

We finally found suitable premises to lease in the middle of the city, in one of the best possible locations in Oxford. The building is in the exact city centre on the first floor of a building on Carfax crossroads, and was recently renovated quite nicely. The floor we proposed leasing would provide us with nearly 2,000 square feet.

We were pleased to discover from research by one of our students, Marcus Roberts, who was studying for his M. Phil. at the time, that this site is highly significant in the Jewish history of Oxford. Our modern centre is only about a hundred yards from the site of the shule that existed in Oxford seven hundred years ago, before the expulsion of the Jews in 1290. In fact, in 1931 the city council put up a plaque across the street from this building, which says that St Aldate's was known before the year 1290 as Great Jewry Street and was the Jewish quarter.

The centre itself is on the same site as a building known in the thirteenth century as 'Jacob's Hall', which belonged to a prominent member of the Jewish community, and there is significant evidence that there was also a yeshivah in the same position. So it was significant that we now deliver extensive courses on Judaism so many years later. Jacob fil Magister Moses, one of medieval Oxford's leading Jews, owned this house, which was at the head of Oxford's medieval Jewish quarter, one of the most important in England. This Jewry was settled from *c.* 1120 until the general expulsion of the Jews.

Jacob's Hall was originally the property of the city itself, being the guildhall of Oxford until 1229. In that year it was sold and given up in favour of a house which had been taken from an important Jew, Moses fil Isaac of Oxford; the house occupied what is now the northern part of the present town hall, just opposite in St Aldate's. Jacob obtained the old guildhall in 1270 from the Stockwell family for a forty shilling 'rent and quit rent'.

This house was one of the best in Oxford. It seems that Jacob both improved and extended his property to the highest standard. It probably had an L-shape plan which overlaps to a significant extent the site of the current L'Chaim Centre and would have formed the west and south sides of our modern site at the corner of Carfax. The main frontage of the house was on St Aldate's, but there may also have been a frontage with *solar* facing Queens Street, which was then called Great Bailey Street. The house also had large and complex cellars which existed until the turn of this century. It had a large, long and irregularly shaped garden which extended south-westwards around the backs of other properties and contained a well, which was a notable domestic facility at that time and indicated the wealth of the owner of the house.

Oxford's First Rabbinical Seminary

It is possible that Jacob's Hall was not only the personal residence of Jacob but also a house of study for scholars pursuing a traditional Jewish education. The evidence for this is tentative, but rests on two grounds. Firstly, Jacob was a member of England's most distinguished rabbinical dynasty. While Jacob was not a noted scholar he was referred to as being a patron of learning, a distinction denoted in the appellation *Ha'Nadiv* (or 'The Benevolent') appended to his name. In addition, Jacob's Hall and another of his houses in Great Jewry are referred to as being 'Aulae', or 'Halls', a technical designation usually meaning an academic school and residence with scholars. Thus it is quite possible that Jacob patronized Jewish scholars in Great Jewry and the balance of probabilities points to his house as the putative yeshivah, given its owner, size and proximity to the medieval synagogue, which was but a minute's walk away across the street.

When Jacob died, his house was inherited by his son Moses, but two years later in 1279 Queen Eleanor expropriated Jacob's Hall and gave it to the vintner Henry Owen, later to be mayor of Oxford. Thereafter the building became a famous inn called variously 'Bates' Inn', 'The New Rentes' and 'The Flower de Luce'. It was also called 'Jacob's Hall' for some time after the expulsion. The inn itself was one of the most prestigious in Oxford and was used to entertain notable visitors, including foreign ambassadors and nobility. Later, in the seventeenth, century it was called 'Baptist Hall', but most or all of the original building was consumed by fire in 1644 in the great fire of Oxford, a fire which was allegedly started by two royalists who were clandestinely trying to roast a stolen pig! Even though all the visible remains of Jacob's Hall except the cellars disappeared in the flames, folk memory seems to have preserved the ghost of Jacob's Hall because a nearby public house listed in 1681 was called 'The Unicorn and Jacob's Well'.

Money Matters

We were very proud to acquire such a prestigious site which, as it turned out, also had a deep significance for Oxford Jewry. We immediately put together a financial package that would make the building viable to rent.

Sponsorship was especially hard. Due to the recent recession, which greatly affected Britain, many people we approached, who otherwise would have agreed to sponsor the visit, could not afford to give the amounts we requested. The Reichman brothers of Canada were approached but had to refuse because they had built a new multi-billion-dollar office complex in London, the famous Canary Wharf; but as a result of the economic situation very few clients went there.

Robert Maxwell Moves in

Then in mid-August 1991 we received confirmation from Mr Robert Maxwell, of the newspapers the *European*, the *New York Daily News*, the *Daily Mirror* and many others, that he was willing to help financially. He said that his newspaper the *European* would like to sponsor the President's visit to Oxford, but not any of our other proposals.

I was very proud of the support which began to pour in. My friend Mr Jonathan Faith took on himself an even larger commitment than the publishing tycoon, and Mr Malcolm Lyons and Mr Tzvi Ryzman of Los Angeles (who own a beauty products company called Original Additions) said they would commit themselves. Mr Meir Jungreis was also willing to help and wished for the shule, which was to be incorporated into the new centre, to be named after his late father.

In addition to the planned talk, we also had a fund-raising lunch arranged. President Reagan refused to accept any honorarium or even funds to cover his own travelling expenses.

All this would have enabled us to move in to our new premises with little or no financial worries. It was imperative that we find new premises since we had outgrown our small accommodation on Cowley Road long ago. The new centre, as it stands now, serves a variety of purposes. It is a large hall for all of our big speaker meetings, daily *shiurim* and Friday-night meals for about forty students a week; it is a full-time shule; and it houses a Hebrew and English Jewish library, offices in which to run the Chabad House and the L'Chaim Society, and a kosher kitchen to serve all our events that require catering, including Shabbat. If any of these facilities were missing we would not be able to provide such a comprehensive service to our students and the community.

The Show Must Go On

After about seven months of intense preparation, sleepless nights and countless phone conversations with the President's Office, and barely two and a half weeks before the event, they phoned us to say that due to 'an unavoidable schedule change the President would not be able to attend on the appointed date'. I received this information at our Simchas Beis Hashoeiva Celebration, one of the most festive of all Jewish occasions, on 26 September, 18 Tishrei.

We were shocked and distressed at this terrible news. Yet I believe that one of the most important things a rabbi and communal leader must train himself to do is not to let personal feelings interfere with work. At that Simchas Beis Hashoeiva we had to use all our will power to show joy at a time of such seeming hopelessness and pain. With one swift move, we were threatened with losing not only an important speaker, but also seven months of hard work and tens of thousands of pounds in addition to our credibility throughout the city. We were shattered; but we had to try to salvage what we could from this disaster.

Our concern throughout this very difficult time was to go ahead with our proposed new centre, notwithstanding the extraordinary amount of funding and sponsorship that had been lost. We spent the next few days trying whatever means possible to secure a speaker to perform the opening so that we could go ahead. This proved to be a real challenge because there were less than two weeks to the appointed date.

A Ray of Hope

When we were faced with the problem of finding a replacement for Ronald Reagan, I thought of inviting Mr Ariel Sharon, but I was not sure that he could come on such short notice. During the summer I had been to Israel and visited Benjamin Netanyahu today the leader of the Israeli opposition Likud party with whom I had become close since the time he lectured for us in Oxford. While I was there he gave me an entry pass for the VIP lounge at the Knesset; I used this opportunity to invite some politicians, including Moshe Arens, David Levy and Prime Minister Yitzhak Shamir, to Oxford. Another minister I spoke to was Mr Sharon, who agreed to come at some future date, but no specific time was mentioned.

In our time of crisis, we turned to Professor Herman Branover, a world-renowned physicist living in Israel, whom we knew had good connections with Ariel Sharon and other members of the government. Professor Branover said he would immediately set himself to work on it. Within a few hours he called back to tell me that Ariel Sharon would probably consent to replace Ronald Reagan.

Smiling through the Tears

Once again we needed to organize the media, security and venue, as the college which had agreed to let us use their hall for Ronald Reagan was not ready to do the same for Sharon. A local Palestinian group announced that they would be bringing in one thousand Palestinian students from London to demonstrate and protest against Sharon's lecture. We therefore had a large security problem on our hands.

At precisely this time, amidst mammoth difficulties and obstacles, we finished negotiating a lease for our new student centre in central Oxford. Unfortunately this triumph was marred by the total collapse of the financial backing which was to have alleviated the pressure experienced in taking on the new centre.

As a result of moving into the new centre and outfitting it with all the necessities (a kitchen, offices, shelving for the library, and the holy ark) we were heavily in debt, with very little prospect of paying for it. We hoped to obtain the support of the community so that we could meet our financial obligations with the least possible difficulty, and to be able to concentrate our efforts on teaching Judaism and retaining an active programme attended by many students and academics. The cancellation did not prove fatal because the support of sympathetic individuals was quickly given to us.

All the preparations for the centre had to be finished in about six days for Ariel Sharon's visit. We had builders working twenty-one hours a day to meet the deadline and, thank God, everything – including the plumbing, electricity and gas – was finished on time.

The Good List and the Bad List

There was a lot of controversy surrounding Mr Sharon's visit. Many of our financial supporters and student officers told us we were making a mistake in inviting him because he was extremely controversial. In the event his speech was moderate and impressed everyone; he is not the devil he has been portrayed as. And if he is, he hid it well when he spoke at the Union. It was certainly one of the largest student lecture ever to take place at the University of Oxford. It was absolutely packed and there was a horde of journalists to record the event. By some strange quirk of fortune, this was the day that the then United States Secretary of State, James Baker, announced that he had finally persuaded the Israelis and the Arabs to sit down and meet each other in Madrid and begin peace negotiations. Mr Sharon was the only Israeli minister who was saying openly that 'this will not be a peace conference, but a war conference'. His point was that if Israel were to cede any land, they would put themselves in such a weak position so as to invite Arab attack.

Extracting Good from Evil

Nevertheless, even before we knew his visit was going to be such a success we decided to bring him. This was based on the following: there is a tendency today to blacklist and character-assassinate people purely because of one or two facets of their personality. We tend to see people as either good or bad, and as soon as someone does something bad they are given the label, A Bad Person. Because of this there are rarely any people we can look up to and respect, because every person in the eyes of the media does something wrong once, and as soon as they do we immediately write them off our Good Person lists.

People Are Not Monolithic

Judaism doesn't see people that way. It refuses to consider complex human beings as monolithic or homogeneous. Judaism maintains that every person has a good impulse and an evil impulse. So when a human does something praiseworthy it is coming from the good side of him or her, and wrongdoing comes from the bad side. In the language of Jewish mysticism, every person has a Godly soul and an animal soul, good being motivated by the former and evil by the latter. So now we can differentiate; when someone does something bad he or she is not bad in totality, it is but one part of them which inclines towards evil. So even if someone does something bad we can still embrace their goodness because it is separate and they are divisible.

The point is that we invited Sharon to show that there was a good side to him which had to be embraced; we promoted the fact that he was a great general. In the opinion of some his greatest mistake was that he went into politics. They contend that he should have remained in the army rather than become a politician. We invited him because of the contribution he has made to people and the deliverance he made time and time again. The same is true of every other human being. We can't just dismiss someone because they do a bad thing. First of all if we do that we would dismiss everybody; secondly it contradicts the whole concept of virtue. Virtue means that human beings have a virtuous side and then a negative side. It is possible to embrace them and promote the side of them that you can agree with. In the case of Sharon what this meant was that although some might criticise his politics, they certainly should acknowledge his great military achievements, and the noble way in which he served the Jewish people.

Unorthodox Jewish Views and Speakers

This is a philosophy that the L'Chaim Society has always adopted. That is why we bring people like Dennis Prager to speak here: a renowned figure in the USA, the author of *Why the Jews? The Reason for Anti-Semitism* and *The Nine Questions People Ask Most about Judaism*. A lot of my Lubavitch colleagues have said to me that we should not bring him because he has written many articles saying that all three denominations of Judaism, namely Orthodox, Conservative and Reform, are legitimate. He also maintains many non-halakhic opinions on Jewish matters which contradict Jewish law; for example, he believes that Jewish law has to be modified in many ways and must be subject to modification in the course of time. Having said this, he has spoken for us twice, and the reason we invite him over and over again is that he has some extraordinary arguments to persuade people why they should take their Judaism seriously, and give it another look. Our audiences were always enthralled by his arguments. That is the side of him we embrace. I told Dennis that of course there will always be things about which we disagree, but there are also matters about which we not only agree, but which are at the forefront of explaining our shared faith.

No Hypocrisy

I encourage students to appreciate that their lack of observance of Judaism cannot contradict the possibility of them doing what they really should do. One of the main things I ask students to do is to keep Shabbat in whatever way possible. I tell them they should try to make Friday night into Shabbat. During term time that is very easy; all they have to do is come to us and they keep Shabbat, and thank God we have regulars who come every week. The problem is that the university term is only eight weeks long and then there is a six-week break between terms and a fifteen-week break over summer. We tell them that in the vacations they should consider, wherever they are and even if they are not religious, how they can make Friday night into Shabbat to keep it holy. It may only be something as simple as a woman lighting a Shabbat candle, or a man making kiddush.

Making Kiddush in a Non-kosher Restaurant

Even if you are sitting with your friends in a non-kosher restaurant or with your family watching television, pick up a cup of wine and say the kiddush for the Shabbat: 'Blessed be the Lord our God who has given us the fruit of the vine.' Sure enough, one of our students came back from vacation and told me he had done this. He was with his parents in France in December, eating in a non-kosher steak house, and he remembered what I had said about making Friday night a Shabbat, so in front of his parents he picked up a glass of wine and said the blessing. A lot of people would argue that this is hypocrisy because he was sitting in a non-kosher restaurant. They would argue that he could not have been keeping Shabbat. What I tried to convey to him was that, because there is a distinct good side and bad side, he can make those few minutes of Shabbat with no contradiction or hypocrisy. His non-observances do not contradict the things he does keep.

When I was a student in Jerusalem I passionately believed in this principle. Every Friday night I would go up to Rechov ben Yehuda, the main tourist thoroughfare in Jerusalem, and I and my friends would put on *tefillin* with people. Once I stopped a man walking up the thoroughfare to ask if he had put on *tefillin* today, and he said, 'No.' I said, 'It is right before Shabbat, why don't you put on *tefillin*?' He just laughed and chuckled. He showed me a pitta bread in his right hand and said, 'This is not just a pitta bread with falafel, this has pork [literally "white meat"] in it. How could I put on *tefillin* when I am holding pork in my right hand?' I said to him, 'Of course you can, because your left hand is free.' So while he was holding his pork sandwich, we quickly put on *tefillin* with him. And there was no contradiction, because man is animated by two distinct impulses.

This is a very important message which we promote. People should keep whatever they can keep; they should not feel themselves to be hypocrites when they lapse, because the side of them which is drawn to Judaism is the Godly soul and the side which is drawn to materialism, vanity and wanting to rid society of religious obligations is a completely different side of them.

This means that nobody is ever a hypocrite, ever a 'bad' person doing good things. Secondly it is an important lesson to us that it is possible to divide and separate out someone's good side without being encumbered with their evil. This is why we decided to host Mr Sharon. Mr Sharon is controversial because he is very right-wing, and people don't like his politics. They consider he is a racist, and that he was responsible for the Sabra and Shatilla massacre in Lebanon in the wake of the Lebanon war (it was proved by the independent Kahan commission that he was certainly not directly responsible, although he was held responsible for not assuming the intentions of the Christian Philangists, who perpetrated the massacre, when they went into the refugee camp). Be that as it may, even if all these terrible things were true, and I personally dispute them one cannot forget what he did for the Jewish people, which is the good side of him that we had to respect. That is why we decided to invite him.

An Inspiration

When Ariel Sharon spoke at the Oxford Union, the room was packed. The debating chamber holds close to a thousand people, and there were about eight hundred in a different hall watching his speech live on video monitors. There was one large demonstration outside, but nothing too significant; the promised thousand students never arrived. Sharon even remarked on the fact that there were so few demonstrators to 'greet' him.

I introduced his speech by reminding the audience of the positive things he has achieved for the Jewish people . . .

'Today indeed is a very special occasion not just for the Jewish residents of Oxford, but for the Jewish community the world over. In medieval times, Oxford was a town with a thriving Jewish community. Many of the venerable buildings that you all know in Oxford today, such as Magdalen College and Christ Church, were actually built on sites which were very significant to the Jewish community. Magdalen College was built where the community buried their dead; Christ Church was built on the site of the Jewish synagogue; and the site of the new student centre in Carfax was actually a Jewish House of Study. All that ended when the Jews were expelled from England in 1290 and their lands were confiscated. And here is the reason for the importance of this occasion; today after 701 years the Jewish community finally returns to a permanent dwelling in the part of Oxford city centre which once was called Great Jewry Street.

'It was very important to us in marking this special occasion that a figure of suitable renown, symbolic of the highest peaks of Jewish courage and the greatest Jewish uprightness, should represent our society and deliver the inaugural address.'

Ariel Sharon's Life

'Ariel Sharon was born in 1928 and was one year old when the slaughter of the Jews of Hebron and the other riots in the Holy Land began. In 1942 he joined the Haganah, the fledgling Israeli defence forces, and in 1948 he fought in the War of Independence and was badly wounded near La Trune in an attempt to break the Arab siege of the old city of Jerusalem.

'With the establishment of the Jewish state, the man who was later to become General Sharon quickly rose through the ranks of the IDF. In 1953, with terrorist attacks raging across Israel, the Israeli Chief of Staff, Moshe Dayan, decided that reprisals were necessary. He commissioned the young Israeli officer Ariel Sharon to put together the first Israeli commando assault unit, soon to become the extraordinary Unit 101. General Sharon, as a commander of Unit 101, has become legendary. So sophisticated and so successful were his military exploits that General Moshe Dayan quickly appointed him Head of Israel's paratroopers, so that the aggressive posture which he gave to Unit 101 would permeate those forces in the Israeli military. Hence you have the fame of the Israeli paratroopers today.'

The Battle Cry: 'Follow Me'

'General Sharon substituted the famous battle cry of all military leaders to their soldiers, "Go out and fight" with "Follow me!" This has become the creed of the Israeli command to this very day. He also taught every Israeli commander that there would not be a single incursion into occupied territory in which a wounded soldier or body was left behind. All Israeli soldiers are returned to their homeland.

'At twenty-nine, Ariel Sharon became Israel's youngest-ever colonel. Just prior to the Six Day War he became a major general, and in the Six Day War he, while commanding an armoured division, broke through the Egyptian defences, opening up the stage that led to the great victory of the Six Day War.'

War and Peace

'But it was not until the Yom Kippur War broke out on 6 October 1973 that Ariel Sharon became the legend he is today. Israel was taken by surprise and the prospects were terrible. I still remember as a young child in Los Angeles the demoralization of the Jewish community around the world when Israel was attacked. On 8 October Israel quickly launched a counter-offensive which failed miserably. The morale of the soldiers was very low; this looked like the final moment for Israel, God forbid. So much so that Moshe Dayan, the Defence Minister at the time, came to Golda Meir with his hands in the air and said, "This is the destruction of the third Temple." But on 15 October General Ariel Sharon, commanding the reserved armoured division, decided to put into effect his great plan of crossing the Suez Canal and opening up a war against Egypt on two fronts, also reasoning that he could threaten Cairo and cause the Egyptian advance forces to pull back hastily to defend their capital. He crossed the canal and quickly out-flanked the Egyptian Third Army, cutting off all of their supplies and opening up Cairo to the Israeli Army. It was then that President Anwar Sadat pushed for a cease-fire, which took place at exactly 101 kilometres from Cairo, thus forever linking the victory with Sharon, original commander of Unit 101. Israel was saved.

'But before I go on, I must say that many people prior to this lecture said to me, "How can you have General Ariel Sharon speak about peace?" I think it is fitting that he should do so: it was because of his actions in the 1973 war that peace negotiations took place at all. General Silasio, the UN observer, who presided over the talks for the cease-fire at kilometre 101 near Cairo, said at the beginning of these talks,

"*A sa ka resh*" – 'The cease-fire is the beginning of the talks of the peace process.'

'This was confirmed by Sadat himself when he came to Jerusalem a few years later. He was greeted at the airport by the Israeli senior representatives, including the Prime Minister Menachem Begin, and the first thing he said when he walked off the plane was, "Where is Sharon? I have to see Sharon!" He did see Sharon, and he said to him, "You don't know how much I wished to capture you when you were in Egypt, when you had the immense courage to break through the canal, right into the ferocity of Egypt." General Sharon's breakthrough frustrated Egypt's plans of ever defeating Israel militarily, and so Sadat was coaxed to the negotiating table.

'General Sharon later assumed many ministerial portfolios, the first being Minister of Agriculture. Then as Minister of Defence in 1981 he initiated the controversial war in Lebanon and now, as Israel's Housing Minister, he is active in settling the land of Israel and making it possible for the huge influx of Russian refugees to be established in Israel.

During his lecture he thanked the Lubavitcher rebbe, Rabbi Menachem Schneerson, on behalf of the government of Israel for all the work he does in Israel and around the world. He also made reference to the terrible rioting which had then taken place recently in Brooklyn's Crown Heights. One of the recurring themes throughout the talk was that the most important thing for a Jew was to be and act Jewishly.

Following his talk, Mr Sharon answered many questions in a professional and convincing manner. After that I presented him with a silver menorah as a gift. Even students who are his detractors later told me that Sharon's dignity and pride was infectious, and made them feel proud too of their Judaism and the land of Israel.

The Opening Ceremony

When Mr Sharon left the hall he walked down the street to our new centre and officially opened our building. He put up a mezuzah on the outside door (this was broadcast on national television), and together with one of the founders of the centre he cut the ribbon, opening the doorway. The ceremony was especially memorable since the police stopped traffic in the city centre for a few moments, a very rare occurrence, and hundreds of people from the lecture followed us back to the building.

After being taken upstairs, Mr Sharon held some interviews with television journalists; then we held a celebratory lunch (also in the centre) which was attended by many leading Oxford professors and academics, as well as Anglo-Jewish businessmen and dignitaries, including the lord mayor of Oxford.

We also held a press conference which was attended by at least thirty different media groups: there were representatives from Israeli papers, British press and television (the BBC and Channel 4) and amongst many others ABC News and the *New York Times*. The MBC (Middle East Broadcasting Company) transmitted the lecture and press conference to seven Arab countries. The entire event turned out to be very successful.

Chapter Thirty-one

REFORM AND ORTHODOX JUDAISM:
ARE THEY EQUAL EXPRESSIONS OF JUDAISM?

The majority of Oxford undergraduates arrive at the age of eighteen or nineteen, but because Oxford is one of the few British universities with no lower age limit, some are only seventeen when they leave home to study. Of course some are even younger, the child prodigy Ruth Lawrence being the most famous case in recent years. She obtained her doctorate before most people even think of applying for a higher education place, and was teaching the most advanced mathematics to people far older than herself.

For the vast majority, the university years bring unprecedented liberty, but those who are particularly young when they come up reveal that freedom to be somewhat of a false idol. Nearly everyone says that it is great to be released from the yoke of parental authority, but what does it mean to be free?

One particular student came to Oxford when she had just turned seventeen. She was from a small town in the West Country and had never left her home county before except for a supervised trip to the theatre in London during her last year of school. Her parents had been very strict with her, and her school had been stricter still, so the freedom of college life was a complete novelty. She went rather wild in her first year, drinking every night in the bar, dating all kinds of unworthy men, and getting into scrapes with the college authorities.

One of her most memorable escapades was her trip out of town one night. Blind drunk, she decided that she had to go for a walk, so she left the college at dead of night. Now most female undergraduates are wary of walking alone in the city after 10 p.m., but she had lost all fear in her drunken state. Fortunately, nothing more unpleasant happened to her than the realization, as she slowly sobered up, that she had no idea where she was. She had in fact walked so far that she had reached the Rover car factory at Cowley, and she had a long walk back to college because there were no buses at that time of the morning.

The sequel to this is more revealing, though. Most students are on some level rather afraid of the choices that face them during and after studying for a degree. But she acted out these fears and made them obvious to all around her. In her second year she rejected all the freedom she had worked so hard to attain. Every night of the week she would stay in studying, and as she spurned her college friends she came to rely more and more on her boyfriend from home, a heavy drinker who lost job after job because he could not keep his temper. In the end, she gave up her degree to live with this man, who was ten years older than her, and she spent all her time running around after him and trying to earn a bit of money to support the two of them. She had been so frightened at the availability of the liberty to do anything she wanted that she decided to reject it completely.

Hers was an extreme case, but it is not unusual. Apparently, the opportunities freedom give are not always the gift they seem to be, and sometimes what we tend to think of as freedom is just another form of slavery. So the idea of liberty is an important one, not least because students tend to complain that the religion they were brought up in is an imposition on them from outside.

Secular Humanism

Some feel the solution is to embrace a watered-down version of their old faith; here I am thinking particularly of Reform Judaism, but sometimes their choice is to use the old faith for the basis of some variety of humanism. To be sure, for many Jews the world over, Reform Judaism offers a means by which to identify with and embrace the ancient traditions of Judaism. Still we must question to what extent Reform Judaism has the essence and not just the flavour, of the original. Although I have no problem with people thinking about what their faith means to them, I am wary of those who call a faith which has radically changed from the original by the name 'Judaism', as though it carries with it the tradition of three millennia. Incidentally, like my seventeen-year-old friend who felt that the freedom to choose was in fact no freedom, I see Reform Judaism as more of a restriction on thought and action than the ancient tenets of Orthodoxy.

So we held a debate in an attempt to get to the heart of the Jewish students' response to their faith and the Torah. This particular Point-Counter-Point revolved around the question of whether Reform and Liberal Judaism are valid alternatives to Orthodox Judaism. As with other debates, I tried to guide the students through their own questions to a better appreciation of what Judaism is really about, but first I gave an outline of the reasons why I feel the Torah, and the faith which interprets it, Orthodox Judaism, are unchangeable.

The External Torah

Maimonides, the great Jewish thinker, codifier and doctor, was the first to set down principles which he distinguished as the cardinal tenets of Jewish faith. The Eternal Torah is Article IX of his thirteen principles: the Torah of Moses will never be nullified, nor will another Torah come from the Almighty besides this one; nothing will be added to it nor deleted from it, not in the written nor in the oral law. As it says, 'you shall neither add thereto nor detract therefrom.'

According to Maimonides, one of the central beliefs of Judaism is that human beings have no right to add anything to or delete anything from the Torah. We should ask what makes this a cardinal article of our faith. It is understandable that believing there is a God should be a basic principle of Jewish faith, and believing that God gave the Torah is understandable too; but why should we not change the Torah? That is the centre of the arguments about the validity of Reform Judaism.

Adaptation and Treatment

Let me play the devil's advocate for a while to point out under what conditions the Torah *ought* to change. First the analogy of a doctor. Any good doctor knows that you must monitor the progress of a patient. You can't rely on information that you picked up two weeks ago, you have constantly to monitor his or her current state. You should change the treatment depending on whether they are getting better or worse, but just to continue a prescription without monitoring its effects on the patient is dangerous and unprofessional.

The same applies in the parent–child relationship. When we speak about 'educating' our children we do not think of using the same process in all situations, because of course not all forms of education are suitable for every child at every age. You have to understand children individually before you can teach them effectively. There is no point in teaching your children not to say rude things to people if they can't even talk yet. You change your approach to your child according to his or her mental capacities, personality, progress and maturity.

Parents and doctors must constantly be in touch with their children and patients to make sure the nurturing or the treatment is right, because medical care and parenting are concerned with the welfare of the recipient, not the donor.

In other words, if the Torah was given for the perfection of humanity and the world, then the Torah would be expected to adapt to the huge transformations we know have happened as human civilization has run its course. If that were the case, surely we should be monitoring the state of the human race constantly, and the Torah should be changed accordingly.

Consider the computer game, *Civilization*. When people are savages, the player has to take a particularly tough line with them: they are ruled by despots because democracy would not get things done which are necessary to survive. All kinds of punishments are apparently acceptable because the people are not necessarily open to a message of morality; perhaps you can't simply speak to them about it, you have to force it upon them. As civilization progresses and matures, then you can speak more about purpose and meaning, and give new kinds of laws which are specifically adapted to the needs of that group of people at that time.

Why People Want the Torah to Change

The Torah completely rejects the strategy of adapting to change, even amidst great social upheaval. The immutability of the Torah seems a flaw in many people's eyes, because it seems to ignore the fact that people are not always the same, and that different ages need different messages. But why do people want to modify the Torah?

I ask this because I believe when we understand this, we can see why people have looked at alternatives to tradition, why people have felt justified in embracing an apparently more human, satisfying and socially appetizing Judaism. The sole premise behind modifying eternal truths is the belief that the Torah was given for our benefit. That God spoke to Moses and to a nation of two and a half million people at Mount Sinai three thousand three hundred years ago because He wanted to develop the human race, because He sought for us to climb the mountain of spirituality and holiness. The underlying premise is that the Torah would not have existed unless we existed before it. These thinkers maintain that the purpose of the Torah was to perfect humanity.

The Creation of the Torah

But the Torah was not given for the human race. Never in Jewish literature does it say so: on the contrary, throughout the Talmud, even in the five books of Moses, the picture painted by our prophets through Godly revelation has always been that we were created to fulfil the Torah, that we must subject ourselves to eternal truths, that truth cannot be modified in accordance with our needs.

For instance, the Talmud says, 'The Torah preceded the world by 2,000 years.' Although the time element is difficult to understand – why specifically 2,000 years? – and there are many kabbalistic answers, there is no question that the Torah preceded the world. People and the world were created as an arena, as a means by which to have the Torah fulfilled.

To be sure, there are many statements throughout the Mishnah and the Talmud such as '*Lo nitna ha'Torah elah letzaref es habriyos*', the Torah was given in order to *letzaref*, meaning to 'connect', humankind together, bring about human understanding. Other pronouncements indicate that the Torah was given to perfect mankind, but that is not the reason it was given, that is the truth of what the Torah does. Still, it is not a central premise, but a mere corollary.

A Tool or a Truth?

Many people believe that Judaism is about self-development. They say it is nice to have a Friday night table on Shabbat because it means all the family can come together once a week. Although that might be a beautiful by-product, and some people might even use that as their main reason for fulfilling the Shabbat, it still doesn't make it the reason it was instituted. Saying that God gave us Shabbat to bring the family together, for instance, that Shabbat is a tool we use to bring about human unity, is like saying that other human beings were created for my purposes. The fact that there is another human being in this world does not mean they were made for me, even though without another human being I could never talk or know love or any other emotion. The fact that the other person develops things which are intrinsic to me as a human being does not mean they were created for me. Similarly the Torah was not created for the expedient needs of humanity.

The Torah might bring about self-development, and living a Torah life might make you a more perfect human being, but those are by-products. The Torah is an end in itself; we try to live according to it because it is truth, and we are supposed to subject ourselves to truth.

If you simply invert the common belief that religion was given for us to better ourselves, and take the opposite view, that we were created so that we could apprehend truth, then you would understand that no modification in civilization, no modification in mankind, could ever change, could ever necessitate a modification of Judaism.

For example, there are two kinds of will known to human beings, internal and external will. Internal will has no ulterior motive. External will has an underlying real reason. Many people go to work, and earn money, but how many people seriously enjoy their work? They work for the pay cheque at the end of the week. That is external will. But internal will is the will to live itself. Can anyone explain why they want to live? You can't explain, it is something intrinsic to our very beings, our very identity. We do everything for that purpose. And that is what the Torah is to God; it is not an external will, He did not give the Torah for humankind, He wanted the Torah fulfilled. He wanted truth to be established for ever, by human beings; His intrinsic will was not for the truth to be used by human beings to better themselves. But the closer we come to truth, the more effort we make to apprehend it, then the more exalted we become.

Why do we automatically assume that Judaism was given for us? I believe that it has much to do with the fact that we are enmeshed in a society that has been dominated for centuries by Christian thinking.

Is God a Means or an End?

Judaism and Christianity have very different orientations towards God and religion. It is summed up in the theory of the seventeenth-century French thinker, Blaise Pascal. He theorized that in a world where no one could know for sure whether God exists, your best bet is to believe in [the Christian] God. His reasoning, called Pascal's Wager, went something like this. Suppose God does not exist; then when I die and enter oblivion (because there is no God-created hell or heaven to punish or reward me), I will have lost very little by believing in a God who turned out not to exist. But suppose God does exist and I omit to believe in Him while I am on earth; what a disaster! Straight to hell for eternity. Obviously, in such a universe, it is best to believe in God on the off-chance, because if not you could be in for a very unpleasant after-life. Of course, Pascal was a man whose thinking was entirely dominated by the idea of reward and punishment.

Christianity tends to emphasize that Jesus is a means to salvation; God is not an end in Himself. And though no one would say it, when you start to speak constantly of the need to find grace, what you are saying is that your God is a path to the real destiny, which is salvation. This thinking led to all kinds of bizarre heresies in the early Church, such as the idea that if salvation was achieved through the forgiveness of sins, the more you sinned the more you would be forgiven, so go out there and sin as much as possible and you could be forgiven even more.

That was never the Jewish understanding of God or Godliness! We believe that God is an end in Himself, and His Torah is an end in itself. This means that the Torah should never be abused by our thinking it exists for our benefit.

Debating Change

At this point the real debate started.

SB: Anyone in the audience who would like to make the case for the viability of an alternative to Orthodox Judaism can by all means do so, because this is not a class, it's a debate.
Q: Surely some things have changed in Judaism over the centuries?
SB: Yes, things have changed, but not the Torah. The reason is that there are two kinds of laws: biblical decrees given by God himself through direct revelation to Moses, and rabbinical decrees, which serve as a fence around

the laws to ensure we don't transgress a biblical command. Distinguishing between the two is extremely important.

According to Rebbe Elizar's commentary on the Talmud, Eve sinned in the garden of Eden because Adam did not distinguish between the fence around the law and the law itself. God commanded Adam, 'But of the tree of the knowledge of good and evil, thou shalt not eat . . .', and if they did 'thou shalt surely die' (Genesis 2:17). But Adam did not prohibit Eve simply from eating; instead he said, *Don't touch the Tree.* He told her that God had forbidden people from touching it. He figured, Look, if she touches it, she'll see that it's good food and she'll eat it. I'll tell her, Don't touch it! He made a fence around the law, which is perfectly accceptable. And praiseworthy. But he didn't tell her that it was his fence around God's law, he told her it was God's command. So later, she sinned. The snake came along and said, 'Why don't you eat from the Tree?' Eve said, 'Eat from it? I can't even touch it or I'll die.' So he pushed her into it, and she touched it, and she was still alive. And so he said to her, 'You see, just as this was a lie, so too if you eat it you also won't die.' And Eve ate from the tree of knowledge of good and evil.

Ever since then, Jews have been very careful to distinguish between rabbinical commands, the fence around the law, and Torah commands, the law itself. For instance, I am not allowed to touch a light switch on Shabbat because I might turn it on – but that is a rabbinical decree. It is nothing to do with the Torah. And wearing a yarmulka is not a law, but a rabbinical enactment. The rabbis are given the authority by the Torah to do so as long as they make it clear that these are rabbinical decrees. The headcovering that a Jew wears, a yarmulka, is a contraction of two Aramaic terms from the Talmud, *yoreh* and *malka*, fear of the king. It is the ultimate sign of humility, telling everyone that your intelligence, the highest human faculty, is dominated by something even higher; you always remember God's law. I believe this is why the Pope wears it as well.

DAN W: These rabbis draw up rules about light switches. I doubt light switches are ever mentioned in the Torah because light switches didn't exist then. Surely they are adjusting the Torah to modern-day circumstances, so why shouldn't Reform rabbis do the same thing? If the rabbis apply that as a new rule of modern-day Shabbat observance, why shouldn't Reform rabbis?

SB: No, no. The rabbis never applied a new principle, the rabbis extended the same principle which prohibits us from lighting a fire to turning on a switch. For instance, when the first heart transplants were performed, the rabbis forbade it because of the principle in Halakha that you may not do anything which could shorten life. The operation was so risky; people were living two weeks and dying, it was better to live for six years with a heart with a hole in it than take a chance and die. So it was forbidden. But later heart transplantation became far more successful, then the pronouncement on heart transplants changed, the law didn't change. The principle that you can't shorten life remained the same. Now, when nine out of ten people live longer after a heart transplant, the principle will dictate that you can have a transplant. That is the point. It is the same principle which follows through in many different circumstances. Of course, I am using this only as an example, and to date heart-transplantation is still forbidden in Jewish law which only recognises cardio-respiratory death as opposed to brain-death as the legitimate criteria for death.

The Torah is an eternal Torah because of its skeletal structure; it deals with principles. And those principles have to be applied to modern-day society without their essential truths being compromised. It is like the USA Congress; there is a constitution, which must be interpreted by the people whom the constitution itself gives authority to, and applied to modern-day dilemmas. For instance, the constitution states that every person should have the right to bear arms, but now in America four hundred people die each week from hand-gun deaths; did they mean the right to bear arms even if it led to a greater danger to American society? You have to take a principle and apply it.

Parenthetically, the difference between the Torah and the United States constitution is that not only is the Torah based on principles, but there are even principles on how to apply principles. Very exact ones, and only someone who is extremely competent in Jewish law can do that. If you are an expert in what you do then you have a right to apply it. And that makes sense; for instance, if a student hadn't gone to medical school for six or seven years, I wouldn't go to see him or her as a doctor. So many people say to me, 'If a rabbi can do this [interpret the law] then I can do it.' Sure you can. If you become a rabbi you can. But it is like saying that because a doctor can write a prescription I can too, and you can't – you'll end up doing more damage than good.

When Moses said we must fulfil the law even when it hurts, he was saying that ultimately it is good for us. It is like a doctor saying to you, 'The pill tastes lousy but I guarantee you it is for your own good.' Although that might be a reason for some people fulfilling the Torah, it is not the definition of what the Torah is. It is not a therapeutic Jewish means by which we can achieve self-development: that is like saying that God is here for our benefit.

At the end of the day, what is the Torah? Its essence is that it is God's wisdom, God's commandments. God is healing, God is meaningful, God gives people purpose in their lives, but that does not mean that God was created to heal us, teach us or make us more whole. God and His Torah are one, and just as you cannot say that God is a means to an end, you can't say that the Torah is a means to an end.

The Torah is an end in itself, but its potency is such that it has the power to enhance the quality of human life. But at the end of the day, that is not its essence. Is the Torah something that God dreamed up to make you a better person? It is like saying, if you have a psychiatrist who helps you, that means that she or he was created for you! That is a dangerous attitude to take to things as important as people or the Torah.

Intrinsic Relationship between God and Humanity

I believe that we have been indoctrinated by our society to believe that religion is about self-development. It is not. Religion is about achieving proximity to God and approaching a truth. And that has always been the Jewish quality of it. Certainly Maimonides explains Judaism throughout his writings as the pinnacle of human attainment, the knowledge of God.

There are many arguments for Reform and Liberal Judaism, but I think the gist is what I have heard from many of the Reform rabbis I have spoken to: we need a more palatable Judaism, a Judaism which is not so strict. It is better to increase our numbers than lose a lot of people along the way because it is too demanding or a bit antiquated. For the sake of preserving the greater whole sometimes you have to forfeit or sacrifice some of the less important features.

The problem with this argument is deciding how to distinguish between an essential feature and a non-essential feature. By whose jurisdiction do you make those decisions? How do you know that when you make a compromise you haven't essentially, irrevocably, compromised something to which you cannot return? For example, when Reform Judaism started in Germany, most Reform temples celebrated the Sabbath on Sunday. They retained Jewish observance but on a different day – and I would call this compromising essence. What is the spirit of Judaism? This is the question that lies at the heart of Reform Judaism.

The Reform approach forgets that Orthodox Judaism has no problem with the Jew who feels that Jewish observance is just too backward and unappealing to one's personal taste. We have no problem with the person rejecting those elements which to him or her are repugnant or unacceptable or which they are too lazy to perform. If you want to put those parts on ice and say this is not for me, then fine, and in the meantime observe what you feel you are capable of, then at least it is something wholesome. If you feel uncomfortable on Shabbat, then keep Passover, if you feel uncomfortable with *tefillin*, so pray without *tefillin*.

We don't believe the Torah to be one massive whole, that if you reject part of it, you reject all of it. It is six hundred and thirteen separate commandments and each commandment is a world unto itself; it is a separate entity, and nothing compromises the other. But to argue, 'Look, I can't keep Shabbat because I work on Saturday, therefore I will keep it on Tuesday,' is keeping nothing at all. That is the difference between compromising essence and just making things more convenient. If you want to make it more convenient and say I cannot keep Shabbat because I work, then keep one hour of Shabbat. I have a friend who got involved in the Chabad House three years ago. He is today working in London. He can't keep Shabbat because he works part of the time; he keeps it when he is not working. He keeps it two hours a day, and for those two he doesn't turn on lights, for those two hours he is absolutely keeping Shabbat and making it holy, just as God commanded him. The fact that the other twenty-two hours he is not has nothing to do with it. We should value the importance of a good act unto itself. But we mistakenly believe that we are hypocrites when we do something like that.

When you pass by beggars asking for money on the street, do you give them money every time? No, no one does. Does that mean that if you see someone who is honestly hungry you say, 'I really want to feed you and I have money in my pocket, but I won't because I don't want to be a hypocrite. I didn't do it yesterday'? There should never be any reason good or bad, even for reasons of self-justification, to prevent oneself from advancing the cause of humanity by doing a positive act or a spiritual act or a Godly act.

So my response to people who feel that Judaism is antiquated, that the synagogue should not have a *mechitza* (traditional separation of the sexes in synagogue) because men and women want to sit together, is this: instead of doing something halfway or modifying it so that you lose its essence, do those things which are acceptable to you and see. Maybe it will grow on you. Judaism believes that one mitzvah creates another mitzvah, one leads to another. But I believe it is a bit of a cop-out to say let us change it and make it more digestible; how do you know you haven't compromised essence?

What are the historical background to and implications of Reform Judaism? Admittedly, it is very difficult to trust any one historian when it comes to questions of Jewish observances and Jewish practices. Depending upon which denomination of Jew is writing the history, the account will lean one way or the other. An Orthodox historian will subconsciously lean towards the wholesomeness of Orthodoxy, a Reform Jew will lean subconsciously towards the enlightenment of Reform Judaism. It is very difficult, and I have read many different books on Jewish history, and each one gives almost a different account on the need that these different strands on Judaism served in any given age. So what I choose to do is quote to you from a highly respectable history of the Jews known to me that was written by a non-Jew. That is Paul Johnson's *History of the Jews*:

> Enlightened Jews are ashamed of their traditional services. The dead
> weight of the past, the lack of intellectual content, the noisy and unseemly
> manner in which Orthodox Jews prayed. In Protestant countries, for
> Christians to visit a synagogue was quite fashionable and provoked
> contempt and pity. Hence Reform Judaism was, in the first place, an
> attempt to remove the taint and ridicule from Jewish forms of worship.
> In 1819 the Hamburg temple introduced a new prayer book and the
> aesthetic changes spread to more fundamental matters. If liturgical
> habits could be discarded because they were embarrassing why not
> absurd and inconvenient doctrines? The mention of the Messiah was
> dropped, so was the return to the Holy Land. The idea was to purify
> and re-energize Judaism in the same spirit as Luther's Reformation. But
> there was an important difference; alas Luther was not constantly looking
> over his shoulders at what other people were doing and copying them.
> Reform Judaism was animated less by overwhelming conviction than by
> social tidy-mindedness and the desire to be more an artificial construct,
> like so many idealistic schemes of the 19th century.

Paul Johnson goes on to demonstrate that everything was done out of
reaction to what the non-Jew would say about the services that were being
introduced. He analyses the pronouncements of Rabbi Abraham Geiger, for
all practical purposes the father of Reform Judaism and certainly its most
important founder. Geiger was just trying to show there was no consistency
in what he was doing because it was a response to some outside external
source, which was gazing down on him. 'He upholds prayers in Hebrew, but
would not eliminate it from the services, he thought circumcision a barbaric
act of blood-letting but opposed its abolition. He sanctioned some breaches
of the Sabbath prohibitions but he would not scrap the Sabbath principle
entirely and adopt a Christian Sunday. He omitted passages on the return
to Zion and other references to what he regarded as out-dated historical
conditions, but he would not bring himself to surrender the principle of
Mosaic law. He tried to extract from the vast accumulated mass of Judaic
belief what he called the religious universal element.'

The point is that Reform Judaism has undergone deep transformation
over the past two hundred years, and it is not a transformation which tries
to retain the essence of Judaism but rather one which tries to create a special
ethos to suit the needs of the time. Even if that will compromise, irrevocably,
the essence of Judaism. For example, anyone who knows anything about
Reform Judaism knows one of the most distinguishing characteristics of
Reform Judaism at the very beginning is that it removed any mention of
the return to Zion, as we just read, from the prayer book. The whole idea
was to be more a part of the European emancipatory societies. How could

you be a good German if every day you prayed to go back to Israel and Zion? The Reform Jews are the ones who fought the hardest against the Zionists. Anyone familiar with history knows the Zionists and the Reform Jews were completely at odds with one another. But now what do you have? I shouldn't say now, let's call it before the *Intifada*: the biggest supporters of Israel, AIPAC, were largely comprised of members of Reform Jewish congregations.

Just down the block from where I lived in Miami Beach is one of the richest Reform Judaism congregations in south Florida, Temple Beth Shalom. They used to raise millions of dollars a year for Israel from their members. That was beautiful, but it was completely at odds with how Reform Judaism began because, and I must say I am not, God forbid, trying to diminish their pride in Israel, which is absolutely sincere, but once Israel became fashionable, it was embraced. In Germany, when it was less fashionable, it was discarded. The proof of this is very sad; since the Intifada, Israel has had largely negative headlines for so many consecutive years, and has commensurately lost much Jewish support, as its fortunes declined. Now of course Israel is getting better headlines due to the current peace agreement with their arch-enemy, the PLO. Orthodox Jews, I believe, have remained steadfastly loyal to Israel, amidst the unfashionability of it all. Whereas less committed congregations are questioning Israel's motives more and more. Surely essence is compromised (and this is a non-Jewish person writing about the history and the beginnings of the movement) 'when you are constantly looking over your shoulder at what people are doing and copying them'.

VOICE FROM AUDIENCE: Surely just because Johnson is not a Jew doesn't mean his book is any less of an interpretation. I mean that book is only a personal view of the whole thing and if he interprets it that way that doesn't make it the final truth on the matter.

SB: Absolutely right, but I think it is very difficult to trust the Jewish historians on emotive Jewish subjects. Because how could they divorce themselves completely from their own personal affiliation and denominationalism. Can you see a Jewish historian, for instance, who is Orthodox writing about the great contribution that Reform Judaism makes. It would be very difficult.

(Background talk)

SB: I can't understand. I mean, Judaism is the mother religion of Christianity. So Christianity looked a lot over their shoulders to develop, but now you are saying we should look back over ours. I'm not saying that we can't learn from Christianity but in this specific situation I highly doubt it. Christianity is an invention of Judaism like . . . Lisa is getting all upset, I'm just quoting Nietzsche. But . . .

VOICE: It wasn't Christianity I was thinking about. I was thinking in the more general view. The value for liberal democracy, it doesn't have much clout in the ghetto, things like that . . .

SB: Look, I'll tell you the truth. If you ask me I will gratefully admit that Orthodox Judaism has a lot to learn from Conservative Judaism and Reform Judaism as well because as a religious Jew I believe there is nothing in this world that one can learn nothing from. But it depends what, and you also have to have guidelines of what you can and what you can't learn. I've got to tell you something, we probably could learn a lot from Nazi Germany!

VOICE 2: Like what?

SB: Like orderliness and efficiency . . .

VOICE 3: Is that all important?

(Background talk.)

SB: Well, I think I would phrase it differently. I would say that Orthodox Judaism has lost, unfortunately, and I don't know how it could justify it on Jewish grounds, it has lost its universal element, its universal dimension. It has become extremely claustrophobic and ghettoized and everything else, but it was never meant to be that way. On the contrary. You know, I knew you were going to ask that, because that is a very good question. Do you accept the premise I have said earlier that God and His wisdom, as embodied in His revealed Divine truth, cannot be a means to an end?

LISA K: Well, why were human beings created . . . through God and His wisdom?

SB: The purpose of what I am saying is not to differentiate.

LK: We don't want to differentiate from God and His wisdom.

SB: No, that they are one and the same. As the Torah says, 'God and His Torah are one.'

LK: Then why was the Torah given?

SB: As a means for humankind to apprehend God. To come closer to God. So the Torah is . . .

LK: 'As a means . . .'

SB: Well, it is a means for Godliness. In other words, that is the end, okay, it is not a means for humankind, it is not for humanity's self-development, it is to point people in the right direction, of where God is. The Torah is God's knowledge; by studying the Torah you come closer to God. That is an end in itself.

Many people come here just for Friday night, some just for social events. A lot of more religious people who visit the L'Chaim Society say, 'Why this waste of money? You get kids just to come for Shabbat? They don't come to study, a lot of people turn up for the meal after the Shabbat prayers have finished so they don't pray.' And I say to them, 'I can't understand what you are talking about. If kids just hear something

Jewish said, just a Torah thought, that is a Jewish experience. That is a Godly experience.' When you study Torah you are close to God, you are apprehending God, because they are one and the same. I always say to them, you guys are such hypocrites, you are saying that Torah is not apprehending God, that it should only serve as a means, it should jump-start them to do *mitzvahs* and behave Jewishly. Torah is not like a shock therapy that gets you up and excited about Judaism. It is an end in itself, that is the purpose. If someone hears something Jewish, something from the Torah, at that moment they are embracing God in their minds.

All I'm trying to say is, and this is not a criticism but something I would actually like to understand, that the Christian concept of emphasizing salvation to such an extent seems – at least from my own ignorance of the subject – at times almost a denigration of God as an end, and makes God the means. Because one of the problems I think religion really suffers from, to this very day, is the idea of reward. It is important that people be rewarded for good deeds. But it is also important that they do not do the good deeds for the purpose of the reward.

For instance, when I was going through high school there was a terrible aeroplane crash. An Air Florida flight took off from Washington DC airport, but the city was covered with snow that day, and the wings had ice; the plane landed on a bridge and broke into two, and passengers were thrown into the Potomac River, which was full of blocks of ice. People were dying of hypothermia. A man was walking by on a bridge and he saw a stewardess dying; without thinking he jumped straight into the river, and saved her life. By this time there were television cameras there, people were watching live as he saved her life. You can imagine what a hero he became. About a month later, President Reagan honoured this hero with a special dinner. When I saw this I thought it was really important to reward someone for an act of kindness, to encourage others. But to say that he would have saved her because he saw the television cameras there and thought he would be famous is nonsense. It is important to reward people but it is ridiculous to encourage people to do good for the sake of a reward; it defeats the purpose.

In Christianity there is an obsession with heaven and hell. Judaism has never had this preoccupation. Who cares where we are going to go? Maybe we will just expire and become nothingness, but if I found out there was no heaven or hell, does that mean forget it, the world becomes a jungle? There is truth, religion is about truth, it is about approaching an ultimate truth. And it is an irreconcilable truth, a truth that cannot be compromised and cannot co-exist with anything false.

QUESTION: Does Reform Judaism serve a purpose in keeping people Jewish in today's society?

SB: I'd say yes and no. On the one hand, there is no question that Reform Judaism keeps millions of Jews Jewish the world over. The question is, what direction? When I was living in Australia I became friendly with a newspaper columnist, Marc Braham. He was friendly with my in-laws, and he wrote an article about Reform Judaism in which he described it as 'something that may be true, but is not necessarily'. He believed that Reform Judaism is a transit camp for people who are on their way out of Judaism. Like the last stop, before you leave. When the previous rebbe of Lubavitch was five years old, he was looking out of the window of his house in the town of Lubavitch in Russia. His father, Rabbi Sholom DovBer of Lubavitch, walked over to him and said, it is better to be on the outside looking in than on the inside looking out; it is better to be on the outside of Judaism looking in, being interested, than being on the inside waiting to get out. So the question is, is Reform Judaism the inside looking out or the outside looking in? I don't know, it is difficult to say, but from Reform Jews I know, the children of Reform Jews, for many it is being on the inside looking out. Maybe not the parents, who have more conviction, but many of the children certainly are on their way out, which is very sad.

DAN WILLIAMS: Can you explain the rationale behind someone having a Jewish mother, and disobeying all the laws but still being called a Jew whereas someone who goes through an Orthodox conversion is expected to keep all of the commandments before their Jewishness can be authenticated. And what do you think about Reform conversions?

SB: That is also a very good question because the answer to that spells out the serious differences between how Orthodox and Reform groups view Judaism. Orthodox Judaism believes that being Jewish is a state of being, not a state of commitment or practice or even belief. Correct me if I am wrong but it is inconceivable that there should be a non-believing Christian, because a Christian is someone who affirms the Christian faith. Whereas in Judaism we have plenty of Jews who are atheists and they are still as Jewish as everybody else.

Just yesterday in *The Times*, a very rich and powerful friend of Amanda's and Piers' said he was Jewish but he was an atheist. Being both at once is very important to him. He doesn't believe that there is a God but he still believes he is Jewish, and that is okay, he is absolutely right. Being Jewish is a state of being; we are a people. And as long as you are part of that people you are Jewish.

On the other hand, Reform Judaism puts much more emphasis on the religious side, on Judaism being something *you do*. The thinking behind this is that really all people are the same; we speak about the religious universal element. That people are part of a collective humanity and then they have their individual beliefs, their individual and ethnic features. But they are merely character traits ancillary to their essential being. And features can be adopted or they can be discarded.

Paradoxically, in the USA at least, the official Reform doctrine of how you become a Jew is either your mother is a Jew or your father is a Jew, but that if only one of your parents is Jewish you are not yet Jewish unless you lead a Jewish life. At least to Reform standards. But if you decide you are not Jewish, Reform Judaism says you are not Jewish and you have to undergo a conversion, which is amazing. Because again it is a state of practice, it is embodying characteristics peculiar to Jews instead of having something at your root essence which is what traditional Judaism believes. A Jew, in our opinion, can never stop being a Jew, and you can't even convert out of it. There is a story, a famous parable by the Dubna Maggid.

There was a crown prince who was supposed to take over the reign of the entire kingdom one day, but he had a real problem: he thought he was a turkey. He used to scrabble around on the floor all day saying, 'Gobble gobble.' He refused to eat from the table or to wear any clothes. It was highly embarrassing, the crown prince running around stark naked with drool all over him saying 'gobble gobble gobble'. The king summoned the greatest doctors in the land and no one could cure him. Until they brought a rabbi.

The rabbi said, 'Look, I can cure him (for the right price).' So the rabbi took off all his clothes, got down on the floor and said, 'Gobble gobble.' The prince said, 'Who are you?' The rabbi said, 'I'm a turkey,' and the prince said, 'Oh really, I'm a turkey too, we could be friends.' They started eating together and the prince was really happy that he had found a companion he could communicate with. Well, the next day, the rabbi came and he had clothes on, and he was on the floor saying 'gobble gobble'. The prince said to him, 'What are you doing, you are wearing clothes!' And the rabbi said to him, 'There is nothing wrong with that, you can wear clothes and be a turkey.' The prince said, 'You can? Okay, I'll put on clothes too.' So now they were running around, clothed, on the floor, saying 'gobble gobble'. The next day the rabbi brought a fork and a knife, he ate from the floor, but with a fork and knife. The prince again asked what he was doing and the rabbi again replied, you can be a turkey and eat with a fork and a knife. Well, the story goes on; the rabbi taught the prince how to be a human being, and all the time the prince thought he was a turkey. And the moral of the story is you can think you are a turkey but you cannot help being a human being, your human nature can always be drawn out of you.

What I mean to say is, if you are Jewish you can behave like someone who is not, you can call yourself an atheist, and believe yourself to be an atheist, and you can call yourself a Christian or a Muslim or a Hindu, but as far as Jews are concerned, as far as ancient Jewish doctrine is concerned, you will for ever remain Jewish. I think there is great beauty to that. It means that being Jewish is something so deep that you can never compromise in any way. If you, God forbid, spit in your father's face, kick him in the shins and humiliate him publicly, would you stop being his son? No. Because being a son is not a matter of behaving like a son; you are a son regardless of how you behave.

Chapter Thirty-two

SINGLES REJECT SYNAGOGUES
WITHOUT SEPARATIONS

I could increase the number of people who participate in our prayer services tenfold if I simply got rid of the *mechitza*, the partition which separates men and women, and allowed them to sit together. But then I would not attract those people to whom prayer is most important and who have the greatest need to pray.

Here I do not refer to the Orthodox or observant Jews who undoubtedly insist on the *mechitza*. Rather, it is the men, and especially the women, who have not yet been fortunate enough, for a variety of reasons, to find a full-time partner in life or start a family. It is to their needs that a Jewish community and hence a synagogue must cater first.

An Invitation to Lecture to Single Women

During my third year in Oxford I became friendly with a woman in her mid-forties who was the programme director of a Jewish organization in London with whom I shared speakers. She told me there were many women like her, past a 'reasonable' age for marriage, who lived in London. A large number were bitter at not having found husbands. She asked if I would deliver a lecture for them and address their frustration. I was happy to comply, and came up with two possible titles, 'Are Nice Jewish Men a Vanishing Breed?, or 'The Place of Single Women in the Jewish Community'. The group chose the latter title and I was surprised to find more than sixty women on the night who seemed eager to hear what I had to say.

I went with the expectation of teaching them something. But as so often happens, I left having learned a great deal myself, especially on a subject which I had not intended to discuss at all: the *mechitza*. Until that time, I, like so many others, was convinced that the only real reason for a *mechitza* was to prevent any interaction between men and women in the synagogue, which seemed not to be conducive to the spirit and environment of prayer. My friend Dennis Prager once stated at a lecture in Oxford that, although not strictly Orthodox, he prays exclusively at a shule with a *mechitza* because, whilst a visible Creator is totally absorbing, more times than not, the invisible God would lose out to a visible man or woman.

Now, I heard something different. Very few of the women present were fully observant Jews, and a tiny number were Orthodox. However, they all told me that when they go to a synagogue service they go to an Orthodox shule with a *mechitza*. I asked why.

Ostracized and Alone

In response they explained: 'Do you know what it is like to go to a shule where the men and women sit together as a family and you are singled out? Instead of feeling part of the service you immediately feel alone and alienated. You begin to pity yourself. The very first thing you are reminded of as you enter is that, while everyone is jovial and happy and surrounded by a spouse and children, you are single.'

But when they attend a shule with a *mechitza* they are made to feel included. No one knows, or is forced to know, the marital status of anyone else, because all the women sit together in unison, as do the men. No one need feel left out.

Before I published this essay, I tested the theory out on an Oxford feminist, with whom I had sparred on many Jewish women's issues in the past. I told her that single Jewish women of advanced years feel uncomfortable in a shule without a *mechitza*. I sat back and braced myself for the rebuttal, but it never came. Instead she began to tell me how her parents were recently divorced. Her father already had a girlfriend but her mother was left alone. She attended services in a large Reform Temple in the United States and came home crying. Everyone sat with their partners, but she sat alone. Her daughter, who had for so long berated me on the inequality of the Orthodox service, told me that after hearing her mother's suffering, she advised her to begin attending an Orthodox service.

To Approach God as an Individual

For me this was a profound awakening. While it was the specific circumstances of the women which shed light on the true quality of the *mechitza*, the light it shed was not limited to their cause alone. What they were really saying is that the essential idea of prayer is to approach God as an individual, and not as a family.

To be sure, we pray as a community, and we require a quorum of ten men in order for the prayers to be even more accepted. We also pray in a synagogue, a place of communal gathering, rather than in the privacy of our own home. And yet that community is made of distinct and separate individuals, all achieving a solitary communion and moment of intimacy with their Creator. It is inappropriate for someone to come before God defined by their familial relations; the only important detail at that moment is that we come before God as His child, His servant, to Whom we must all pay homage, on Whom we are all dependent, and for Whom we all await the answers to our prayers.

While the synagogue social hall is a place for women to introduce their husbands to a new acquaintance, and for the rabbi to stand alongside his wife as they greet their congregants, the synagogue is no such place. On the contrary, it is the supreme forum for a person, surrounded and in unison with other individual members of the world Jewish community, to approach and meet their Creator.

Celebration of the Individual

In this way, what these intelligent women, whose wisdom sprang from deep pondering on their single status, were saying was that praying in a synagogue with a *mechitza* celebrated their individualism. Whereas at the synagogue family picnic they would feel out of place; within the closed doors of the House of Prayer their Creator embraced them and made each feel special and not in any way deficient for not having (yet) found a spouse.

Shortly afterwards a Jewish Nobel Prize laureate came to Oxford for a short time with his wife. I went to introduce myself and invited them round. His wife was extremely friendly, but she made it clear they would not be attending our prayer services. 'When we married, my husband was Orthodox and we prayed at a shule with a *mechitza*. I got tired of sitting alone behind the curtain,' she told me. Ever since then they had been praying at a Conservative Temple in the United States where couples sat together. 'But what of the men and women who cannot remedy the problem of sitting alone?' I asked her. 'Should they be reminded of their loneliness every time they enter the synagogue?' And to this she had nothing to say. 'I never thought of that,' she admitted. And neither had I, before that evening.

The point is that if we are to thrive as a community then we must make room for all members of the community.

Proper Focus for the Synagogue

Some have told me that the way to get round this problem is by setting up singles' *minyanim*, and indeed many synagogues have done just this. But this just begs the question and inflames the wound. A synagogue is not meant to be a cattle market. It is a place of intimacy between the individual and their Creator where the individual pours out their most intimate wishes and secrets and begs the Divine One for compassion and grace. It should never be reduced to the kind of place where greater thought is given to the colour of lipstick one wears, or to whether one's suit has been pressed for the festival, than to the state of one's heart as we prepare to bare our souls before our Maker.

337

To repeat: shules are not picnic grounds, nor are they meat markets or places for men and women to feel warmed by each other's presence and hold hands. Rather, a shule is the ultimate place for humility and a denial of self-assumption, where one man and one woman both endeavour above all to make themselves vessels worthy of Divine presence and blessing.

And so they should remain. Long live the *mechitza*.

SECTION THREE

====

JUDAISM AND OTHER
RELIGIONS IN OXFORD

Chapter Thirty-three

HOW KOSHER WAS KHOMEINI?

===

Few people realize that Oxford is the home to two distinct universities. The one that is officially the University of Oxford is probably the most famous in the world and is what everyone is referring to when they speak of Oxford. The other, Oxford Brookes University (formerly the Oxford Polytechnic), is not so widely known even in England.

The tertiary education system in England and Wales has for decades been a dual system. Polytechnics, as they were known, were intended to provide good teaching in technical subjects from diploma up to degree level. Universities were seen as providing both undergraduate and graduate degrees in a more rarefied atmosphere of teaching coupled with research. Over the years the distinctions became blurred: many university departments withdrew from research while many polytechnics became world leaders in specialized research. In 1992 the government reorganized the situation: all polytechnics were redesignated as universities, and the two-tier system of funding (for teaching and research, or for teaching alone) was applied to all universities, old and new.

For a long time polytechnics had been regarded as the poor relations of their older cousins, the universities, providing a slightly inferior way of obtaining a degree. Obviously this attitude had some effect on the relations between the two Oxford institutions, an ill-defined alignment of 'the Poly' with down-to-earth youth and vanguardism, and a reactionary affiliation between the university and all things traditional. If big bands come to Oxford they play at the only half-decent venue, the former Poly: if major works of art are shown in Oxford they tend to be owned by the colleges.

The two universities are separated by a distance of about two miles and, as one might imagine, when two institutions of such seemingly disproportionate importance, with students of similar age, confront each other in proximity, there is bound to be some enmity. For the most part, the two universities have almost no contact and therefore there is little space for the two to come into conflict. The Oxford Brookes students have their own pubs while the Oxford university students have their college JCRs (Junior Common Rooms) which serve as pubs, game rooms and meeting places.

The other main segregating factor is the fact that many of the university's greatest student haunts, most notably the Oxford Union, are open for membership to Oxford University students only. The Oxford university students tend to gather in the older pubs in the centre of town, such as The Turf, The King's Arms and The White Horse, whereas Oxford Brookes students are most likely to be found in pubs aiming at a younger clientele – The Brew House is a notable example.

The exception, however, is among the Jewish students. The University of Oxford has about one thousand Jewish students, the Oxford Brookes between two and three hundred. Because the numbers are so small, the students must and do share many of the same amenities. Firstly, there is only one synagogue, and although Oxford Brookes has its own Jewish Society of students which is active mainly in organizing social events, the students there are also heavily involved in Oxford University's Jewish Society and L'Chaim Society.

An Elitist Tradition

It can sometimes become a source of friction. Oxford University has a tradition of being somewhat élitist, and while this has changed dramatically over the years, one still finds those who will corroborate that view among Oxford Brookes Jewish students. When they attend Friday-night meals at the Jewish Society, they complain of feeling rather left out. Firstly, they are a small minority amongst the Oxford University students, who always sit together, leaving them to fend for themselves. Secondly, I have heard the complaint from many students that some of the Oxford University students treat them as half-citizens. Now there are always bound to be some problems when students of a university such as Oxford, who have worked for years and achieved the best results in order to get into Oxford, confront students of an institution which, in their minds, is of a significantly lower academic standard. The problems, of course, are on both sides. The Oxford University students may treat the Brookes students as somewhat inferior; and for the Brookes students there is the possibility that even if the Oxford University students treat them as equals, they will always have a chip on their shoulders, imagining slights.

The slights are not always imaginary, however. Our L'Chaim Society has always been open to both groups of students: we have shared a close association with the Brookes students, several of whom have served as presidents and officers of our society. This association reached its strongest when, in the years 1990–92, the leaders and most active members of the former polytechnic's Jewish students were sharing a house in Howard Street, east Oxford. These students became some of my best friends, as a result of which we arranged many joint events and programmes. Among the students sharing this house were two girls, both of whom were dating students from Oxford University. I remember on a few occasions how, in the course of general gossip, students from the university remarked what an anomaly it was that Oxford University students were taking out girls from Brookes. And, truth be told, there have not been a great number of occasions when Brookes students have significantly penetrated the ranks of the Jewish university students. There have also been many occasions when the Brookes Jewish Society has complained that they were accorded secondary status by the University Jewish Society when it came to resources, such as the distribution of the University Term Cards and generally the publicizing of events.

Elitism in the United States

I first became aware of the potential for élitism before I even arrived at Oxford. While still living in New York, my wife and I visited some Chabad Houses on campuses around the north-eastern United States in order to gather some ideas. I am a great believer in not having to reinvent the wheel, and if there were some successful programmes for students already being carried out, I wanted to implement them at Oxford. We thus visited one of the more successful Lubavitch campus operations, among which is the Chabad House at Boston. At their Friday-night dinner there was a mixed crowd from many different universities, some of them the cream of the Ivy League such as Harvard, and others more ordinary, such as Northwestern University. In a general conversation about student life in Boston, it was two of the Harvard students who told me about the air of élitism which the Harvard students had towards other university students in the vicinity. This was why most of them 'hung out' at the Harvard Hillel, where there was an exclusively Harvard crowd on Shabbat, instead of coming to Chabad House. I resolved to try not to perpetuate a similar incongruity in Oxford.

Yet when we did arrive two months later there was much talk about why we were in Oxford, amidst its relatively small Jewish population. Also, as the influence of the university students was disproportionate to their numbers, I naturally found myself at first being pulled in that direction. We were spending most of our time and money on them and insufficient on the then polytechnic students, whom I barely knew at the time.

The Hand of God in a Broken-down Mitzvah Tank

All this changed via what may seem a strange encounter but which had the undeniable marks of Divine intervention. Lubavitch Foundation in London had an old *mitzvah*-mobile, a converted bakery truck, that was on its last legs and was not being used. In its glory days it roamed all over

London, distributing Shabbat candles and getting men to don tefillin. But it was now a miserable heap. I proposed to bring it to Oxford to set up a roving kosher kebab van. Now, every night after hours in Oxford, the students' prime source of food is a few doner kebab vans which park in the High Street and in George Street. Nothing else is open and they have little choice. Our idea was to offer Jewish students twice-weekly food of different quality. It would be a great chance to meet new Jewish students, as well as to offer them the same amenities available to non-Jewish students, but of the kosher variety. (I have always been a great believer in making Judaism as easy as possible. The sacrifice philosophy was perhaps more appropriate in earlier generations.) Now, we knew we wouldn't be able to fit a kitchen into this *mitzvah*-mobile, but we did have ways of keeping ready-made kebabs warm so as to sell them in the street.

I and a dedicated group of students drove the mobile down from London and it plumed smoke in our faces through the entire trip. It was in really bad shape. Undaunted, when the Sunday evening on which it was advertised to begin trading arrived, I fearlessly boarded the truck with five students who would serve as helpers. The van belched forward and, as we travelled towards our destination at the High Street, we had scarcely made it down the road when it came to a complete halt. We tried to restart it . . . nothing. This truck had died a complete and miserable death right in the middle of St Clement's, one of Oxford's busiest streets, with no hope of a resurrection. After about fifteen minutes of kicking and verbally abusing the engine to get it to start, we had a line of fifty cars behind us honking and demanding we move the mobile immediately. But we just couldn't do it; and there was no mechanic available on this Sunday evening to rescue us. The situation was desperate and miserable, when suddenly a miracle occurred.

There was a group of Jewish students from Brookes University drinking at the pub when they saw what was happening and all came out to rescue us, headed by the president of the Brookes Students Union, a Jewish student called David Israel. David approached and said to me, 'What's the problem, Rabbi?' I explained our forlorn situation to him and how God had forestalled our attempt at empowering the Jewish population of Oxford with kosher kebab. By this time the police had arrived. They didn't speak much at first. They just stared at the deceased, hulking monstrosity which was clogging their roads. They were clearly confused. 'What the . . . is this [expletive deleted]?' they asked inquisitively. But David, clearly having witnessed this odd Lubavitch creation previously, answered for me, 'It's a *mitzvah* tank.'

'A what? What does it do and what is it doing here?'

'Well,' David continued, 'it goes around doing *mitzvahs*, only this time it's selling kebab and it's stuck.'

By now the police were sure we had all had some very funny tobacco. How else could we account for this bizarre story of a converted religious vehicle, originally a bakery truck now selling kebab, being left forlorn in the middle of an Oxford street? 'Look,' the policeman said, 'I don't know what the hell this is, or what it is meant to do. But whatever it is, it had better not do it here. Move it at once.' And here all the Jewish students, about fourteen, began to push our (im)mobile-kebab-*mitzvah*-mobile through the streets of Oxford until it reached the Chabad House.

It was from then on that I became friends with David and company, and especially with the then leaders of the Brookes Jewish Society, Stephen Portnoy and Andy Tilsiter.

A Clash of Jewish and Arab Students

About a month later, David, as Student Union president, organized a multi-cultural fair at Brookes. Stephen and Andy, as presidents of the Jewish Society, asked me to come and help man the Jewish stall. They would provide the cultural dimension and they were hoping that I would answer any religious questions which arose.

By the time I arrived at the stall, the Jewish students were furious. There was an Islamic booth just across from them which was distributing literature very hostile to Israel. Some of the literature blatantly called for a holy war against Israel. There were some tracts of speeches by Ayatollah Khomeini, translated into English, which were also vitriolically opposed to the 'satanic Zionist State'. This was certainly not the kind of multi-cultural fair that David Israel had called for but he felt powerless to stop them from distributing their literature as he felt it would lead to accusations that he was practising favouritism. The problem was left for us to handle.

Oxford is very interesting in this respect. There are many Palestinian and Arab students here and by and large we get along well with them. There are even many Arab students with whom I am friends and who frequent many of our events. These students include offspring of the élite of Arab life – sons and daughters of Saudi oil sheiks and businessmen. But in Oxford we respect each other in the spirit of equality in a city where there are many disparate groups, although we are acutely aware of the differences which separate us.

L'Chaim and the Middle East Societies

To be sure, the L'Chaim Society, which hosts a number of distinguished Israeli politicians and representatives, has a fierce competitor in the form of the Oxford University Middle East Society, run primarily by Palestinian students who attempt to bring an equal number of Arab diplomats to respond to our speakers. Some of their events are spectacular, such as when they hosted Jimmy Carter in October 1988. But even here the relations between our two groups are amicable and their leadership offers ours free entry to their events; we reciprocate. Every year, in fact, at the University Freshers' Fair, L'Chaim is placed in a room with other societies with a religious orientation. We are usually next to the Middle East Society and the Islamic Society, often sandwiched in between them, and we are always helpful and co-operative with one another, sharing materials and supplies and, of course, discussion.

So when the students asked me to speak to the stall holders, I had no intention of disrupting these friendly relationships. Rather, I wanted to ask that they promote their own cause without the need to denigrate or scorn the cause of the Jewish students just across from them. Surely there were aspects of Islam that were not militantly opposed to the existence of the State of Israel. But I met with a hostile response. We were told categorically that we had no right to interfere with what they were distributing.

When we pointed out that we felt we did have a right to oppose literature which could be used to incite hostility, even violence, to the Jewish and Zionist organizations at the university, one of their representatives picked up one of the tracts by Khomeini and began to read aloud about the Zionist 'crimes and vices which had to be eradicated'.

Familial Origins in Iran

I told this student that my father was born and brought up in Iran, specifically from the city of Isfahan. Although he had lived for many years in the United States, all his culture and mannerisms were still distinctively Iranian. I therefore could not support the views of the new Iranian leader which were so blatantly hostile towards the many similar Jews around the world who loved Iran and had contributed so much to its society.

The student looked at me quizzically. 'You're a rabbi, are you not?' I replied in the affirmative. 'Are you observant of your religion?' the Palestinian student inquired, to which I again responded in the affirmative. 'Then how could you not support this cleric who had done so much to rescue Iranian culture from western atheism and the systematic destruction of religious belief that pervaded Iran before his rise to power?'

Divide and Conquer

This was a classic tactic. Divide and conquer. This clever student, of course, noticed that the six Jewish students surrounding me were not observant; they weren't wearing yarmulkas. So, he thought, better to establish how he had more in common with me than them, and thus obscure the real issue of his distribution of offensive material.

But the Jewish students standing in the wings seemed uneasy with his question. Perhaps I, as a Chasidic Jew, indeed shared the goals of my Arab counterpart. Did I too not share this zeal for religious observance spreading and dominating secular culture? I did not want to debate that question here when the issue was clearly a different one. But when we got back to our stall, defeated because they did nothing in response to our protests, I told the students I would address his question that Friday night at our centre. Ever since, on many occasions, I have been forced to return to the issue of religious coercion and explain the Jewish view on the subject.

Khomeinism in a Jewish Guise

I should say that it not only serves as a response to Khomeinism and religious coercion in general, but to Israeli politics in particular. Anger at the Israeli religious establishment has been quite vociferously expressed at Oxford since I arrived. The idea that small religious parties should blackmail the Israeli government into enacting religious measures so they could join a ruling coalition is one of the greatest sources of anger regarding Jewish matters that I have seen in friends and acquaintances. Even those who are most sympathetic to the Jewish religion in general, and to traditional Judaism in particular, feel that these efforts are counter-productive, and I tend to agree. While I would support enforcing the closure of businesses on the Sabbath, because every society requires a family day of sanctity and rest in which business is not paramount, I completely oppose the mixing of religion and politics, for the reason this chapter demonstrates.

Rabbi Meir Kahane's Legacy

When I first arrived in Oxford I became friendly with an extremely left-wing Israeli doctorate student who was writing a paper on Kahanism. While he despised everything Rabbi Meir Kahane stood for, he had a soft spot for religious tradition, and once asked me to explain the differences between the policies of the Lubavitcher rebbe, who clearly would like to see a more observant State of Israel, and those of Meir Kahane. 'It appears to me,' he told me, 'without wishing to be offensive, that the goals of your rebbe and Rabbi Kahane are similar.'

'In many aspects,' I retorted, 'that may be so. But there is a fundamental difference which separates them. Whereas Kahane has set out to change governments, the Lubavitcher rebbe has set out to change people, one at a time.' This answer was sufficient for him.

(I should mention that I had a great deal of respect for this student because he didn't just talk about liberalism, but embodied it completely. He may have hated Kahane for his policies but he was mature enough to separate that from any hatred of the man. When, two years later, I awoke to the BBC headlines that Rabbi Kahane was mercilessly gunned down by a Palestinian assassin, I phoned this student, who today teaches politics at Tel Aviv University, to tell him what had happened. He was genuinely saddened. 'Shmuley,' he said, 'I did not support a word he uttered. But he did not deserve this. Nobody deserves this.' Other students, who preach of how they value human life, and criticize the Israeli military for shooting Palestinian stone-throwers, openly chuckled and told jokes to each other, in my presence, when they heard the news.)

Khomeini is a Serious Force to Reckon With

For more than a decade an elderly sage with long white beard, traditional black headdress and passionate religious zealotry dominated world news in a manner equalled only by the State of Israel. He challenged the technologically advanced world we live in, our appraisal of modern society and its meaning, by showing that a theocratic state, steeped in the uncompromising ways of ancient tradition, could sustain itself in relative stability despite its turbulent revolutionary beginnings. His name, of course, was Ayatollah Ruholla Khomeini, and although he is now gone, the legacy he left his people remains as strong as ever.

On hearing of his death, I myself breathed a sigh of relief even while watching with sympathy the intense grief and anguish of the Iranian people as they abused their bodies at the funeral processions for the Imam. While I observed this spectacle, a powerful question overcame me. Why was I, an observant Jew, along with the entire body of traditional Jewry, not more sympathetic to his cause? Here was a man, as the Arab student at the former polytechnic had argued, who had rescued the mores and zealotry of religion from the secular and acculturated values of the Shah's regime. He acted like a modern-day Maccabee, rescuing a traditionally religious people from the smouldering cauldron of hellenism, the by-product of which is often the moral decadence of an atheistic melting-pot. He took what was, in his mind, a westernized society committed to the spiritual suicide of the people and delivered religious belief from systematic liquidation. Are these not values to which Judaism also aspires?

Khomeini's Reform and Transformation of Iranian Society

A brief examination of the Ayatollah's legacy will help clarify my inquiry. Khomeini denounced the immorality of western civilization to the point where 'western' and 'immoral' tended to become synonymous. 'Westernization', in his vivid language, meant '[a man] parading around the streets with a European hat on [his] head watching the naked girls' (that is, the women in provocative western dress).

The IRP programme is required reading in Iranian schools and argues:

'For decades our society has been consuming imported culture and education. In order to strengthen their political and economic imperialism, the world-devourers have used cultural imperialism.' Therefore, western patterns of life had to be eliminated in all areas: food habits, clothing fashions, architecture and city planning, education and manners.

In order to gain 'cultural independence' Khomeini declared a 'cultural revolution' in the spring of 1980 (Khomeini's speech on 26 April 1980) and established the 'Headquarters of Culture' to co-ordinate the effort. To date, the government Islamization programme has indeed affected nearly every area of life in Iran. Media, art and entertainment, clothing and the family all became subject to moral regulations. Prostitution and pornography were of course totally outlawed, carrying with them severe punishments. The fundamentalist regime also imposed *hijab* (the Islamic code of dress) on women so that none could be immodestly attired. Western-dressed Iranian women were denounced as 'cabaret dancers' by Khomeini. Even co-educational schools were outlawed, having been classified as 'houses of prostitution', and thought of as adversely affecting the concentration of the student due to the 'emotional appeal of the opposite sex' (*New York Times*, 22 April 1979).

Khomeini's regime converted the media, artistic expression and films into morality exercises promoting religious culture and values. The IRP characterized the media as a 'university' for the education of the population. It declared that 'printing anti-religious ideas and beliefs is not permitted in Islamic society'. Radio and TV programmes were changed to reflect 'the true message' of religious life, as was art so that 'it be in conformity with genuine Islamic and religious themes'.

Iranian television on Channels 1 and 2 on a typical day could include Verses of the Holy Koran, Calls to Prayer and Lessons in Arabic as well as several news programmes. The regime also monopolized all means of mass communication, banning secular papers, in an attempt to prevent sexual perversion from infiltrating the country's consciousness. Religious songs became the principal musical expression, replacing rock and disco; mixed dancing was forbidden.

No one in Iran seems to doubt that since the revolution and the introduction of its fierce penalties, crime rates, and violent crime in particular, have dropped considerably. Iran at present enjoys one of the lowest urban crime rates of any country in the world.

Consonance with Jewish Goals

In striking similarity to the rudimentary principle of Judaism being a complete way of life, Khomeini's Iran represents a return, not simply to the ideals of Islam, but to the maximalist conception of it as a guide to the details, great and small, of everyday living. As it happens, Khomeini published his own commentary on these matters. In the 1950s, at the Faizieh Theological School in Qom, his reputation as a teacher was growing and people would write to him from all over Iran to ask his opinions on points of religion. These opinions were collated and turned into a book which he published in 1960; after this he was entitled to refer to himself as an ayatollah.

The book, *Towzhih al-Masa'il*, or 'Explication of Problems', is a bestseller in Iran, an immense volume which contains more than three thousand rulings on the conduct of daily life and religious observances, from laws on inheritance to matters of personal cleanliness and the right way to slaughter animals.

Nothing was private enough to prevent Ayatollah Khomeini from laying down the law on it. In western eyes, at any rate, it seems intrusive to describe the varieties of bleeding in a woman's menstrual flow, or to prescribe the correct way to face when defecating and the correct way to clean oneself afterwards. And yet, even the Torah will at times discuss such matters espousing laws which govern all our actions, encouraging one to know God 'in all thy ways' (Proverbs 3:6).

A further significant point is that Khomeini did not only heighten the observance of Islam in Iran, but in many cases he coerced Jews into observance of Judaism. In one instance, told to me by one of the individuals who witnessed the event, he summoned a group of wealthy Jewish industrialists to his chambers. All of them had factories that were working on Shabbat and, to their amazement, he condemned them for forsaking their commandments. He declared that in an Islamic country, just as Friday was revered by Muslims, Saturday had to be revered by Jews. He concluded by ruling that henceforth, if any Jewish factory opened on Shabbat, the owner would be punished by a firing squad. All present complied.

Clearly, ideologies differ in complexity, and although it may not be as complex as others, Iranian fundamentalism, like many totalitarian ideologies, provides its adherents with a sense of mission and a holistic concept of persons and society, and it has its own distinctive style and rhetoric. The original question posed to me, then, returns: in light of the moral, ethical and religious achievements of this man of faith, why was no voice heard from within the camp of traditional Jewry to applaud this religious leader while alive, or eulogize him upon his death?

Khomeini's Brutality

No doubt Khomeini's brutality repels us from praising the Imam's achievements, and it may well be argued that the results in Iran may not owe as much to the vigilance of the *Komitehs* as to the punishments that are inflicted. But in the quest for intellectual maturity, humans should have learned to extract good from evil. If the Imam's goals were good but his means evil, we should at once commend his ambitions and achievements, yet remain able to decry his methods.

When Politics Ousts Religion

I suggest that Khomeini was rejected not merely because of his use of force to accomplish religious ends. Rather, it was how this use of force seemed to reveal the Imam's very perception of religion as a whole.

There are those who believe that religion is a mountain to be climbed, a goal to be reached. To them, a person's status in the eyes of God is ascertained solely by where he or she now stands. If any actions manifest any tendency towards evil, then, in essence, the person has accomplished nothing. It is only the one who arrives at the peak of the mountain, whose journey has reached its climax, who has banished all evil from within him, who may justly be referred to as 'a religious individual'. In the minds of the leaders of this school of thought, it is not a person's slow progression in affinity with God which is commendable, but his rapid rise to the throne of the Creator.

Judaism does not subscribe to this outlook. In the eyes of Jewish thought it is not the *goal* which is significant, but the *path*. The distance a person has traversed, how far they have progressed, is what God measures. Of the Talmud's most central themes is the idea that a returnee to Judaism (*baal teshuvah*) is far greater than a *tzadik* (saint). The reason is that the returnee has come much further, and travelled a far more tortuous path. The Talmud even declares, 'In the place where a *baal teshuvah* (returnee) stands, a *tzadik* (saint) cannot stand (Berachot 34b; Sanhedrin 99a). The *tzadik*, whose righteousness and good deeds by far outweigh those of the returnee, may indeed be standing at the mountain's summit, and from his vantage point he may gaze down at the struggling climb of the *baal teshuvah*, as he slowly rises from the ash heap in search of sublime and transcendent meaning. Yet the *tzadik* is pronounced inferior, for he did not travel any great distance to reach the mountain's top. Everything was handed to him on a silver platter, from the *cheder* (school) he was sent to by his parents, to the yeshivah (college) he attended with the rest of his friends. The *baal teshuvah*, on the other hand, has clambered from the abyss of spiritual despair and has, at the very least, started back on the proper path by his or her own efforts.

Not Righteousness But Transformation

Stated in other words, what the Almighty searches for in humanity is not righteousness, but *transformation*. A person's gradual change from being a materialistically inclined, indulgent organism governed by physical needs and tendencies, to a being with spiritual foresight and disposition is the purpose of religion and God's calling to humankind. What the Almighty desires is that we make an effort to change ourselves for the better, not that we merely become good. He desires to see a significant expenditure of energy on our part. He wants to see that we 'give a damn'. Therefore, if one is born righteous and is reared in a religiously wholesome environment, one will not be judged by how good one is, but by how much better a person and more righteous an individual becomes.

Becoming an Outwardly Oriented Individual

Torah and *mitzvot* (commandments) are the critical ingredient in the development and growth of humans. With every passing *mitzvah* one slowly becomes an outwardly oriented individual. Whereas a child's first words on learning to speak are often 'Mine!', or 'Give me', each *mitzvah* is a lesson in reorienting this natural state to one of *giving* rather than taking. As a living organism man first learns to take rather than give. It is vital to his existence. One needs to be clothed, fed, bathed, nurtured and loved if one is to survive. Our initial stage of life is almost completely passive; as our first lesson about life we internalize the idea of drawing in all that others are prepared to do for us. What changes this process of taking and being inwardly inclined is of course responsibility. People become older and they learn that their contribution on a microcosmic level, such as to family and friends, and on a macrocosmic level, to community and the world at large, is very much needed if the world is to continue.

But before life makes any demands of the human, the very first calling to which he must respond is to that of his Creator. Before children are old or responsible enough to help Mother around the house, they first learn they must say a blessing before eating food, and must give a coin to charity every day. The reason: because God needs them, and they must therefore learn to give, and not just to take. In gradual increments, then, humanity learns, through a religious education, to transcend physical necessity and to focus on the needs of others.

Further still, the spiritual individual learns to utilize their own physical desires for the purpose of understanding another's needs as well. When one understands how vital it is to feel loved, one understands how critical it is to display love to someone else, for their needs are the same. As in the process of learning how to give and in the process of becoming an outwardly oriented individual, man learns to discover God and simultaneously emulate His ways. In the words of the Talmud, 'Just as He is kind, so too should you be kind.'

It is Not Good for Man to Be Alone

Marriage serves as the classic illustration of the principle of outward growth to reach others. While a *mitzvah* exists in its own right, marriage is also the premise for the fulfilment of many other *mitzvot*, not least among them being the perpetuation of humanity and the Jewish people. Why did God choose the framework of marriage as necessary for human existence? To paraphrase the Bible, why indeed is it not good for people to be alone?

Marriage serves as the classic illustration of this principle and as the ultimate institution designed to educate an individual away from his or her natural predisposition. Even the mechanical structure of marriage is such that one must learn to give constantly, from the highest things, like comforting a husband during tragedy, to the seemingly insignificant, like refraining from eating until one's wife comes to the table. It is precisely these 'mechanical' matters which are of pivotal importance to the success of every marriage.

Children Continue a Process of Reorientation

Children soon follow and every parent is faced with a new challenge in the art of generosity: giving without receiving in return. An infant is born with no saving grace, save that of the parent's intuitive love for the child. They have not yet become doctors or lawyers, or generated any *nachas* for their parents. Yet their dependence on their parents is absolute, involving everything from food to mobility. There are no guarantees that the child will ever reciprocate. Indeed, many adult children abandon their parents to nursing homes in their old age. Nevertheless, the idea of a parent coercing his offspring to sign a contract at birth, mandating that child care will be provided only on the condition that the children agree to aid their parents in their hour of need, is laughable. No mountain is too high, no sea too vast, to impede the unrestrained love of parent for child. But why is this all so important?

Because through the love, giving, kindness and compassion of everyday experience, a married man or woman learns to find God. People slowly transform themselves to become outwardly oriented; they transcend their natural selfishness and become humanitarian and philanthropic. They learn to perceive an Existence higher and greater than themselves. And one learns to obey the commands of that Being. Not for the prospects of reward, but out of deep-seated love and conviction. Humans become Godly.

God's Laws Are for People, Not States

When religion is practised for any external consideration, force being the extreme among them, inner transformation cannot follow. Nothing changes, no one becomes spiritual, and the purpose of religion is defeated.

Ayatollah Khomeini changed *government* without changing people. His theocracy was not merely tarnished by the methods it pursued in procuring religious observance, but was supplanted by those methods. He succeeded in bringing about a religious *government*, but not a religious *society*. And although, it may be argued, Iranian society today may indeed exist at the summit of the spiritual mountain, officially void of sexual deviance, theft, rape or impropriety, the population did not climb that mountain. Rather, they were like a cannonball shot there by the religious zeal of the Iranian National Guard, with fear and intimidation serving as gunpowder. The population did not traverse any distance; no one struggled with internal self-doubt, none felt the terrible tension of religious turmoil that tears the soul asunder, and the internal dialectic that makes up the religious experience. In short, they were not personally touched by the sublime hand of God which can only be felt when one works with oneself for decades to reshape oneself into a vessel for God. Time will tell whether the changes Khomeini brought to Iranian society will have any permanence, but one suspects that if the constraints were removed the people would naturally fall back to their previous existence.

Khomeini's Objective: Seize the Reins of Government

The transformation of government, irrespective of whether the people kept pace, was Khomeini's intention all along. It accounts for his infatuation with absolute governmental control. He always argued the importance of politics and domination of the political and social systems by 'true believers'. In his own words:

> If in a society all its members are Muslim and they observe Islam in their personal lives while their social relations are not governed by pure Islamic laws, it is not an Islamic society. On the other hand, if in a society all its members are not Muslim ... or some of its members are weak Muslims and do not behave according to Islam in all their personal obligations, while the values and laws governing social relations are Islamic, that society is Islamic.
>
> (*Mavazihi-Ma* page 26)

In yet another of Khomeini's works, *Al-Hukumat-ul-Islamia*, he states:

> When a Mujtahid who is just and learned stands up for the establishment and organization of the government, he will enjoy all the rights in the affairs of the society that were enjoyed by the Prophet, and it will be the duty of the people to listen to and obey [him] and this Faqih and Mujtahid

will hold the supreme power in the government and the management and control of social and political affairs of the people in the same way as the Prophet and Hazrat Ali [used to do].

Clearly, to Khomeini the exercise of governmental control was the highest religious achievement, a position which Judaism cannot embrace. The Jewish world-view is about changing people through direct exposure. It sees religion ultimately growing from the grass-roots level of the human condition and human experience.

Religious Conviction and Governmental Control Become Synonymous

Samuel Huntington has commented that 'the most important political distinction among countries concerns not their form of government but their degree of government' (*Political Order in Changing Societies*). The main characteristic of Khomeini's fundamentalist ideology is its totalitarian approach to politics. The regime sought to promote the politicization of all spheres of social and even private affairs: its world-view is in fact predicated upon a removal of these distinctions. In Islamic government, Khomeini had asserted, 'There is not a single topic in human life for which Islam has not provided instructions and established norms' (*Islamic Government in Islamic Revolution*, page 80). The IRP programme states that it aims at establishing a '*tawhidi*' (unitary) society, 'a society in which Islamic values, commands, and laws govern all social relations' (*Mavazihi-Ma*, page 26).

What this has led to is the politicization of religion itself. In his many fiery speeches, Khomeini favoured violence and oppression to bolster religious observance, but did not offer a convincing, positive argument for the beauty and necessity of religion. The lack of explanation was not due to personal ignorance; after all, he was a recognized scholar. Rather, it is fundamentally inconsistent with his view of religion. In his eyes the only matter which was of importance was that the people should adhere to Islamic living standards and values. As government serves this purpose well, it has become the personification of Khomeini's religious zeal. He had no desire for the inner transformation of his people. Shiite fundamentalism has abrogated its intellectual dimension, and when this happens, fanaticism is sure to follow.

Suppressing Human Development

Khomeini had indeed expressed a distaste for the natural state of humanity, preferring to stunt it rather than allow it to develop fully. 'An Islamic regime must be serious in every aspect of life,' the Imam said in a broadcast on Iran Radio six months after the revolution. 'There is no fun in Islam. There can be no fun or enjoyment in whatever is serious.' To Judaism, happiness is

representative of extraordinary energy and fervour which should be culti-
vated and nurtured for the service of God. Like everything, it can be utilized
for evil or for good. Judaism thrives on our constant use of material existence
for beneficial and goodly consequence, despite the temptation that it be
used otherwise. In this manner one constantly reaffirms that everything
is in God's possession, thus substantiating His absolute sovereignty over
creation.

Thorn in the Side of Khomeini

This uncompromising outlook on life led Khomeini to oust his self-
appointed successor, Ayatollah Montazeri, only months before he died.
Montazeri saw the capture of political power by the clergy only as a
means which ought to be used in order to improve the material and
spiritual conditions of the people. Khomeini maintained that, if need be,
people should be forced to behave in an Islamic way. Montazeri, for his
part, argued in favour of persuasion through setting good examples.

Both men advocated a return to the simple life and helped popularize
such notions as frugality, a reduction in one's expectations from life, a cut
in consumption and a distaste for luxuries. Both wanted the Iranians to
sleep on the ground, sit on the floor, eat only one or two simple meals
a day, make do with very few clothes and be content with living in one
or two rooms (Amir Taheri, *The Spirit of Allah*, page 294).

The difference was that Montazeri believed that human nature of itself
tends towards good if given the chance. Khomeini, however, pinpointed
the little devil he saw hiding within every person, and thought nothing of
enforcing the good at bayonet point if necessary. Between 1981 and 1985
the two leaders adopted basically contradictory positions on almost every
major issue, with Montazeri playing the liberal and Khomeini remaining
true to his image of the uncompromising radical.

Good Cop/Bad Cop

Opponents of the regime accused the two men of offering an Islamic
version of the soft-cop/tough-cop interplay in order to confuse the people. This is almost certainly unfair: the two men genuinely had variant
approaches. The difference between Khomeini and Montazeri extended
to the important issue of exporting the revolution as well. Montazeri
emphasized proselytization and propaganda; Khomeini inclined to see an
effective answer only in the use of force. In 1981 the Imam ordered the
creation of an 'Army of Twenty Million' which, when fully ready, would
fight to hoist the flag of Allah in every capital of the world.

Judaism does not believe in people being banged into shape so that
they fit the spiritual puzzle. Rather, it advocates an inner transformation

so that the human pieces fit the puzzle both in shape as well as content, in deed as well as in heart. The result is a truer, more beautiful whole that will no longer be a jagged, uneven puzzle.

Attacked by Colleagues

When I first expressed these ideas in print, in an American Jewish magazine, *Chai Today*, I received several letters of disagreement, one of which was exceedingly abusive and was subsequently published in an alternative Jewish periodical. In the letter, the author attacked me for my 'misrepresenting Judaism' and accused me of possessing 'a severely misguided understanding of Judaism at best, and a liberal mind-set at worst'.

The author, who is an Orthodox rabbi from California, made the following argument, which I shall summarize.

He maintained that I had misrepresented Judaism because indeed Judaism did possess many of the mechanisms employed by Khomeini. Judaism calls for very severe physical punishment, in many cases capital, for religious transgression. For example, one who breaks the laws of Shabbat can be put to death if all the criteria are met, such as the presence of witnesses and warning, and so on. Moreover, for even the slightest religious infringement, the offender would receive lashes from a Jewish court, in Temple times. 'What Rabbi Boteach is seeking to do,' he concluded, 'is to whitewash Judaism of its similarities to the Khomeini regime, so that it conforms with today's liberal values.'

To be sure, the good rabbi, whose attack saddened me because of its hostile tone, is correct. Indeed Judaism does mandate physical punishment for religious offenders. Where he grossly errs, however, is in his understanding of the purpose of these warnings and punishments, and what the Torah is seeking to achieve by stipulating them.

One Apple Should Not Infect Another

The purpose of the punishments delineated in Scripture is not to make the population religious. Rather, their purpose is to preserve the religious observance and devotion of a population that is already religious.

To explain: God wishes that people approach religion from a stance of joy, interest, personal involvement, choice and conviction. There are numerous statements throughout Jewish literature which show that these qualifications are not just preferable in serving God, but rather they are in essence. If so, the question may be asked, why did God institute such severe punishments for religious infraction? The answer is that these laws were instituted for a society which used to be the norm, that is, the majority of the population were observant and devout. The problem was, what if a few rotten apples began to appear within the group? In order to prevent them from infecting everyone else with their faithlessness, and to protect the offenders themselves from acting upon their faithlessness, the Torah instituted punishment primarily as a deterrent but also as a way of weeding out those who could adversely affect the faithful, as Maimonides explains at length in the *Guide to the Perplexed*.

The Sanhedrin Exiles Itself

That this is true is easily demonstrated by a passage from the Talmud, which tells of how forty years before the destruction of the Second Temple, when the terrible suffering which was being visited upon the Jews caused them to be a lawless people, many of whom incurred a capital penalty under Jewish law, the Sanhedrin, the high Jewish court, exiled itself from its chambers on the Temple Mount. The reason: they were only allowed to pass capital judgements when they were in the chamber, and there were so many who were deserving of it, they did not wish to put vast numbers of people to death.

In other words, once the death penalty no longer proved an effective means of retaining and preserving the spiritual devotion of the people, it was abandoned. And although the Sanhedrin could have used it as a means to reinstall fear into the population and thus make them religious again, this is not what Judaism is about. It is not engendered by fear or intimidation, but by love, allegiance and an inner desire on the part of humanity to reach out to their Creator, like a child who lovingly seeks out his father.

Chapter Thirty-four

IS THERE A DEVIL IN JUDAISM?

The joke goes that of all the Oxford and Cambridge colleges, there are only two names found in both places, and both these are named after Jews. What are they? Wolfson College, established by Lord Wolfson's charitable Trust (one of Anglo-Jewry's leading Jewish philanthropists), and Jesus College. Unfortunately this is not true as there is of course a Magdalene, and a Trinity at 'the other place' as well as in Oxford, but that does not spoil the point of the joke, which is usually told by Jews and is designed to make the Jews feel slightly more at home and comfortable about their place at Oxford.

Bearing in mind the links as well as the vast gulfs between the Christian tradition and Judaism, it is worthwhile exploring what some of the differences really mean. The following explores one fundamental aspect of the contrast between Christian and Jewish doctrine, and its major ramifications for everyday living.

The Power of One Good Deed

If there can be said to be just one devastating social ill which is wreaking havoc in today's world it is that we have lost an appreciation for a single good deed. Every time we are about to undertake a new deed of goodness, we look at the state of the world and it seems futile. But there are other reasons why we have denigrated the power of a single act of kindness or goodness, and it may have something to do with the penetration of Christian thought into society at large and the Jewish community in particular.

One of the major points of departure between Christianity and Judaism is the belief in the devil. In the Christian beliefs, there is God, but opposing Him is Lucifer, a rebellious and fallen angel, also known as Satan. He has set up for himself an alternative kingdom. In the same way that God promises rewards for good deeds, the devil promises material plenty for invoking his will instead of the Divine. The two powers compete against each other, and although ultimately it is God who will prevail, and the devil and those who basked in his glory will be punished on Judgement Day, until that time comes he operates an autonomous kingdom in which evil is allowed to flourish unhindered.

There Can be Only One Kingdom and One Ruler

Of course, this type of thinking is anathema to Judaism, which can accept no all-powerful existence save that of the Almighty. Although Judaism also speaks of a 'satan' which lurks in the heart of each individual, the Zohar explains that this satan or evil inclination should be seen as a hired agent of the Almighty who, while attempting to lead a human away from the path of righteousness, secretly prays that the individual will not follow. The Zohar gives the analogy of a king who, in an effort to test the character of his son, the crown prince, hires a prostitute to seduce him. Although she uses all her charms to cause the prince to stumble, her inner desire is that he will not succumb to her temptation.

The ramifications of these contradictory Jewish and Christian beliefs transcend by far the mere understanding of whether God is all-powerful or has any competition. It is from these divergent beliefs that the Christian and Jewish understanding of good, evil, sin and repentance part ways as well.

In Christian beliefs, but most markedly in Catholicism, sin is taken very seriously indeed. If one has sinned, it is not sufficient just to turn one's head from the lapse and continue on the path of righteousness. One must first obliterate the sin, through various means, among which are confession, deep remorse, and perhaps even denial of the body and self-flagellation.

Continuing After a Terrible Fall

But in Judaism the opposite is true. The Jewish attitude towards the person who sins can be summed up in a story of what took place between the Belzer rebbe and one of his Chasidim. The man came to the rebbe and told him that he had had sexual relations with a non-Jewish woman who was not his wife. The rebbe looked him in the eye, raised his eyebrows as if to say, 'Why are you wasting your time and making a big deal out of this?' and said just two words, 'Go further.' Of course, the rebbe was not condoning the man's adultery or the hurt it would cause: he was not saying the man had committed a very grave and serious offence. Rather, he had indeed stumbled. But what was most important was that he should get on with his life.

Judaism deals with sin by drowning it in good deeds. The sin is not given the status of being an independent entity. Rather, it is seen as a void of goodness, a blackness that must be filled with light.

Evil as an Entity

The divergent approaches of two of the world's leading religions are predicated on the way they see good and evil. In the Christian conception, the devil has his own domain. He has almost unlimited power in the perimeter of evil. As such, anything connected with him, any sin or evil act, is also an independent creation. He who sins, in the Christian view, has brought into being a grotesque, rebellious act which, if not dealt with and eradicated, will stand on its own merit and haunt the evildoer for aeons to come. It is not enough to drown it in light, because its blackness is an independent entity which actively opposes goodness, just as the devil himself does.

Evil as the Absence of Goodness

However, in the Jewish conception of things, evil is defined, not as an independent domain, but as an absence of Godliness. Only in those places where Godly light does not shine, or where the individual creates an obstruction to Godly light by sinning, can evil exist. It is not a real or independent entity, but simply a void. There is no devil in Judaism, and consequently there is no independent arena in which evil can thrive or stand on its own. Rather, evil is the lack of Godly illumination.

In Psalm 34, verse 14, King David says, 'Depart from evil, and do good . . .' It is important to note that King David does not say that in order to turn away from evil one must first destroy, or wage a pitched battle against, one's sin. He does not treat evil like a fiery dragon which one has brought into being through one's un-Godly activities, that must be slain before one can re-embark on a path of goodness. Such an approach would give sin far more credit than it deserves. Because evil is an absence of goodness, one counters it by an abundance of goodness. Evil is nothing, and one destroys a 'nothing' by replacing it with something tangible and real.

. . . and Darkness as the Absence of Light

To illustrate better this concept, imagine walking into a room which is pitch black. One cannot see anything, but one needs to see. There are two ways of going about generating illumination. The first is to attack the darkness. You reach for your sword to slay the blackness which dominates the room and all its environs. Of course, this would just prove a futile battle against a non-existent enemy. It is far easier and productive to switch on the light: all the darkness is automatically dispelled. What is even easier is to light a small candle. The quality of light is such that, even in the tiniest quantities, it still dispels an amazing amount of darkness.

The same is true of goodness. To destroy even the gravest sin, one must simply do a *mitzvah*. By doing so one achieves two purposes at once. The performance of a good and righteous act, and the automatic cancellation of those previous deeds which stand in contradiction to Godliness and goodness.

This is a profound lesson to those who are intent on undertaking a religious life at an advanced stage in their career. The clearest and greatest obstacle to Oxford students becoming seriously involved in the study and observance of Judaism is that they say to themselves, 'I've missed the boat. It is too late for me to begin.'

What one must recognize is the power and transcendence of even one good deed 'which dispels much darkness'. Twenty-five years of not living a Jewish life pales into insignificance when one performs even one *mitzvah* and allows the light of the human soul to illuminate one's life.

Chapter Thirty-five

MESSIAHS CAME MARCHING ONE BY ONE

For many students, the Oxford environment provides the opportunity to look critically at one's deepest beliefs. However, the intellectual milieu is far from being neutral. It is currently biased towards atheism, and the spiritual contexts that do exist are naturally strongly influenced by the university's long and prestigious heritage as a Christian institution. This of course makes it more difficult for those from any other tradition to maintain their beliefs, even in apparently small matters. For instance, out of respect for the Christian Sabbath, the university examinations are never held on Sunday. Of course, there is no similar automatic respect for the Jewish Sabbath, which presents a problem for many of the Jewish students who refuse to sit their exams on Saturday. Christians do not have to decide whether they will sit a paper on their Sabbath or not. For a Jewish student, it *must* be decided whether an examination on Saturday will be taken or delayed. If it is delayed, the student must be invigilated in the house of an Oxford don to ensure that he does not come into contact with other students who have sat the exam. Being virtually locked up in the home of someone you may not even know well can be a real encumbrance. Since the environment is geared towards a certain way of thinking, it takes commitment and motivation just to stay still in one place: to advance spiritually then takes a great deal of effort.

The Christianity which is to be found in Oxford is for the most part quite passive, and accepts the existence of other faiths. There is, however, a growing evangelical element. This affects the Jewish student community in that approximately once a year there is a concerted effort, on the part of the evangelicals, to convert others to their faith. The event is known as mission week and has become notorious among the Jewish students. It is not uncommon for Jewish students to be specifically targeted in these efforts. The most distressing episode took place just as I arrived in my first year; four young Jewish students during mission week converted to Christianity. These four were all students of Oxford University, and all had particular emotional vulnerabilities at that time, one especially so. They were unable to counter the arguments of the Christian missionaries with anything like the vigour which would have been available to them if they had had all the arguments at their fingertips or, more importantly, if they had been emotionally secure.

Preying on Emotional Weakness

To be truthful, this event angered me. I have no objection whatsoever to Christian missionizing, even aggressive missionizing so long as it is done with respect for another's faith and integrity. Any human being has the right to promote what they see as the truth. What is significant, however, is how one goes about disseminating one's beliefs. What I object to is targeting specific candidates and particularly students who are vulnerable due to deep personal problems. In this instance, what these students needed was of course attention and caring. When such caring is provided with the express purpose of introducing someone to a faith foreign to his own and to his people's, I consider that to be very dishonest and disheartening. I expressed these sentiments to many of Oxford's Christian college chaplains with whom I am friendly, and all of them agreed that if there were a Jewish student who came to them with a problem, they would first encourage him or her to come to see me or another Jewish cleric. They said they could not countenance the actions of these evangelicals, and distanced themselves from these people, who incidentally were not connected with the university.

One incident was particularly repugnant. A truly brilliant Jewish philosophy student, who came from an observant home but was deeply estranged from her parents and a manic depressive, was 'love-bombed' by a Christian missionary who became her boyfriend. After three weeks, she was baptized, gave up her degree and left the university to do a mission with him in Eastern Europe. Her parents were aghast and asked me to intervene, but there was nothing I could do. After a few months he had to leave her to do a mission on his own. He left her in the care of his Christian group. It was at that moment she discovered his emotions for her were feigned and the only thing which interested her 'boyfriend' was that she be a good Christian. Luckily, she came back to be comforted from heartbreak by her parents and rejoined the university and the Jewish community.

Australian Antics and a Jewish Bishop

But I have seen worse. When I was sent to Australia with nine colleagues by the Lubavitcher rebbe at nineteen years old in 1986 to serve as founding member of a higher Jewish educational facility in Sydney, we arrived to discover that Christian missionaries were converting large numbers of Jewish students. They even had a messianic Jewish congregation barely one mile from our dormitory. There was nothing being done to combat it, and I found myself reluctantly accepting the responsibility. So I became a one-man anti-missionary unit, and I would go out at night to meet Jews who had been converted to Christianity, to discuss why they had done it. My purpose was not to get them to drop Christianity, especially if they felt that they had embraced it sincerely and I had no right to disrespect their decision. What I did seek to accomplish was to discover whether they had seriously explored Judaism before opting out, and to tell them that what they owed their people and three thousand years of tradition, at the very least, was to examine whether Judaism could offer them whatever it was which they discovered within Christianity. In every case, the Jews I met who had converted to Christianity had two things in common: firstly, they were grossly ignorant of Jewish tradition. Secondly, they had embraced Christianity primarily for emotional reasons.

My student rabbinical garb was not very conducive to conversations on this subject, and so I would don jeans and T-shirt and a knitted yarmulka with my name on it. My colleagues loved taking pictures of my escapades, until one day it did me in. The head of our Rabbinical College, the Rosh Yeshivah, got hold of the pictures and was perplexed. He then casually walked one day into a regular afternoon study session in the study hall. He found my colleagues studiously occupied with the Talmud, but the book I was using drew considerable attention on his part because it was so much smaller than the large volumes of the Talmud. Clearly I was studying something different. He nonchalantly made his way over to my table and discovered I was memorizing passages from the New Testament. He was not pleased.

Journeying Along the Priest Path

That night he summoned me to his house, and for two hours told me a long convoluted tale of how one of his colleagues in yeshivah years earlier was today a priest. I took the hint. He was really under the impression that I was studying these things and speaking with these Jewish individuals because I had developed a strong attraction for Christianity. I desperately tried to explain the real situation, but he would not listen. He was convinced I had embarked upon what he called 'the priest path'. He forbade me from further studying any Christian texts, at least until I demonstrated to him that I was as interested in studying Judaism. He even confiscated my borrower's card from the library down the road to ensure that I would heed his word.

But there was an outcry. Parents of those to whom I spoke, as well as secular Jewish benefactors of our yeshivah, protested at my activities being halted, and I was allowed to continue. I was amazed and here I learned something very significant. There is probably nothing in Jewish life that arouses greater hostility among even the most assimilated of Jews than a Jew who converts to another faith. In all my years in Jewish communal work, I have met parents whose children have married non-Jewish partners, whose children have completely abandoned them, and whose children have become Christian, Hare Krishna, or Buddhist. It is the final category of parents whose lives are most torn asunder. They can have no peace. The thought of their Jewish children forsaking their people is what hurts most.

The Ethics of Evangelism under Debate

The same is true of students at Oxford. Even those who attend Jewish activities minimally and who are on the periphery of Jewish life at the university still turn out in great numbers whenever we organize an event rebutting missionary claims.

In November 1990 we staged a formal and prestigious event exploring Christian missionizing, and we had a debate in the Gulbenkian Lecture Theatre in the university's St Cross building, entitled 'The Ethics of Evangelism'. In the past this lecture theatre has been used for such prestigious events as the Professor of Poetry's annual lecture to the students, as well as our two debates on science versus religion, both of which attracted over a thousand students. The panellists included the religious affairs correspondent of *The Times*, Clifford Longley, Rabbi Dr Jacob Immanuel Schochet, the well-known Jewish philosopher and probably the most famous Jewish anti-missionary in the world, and the leading Christian cleric and theologian Bishop Kenneth Cragg, formerly the Anglican Bishop of Jerusalem. It was the first time that Oxford saw a debate on this issue which included prominent representatives of the church, media and the Jewish religion. Each panellist had the opportunity to express their point of view, and then questions were asked. The unanimous conclusion of all of the panellists was that Christian missionizing must proceed only along the most honest and ethical lines, and was repugnant if it specifically targeted Jews or those in a dire emotional state.

The driving force behind that debate was not to attack Christianity, but to put it into perspective. Nevertheless, the response of the Jewish students was very strong, and conversion to Christianity is something which even the most liberal of Jewish students exhibit hostility toward.

'As Long as She Has a God'

The only exception to this I have encountered occurred with one of the students I was closest to. He was an Australian studying on a scholarship. His father had died four years earlier, and this had left a strong impact on his life. He examined and was touched by everything. Deeply emotional, he was also extremely lonely. But his father's passing impelled him to a deeper commitment to Judaism, which was almost entirely lacking from his life before the death. He became a very spiritual person.

After a few months at Oxford he began dating a Jewish girl I knew only fleetingly. It became serious, and he was very happy. After a few weeks, a number of my students came to warn me that his girlfriend, who was not at all an observant Jew, was attending Christian meetings, and I should step in. But before I even had that chance, it was Shavuot night and a group of about fifty of us were staying up the entire night to study as part of the L'Chaim Society's *Tikun Leil Shavuot*. While I was studying with this student, a mutual friend of ours said to me, 'Did he tell you? His girlfriend was baptized. She became a Christian last week.' I was astonished. 'How could you have kept this from me?' I asked him. 'I am your rabbi, and you are one of my closest friends. You are also someone to whom Judaism and spirituality are of supreme importance. A Jewish girl who is your girlfriend, whom you are even contemplating marrying, develops an interest in Christianity and subsequently converts, and through the whole ordeal you do not utter a single word?' I could not contain my indignation.

His response: 'Listen, Shmuley. I agree that you have a point. But I waited so long to find a girl who didn't just pursue her degree or materialism that I concluded, so long as she has a god, any god, is the only thing that matters.'

(Fortunately, he later came to see my point of view and brought his girlfriend around to hear me lecture on a Friday night. Ironically, and I mention this only to tell the story as it happened, she was so impressed by what I had to say that particular Shabbat that the next Sunday at church services she quoted me by name and repeated the entire speech. Evidently this was a form of evangelical congregation where any congregant could get up and say something of inspiration.)

It is to counter innocent misconceptions such as these that I began to teach the students, even those who take Judaism seriously, why Christianity is inappropriate for the Jew and incompatible with Jewish tradition.

The Need for Mutual Respect

I should mention that the present purpose of this exposition is not in any way to undermine the faith of Christians, which I respect and encourage. I am often approached by intelligent Christian students who feel disillusioned with matters of faith, or wish that Christianity would embrace a particularly Jewish perspective on a given matter. My response to them is always that they must live within their tradition and do their best to make it work. Christianity brought the knowledge of God to billions of people throughout the generations, in the most distant isles and shores.

Rather, the following is an attempt to demonstrate to those of the Jewish faith why the rabbis never embraced Jesus as the Messiah, and why they rejected many of the religious tenets which are taught by those who believe that Jesus of Nazareth was indeed the promised Jewish redeemer. I aim to present the facts as the Jews know them in order to contrast them with the assertions made by Christians, and so to redress the current imbalance of information.

For centuries, there has been a tradition of Christians reinterpreting the Hebrew Bible (called the Old Testament) and telling Jews what it *really* means in the light of their knowledge of the New Testament. This essay aims to provide a more rounded picture, to provide a firm basis for intelligent discussion of the matter. The main thrusts of the argument are twofold: that Jesus could not have been the Jewish Messiah from various proofs in the Hebrew Bible, and that the interpretations which have been accepted as fundamental to Christian doctrine are missing from the Jews' understanding of their own Messiah. Rabbinical teaching places an entirely different interpretation from that of the Christian churches on the prophecies about the redeemer.

Part One

The Blood of the Messiah

It is an integral part of both the Christian and Jewish faiths that the Messiah must stem from the House of David. That the Messiah must be the scion of the Davidic dynasty is repeated many times in the prophets:

> Isaiah 11:1–2 – And there shall come forth a rod out of the stem of Jesse, and a Branch shall grow out of his roots:
> And the spirit of the Lord shall rest upon him, the spirit of wisdom and understanding, the spirit of counsel and might, the spirit of knowledge and of the fear of the Lord.

> Jeremiah 23:5 – the days come, saith the Lord, that I will raise unto David a righteous Branch, and a king shall reign and prosper, and shall execute judgement and justice in the earth.

However, the Gospels relate that Jesus was not a male descendant of the House of David, but was the alleged son of God, born of a virgin. To be sure, the idea of a God-man, born of a union between the Creator and a human mother, has always been foreign to Judaism. One might even say that it is anathema to Judaism, whose greatest contribution to the rise of religion was to remove any anthropomorphic or bodily features

Simon Wiesenthal having tea with Jewish Rhodes and Marshall scholars at the Chabad House in Oxford.

Benny Begin (M.K.), son of the late Israeli Prime Minister, Menachem Begin, and leading Israeli politician, addresses L'Chaim on security issues and the legacy his father left the Israeli people.

Academy Award winning actor, Jon Voight participates with Oxford students at a Bible class with Rabbi Boteach in his study.

Actor Jon Voight addresses L'Chaim Society students at the beautiful eighteenth-century University Examination Schools, a most fearsome place for the students as their futures are decided here.

Lord Immanuel Jakobovits, Emeritus Chief Rabbi of the UK and Commonwealth, debates with heart transplant pioneer Dr Christiaan Barnard on euthanasia.

Dr Christiaan Barnard debates with Lord Immanuel Jakobovits at the Oxford Union Society. In the background, to the left, is Celia Rothenberg, a Marshall scholar and student president of L'Chaim Society during that term.

Godfrey Bradman, leading British property developer and environmentalist, addresses hundreds of L'Chaim students on the importance of commerce and the environment.

Brian Glasser, a Jewish Rhodes Scholar from West Virginia and first student President of the L'Chaim Society, introduces Elie Weisel to the Oxford Union.

Elie Weisel, writer and Nobel Peace Prize Laureate, converses with Lord Jenkins, Chancellor of Oxford University, at a dinner L'Chaim held in Mr Weisel's honour.

Elie Weisel conversing at the L'Chaim dinner held in his honour with Sir Claus Moser, former Warden of Wadham College, Oxford and former Chairman of the Royal Opera House, Covent Garden.

Elie Weisel addresses 1,500 Oxford students on the subject of the 'Joys of Purim', in a world that witnessed the Holocaust. This lecture took place one day after the most joyous of all Jewish festivals, Purim.

Dr Richard Judd, keeper of the Bodleian Library Hebraica collection, shows the first ever printed copy of the Talmud, censored by a fourteenth-century Jewish convert monk.

Senator Rudy Boschwitz of Minnesota, nicknamed the Rabbi of the Senate. His Friday night lecture at Oxford was accompanied by the first ever Shabbat dinner at the Oxford Union.

Rabbi Boteach officiates at a Jewish wedding of two Oxford students, an all too rare occasion at the University.

Rabbi Boteach and former L'Chaim President Dan Williams in the traditional celebrations for the completing of Finals — the last exams to be taken by undergraduates — when friends and colleagues regularly douse the finalists with champagne and shaving cream.

Rabbi Boteach with Cory Booker (far left), American Rhodes Scholar and President of L'Chaim Society 1993 and Michael Benson, grandson of the President and Prophet of the Mormon Church. L'Chaim attracts many diverse non-Jewish students who remarkably find a home away from home at the L'Chaim Centre.

from the Creator. This was the essential difference between Judaism, progenitor of monotheism, and the primarily pagan cults which preceded it.

Some Christian theologians have attempted to respond to this inconsistency by saying that Jesus's mother, Mary, stemmed from the House of David, and thus Jesus can trace his lineage back to King David. However, the Gospels of Matthew and Luke state specifically that their genealogies trace Jesus through *Joseph*, not Mary. It even lists it as such, mentioning Joseph directly. But even if we agree to contradict the verses and say that Mary was a descendant of David, Jesus is excluded from being the Messiah. According to Jewish law, the law by which claims to being the Messiah must be tested, all genealogies are traced *only* through the father, not the mother. This is clearly seen throughout the entire Bible, and requires no elaboration.

Conflicting Genealogies

This problem is further compounded by the fact that the two genealogies of Jesus recorded in the Gospels (Matthew 1, Luke 3) are inconsistent and contradictory. So different are they that they disagree even concerning which son of King David from whom Jesus stemmed. Matthew states that he came from *Solomon*, while Luke states that he stemmed from *Nathan*, the son of David.

Matthew 1:
1 The book of the generation of Jesus Christ, the Son of David, the Son of Abraham. 2 Abraham begat Isaac; and Isaac begat Jacob; and Jacob begat Judas and his brethren; 3 Judas begat Phares and Zara of Thamar; and Phares begat Esrom; and Esrom begat Aram. 4 Aram begat Aminadab; Aminadab begat Naasson; and Naasson begat Salmon; 5 And Salmon begat Booz of Rachab; Booz begat Obed of Ruth; and Obed begat Jesse; 6 And Jesse begat David the king; *and David the king begat Solomon of her that had been the wife of Urias*; 7 And Solomon begat Roboam; and Roboam begat Abia; and Abia begat Asa; 8 And Asa begat Josaphat; and Josaphat begat Joram; and Joram begat Ozias. 9 And Ozias begat Joatham; and Joatham begat Achaz; and Achaz begat Ezekias; 10 And Ezekias begat Manasses; and Manasses begat Amon; and Amon begat Josias; 11 *And Josias begat Jeconias and his brethren, about the time they were carried away to Babylon*: 12 And after they were brought to Babylon, Jeconias begat Salathiel; and Salathiel begat Zorobabel; 13 And Zorobabel begat Abiud; and Abiud begat Eliakim; and Eliakim begat Azor; 14 And Azor begat Sadoc; and Sadoc begat Achim; and Achim begat Eliud; 15 And Eliud begat Eleazar; and Eleazar begat Matthan; and Matthan begat Jacob; 16 And Jacob begat Joseph the husband of Mary, of whom was born Jesus, who is called Christ. 17 So all the generations from Abraham to David are

fourteen generations; and from David until the carrying away into Babylon are fourteen generations; and from the carrying away into Babylon unto Christ are fourteen generations.

Luke 3:
23 And Jesus Himself began to be about thirty years of age, being (as was supposed) the son of Joseph, which was the son of Heli; 24 Which was the son of Matthat, which was the son of Levi, which was the son of Melchi, which was the son of Janna, which was the son of Joseph, 25 Which was the son of Mattathias, which was the son of Amos, which was the son of Naum, which was the son of Esli, which was the son of Nagge, 26 Which was the son of Maath, which was the son of Mattathias, which was the son of Semei, which was the son of Joseph, which was the son of Juda, 27 Which was the son of Joanna, which was the son of Rhesa, which was the son of Zorobabel, which was the son of Salathiel, which was the son of Neri, 28 Which was the son of Melchi, which was the son of Addi, which was the son of Cosam, which was the son of Elmodam, which was the son of Er, 29 Which was the son of Jose, which was the son of Eliezer, which was the son of Jorim, which was the son of Matthat, which was the son of Levi, 30 Which was the son of Simeon, which was the son of Juda, which was the son of Joseph, which was the son of Jonan, which was the son of Eliakim, 31 Which was the son of Melea, which was the son of Menna, which was the son of Mattatha, which was the son of *Nathan, which was the son of David.*

Christian theologians tend to explain these inconsistencies by asserting that one describes the genealogy of Joseph, while the other describes that of Mary. If this is accepted as the case, though, both of the genealogies respectively exclude Jesus from being the Messiah.

Completing the Genealogy

Luke testifies that Jesus was descended from Solomon's son Nathan. The Hebrew Bible states specifically, and then reiterates the point, that the messianic King must stem from *Solomon* and from no other son of David.

1 Chronicles 17:11 states: And it shall come to pass, when thy days be expired that thou must go to be with thy fathers, that I will raise up thy seed after thee, which shall be of thy sons; and I will establish his kingdom. 12 He shall build me an house and I will establish his throne for ever. 13 I will be his father, and he shall be my son: and I will not take my mercy away from him, as I took it from him that was before thee: 14 But I will settle him in mine house and in my kingdom for ever: and his throne shall be established for evermore.

Clearly, these verses are referring to the son of David who will succeed him on the throne and whose kingdom shall last for ever. Who is this son? We find out a few chapters later, where he is mentioned quite explicitly.

1 Chronicles 22:9: Behold, a son shall be born to thee, who shall be a man of rest; and I will give him rest from all his enemies round about: for *his name shall be Solomon*, and I will give peace and quietness unto Israel in his days. 10 He shall build an house for my name; and he shall be my son, and I will be his father; and I will establish the throne of his kingdom over Israel for ever.

Filling in the Missing Kings

The genealogy of Matthew does indeed state that Jesus stemmed from Solomon, and it might be argued that the genealogy of Jesus could therefore allow for him to be the messianic king. In Matthew verses 6–11, the kings of Judah are recorded as part of the genealogy. After Joram (verse 8) this genealogy is incorrect. Four kings have been omitted in order to fulfil the numerology in Matthew 1:17, 'So all the generations from Abraham to David are fourteen; and from David until the carrying away into Babylon are fourteen generations; and from the carrying away into Babylon unto Christ are fourteen generations.' The four omitted kings are Ahaziah, Joash, Amaziah, and Jehoiakim: with these four added back, this genealogy is identical to the Hebrew Bible's genealogy of the kings of Judah in 1 Chronicles 3:10–16.

With this correction it will be noted quite clearly that Jeconiah was the son of Jehoiakim. This is stated explicitly in Jeremiah 27:20 '. . . when he carried away captive Jeconiah the son of Jehoiakim king of Judah . . .' Jeconiah was the same person as Conia. As it is stated in Jeremiah 37:1, 'Zedekiah the son of Josiah reigned instead of Coniah the son of Jehoiakim'.

Jeconiah is Cursed

The genealogy in Matthew that describes Jesus as a descendant of Jeconiah also excludes Jesus from being the Messiah. This is because Jeconiah and his descendants were cursed by God to exclude them from succeeding to David's throne.

In Jeremiah 22:24–30, a condemnation is recorded in which God curses Jeconiah and his descendants terribly: God vows that, 'no man of his seed shall prosper, sitting upon the throne of David, and ruling any more in Judah'. If Jesus was descended from Jeconiah, he is included in this curse and it is therefore not possible for him to be the King Messiah described in the Hebrew Bible.

Accordingly, both New Testament genealogies record that Jesus could not have been the Messiah. Luke because Scripture clearly indicates that the Messiah must be born of Solomon, and the disciple's testimony says he was from Nathan. Matthew because it lists Jesus as having stemmed from Jeconiah, from whom God swore he would remove the sceptre.

Errors in Interpretation of the Hebrew Bible

The central key in understanding the rabbinical rejection of Christian missionary claims is this: the Jewish people are the possessors of an oral tradition of transmission and interpretation of Scripture which goes back to the time of Moses. Verses in Scripture, even the most explicit, are highly ambiguous, and are thus susceptible to multiple interpretations. How then are we to know which is the correct rendition? The answer is that intrinsic to the Jewish religion is the belief that God not only gave a written law, but an oral explanation as to what it all meant. This was never intended to be written but transmitted mouth to mouth, father to son, master to pupil. When the Sages, however, feared that it might be lost, it was written and systematized into what we today call the *Mishna, Talmud* and *Aggada*, and *Midrash*.

Thus the written law, the Five Books of Moses, was given at Sinai along with an oral tradition for understanding it fully. Acccording to Jewish belief, it is the rabbis and Sages who possess the legitimate system of interpretation. No one else can approach the Jews with a new system of interpretation because it would be mere speculation, and completely outside what we believe God told Moses was the correct meaning of each verse. Thus the Christian understanding of our Scripture, notwithstanding its merits, is of little practical value to the Jew when it contradicts our established rules of interpretation.

Hundreds of Christian Denominations

Christianity falters on this foundation upon which Judaism thrives. At present, there exist literally hundreds of denominations of Christianity, because although all these denominations possess the same *written* New Testament, they cannot agree on how to *read* it. The New Testament has no accompanying tradition for interpretation, so each denomination translates it as they see fit, resulting in bitter confrontations between those with different ways of reading it. Even in the first few centuries of Christianity, consensus of interpretation was not the case, as the bitter rivalries between various sects indicate. Once the Catholic Church was established as the arbiter of interpretation in western Europe, the problems were not over: control of access meant simply that it was the ordinary person who had no contact with the supposedly life-giving text, not that misreading was avoided altogether. Of course, the Reformation opened the doors for the ordinary Christian to enjoy the New Testament, but it also allowed all kinds of variant and divisive interpretations to gain hold of the general population.

The Singularity of Judaism

On the other hand, since the Torah was originally given along with its interpretation, there is therefore only one Judaism, the written texts correctly rendered for all time within an oral framework. Evangelical Christians, who are missing that framework of interpretation, often come to Jews to 'enlighten' them as to what their Hebrew Bible 'really' means. Yet it is reported in Mark that Jesus himself said explicitly that the rabbis and only the rabbis had the authority to interpret the Law of Moses, for they occupy the seat of Moses: 'The scribes and the Pharisees sit in Moses' seat. Therefore whatever they tell you to observe, that observe and do, but do not do according to the works; for they say, and do not do.'

This also means that only the rabbis may decide who the Messiah will be. The Torah prescribes precisely what qualifications must be possessed, what is to be accomplished, and many other criteria for the identification of the real Messiah. As the rabbis are the only ones who possess the tradition for interpretation of the messianic prophecies, they are the only ones who are in a position to judge just who has fulfilled these prophecies.

Jesus Rejected by the Rabbis

Jesus himself was never accepted by the rabbis of his generation, the Pharisees. The great majority of the New Testament relates that he constantly battled with the Pharisees, castigating and accusing them because they would not accept him. He called them by names that perhaps did not suit 'the Prince of Peace'. In Matthew 23:33 he refers to the rabbis as 'Ye serpents, ye generation of vipers', and very frequently throughout the Gospels he referred to them as 'scorpions' and 'vipers'. He was not this malicious to any other party or persons, but only to the rabbis. It seems that he took their rejection of him quite personally and recognized that they posed a threat to him.

Such incessant personal attack against the rabbis is a phenomenon found in virtually all messianic pretenders throughout history, an important example of which was the now infamous Shabbatei Tzvi, easily the most accepted false 'Messiah' among Jews in history. In every case the attacks are a result of the rabbis' refusal to support the would-be Messiah.

The Apostles are Unlearned

According to the New Testament, Jesus was never given the backing of the Sages and Pharisees. Also, not one of his disciples was a person learned in the Torah. The New Testament attests the fact that many of Jesus' original disciples were ignorant. Peter and John, two of his most acclaimed apostles, are quoted in Acts 4:13 as being 'unlearned and ignorant men'. Matthew, before joining the ranks of Jesus' believers, was a tax collector: Matthew 9:9: 'And Jesus passed forth from thence, he saw a man, named Matthew, sitting at the receipt of custom; and he saith unto him, Follow me.' (The Talmud has a very low opinion of this profession, stating repeatedly that the tax collectors of the Second Temple era, who served as agents of the occupying Roman authorities, were thieves and crooks, and often even murderers. Even in the New Testament, when Jesus wishes to rebuke his students, he often refers to them as being 'worse than the tax collectors'.) The remaining apostles were fishermen and other men without access to traditional knowledge (Matthew 4:18, Mark 1:16, Luke 5:2–11), including many women who some traditions maintain were of ill repute. This is not to say that above-mentioned individuals were not highly meritorious. But whatever virtue they possessed, it seems undeniable that they were not scholars of Jewish law and thought.

The point in all this is that the founding followers of Jesus would not have had the necessary knowledge to render correctly the Hebrew Bible: in addition to the fact that they were ignorant of traditional interpretation, their professions too made the possibility of mastery of the Torah highly improbable. So they would have been particularly vulnerable to misinterpreting their fellow man, Jesus, as the Messiah.

Paul and His Interpretation of the Law

The New Testament states that the Apostle Paul was a learned man who converted to Christianity on the road to Damascus. As he was the most learned of all Jesus' followers we would expect him to be able to interpret the Torah correctly. There is no individual in the history of the Christian religion who is more responsible for the differences that separate Christianity from Judaism than Paul. It was he who argued for the abrogation of the law, and incurred the wrath of his fellow apostles in doing so. His interpretation of the law, then, must be subjected to critical examination.

A fundamental teaching of Christianity is of course the dissolution of the commandments of the Torah. This abolition was enacted by Paul, and his grounds for so major a change are allegedly based on a verse from the Torah.

Concerning the hanging of a body after capital punishment by stoning, the Torah warns that it is not to be left overnight: rather, the corpse must be removed from the tree on the very same day as the stoning, and buried. The reason given for this in the Law is this: 'for he that is hanged is accursed of God' (Deuteronomy 21:23). The reason that it is a curse unto God when a person is left hanging, as the Rashi and other classical Jewish commentators explain, is because God created Man in His image. So, when a human resembling the Creator hangs on a tree, it is an affront unto God, for the person possesses His likeness. Rashi makes this analogous to a king who has an identical twin brother who is a murderer. The law eventually catches up with him, and he is hanged. All who see the hanging corpse remark, 'Look, the king has been hanged for an offence.' Thus, so as not to serve as an insult to the Creator, the body must be removed.

Cursed are Those Who Hang on a Tree

Yet Paul misread the verse. In Galatians 3:13 he interpreted the verse as saying, 'cursed is every one *that hangeth on a tree*'. Paul understood that the curse is on the *person hanging* and not as the verse itself says, a curse, a disgrace, unto God. Any student of Hebrew can obviously spot the difference and render the interpretation I have offered above.

But following his own premise, Paul interpreted the verse to mean that the tree referred to in this verse is the law, the Torah. All who hang on a tree, in other words those who are dependent on the Torah for salvation, are ultimately cursed. For Man is condemned to sin and cannot keep the law in its entirety. So Paul taught that Jesus, by dying and becoming a curse *for us*, has relieved Man from the curse of the law.

Paul's interpretation is completely invalidated because of his misreading of the verse. The verse never says that Man is cursed, but that God is cursed or *disgraced* when a man is left to hang on a tree.

Eternity of Torah Law

Paul knew that to make Christianity attractive to the Gentiles it was necessary to distance the new religion from the practices of the Jewish faith that Gentile converts would find unacceptable. In his missionary zeal, he overturned the promise of God in Deuteronomy 29:29 that, 'those things which are revealed [meaning the Torah, as the verse itself explicates immediately afterward] belong unto us and to our children for ever, that we may do *all the words of this Torah* [law].' This means that God swears that the Torah and its laws are for ever, applicable at all times and in all situations. If God knew that He would eventually abrogate the laws of the Torah and replace it with a new covenant in Jesus, He would not have stated that the Torah is for ever.

Jesus himself proclaims in Matthew 5:18–19 that 'till heaven and earth pass, one jot or one tittle shall in no wise pass from the law, till all be fulfilled. Whosoever therefore shall break one of these least

375

commandments, and shall teach men so, he shall be called the least in the kingdom of heaven'.

The reason this is all so significant, especially for young students who wish to abandon Judaism and embrace Christianity, is that by doing so they are essentially moving from an action-based religion to a religion whose most important premise is faith. This transformation from God's calling to humanity found in the Torah being primarily one of action, to the New Testament's call for faith is, of course, predicated on the above.

The Virgin Birth: How Could We Know?

The early Christians rapidly withdrew from the Bible written in Hebrew, substituting instead a Greek and then a Latin version, and finally a plethora of vernacular editions, for the new religion. Many key words suffered in the translation and compounded with other original errors of interpretation to create an unreliable alternative to the original Hebrew Bible and its complete meaning.

In the first chapter of Matthew, the concept of the virgin birth is introduced. Mary is said to become pregnant by the Holy Ghost, fulfilling what the prophet spoke in Isaiah 7:14: 'Behold, a virgin [almah] shall conceive, and bear a son, and shall call his name Immanuel.' In Matthew 1:23 this is rendered as, 'Behold, a virgin shall be with child, and shall bring forth a son, and they shall call his name Emmanuel, which being interpreted is, God with us.'

Virgin birth is a concept completely foreign to Judaism, but even more so in relation to the Messiah. How could one imagine that God would cause the long-awaited, promised redeemer to be born in such shame? After all, the book of Matthew reveals that Joseph, Mary's husband, knew the child was not his. That can leave only one of two possibilities: either he nevertheless told people the child was his own, or he denied that he had fathered the boy. In both possibilities, people would still never know that it was of God. In the eyes of the public, then, Jesus was a child conceived by someone other than Mary's husband; born to a newly married woman, but her husband had not fathered the child.

Although Mary could tell everyone that she had not had intercourse outside of marriage, but that God caused her to conceive, she would not be believed. Let's face it, this just does not happen every day. The Messiah would therefore be viewed by everyone as being illegitimate. Legally, he would also be judged as a 'mamzer', for the Torah decides all legal matters by the word of *two* witnesses. So once Joseph denied the child was his, even though he might testify to the fact, as the New Testament records, that he experienced a revelation by an angel in which it was told to him that the boy was conceived by the Holy Spirit, the Jewish court would rule the child as being illegitimate. For they could not rely on the testimony of Joseph since (a) he was only a single witness, (b) he was Mary's relative (husband) and therefore could not testify for, or against, her, (c) the court would reject his testimony for it possessed no substantial evidence. There are many people in the world who claim to have experienced Divine revelation, but we would not be prepared to believe them without proof.

The Maiden and the Virgin

At this point it is useful to investigate how the notion of a virgin birth came about. As mentioned before, it is based on a verse in Isaiah which states that an *'almah'* shall conceive a child. The authors of the New Testament mistranslate *almah* to mean exclusively a virgin, and therefore say the prophet foresaw a virgin birth.

But this is a complete distortion of the true meaning of this word. *Almah* simply means a *young woman*. It is derived from the root word of *alam* meaning young. It does not mean virgin. Although a young woman may of course be a virgin and the connotations of the word do not exclude this possibility, the word *almah* by itself does not imply at all that the woman has to be a virgin.

In fact, there is even a verse in scripture in which *almah* cannot mean a virgin. In Proverbs 30:19, King Solomon discusses four common ways, or paths, 'The way of an eagle in the air; the way of a serpent upon a rock; the way of a ship in the midst of the sea, and the way of a man with an *almah*.' The common characteristic amongst these 'ways' is that they leave no *trace*. Therefore, the next verse continues, 'Such is the way of an adulterous woman; she eateth, and wipeth her mouth, and saith, I have done no wickedness.' King Solomon is lamenting the fact that the adulterous woman can get away with her infidelity. Here is a clear example of a place in scripture in which *almah* cannot mean virgin. If it did mean virgin, then there would be a trace, since the woman in question would lose her virginity. Thus, the adulterous woman, if she had previously been a virgin, would be found out.

The mistranslation must have arisen because the Hebrew Bible had been read in Greek. The authors of the New Testament and the apostles were apparently Hellenized Israelites, very prevalent among the Jews of the time, a group who were somewhat estranged from Jewish ideals and lifestyle. In the Septuagint, the Greek translation of the Bible, the concepts of a young woman and a virgin are rendered by the same word, unlike the Hebrew original which allocates a distinct term for each. The authors of the New Testament then understood that the prophet was foretelling the birth of a child from a virgin, and applied this prophecy to Jesus. Thus a cardinal principle of Christianity is based on a Greek rendering of the Hebrew Bible by the apostles, which is clearly suspect.

Errors in Scripture

Another classic example of a New Testament misreading of the Hebrew Bible is in Acts 7:14–16, 'Then sent Joseph, and called his father Jacob to him, and all his kindred, threescore and fifteen souls. So Jacob went down into Egypt, and died, he and our fathers. And were carried over into Sychem, and laid in the sepulchre that Abraham bought for a sum of money of the sons of Emmor, the father of Sychem.'

In these three short verses there are five mistakes: seventy, not seventy-five, souls descended down to Egypt; Jacob was buried in Hebron, not Sychem; the plot of land in Sychem was purchased by Jacob, not Abraham; Chamor (Emmor) was the son of Sychem, not the father; Abraham bought his burial site from Ephron the Hittite, not from Emmor.

Saul as King

In Acts 13:21, simple facts of the Torah are distorted. There it is stated that Saul was king over Israel for forty years. Yet in truth, he was king for only two years, according to 1 Samuel 13:1. Incidentally, the New Revised Standard Version maintains that this verse mentioning how long Saul reigned is lacking in the Septuagint, and this may be the cause of the error.

A New Order of Twelve Tribes

The seventh chapter of the book of Revelation purports to enumerate the twelve tribes. Verses 5–8 list: Juda, Reuben, Gad, Aser, Nepthalim, Manasses, Simeon, Levi, Issachar, Zebulon, Joseph, and Benjamin. They do not correspond with the twelve tribes of Israel. The tribe of Dan is not mentioned at all, and the tribe of Manasses is mentioned in his stead, even though the tribe of Joseph is also mentioned. Manasses was Joseph's son, and they are therefore of the same tribe. When Joseph is counted along with the tribes, Manasses should never be mentioned, and vice versa.

Part Two

Jesus' Teachings Contradict Fundamentals of Jewish Religion

The Messiah is to be one of the greatest (if not *the* greatest) Sages ever to live. The prophet Isaiah has foretold concerning him that 'the spirit of the Lord shall rest upon him, the spirit of wisdom and understanding, the spirit of counsel and might, the spirit of knowledge and of the fear of the Lord' (Isaiah 11:2).

It is against this backdrop that the candidacy of Jesus as Messiah must be considered. The New Testament itself relates in John 7:15 that Jesus had 'never learned' letters. Indeed, the statements and misquotations attributed to him in the New Testament testify that either he himself erred in his interpretation of many aspects of the Jewish faith, or that the New Testament has incorrectly recorded his words.

Misquoting Basics of Jewish Belief

Twice in the New Testament, in Matthew 22:37 as well as in the gospel of Mark, Jesus is quoted as referring to the She'mah, the most famous and basic prayer in the whole of Jewish liturgy. This is a prayer which the observant Jew recites thrice daily, and is also meant to serve as the final prayer recited by a Jew before he dies. But in both instances Jesus misquotes the She'mah, stating, 'thou shalt love the Lord thy God with all thy heart, and with all thy soul, *and with all thy mind*, and with all thy strength' (Mark 12:30). The real She'mah, found in Deuteronomy 6:4, omits the words 'with all thy mind'. It is clear from the New Testament that Jesus is repeating a direct quotation. Something is undeniably wrong if the Messiah cannot quote the most classical testimony of Jewish faith.

The Murder of Zacharias

In Matthew 23:35, Jesus accuses the rabbis of murdering Zacharias ben Barachias between the Temple and the Altar. However, the real prophet who was killed in the Temple was Zacharias *ben Yehoyadas*, who lived 324 years later. Jesus' confusion of the two is troubling.

Picking Corn on the Sabbath

A story is related in Mark 2:23–26 in which Jesus' students were found picking corn on the Sabbath because they were hungry. When the rabbis protested to Jesus that his disciples were desecrating the holy day, Jesus retorted by saying, 'Have ye never read what David did, when he had need, and was an hungred, he, and they that were with him? How he went into the house of God in the days of *Abiathar* the high priest, and did eat the showbreads, which is not lawful to eat but for the priests, and gave also to them which were with him?'

Firstly, the event, which can be read in 1 Samuel 21, took place when *Ahimelech* was the High Priest, not Abiathar: 'Then came David to Nob to Ahimelech the priest' (1 Samuel 21:1). Secondly, as in David's case it was a life-threatening predicament, he was permitted to eat of the Temple's holy bread. (In case of danger to life, all of the Torah's prohibitions are cast aside, except three: murder, idolatry and sexual immorality.) In the case of Jesus' disciples, the New Testament itself relates that the circumstances were not life-threatening at all: his students were not dying of hunger, rather they were just hungry, so the laws of the Torah are not allowed to be broken especially those of Shabbus. The two events are simply not analogous.

Standing up to Evil

In Matthew 5:39–42, Jesus teaches, 'But I say unto you, That ye resist not evil: but whosoever shall smite thee on thy right cheek, turn to him the other also. And if any man will sue thee at the law, and take away thy coat, let him have thy cloke also. Give to him that asketh thee, and from him that would borrow of thee turn not thou away.' This is repeated also in Luke 6:30, and Jesus adds, 'of him that taketh away thy goods ask them not again'.

This argument rejects the whole of Jewish teaching in matters relating to combatting evil in that it actually encourages evil. By teaching people not to resist evil, all murderers, rapists and thieves are encouraged to continue their actions. Contrast Jesus' statement with this one from Moses, 'That which is altogether just shalt thou follow' (Deuteronomy 16:20). Judaism is not a pacifist religion, and can often view pacifism as a refusal to fight wickedness. The work of God is to promote a better world, not allow those who oppress the weak to trample on them even harder.

Miraculous Powers of the Believers

In Mark 16:16–18, Jesus declares, 'He that believeth and is baptized shall be saved; but he that believeth not shall be damned. And these signs shall follow them that believe; In my name shall they cast out devils; they shall speak with new tongues; They shall take up serpents; and if they drink any deadly thing, it shall not hurt them; they shall lay hands on the sick, and they shall recover.'

In the same way he is quoted in Luke 17:6 as telling his disciples that 'If ye had faith as [big as] a grain of mustard seed, ye might say unto this sycamine tree, Be thou plucked up by the root, and be thou planted in the sea; and it would obey you.'

It would seem to me that even devout Christians would find these teachings difficult to live by. What the Jew must therefore question in deciding whether Jesus is the Messiah is whether or not his teachings demonstrated the sublime quality of wisdom which the prophet foretold the Messiah would possess.

Part Three

The Messianic Prophecies Remain Unfulfilled

The soundest way of knowing whether or not Jesus was the Messiah is to determine if the messianic prophecies were fulfilled in him. Throughout the generations there have been many individuals who have fulfilled the qualifications for the Messiah, the result of which has been confusion among the masses causing horrible consequences. Therefore, the only way of truly knowing, beyond the shadow of a doubt, who is the Messiah is by seeing whether the individual accomplished that which the Messiah is sent to accomplish. God has outlined for the Messiah a clearly defined purpose within the Torah and an individual's failure to fulfil that purpose identifies him as a false Messiah. Let us examine how Jesus fits into the prophecy picture.

The Wolf and the Lamb

In Isaiah 11:6–9 we are told that when the Messiah arrives, 'The wolf also shall dwell with the lamb, and the leopard shall lie down with the kid.' The verses go on to describe how all animals will live in harmony with one another. Then the prophecy ends with the beautiful words, 'the earth shall be full of the knowledge of the Lord, as the waters cover the sea.'

Where is this era of great peace which is promised, or that of an openly Godly world? Our world is lamentably only too far from any of these ideals. If a Christian missionary should answer that these things will be fulfilled in a second coming, the response of the Jew should be that we will also wait for that moment to decide whether we will embrace and follow Christianity. Until then, Jesus' candidacy is rejected because he filled none of the criteria to be crowned Messiah.

Since the times of Jesus until the present, animosity and struggle remain amidst animals and people. The world is only too far from being full of the knowledge of the Lord, with atheism and even pagan idol worship running rampant. The prophecy has not yet been fulfilled.

Elijah Heralds the Messianic Coming

In Malachi 3:23 it is foretold, 'Behold, I will send you Elijah the prophet before the coming of the great and dreadful day of the Lord.' Before the arrival of the Messiah, Elijah will appear and herald his coming. (This is found in Malachi 4:5 in the Revised Standard Version.)

Elijah did not appear before the arrival of Jesus and announce his arrival. In the New Testament, Jesus says that John the Baptist was

Elijah, and John had heralded his coming. But the same New Testament, in John 1:21, says, 'And they asked him [John the Baptist], What then? Are thou Elias? And he saith, I am not.' Either John was not Elijah, or Jesus was right and John was Elijah. And if he was Elijah and his mission was to herald Jesus' coming, why did he deny it?

An Age When the Righteous Shall Flourish

In Psalms 72:7–11 it is stated that in the epoch of the Messiah, 'shall the righteous flourish; and abundance of peace so long as the moon endureth. He shall have dominion also from sea to sea, and from the river unto the ends of the earth. They that dwell in the wilderness shall bow before him: and his enemies shall lick the dust.' Daniel 7:14 expresses similar ideas, 'all peoples, nations, and languages should serve him'.

There is no form of real peace in our own times, nor has there been any since Jesus was alive. Many who purport a belief in Jesus have brought destruction and persecution, killing people who would not embrace Christian belief.

The Messiah's Dominion

The New Testament itself relates that Jesus never had any real form of dominion over any nation or people, as Isaiah predicted the Messiah would. He was very much abused throughout his life, even being put to death by the Romans.

Considering the messianic prophecies were not fulfilled, there is no reason, therefore, to believe he was the promised one.

Jesus in a Second Coming

The Christians, realizing this as a serious dilemma, claim that Jesus will fulfil them all in a 'second coming'. Yet there is no mention anywhere of a second coming in Scripture. Furthermore, even if the Christians rely on a second coming to fulfil the necessary prophecies, they still must admit that Jesus has not as yet fulfilled them, and therefore has not so far met the criteria for being the Messiah. If so, there exists no reason for us to believe that he was the Messiah.

A Prophet Like Moses

The Christians claim that God's promise in Deuteronomy 18:18 that He will raise up to the Jews a prophet like Moses – 'I will raise them up a Prophet from among their brethren, like unto thee, and will put my words in his mouth; and he shall speak unto them all that I shall command him' – was a reference to Jesus. It is important to note that immediately afterwards God warns the people of Israel, 'But the prophet, which shall presume to speak a word in my name, which I have not commanded him to speak, or that shall speak in the name of other gods, even that prophet shall die' (Deuteronomy 18:20). In addition to all the prophecies which Jesus did not fulfil, there are many prophecies he predicted would come to pass that never transpired.

Arriving Soon

In Matthew 24:34 Jesus says, 'Verily I say unto you, this generation shall not pass, till all these things be fulfilled.' He further says in Mark 1:15 that 'the kingdom of God is at hand: repent ye, and believe the gospel'. In Revelation 22:7, Jesus again states, 'Behold, I come quickly'. It is now nearly 2,000 years later. We are still waiting.

All the above leads us to question seriously whether Jesus could have been the promised Jewish Messiah. Current Christian theology reiterates this view, with many theologians of the opinion that he himself did not in fact ever claim to be the Messiah: the words in the New Testament that express this idea were in fact later interpolations by the early Christian Church. The Jew therefore who is approached by Christian missionaries with little respect for Jewish faith, and who seek to convert as many Jews to their own beliefs as possible, should find it necessary first to explore his own roots. I know of few who after doing so ever found the need to search elsewhere for spiritual fulfilment or meaningful existence.

Christianity offers a unique sublimity and spirituality to its adherents and as such should be respected and embraced by those raised by its traditions. The Jew, however, must remain steadfastly attached to his traditions and people.

Chapter Thirty-six

CAPITALISM, COMMUNISM
AND COMPUTERS IN JEWISH THOUGHT
═══

In every major university, to which Oxford is no exception, research comes hand in hand with technology nowadays, even in the humanities. So it is surprising for many students from overseas to discover, on coming to Oxford, that computers hardly exist here outside the sciences and mathematics faculties.

Those who regularly use the Bodleian Library are delighted that the millions of books it holds are at last being catalogued by computer, but the process is slow. Often the most sought-after books are still only available after a long search and even longer wait, because there is no single complete catalogue of their collection, and the computer-held entries cover only the most recent years.

No Room for Computers

One fresher came to Oxford from a home that had been filled with modern gadgets. Since the first home computers had arrived in British shops in the early 1980s, there had always been one in her home. She felt very comfortable writing notes straight into a computer and writing essays with a word processing package. So she bounced into Oxford full of enthusiasm for the benefits that working with modern technology could bring, but the problem was that she was not studying a subject seen to need the help of a computer.

She was in Oxford to 'read English' – and as her tutor kindly (and erroneously) pointed out to her on the day of her first tutorial, 'One cannot read from a machine, one needs the look and the feel of books.' She had told him, in passing, that she intended to use a computer for the bulk of her work, and his response was derisory, almost hostile. In his opinion, those who use the keyboard all day lose the ability to write legibly, and he warned her that he would not approve of a tutorial essay that had been produced by word processing.

So she joined the ranks of the essay-writing masses of Oxford. These students are often in my office on the day of their tutorial, telling me that they have had to stay up all night to finish their week's work. This feat is

384

clearly very important to them, so I ask them to show me what they have produced. They fumble about in their pockets and at last produce a few sheets of crumpled paper that comprises their offering to their tutor. The essay is invariably scrawled in biro, and the numerous crossings out make it look horribly untidy; I find it hard to see how this can be superior in even the crustiest old don's eyes to the neat and well-structured papers that can be produced on a computer. But still, Oxford has managed for centuries without the benefits of on-page editing, so a significant number of college fellows really don't see why they should take any notice of these new-fangled contraptions.

However, the right balance between irrationally eschewing technology and revering it for its own sake is hard to find. As we shall see, for many people technology can usurp the important place we should naturally give to other people.

But we are not alone in this struggle, purely modern though this problem might seem. The Torah passage in which the richly symbolic story of the Tower of Babel is found is filled with many surprisingly astute allusions to problems and issues we often assume are only recent discoveries of the 'modern' world. Amongst other things, it discusses what is probably the earliest reference to possible colonization of the moon, the modern infatuation and obsession with technology, and the battle between the world's prevailing economic systems, capitalism and communism.

The Earliest Space Vehicle?

Rabbi Yonasan Eibshitz comments on the reason the Tower of Babel may have been built, especially by the generation immediately following the flood. He maintains that the Tower served as a launching pad for people to fire a projectile, a capsule, with which humankind could settle on the moon, where they would find refuge from the natural calamities of the world and escape future destruction from a flood or the like. The builders of the Tower had just witnessed God's near destruction of mankind through the flood. They would thus have had to get off the planet if they were to survive.

An Ancient Equivalent of 1984

Haamek Davar explains that the Tower of Babel was built to serve as a watchtower; its builders wished to supervise everyone's actions, rather like Big Brother in Orwell's *1984*. This broadly corresponds with the Soviet experience of the KGB and electronic listening devices, the Germans with the Stasi, and Saddam Hussein with his intelligence network. In the Talmud, God was concerned for the welfare of his human creatures and objected to people being treated like sheep. The plan was destroyed when people were later scattered and there was no possible way that a single tower could watch over all of them, or understand their many languages: only God could do this.

The Individual vs the Community

Perhaps most importantly, the Torah discusses Communism. It is contrasted with the evils of capitalism. But first let us digress for a moment to discover what capitalism and Communism might really mean.

How could one sum up the whole of human history and existence in a single idea? For me, the human condition is primarily characterized by the struggle between the self and the community. When we are born, we feel at one with the world: when the room is cold it feels as though the whole universe is cold, when we are hungry we think the whole of creation is hungry, and when we are loved we feel that everything is loved. It is only through the process of learning how to cope with the world that we come to see ourselves as disconnected from those people and things which surround us. We learn to categorize and we learn to separate, and in doing so we learn to be selfish. The rest of our lives is the journey back to feeling part of a community, but through choice and not unawareness, through knowledge, not ignorance.

It is not surprising that the journey to community is a difficult one. We are afraid to be alone, but are somewhat uncomfortable depending on other people. We like ourselves more than anyone else, but we feel guilty if we are discovered behaving selfishly. I may like the social benefits I receive from living in Britain (free higher education, the welfare state, the National Health Service), but that does not mean that I actually enjoy paying my taxes.

The major political systems of the world express this internal struggle: reduced to an almost absurd essence, capitalism thinks that the community is served by focusing on the individual, while communism thinks the individual is served by putting the rights of the community first.

Of course this struggle was not discovered by Marx; he was simply the one who expressed it for the modern secular world. Thousands of years before, the Bible had focused on this issue.

Communism in the Bible

Don Isaac Abravanel, the great Spanish rabbinic exegete, who also served as Minister of Finance first to Ferdinand and Isabella of Spain, and later to King Manuel of Portugal, sees the Tower of Babel as evidence of the earliest corruption of the human community. The builders of the Tower urged urban settlement and the abandonment of the tilling of the earth.

Abravanel explains that the sin of those who built the Tower of Babel was that they wanted to create a state, the root of all evil. 'They wanted to put their hands and minds to perfect the tasks needed for building a city, which includes all types of tasks; and a tower with it, so that they could join together there and make themselves urban people rather than people of the field, thinking that it was a special sign for them to have a state ... and violence and theft and murder, none of which existed when they were in the field.'

This passage in the Talmud is therefore seen as an extremely early reference to the problems of the big city, and especially the inner city, currently wreaking such havoc even in countries as rich as the United States.

Even worse, in the opinion of Abravanel, the builders of the Tower attempted to establish a regime in which each person would have private property, which opposed the purpose of creation:

> At the time, everything they had was owned by all equally, because no person had an inheritance or anything else private for his own use, because everything belonged to all ... When they began to build the city and the tower, they removed themselves from comradeship, and their possessions and inheritances became private. And they came to exchanging things and setting them aside, because of their desire for each to have his own things, saying: 'What is mine is mine, and what is yours is yours', to the point where because of this they separated from one another.

Abravanel addressed this very pressing question: If this type of regime is forbidden and deemed to be evil, why did God not forbid it to the Jewish people? After all, capitalism is deeply embedded within Judaism! In answering this question, Abravanel seems to offer a perspective on the purpose of a capitalistic world and the manner in which we are meant to cope with it.

A Jewish Approach to Capitalism

'When the Almighty saw that Adam and his descendants had immersed themselves in all the lusts for luxury and had defiled themselves with them, He did not forbid His people ... but encouraged the Children of Israel to behave in those matters with justice and in a proper manner, not in a despicable manner.'

According to Abravanel, the purpose of humankind in the generations following the Tower of Babel is to return the world to the way it was, before humanity ruined it by 'progress' and by building the city and the Tower.

Machines before People

Thus Abravanel sees the sin of the generation who built the Tower as due in part to the fact that they saw technological advance and the building of civilization not as a means of enhancing the quality of human life, but as an end in itself. The generation prided themselves on their ability to overcome nature, but in the process they denigrated human life by putting the machines they created and the art forms they produced ahead of human values.

The rabbis express this thought aptly. They explain that while the Tower was under construction, if a person dropped dead, no one cared. On the other hand, if a single brick fell and broke they would all cry out saying, 'When will there be another like it?' Technology became the goal instead of the means.

The Computer Generation

Today's computer generation aptly demonstrates the same point. The purpose of a computer is to minimize the time it takes to perform a given task and to store, classify and present information in a manner not readily capable by an unaided human. Thus, this book was produced on word-processing software, and if it had to be done with paper and pencil the editing process and the production time would quadruple, and the final product would be untidy.

Yet most computer owners, this author included, become emotionally attached to their machines. They see a computer not as a tool for producing results, but as an end in itself. Suddenly, they're out ordering computer magazines and spending thousands constantly upgrading their hardware and software to acquire only the most marginal performance enhancement.

We should consider whether giving such priority to anything other than people tends towards evil. Rabbi Abravanel's comment on the Tower of Babel can easily be adapted to computers; people can sometimes be far more concerned with the state of their hardware than the state of someone else's health. Or users can get a far bigger buzz by playing with their computers than conversing with a fellow human being.

Computers as Modern-Day Mistresses

This may sound funny, but in real life it is not. In July of 1991 a friend of mine in his fifties bought his first computer. He has always been a happily married man and a good father. When I visited them recently his wife grumbled about the numerous fights they were now having. Something was coming between them. When I asked her what the matter was, she referred to their problem as *It*. Her husband was spending far more time with, and was far more attached to, his computer than to her. She became particularly annoyed when he insisted on bringing the computer into the bedroom at night. She was completely serious when she later designated her husband's PC, 'the modern-day mistress'.

Yes, husbands, and I am sure that this applies to wives as well, can be just as devoted to and interested in their computers as in their families, and perhaps more. A hard-disk crash can at times be felt to be almost as devastating as the deterioration of a family member's health.

A Passion for Cars

This is also true of other objects. Cars were initially designed to get you from one place to the next. Yet among many people today they are an end in themselves. People sometimes stop their children getting into their car because their feet are dirty, or because they might destroy it in some other way. Houses are also sometimes treated like that. Although a house is a modern person's greatest material blessing, and should be used for good purposes, often a householder will not allow their home to be used for a charitable cause or as a venue for a weekly study group because it is feared that too many guests will ruin the home.

A Substitute for People

Although this principle of mistaking the means for the end can apply equally to most material possessions, it appears to me that the problem is especially acute in relation to computers. Some people forsake human company for that of a computer because the machine takes orders and people very often refuse. Is it because the computer does everything it is told, bar those annoying crashes? Or perhaps it is because computers are so much more intelligent than cars and stereos, and they seem to reflect human creativity better than any material item. I am not sure what the reason is, but this does not mean the problem is not a serious one. Still, the current trend is for more and more anthropomorphism in computers that can perhaps be interpreted as pandering to our ideal of a perfect companion.

There is a famous *Star Trek* episode in which the Enterprise's computer malfunctions and starts to talk to Captain Kirk in the most caressingly feminine voice. Kirk is embarrassed at the change from businesslike tones to a voice expressing emotion, and the viewer finds the scene highly amusing. However, this idea from sci-fi has rather less amusing parallels in the modern world of computers. Many users are given choices over the prompts their computers use: given the choice of a perfunctory bleep or a feminine voice drawling 'Goodbye' in tones of regret, what does the (male) user choose? The sexy voice, of course, which makes the endearingly obedient computer into a substitute for an endearingly obedient person.

The point is that in the real world other humans inhabit, the computer lover has to negotiate and interact in a two-way process to get things done: quite a culture shock! It is a dangerous thing to lose the ability to see people as the most important in this world and to start wishing they were more like computers, the tools we use to make the world a better place.

Culture and Arts as Ends in Themselves

Of course, this discussion pertains to culture and the arts as well. Asked to determine between having the products of a manic artist such as van Gogh and allowing him a sane but uninspired life, which would you choose? In the Second World War, when the Nazis were marching on Paris, one of the first orders given to the civil administration in Paris was to remove and hide the national treasures, the *Mona Lisa* and the like. Meanwhile, thousands of war refugees without any shelter or food were left stranded by the wayside. Unfortunately, they were not designated as national treasures. The paintings which were created to enhance the beauty of their lives replaced them in importance. By insisting on these false priorities we make art into a foreign god.

Walking through the streets of Oxford, especially in the tourist season, one can expect to see a score of beggars attracted to the city by its relative affluence. It is easy to lose one's humanity and complain about such people, although there must be some underlying reason for their poverty, or lack of motivation or of self-respect, that would be more useful to attack and eliminate. Somehow, we rarely seem to do this, and we end up ignoring them or seeing them as a blight on a beautiful historical city.

We must be careful not to repeat the mistakes of those who built the Tower of Babel. We must never allow objects made by us, synthetic creation, to replace those objects which are precious because of their Divine creation and their reflection of the Godly image. This applies not only to the lives of humans, which are of infinite quality and sanctity, but to the rest of the planet, too: we cannot re-create the art forms of the coral reefs, rain forests and wonderful species that inhabit this earth which has been given to us to protect, and which are rapidly disappearing.

The same beauty which we seek to find in a Rembrandt or a play by Shakespeare we must also find in human life and human form, and in animal and plant diversity.

A Jewish Approach to Communism

Still, Abravanel's comments on the nature of capitalism as evil must make us think again about the typical Jewish reaction to Communism. Since Marxism has often taken the form of an extremely Godless totalitarian tool, it has been easy to dismiss such an ideology as something that Judaism could never embrace.

However, Godlessness is not a necessary characteristic of Communism. Communism can even be described as a moral alternative to the material excesses of capitalism. To cite a contemporary Jewish example: there are many kibbutzim in Israel who live by the standards of economic collectivism, while religious kibbutzim uphold the banner of Jewish observance. On the other hand, many kibbutzim are not only non-religious but even violently anti-religious, such as the Shomer-Haztair movement. The fact that a community in Israel adopts the kibbutz way of life does not force a person in either direction, and the adoption of Communism is not necessarily linked to atheism either.

So why doesn't Judaism adopt a collectivist economic system?

The question is a good one. It seems preposterous that a Godly system by which to live one's life should allow a situation in which some people pursue wealth and buy homes with many bedrooms when others remain homeless in the streets. How could all this happen and even be sanctioned by religion?

The Failure of Communism

The most common response in the west has been that the answer lies simply in the failure of Communism. Communism failed, therefore capitalism must be right.

According to capitalism, what led the Soviet Union to its final collapse more than any other reason was the complete failure of its economic system. The Soviet economy, industry, harvest and produce were all in a shambles. People simply got tired of walking into a store in which all the shelves were empty. The reason for this complete breakdown was surely the lack of impetus and motivation on the part of the workers. When each is paid according to what the need is and not according to how much he or she produces, it becomes foolish to put in a harder day's work than one's fellow. 'Why should I? Will my family benefit as a result of my being a more devoted employee? Will that family vacation I have always dreamed about become any more of a reality?' The people could see that the ideals of Marx had not been achieved, and were dissatisfied. So the Soviet Union stagnated, whereas western materialism flourished – at least for those empowered economically.

Lubavitch as a Socialist Collectivist System

The standard capitalist approach is vastly incomplete and even un-Jewish because it assumes, as its basic premise, that people can only be motivated by reason of material gain. Surely there are motivating factors, advocated by Judaism itself, which could serve as an impetus for the enhancement of human productivity and the pursuit of excellence?

The Lubavitch movement can serve as a case in point. In Lubavitch there are tight controls on what a Shliach, or emissary, is paid. Pay is determined almost exclusively by necessity, not by productivity or seniority. Thus one begins at what is a basic starting salary, and although there is a simple annual pay rise to compensate for the rise in the cost-of-living, the only real increases in salary are given on the birth of children. So if a Shliach has a new child, he would be paid, say, $50 more a week. Now, how can Lubavitch survive and thrive as a movement when it uses a payment system whereby, notwithstanding one's talent or devotion, one is paid the same as one's less productive colleagues? Simple. The success of Lubavitch is predicated on the ideological devotion of a group of people to the Jewish religion and the continuity of the Jewish people. The motivating factor is wholly independent of material gain. Although every young ideological Shliach is, of course, human and would no doubt respond to a material impetus, the reason he performs his work is because he believes in his mission, not just in the dollar.

This seems to be the kind of thing that Judaism should be encouraging everyone to do, not just Chasidic Jews. Instead of having capitalism ingrained into our religion, surely Judaism could have set up a system whereby everyone is paid according to their needs, while encouraging everyone to exert themselves to the utmost in order to bring about a better world?

The same applies to an academic lifestyle. None of the many academics I know sees him or herself as the inferior of those who engage in commerce. In fact, the opposite is probably true! Academia can sometimes be accompanied by arrogance. So why are they willing to work just as hard, and often much harder, than business people to be paid so much less? The impetus is beyond material gain.

Teachers and Independents

At times that impetus is a pure and genuine love of knowledge, or a desire to chance upon the discoveries which will change the lot of all humankind. But academic work often also has at least as much to do with establishing a reputation. Business people look to achieve prominence through wealth and position within the established order of a corporation; academics look to accomplish the same by way of reputation and their contribution to society. In studies cited by Deborah Tannen in her best-selling analysis of speech, *You Just Don't Understand*, academics mentioned two main reasons for choosing their profession. Men tended to say they needed independence, that is, having status accorded to them for themselves rather than because of their place in a company hierarchy; and women said they wished to teach, that is, have status accorded them from assuming the role of one who imparts information. These motives were enough to keep them teaching on pay vastly inferior to that of their peers who had gone into other employment.

The Lure of Money

The Torah is obsessed with the notion that we must strive to better the world in which we live and improve the lot of humankind itself. But it could have made non-material gains much more of a priority if it had removed the distracting motivation of financial compensation, and support for a capitalist economic system, from the picture. Surely the Torah should have focused exclusively on religious fervour as a means of motivating people?

This question becomes particularly acute in the light of the fact that Judaism, like no other religion before it, criticizes human involvement in business affairs, especially when this concern serves to blur our vision of higher matters. Judaism equates business concerns with violence in metaphors from the Torah such as 'turbulent waters', 'stormy seas', and the like. This is wholly understandable, especially in the light of today's references to business and the 'stormy seas' of high finance. Business occupies, even consumes, one's thoughts, passions and a great deal of one's time.

Nothing absorbs a person's mental faculties as much as business worries; the most efficient hindrance to one's attention to religious matters is having to deal with outstanding bills and feeling apprehensive about the financial welfare of one's family.

We could have avoided all this if the Torah had simply advocated an alternative economic system whereby no one takes individual responsibility for a company's success or failure, because there is no private ownership. Rather, each is paid enough to feed the family, pay the electricity bill, live in a comfortable enough house, and get on with the truly serious things in life. So why is Judaism not purely collectivist?

Prematurely Perfect

Communism is not wrong, because the ideals of sharing and community are right; nor is it an inherently un-Godly regime, as we have seen in the case of the religious kibbutzim, but nevertheless it is not embraced by Judaism. Communism is rejected because it is the easy way out. Chasidic Judaism is quite clear on the point that the perfection of humans is not a question of withdrawing from the world, but of sublimating it. My point is that Communism creates a situation whereby the state is in a more advanced mode than the individuals that comprise it, and this is an inherently regressive and unstable situation unless great control of the people is used.

For example, what are the consequences of the state taking on all responsibility for those who are unable to cope with the modern world?

Suppose that, before the whole country as a group of individuals learns to look after those in need, the state steps in and says, 'No, there's no need for charity. The state will look after those who need a helping hand, you just get on with producing goods for everyone.' If we as individuals were to lose all direct obligation for the welfare of others, our charitable nature would wither. And if charity is forced out of everyone by a state's tax system, how does the spirit of giving grow? No one voluntarily pays more taxes, but when giving charity is an act of free will it can lead to great rewards for both the receiver and the giver.

Communism as it was practised in the USSR ignored a side of human nature. The need to make a mark on the world and express one's personality through success was denigrated and driven underground, although of course there were plenty of powerful people prepared to disregard the ideals of Communism for personal gain.

Suppressing a part of ourselves as humans leads us to be weaker, less perfect individuals who will then be unable to go on to help others to the fullest extent. Judaism advocates that one sublimates one's need to compete so that it is not used selfishly but for the benefit of others. We should aim to move from saying, 'I will not respect you because I want to be the only one to succeed', to saying, 'I applaud my brothers and sisters for their achievements, and I'll strive to help others to climb this mountain, too. Their success will be part of my reward.' If all competitiveness were to be stifled, from where would the benefit to others arise?

The problem with Communism is that, although we can imagine a perfect Communist state in which wealth is distributed evenly and fairly, the mechanisms that achieved this would be impersonal. It would be a perfect state made up of imperfect individuals who were unable to relate to their fellows beyond the state-controlled mechanism for redistributing wealth; so if enough people decided they wanted to be selfish again, the state would be unable to stop them. The ideologies of the state and of the people would be at odds. Stated in other words, it is far better for the individuals to choose to be charitable through voluntarily offering a percentage of their income to those less fortunate than they, than to have the money forcibly extricated from them, as in a socialist collectivist system. In the former scenario, the individual is transformed. He becomes charitable and embodies human goodness. In the latter, he remains unchanged as a mere vessel of the State.

But if the citizens of a country collectively elevated their human capacity for ambition and competition so that they shared equally, then the whole society would be perfect in all ways. It would also be remarkably stable, because state and people would be striving for the same goals. Let us strive for a perfection of both people and the regimes they live under, so that both march forward together.

Chapter Thirty-seven

MORMONS AND JEWS AT OXFORD

====

One of the most interesting things about the city of Oxford is its multi-culturalism. Like most British cities of a reasonable size, Oxford has attracted a number of people from various cultures to work and live. Some areas of the town have a particularly fertile mix of cultures, and the Cowley Road where the Chabad House can be found is certainly one of these. Simply listing the places that sell food will show the variety of people who live there; there are a number of Chinese and Indian take-aways, Halal stores, spice emporia, homely Italian eating houses, and of course the very popular restaurant offering Jamaican food to hungry students. But the interesting mixture of cultures is not confined to a few areas of the town.

Because the university attracts the intellectual high-fliers from all over the world, very few faiths are unrepresented here, although as I have said in the 'Race Relations' chapter, the university is extraordinarily lacking in ethnic diversity at least in great numbers. Although the history of Oxford itself is overwhelmingly Christian, the modern university is renowned as a centre for learning, not of specifically Protestant or even Christian learning, and people are unlikely to come here specifically for its religion. Perhaps the biggest draw for students of all faiths is that Oxford University tries to make its learning a neutral activity, and academics are genuinely interested in the insights that all cultures and systems of knowledge can contribute to the knowledge taught here.

Living in New York, or even in north-west London, which in England is joked about as the Jewish ghetto, I would not have had the opportunity to meet the diversity of people and become their friends as I have in Oxford. One of the most unusual situations I find myself in is that for over three years now I have had as one of my closest student friends Michael Taft Benson, who is the grandson of the man who has been president of the Mormon Church since 1986, Ezrah Taft Benson.

Now the Mormons believe that the president of their Church is a living prophet, so Mike's grandfather has unequivocal authority within the movement. Ezrah Taft Benson is also a powerful man in the secular world, having served eight years as the Secretary of Agriculture during the Eisenhower Presidency. Mike himself is a very devout Mormon. He served on a mission for two years, as most male Mormons do, trying to bring converts to his faith. Here at Oxford he is doing a D.Phil. in International Relations with specific emphasis on Middle Eastern affairs. One of the reasons we became friendly is that although Mike's faith is different from mine, and Judaism and Mormonism are extremely dissimilar in their orientation as well as in their general beliefs, he found he fitted well among us. When he arrived he was the only Mormon at Oxford, and the fact was that we were religious Jews and he wanted to be part of a religious community.

We also discovered that there was much in common in our faiths. For example, Jews have a very strict dietary code and so do Mormons. Mike in his entire life has never drunk coffee, smoked a cigarette or had any wine or other alcoholic beverage. I also at nineteen years old was sent by the Lubavitcher rebbe, I wouldn't call it on a mission, but to help bolster Jewish education and awareness in Australia, and to help found a rabbinical college, which I did with nine of my colleagues; this too was for a two-year period. The Mormons have very large families; the average Mormon family has between six and eight children, which is roughly the same as the average Chasidic Jewish family. When they are not on a mission, Mormons tend to live in close-knit groups as do Chasidic Jews; they also have a concept of a very tight and unified leadership, although the rebbe is quite different from Mike's grandfather. Mike thrived on our recognition of what we shared and we became close friends.

This is interesting because when I lived in Crown Heights in New York, Mormon missionaries would come knocking at our door, asking if they could speak to us about the book of Mormon. We took great offence because we knew that they knew we would never convert, and we felt that they were just going to offend and insult us by trying in a Chasidic neighbourhood. As a result I had a low opinion of Mormons. This feeling was reinforced because of my experience when I was in rabbinical college in Jerusalem. There was a great controversy raging at the time because the Mormons were building a new campus of Brigham Young University on Mount Scopus; a multi-million dollar facility, which was very beautiful. All the Jewish religious organizations were claiming they would use it to prey on secular Israelis who were not aware of their culture, and then convert them to Mormonism. There was a great outcry in the Jewish community against the building of the centre: the controversy was terrible, and there were huge demonstrations with tens of thousands of Chasidic Jews in the street, and accusations about how the Centre had been allowed. I myself attended some of these rallies. Here in Oxford I suddenly found myself becoming closest friends with not just a Mormon but the grandson of the head of the Mormon church, and a deeply religious Mormon at that.

Mike had become so close to me that he was in my office virtually every day, we took long drives together, we went to a lot of Jewish events. He even travelled with me to the USA for the AIPAC, the American-Jewish lobby, conference. (Every year I attend the AIPAC conference because we are friendly with some of the vice-presidents who have children at Oxford and they assist us in bringing speakers to come under our auspices at the university.) He went with me and other Jewish students in March 1992. The day after the conference, the Lubavitch movement hosted a beautiful gala dinner at the Ramada Hotel in Washington D.C. in honour of the Lubavitch rebbe's ninetieth birthday. It was attended by twenty-six senators, the presidents of major Jewish organizations, Elie Wiesel was the guest speaker, and it was chaired by Ronald Pearlman, the chairman of the Revlon Corporation. I brought Mike to this as well. There he introduced me to Senator Oran Hatch, who is a close friend of his family. Senator Hatch, from Utah, has great respect for Lubavitch in that state and said many graceful things about the rebbe. This was the pattern of relationship that Mike and I enjoyed.

Standing up for Belief

Mike is a true ambassador for his religion. I think it is fair to say that every person he encounters at Oxford has in some form or another a negative or at least suspicious opinion of Mormons, and he completely changes their stereotyped image. While I cannot embrace his beliefs, I have great respect for him and his total commitment to his faith. He has brought credit and dignity to Mormonism in this city and I respect how his belief system has made him into such a kind and caring human being.

For example, Mike has told me some of the central principles of the Mormon religion, one of which is that we are today what God once was; God was once human, and every human being if they lead a virtuous life can one day become a God, and have their own planet. Also since they believe that marriage is eternal, not just in this world but in the world to come as well, God probably today has a wife. In addition there are other beliefs which Judaism would find hard to swallow, such as that Mormons baptize people posthumously. That is why many people will be familiar with the fact that the Mormon Church in Utah has the best archives of any people in the world. They search for people's ancestors to convert posthumously and baptize them by proxy. A Mormon will stand and say the person's name and be baptized by proxy for them. Nevertheless I was deeply impressed by the fact that Mike stands by his convictions and, as I said, we found many things in common. Since meeting Mike I can honestly say that I have found Mormonism to contain strong human and family values and every Mormon that I have met through Mike is kind, loving and leads a holy and spiritual life.

He introduced me to a friend of his, Brock Oaks, a sensitive and highly intelligent young man, who at the time was a Mormon missionary at Oxford, and we also became friendly. I think he understood he should not try to missionize me. There was a sense of camaraderie between us because Mormon missionaries are not much appreciated. He stood on the street all day speaking to people about his faith; most of the time he would be abused or people would shout at him. He had doors slammed in his face. I have been very much in the same situation; even Oxford people can sometimes be nasty, but people can be especially harsh on the streets of places like New York, Jerusalem, Sydney and Los Angeles. I had a natural sympathy for his dedication and commitment.

Religion and Ambition

One day Brock came into my office to tell me he would soon be going to the Air Force Academy. When I asked why, he said, 'Because my father and my mother went there.' I asked what his parents did; he looked completely amazed. I soon realized he was not used to having to explain who his father was. He told me that he is the Commander of the US Air Force in Europe, a four-star American general, Deputy Commander of all NATO forces in Europe, and Supreme Commander of all Allied Air Forces in Europe. When I asked him if General Oaks would agree to come to speak for us, he told me his father doesn't do a lot of public lectures; but then he asked me what we would want him to speak about. I said that for such a deeply religious and devout man it would be appropriate if he would speak about the synthesis of religious convictions with professional achievements. How often does someone with strong religious scruples rise to that level?

A week later I received a telephone call from General Oaks himself, preceded by a briefing from a Colonel Murtah. I began to see just how powerful this man was. The colonel explained who the general was, and that he commanded over half a million troops in Europe, and then I spoke to the general. You can imagine how happy I was when he agreed to speak to us.

He arrived with his motorcade a few weeks later. We arranged his lecture at the Oxford Union, which was preceded by a dinner where I spoke about how beautiful it was that, although we were from two completely different religions, I and his son got along as the closest friends, and our friendship had culminated in this lecture. General Oaks for his part said he was humbled by the dinner which we held in his honour; there were a lot of famous academics and professors there, from all fields, who were interested in meeting an American general. He came with bodyguards and an armour-plated Mercedes; he had just flown to the Air Force base near Oxford, and was here for the evening.

The Beardless US Air Force

He told a fascinating story dating from the time when he had just one star, and was working in the Pentagon. Lubavitch was taking the US Air Force to court over the case of a Jewish airman who had become a *baal teshuvah*, a returnee to Judaism. Now Lubavitch had earlier fought the Air Force on the subject of a yarmulka. The Air Force was arguing in court that it was against the conventions of the service and the uniform; if one man started to wear his yarmulka the whole idea of the uniform would fall apart, and after that discipline would collapse. Lubavitch fought this, and they succeeded. At the time of his story, Lubavitch was fighting about someone who wanted to wear a beard, which is also contrary to the Air Force code. Again the Air Force were afraid that all discipline would fall apart if this one man wore a beard. The commander of the Air Force went to General Oaks and said to him, 'Oaks, we want you to go out to Capitol Hill, and fight our battle for us. If you win, you get another star.' General Oaks said he went out and fought, and won, and the Lubavitcher man was not allowed to wear a beard in the Air Force. He said now that he had met Lubavitch and seen the good work they were doing in Oxford and how they were hosting him, he felt so ashamed he wanted to take that second star off. The comment was said tongue-in-cheek, but displayed the level of attachment we had achieved between the Mormon and Jewish communities.

The Advantage of Religion

At the Oxford Union, General Oaks gave a wonderful speech. He told us he had entered the Air Force as an insignificant junior officer like everyone else, and then gone to the Air Force Academy to train as a pilot. He was a religious Mormon and so of course he would not drink alcohol, and he would not smoke. When he first arrived at the academy, his commander said to him, 'Oaks, if you don't smoke or drink that means you won't be part of a group, you won't be buddies with anyone and you'll never get ahead in the Air Force.' He told his commander if that is what it meant then 'I'll leave the Air Force but I'll never compromise my religious convictions.' Many people told him the same thing, and yet because of his diligence, his intellect and his devotion, he kept being promoted until he became Commander of all US and Allied Air Forces in Europe.

His point throughout the speech was that religious convictions are not incompatible with professionalism. On the contrary, he listed a number of important items within religion which give people the ability to succeed: discipline, family values, a belief in a higher goal, and knowing what is important and what is unimportant, what one should legitimately become upset over, and what to forget. Religion helps you to know that if you don't get the promotion it is no big deal because that is not what life is really about. He deeply impressed his audience, and they understood how amazing it is that a Mormon rose so high. Even when he had flown over sixty combat missions in Vietnam, he never felt the need to succumb to any of the substances or vices forbidden by his religion. This was an important message for our students to hear, and I deeply respect General Oaks for saying it. Of all the great men that L'Chaim Society has hosted over the years, he is truly one of the greatest.

A Sign of Faith

One of the biggest problems with our students is that they feel they won't get ahead unless they conform to the conventions and rules which operate in society. There are two highly visible areas in which this happens. Firstly, male students who come to Oxford wearing yarmulkas often feel they have to take them off here. They are afraid of not being treated as equals by their fellow students, and they also think their own tutors will discriminate against them and won't give them the marks they deserve.

Secondly, even if they go through Oxford wearing a yarmulka, when it comes to leaving, and working in other places, they say you can't work in banking, as an accountant, or as a lawyer, in a yarmulka. In New York, for example, it seems to be acceptable, but in places like London it is quite rare for men to wear yarmulkas to work. I found this out especially when I once had to go to visit an ex-Oxford student who now works in Goldman-Sachs, the American investment banking firm. Imagine the huge trading floor with the most modern technology and thousands of phone lines, PCs and people – bond traders, equity traders, futures traders, options traders, all screaming – and when I walked across, everything came to a standstill. It was as though a man from the moon had walked in, instead of a Chasidic rabbi with a yarmulka and a beard; it was quiet for about thirty seconds until I went to the trading desk of my friend, who looked around. Even he was taken aback by everybody's reaction.

People feel that religious conviction is incompatible with success, and that is why it was so important that such a powerful but religious general was willing to come to Oxford to talk about his success.

Discrimination is No Excuse for Failure

A world-famous medical researcher and Nobel Prize Laureate, Dr Baruch Blumberg, is the Master of Balliol College, which is often said to be Oxford's most academically prestigious undergraduate college. Balliol has already produced six British prime ministers, it is perhaps the most difficult college to get into, has the highest percentage of Rhodes Scholars and so on. Dr Blumberg is the first ever American master of Balliol. Until his tenure there had only been British masters. He is also the first scientist to be master because usually someone from the humanities is appointed.

His background is interesting. He grew up an Orthodox Jew, was educated in the Flatbush yeshivah in Brooklyn, New York, and in 1976 he won the Nobel Prize for medicine for developing the Hepatitis B vaccine, which has saved millions of lives worldwide. When he first arrived I phoned him and his wife to welcome them to Oxford, and I spoke to him about how impressive it was to me that he had maintained this name Baruch in all his official publications. If one looks in the Encyclopaedia Britannica one will see that the citation for the Nobel Prize given to him also says Baruch, which is of course a visibly Jewish name. I said to him, 'It's funny that you have retained this name; most scholars in Oxford are afraid that if they retain a Jewish name or identity they will be discriminated against.' His wife said to me, 'My husband was very good, the best at what he did, that is why he won the Nobel Prize. If people don't use their Jewish names and identities because they think it will hold them back because of discrimination against them, that is just an excuse.'

And this is what I always tell the students to emphasize that achievement and religious conviction are not incompatible. It is only an excuse for not getting ahead. Like the famous joke: a Jewish man goes for an interview at a radio station to be a disc jockey. He comes back and his friend asks him, 'Did you get the job?' and he says, 'N-n-n-n-no, th-th-th-they dddd-d-didn't g-g-give it t-t-t-t-to me those anti-sss-s-s-s-s-s-s-Semitics!' And of course the joke is that he is a stutterer and he blames it on anti-Semitism. This belief among Jewish people that they are being discriminated against is something we have to uproot from students and prove it is not what the the outside world really thinks and what it really believes. Because it is not something we can embrace. We must bring pride to Jewish affirmation.

Conversations with an Oxford Pagan

I believe many people who know Oxford University would be surprised to hear that it is also a home to a small but significant subculture of student naturists who profess pagan beliefs and enact pagan rituals. I had many interesting discussions – and differences – with one articulate Jewish girl student who became involved with Oxford pagans and even became one of their priestesses. But I hope we eventually agreed that the world has a common origin and unity, which is best expressed through monotheism, the single greatest contribution the Jews have given the world.

SECTION FOUR

═══

RELATIONSHIPS

Chapter Thirty-eight

WHEN MEN AND WOMEN
CANNOT UNDERSTAND EACH OTHER

The people from many different cultures and religions I come across in my work in Oxford often say to me that they envy the deep sense of community which Jews traditionally have had: we are intrinsically connected with one another and feel for each other in both the saddest and happiest occasions of life. In a pressurized environment like that found in the University of Oxford, this closeness becomes especially important. When the rest of your peers, even your nearest friends in college, are in direct competition with you, it is refreshing to have a retreat where the only contest is how to be the most companionable person.

Having said that, it is important to be able to know the real reason for this close relationship. It is partly founded on the recognition of a shared culture, a shared history and language. It is also because we all may be labelled 'Jew' in the same way. But these reasons fail to encapsulate the essence of Jewishness. As we see elsewhere in this book, being a Jew is a matter of intrinsic identity, an identity that is defined by our relationship with God, to each other and the world. It is an existential fact, a statement of essence. This is something that we can deny or accept, live our lives by or fight against, but it is always a fact. Because it is so, our whole lives are shaped by it, but especially our relationships with those who share this relationship with God.

This fact is essentially supra-rational, but wonderfully true. Our relationship with God at times demands a great deal of self-sacrifice, but it is a joy to us as well.

A large part of my work here in Oxford is to try to convince people of this. I do not pit the ancient wisdom of the Jews against such a sophisticated centre of knowledge and culture, and people's natural desire to fit in. Rather, I assert the connections and opportunities for integrity that exist on both fronts.

In the final analysis, this world is about relationships, and the more we put into them, the more we get out. However, we also have to be prepared to be committed to relationships that we do not, indeed cannot, understand. In my experience it is specifically the irrational, or supra-rational, elements within a relationship that hinder it most. But this is completely unnecessary. One student's story illustrates the value of this way of approaching relationships.

A Crisis in Faith

Since my arrival in Oxford, I have been touched to discover that a large number of non-Jewish students are keen to frequent our events. This of course occurs in the areas where it would be most expected – when we host the likes of Mikhail Gorbachev, Leonard Nimoy and Elie Wiesel, or an Israeli minister – but we also enjoy the presence of non-Jews in core Jewish functions such as Friday-night Shabbat dinner, classes on Talmud, Jewish law, and mysticism.

These non-Jewish students certainly do not come to the L'Chaim Society simply because they have no faith of their own. A number of devout Catholic, Protestant and Mormon students come to us, and sometimes they even want to discuss a crisis in their own faith. I must always tread very carefully in offering guidance and counselling to these students. In promoting a Jewish view of life and God I do not look to increase their disenchantment with their own religion, or to consider conversion to Judaism. On the contrary, my purpose is to have them leave my office with greater determination to make their faith work.

So it was with more than a little trepidation that I welcomed a new non-Jewish student into my office to discuss his faith; some time ago a Jewish tutor at one of the colleges had introduced him to me.

This student was a Rhodes Scholar and a deeply committed Christian. Although he had been brought up as a Unitarian from birth, as soon as he arrived in Oxford he tried out different denominations of churches; the problem was that he found them all equally unsatisfying. This led to a terrible crisis in his faith, in which he began to feel disillusioned with Christianity as a whole. He was aware that it was not Christianity that had changed, but himself, and his greatest fear was that he might have lost the faith which used to be so natural and central a part of him.

After enjoying two Friday-night dinners with us, which were very lively and carefree, he came to me to discuss his faith. He explained why he had chosen to speak to a Chasidic rabbi, rather than a member of the Christian clergy: he said, 'You seem to take religion very naturally and rejoice in it.' And it turned out that this was the key to his problem.

He proceeded to tell me over the course of two and a half hours, at times with tears in his eyes, that he felt Christianity demanded he should stop being himself before he could begin to be religious. He felt it was making unnatural demands of him: 'There is almost a sense that I must vacate myself, be rid of my essential being, before I can become a

Christian. Am I really that unholy that the only way I can approach God is by first discarding my essential identity?'

Am I Really That Unholy?

Although I hear this complaint very often from Christians, there is a reason why students are particularly hurt by the idea that they are intrinsically wicked. Young people, who have not yet developed a lust for money or power, whose greatest ambition is to bring love and equality into the world, cannot fathom what could be so naturally wrong with them that it necessitates a rejection of all that has gone before in their lives. This feeling was especially strong in this particular student, who had an innate sense of spirituality, a feeling that he loved God, but wanted to draw nearer to Him without ceasing to be who he was.

First I told him that if every religion were perfect there would be no room for the believer to make their contribution: perhaps his deep sense of the goodness of humanity would make an irreplaceable contribution to his Christian community. So, rather than being disillusioned with his faith, I asked him to rise to the challenge of enhancing it on behalf of others, as well as for himself.

Faith and Action

I then mentioned to him my belief that true redemption does not only come in the form of an absolute faith in the Divinity, but in a further step. Faith should empower one to goodly, and hence Godly, activity. Here is the main point of departure between Judaism and Christianity. Most people are under the impression that the distinguishing characteristic between Judaism and Christianity is belief in the Divinity, or Messiahship, of Jesus. But in practice, the main point of departure between these two great world religions is Christianity's emphasis on faith, and Judaism's insistence on action. Judaism's passion is for the performance of *mitzvot*, Divinely motivated actions, whereas Christianity promises salvation through belief in the redeemer. Judaism promises a better world if we all undertake positive steps to make it happen: we must never relegate the task of perfecting the world to another party or generation. In essence, we must never allow belief in a world of faith or thought to exclude us from concern for the empirical world in which we live.

Interestingly, the student found this too radical and novel an approach to accept. Firstly, it did not fit in with the ideas to which he was accustomed. Secondly, it seemed to him to contradict the logic of his belief: for someone trained to understand that faith is everything, action must appear to be a very inferior goal. It seems that human beings living in the post-Romantic world naturally presume that ethereal subjects like faith are superior to mundane and physical items like deed.

The student's argument for faith's superiority to deed was straightforward. Faith clearly uses our highest and most uniquely human faculties: intellect and emotion. On the other hand, deeds need nothing higher than the ability to listen and take orders, as all animal trainers recognize. It seems that faith, employing the highest faculties that human beings possess, should necessarily be superior to action. Furthermore, believing in God serves to connect us to Him on a far higher plane than action, since through the former we may come to apprehend God in toto and connect ourselves to Him, whereas action embraces only a single aspect of God's will.

The Intrinsic Will

Taking my cue from these points, I entered into my polemic. In Jewish mysticism, will is always considered to be greater than intellect or emotion. It reigns supreme. The proof of this is that we hear people constantly saying things like, 'I know that this sounds crazy, and I would usually say I hate the idea, but I'm going to do it anyway.' In other words, our intellect, even our emotions, are sometimes powerless to prevent actions which we recognize as foolish. How can this happen? The answer is that each one of us possesses what can be referred to as Intrinsic Will, which dictates both who we are and what we do. It is intrinsic because it exists at the deepest level of ourselves, far transcending our logic, intelligence or emotion and ruling over them from above.

In the language of the Kabbalah, will is referred to as *keter*, the crown which sits on the head. In other words, it transcends and overrides the intellect and emotions. While the study of the Torah itself represents Godly wisdom and intellect, the Intrinsic Will of God is expressed in the *mitzvot* which are ordered by the Torah. It follows, therefore, that when we study the Torah we are connected with the consciousness of God, but when we keep the *mitzvot* we are fully connected with Godly Will, which by far transcends consciousness. It is for this reason that Judaism has always emphasized the fulfilment of *mitzvot*: they even take precedence over studying the Torah, and are codified as such in the *Code of Jewish Law*.

To identify briefly some of our intrinsic human desires, take for example the will to live. Even if one rationally and coherently argues to one's neighbour that their life is not worth living, they will nevertheless continue to live. Even if they are convinced that they are better off dead, this will not prove sufficient to impel them to suicide. The reason: because the will to live and survive is intrinsic to the human condition. It therefore cannot be acted upon by intellect or rational thought.

Another example of intrinsic human will is the will to succeed and find meaning in life. Each and every one of us possesses a deep-seated desire to achieve things in life and thus lend significance and importance to our being. In fact, I would contend, based on experiences with students at Oxford, that the number one reason for depression is a feeling of a lack of direction, that their lives are not leading anywhere productive. Thus, often when a student comes into my office seeking comfort from depression, providing it is frequently as easy as getting them to devote greater time to their work. When they do not study hard enough, it bothers them immensely, and this then leads to a vicious cycle of depression and more time away from their books.

The concept of Intrinsic Will is absolutely central to a true understanding, not only of God, but of ourselves. There is a part of us, deep down beneath all the conscious and revealed layers, which constitutes a glimpse of the true totality of our existence and what we are. The less it can be revealed in thought or expressed in words, the more powerful and essential it is. It is only when the people around us come to terms with that part of us that they can truly become connected with us.

Slaughtering Animals for God

A careful study of the most enigmatic aspect of the God–man relationship will yield much fruit. Throughout the ages, the sacrificial service in the Temple has generated consternation and anxiety among many Jews. This difficulty seems to be increasingly common as the years go by. There are those who feel that, at best, it resembles ancient pagan practices, and at worst is anachronistic and offensive. If we are honest with ourselves, how many of us genuinely long and pine for the rededication of the Temple in the messianic era, so that the sacrificial service can be restored and resumed?

The sacrificial service is clearly not part of the panoply of ideas to which modern Jews are accustomed. A sacrifice apparently contradicts the logic of our belief. For anyone groomed in the idea that Judaism is about doing kind deeds and being good, slaughtering animals to one's God seems inappropriate. As in the point made above, it seems that human beings living in the post-Romantic world naturally presume that ethereal subjects such as faith should not be concerned with grossly mundane and physical practices like animal offerings.

However, the reality of Judaism is such that one must accept that just as there are beautiful ideas advocated by our religion, such as behaving charitably and visiting the sick, so too there are Godly elements which are completely beyond human understanding, and are a part of a transcendent Divine Will. Only an observance of both types of precepts establishes a meaningful relationship with our Creator.

A Partner Who Can't Appreciate Flowers

As an example, consider a couple who marry. She says she loves flowers and asks him, if he plans to buy her anything, please to put flowers at the top of his list. He replies that flowers die quickly. 'I can't understand why you're insisting on me buying things with such a short life; they're a waste of money!' Instead, he agrees to buy her silk clothing and sparkling jewellery, but she insists that he cannot love her until he does what she has asked. He then demands that at the very least she should explain herself to him, but she cannot. Where is the woman who can truly explain why she loves flowers more than so much else? Yet he insists that he cannot appreciate or respond to her request unless she can rationalize it for him.

In this, the husband is making a twofold mistake. The first part is only a mistake because of the specific context of his being in a relationship. The true meaning of a relationship is that one accepts and entertains the wishes and the desires of the other partner. If you choose to fulfil only those desires of your partner that make sense to you, then your relationship is de facto merely a relationship with *yourself*. There is no room for a partner to exist as him or herself in such a relationship, since only when they comply with the wishes and understanding of the other partner are they and their desires taken seriously.

This could be understood in another way: a relationship is about two people making room in their lives for each other. In the fullest sense, this means another person, not just a clone of yourself. If there is nothing in your life which gives space to another person, if you cannot generate the sensitivity or discipline merely to execute another's most basic needs, then for all practical purposes you are not involved in a genuine relationship. Although you and your spouse may share the same house, and you may even have had children together, you are still as distant as the sun and the moon: there is no real harmony or correspondence, even though the view we have from earth may show up superficial similarities. If this is the case, you are not genuinely looking for another person with whom to share your life, but rather you are looking to duplicate or, in mathematical terms, to square yourself. One man and his *doppelgänger* do not constitute a relationship.

Denying a Woman's Femininity

However, the second mistake that the husband makes is far more significant. When he only carries out those wishes of his wife that make sense, or alternatively when he says that he will do whatever she wants as long as she explains herself, he is insisting that he be connected only to her intellectual, rational side. Her deeper, truer self not only remains a mystery to him but forever remains a domain with which he refuses association. He connects himself with the part of her he understands and appreciates, but rashly neglects the part which is a far more holistic statement of the person his wife really is. Due to this shortcoming, he ends up being only partially married to his wife.

In other words, there is an essential femininity in his wife which, since he is male, he will never understand: thus it will always remain undisclosed to him. It is that femininity which expresses itself in the kind of things he cannot appreciate; in this example, flowers. She cannot explain those desires for the same reason she cannot truly explain what it means to be female as opposed to male. It is a quintessential point of existence, not a revealed or expressed mode of behaviour. So there is nothing she can possibly do that can convey to her husband her intrinsic desire. He is not her, therefore there is a part of her that he will never understand. It completely transcends logic, *but this does not invalidate its importance.*

The Woman in Your Wife

When the husband insists on an explanation, or insists that he will only purchase those things for her which even he can appreciate, he renders it impossible to be truly married to the woman in his wife. He may be married to the part of her which is the same in all humans, her capacity for emotion and intellect, but the part of her which should most attract and stimulate him, her femininity and womanhood, is something which he has dismissed completely.

From all this, it is clear that his relationship with his wife is at best superficial, at worst merely comparable to any relationship he has with his other friends, barring the sexual element. Although his wife is a woman and an individual, he consciously excises this element in her from his relations with her. His demand that his wife be intelligible to him attempts to create her in his own image, not that of God, and dismisses her intrinsic identity as a separate person.

On the other hand, when he actually executes her every desire, whether or not he understands it, he ensures that he is connected with her innermost self. Only now is he married to his wife, to the whole of his wife.

Of course, the above is just an example from many that we can draw on. The point is that in each relationship there will always be at least one attribute of one's partner which will forever remain an enigma.

Understanding the Infinite

In the same manner, there are people today who insist on understanding God. They want to humanize Him to the extent that He becomes intelligible, instead of accepting that the most basic definition of a God is a Being unlike anything human, transcending all comprehension and apprehension. By refusing to embrace any element of Divine Will which cannot be grasped by human logic, they insist that their God must make sense, otherwise they will ignore Him.

Judaism is Not Religious Humanism

A predominant modern attitude to Judaism is to see it as nothing more than religious humanism. Jewish people everywhere take pride in revealing to the world the beautiful ethics and morals of Judaism; how Judaism cares for the downtrodden, the hungry, the widows, the orphans – all those less fortunate than us. It is true that one of the beauties of Judaism is its extensive human dimension. However, pretending that this is the sum total of Jewish belief is a self-imposed fallacy, a fallacy conjured up by those who want Judaism to reflect best whatever impresses the world most at any given time.

The essential essence of Judaism is, and shall always remain, hidden: the reason for this is that God is not human. Insisting that we want to understand Him in the same way we understand humans divorces us from any real connection we could ever have with the truly Divine.

Unease at the Mysteries of Creation

The point should also be raised as to why we feel it is in our interest to apprehend the Divinity. Why do we feel such a profound sense of unease when confronted with the mysteries of Creation? We appear to have lost all sensitivity to the need for awe and wonder. In secular terms, why should a husband dismiss his wife's femininity?

When a human being fulfils the Will of the Creator he or she is directly connected to the Creator's intrinsic Will and essence. That person draws life from the source of all life, draws strength from the fountain of strength, and is uplifted to lofty and infinite heights. For this reason, when a human being makes use of a physical article, such as leather, in fulfilment of the mitzvah of *tefillin*, the physical article retains that holiness and is transformed into a consecrated, ineffable object. The reason being that it served at the point of contact between that person and God. It was touched by the Divine.

In our lives, we must be as the leather article: not merely fulfilling, but transformed by, subsisting and thriving on, the commandments of our Creator. There can be no greater method of celebrating our ability to be connected to the Master of the Universe than by executing his Intrinsic Will. There can be no better means of entering into a meaningful relationship with our source and Creator than by attaching ourselves, not just to Godly consciousness, but to Godly essence.

Chapter Thirty-nine

WHY DO WE MARRY?

God commanded Moses to build a brass basin in the Tabernacle for the *kohanim* (priests) to wash their hands and feet before undertaking work in the Sanctuary. Tradition maintains that this basin was made from the daughters of Israel's brass mirrors which they would use to beautify themselves for their husbands. Moses had felt they were inappropriate to be used in the tent of God, but God overruled him and instructed him specifically to make the basin from the mirrors since it was objects like these which promoted love and intimacy between husband and wife. God was telling Moses that even humble objects which make the bond between husband and wife stronger are holy. And I am sure that we moderns can learn from this ancient lesson.

On Sunday, 14 March, the L'Chaim Society celebrated its final event of Hilary Term 1993 in the form of a book launch, coinciding with National Jewish Book Week, of my publication: *The Wolf Shall Lie With the Lamb: The Messiah in Hasidic Thought.* Of the many emotions felt by an author on the publication of a book, I would like to convey what I believe to be the most important, and it also has to do with marriage.

The Problem with Marriage

One of the largest retailers in Britain has just started an experimental scheme to sell 'divorce cards'. Many people, including the Bishop of Birmingham, were outraged at the idea of congratulating someone on the break-up of their marriage, but this misses the real issue. Divorce has entered the centre stage of modern society, not as the villain of the piece, but as a stock character; apparently it is an occasion to be expected as much as the birth of a child or a marriage.

The staggeringly high number of divorces in today's society seems to indicate that something is fundamentally wrong, either with the institution of marriage as it exists in the modern world, or with our current conception of it. A common notion is that the way in which married people behave leads to the breakdown of marriages, but I would like to suggest that this is not the central issue. A far more deep-rooted

413

problem is the motive that prompts us to marry in the first place: it leads to our inability to deal with marital difficulties once they arise, as they inevitably do.

The Respectable Thing to Do

I would contend that few of us today can fully understand the reasons why we marry. Most people say their reason is love, but surely the need to solidify or eternalize one's love for another human being in the form of an established institution like marriage seems to hint at a deficiency or insecurity in that love. If you truly love each other, the feelings you have right at this moment should be sufficient to maintain the two of you together for the rest of your lives, without the formality of a public ceremony. If not, it is foolish to think that marriage will hold you together. Nobody wants to remain in a loveless marriage.

A variation on this theme is that because you love each other so much, you naturally want to build a home together, and live within a framework that everyone can recognize as uniting the two of you. This can be done, though, without getting married; by simply living together. In today's society this is becoming an increasingly viable and widely accepted alternative. When children arrive, many couples then get married because they prefer not to incur the disapproval of society by having children out of wedlock.

I would hope that there must be some deeper reason for marrying than simply because it is the accepted and respectable thing to do. If there is no deeper reason than social conditioning, then perhaps this accounts for the high percentage of marriages that end in divorce. Having no deep reason for marrying, especially if we don't know why we marry at all, must vastly increase the chances of not remaining married.

No Man is an Island

In today's world we look upon ourselves as being whole individuals. Although we readily acknowledge our deficiencies or character flaws, we never see ourselves as being incomplete or deficient in any deep-seated way. We see ourselves as good people, perhaps not perfect, but none the less not missing anything vital. That cosiness and sense of unity is further enhanced by a good education, a well-paid job, and general financial security. The assumption of completeness implies that there can be no fundamental reason for marrying at all. If we are not missing anything in life, why search for a life-long partner?

Only if you feel you are a complete human being can you ask why you should share the rest of your life with, and acknowledge a dependence on, another human being. This question is asked because we habitually misunderstand ourselves when we see each person as a whole being. The Jewish understanding of the human condition completely rejects this outlook.

Adam and Eve

Judaism sees a man or woman as only one half of a potentially whole being. Each person is simply incomplete. No job, acquisition of knowledge, or praise from other human beings can ever change that. It is an anatomical and spiritual fact. And this lack of completion is rooted in the very constitution of humankind. Most people interpret the Bible as saying that Adam was male, and that he searched for a female who was later given to him when God caused him to sleep and removed one of his ribs from which He built Eve. Such an interpretation places a wholly negative light on the female qualities by implying they are not in some way intrinsic to the concept of a human being, since God did not at first create any of the traits we value in women. Judaism maintains that God created Adam in the Garden of Eden as a *hybrid* of both male and female. The original Adam was whole, embracing both masculine and feminine traits. God then separated Adam into two distinct parts.

The traditional Jewish interpretation of these verses in Genesis suggests that the word, *tzela*, interpreted usually as 'rib', here means a side. When Adam fell asleep, God removed an entire side, the feminine side, from His creature, and the result was the splitting of the first human into the newly male Adam and the female Eve. The result also was that each side was no longer complete and now depended on rejoining, reuniting, with the lost half in order to achieve wholeness.

Searching for the Lost Half

This is the real reason we marry. We do not unite as one to achieve happiness, nor to substantiate our love within an institution. The reason we marry is that every single one of us is only a half of what was once a whole. Via a recognition of that fact we can begin to appreciate how lucky we are to be married in the first place, and continue to strive to remain married. We marry because long ago the Creator of the world separated the original human into two halves, and instituted that we should search for our lost half and rejoin through a holy state of matrimony. It makes sense to assume that He who created and separated us in the first place is He who is capable of reuniting us. Therefore, it is insufficient to live together. While that can serve as a profound statement of love and commitment, it still falls far short of the necessary effect. Humans must not only love, but achieve a literal 'wholeness', which is achieved through the *spiritual* unification brought about by marriage.

A Spiritual Bond

It is this understanding which can radically alter both our view of marriage and our commitment to making it work. If one's attitude is that 'I am a whole person, my life is fine, but it would be enhanced by having someone share it with me', the spirit is essentially the same as wishing to have an optional extra such as a comfortable home or a car. Marriage should not be seen as something that is merely an addition to one's existence, but rather as an absolute essential, intrinsic to a human being. If not, then the first time something goes wrong, one's attitude will be, 'What do I need this for?' If I own a car that breaks down every day, I dispose of the car; similarly, one tries to sell a house on which costs are too high, and so on. Even though someone with the shallowest views of marriage acknowledges that a spouse is far more important than a car or house, nevertheless the underlying philosophy of all the above is the same. They are all seen as things which are *in addition* to one's existence, and not fundamental or intrinsic to it.

Divorce becomes a helpful recourse only in the most acute circumstances. To see one's spouse as a part of oneself, as it were a limb, and even much more so, reveals the impossibility of divorcing. Divorce is essentially a separation of oneself from oneself. Although I am readily prepared to dispose of a car which causes more anguish than pleasure, the same is not true of my arm. One is fully prepared to stay the course in order to fix problems with a limb, however serious, since to hate one's arm or leg is to hate oneself. If husbands and wives develop an appreciation for the fact that their spouse is a part of themselves, then even when they are sure that their spouse is behaving unreasonably, or possesses undesirable character traits, they will work to see the situation improved since they understand that they are fortunate to be married in the first instance.

The Marriage Missionary

I was once speaking with an Oxford student whose parents are divorced. Most of her friends also come from broken homes. She was intensely hostile to marriage and was persistent that living together provided a far better alternative. As far as she was concerned, the only genuine and coherent argument for marriage arises if someone is religious. But because a person like her does not live by religious tenets, then they by definition cannot live in sin. So basically the only argument according to her for marriage is a negative one: to prevent religious people from living in sin. Her group of friends added that the only reason people still marry is social convention. When I asked what the original purpose of this convention was, the first reason they gave was to dominate women, and trap them in a patriarchal male-centred institution. The second reason they gave, however, was that society imposed marriage on people as a glaring sign that they are together.

It may surprise the reader to hear that so many of today's students have no confidence in marriage, but I am increasingly convinced that it is a fact. I myself was surprised at the unmitigated hostility that most young people have towards marriage today. They simply have never heard any convincing reason why people should marry. After all, according to this student and her group of friends, all the people they knew who had been married for more than five years were miserable or divorced.

Because they needed strong reasons to see marriage as anything but strife, even with someone they were in love with, I asked them to assess the difference between a parent's relationship to a child and the relationship between partners, whether married or not.

My Spouse, My Child

'Suppose one of you can't have children, and would like to adopt. But before making the decision to adopt, you think that if things do not work out you have the right to return him or her to the agency. Could any of you condone that kind of attitude?'

They all shook their heads. I asked them why. They answered that by considering this condition they would not be treating the baby as their child, but rather as some sort of employee with a dismissal clause in its contract. Exactly! When you fail to commit yourself before a given relationship, this is a statement of the relationship being meaningless. A parent who refuses to commit themselves to their children prior to their birth is saying that this will be my charge, but not my child.

As a rabbi I am often cast in the difficult role of being an ear to marital dissatisfaction. The first advice I always offer is to treat your spouse, at the very least, the way you treat your own child. If a severe character flaw, such as a violent temper, is discovered in one's child, one should not immediately think that he or she is not worth cherishing and should be discarded, because a child is a part of the family, indeed a part of oneself. A parent thinks, 'I'll work to make him or her better.' Well, this is your husband, or your wife. Why not give them the same level of commitment?

Living Together or Marriage

Living together and marrying are two different statements altogether. When you live together you are saying that if it works out, great, and if not, I'm fine the way I am and I can therefore walk straight out of this relationship without it having any, or only minimal, long-term adverse effects. I am a whole human being, it is just nicer to share one's life with someone else. But when you marry before you begin living together, it is a statement that we are much more than merely living together, we are one. Marrying is the exact equivalent of the statement of unconditional love that a parent feels toward their child the moment the child is born. When a child is born a parent feels that no matter how the child will turn out, for good or for bad, they will always love the child. And there is a reason for this, and it's quite simple. One's child is a part of one's being. To love the child is like loving oneself. We are fundamentally changed when our children are born, because there is no such thing as being a parent without a child. Having a child makes us into parents, and their existence is intrinsic to our identity.

And the same is true of marriage. It is getting married that makes you whole. We are incomplete without our destined partners. Just as a parent is not a parent without a child, we are not complete people without being forged as one with a spouse. When we agree to marry, instead of merely living together, we are making a statement that we recognize that we need to be 'sown together', as it were.

This is beside the fact that logic dictates commitment is the only possible way in which a relationship can flourish. If two people share an apartment with nothing holding them together save their deep love for one another, when they have their very first fight and they no longer, even momentarily, feel the same affection, their first instinct will be to question if the relationship is worth preserving. They will not first feel that they must make this work at all costs and make the effort to keep what they have together. Rather, they will first inquire, 'Do I really need this?' And if they can justify the relationship, then they will make up, apologize, and seek reconciliation. But if not, they will simply get up and walk out. No strings attached.

On the other hand, a married couple, who have committed themselves to each other for eternity, whenever something crops up that can indeed affect the relationship, are committed to compromise. They are married. They can no more walk out on one another than they can unzip themselves and jump out of their own skin. The attitude now becomes, 'This is not just any woman with whom I am living. This is my wife. And this is not just a shared apartment. This is my home.' And both exercise the maximum effort to make their lives together work with harmony and love.

Marriage and Money

In a telling comment, when I asked the young woman mentioned above why she felt that marriage was nothing more than an institution designed to subjugate women, she told me, 'All marriage means is that you now have mutual financial obligations, economic dependence.' She told me that what I call commitment in marriage expresses itself only in economic factors and the most practical measures of life. It is not any higher commitment of the emotions. 'So what kind of love is that?' She said, 'I could make a case that love is much stronger when it does not need that kind of mutual financial gain, or the framework of an institution, in order to remain constant or even flourish.'

Love in Action

That the commitment in marriage is primarily demonstrated in economic and very practical matters is true. To think that this fact displays a weakness in the love is ridiculous and betrays a lack of understanding of the relationship between emotion and the true meaning of love. No emotion is true or real unless it translates itself into action. If a person feels something but does nothing about their emotion, it is safe to predict that even the feelings are merely ephemeral and will not last all that long.

For example, the rich countries of the world are full of 'hollow men'. These are the people who complain about children who are starving in Somalia, and the plight of youth in our inner cities, speaking as though they were emotionally tortured by these tragedies, but then refuse to do a thing about it. When they are approached by charities, they give nothing, or a mere fraction of their wealth. I know many such people in my work at Oxford. We are financially self-sufficient, which means that although we receive no money from the government or from any Jewish foundations, we do a hell of a lot of fund-raising. I regularly witness Jewish businessmen telling me that 'with such high assimilation and intermarriage rates, I fear for the very continuity of the Jewish people'. But when I then ask them to support our activities, which are dedicated to reversing these trends, they give me a cheque for a sum that means nothing to them. How much do they really feel if this is what their hearts prompt them to give?

And this is where this student erred. The commitment in marriage does indeed express itself precisely in the most practical things, because when you love someone completely, the love expresses itself, not only in the loftiest things, but in the lowliest as well. You not only write poetry to one another, but you also take out the rubbish so your spouse does not have to do it. And perhaps taking out the rubbish and saving them the burden is an even greater statement of love than poetry. Because it is saying that 'I love you so much that I am even willing to do those things that I would never naturally feel compelled to do, or want to do.'

Chasidic thought asks why, when lovers have not seen each other for a very long time, the first thing they do, before conversing or looking each other over, is embrace. Why not engage in passionate conversation, telling each other how much they love one another and how much they missed each other? The reason is this: they are making a subconscious statement, 'I love even your back. I love you so much, not just your face, which is the highest part of you, not just speaking to you, in which I can embrace your loftiest faculties. But even your back I love. Even that part which possesses no intellect and no emotion is what I love. I love all of you.'

A Shared Life

And here I return to the subject of the book launch. Recently I was invited to Aylesbury Grammar School to deliver a lecture to sixth formers on Judaism. It was part of a series on world religions organized by their teacher. I arrived with high hopes of usefully addressing four hundred non-Jewish students on Judaism, but left with my idealism crushed. The lecture was straightforward enough, but when it was time for questions, I was appalled by the misinformation about Israel and the Middle East that had been fed to these kids. Although my lecture was purely religious and made no mention whatever of Israeli politics, virtually all the questions revolved around this theme. I was asked why Israelis enjoy breaking the bones of the Palestinians; why Israel is so belligerent and expansionist; is it right that the Israelis should expel the Palestinians from their homes? It was capped by repeated questions on why Jews did not believe in the divinity of Jesus.

After this continued for some time, I looked at the boys and told them that if they were living in Israel right now, they would not have the luxury of sitting in a classroom asking a rabbi questions. Rather, at their age they would have just begun army service and would be hiking in the desert with forty kilogrammes of equipment on their backs. Do you think the average Israeli enjoys this? No, but they do it because just forty years ago, in the lifetime of all of their parents, six million Jews went to the gas chambers with no one to defend them and no country to take them in. Jews learned then that they must rely on themselves, notwithstanding how young they might be.

I then proceeded to ask them simple questions such as in which years did the major Arab–Israeli Wars take place; what year Israel was established; who was Nasser. Not a single boy could answer even one of the questions. Having demonstrated their ignorance of Middle Eastern affairs, I encouraged them to become more knowledgeable before they made judgements.

I have always dismissed as utter rubbish the notion, promoted in obscure Jewish quarters, that non-Jews are natural anti-Semites. But this event shook me to the core. I was not the only one shocked; the teacher was profoundly apologetic, and told me that most of the time religions other than the Church of England received a warm welcome in the school.

Changing the Mind Set

The drive back to Oxford from Aylesbury takes about forty minutes and I spent that time thinking about the dangers of not promoting a Jewish message more frequently in rural areas such as the place I had just visited. These were good kids, but they had been subjected to an incessant media-bashing of Israel without anyone to defend her. I drew two conclusions. The first was that Jewish insularity did no one any good and Jews the world over must be encouraged to become ambassadors for their people. Secondly, Israel herself was losing an important propaganda war in which the minds of the world's young generation were being set against her. Something had to be done.

While most people celebrate Israel's remarkable defence structure and military achievements, few would say the same of her diplomacy. There have been only a handful of articulate Israeli spokesmen in English, and today I know of only one, Benjamin Netanyahu, who twice made beautiful and eloquent defences of Israel when he spoke for us at the Oxford Union.

I arrived home from my trip to Aylesbury disillusioned by the immense task that loomed before us. There was so much to be done in this genera-tion after the Holocaust, and who was prepared to do it? When I returned home for lunch, my wife greeted me with an immense smile and these words, 'You're not going to believe how beautiful this is!' She picked up a handsomely bound red book entitled *The Wolf Shall Lie With the Lamb*. It was the first copy of my book to be sent from the United States by the publisher, and a *mazel tov* card had arrived with it. I had waited two years since the completion of the manuscript to see it in its published form and I was understandably ecstatic. But I focused more on the joy of my wife than my own and something puzzled me: she was just as elated and excited as me, and yet it was I who had written the book! It was then that the full force of what I described above finally materialized in my mind. It was not my book, or a book that my wife could celebrate because it had been written by her husband. It was *our* book. She was just as happy as I was because we are married and my joy was equally her joy. When she showed people the book she was showing something that was hers.

And this is an important point to make. Because most people embrace the ideology that a husband and wife are engaged in some kind of intense partnership and are not really one, they believe that only the things in which both are equally involved, like children, should be shared equally between husband and wife. We commonly reject the notion that every area of marriage, even where one partner is more involved than the other, should be equally shared. So people think that if the husband has a career, it is his career. Although he may accept that the money generated by his being a lawyer, for example, belongs to both equally, the means for making the money is his.

What he denies by expressing this kind of attitude is, first, that he and his wife were united at marriage to become one in all things. Secondly, he fails to recognize that without his wife he would not be a lawyer and her presence is an integral part of his success. She is just as necessary in this endeavour as she is in having a child.

Part-time Marriage

The horror stories of not viewing it in this way are well known. Because a husband or wife can believe their career belongs to themselves and not to each other, then often he can justify behaving like a bachelor while away from home. When he goes to a law conference, he may justify a casual fling to himself because he almost forgets he is married while he is away. However, if he felt his wife's presence within his career, he would find it much easier to resist any temptation while he was away.

Chapter Forty

CAN ONE LIE TO PROMOTE PEACE?

═══

Unlike Cambridge, Oxford University's reputation is currently said to rest largely on its standing in the field of the humanities. There is intellectual tension between the devotees of *logos*, or science, and those who believe there is more to the human condition than a collection of randomly accumulated chemicals that will one day be completely explained when the Grand Unification Theory, historically so elusive, is finally formulated. Of course, scientific reductionists are not just those studying or teaching science, and those with faith in a meaning beyond equations and theorems are not confined to the field of humanities.

However, there is a strong perception amongst many undergraduates that the realm of truth in its purest form does indeed belong to the philosophers and scientists, while those who study literature, art or music are in some sense only toying with an alternative world of aesthetic meaning and beauty which is essentially less reasonable than the 'real' world of facts.

In this respect, it has always remained curious to me that students of science in this university tend primarily to socialize with their own kind, and have interests which are peculiarly limited to the sciences and empirical fact. In terms of their interest in Judaism, it rests almost entirely within the legal realm of Talmud and Halakha, or Jewish rationalism like Maimonides' philosophical tract, *Guide of the Perplexed*, much applauded by and attractive to Oxford intellectuals. But they have little interest in or appreciation for the more esoteric, as opposed to exoteric, and mystical element of Judaism, such as Chasidic thought or Kabbalah. There is little appreciation for the need for mystery or wonder in human life, and especially in man's relationship with the Almighty.

On the other hand, the secular era of the Romantics certainly infused a great deal of respect into European culture for the ideals of sublime love and beauty, which has not entirely worn off, even in the aftermath of the sexual revolution. And while pre-marital sex is widely available and practised at Oxford, as in almost all college campuses, there remains a feeling among the students that something essential is missing. The obviousness of it all never quite strikes them. Yet the very idea of the kind of arranged marriage that was once mandatory here, and is still a viable option in many cultures, is anathema to modern western thinking. Similarly, scientific reductionism, which was and still is an Oxford tradition, as well as utilitarianism, are often frowned upon because it is said they reduce the richness and diversity of life to the lowest common denominator so that it eventually means nothing, even though we may understand it completely. The individual with faith in God or beauty often feels entitled to express condescension for those who work to understand life by reducing phenomena to their simplest elements because the aesthete or religious person has a grasp of the 'real' meaning of life that is necessarily indefinable.

The Quest for Truth

Clearly, the debate as to which human values are considered the greatest is still not resolved. A complicating factor is the common perception of where theology and religion stand in this debate. For centuries, religion and the quest for the knowledge of God was unquestioningly considered to be the ultimate aim, uncompromisingly and ultimately true. Indeed Maimonides listed disinterested worship of God as the ultimate aim of Jewish messianic fervour.

The ramifications of this acceptance in western Europe was that if the Christian Church said a thing was so, scientists were to accept it as axiomatic. Otherwise they were liable to religious and secular sanctions. Hence there was a profound crisis when the Church's teaching that the earth was flat was finally proved to be wrong. (The Talmud had said this explicitly fourteen hundred years previously.) This was perhaps the beginning of the whole cultural swing from believing the truth of religion before any other truth was considered, to the present when scientific truth tends to control our reaction to all other interpretations of life.

The great world religions are traditionally placed in opposition to Romantic thinking: Romanticism is often perceived as atheistic, humanistic or deistic, as denying the presence of a benevolent and interested God, and therefore throwing responsibility for human welfare on to human effort alone.

The Romantic idea that love creates its own reality might easily be interpreted as fundamentally opposed to the belief in an eternally true God who wishes us to understand the world as it really and eternally is. It is not surprising that the great English Romantic poet, Percy Bysshe Shelley, a student at University College, was expelled from Oxford in 1811 for his part in the pamphlet *The Necessity of Atheism*: at that time the university was a religious as well as an educational institution and it could not be seen to be associated with such ideas. However, since that time Oxford has proudly re-embraced the memory of its son and the beautiful Shelley Memorial stands in University College as a monument to the ideals of the Romantic movement. In many ways his memory was ensured rehabilitation largely because of the dearth of romance and the pre-eminence of unromantic sex in modern western society.

However, religion is also seen as standing in opposition to the world of scientific truth, not because it is supposed to reject truth, but because it dares to posit an alternative truth of its own. This is remarkably similar to the position taken by the Romantics: a different kind of reality to that of empirical science was suggested by concentrating on the sublime rather than the everyday modes of human existence.

Here I will argue that religion and its attendant science, theology, are in a unique position to interpret the battle between different perceptions of reality. The Jewish religion has not thrown its lot in with objective or sublime truth, but rather prefers to take the best of both to create a truth that is greater than either alone. Literal truth as promoted by the sciences is at times remarkably restricting and unable to deal with practical problems, and the truth created by a world of love and beauty can be unwieldy and impractical in its own way. A real understanding of the values to which Judaism wishes humanity to aspire serves to cut straight to the core of eternal and real truth, and present them to the world in intellectually and emotionally satisfying ways.

Is Love Greater Than Truth?

Judaism has always emphasized the need to serve God with joy. Ironically, though, the Torah itself does not end on such a positive note: it concludes with an account of the death of Moses, the great law-giver, and how the Jewish people mourned his passing. 'So Moses died there, the servant of the Lord, and He buried him in the valley, in the land of Moab, over against Bethpeor; and no man knows the whereabouts of his sepulchre unto this day' (Deuteronomy 34:5).

The Talmud maintains that God Himself buried Moses, and this gives us the reason why the place of his burial is unknown. Yet this extraordinary distinction accorded to Moses by the Almighty on his passing does not seem to have been given by the Jewish people themselves. On the contrary, although they mourned and missed their fallen leader who had done so much for them, we know they did not miss him as deeply as they did his elder brother, Aaron, who had died slightly earlier.

The Torah relates, 'And the sons of Israel wept for Moses in the plains of Moab thirty days; so were ended the days of weeping (in the) mourning of Moses' (Deuteronomy 23:15). Commenting on this verse, Rashi observes that the Torah expressly states that the 'sons' of Israel wept, but not that everyone wept. On the other hand, 'for Aaron, since he pursued peace and made peace between man and his neighbour and between wife and husband, it is stated, *all* the house of Israel', that is male and female, mourned (Numbers 20:29).

The system of government for the Jews as they were led through the wilderness was a triarchy, and their leaders were the triumvirate of Moses, Aaron and Miriam. Moses was the 'king' or leader, the one who ruled with supreme authority: his authority emanated from God and not from democratic consent, and could not be questioned by the people, as Korach and his followers harshly discovered. Miriam, Moses' sister, appropriately, led the women: the women were given the opportunity to relate to another woman, someone who was more in tune with the particular dilemmas and hardships they encountered in the desert. Finally, Aaron filled a unique gap: his was the face of humanity in the leadership of the Jews. We know that he personified goodness, warmth and human understanding. As a part of their leadership, the Jews needed someone who could empathize with both their physical and spiritual hardships.

At that time, the children of Israel were confronting difficulties on all sides: they travelled in a harsh physical terrain, a desert in which nothing grew and no water was to be found. They were also encountering for the first time a new moral and ethical code, as well as a whole spiritual way of life radically different to what they were accustomed to in Egypt. Of course, all this required a great capacity for adaptation: to adjust, they needed not only Moses' authority to reveal their new role to them, but also the compassion and love of Aaron to ease them into that new way of living.

Two Versions of Truth

Moses lived by the letter of the law, enforcing it to its fullest extent. He certainly did not lack warmth or compassion: the Bible states that on more than one occasion he saved the lives of all of the children of Israel from God's justifiable wrath. Yet Moses lived by truth, and truth alone: to him there was no greater human endeavour than the pursuit of truth, and in this he was not willing to make compromises. Moses would never allow his warmth and compassion to muddle his thinking. For him, the law was the law. Aaron, on the other hand, believed that peace and brotherhood always preceded, indeed superseded, truth, and such was his legacy to us. In his eyes there was nothing loftier in existence than virtuous love and the pursuit of peace among men, and he lived by this creed.

For this reason, we have the surprising circumstance that Aaron enjoyed greater popularity than Moses within the camp of Israel. Moses, after his death, was missed, but he was not missed as an individual so much as an institution: the people had appreciated the strong leadership he provided, and all that he had wrought on their behalf, but their lives had not necessarily been touched deeply by him as a person. When the nation of Israel mourned the passing of Aaron they were mourning someone who had entered their lives. They were not mourning the office of the High Priest, but the man, Aaron.

The conflict in ideology waged between Moses and his elder brother Aaron has, throughout the ages, continued to hold both philosophers and lay community in its grip. After all, which is the greater virtue, truth or love? Which is most important: the law, or something beyond the law, to which the law brings us?

Although even to ask this question might anger those who have witnessed abuses of the law and the Halakha by people who subordinate them to an alternative and more 'modern' moral and societal code, the question still must be asked. It must be asked because today's generation is no longer satisfied with the 'what?' and the 'how?' of Jewish life, but desperately seeks to know the ultimate 'why?' They not only ask 'Where is Jewish life leading me?' and 'What can I aspire to if I lead a Jewish life?', but 'Is there an ultimate purpose, a destination, which we will reach if we observe God's commandments?'

The Beauty of Peace and Love

Aaron believed that peace and brotherhood superseded bare truth. The Talmud relates that he would even bend the truth in order to bring people back together again. On one occasion, Aaron saw a husband and wife quarrelling, each one refusing reconciliation. Aaron approached the estranged husband and inquired about his wife. Of course, the man launched into a tirade of bitter complaints about his wife's behaviour. He would insult and abuse her, saying he never wanted to see her again. Later, Aaron approached the wife, and she too abused her husband incessantly. Breaking into her monologue, Aaron stated that he had just spoken to her husband, how with tears in his eyes the man had told Aaron that he longed for his wife to return. He said her husband had spoken of her beauty and charm, and had deeply regretted any fights or arguments they may have had. Similarly, he returned to the husband and told him of his wife's praise of him and how she longed for a reconciliation in their marriage.

We may well ask what becomes of the truth in such an exchange. A saintly individual had clearly and deliberately lied. Notwithstanding one's motives, does the Torah condone behaviour that has such a blatant disregard for truth? Perhaps the couple's relationship would be jeopardized by accepting Aaron's distortion of the truth, and their chance of being reunited permanently blighted because of his misinformation? Is there no danger in basing such an important enterprise on such wrong foundations?

427

To all the above, Aaron would respond by asking, is divorce true? If the couple divorce, could this be a truer state of affairs? The fact that two people who once loved each other now entertain irreconcilable differences, or can no longer live together, is the greatest lie of all! Two friends who once trusted each other with their most intimate secrets, but who now refuse to talk to each other, is the greatest falsehood! To reverse these situations must therefore be the greatest truth, a higher truth than merely sticking to the facts. There would be no purpose at all in Aaron's conversations with the husband and wife if he told them what they already knew or suspected: the purpose was to reconcile, not bear witness to quarrelling. Aaron sought to elevate the couple to a higher reality, the most sublime of which is loving kindness between all people, especially between husband and wife.

The World as a Showcase for Unity

Since God created the whole world, all the components in creation are a manifestation of His unity. The finest demonstration of this is when two human beings, notwithstanding how different they may be, even as different as male and female, can still live together in harmony. When people find the need to communicate with each other, live together, and care for one another, they demonstrate that in fact they are of one essence, emanating from the same source. However, when animosity, or even hatred, reigns between them, it then appears as if they truly are disparate and irreconcilable. In this case, they do not appear to share one Creator: for if they did, they would be able to get along despite their differences, just as the members of a family can live harmoniously.

That the many and various components of the world are all parts of a single creation is true. That all human beings can come together as one is true. That the diversity in creation reflects a diversity in God, heaven and earth, or a multiplicity of origins, is false. That people must feel contention instead of brotherhood is false.

So we can say, with Aaron, that peace is true. Not only is peace beautiful and true, it also reflects the ultimate truth. We can appeal to no higher value than peace in our search to capture this sublime theme of Divine unity. The familiar phrase, 'Truth is beauty', should prompt us to know there is nothing more beautiful or true than the harmony of peace and love.

Aaron understood this. His willingness to bend the facts when people fought was not a perversion of the ultimate truth. Rather, he chose to distort a version of reality that was masquerading as truth: the reality of a husband and wife fighting should *never have been* a reality. In most cases, a willingness to compromise on both sides will lead to a harmonious ending. Inability to compromise, or emphasis on individual desires over and above the needs of the marriage, is the ultimate untruth. For this reason, Aaron not only felt it proper, but mandatory, to tell 'white lies' to make peace between people. Hillel, the great Sage of Israel, proclaimed, 'Be of the disciples of Aaron, loving peace and pursuing peace, loving your fellow creatures and bringing them near to the Torah' (*Ethics of Our Fathers* 1:12). Aaron did not simply love peace in the abstract, he promoted peace in the here and now by doing everything in his power to bring people together.

And we must emulate him. Because students live together in such a close-knit environment, close friendships, because of their unusual intensity and its incessant exposure, this can often lead to tension. I have frequent experience of students coming to complain about a friend who was insensitive or said the wrong thing. The same can be true of parents. I tell them that friendship and kinship are too precious to forfeit over a single comment, and encourage them to apologize. 'Why should I apologize?' they ask. 'It wasn't me who said it.'

Learning Not Just to Love but Pursue Peace

But who did you think Hillel was speaking to when he encouraged the *pursuit* of peace. Life should not be about feeling wronged or slighted, and no moral superiority which can be garnered from being wronged can ever be the equal of harmony between people. Surely in our present century, which has been riddled with demonic hatred and stupid wars and conflicts, the single most important precept, and the only one capable of redeeming mankind from itself, is the imperative to pursue peace.

We must do whatever we can, in every single situation, to ensure that we quarrel with no one. Even if it means belittling ourselves at times and falsely admitting that we, and the other party, were to blame for the argument.

Shabbat Candles Before Chanuka

That peace is the ultimate objective of a Torah life is reflected in many areas of Jewish law. Maimonides writes, in *Laws of Chanuka*, what the law would be if a person has only enough money to light either the Chanuka lights or the Shabbat candles. He rules that the law would be that he or she should light the Shabbat candles rather than those for Chanuka because the Shabbat candles are designed to bring peace into the world, and peace constitutes the reason for creation. Before the invention of gas or electric light, the only method of illuminating a house on Shabbat was the Shabbat candles lit immediately before the start of the Shabbat evening. The candles' illumination ensured that no one would destroy the Shabbat atmosphere by tripping or falling over furniture or the like. Not even the annual public proclamation of Divine intervention (to save the Jews from the hands of their oppressors in the Chanuka battle) can supersede the weekly need for these lights of peace in the home.

An Era of Peace

In truth, though, there is really no need to find examples of the importance of peace from the codes of Jewish law: the Torah and the prophets have already established peace as the ultimate virtue to which the entire historical process is leading. The end of days, the messianic era as foretold by the prophets, will be an age when peace will reign throughout the world. Two and a half thousand years ago, Jeremiah, Isaiah and countless other prophets stood in public squares and heralded an era of eternal peace and brotherhood; an era of conciliation and kinship; an era lacking contention and jealousy. We still look forward to an age when all people will join together to serve God as one community.

To appreciate the staggering importance of this prediction, we must consider what the opposition to this idea would have been. It came in an age when men were judged almost entirely by their ability to do battle; an age when war was glorified and the greatest poets of the day devoted their literary creativity to praising the brave combatants; an age when a political leader was chosen not for wisdom and vision, but for a previous record of vanquishing the enemy. Despite this, the Jewish prophets foretold of a truly righteous redeemer, whose greatness would be his ability to make peace, one who would usher in an era when 'the wolf would dwell down with the lamb'.

Indeed, all of Judaism is designed to bring disparate entities closer together; husbands to wives, brothers to sisters, nations to other nations – and ultimately to bring humankind closer to their Creator. This is the goal of a messianic age. Aaron, who 'loved and pursued peace', was pulling us toward that destiny. We will follow him.

Chapter Forty-one

ARE WE BORED WITH SEX?

I typically spend eight hours a day counselling, studying and talking with students who drop by at my office in the L'Chaim Centre. The average student will pass by our office four or five times daily, making it easy to come up for a quick shmooze. Often the talk is fairly ordinary; how the students are faring in their work, tutorials and exams, or light political discussion. But whenever a student comes to see me specifically to receive my advice on a given matter, it invariably revolves around their current relationship. The reason they come to me is threefold. Firstly I am married with children and they wish to speak to someone who is experienced in a stable, long-term relationship. Secondly, I am a rabbi and as such they assume (often incorrectly) that I must have some wisdom to impart. Thirdly, I am their friend. Now, one may counter that surely they have many other friends with whom they may speak. This is true. But I am the friend who is not a student, and so not in need of extricating myself from the various snags of student life. One sinking ship cannot save another, and most students assume their colleagues are going through the same problems as they.

The Obsession with Relationships

From what I have witnessed over these last few years, the average student goes through no less than four to five relationships over a three-year period at Oxford. These relationships are of varying intensity, some lasting a week or two, and some lasting several months. Often they are serious indeed.

Most students today feel rather incomplete if they are not in a relationship, however tortured. It is not as important necessarily to be *in* a relationship, as much as it is at least to be *preoccupied* with being in one and with the concept as a whole. Thus most students, even if they are not in a relationship, can be said to be in a constant state of being 'between relationships'. Indeed, it is not unfair to use the word relationship as the most descriptive of all student life and activities.

To be sure, this preoccupation, even obsession, with relationships is a very time-consuming affair. The question may be asked why students, whose principal interest in coming to Oxford is of course to obtain a good degree, are willing to expend such vast quantities of time and effort all in the name of sharing their lives *temporarily* with others?

A Cure for Loneliness

The simple answer is that Oxford can be a very lonely place, more so, I believe, than many other university towns. There is such fierce competition to obtain a first-class degree, and such immense pressure to succeed, that many of the students begin to have an existential feeling of loneliness. They do not feel they are something unless they excel, which is what got them into Oxford in the first place. Thus their identities are largely defined by their work and after a prolonged period of time this falters. Immersing oneself in one's work no longer seems as satisfying and the students long desperately to love and be loved.

To be sure, nobody likes to be alone. But the pressures of modern life will often force a young student to make a difficult choice between immediate personal aspirations for love and warmth, and more long-term ambitions for great achievement, prestige, power and money. Students understand that success can often entail extreme loneliness and it is specifically the most successful people who often appear as the most ruthless. While they may be admired, they are rarely liked. On the other hand, we are all too familiar with the stereotype of the lovable man or woman who just won't stand up for themselves, and so is trampled on by all the more vicious people who surround them. Surely a compromise or middle ground must be found.

Well, the students find it in the form of someone with whom they can share their feelings, hopes and ambitions without considering that every sentence is a contest and an attempt at one-upmanship, which is what intellectual life at Oxford can sometimes become. Stated in other words, what a boyfriend or girlfriend can often provide is someone whom you trust implicitly and who is not part of the rat race to outdo you, at least, that is, until the relationship sours.

I often tell the students that the individuals most likely to succeed in life are those who embody characteristics often ascribed to either men or women, but rarely to both: those who are both keen to relate to others on a level of community, and are also keen to impart their valuable knowledge to friends and colleagues, but without any hint of condescension. One can always identify this type of student primarily by one unmistakable and rare character trait: they never cut into the words of their colleagues during conversation. Sometimes, the most difficult thing to accomplish at Oxford is just to get a word in edgewise. Those who want to learn will listen, and those who are prepared to learn from anyone and everyone are guaranteed success in all areas of life. In addition, they will never be confronted with having to choose between humane values and the values of the market place since they have already acquired the best of both.

Baseball Before Judaism

To be whole means to enhance oneself through every experience in life. Shimshon Stock, who is today a Lubavitch communal activist, was privileged with a private weekly Torah class with Rabbi Menachem Schneerson before the latter became the rebbe of Lubavitch. One week he did not appear for class. The rebbe inquired about his absence. He made various excuses. The rebbe pressed him for the real reason. Shimshon admitted he had gone to Ebbetts Field for the Brooklyn Dodgers baseball game.

The rebbe asked him what he had learned from the game.

Shimshon replied that he did not learn anything. He had gone purely for pleasure.

The rebbe told him that one must learn something from everything one sees and proceeded to tell him one may learn from baseball.

In a baseball game there are two groups of people, the participants and the spectators. If the game is going badly, and the home team is losing, then the spectators can leave early and go home. They need not stay to the bitter end. However, the participants have to stay and play. Their team can be ten runs behind with only one innings left. Nevertheless, since it is their game, they must continue. And there is always the possibility that through their efforts they will succeed.

This story demonstrates the classic adage of the Mishua that from every event there is something wholesome to be learned.

Long-Term Relationships are Rare

But amidst this yearning to be in a relationship, there can be no doubt that long-term relationships, such as those extending over an entire three years at Oxford, are very rare indeed. Of the thousands of students I have encountered in my time here, less than ten relationships I am aware of have lasted that long, and half of those have gone on to marriage.

Why is it that relationships among students today are so short-lived? There are many reasons. But the two I have found to be most common are: one of the people in the relationship begins to feel too claustrophobic, having to spend all their free time with their partner; and sexual boredom and indifference.

To elaborate on the first, there was a guy and a girl who dated for over five months, only to break up with acrimony. When I asked the girl what had

433

happened, she told me he was not giving her enough time and too often wished to do things on his own. But when I questioned him concerning the cause of the break-up, he was much more candid. 'Shmuley, I don't mean to be offensive to a rabbi. But right now one of the principal wishes in my youth is to bed as many women as possible. And this relationship began to feel like a straitjacket.'

Given that feelings of claustrophobia or being trapped have existed as reasons for break-ups from time immemorial, it is the latter reason, that of sexual boredom and the inability of intimacy to hold a young couple together, which is far more alarming.

The Case for the Demise of Sex

Recently, two students who had been dating for over half a year, and seemed to be quite serious about their relationship, broke it off abruptly. As I am quite friendly with them, they candidly replied to my question when I asked why it had puttered out, 'We quite literally *screwed* the life out of our relationship.'

All around the world, it seems, the jury is out and the verdict is in: people are getting bored with sex. From magazines to movies, flesh and erotica are out, while modest dressing and subtlety are back in fashion. It seems we have all suffered a dreaded sexual disease that is a more potent turn-off than any health considerations: we're being bored to death by sex. The *Sunday Times*, one of Britain's leading Sunday papers, reported on 11 April 1993 that *Penthouse* magazine, 'the men's magazine that was the first to bare all, is asking its models to put their clothes back on. Skin, it seems, is no longer "in".'

What has led to this sudden exercise in modesty on the part of so famous an exhibitor of flesh? Could it be the Christian 'decade of evangelism' heralded by the Archbishop of Canterbury, or Chief Rabbi Sack's call for a 'decade of renewal'? No. Nothing quite as profound as that. It is simply a commercial decision. The *Sunday Times* went on to say, 'The plunging sales of "girlie" magazines have led to a catharsis in Britain's publishing industry . . . *Penthouse* once boasted 500,000 readers; now it claims 120,000 a month . . . The number of naked women is being reduced in favour of serious features . . .'

Similarly, *Newsweek* magazine reports that France's longest established nudist colony is experiencing a rebellion amongst its new generation of sunbathers. They are wearing clothes at the beach. When the reporter asked a sixteen-year-old who was wearing a swimsuit why she was rejecting the nudist principle, she responded, 'Unless I put on clothes, the boys won't even look at me.'

Neither have films, the leading exhibitor of naked flesh, been immune from this indifference of the masses. Madonna, high-priestess of sex and erotica, has released her latest 'bare-all' film, *Body of Evidence*, which has the absurdly funny story line that she murders her boyfriend through sexual intercourse, in what one Oxford film critic correctly describes as a desperate attempt by the publicity-seeking star to leave 'no stone unshagged in the twilight of her career'.

Meanwhile, films like Disney's *Jungle Book*, a cartoon in which the only unclothed characters are the animals of the wild, has been re-released after three decades, and is packing the houses with viewers of all ages. Has sex suddenly become powerless, or is it merely a case of severe over[s]exposure? By gaining an insight into the essential nature of the male–female attraction, we can search for a remedy for this situation.

Donor and Developer

In the beginning God created the heaven and the earth (Genesis 1:1). Thus, in its very first verse the Bible reveals that, at the onset of creation, and before the advent of Adam and Eve or their animal counterparts, the Creator had already introduced into His creation the dual components of male and female, donor and developer. The earth would materialize the necessary life-giving substance provided by the heavens, receiving it and allowing it to undergo subsequent development. The heavens would shower water and nourishment onto the land, which the land would transform into lush greenery bursting with life.

Later, this trend of a two-part world, a duality of existence, continued with the creation of male and female life, beginning first with the plants and animals, and culminating in the creation of Man and Woman. Theologians of all denominations and creeds have been eternally perplexed by the mystery of the need to fragment the inhabitants of creation into male and female. It seems impossible for the monotheist to reconcile belief in the oneness and indivisible unity of God with God's pluralistic creation. The ways of God are meant to emulate His being: if He is One, then Man, who was created 'in His image', should be uniquely singular as well. And if the need to fragment humankind into male and female was for reproduction, then the Creator, in His infinite wisdom, could have caused the world's inhabitants to reproduce by asexual means.

An Arena for God's Unity

Man erroneously tends to view the world as a separate and independent entity, divorced from God's all-encompassing unity. God is not readily seen in this world and the mistake of dissociating Him from His creation is easily made. Notwithstanding this weakness in Man's perception, the purpose of the creation was to demonstrate, not to compromise, the unity of the Creator. To this extent, our mundane and physical world, whose very existence seems to negate that unity, was chosen as the showcase for this manifestation.

Real and False Unity

There exist many differing degrees within the concept broadly termed 'unity'. Two individuals may 'unite', yet all the while remain autonomous, and even somewhat antagonistic to each other. The peace treaty between Israel and Egypt and especially that between Israel and the PLO, for example, stand as classic testimonials to this phenomenon, as does the current crisis in the 'united' European Community now that their common enemy of the USSR has disappeared. This is obviously not real unity at all. Two nations may indeed forge a peace or trade treaty, but that may do nothing to unseat the underlying antipathy felt for one another. True unity can only exist when two entities become synthesized and orchestrated together as a single unit through a process of mutual fusion, to the extent that each becomes only half of a distinct whole.

For this reason, the Creator chose to create male and female. Had He created only a single sex in each species, no manifestation of unity could have been accomplished. For 'one' in turn to give rise to and equal 'one' is no great mathematical feat. On the other hand, for two separate beings to unite and, notwithstanding their own individuality, equal 'one' is an astounding achievement. For male and female to unite and give birth to a child is a demonstration par excellence of how two separate entities, while being fragmented and dissociated, may none the less combine to equal 'one'. Thus the equation at which we arrive and which has no equal in the empirical world is '$1 + 1 = 1$'. Here it is demonstrated how male and female are indeed only halves of a single whole and reunited when they join to create 'one flesh'.

Covenant Between the Parts

When God desired to forge a covenant with Abraham, He instructed him to bring a heifer, goat and ram, and to cut them in half as a sign of the covenant. The event came to be known as 'The Pact Between the Halves'. It seems curious that in forging a covenant expressing unity the Almighty required Abraham to halve the sacrificial animals. Why use division as a sign of unity? The explanation is that God desired that the animals signify a higher form of unity, namely that henceforward God and the descendants of Abraham would be two halves of one whole. It symbolized that just as the two halves of the animal were really one, so the people making the covenant were one with God. Just as one side of an animal cannot live without the other, so the two cannot continue without each other. The applicability of this analogy to the Creator and His world is self-apparent. When the elements of God's world, all of which may be subdivided into male and female, or donor and developer, unite and become one, the false illusion of the plurality and disharmony of God and His world is torn asunder. God and His world are one and that oneness is best demonstrated when man embraces his fellow human beings and creates another human being in his own image through that unity. In this way, every individual acknowledges how all of humankind emanate from a single source. The underlying unity of everything in the creation is observed and God and His world are reconciled. Once this is established, it is just a short step until humanity comes calling upon their Creator acknowledging their dependency and roots.

In this respect, it may be appreciated that the association between husband and wife is unique and substantially greater and more intense than all other forms of unification found in the empirical world. However, the sublimity and uniqueness of the union of marriage is not only demonstrable from a theosophical perspective. The union between husband and wife is of course unique in the very chemical structure of the relationship.

Fire and Water

Chasidic thought maintains that in the emotional attractions found among humanity we observe two kinds of powerful love. One love is analogous to water and the other to fire. The love which uses water as its metaphor is that which exists, for example, between brother and sister: as they are relatives by birth, they feel comfortable with each other and experience an innate closeness from early infancy. Their love is therefore strong, steady, predictable and calm. It does not thrive on interruptions, and an extended period divorced of one another's company will not serve to enhance the relationship, but to hinder it. Rather, their love flourishes on a consistent interaction, for this defines the very nature of the love from its inception.

Conversely, husband and wife enjoy a *fiery* love. It is fiery because of the extreme distance between them before they were married, when they were complete strangers. In some ways, this distance continues throughout their lives together due to the disparities between male and female. There is no commonality between them provided by the same family background as there is for a brother and a sister, and so they cannot enjoy a casual and calm love. Rather, their attraction to one another must serve as the agent through which they transcend their differences and unite to become one. The love must be aggressive enough continually to overleap divisive bounds. As the flames of a candle stretch up despite their being bound to the wick, likewise, husband and wife, irrespective of the fact that each is constrained by his or her fully formed character, must stretch out over the vast distance to fuse together. So in the relationship between husband and wife there is a constant flux: separation and distance are followed by affinity and closeness.

It may therefore be said that husband and wife live in a constant state of separation and reunification. If a brother and sister were to experience this kind of fiery love, it would consume them. It is not the appropriate emotional interaction as it does not suit or support their relationship. Similarly, the reverse is true: if husband and wife were to experience a calm, casual love, their relationship would suffer. If husband and wife become, to use the contemporary adage, 'the best of friends' but nothing more, then the death knell for their marriage has already been sounded. There would not be a force significant enough either to contain the originally separate individuals or to nurture the unity. Marriages thrive on their single most important ingredient: passion.

Unity Which Thrives on Separation

By recognizing the eclectic nature and necessities of the husband–wife relationship, one may begin to appreciate the practical importance of the laws of family purity and going to *mikvah*, the Jewish ritual bath of immersion. Among other things, these stipulate a period of about two weeks each month, during and following the wife's menstruation, in which husband and wife may not experience physical union. Much has been said and written regarding the beneficial outcome of such abstention. It has been argued that the abstention involved in family purity produces discipline in the marriage, keeps it fresh and vibrant, provides for a mini 'wedding night' every two weeks upon reunification, and allows a couple to communicate on something other than on a purely physical plane. All of these outcomes are indeed beneficial, and yet when proposed as a 'reason' for the observation of the laws they remain somewhat superficial.

Far from being an artificial imposition, married life as regulated by the *mikvah* is a natural reflection of the type of love which exists between husband and wife. The love is one which constantly explodes like a glowing fireball, subsequently receding and subsiding only to burst forth once again with added zest and enthusiasm. To nurture this love, the lifestyle of husband and wife must in turn correspond to that emotion which they are attempting to cultivate and enhance. Their physical behaviour must reflect that emotional state in order to support it, so that even when physically separate husband and wife are reunited.

The Fire in Men and Women

This fiery dimension of the love which exists only between husband and wife is alluded to in the Hebrew terms for 'man' and 'woman', 'Ish' and

'Isha'. When written in Hebrew, 'Ish' is spelled 'aleph', 'yud', 'shin': 'isha' is spelled 'aleph', 'shin', 'hay'. The common letters are 'aleph' and 'shin', which together comprise the word 'aish' or 'fire'. When we combine the two letters that are unique to each one, 'yud' from 'Ish' and 'hay' from 'Isha', we form one of God's names. In this way a remarkable insight can be achieved. The love between husband and wife is meant to be of a fiery, passionate nature. On its own, however, fire is totally unpredictable. At times, it is positive and useful, but if it is left unenclosed for long it goes out of control and can suddenly become destructive and dangerous. It is, therefore, imperative for us to realize and respect the sanctity of this fiery relationship. By heeding the practices of *Taharat Hamishpacha* we make God an active partner and both 'Ish' (man) and 'Isha' (woman) realize their full potential to regenerate by sexual reproduction, forge a bond and unite, even if they are overtly hostile toward one another. Their sexual life together becomes deep and meaningful, all the while retaining its passionate nature.

The Sexual Society

The same is true on a collective level. As a candle that burns too brightly consumes its wick and sputters out, a society which has no respect for modesty, and is sexually over-explicit, consumes the sexual passion of its members. The result is the utter demise of our sexual interests, which spells disaster for all intimate relationships. There is simply no physical relationship which can thrive without passion. Therefore, the society which we help to nurture must, of necessity, encourage modesty in dress, speech and action. By expressing our sexuality in conformity with Judaism, which above all maintains that human sexuality be manifest only in an intimate setting, and only with an individual who has demonstrated their love for us through solid commitment, we ensure that the candle which represents our sexual selves always burns brightest, and is not exhausted by a heat that is too intense, or dulled by the presence of so many other candles that its light becomes ineffective and meaningless.

Sanctity Means Moderation

It is with this insight that we can understand the definition which Judaism has traditionally given holiness. Surprisingly, it is 'moderation'. The way in which humankind achieves holiness is not only through abstaining from those things which are prohibited, but especially through 'sanctifying ourselves through that which is permitted to us', meaning, taking everything in healthy measured quantities, so that they work best for us when we most need them. Sexual promiscuity is not wrong because it contravenes puritanism or prudishness. Judaism is not prudish. It is wrong because sex with too many partners dulls our ability to remain passionate and committed to our partner.

The medieval rabbinic commentator, Akeidas Yitzchak, explains at length the concept of holiness, seeing it as an 'intermediate step' in Judaism. There are certain things for which we have no concept of a middle way, such as day and night. In regard to cold and hot, though, there is an intermediate step, that of lukewarm. The same is true of black and white. Holiness, too, is an intermediate stage, between what is permitted and what is forbidden, being neither one nor the other, but rather 'sanctifying yourself with that which is permitted to you.' It is all a matter of degree.

Similarly, Hakesav Vehakabalah explains that the concept of *kedushah*, holiness, means being holy even when engaged in physical activities. This means not merely seeking pleasure in our actions, but rather involving our intellect and emotions and dedicating ourselves to our Creator and fellow creatures. With respect to sexual relationships this would mean accompanying sex with real love and romance rather than just base instinct and actions motivated by hormones. In this way, the individual subliminates and consecrates his actions so that they are not merely the orgiastic pursuit of materialism. The physical thus becomes a vessel for the Divine.

With respect to intimate relationships, this kind of devotion makes the difference between 'having sex' with someone, and 'making love', in a committed, holy partnership like marriage. The difference between them is quite subtle, but then subtlety and modesty, as opposed to coarseness and impropriety, is what holiness is all about.

Chapter Forty-two

TWO APPROACHES TO CONTEMPORARY
JUDAISM AND A NEW APPROACH
TO INTERMARRIAGE

Unlike any other university, Oxford has had a pervasive impact on society and culture. That the name Oxford is synonymous with a definitive standard of academic excellence and lends unequalled credence to such things as 'the Oxford English Dictionary' is to be expected. But what is remarkable is that London's busiest shopping thoroughfare, and the highest-priced retail real estate in the entire world, for example, is Oxford Street. Similarly, one can buy Oxford shoes, a shirt with an Oxford collar, and there are literally thousands of businesses throughout the world that incorporate the name Oxford somewhere in their titles. Whenever I travel abroad I am astounded how many cities have an Oxford something or other. The very name seems to invoke reverence, and however one looks at this, history has it that Oxford remained immune to Hitler's bombing of Britain because of his great love for the city. After the intended invasion of Britain, he even planned to establish it as the new capital of a Nazi-dominated Europe. The American students, many of whom find Oxford cold and unwelcoming, cite this as proof of the evil of the city, while those who grow with Oxford, and there are many, cite it as irrevocable proof of Oxford's adorability. Even a monster could appreciate it.

The Oxford of Israel

Nor is the Jewish State above being taken with Oxford. Israel's first Prime Minister, David ben Gurion, sought to create an élite academic centre in a small agricultural settlement in the Negev desert by the name of Sdei Boker, which he said he hoped would become 'the Oxford of Israel'.

Whether or not he succeeded can be debated. Sdei Boker does have a small university which is said to carry out important research, although its fame never seems quite to have equalled that of its original model. The day may come one day when there will be a Sdei Boker shoe and a Sdei Boker necktie, or perhaps even the Sdei Boker Hebrew Dictionary. Only then can Sdei Boker be said to have arrived.

Between the ages of sixteen and nineteen, I was a rabbinical student in Jerusalem and, on weekends, would often visit my aunt and uncle who live in Sdei Boker. My uncle is an American scientist who had been living in the settlement for over twenty years, and through him I became well acquainted with Sdei Boker. In this respect I can be said to have had my first exposure to Oxford, a foreshadowing of things to come, through the Israeli Oxford.

A Touching Reunion

The residents, many of whom were immigrants to Israel, specifically from the United States and Britain, often spoke of the real Oxford, comparing and contrasting their achievements and impressive progress with their glorious counterpart. They were a motley collection of secular scientists and professed atheists. Yet every Shabbat ten of them would get together to make a *minyan* and read the Torah and every time I came, although I was the 'religious enemy', they made me feel at home. I once asked my uncle why it was that people who could be so hostile to religion still came to religious services. My uncle told me it came down to this: if they had not come, there simply wouldn't be a single Jewish service in the entire city. And this was Israel. Their conscience would not allow them to be the only city in Israel where the Jewish Sabbath had no foothold whatsoever.

And it was here, amidst these religious antagonists, who prided themselves on being Jews in the cast of Ben Gurion who were not defined in ancient religious terms, that I had one of the most significant and heartfelt religious experiences of my life.

We were reading in Genesis of the beginning of Joseph's odyssey, his journey from being the youngster in a family of twelve, to viceroy and ruler in Egypt. The Torah speaks graphically of how Jacob favoured his second youngest son, Joseph, over his older children. As the biblical narrative unfolds, it is revealed that Jacob's favouritism resulted in the older brothers envying Joseph. By the end of the first phase of Joseph's incredible adventure, this destructive sibling rivalry had led Joseph's brothers to sell him as a servant to Egypt.

But later, when they come to buy food in Egypt in a terrible famine, Joseph at first subjects them to agonizing remorse for having sold him. They cannot recognize him and he becomes to them a mean Egyptian overlord. But then the moment comes when Joseph forgives them and reveals himself to his brothers. When we reached this point of the reunion, the reader of the Torah, whose Bar Mitzvah Sidra it was years earlier, broke into uncontrollable tears as he read of the reunion. He could not continue reading. We even had to move him away from the scroll for fear that his tears might cause the letters of the Torah to run. His reaction deeply affected all those present. Ever since, whenever Parshas Vayigash in which the story is contained, is read, I feel myself getting goose bumps. It is a powerful tale, its effect undiminished even after over three millennia.

Are Some Things Unforgivable?

Much has been made of the subsequent reunion between Joseph and his brothers. For many it is the most moving and heart-warming event of the Torah. Joseph himself is described as so overcome by emotion that 'he could no longer contain himself.' He then cried with such a mighty thunder that its echo was heard in the Palace of Pharaoh as well as throughout Egypt.

The tear-jerking beauty of the story centres on the forgiveness Joseph chose to extend to his brothers. The reader or listener to the tale cannot help wondering why Joseph was so magnanimous. After all, these were the same men who just two decades earlier tried to murder him, lied to his father about his death, and sold him to a life of servitude and bondage.

The puzzle is not easily solved by assuming that because they were his brothers he could not help feeling compassion and forgiveness for them. When Joseph's saintly father Jacob had earlier faced a very similar predicament with his twin brother, Esau, he gave a clear precedent for remaining hostile to a vindictive sibling. Esau had pledged to murder his younger brother for stealing the blessing of the firstborn, and this intent to harm was something which Jacob never forgave and never forgot. Jacob, after not seeing his brother for over twenty years (similar to the period that Joseph and his brothers were separated), did not in any way look forward to the necessary reunion as he passed through Esau's land on the journey back to Isaac's home. On the contrary, Jacob took ample precautions to protect himself and his family, even preparing to wage war on Esau, in case the latter retained his intention to carry out his earlier pledge to destroy him.

The reader may at this point be misled into assuming that the two incidents must be dissimilar, and that Joseph forgave his brothers because they had repented their sin, indicated by their willingness to lay down their lives in protection of Benjamin, whereas Esau maintained his loathing of Jacob. However, the narratives of the Torah seem to vindicate Esau of his earlier treatment of his brother to a much greater extent than Joseph's brothers are allowed excuses. The Torah relates at length how Esau embraced his twin brother, cried on his shoulder and even offered to escort his sibling and his family with great pomp and ceremony to Mount Seir. It is Jacob who declines, offering an excuse that his party, incorporating young children and many cattle, could not keep up with Esau's pace. There does not seem to be any air of forgiveness or trust about Jacob, nor does he exhibit a willingness to be reconciled with his brother. The man who vowed to murder him and his family, brother or not, is not to be trusted. Although Esau has never yet acted on his pledge, Jacob eschews his brother. He is *persona non grata* among the nation of Israel.

Joseph's brothers, however, not only pledged harm to their younger sibling, but actually carried it out. They would easily have killed him had it not been for Reuben's, the eldest brother's, interference. In the event, they flung Joseph into a pit filled with scorpions and serpents, and eventually traded him to Ishmaelites who sold him into slavery in Egypt. This is not the kind of action which automatically warrants forgiveness, however sincere the repentance. Why, then, was Joseph so much more forgiving than his father, far exceeding the call of duty?

The answer is that Jacob and Joseph represent two opposite extremes in Jewish affirmation and identity. In contemporary times they represent the difference, broadly speaking, between Jews prior to and after the Second World War.

Isolationism vs Universalism

There are those who have always maintained that Jews and Judaism can only exist in a spirit of isolation. Jews must settle in self-imposed ghettos that insulate them from the adverse effects of secular culture and contamination. Jewish children and adolescents must grow and prosper in a uniquely Jewish environment where they are protected from any transient winds of western acculturation.

Jacob was of this philosophy, living much of his life as a spiritual hermit. From the beginning of his adult life he isolated his family from the perverse and degenerate ways of the Canaanites and Philistines. Jacob found comfort and solace in the words of the Torah. There was nothing so exciting, stimulating, or urgent outside the haven of Torah that it could take precedence over Jacob's glorious world of intellectual and spiritual escape. He found protection from the world of barbarity – womanizing, hunting and material obsession – that his twin brother Esau inhabited. Jacob shut out the world and was thus ensured profound spiritual and character development. The Torah describes him as 'a complete man whose [main preoccupation was] study in tents'.

This approach to life set a whole later trend. When he was confronted with Laban's trickery, Jacob reacted to the treachery and double-crossing of his father-in-law by reaching into himself and his family for safety. He learned to live apart from the wicked Laban and his clan. Most importantly, he guaranteed the goodness and Jewishness of his children by refusing to expose them to the moral turpitude of the world. Again, after fleeing his father-in-law to return to the Godly aura of his father Isaac, Jacob chose to insulate himself from the evil influences of Shechem and their environs.

A Self-imposed Ghetto

When Jacob finally moved down to Egypt, he and his sons did not live among Egyptian society. Instead, they moved to Goshen. The Torah commentators go so far as to refer to Goshen as the first Jewish ghetto, since it was specifically chosen to shield Jacob and his retinue from perverse Egyptian influence.

It is fair to say that Jewish history has been dominated by this philosophy and spiritual outlook. Far more frequently than wicked anti-Semites forcing the Jews to live in ghettos, the Jews have chosen them of their own accord. The ghetto protected them from the negative influences of their Gentile counterparts. Jews found spiritual and physical security in numbers. Their co-religionists who were of similar mind and conviction were the only ones to be trusted with exposure to their children.

While this was true of Jewish communities of all denominations, it was especially true of the Orthodox. An attempt was made to surround oneself with co-religionists. Thus one's neighbours, business partners, seamstresses and milkmen were not only Jews, but Jews of similar commitment and observance.

In the aftermath of the Second World War, the world of the ghetto was lost. The Nazis first enforced and confirmed, but later tore down for ever, the ghetto walls through their destruction of European Jewry. The war was the most severe and catastrophic upheaval to afflict the Jewish people in their long and tormented history. The Jews could never return to their old ways since a thousand-year-old domicile of Jewry was burnt to the ground. They were now forced to confront the world, for better or worse. Due to economic and social concerns, the Jews had to find their sustenance on the other side of the ghetto wall. They came to places in the west where a life of isolation was not only inconvenient, but impossible. In the mid-twentieth century Jews entered and excelled at universities and professions. In those short years a new breed of Jew emerged: a Jew like Joseph.

One Flew Over the Ghetto Nest

Joseph was the antithesis of his father. Although he was his father's son, his circumstances forced him, a Jew, to fully engage with the world and prosper. Torn away from a Jewish domicile and environment while still in his formative years, Joseph's Judaism was put to the greatest test. His Judaism had to face the challenge of secularism in a philosophical age, questionable business practices and Egyptian permissiveness and promiscuity.

Joseph was the first to reverse the tide of Jewish identity. The first Jew whose convictions were tested through fire. Abraham, like his grandson

Jacob, but perhaps not to the same degree, was also an isolationist. The Torah narratives which depict the life of Abraham tell of a man who lived alone, flanked by his faithful wife and servants, and the 'many souls', or converts, 'which they had made in Charan'. Abraham set a precedent by taking special precautions to ensure the spiritual life of his fledgling community and family. He lived and prospered alone. While he left a noticeable impact on those around him, converting many and establishing the tenets of monotheism, this was all done with momentary intrusions into secular life made with the intention of leaving an indelible mark of Godliness on the world. Abraham and his retinue would make forays into cities and civilizations, not to become permanent members of their communities, but to influence them towards abandoning pagan idolatry and embracing the one true God. This was as far as he would go, though: he did not live among the people whom he was seeking to influence as he could not risk all that he was attempting to establish. There is, therefore, a stark contrast between Abraham and his nephew Lot, who chose to live amidst the decadence of Sodom and Gomorrah while Abraham pitched his tents far away. Lot however was not entirely immune to their influences and practices.

The pattern continued with Abraham's son Isaac, and again with Isaac's son Jacob, as mentioned above. It was only broken by the profound success of Joseph's life in the world. Joseph emerged in Egypt not only as viceroy to the king, but as a spiritual master. He triumphed in the face of tortuous adversity. When Potiphar's wife flung herself at his knees demanding that he sin with her, he fled. He preserved his spiritual character and set the standard for Jews of all subsequent generations to follow.

The First Tzadik

For this reason Joseph is the first and only one in the Bible to be awarded the accolade *Hatzadik*, the righteous. The fathers of the Jewish nation, Abraham, Isaac and Jacob, could justly be called 'saintly', and indeed they were. They led exemplary lives. However, it would be misguided to refer to them as righteous, for their upright characters had neither been tested nor found to flourish and prosper in an unrighteous environment such as Egypt and in the face of adversity. To be sure, Abraham suffered terribly for his denial of idolatry and Nimrod's deity. But thereafter he largely retreated into the confines of his own faith – community. He was a man who stood alone.

Joseph, then, is the paradigm of the contemporary Godly Jew. The Jew who finds himself immersed in secular society and western culture, but struggles to remain loyal to his God and his people. The Jew who attends university, pursues a professional career, but never compromises on his tradition and values. This is the Joseph-Jew and it is to this pinnacle that we must all strive.

What Makes Joseph Tick?

If Joseph is the pattern we should be following, then it is pertinent to investigate the secret of his strength, the factors that gave him the fortitude and tenacity to withstand the acculturation of Egypt and emerge a whole Jew.

The Talmud tells of two pivotal factors. When Joseph was tempted to the bed of his master's wife, the Talmud declares, 'He suddenly saw the image of his father Jacob' and abstained from sin. In other words, he remembered his link to the Jewish tradition, the firm Jewish education he had received. His father had held him on his lap to impart the words of the Torah, had been patient with him, had been proud to witness his young son repeat the words of the *modeh ani*, the first words on the lips of a Jew as he awakes, and the *Shemah*, the most sublime formulation of Jewish faith and belief. Joseph felt himself incapable of repudiating that tradition: it would mean completely rejecting the love, sweat and tears that had been invested in him. Joseph's lesson to us is that there can be no substitute for this integral part of a child's spiritual development.

To Impart Rather Than Absorb

The other secret of Joseph's triumph was his desire to leave an impact on, rather than just receive impressions from, his surroundings. There is the old story of the farm boy who moves to the big city, says, 'Wow! What have I been missing?' and begins to pursue all the treasures and pleasures of 'civilization'. If Joseph had resembled this boy, there can be no doubt that he would have vanished into oblivion. Rather, amidst all the wealth and splendours of Egypt, Joseph arrived with a firm conviction that his Hebrew tradition could impart spirituality and morality to a country that desperately needed it. Regardless of Egypt's cultural, architectural and scientific achievements, he understood that the country desperately required a *soul*, and he was there to provide it. As a believer in Divine providence, Joseph accepted that God had sent him to Egypt for a Godly purpose.

I too have employed this tactic successfully here in Oxford, both on a personal and collective level. When Orthodox Jewish students arrive in Oxford and inevitably their Judaism begins to slip, they defend themselves by telling me that it is impossible to remain on the same spiritual plane in Oxford as in New York, Jerusalem and London. In every case where I have discussed this with students, invariably the word they use to describe their declining observance is the same: inevitable. What then, I ask them, sustains my wife and me, as well as countless Chabad emissaries throughout the world who find themselves in places where there is no communal support for their Jewishness? The answer, I tell them, is that we have come to impact rather than be impacted upon. When a person is so preoccupied with being an exponent, he has no time to be influenced by his environment. Stated in other words and by way of metaphor, if a sponge is expelling its water, then it cannot simultaneously absorb outside water as well. It cannot enact two directions at once. Thus what I tell the students is that to survive in Oxford and maintain one's spiritual integrity, one must teach other students Judaism and serve as a living example of integrity and goodness. Whenever I convinced a student to spend at least three or four hours a week teaching, I have seen that that student's dedication to Judaism has not wavered.

It would be so satisfying to see more 'Josephs' in Oxford today. It may sound surprising, but the goal of the Oxford fresher who also happens to be a Jew is not solely to learn, but also to teach. It is good to be impressed with what the city has to offer. It is desirable that young minds see the need to acquire the best possible secular education, which is essentially why a student comes to Oxford in the first instance. However, it is also imperative that the student understand that there is a wealth of benefit which a Jewish education can offer to Oxford as well. Learning is most satisfying when it is a two-way process, so not only does Oxford leave its mark on the student but the student leaves a mark on Oxford. If a student concentrates as much on giving as taking, especially in those areas where his contribution is vital and necessary, then there can be no danger of losing identity in an avalanche of Oxford culture. All too often I have witnessed Jewish students of varying degrees of Jewish observance arrive in Oxford with their eyes open to the bad as well as the good in Oxford: they talk of 'experimenting' with various lifestyles that were not previously afforded within the framework of a Jewish education or a committed Jewish home.

The Role of the Lamplighter

This is why Joseph remained Jewish in Egypt. He had highly focused goals and ambitions. He knew that his mission in life was to be a 'lamplighter'. Understanding that he had been fortunate to have had a moral and spiritual upbringing, he felt a duty to impart that knowledge to others in order to negate the suffocating selfishness that can abound in a world without God, or with too many gods.

Learning Jewish Tolerance

Returning to the original point, Joseph's emergence from his trial by fire in Egypt was also the secret of why he was able to forgive his brothers, in contrast to the example set by his beloved father. Joseph learned tremendous tolerance from his vast experiences. Having been through hellish psychological torture and torment, having had his character and identity threatened by myriad trials, he was sympathetic to others' tribulations as well. Perhaps he was particularly sensitized to the crisis of identity that must have afflicted his older brothers when his father began to treat him with such favour, and when they would have expected their status in the family to be secure. He was not the same person as the Joseph who had been thrown into the pit by his brothers, who had been unable to empathize with, or even show interest in, his brothers' feelings. At seventeen, perhaps rightfully, his only response was hatred.

The Joseph who had been through the cauldron of Egypt had changed and was able to commiserate with his brothers' sense of loss, pain and hurt. Here was a Joseph who attempted to fathom the level of distress and neglect his brothers must have suffered as a result of his father's partiality towards him. Having lived through such adversity, he was sympathetic to the suffering of those around him as well.

In this way, he was able to feel compassion for his brothers. He understood that it was not natural for brothers to conspire together to murder one of their own. Only siblings who feel jealously hostile towards a preferred favourite could pursue such a vindictive action. The Talmud itself criticizes Jacob for his favouritism, whatever his motives. Joseph was now able to empathize with those who had hurt him.

Insularity Obstructs Tolerance

The manifest characteristics of the Joseph-Jew are love, compassion and, above all, tolerance. It is no coincidence that the most intolerant of all Jewish groups are those who live in isolated, self-imposed Jewish ghettos. They look down from what they consider their spiritual perches of excellence at those Jews whom they judge to be misguided and sinful. Instead of living in their midst and loving them enough to teach them in a spirit of brotherhood and equality, they condemn them and in some cases even throw stones at them.

One of the most significant Jewish teachings for this generation is the lesson in *Ethics of Our Fathers* that one should never judge one's fellow until one has been in a similar predicament. Who of us who has not been in the hell of Auschwitz could condemn a survivor for blasphemy? Are we sure that had we been in the same predicament we would not have reacted far worse? Judaism came upon the earth to remove judgementalism from the planet. Man cannot unite with his fellow and create a true faith-community if he is constantly looking on him condescendingly. And while we are expected to deplore and condemn ungodly and evil acts, we are simultaneously expected to explore the motives and special circumstances of the perpetrator, ultimately showing him our compassion.

Looking on Others Favourably

This means changing some of our most basic attitudes. There are those of us who attend synagogue regularly who witness someone who attends only to say *kaddish* after a death in the family, or in the few months prior to a son's Bar Mitzvah, scornfully. Instead of inviting him in and making him feel as if he has come home, we turn our noses up and make him feel as though a sin has been committed. 'Suddenly, when he needs us and the shule he shows up!' Sadly, this attitude will only drive such a person further away and make attendance more irregular.

Who of us has experienced the hardships of life and is prepared to judge our fellow man over his lack of religious commitment? Judaism is meant to be inviting and inclusive, at all times, and never divisive or exclusive.

As Jews of a new era we must strive to be as much like Joseph as possible – professional, successful, but always retaining an unyielding and unswerving devotion to our roots as well as to our Jewish brethren.

Reversing Condemnation of Intermarrieds

An example of the need for this tolerance is in our approach to those who marry partners outside the Jewish people. Traditionally, the Jewish community's attitude to those who intermarried was to ostracize them and their families. They were treated as if they had committed a cardinal sin within Judaism, never to return. Their parents often mourned them as if for the dead, and other family members felt the need to limit contact as much as possible.

In such cases it is tolerance that must prevail. There is no cardinal offence in Judaism which marks a point of no return. There is no single act that can be committed by any Jew which warrants their co-religionists treating them as if they were foreigners. If God did not stipulate a cardinal offence or a point of no return, far be it from us to invent it. It is a crime to treat someone who has married out of the faith as anything other than an equal, an integral member of the Jewish people.

To be sure, even those who advocate hostility to those who marry out do not themselves argue that intermarriage is a cardinal offence and therefore the perpetrator must be ostracized. On the contrary, their argument is that the only way to prevent others from doing likewise is by placing the culprit in a state bordering on excommunication so that if others see the scorn shown by family and friends, they will refrain from doing likewise.

The Failure of Ostracization

But this approach has proven a colossal failure. For five decades Jewish men and women who intermarry have been banished, sometimes in the strongest and most uncompassionate ways, by parents, siblings and friends. The result of this most unJewish response is that those who did intermarry used their ostracism as a licence to rid themselves of any sense of responsibility or filial attachment to the Jewish community. It is no coincidence that even those who are brought up in Orthodox Jewish homes and attend traditional synagogue services sign up as members principally with reform and liberal congregations after they intermarry, simply because they feel themselves to be anathema to Orthodoxy. Can this be construed as progress?

No Jew ceases to be Jewish as a result of intermarrying and even those who cannot be persuaded to break a relationship with a non-Jewish partner must still be told, in the most loving yet forceful terms, that they are still Jewish and that nothing they ever do will change that. They are Jewish for all eternity, regardless of who their spouse is, and they have responsibilities to the Jewish community. They must try to attend synagogue and perform *mitzvot*. Marrying out is not a licence to cease all Jewish activities or affiliation, and far be it from any Jewish communal leader to promote this erroneous and destructive mind-set. We must reach out and welcome as family every Jewish individual regardless of their choices in life.

Looked at pragmatically, this attitude of treating the Jew who marries out as a leper and outcast has yielded no benefits at all. It has not stemmed the tide of intermarriage. Those who employ the technique are aware of its negative consequences for the person in question and how it will doubtlessly make him feel as though the Jewish people are no longer his home. Yet they justify this attitude in the hope that the many who witness the intermarried's ostracism will take heed and fear the consequences of marrying out. But the statistics prove this method has had no impact and has not served to curb the tide of intermarriage. If anything it has caused us to lose twice as many Jews because now we do not only risk losing the offspring of those who intermarry, but we alienate Jewish partners themselves by unjustly pushing them from us with both hands.

Being Consistent about Homosexuals and Bachelors

The final proof for the folly of this method is that no one would advocate that the same be done with confirmed Jewish bachelors or homosexuals, both of whom are guilty of virtually the same act as one who marries out. The lifestyles of all three lead to the decimation of the Jewish people through the neglect of procreating Jewish offspring, yet it is only the intermarrieds who are made to feel they have ridden into Jewish oblivion. As shown above, this method of castigating and vilifying them has proven fruitless. Worst of all, it is un-Jewish behaviour and must immediately be ceased.

The time has come when we must expend every effort in welcoming back all those who may not have married Jewish partners and confirm and encourage their obligations to the Jewish community. Through this we will be acting in a spirit of love and righteousness in emulation of Joseph our compatriot.

Chapter Forty-three

REJECTING JUDGEMENTALISM

Students tend to be something of a judgemental lot, and that should not surprise anyone. In any educational institution where idealism often outweighs pragmatism, one is bound to find its participants looking askance or condescendingly at others who may not share their morals or indeed the same untainted sense of idealism. What is interesting, however, is the areas in which students are prepared to judge others. In some ways, as stated above, they tend to examine and rate a person's actions and decide whether or not they wish to be that person's friend. But then there are categories which they ignore completely. No judgements are ever made about someone's sexual habits, for example, or promiscuity, unless of course their practices 'are hurting someone'.

In fact, from my experience this is the only criterion on which students are prepared to judge someone else and question their morality. If someone complains about another's behaviour and asserts it has offended them or intruded on their rights, students conclude that that person's actions are objectionable. Everything else is forgiven.

Boy Leaves Girl

Case in point: a few years ago a young man and woman met at the L'Chaim Centre. They had much in common and began to date.

For me such an occurrence is always a mixed blessing. Undoubtedly the primary function of the L'Chaim Society is to give rise to and perpetuate Jewish observance and the Jewish nation. There can be no more effective method of achieving this than to have Jewish men and women meet in a committed Jewish environment which promotes Jewish values. Indeed, in the field of matchmaking, both active and passive, we have had several triumphs. To date, there are sixteen marriages which resulted directly from the L'Chaim Society, over a period of five years, and many more long-term relationships which are stable but have not yet culminated in marriage.

One of my most cherished and memorable moments at Oxford was when I witnessed the marriage of a student who, when I met him, had not even been circumcised and was so innocently ignorant of Judaism that he believed Judaism was still polygamous – he was convinced I had two wives and refrained from addressing my wife for fear he would insult the other. But he married under a chupa, after becoming fully observant, to a wonderful young woman he had met at the L'Chaim Society. I am not the sentimental type, but as his bride circled him seven times under the wedding-canopy to the tune of '*Eishes Chayil*', a woman of valour, I broke down in tears, much to the amazement of the assembled crowd. Furthermore, of all the many photographs of various past activities and famous speakers adorning the walls of our L'Chaim Centre in Oxford, it is the pictures of former students' weddings that are most prominent.

However, if a new couple meet at L'Chaim and subsequently break up with acrimony, it can cause me great troubles. Often they subsequently will not want to see one another and all too often we will have students who refrain from attending synagogue services or the Shabbat meal to avoid their former boyfriend or girlfriend. So my general policy is to stay out of the way as much as possible.

Pressure to Cast Out a Student

Well, the man and woman with much in common, mentioned earlier, became too close too fast. The mechanics were completely wrong. She was from a very religious Jewish background and so had little experience of men. When she arrived in Oxford she often spoke of 'experimenting' with things denied her by virtue of her strict upbringing. After their first intimate encounter, he broke it off and she was devastated. The experiment had failed, at least for her. He had what he wanted and moved on. She was so hurt by what she described as 'having been used' and taken advantage of that she demanded I intervene to prevent him from attending the L'Chaim Society, or at the very least that I severely rebuke him for his deed. I refused to do either. I told her if he brought up the subject with me, then I would address it. Otherwise I cannot enter people's personal lives without being invited. For her part, she was mortified, and so were all her friends who got wind of the story. They could not understand how I could respect him after what he had done. Finally, one of the Jewish students approached me and told me that I was being strongly criticized for my refusal to take punitive measures against this student, with whom I was particularly friendly. 'And what did he do wrong, that I should punish him?' I asked. 'Well, he hurt her. He just left her after he had finished with her.'

This I just could not understand. 'But it was she,' I countered, 'who kept speaking of experimenting.' In other words, the promiscuous side of 'experimenting' is something about which the students refused to cast any moral judgement. It was only that in this case someone had got hurt. But the very meaning of experimenting is that things will remain casual. Someone is therefore bound to get hurt. One cannot argue that religious mores are too constraining and therefore abandon them, and then complain that they have been hurt by the very causes those religious laws are meant to protect the individual from in the first place.

Still, I have always had trouble determining when I have the right, perhaps even the necessity, of judging a student's actions, while remaining a concerned and caring pastoral guide.

Organizations Who Will Not Judge

There is a case for saying that one should never be judgemental. Two established and distinguished organizations will demonstrate this point. The charity Oxfam and the Citizens' Advice Bureau (CAB) were both set up many years ago in Britain and are still recognized as doing vital work in the community on a national and international level.

The prime characteristic of both these organizations is that they refuse to judge the people they try to help. Aid or advice is not given on the basis of whether the agency feels the person is living his or her life correctly and in accordance with pre-judged norms. Oxfam and the CAB are not content with simply being passive, though, as this approach might imply. Rather, they lobby parliament and other interested parties to change their social policies for the better, with the aim of helping even more people. So their work is twofold: they provide help and assistance in a neutral environment where people are respected, whatever they choose to be. At the same time, though, these organizations refuse to see institutionalized wrongs as unchangeable: they openly speak out about them and actively work against them. It can be argued that it is specifically their policy of offering assistance, irrespective of the beneficiaries' morality, which has served as the source of their success.

To be honest, I tend to agree with the above in many everyday circumstances. But as mentioned earlier, I have experienced significant criticism at the hands of the students specifically for my policy of non-judgementalism. Sometimes, of course, personal judgements are essential, as I shall show.

A Case of Infidelity

One severe case was when a student recently came to see me with a 'retroactive complaint'. When something has already transpired and the complainer is logically forced to accept there is nothing to be done about it, he or she may nevertheless feel it necessary to make a protest; I call this a 'retroactive complaint'. Students are an idealistic lot and they feel the need to make complaints to promote or preserve a cause, even when the protest can have no bearing on practical reality.

A world-famous speaker and politician had just delivered a public lecture for the L'Chaim Society at the Oxford Union, attended by over one thousand students. Four weeks later the speaker revealed on national television in his own country that he had had an affair and was unfaithful to his wife. The student wanted it to be known that he strongly objected to this man having appeared under the banner of a Jewish religious organization. He understood, of course, that at the time when the politician spoke for us we were unaware of his infidelity, but nevertheless the objection to his presence had to be made.

Clinton's Election Sets New Standard

I thought long and hard about this. First of all, it had come in a year in which I applauded the election of Bill Clinton, in spite of the allegations of his marital infidelity. My own opinion is that President Clinton would have been indefensible had he lied and denied the charge, as did Gary Hart four years earlier, or had he announced that he could not imagine what was so wrong with a little fling on the side and why people were making such a furore. In the event, what Clinton did say was that there had been problems in his marriage; his wife then publicly announced that she had forgiven him and that she was standing by him. When a person commits an offence such as adultery, it is an issue between that person, their spouse, and God. The adulterer must ask forgiveness from both of those parties with all his or her might and soul. If they choose to forgive, it is nobody's business to know of the offence or to hold it against either the adulterer or the injured spouse who has so magnanimously forgiven such a grievous hurt. What Clinton's election showed, in spite of the Jennifer Flowers affair, was that good, common, decent people proclaimed to the world that if people err and commit an offence, but then ask to be forgiven and allowed to get on with their lives, we must not only allow them to do so but encourage them. Clinton's election taught the world that there is no offence we can commit which is either beyond repentance, or which suddenly just ends one's life. The future president did not have to hang up his boots and withdraw from the running once it became known he had made a terrible mistake. Rather, he could sincerely regret his tragic error, make amends, and achieve future greatness, unimpeded by his previous misjudgement.

If this is not the case, then the innocent spouse could be hurt even more. Supposing a husband injures his wife and marriage with a terrible act of infidelity. The wife, despite the hurt inflicted upon her, finds it within herself to forgive him and love him again as before. She wishes to continue living with and loving him. At this point, the public intrudes, telling her, 'No! You may have forgotten the incident, but we will take up your cause for you.' In their arrogance they intrude into her life, assuming she is too weak to fight her own battles, rather than that she is strong enough to forgive. They reopen old wounds with their misplaced concern. They effectively tell her she is wrong to forgive her husband.

It is a different case altogether if a candidate for public office is actively promoting adultery as something that is tolerable and 'no big deal'. Such an attitude shows the nominee's values are terribly askew. Adultery is a serious offence and should be treated with scorn and contempt. People are not perfect, though, and when they make mistakes they should be granted the latitude of picking themselves up. This is especially so when the spouse against whom the crime was committed shows the way forward by extending forgiveness in return for hurt.

Putting Oneself in Someone Else's Shoes

My initial reaction to the student's complaint was that it was not justified. Publicly admitting to a grave mistake should not end your public life at a young age. If it did, people would become even less willing to admit their mistakes than they already are. I told the student that one of the most important teachings in Judaism, found in *Ethics of Our Fathers*, is, 'Judge not your fellow until you are in his place' (Avos 2:4).

The politician in question is uncommonly handsome and charismatic. Furthermore, as a prime ministerial hopeful, he leads a life of enormous pressure and stress. He must travel constantly in the presence of young female aides who look up to him as to a Greek god. I asked the student whether he would have committed the same mistake, or even done worse, given the same temptation. 'Perhaps, in the same circumstances, you would not only have had an affair with a young aide, but left your wife altogether and destroyed your family for her?' Surely until you are in this man's shoes, there is no possible way that you can say you would not match his behaviour with the same or worse.

Mitigating Circumstances in People's Lives

In a discussion of this matter in his ground-breaking opus on Chasidic thought, *Tanya*, Rabbi Shneur Zalman of Liadi expresses the idea in this way:

> This also a person must relive in his heart, to fulfil the instruction of our rabbis, of blessed memory: 'And be humble of spirit before all men.' This you must be in true sincerity, in the presence of any individual, even in the presence of the most worthless of worthless men. This accords with the instruction of our Sages: 'Judge not your fellow until you are in his place.' For it is his 'place' that causes him to sin, because his livelihood requires him to go to the market for the whole day and to

be one of those who 'sit at the street corners', where his eyes behold all the temptations; the eye sees and the heart desires, and his evil nature is kindled like a baker's red-hot oven, as is written in Josea: 'It burneth as a flaming fire ...'

It is different, however, with him who goes but little to the market place, and who remains in his house for the greater part of the day; or even if he spends the whole day in the market but is possibly not so passionate by nature – for the evil inclination of all people is not the same ...

As the Great Ones Fall

Sitting on our high pedestal of moral superiority, it is easy for us to pass judgement on those who fail in areas of life which society sees as important. It is relatively simple to ignore the many accomplishments of great people when they submit to one big blunder. If it is true that mankind in general, and certain civilizations in particular, have always needed heroes, then it is even more true that as much as we need heroes we also seem to delight in their fall. When a great person falls it partly lessens the burden on us to emulate greatness. Instead of being forced to confront the challenge the great throw out to us and follow in their footsteps, we are able to turn back to our own pathetic lives with a sneer against them, 'There! He wasn't very special after all!'

Judgementalism as the Equivalent of Arrogance

Judaism vigorously opposes this casual dismissal of people and the greatness they struggle to achieve. There is virtually no emotional vice that is not associated with judgementalism. Passing judgement on another person involves the greatest statement of arrogance. Firstly, the one judging believes he has the moral right, even the moral imperative, to place himself higher than another human being because of that person's actions. The person sitting in judgement assumes the offender is inherently evil or bad, for example that the adulterous husband is a born womanizer rather than the victim of circumstances that made infidelity very difficult to resist. Secondly, the one who sits in judgement believes he does not embody the same evil, or tendency for evil, as the person on whom he is passing judgement: he assumes that if he had been in the same situation, he would have behaved in an altogether more virtuous manner.

In this respect, often the judgementalist is either a prophet or a fool. After all, only if he is a prophet can he know for certain that he would not have behaved in a similar manner. Even if he argues that he has been in a similar predicament and so he has the right to pass judgement, it cannot be assumed he and his fellow are exactly the same. It was to forewarn against this misguided assumption that Rabbi Shneur Zalman stated that 'the evil inclination of all people is not the same'.

The judgemental person is also, in many cases, guilty of envy and vindictiveness. Otherwise, why does he suddenly find the great need to be the world's moral arbiter? Unless God has entrusted him with some great mission to preserve mankind's integrity, or he himself is so perfect that he no longer needs to concentrate on his own faults, he is wrong to devote all his time in condescension towards others.

The Talmud expresses this idea succinctly when it mentions that every time a person wishes for God to judge his fellow man, by saying to his colleague, 'May God judge between us', what the Almighty does first is to judge the person making the statement. After all, only a person who believes himself to be completely righteous would have the arrogance to damn others for their imperfections. Thus, God is out to determine whether this is indeed the case.

The Lessons of Imperfection

No human is perfect. To an extent, there is a very positive lesson to be derived from our own imperfection. From consistently pondering why it is that humanity is so imperfect, I have drawn the conclusion that our flaws should teach us sympathy and humility. If indeed perfection were attainable, it would be rather easy to judge other people for their imperfections. Since no one is perfect, though, we should be reminded of our own faults whenever we witness someone else's imperfection, and so be able to be forgiving and loving towards them.

Where We Draw the Line

However, some crimes are so repugnant that they seem to defy any consideration of circumstances. Witness the public outcry when the notorious Judge Pickles gave a lenient sentence to a man who had abused his young daughter because of the 'mitigating circumstances' that his wife was pregnant. There are certain things which (nearly) all of us accept to be just plain wrong, regardless of any external considerations. For example, a husband beats his wife. Maybe his wife was verbally abusive, humiliated him publicly and wasted all their money. Still, none of the above is any excuse for beating her. Even if he was given a bad example because his father had beaten his mother he is not excused, because witnessing his own mother, or his father's wife, being beaten should have filled him with a deep sense of revulsion and rage for this most cowardly act.

We Need to Judge within a System of Justice

This does not imply that no one ever has the right morally to censure certain forms of behaviour, nor does it argue for the complete dissolution of any justice system or meting out of punishment. To be sure, some crimes are so heinous that we must cast moral censure upon them. Such denunciation serves as an absolutely central element of any decent civilization: if we cannot pass judgement on our fellow man, then how can the criminal be punished for crimes?

We cannot follow a path of moral relativism whereby all immoral actions are excused because of mitigating circumstances. That would create the intolerable situation in which all notions of right and wrong are cast aside because to all practical purposes it is impossible to apply them because of unknown influences on the criminal. For the good of society, there must be some sense of a moral norm, departure from which will bring condemnation or retribution.

How, then, can we reconcile this need to identify certain modes of behaviour as repulsive and evil, with the Mishnah's dictum that one must never judge one's fellow 'until he has reached his place'?

'Sins and Not Sinners'

The answer is to separate the perpetrator of the crimes from the crimes themselves. By doing so, we are able to focus on the real problem – the evil of man's deeds.

In the book of Psalms, King David proclaims, 'May sin be eradicated from the earth . . .' The Talmud comments, 'Sins, and not sinners.' It is perfectly justified to decry the existence of sin and aberrations in our world. We are not only permitted but obligated to cast moral judgement and upbraid improper behaviour. We must expend every effort to eradicate any destructive behaviour. But this does not include eradicating the offender from the earth.

Thus we can decry the commitment of adultery and simultaneously preserve our compassion for the perpetrator of the crime. The reason for this is that indeed the two are separable.

An Evil Act But Not an Evil Man

People at times act evilly, but this does not make them evil. In the Jewish scheme of things, a person is born innocent with the possibility of goodness or evil set before him or her. When a man chooses either path, he is essentially not an evil or even a good person, but a person who has *chosen to act* in a good way, or to act evilly. The deed is not intrinsic to one's character.

This, of course, has a positive as well as a negative dimension. The positive dimension is that even if someone behaves wickedly, the deed is not intrinsic to his or her personality and is thus potentially reversible. Of course, the more they behave in this way, the more it becomes ingrained into their personality. In Tanya, Rabbi Shneur Zalman re-asserts an earlier Maimonidean dictum that when a deed is repeated many times, 'it becomes second nature'. The negative side follows this same logic: notwithstanding how many times a person chooses to behave in a commendable and praiseworthy way, there is no guarantee that they will repeat this laudatory behaviour. Although of course it is true that the more goodness one practises, the easier it becomes to continue the pursuit of goodness, and to make the sacrifices necessary for the welfare of others. However, this does not in any form constitute an assurance that one will continue to be good. Everyone must constantly be on guard because one can never take solace from having made the right decisions in the past. We must never allow our moral guard to slip even infinitesimally.

In this way, we can simultaneously condemn a worthless or harmful transgression while upholding the intrinsic value of the man. The justice system reprimands him for his evil deed, but encourages him to do better, because his inner potential remains unaffected by the offence. He is not an evil man, but a man who has acted evilly.

Character Traits That Become Ingrained

There is, however, an important exception to this rule. As above, the more one behaves in a certain pattern, the more difficult it becomes to separate the person and the behaviour. Repeating the same act, for good or for bad, becomes a part of one's personality. This does not mean that it cannot be reversed, but it is just far more difficult to do so. When the same action is repeated often, it becomes more and more difficult to distinguish between the person committing the act and the act itself.

For example, Jewish law stipulates that the best way for charity to be given is not in one lump sum, but in smaller, daily dosages. Even if an annual charitable gift will equal the daily sum, one must still give it in a regular way rather than on a one-off basis. If the net effect for those receiving $1,095 a year or $3 a day is the same, what could possibly be the difference?

Becoming a Charitable Person

The answer is that while it may not make any difference to those receiving the funds, it does make a difference to the one who is contributing the funds. When one gives charity on an annual, one-off basis, that donor can be categorized as a person *who practises charity*. If one gives on a daily basis, however, one is no longer someone who practises charity, but a *charitable person*. The action becomes intrinsic to the contributor's being. The possibility arises of behaving intuitively with respect to an act of charity. Whereas one may not have been a naturally charitable individual, and indeed many are not, the habitual giver will find it virtually impossible to walk down the street and turn down a person who is in legitimate need. Charity will begin to flow as part of a natural effusion from deep within one's nature.

Innate and Acquired Nature

Maimonides writes in his *Laws of Character Dispositions*, in which he discusses the kind of people we ought to be, that there are two kinds of human nature, that with which one is born, our innate selves, and that which we acquire. In the modern vernacular, there are those human quality traits which result from *nature*, and others from *nurture* (Ibid. 1:2). Elaborating on this important principle in the Tanya, Rabbi Shneur Zalman of Liadi explains that the acquired nature is brought about through a process of repeating the same activity over and over again until it becomes ingrained into the psyche. So, even an inborn trait for evil can be eliminated by acting in a manner contrary to one's nature. It is all a matter of discipline and repetitiveness. Maimonides adds that the most effective way in which to dispense with an undesirable character trait is to go to the opposite extreme for a certain period of time, until the person naturally begins to fall somewhere in the middle. Thus, if one is too stingy, they should become overly generous and dispense large quantities of money, so that they can settle comfortably into a healthy balance. And although Maimonides is vociferously opposed to any extreme emotions or character traits – with the exception of anger, from which, he maintains, one must distance oneself completely – he allows extremism for a temporary period in that it helps the individual achieve a healthy equilibrium.

Similarly, when the perpetration of evil becomes so ingrained within a person's character that he or she intuitively behaves meanly, vindictively, and with total disregard for human life, then that person can be said to have acquired an evil nature. This does not mean that he or she cannot reverse the habit. It does, however, mean that it is exceedingly difficult and for some borders on the nearly impossible.

Eichmann Seeks Repentance

A case in point was the famous trial of Adolf Eichmann in a Jerusalem courtroom for crimes against humanity. After being found guilty of unspeakable crimes against humanity in general and the Jewish people in particular by the special Jerusalem Court, Eichmann tried desperately to save his life. He made the following appeal to the judges in his defence: 'I abhor the atrocities committed on the Jews as the greatest crime, and consider it just that the people responsible should be brought to justice now and in the future ... I pray you, Mr President, to commute the death sentence!' (*Justice in Jerusalem*, by Gideon Hausner, page 444). His argument was that now that he had recognized the horrific nature of his crime, and expressed this remorse and regret, his death sentence should be commuted. He entreated the court for compassion and mercy.

Given that there is no possible way to ascertain whether or not his statement was sincere, but assuming that it was, can we then proceed to forgive him for his crime? Can we apply the above principle of separating men from the crimes they commit?

The answer is an emphatic, NO! We cannot forgive such evil people. When someone is both directly and indirectly responsible for the murder of millions of people, they have become the personification of evil. What this means is that millions of times over they have deadened themselves internally to another human being's anguish and suffering. They have ensured that they are and will remain completely insensitive to any humane feelings welling up within them. For all intents and purposes, they have murdered the source of all brotherly love, the 'image of God' within them, and what remains is only the husk of an animal.

There are indeed moral absolutes, the greatest travesty of which is to take the life of another human being. This constitutes a point of no return. Thus, Eichmann and others who have committed similar atrocities are indistinguishable from the crimes which they commit. They are evil. Just as it is entirely appropriate to weigh and condemn their evil actions, likewise it is appropriate to condemn them as well.

A Student Challenge

Once, when I was delivering a lecture in Oxford on this same subject, I asked the student audience if they felt that Eichmann should have been forgiven, especially since, had he lived, he could have served as the ultimate witness to the evils of the Holocaust, so helping to prevent it from happening again. A student's hand went up. 'Absolutely,' he said. 'He should have been allowed to live.' I asked why. 'Because,' he responded, 'it was far more important for the world to hear about the Holocaust from his lips than it was to carry out justice.'

I disagreed with him. 'The only message that the world will hear if Eichmann is forgiven and allowed to live is that one can murder millions of innocent victims and still atone for one's sins. That there really is nothing in this world that is so terrible that it leaves an indelible mark on one's person, on one's soul. And that,' I concluded, 'is the wrong message.'

Pharaoh is Punished Amidst a 'Hardened Heart'

Maimonides discusses this theme in his treatment of Pharaoh and the biblical enigma of God hardening his heart. Certainly, central to all Jewish tenets is the belief in our freedom to choose between good and evil. So why did Pharaoh not have any choice? Why did the Almighty constantly harden his heart so that he would not allow the Jews to leave Egypt?

The answer, as above, is that by enslaving and brutally torturing a helpless nation, Pharaoh's evil had become intrinsic. He was evil in his essence, and thus it was not God who had removed Pharaoh's ability to repent and do good, but rather Pharaoh himself who had obliterated any hope of that possibility by living in a perpetual state of evil action. What the Almighty merely did was use this wretched criminal as an example to the rest of the world of the fate of such inhumanity.

But what is pivotal for today's students to understand, and others who are fortunate enough to live a privileged life, is that under normal circumstances it is forbidden to judge our fellow man since men are good, and sometimes the things they do are not so good.

This is said, though, with regard to the perpetration of some crimes which would indeed be influenced by some kind of circumstance, such as the predicament of the politician described earlier in this chapter. But some crimes are seen by Jewish law as being so heinous that we dare not excuse the action or the man. Certainly, gross physical violence is at the top of the list.

Chapter Forty-four

A DEFINITION OF LONELINESS
AND HOW TO OVERCOME IT

Coming to Oxford can be a daunting experience for all but the most annoyingly self-confident students. First of all, there are the new terminology and social conventions to get to grips with, and although these are not as obscure as they once were it can at first seem impossible that you will ever understand what the students who have been here a few years longer are actually talking about.

Why does everyone insist on calling the High Street 'The High'? Do you take the college dean (disciplinarian) seriously when he or she fines you £15 for walking on a lawn? The answer most certainly is, yes, except in a very few colleges. Do you take your neighbour seriously when he says you are to be 'sconced' for talking about the paintings in hall? Rarely, except in some colleges. When the college regulations stipulate that gowns must be worn to tutorials and lectures do you actually don what the students consider to be a ridiculous-looking thing and parade about the quad and town in it? No, except in one or two colleges. Finally, be wary of digging into your pocket to give a few pennies to the hard-up master when you are told that Master's Collections are coming up: this is an oral report to the head of the college on your progress so far, not an opportunity to show your capacity for charity.

Loneliness Sets In

One of the most difficult emotions experienced by students when they first arrive in Oxford is loneliness. For many it is the fact that they are leaving home, often for the first time. Those who have been to boarding school have often been away from home since they were seven, but even for them there are many reasons for feeling lonely. Some feel loneliness and a sense of isolation because of the large workloads greeting their arrival: there seems to be no time for finding new friends when there is so much work to do. Often, this will lead to the terrible yet recurrent Oxford tragedy of student suicide.

Others feel lonely because Oxford's emphasis is on intellectual achievement rather than emotional bonding: students are forced to compete with their new friends and acquaintances before they have begun to connect with them and know them as people. The Oxford myth can be so daunting that although one may have won a much coveted place at the university and have access to the reality of Oxford, it still seems easier to assume there was some mistake made when the college admitted you. The majority of students presuppose that all the other people they meet here will be brilliant, yet the fact is that most people are interesting but also fairly ordinary, and not at all frightening. This is not to say there are not some truly brilliant students to be found in this university, but it is also true that the reason a particular student makes it to Oxford has often more to do with hard work than braininess.

Perhaps the most painful loneliness is felt by those who see around them other students who seem to have broken into new friendships and communities, while they themselves feel unable to participate. Cliques easily form in the small, intense and enclosed community of an Oxford college, and the existence of these almost tribal bands of friends can be a source of a profound sense of being the only one who is alone.

Humans as Social Creatures

The reasons for loneliness are varied and complicated, but a common realization after a few months at Oxford is that there really is no need to be alone in a city so full of vibrant and fascinating individuals. Loneliness is so often more a question of the perception of a problem rather than a problem really existing, but it takes time to see this. After all, loneliness is not a natural state for a human being. We are social creatures and exist in communities. University is a wonderful opportunity to create your own community rather than having it entirely imposed on you: the choice of what to make belongs exclusively to the students.

The first few weeks at college are characterized by a wonderful opening up of personalities: it is easy to talk about interesting ideas and intimate problems because everyone else is in the same situation. Later, people tend to close up a little against people they have not already initiated as new friends, but there is no reason for the process of connecting with people and making friends ever to cease. Some people retain the happy knack of being intimate with people that most others find difficult or repellent: these are the ones who hold a community together.

But whatever the causes of loneliness, for each there must be a cure.

Adam's Loneliness

In the unfolding narrative of Genesis and the creation of the first man, Adam, the Torah discusses the fact that immediately after his being was called forth into existence, Adam became lonely. God, in his kindness, creates him a partner. 'And the Lord God said, It is not good that the man should be alone; I will make him an helpmeet for him' (Genesis 2:18). But why was Adam lonely? After all, he was living in the Garden of Eden and had all the angels to converse with.

According to the rabbis, the reason for Adam's loneliness was that the angels did not need anything in their turn from Adam. They were perfect and not in need of companionship. Adam was lonely because he could not give. With the creation of Eve, however, he had someone who needed him, someone whose life he could touch. This made him feel necessary and cured the pangs of his loneliness. He in turn could do the same for Eve.

No parent is completely happy at the prospect of their children growing up and assuming independence, and parents are thrilled when their children still phone them for advice, even after they have moved from home. Everyone wants to feel needed.

Last year, a student with whom I enjoyed a close relationship came to see me, very late at night, ashen-faced. His father's closest friend, someone who had been like an uncle to him through the years, had just taken his own life. He had been made redundant from work a year earlier, and although his wife earned a comfortable living from her occupation, he could not live with the loneliness of being unable to contribute to his family's financial well-being.

Living Life By Oneself

In Judaism, and especially at the L'Chaim Society, when we toast our fellow human beings over wine or other alcoholic beverages, we say, 'L'Chaim' which literally translates as 'To life' in the plural, that is 'To many lives', lives which are lived together. But no one could live life by themselves. We all need someone else, but even more important, life only has meaning when we can share our lives with others, and we can strengthen and enrich their lives, not in any patronizing way but on a genuine level of community.

When our matriarch Sarah died in the book of Genesis, the Torah reads, 'And these were the years [shnei] of Sarah, one hundred, and twenty, and seven.' Yet the word shnei literally means 'two': it is as if the Torah is saying, 'These were the two lives of Sarah.' In the words of Rashi, 'All her years were good': the reason she lived a full and complete life was that she lived two lives, one her own, and the other the manner in which she enriched the lives of others.

Here we have a new, and perhaps more profound reason, for the loneliness experienced by many on arriving at Oxford. With such illustrious predecessors in this university, and so many parents and tutors who have high hopes and are pushing us to be a success in our studies, our confidence in our ability to make a significant contribution, to leave any mark on Oxford at all, is called into question.

As part of a comprehensive solution, I suggest that students try to the best of their ability to get involved in Oxford Jewish and humanitarian life, not just in attending Jewish functions, but in contributing to their organization. Even if it is something as straightforward as encouraging a colleague to attend on Friday night, or helping to put up posters or to prepare our weekly mailing, or something as difficult as helping with the logistics of some of L'Chaim's extraordinary events, such as the Science/Religion or Middle East debate, or helping organize the security for the visit of Yitzhak Shamir – at any level we are immensely appreciative of help from our student members. There is a whole group of dedicated members of the JCR, MCR, and SCR (undergraduates, graduates and faculty) who would benefit from their contribution, and another group, who have not yet been given the opportunity to become involved, are waiting for members of L'Chaim to touch their lives. On a broader, more universal level it means becoming involved in global projects that benefit all humanity, and Oxford has many such organisations. But the important thing is to start somewhere. Perhaps with a single good deed which will benefit one's fellow man.